SQUARING THE CIRCLE IS THE KEY TO JOHN DEE'S DESIGN FOR THE 1599 GLOBE THEATER

ISBN-13: 978-1500684600

ISBN-10: 1500684600 :

Published by:
Cosmopolite Press
James Alan Egan
152 Mill Street
Newport, Rhode Island 02840

For more information, visit:
newporttowermuseum.com

Printed in the United States of America

SQUARING THE CIRCLE IS THE KEY TO JOHN DEE'S DESIGN FOR THE 1599 GLOBE THEATER

BY
JAMES ALAN EGAN

"CITIZEN OF THE WORLD"
(COSMOPOLITE, IS A WORD COINED BY JOHN DEE, FROM THE GREEK WORDS COSMOS MEANING "WORLD" AND POLITÊS MEANING "CITIZEN")

COSMOPOLITE PRESS
NEWPORT, RHODE ISLAND

This book is dedicated to Joy Hancox, who has enthusiastically shared the Byrom Collection drawings and her perceptive insights with the world.

TABLE OF CONTENTS

THE JOY OF DISCOVERY

Joy Hancox
researcher and author

In August of 1965, Joy Hancox bought a converted farmhouse on the old Roman road heading north from Manchester, in the northwest of England.

While researching, she found that the farm was owned from 1729 to 1745 by Thomas Siddal Jr.

In 1715, Thomas father, Thomas Siddal Sr. was executed because of his support for James Stuart, the "Old Pretender" to the throne of England. At age seven, Thomas Jr. had to witness his father's head being displayed on a pike in Manchester for all to see.

Thirty years later, in 1745, Thomas Jr. took part in the second Jacobite rebellion. Like father, like son, he was similarly executed.

Digging up this family history, Joy Hancox came across one of Siddal's friends, John Byrom, a man whose life was shrouded by mystery and intrigue.

John Byrom at an early age
(1692-1763)

This Day are Publish'd,
PROPOSALS *for* Printing *by* SUBSCRIPTION,
A New and Compleat METHOD of SHORT-HAND.
By JOHN BYROM, *A.M.*
Sometime Fellow of Trinity-College, Cambridge.

Whereby any Person may, in a few Weeks, learn to write a Short-Hand, which is perfectly Neat, Distinct, and Exact, free from all Ambiguity and Arbitrary Characters, consisting entirely of the Letters of its Alphabet, easy to be written, read, and remember'd, capable of the greatest Contractions and utmost Expedition, applicable to all Kind of Business, Arts and Sciences, and calculated FOR UNIVERSAL USE AND BENEFIT.

Proposals, with a general Description and Recommendation, drawn up by some of Mr. Byrom's Scholars, are deliver'd, and Subscriptions taken in,

By the Author himself, at Manchester in Lancashire.

Mr. William Chaddocke, Merchant, in Catteaton-street, fronting Basinghall-street, near Guildhall, London.

Francis Fauquier, Esq; at Bath.

Dr. Hartley, in Prince's-street near Leicester fields.

George Lloyd, Esq; at Mr. Murray's, Apothecary, in Henrietta-street, Covent-garden.

George Weller, Esq; at his Chambers No. I. in Elm-Court, Temple.

And by the following Booksellers.

Mr. Stepeen Austen, at the Angel and Bible in St. Paul's Church-yard. Mess. Ward and Chandler, at the Ship without Temple-Bar, and at York and Scarborough. Mr. George Hawkins, at Milton's Head between the Temple-Gates, and at Tonbridge-Wells. Mr. James Hutton, at the Bible and Sun without Temple-Bar. Mr. William Thurlbourn, at Cambridge. And, Mr. William Frederick, at Bath.

John Byrom's advertisement
for his short-hand lessons

Like his friend, Thomas Siddal Jr., John Byrom was a Jacobite. But somehow Byrom managed to keep his head.

He was a member of the Royal Society, and invented the efficient "New Universal Shorthand," which he taught to wealthy patrons.

He wrote poems, epigrams, and even coined the phrase "Tweedledum and Tweedledee," while critiquing two composers, neither of whom he particularly admired.

Fascinated by this Byrom character, Joy dug deeper into his life (and particularly his connections to people in high places.)

In June of 1984, a family which Joy had contacted in her research provided her with two large envelopes containing over 600 skillfully drawn geometric drawings. The owners had found the drawings in the cupboard years earlier and thought they might be useful to Joy in her Byrom research. Indeed they were.

Joyous books

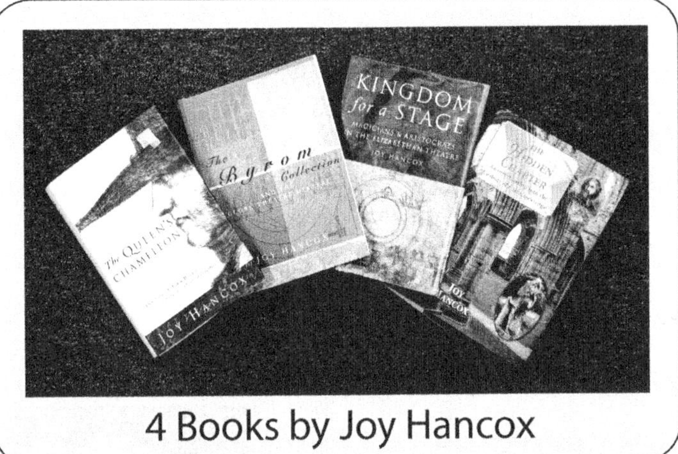

4 Books by Joy Hancox

Joy Hancox has now completed four amazingly-thorough books about John Byrom and 516 pieces she calls the "Byrom Collection."

The Queen's Chameleon: Life of John Byrom: A Study in Conflicting Loyalties (London, Jonathan Cape Ltd., *1994)*

The Byrom Collection: And the Globe Theatre Mystery (London, Jonathan Cape Ltd., 1997)

Kingdom For a Stage: Magicians and Aristocrats in the Elizabethan Theatre (Stroud UK, Sutton Pub. Ltd., 2001)

The Hidden Chapter: The Investigation into the Custody of Lost Knowledge (Manchester, Byrom Projects, 2011)

The 4 drawings of the original Globe theater

My book focuses on only a few of these 516 cards/papers. They are the ones Joy Hancox believes were the blueprints of the Globe theater, which was built on the south bank of the Thames River in London in 1599.

Joy discovered that these **four** specific drawings integrate with each other to provide the proportions and dimensions of the original Globe theater:

1 The "overview" plan
2 The "close-up" plan
3 The "parametric" plan
4 The "Tiring House" plan

(Joy Hancox has kindly agreed to allow me to use the four Byrom geometric drawings for the purposes of scholarship and further understanding of this book.)

1 The "overview" plan

The "overview" diagram of the Globe Theater has drawings on both sides.

The two sides are mates. They are identical in size. They share several features, like a central point, central square, large diamond, and a large outer circle.

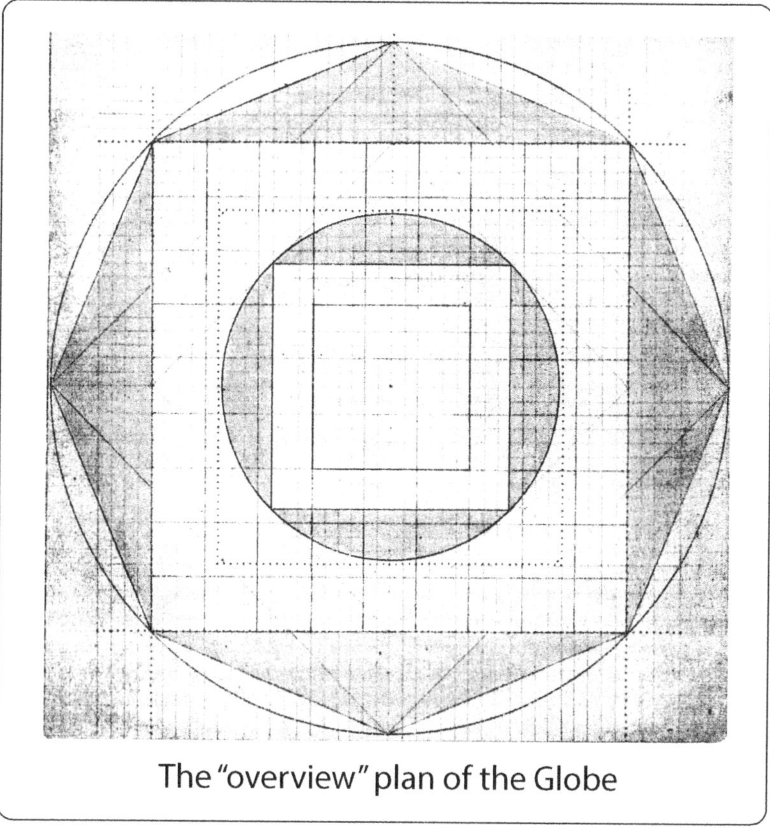

The "overview" plan of the Globe

They are based on the same underlying geometry, but each side emphasizes different aspects.

At first glance they might appear to be confounding Pop-Art mandalas, so we will break them down into their component parts.

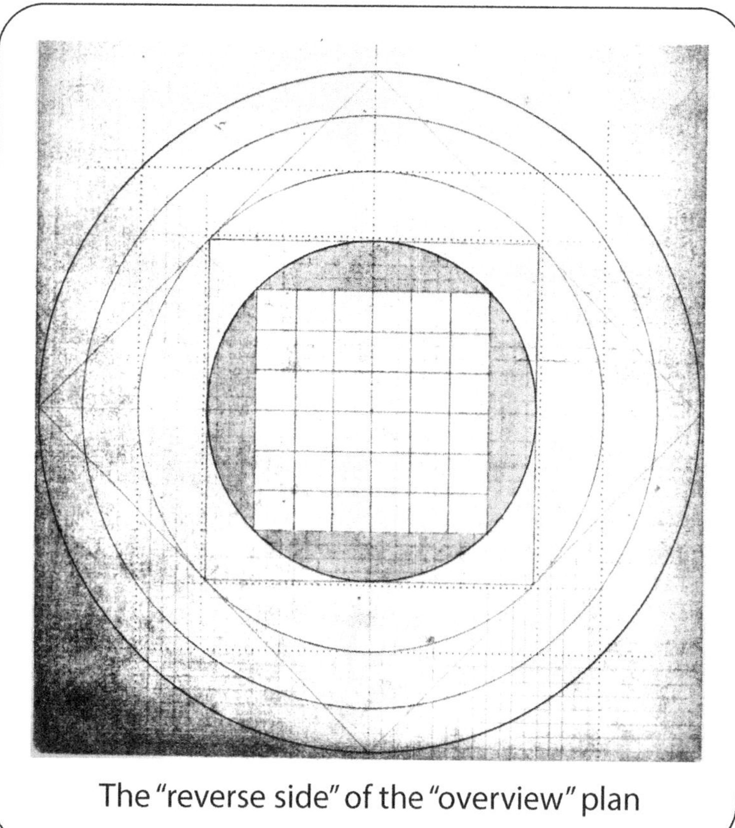

The "reverse side" of the "overview" plan

2 *The "close-up" plan*

The "close-up" plan shows just central area of the Globe and provides what I call the "design seed" for the "overview" plan.

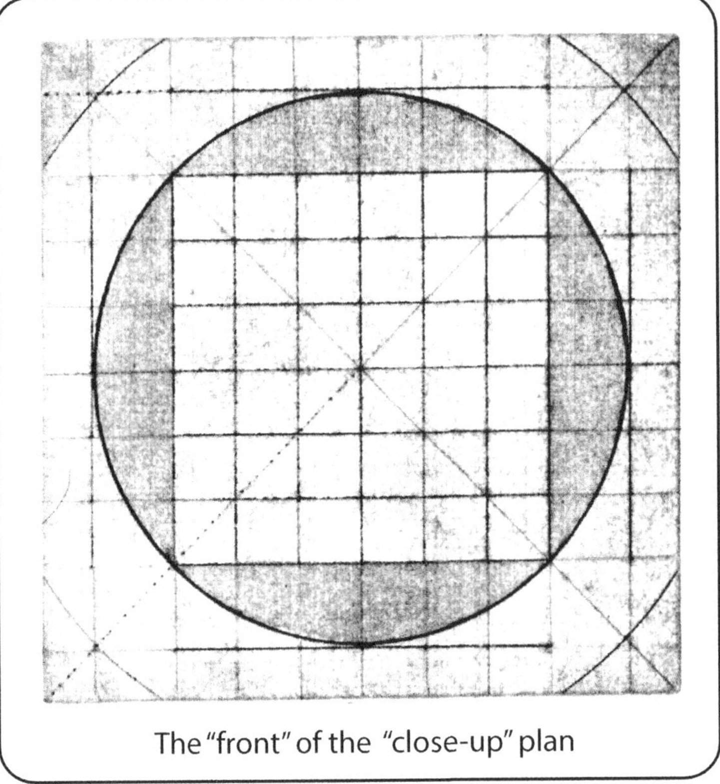

The "front" of the "close-up" plan

On the "reverse" side of the "close-up" plan are 6 concentric circles. Strangely, there are no squares or octagons.

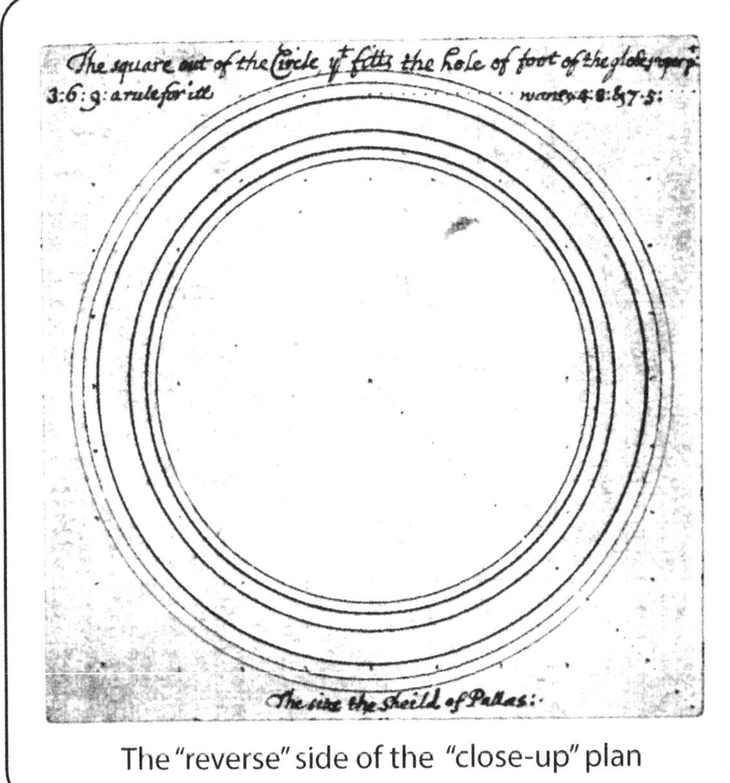

The "reverse" side of the "close-up" plan

3 The "parametric" plan

The "parametric" plan combines an "overview" plan with a "side-view" plan, indicating the heights of various features.

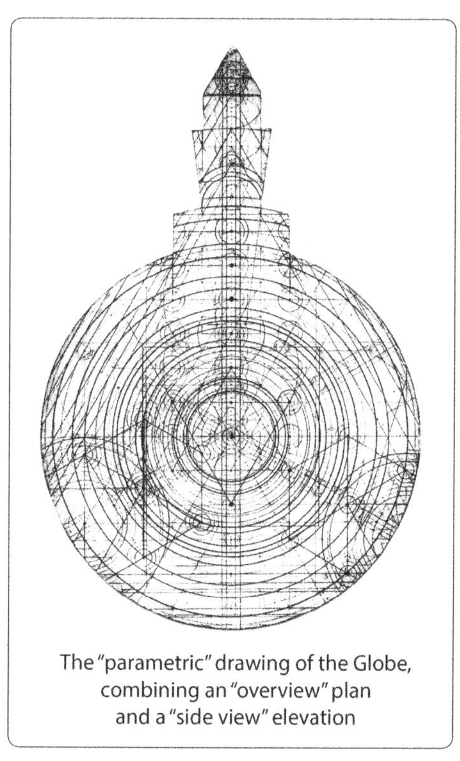

The "parametric" drawing of the Globe, combining an "overview" plan and a "side view" elevation

4 The "Tiring House" plan

The "Tiring House" plan is an overview of the first floor of the "backstage" rooms, where the actors got dressed and props were stored.

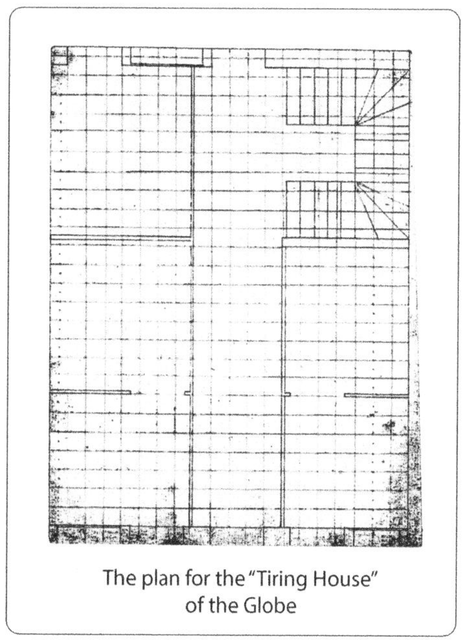

The plan for the "Tiring House" of the Globe

Warning: There will be a Magical Mystery Detour

In this book, we'll first investigate the underlying geometry of the "overview" plan and the "close-up" plan of the Globe theater.

Then we'll go on a short ***vacation*** (or "go on holiday," as the Brits say). It's more like what the Beatles called a "Magical Mystery Tour," a trip that will take us many places, far from the Globe theatre in London. We'll decode a cryptic book that has remained undeciphered for 450 years. We'll visit a building in America, which I consider to be a "sister" of the Globe Theater. We'll learn about "Nature's Operating System" from Buckminster Fuller, one of the greatest geometers in the 1900s. And will learn from Pythagoras (ca. 525 BC) and Nicomachus (ca. 125 AD) about "The Greatest and Most Perfect Harmony."

Refreshed from our "Sacred Geometry Vacation," we'll apply what we have learned to the four Globe theater drawings.

So, hang on for a rollicking adventure through shape and number. But don't feel intimidated. The math and geometry involved is so simple a sixth grader could understand it. All it takes is an open mind.

The "front" side of the "overview" diagram consists of:

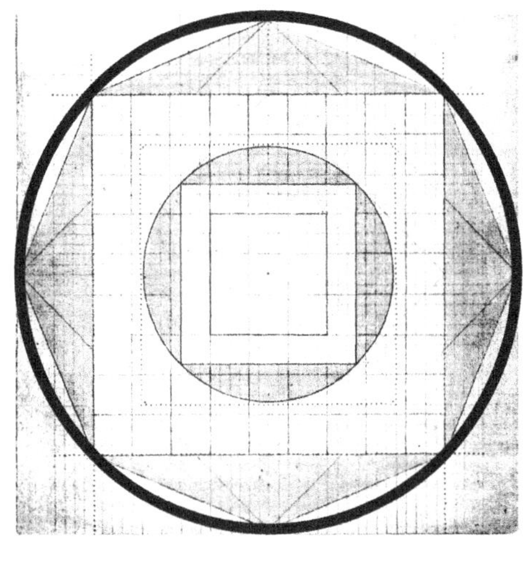

1 The outermost circle, about 102 units in diameter

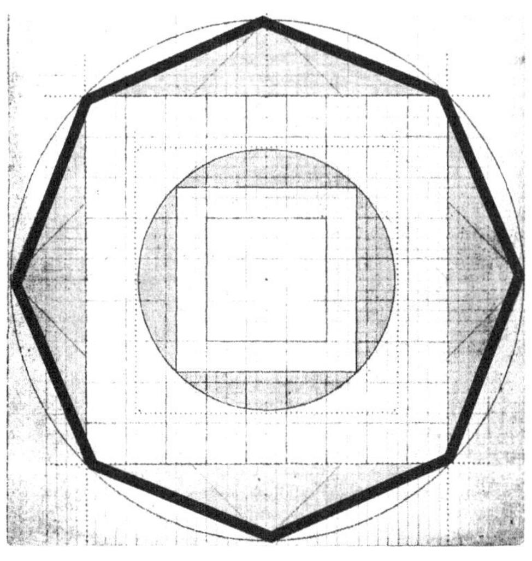

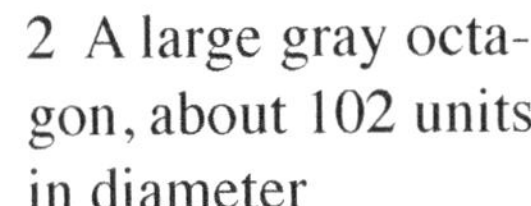

2 A large gray octagon, about 102 units in diameter

3 A large white square which is 72 by 72 units square

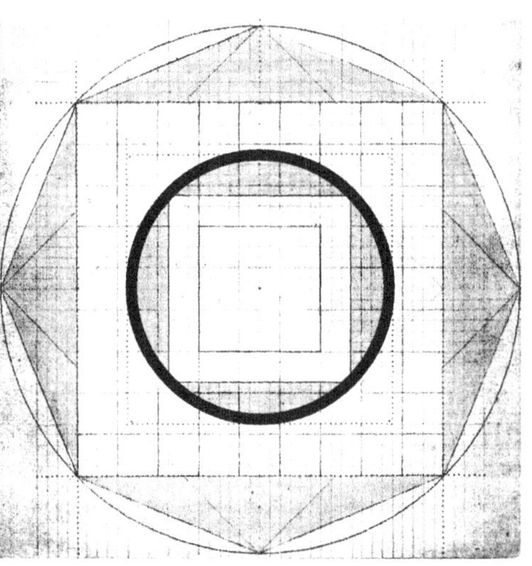

4 A small gray circle, about 51 units in diameter

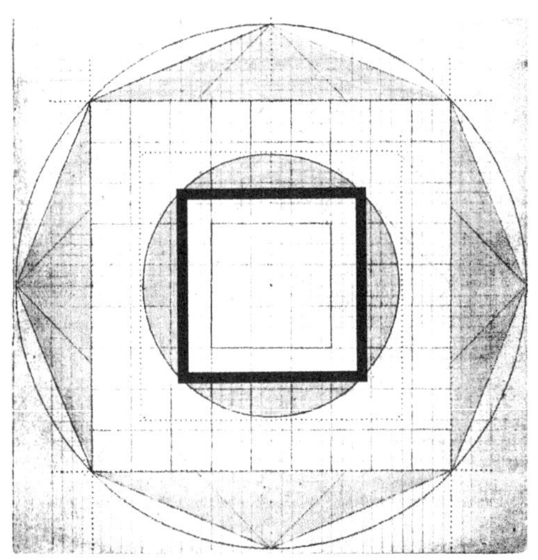

5 A small white square which is 36 by 36 units square

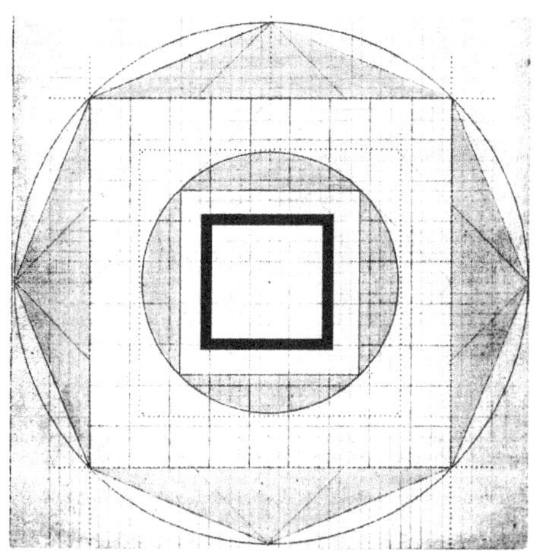

6 A very, small 24 by 24 unit square, within the small white square.

7 A faint-lined, large diamond shape. Its four corner points, plus the four corner points of the large, white 72 by 72 square all "point" to the eight corners of the octagon

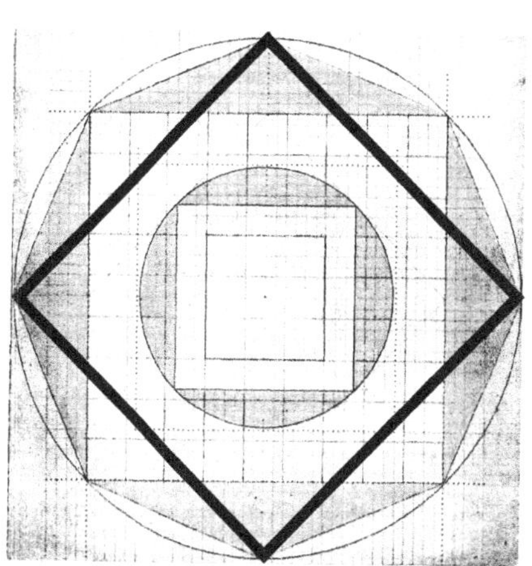

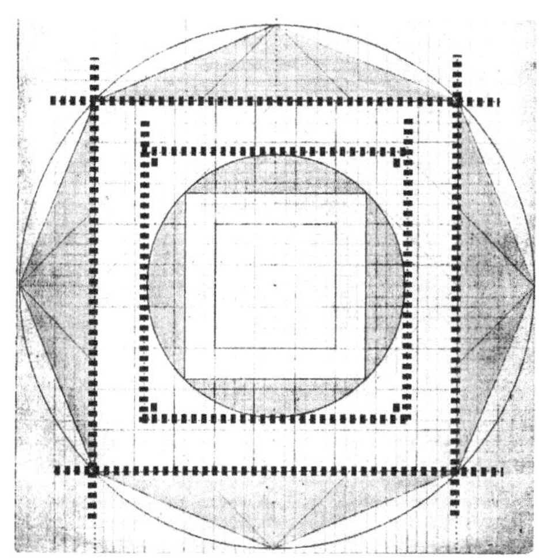

8 And finally, the pin-pricks. Though they visually connect to look like a dotted line, the pin-pricks are the "measuring tool" to indicate dimensions. (They're like built-in rulers.)

As the pinpricks pierce the card, the same measurements apply to both the front and the back of the card.

Pinprick clues

Inspect the pin-pricks that coincide with
the edges of the large white square.
They extend beyond the corners,
looking like printers' registration marks.

The large, white square is 72 units tall by 72 units wide.
Thus, its area is 5184 square units.
Why 72? Why not 70 or 75?
Or why not just make the drawing larger and use 100?

Joy Hancox found so many references to 72 in the Byrom Collection drawings, she calls it "**the rule of 72**."

Why 72?

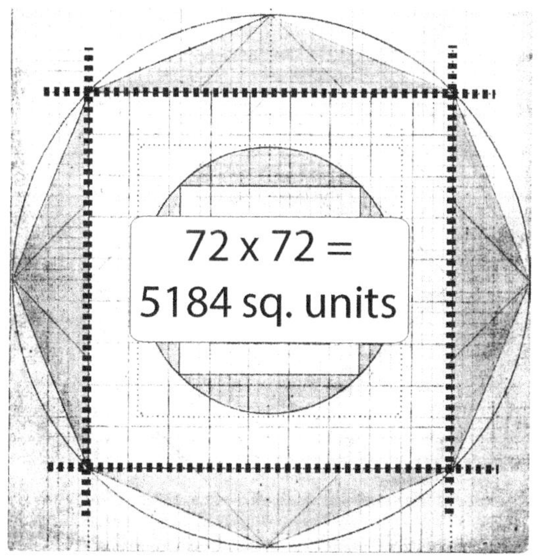

(The short answer is: It's a Metamorphosis number.
We'll explore the Metamorphosis sequence on our upcoming journey.)

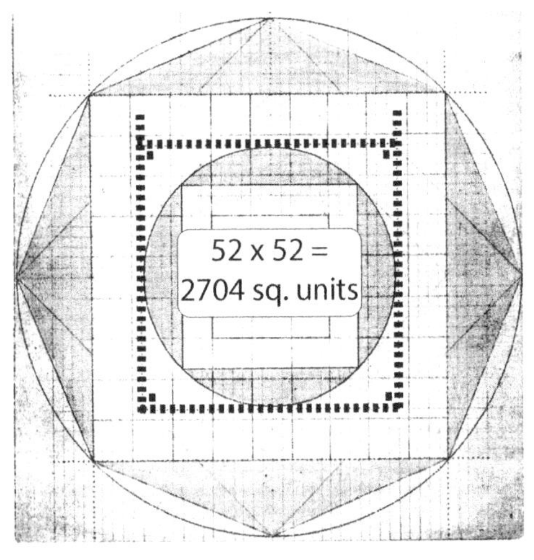

Further inward, four other lines of pinpricks form a "dotted line" square, which is 52 units tall by 52 units wide. Thus, its area is 2704 square units.

One might suspect that this 52 x 52 square is "half the area" of the 72 x 72 square.

But it's not.
Doubling 2704 results in 5408, not 5184.

Something else is peculiar. Why isn't the small gray circle tangent to the 52 x 52 pin-prick line? It's not because of "sloppiness." The small gray circle is clearly "shy of the dotted-line" by the same amount north, south, east, and west. The circle seems as though it fits in a square 51 x 51 units wide, not 52 by 52.

There's another curious detail. Just inside each of the corners of the 52 x 52 dotted line is a single pin-prick. Notice that it seems to mark where the "faint-lined" large diamond clips off the corners of the pin-prick square.

What's going on here?

Well, the "reverse" side of the card provides some clarifying clues.

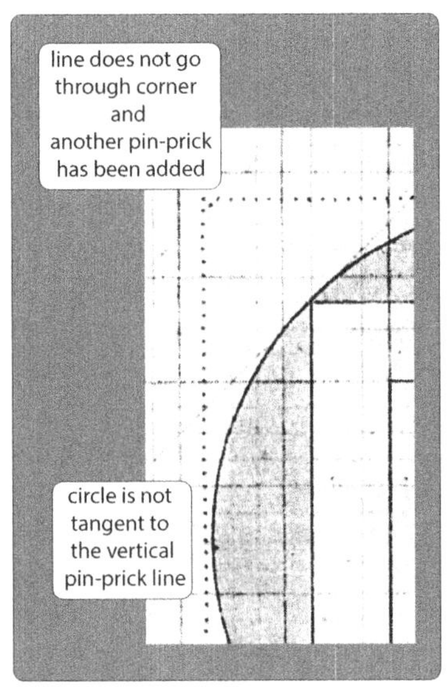

The "reverse" side of the "overview" plan consists of:

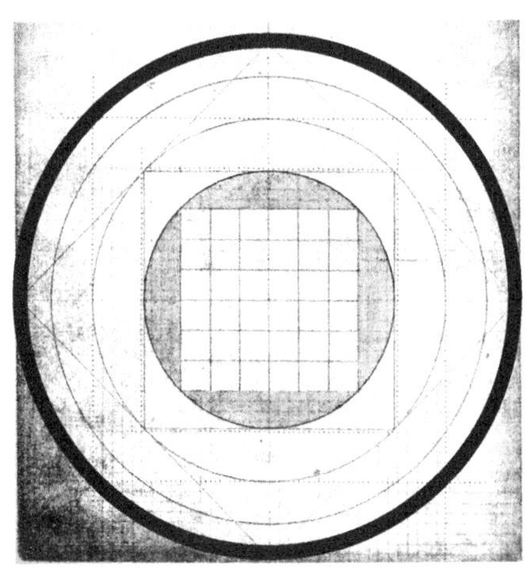

1 An outermost circle about 102 units in diameter.

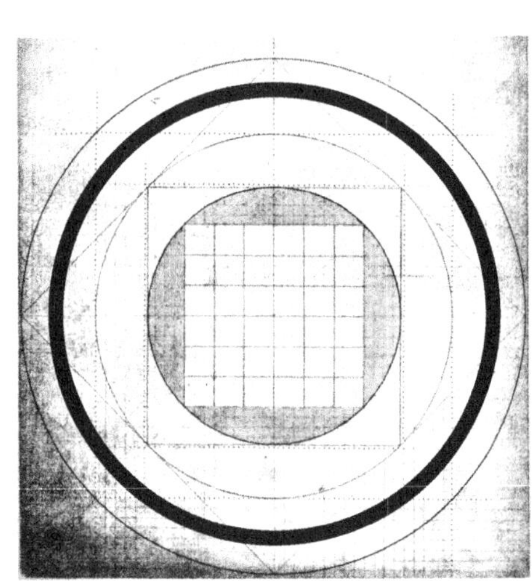

2 A circle about 88 units in diameter.

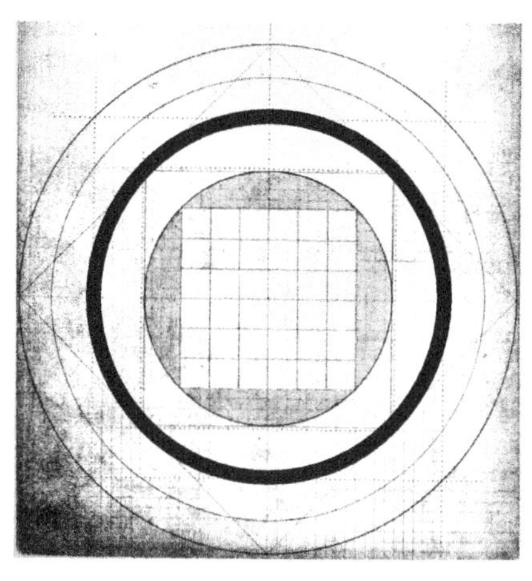

3 A circle about 72 units in diameter.

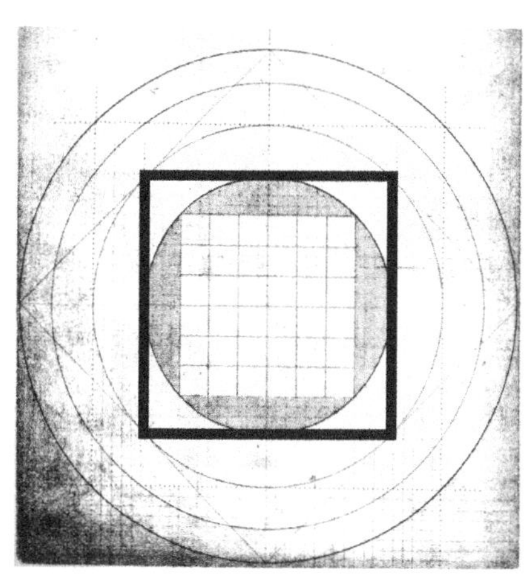

4 An approximately 51 unit by 51 unit square

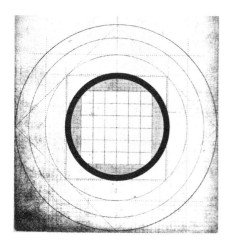

5 A gray-filled circle about 72 units in diameter.

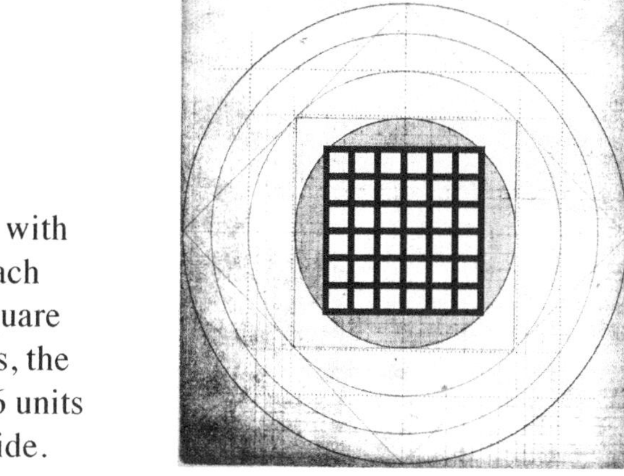

6 A white square with a 6 x 6 grid. As each individual grid square is 6 units x 6 units, the white square is 36 units tall by 36 units wide.

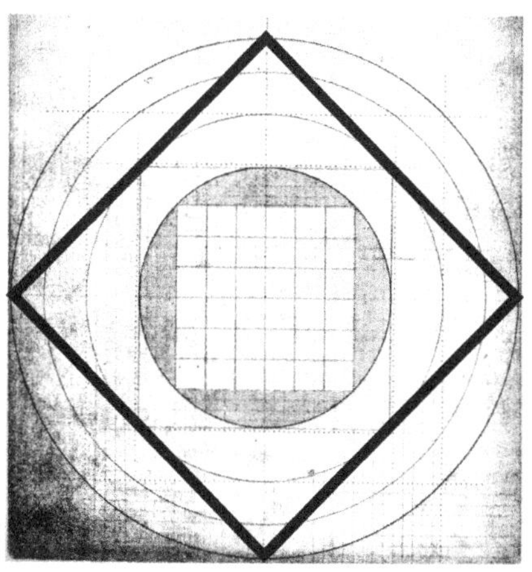

7 There's also a single "diamond" shape which points north, south, east, and west. Notice that this diamond intersects the corners of the square which circumscribes the gray circle.

Again the question arises: Why didn't the illustrator simply reduce the 52 x 52 square of pinpricks so that it coincided with the 51 x 51 square in the first place?

The answer has to do with geometry and arithmetic. It's simple math.

(Don't worry, there will be no quiz. And I'll summarize all the calculations.)

Here's how inscribed squares and inscribed circles interrelate (in terms of percentages):

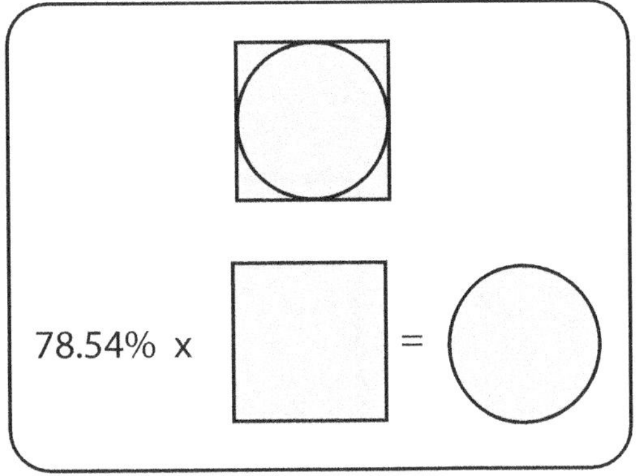

To find the area of a square inscribed in a circle, multiply the area of the circle by 78.54%.

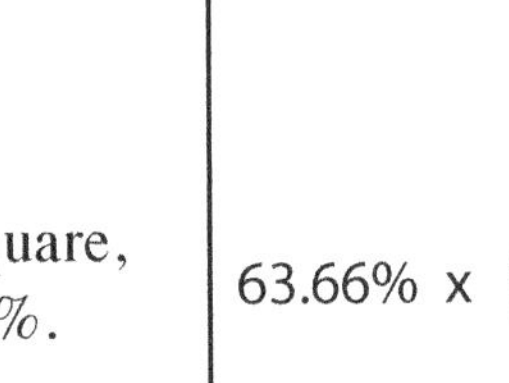

To find the area of a circle inscribed in a square, multiply the area of the square by 63.66%.

(For you mathematicians, $\pi/4 = .7854$
And $2/\pi = .6366$)

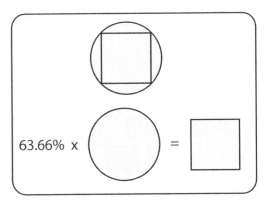

When you alternate inscribed circle and inscribed squares, something interesting happens.

(Hint from Macbeth: "Double, double toil and trouble; Fire burn, and caldron bubble.")

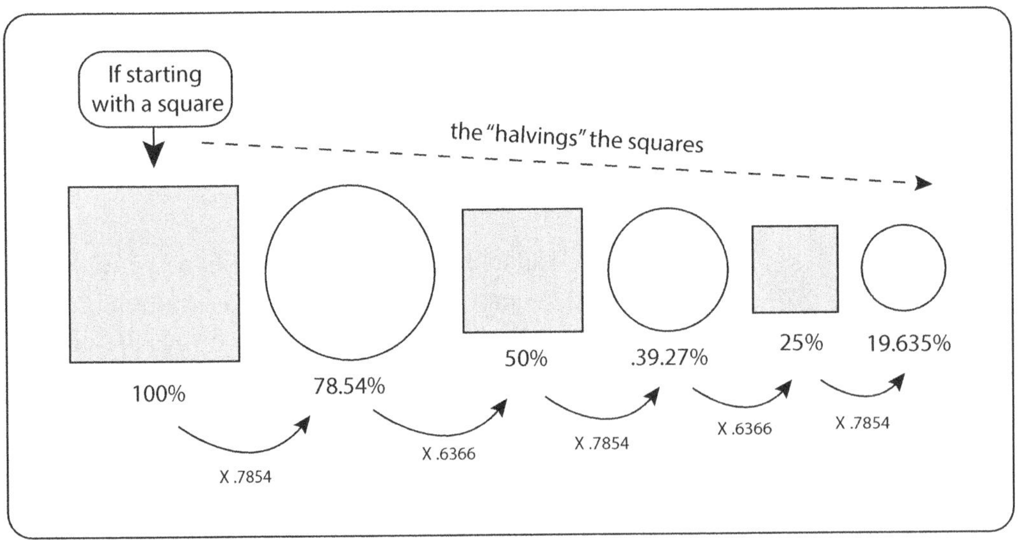

Starting from a square which we'll call 100%, let's apply these percentages (78.54% and 63.66%).

Look what happens!

The squares follow a "halving" pattern.

And the circles follow a "halving" pattern.

That's pretty cool!

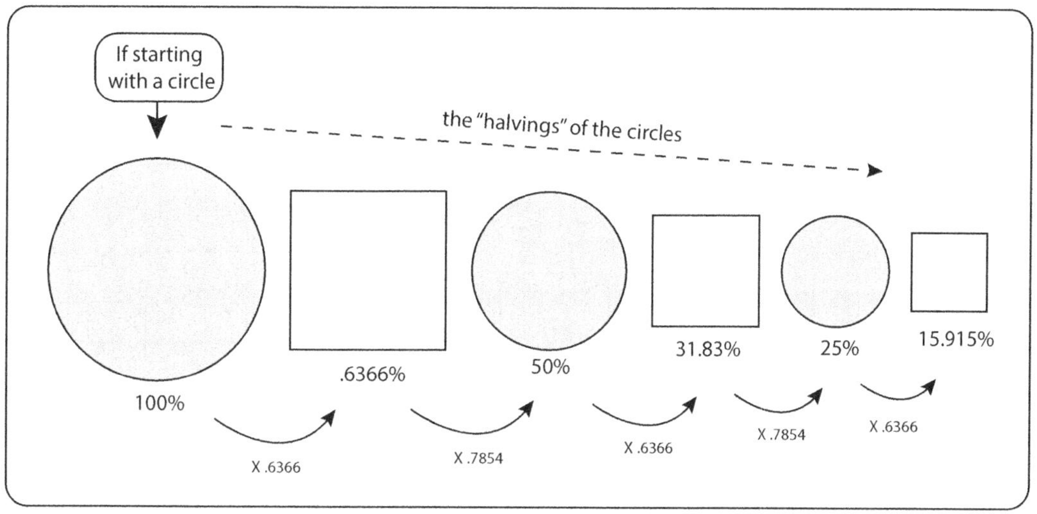

When we apply these percentages (63.66% and 78.54%)
starting from a "100% circle," it follows a "halving" pattern.

That's double cool!

Interrelationships of the various areas of the squares and circles

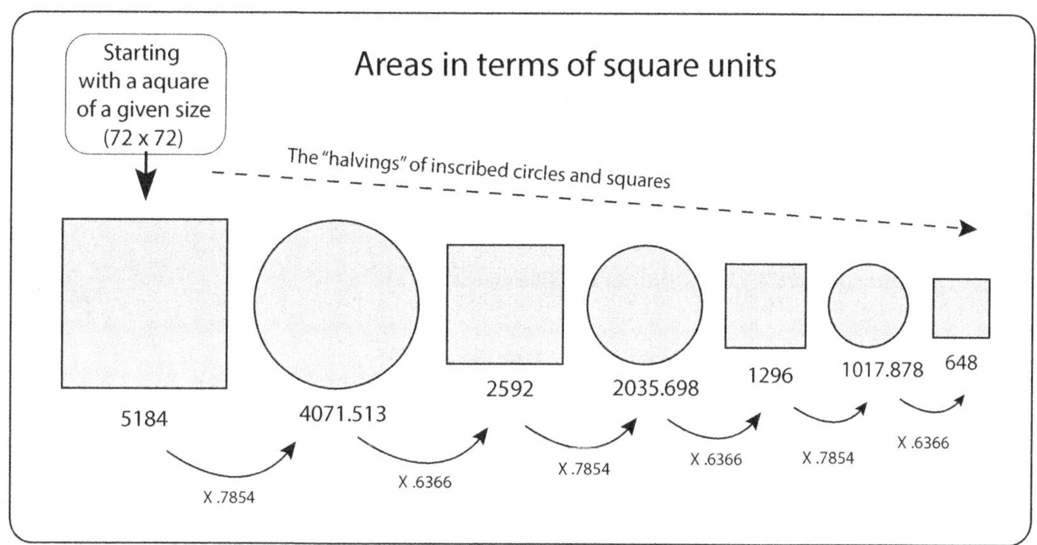

Now let's apply these percentages to the known size:
the 72 unit x 72 unit outer square.

The "halfings" are more obvious in the progression of
the squares because the results are whole numbers.

(The areas of the circles are calculated using π, which is an
irrational number. Thus, all the results are irrational numbers,
which I have truncated to three digits after the decimal point.)

Interrelationships of the various "diameters and diagonals"

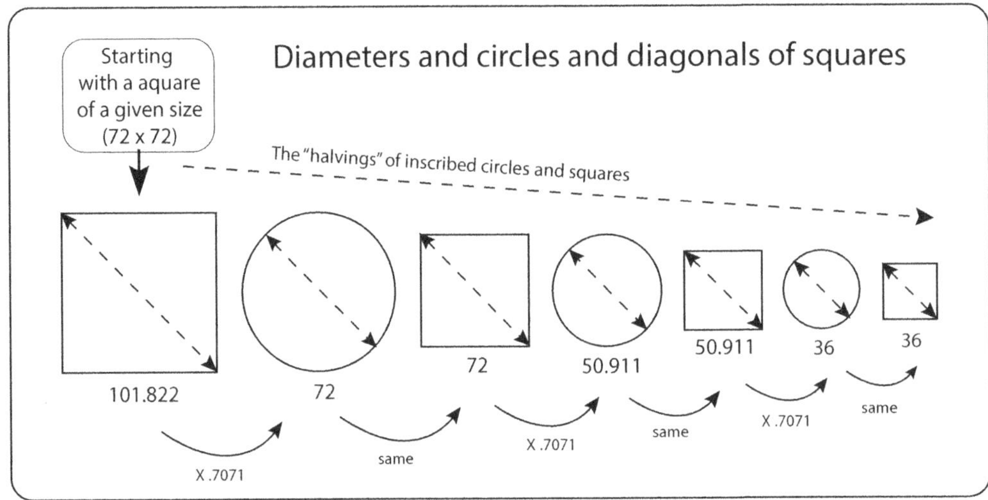

Let's look at the progression in terms of the "diameters" of the circles and the "diagonals"of the squares.

First, the 72 x 72 square has diagonal of 101.822 square units. Next, the circle inscribed in the 72 x 72 square has a radius of 72. The reason its inscribed circle is 72 units, can be easily seen if we choose a horizontal (or vertical) diameter for the circle. (Mathematically, √2/2=.7071, and 70.71% of 101.822 is 72)

Next, the square inscribed in that circle has a "diagonal" of 72 because the corners of the inscribed square touch the circle.

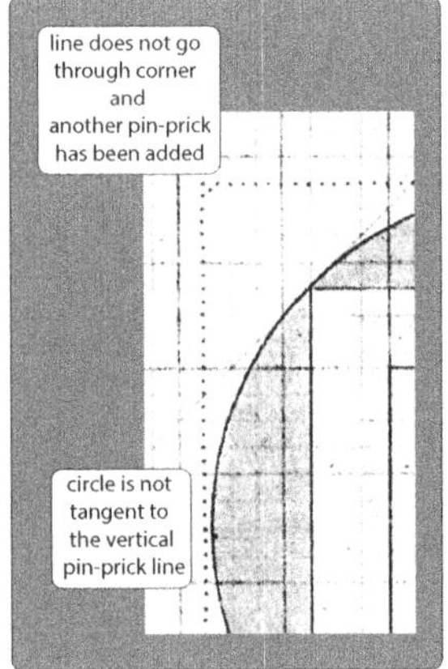

Continuing inward, the next inscribed circle, and its inscribed square have a diagonal (or diameter) of 50.911.

This is why the drawing's gray circle curiously was smaller than the 52 x 52 square of pinpricks.

It's also the reason for that extra point just inside the four corners of the 52 x 52 dotted-line square of pinpricks.

This 50.911 x 50.911 square is easier to see on the "reverse" side of the drawing. If the diagonal of a square is 50.911, the sides of that square will be 36 x 36 units. (36 x√2 = 50.911)

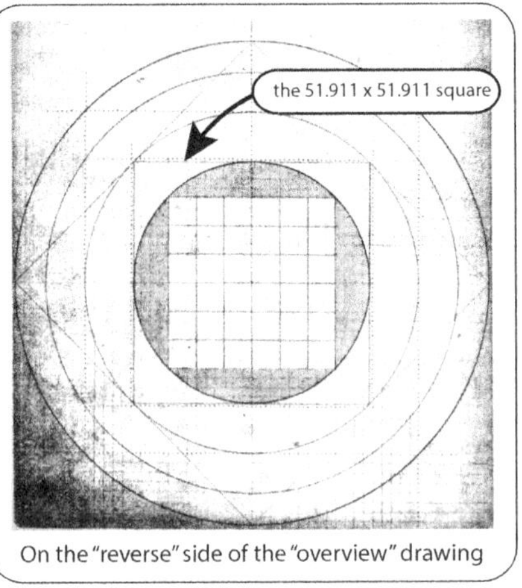

On the "reverse" side of the "overview" drawing

Next inwards, are an inscribed circle and an inscribed square with a diameter (or diagonal) of 36.

And finally, there's an inscribed circle and an inscribed square with a diameter (or diagonal) of 25.445.

Interrelationships of the various "radii and half diagonals"

Finally, here's a look at the progression in terms of "radii" of the circle and the "half-diagonals" of the squares.

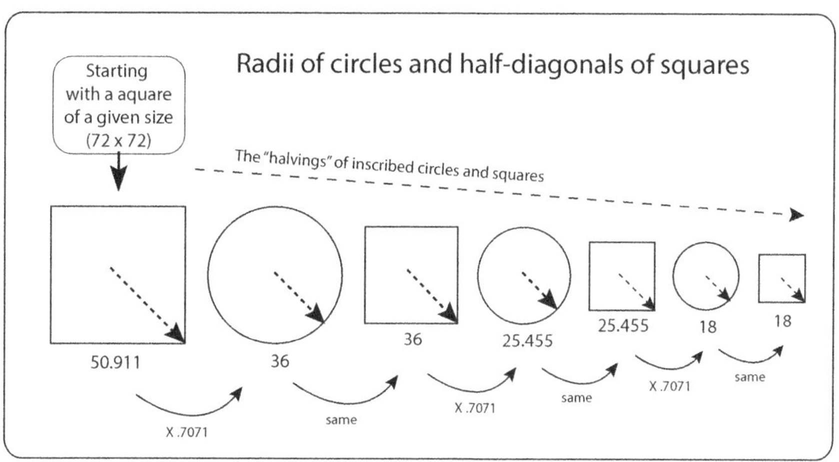

Summary

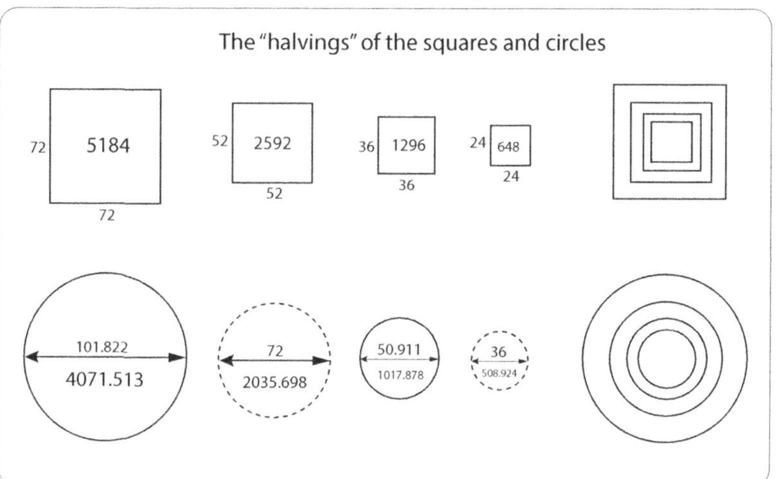

In short, the "overall" plan is alternating "halvings" of circles and squares.

If we start from the center and go outwards, the diagram displays alternating "doublings" of circles and squares.

(I actually prefer to call this rhythm as "doublings," as it connotes growth, whereas "halvings" implies reduction.)

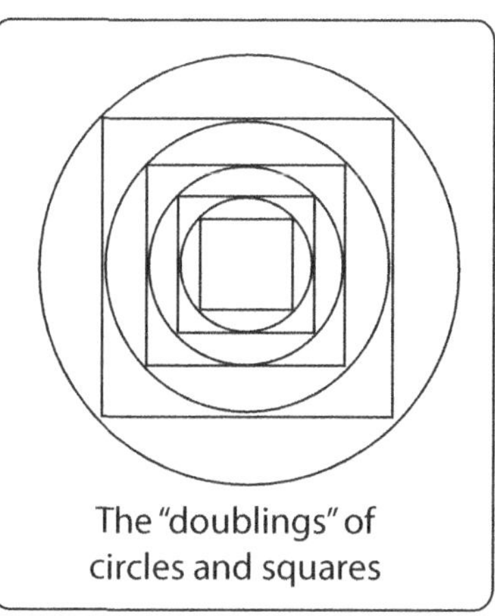
The "doublings" of circles and squares

Here are all the "doublings" of the circles and squares superimposed.

And here they are with a little tone to make it more graphic (and hypnotic).

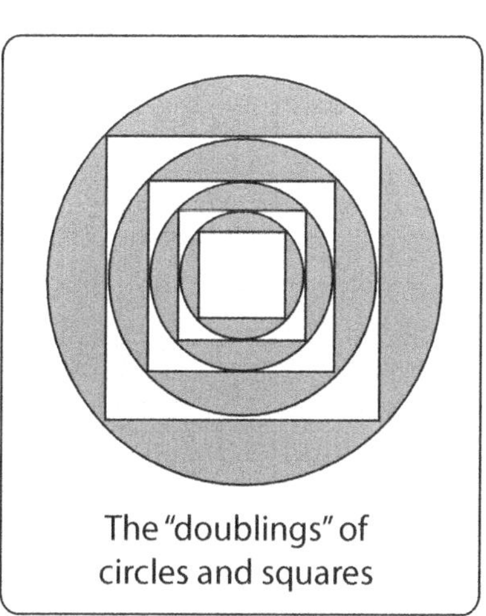
The "doublings" of circles and squares

But wait, there's more!

As the pointy stellations of the octagon touch the outer circle, there's also a progression of the "doublings" of the **octagons**.

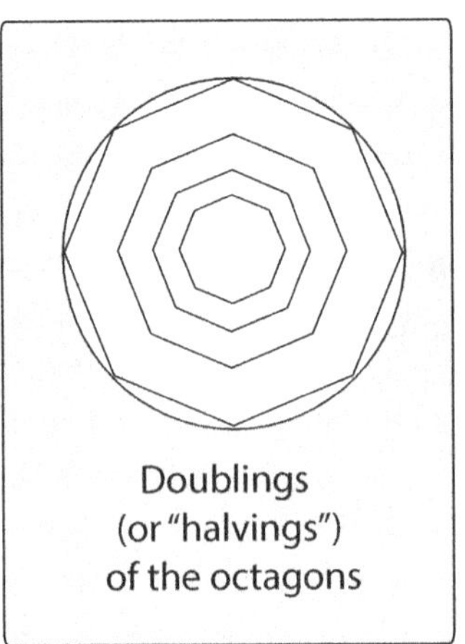

Doublings (or "halvings") of the octagons

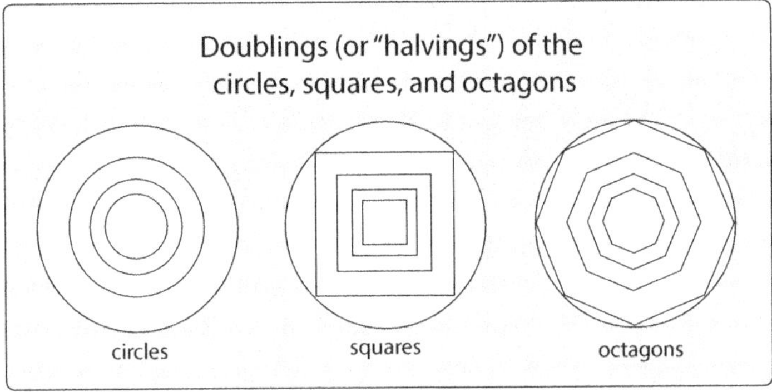

Doublings (or "halvings") of the circles, squares, and octagons

Here are the "doublings" isolated from each other.

Here they are in pairs.

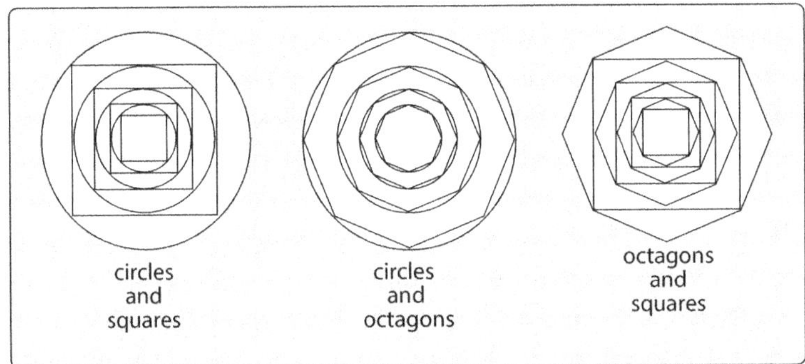

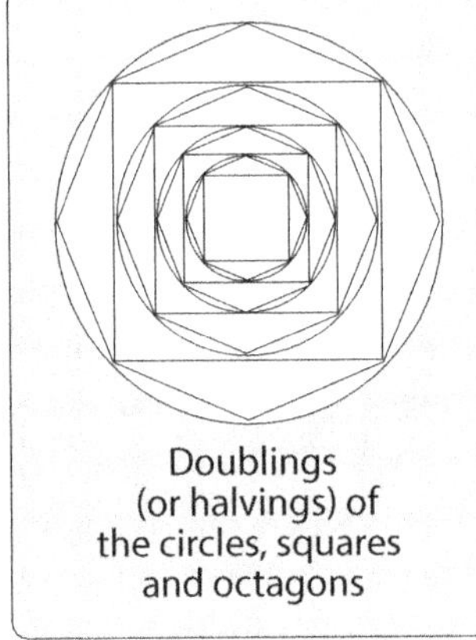

Doublings (or halvings) of the circles, squares and octagons

And here they are all together.

Adding a little tone, it looks like a blossoming flower.

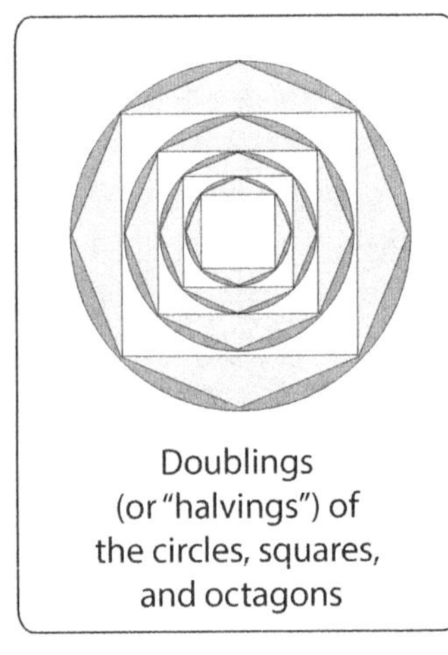

Doublings (or "halvings") of the circles, squares, and octagons

This is all pretty exciting, but what does it mean?

The front of the "close-up" plan

To find out, we must investigate the diagram that Joy Hancox determined was the plan for the Starr's Mall or the central open-air section of the Globe Theater.

I call it the "close-up" plan.

The front side looks like a bull's-eye target centered on a checkerboard.

Let's examine the parts by starting in the center and working our way outwards.

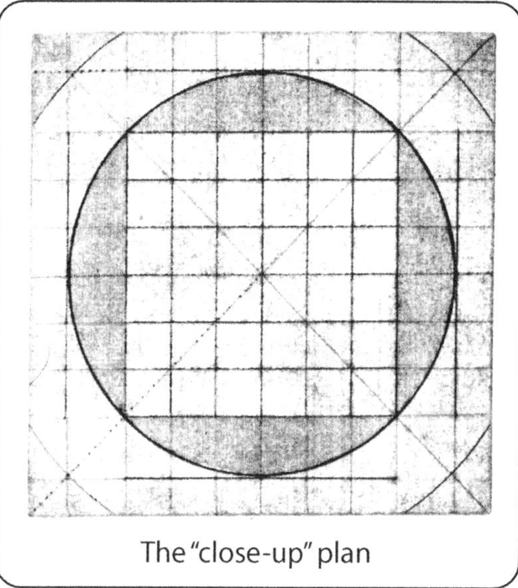

The "close-up" plan

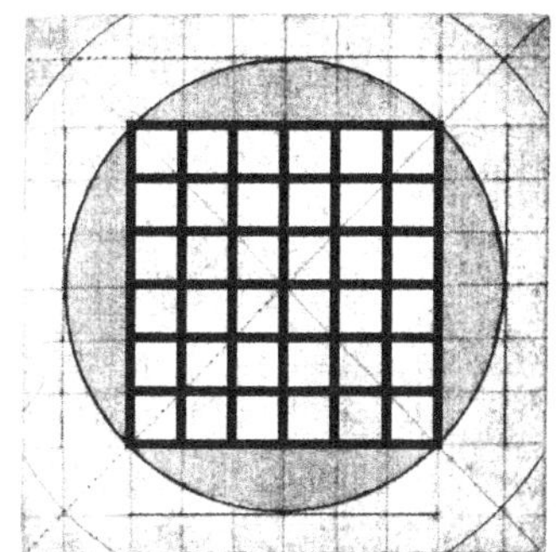

1 A white square with a 6 by 6 grid.

2 A gray circle circumscribed around that square.

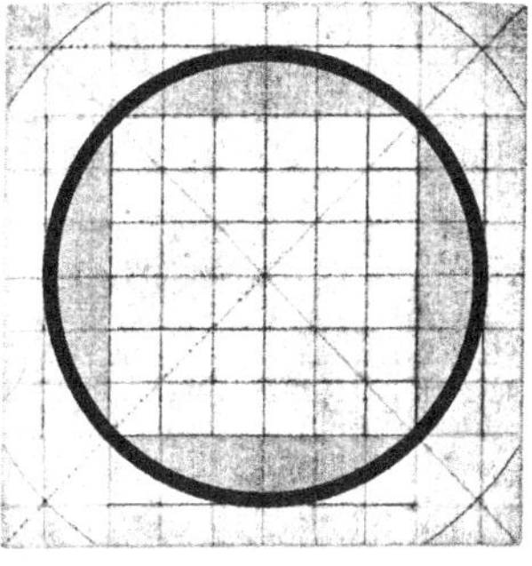

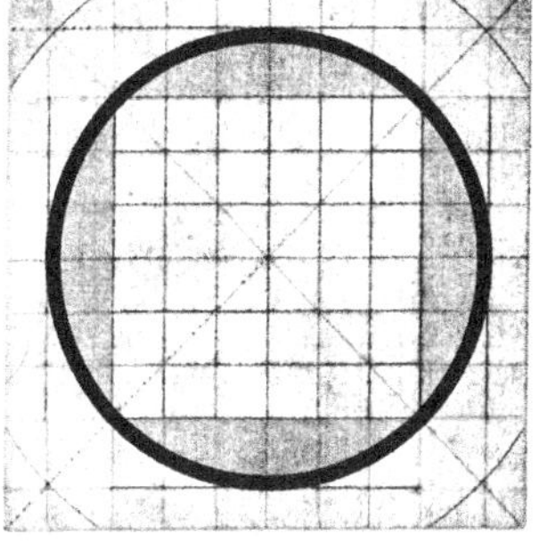

3 An outer circle, so big that it runs off the page.

4 A giant X that is made from the two diagonals of the square drawing.

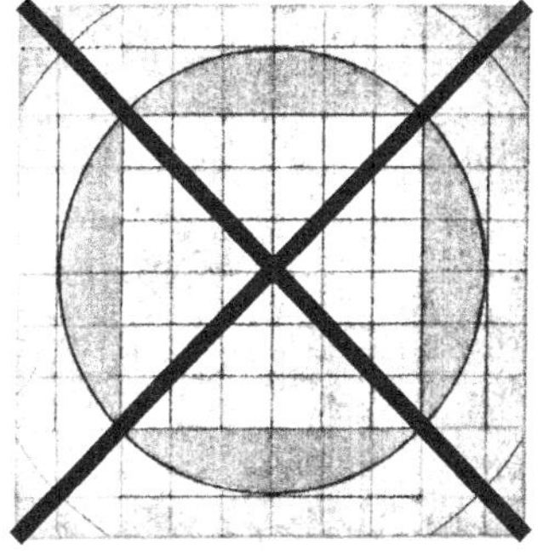

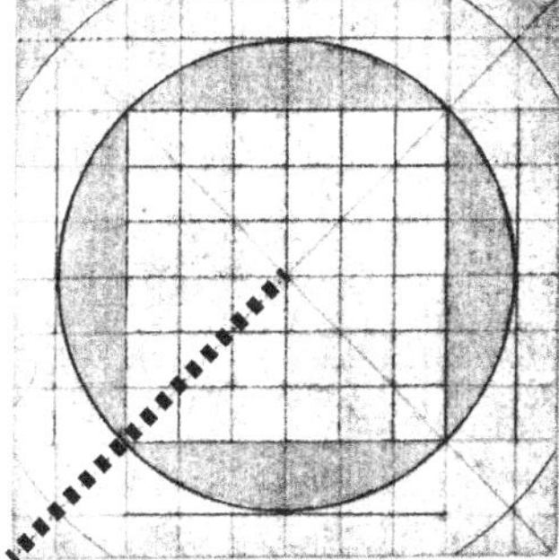

5 The lower left leg of the giant X has a pin-prick "measuring ruler."

6 There are also pinpricks along the upper left side of a partially drawn square, which circumscribes the gray circle.

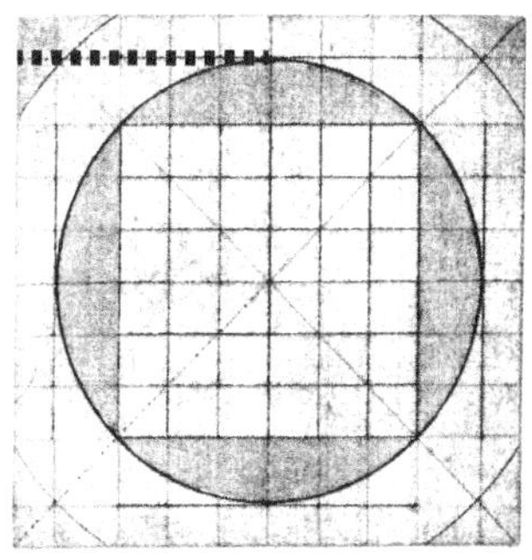

The reverse side of the "close-up" plan

The "back" side of the illustration has **no squares** at all!

There are simply **six concentric circles,** radiating in what seems to be a random fashion.

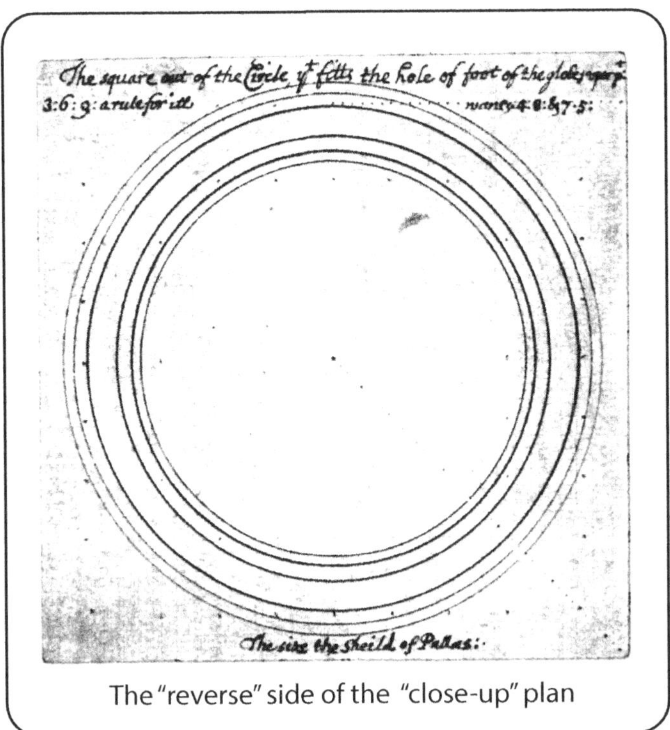

The "reverse" side of the "close-up" plan

The handwriting across the top reads:

"The square out of the Circle, yt fitts the whole of globe's uper pt. 3:6:9: a rule for itt.................................... varies 4:8: & 7·5:"

And along the bottom is written:

"The size the Sheild of Pallas:·"

This is a curious jumble of geometry, instructions, and numbers. What does it have to do with a shield named after a Greek goddess?

Well, I'll give you a hint. The caption and drawings coalesce into one brilliant geometrical riddle.

But you'll never solve it in less you first understand the mathematical cosmology of the person who drew the illustrations and wrote the words.

This is why, in a moment, we're going to take a little vacation and later return, equipped with the tools to solve these geometric riddles.

Bottom Line: I believe John Dee designed the original Globe theater

My conjectured illustration of John Dee designing the four plans for the Globe theater

The purpose of this book is to explore more deeply the geometry involved in these specific drawings and to provide support for Joy Hancox's conclusion that these drawings of the Globe Theater were created by John Dee:

I've been studying John Dee for over 20 years and have written 12 books on his mathematical, scientific, and philosophical works.

Title page of John Dee's 1558 *Propaedeumata Aphoristica* (*Preparatory Aphorisms*)

I've translated and substantially decoded several of his books, which were written in Latin: his 1558 *Propaedeumata Aphoristica* (*Preparatory Aphorisms*) and his 1564 *Monas Hieroglyphica* (*Sacred Symbol of Oneness*).

I have transliterated from Elizabethan English Dee's 1570 Preface to Euclid's *Elements*, and his 1594 *Discourse Apologetical.*

Title page of John Dee's 1564 *Monas Hieroglyphica* (*Sacred Symbol of Oneness*)

Some great books about John Dee

John Dee
1528-1608

The best biographies of Dee are:
The Queen's Conjurer, by Benjamin Woolley, (New York, Henry Holt, 2001)

The Arch Conjurer of England: John Dee, by Glyn Parry, (New Haven and London, Yale University Press, 2011)

The best book on Dee's philosophy is:

John Dee's Natural Philosophy: Between Science and Religion, by Nicholas H. Clullee, (London and New York, Routledge, 1988)

The best book on Dee's writings is John Dee: *The Politics of Reading and Writing in the English Renaissance*, by William H. Sherman, (Amherst, University of Massachusetts, 1995)

An excellent compilation of excerpts from Dee's writings is:
John Dee: Essential Readings, by Gerald Suster, (London, Crucible, 1986)

To really understand Dee, read his diaries:
The Diaries of John Dee, edited by Edward Fenton, (Oxfordshire, Day Books, 2000)

Queen Elizabeth I called John Dee "my philosopher"

John Dee performing an experiment before Queen Elizabeth I, by Henry Gillard Glindoni, (ca. 1880 original at the Wellcome Library, London)

John Dee was an English polymath who lived from 1528 to 1608, through the tumultuous reigns of Henry VIII, Edward VI, Mary I, and Queen Elizabeth I.

In 1558, Dee was asked by Elizabeth to determine the most propitious date for her coronation, which he did: January 15, 1559. Elizabeth called on Dee quite frequently to help her decide important matters of state and referred to John Dee as "my philosopher."

John Dee Tower of 1583

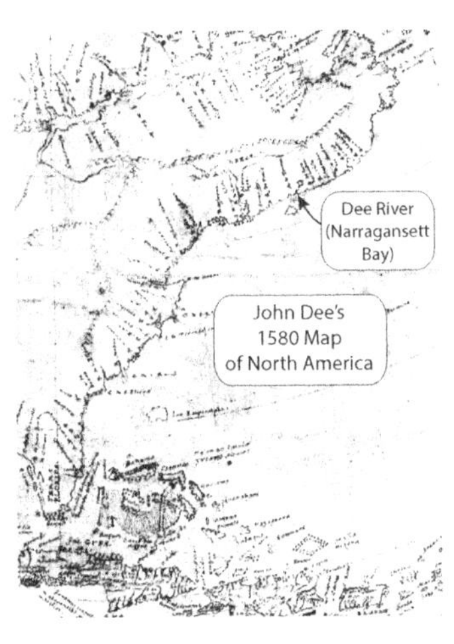

My own interest in John Dee started when I found that Narragansett Bay, in Rhode Island (where I live) was called the "Dee River and port" in the year 1583.

Yes, that's 37 years before the Pilgrims of 1620. It's hard to believe, but it's written in a deed in the Elizabethan State Papers and has been written about by David Beers Quinn and Samuel Eliot Morison, two of the most noted authorities on the Elizabethan exploration of the New World. Dee even drew the bay in his 1580 Map of North America.

The 28-foot-tall stone-and-mortar Tower that still stands in Touro Park, in Newport, Rhode Island

The thrust of my research is that I believe John Dee designed a circular building to be the city-center for this first Elizabethan colony in the New World.

The building got built, but the colony ultimately failed. However, what's amazing is that the building still stands today!

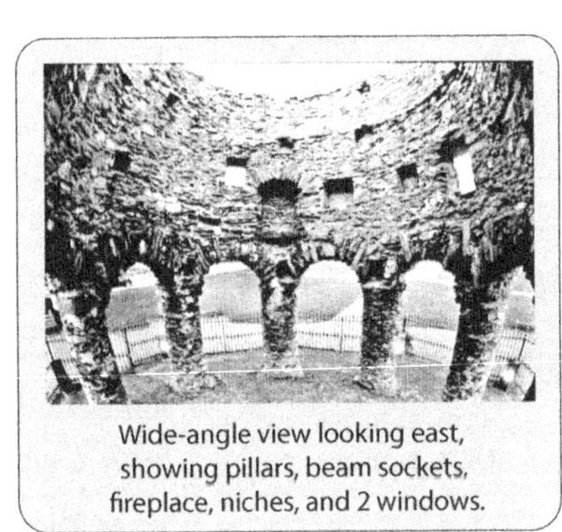
Wide-angle view looking east, showing pillars, beam sockets, fireplace, niches, and 2 windows.

At the base of the Tower are eight sturdy (3 foot in diameter) pillars supporting eight semicircular arches.

Above that rises a cylinder about 24 feet in diameter. Inside you can see numerous beam sockets, windows, niches, and even a fireplace with two flues.

In short, the Tower is an octagon down below, and a circle above.

The 28-foot tall stone and mortar tower that stands in Touro Park today once had a panoramic view of Newport Harbor and the mouth of Narragansett Bay. Historians can't agree on who built it. Over the years there have been five other main theories:

1 A Round Church built by the Vikings around 1150 AD
2 A pagoda-lighthouse built by the Chinese in 1421
3 A temple built by the Templars in 1398
4 A watchtower built by the Portuguese in 1501
5 A windmill built by the first governor of Rhode Island, who owned the Tower in 1667

Title page of John Dee's 1577 *General and Rare Memorials to the Perfect Art of Navigation*

I think all those theories are incorrect. I think the Tower was designed to be the city-center of the first Elizabeth Colony in the New World.

In 1570, Dee had written eight books entitled *General and Rare Memorials to the Perfect Art of Navigation.*

In one book, Dee declares Queen Elizabeth has a legal right to all of North America (except for Florida which the Spanish occupied) based on earlier claims by King Arthur, Prince Madoc, and John and Sebastian Cabot. In another book, Dee coins the term "British Empire," which later grew to be the largest empire the world has ever known.

In 1583, Sir Humphrey Gilbert and his 5-ship, 260-man expedition set out to colonize the Dee River. Unfortunately. Sir Humphrey died on the mission, and since the letters patent to North America were in his name only, they became void. The colony failed to take root.

But a year earlier, in 1582, an 80-man expedition led by preliminary expedition led by Anthony Brigham came to the New World, stayed here for nine months, and I claim built the tower to be ready for Sir Humphrey when he arrived.

John Dee was the cartographical, navigational, and legal mastermind behind this whole effort and I believe he was also the architect of what I call the John Dee Tower of 1583.

(Dee himself never crossed the Atlantic, but would have provided precise blueprints and probably a scale model of the Tower.)

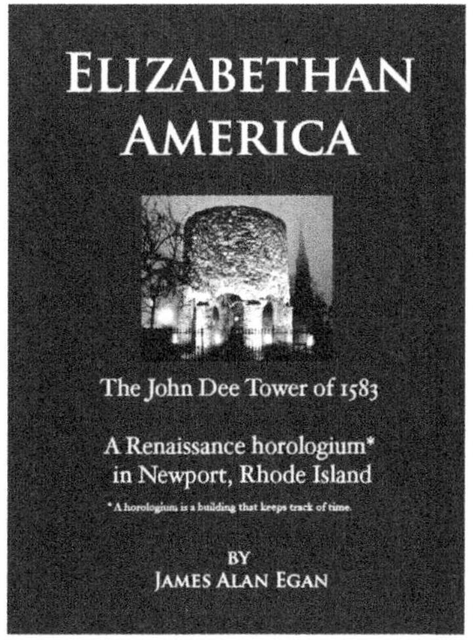

I've written all about the 1583 colonization effort in my book, Elizabethan America, so I won't go into all the details of the architecture, the expedition, and the cast of characters involved.

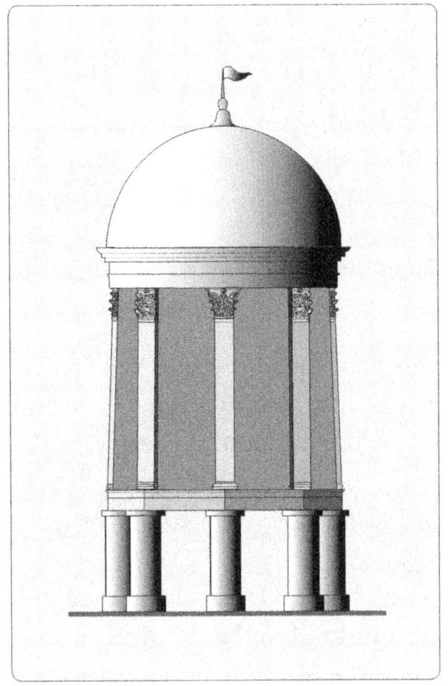

But I will show you a depiction of what I feel the building originally looked like.

I believe it stood 48 feet tall and had a gold dome topped by a 6-foot finial.

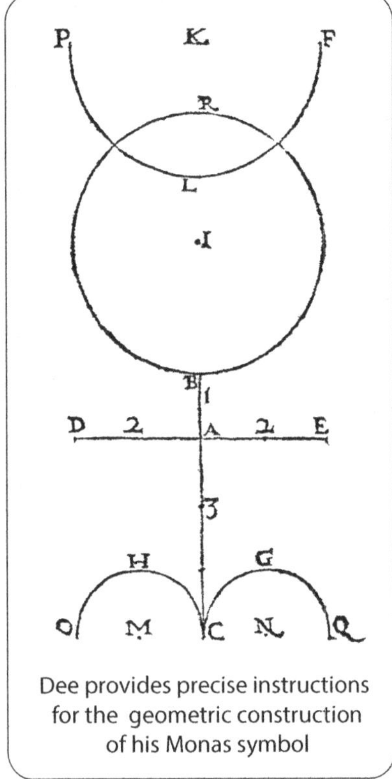

Dee provides precise instructions for the geometric construction of his Monas symbol

In 1564, Dee wrote his most cherished work, the *Monas Hieroglyphica,* dedicated to the Holy Roman Emperor Maximilian.

The book consists of 24 cryptic theorems, most of which analyze the "Monas symbol," a figure John Dee invented, which is comprised of four parts:

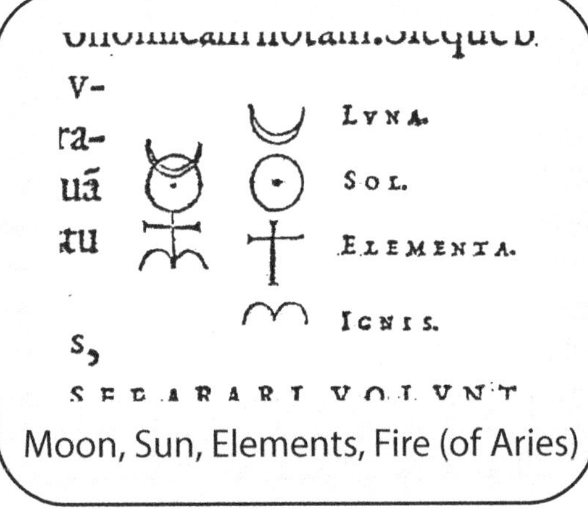

Moon, Sun, Elements, Fire (of Aries)

1 The Moon (a semicircle)
2 The Sun (a full circle)
3 The Cross of the Elements (Fire, Air, Water, and Earth)
4 The Sign of Aries (the zodiacal sign that starts on the Spring Equinox, March 21)

To summarize my thesis, I believe the John Dee Tower of 1583, was a city center, a church, and a horologium, a building that keeps track of time.

I think each of the 3 floors contained a "camera-obscura solar-disc calendar-room. These rooms were used by Italian astronomers to prove the Julian Calendar was 10 days out-of-sync from the sun, leading to the Gregorian Calendar Reform of 1853. In England, Dee wrote a 60-page treatise for the Queen recommending the reform of the English calendar.

Each floor of the Tower was a "camera obscura solar disc calendar room"

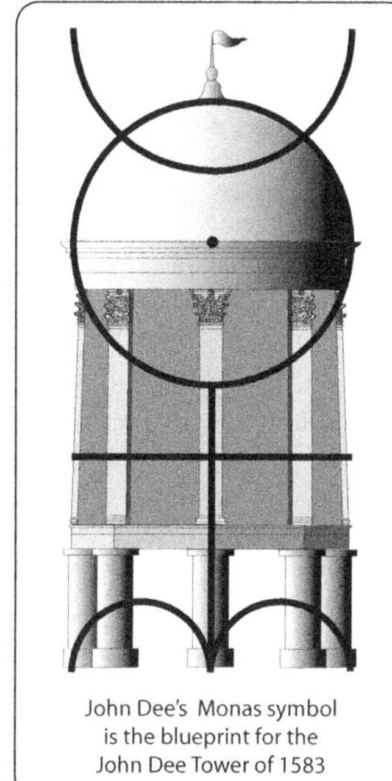

John Dee's Monas symbol is the blueprint for the John Dee Tower of 1583

And the punch line is this: The Monas symbol is the design "side-view" plan for the John Dee Tower of 1583.

And the text of the *Monas Hieroglyphica* cryptically explains the Tower's function, not just as a horologium, but also as a building which is proportioned using mathematical harmonies.

In short, what we see today is the skeleton of a classical Vitruvian circular temple, designed by John Dee to plant Christianity and his mathematical cosmology in the New World.

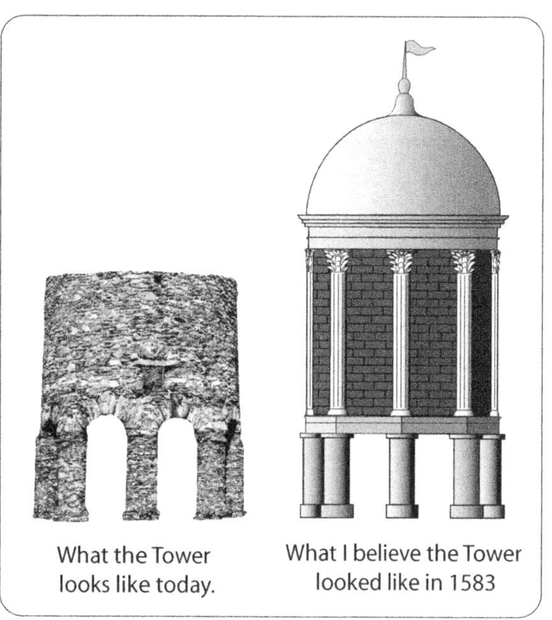

What the Tower looks like today. What I believe the Tower looked like in 1583

And Dee applied the same mathematical cosmology in his designs for the Globe theater. To me, the John Dee Tower and the Globe theater are "sisters." They were both born from the same father–John Dee.

Title page of John Dee's 1564 *Monas Hieroglyphica*

The Monas Hieroglyphica
(Dee's most cherished work)

The *Monas Hieroglyphica* (Sacred Symbol of Oneness) has puzzled scholars for centuries. Gerald Suster, in *John Dee, Essential Readings* writes:

"Certainly Dee regarded it as his masterpiece, the summary and crowning synthesis of all the knowledge and wisdom he had acquired."

But in the past few centuries, no one has been able to figure out what it all means. Dee scholar Francis Yates writes that Dee's explanatory text **"leaves the reader thoroughly bewildered."**

Suster adds:

"Commentators agree that the key is no longer with us, that key being Dee's oral explanation; or perhaps we are too far removed from sixteenth-century intellectual sensibilities to perceive implications deeply significant to intelligent men of that time."

This wasn't about to stop me. The wise John Dee was expressing something very important in the *Monas*. If I could figure out Dee's cosmology, the design of the Tower would become clear. I literally had to think like a Renaissance guy.

I tracked down and studied all the existing translations of Dee's work. A library in Edinborough, Scotland sent me a copy of a handwritten translation done in 1691. A library near Prague provided me with a copy (in Latin) handwritten by Dee in the late 1580's. Then, with the help of a Latin expert, I made my own translation.

Most scholars see the *Monas Hieroglyphica* as an alchemical text that somehow involves numbers. To me the *Monas Hieroglyphica* was a mathematics text written in alchemical language to slightly obscure some kind of important math concepts he had discovered. He wanted to share his wisdom but only with those wise enough to figure out what he was talking about.

Dee's discovery must be important because he dedicated his book to King Maximillian, the Holy Roman Emperor. In the *Letter to Maximillian* that preceeds the 24 Theorems of the *Monas*, Dee says he has a "**rare gift**" for the King.

Now, you don't promise the King a rare gift if you don't have one to give. The King had all the riches he wanted. What did Dee have that's so special it was fit for a King?

(I'll give you a hint. It's a number. But I could give you 12 million guesses and you still might not guess it.)

Dee flatters himself by suggesting that only one in a million philosophers could have discovered what he has found. But he adds that his findings will be useful to 14 different professions.

(His admonitions to the 14 professions are each little riddles.)

Dee tells Maximillian that "his mind was pregnant with the *Monas Hieroglyphica* continuously for the past 7 years."

(This is actually a numerical clue.)

Dee even informs the reader that he likes to use Gematria, Notariacon and Tzyruph. Don't be put off by these strange words. They're really quite simple (and fun).

Gematria

certain letters represent certain numbers

Notariacon

the first letters of a phrase combine to spell a new word (like an acronym)

Tzyruph

certain letters, jumbled, form different words

14 professions
(that Dee claims will find the information in the Monas Hieroglyphica useful)

1 Grammarians
2 Arithmeticians
3 Geometers
4 Musicians
5 Astronomers
6 Opticians
7 Experts on Weights and Measures
8 Experts on Matter and Space
9 Cabbalists
10 Magicians
11 Physicians
12 Scryers
13 Refiners of Gold
14 Alchemists

In short, Dee's book is an amalgam of word games, number codes, metaphors, parables and brain-teasers. I call it a "The Book of 100 Riddles."

When it was published in 1564, **Queen Elizabeth** summoned Dee to court to explain it to her. When he journeyed to Prague, he explained it to Maximilian's son, **King Rudolph II**.

[I have explained the riddles more thoroughly in 3 other books, but what follows is the gist of Dee's work, enough to explain what it has to do with the Tower, and of course Dee's "rare gift" to the King. I encourage you to read a translation of Dee's work first and try to solve it yourself. At least you'll see that it's Dee who sounds esoteric, not me.]

Dee encapsulates his cosmology into one simple graphic figure: the **Monas symbol**.

At first glance it may look like just a stick figure of a one-eyed person, squatting, with outstretched arms, and horns or a crown. But it's so much more.

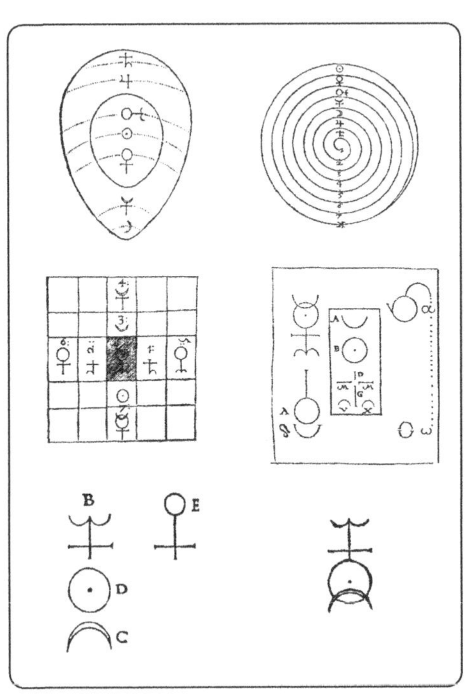

Dee writes that the **astrological symbols the 7 planets**

(Saturn, Jupiter, Moon, Mercury, Mars, Venus and Sun)

can be made from various parts, and presents them in an egg, in a square, and on 7 circuits of a spiral.

He fashions several parts into a mortar and pestle, and other parts into a distilling vessel and collecting bowl.

He even **inverts** the symbol, and **separates** its parts in various ways.

(These are all riddles, with cryptic hints in the text.)

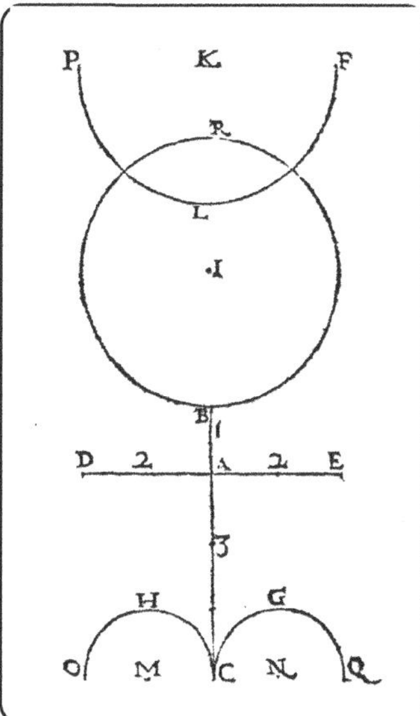

Proportions of the Monas Symbol

Dee insists all component parts be drawn
in the proper geometric proportions.
There is only one correct way to draw the symbol.

He starts in the middle with the short line AB.
If that is 1 unit, the lower part of the vertical line of the Cross is 3 units.
And the arms of the Cross are each 2 units.

The diameter of the Sun must equal the diameter of the Moon.
The diameter of each of the Aries half-circles equals the radius of the Sun.

The entire shape works out to be a 9:4 height-to-width proportion.

He is also gived a detailed description
of how it should look "for Ornament,"
like when it is engraved in a ring or a seal.

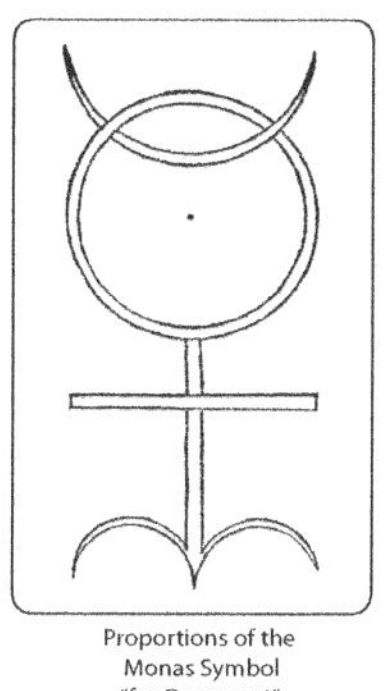

Proportions of the Monas Symbol "for Ornament"

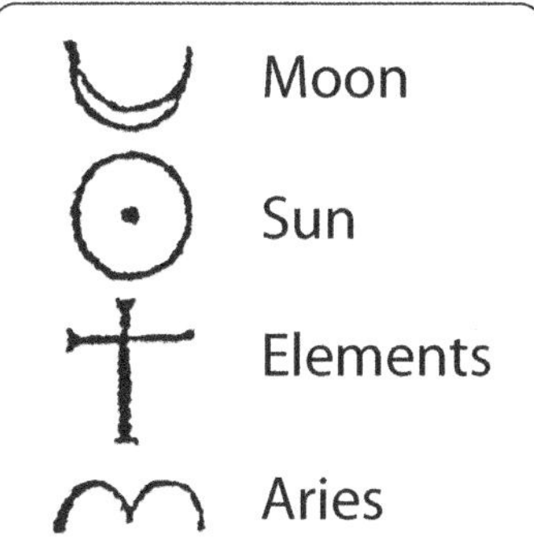

The Monas symbol has four main parts:
At the top is the half-circle of the **Moon**.

Below it is the symbol of the **Sun**. Dee explains
that the point in the center represents earth.

Below that is what Dee calls the **Cross of the Elements**.
The cross obviously has theological meaning, but Dee
emphasizes its geometry. The cross is "offset,"
the horizontal arm crosses the vertical spine
exactly one quarter of the way up from the top.

At the bottom of the Monas symbol is Dee's
sign for **Aries**, the zodiacal month that begins
at the Spring Equinox, around March 21st.

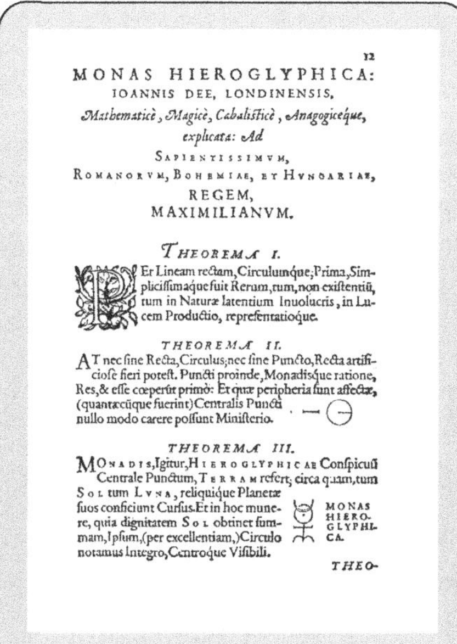

12

MONAS HIEROGLYPHICA:
IOANNIS DEE, LONDINENSIS,
Mathematicè, Magicè, Cabalisticè, Anagogiceque, explicata: Ad
SAPIENTISSIMVM,
ROMANORVM, BOHEMIAE, ET HVNGARIAE,
REGEM,
MAXIMILIANVM.

THEOREMA I.

PEr Lineam rectam, Circulumque; Prima, Simplicissimaque fuit Rerum, tum, non existentiũ, tum in Naturæ latentium Inuolucris, in Lucem Productio, representatioque.

THEOREMA II.

AT nec sine Recta, Circulus; nec sine Puncto, Recta artificiose fieri potest. Puncti proinde, Monadisque ratione, Res, & esse cœperũt primò: Et quæ peripheria sunt affectæ, (quantæcũque fuerint) Centralis Puncti nullo modo carere possunt Ministerio.

THEOREMA III.

MONADIS, Igitur, HIEROGLYPHICAE Conspicuũ Centrale Punctum, TERRAM refert; circa quam, tum SOL tum LVNA, reliquique Planetæ suos conficiunt Cursus. Et in hoc munere, quia dignitatem SOL obtinet summam, Ipsum, (per excellentiam,) Circulo notamus Integro, Centroque Visibili.

MONAS HIEROGLYPHICA.

THEO-

The first 5 short Theorems will
give you a feel for Dee's writing.

SACRED SYMBOL OF ONENESS

JOHN DEE OF LONDON

Mathematically, Magically, Cabalistically, and Anagogically
Explained To

MAXIMILLIAN

Most Wise

KING

of The Romans, Bohemia, and Hungary

THEOREM 1

The very First and most Simple Representation, of not only existing things, but also things hidden in the Folds of Nature, and also in the exhibition of the Bringing Forth of Light, is made by means of a straight Line and a Circle.

THEOREM 2

However, a Circle cannot be skillfully crafted without the Line. Likewise, the Line cannot be crafted without the Point. Thus, Things come into being by way of the Point and a Monad. And things related to the circumference (regardless of how big they may be) cannot exist without the Service of the Central Point.

THEOREM 3

Thus, the Central Conspicuous Point of the HIEROGLYPHIC MONAD refers to the EARTH, around which both the Sun, as well as the MOON, and the rest of the Planets complete their Courses. And in this gift, since the Sun possesses the greatest dignity (because of its excellence) we represent It by a Complete Circle with a Visible Center.

THEOREM 4

The Semicircle of the Moon is shown here to be Above the Circle of the Sun. Nonetheless, the Moon obeys the SUN as her Master and King.

The Moon seems to rejoice in the Sun's Shape and proximity so much that she emulates him in the Size of her Radius (at least, as it appears to the common man). Finally she longs to be imbued by the SOLAR RAYS so much that she becomes Transformed into him. Then she disappears from the Sky altogether. After a few Days she reappears as a horned-shaped figure, exactly as we have depicted her.

THEOR. 5

And most certainly, one Day was Made out of Evening and Morning by the joining of the Lunar Half-Circle to its Solar complement. Thus, it was on this first Day that the LIGHT of the Philosophers was made.

(Dee's word "Anagogically" means "making a spiritual interpretation from a literal statement." Medieval scholars interpreted the Bible in 4 ways: "Literally, Allegorically, Morally, and Anagogically." Dee had created his own "4 ways." Most significantly, he has replaced the first word, "Literally," with the word "Mathematically.")

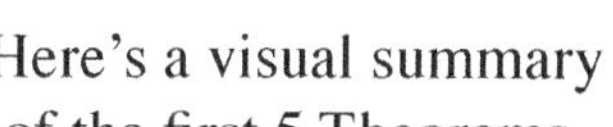

Here's a visual summary
of the first 5 Theorems.

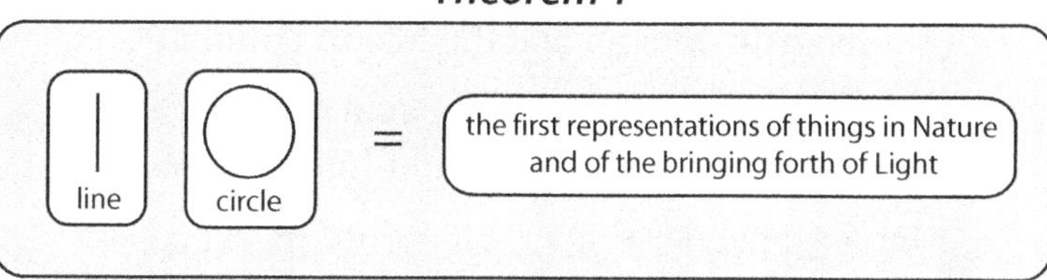

The first two Theorems read like the beginning of a geometry text, explaining "point, line and circle."

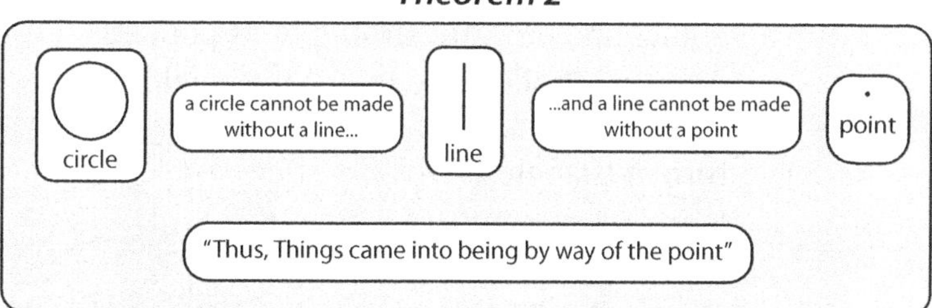

Dee was well-versed in Copernicus' sun-centered ideas, and probably knew Copernicus was right, but he wasn't about to get embroiled in such a sensitive issue.

[However, one of Dee's best students, Thomas Digges, was not afraid to espouse his own heliocentric beliefs.]

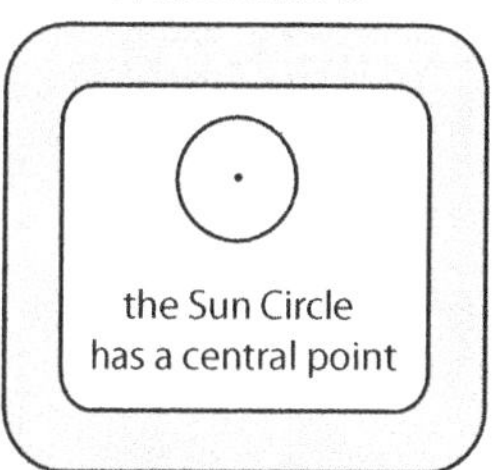

In Theorem 4, Dee explains that the Moon emulates the Sun and, during the full Moon, they appear to be the same size.

(To show this, I have added a dotted line to the top of the Moon.)

Indeed, even though they are at dramatically different distances from earth (250,000 miles verses 93,000,000 miles), the moon and sun each appear to subtend or angle of about a half of a degree.

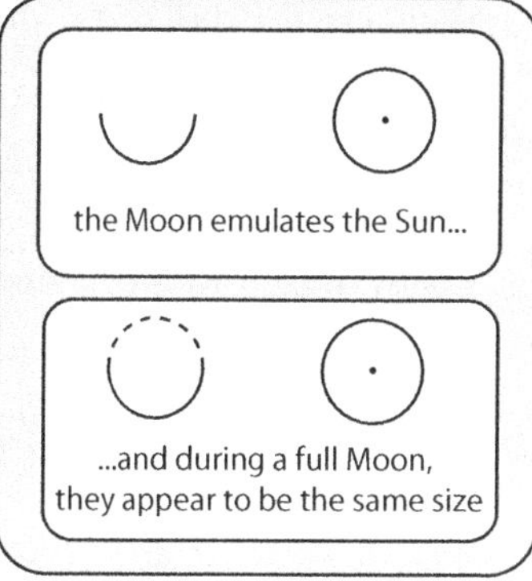

Evening and Morning, light and dark, Moon and Sun. These are all opposites. Can you guess what Dee means by the "Light of the Philosophers"?

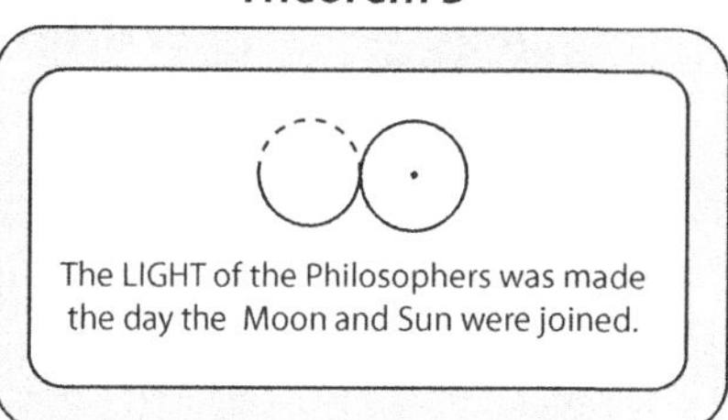

It's a camera obscura.
Light on the outside, dark on the inside.

(In a dark room with one small hole, the image of what's outside appears on the opposite interior wall, upside-down and reversed left-to-right.)

Even if humans weren't around to observe it, on the very "first Day," when the sun first started to shine, a camera obscura would have been be created in a cave that had one small hole.

All it takes is light. In fact, in any dark room with a small hole, you can't get the camera obscura effect **not** to happen.

The Title page has two columns,
the **Sun** column and the **Moon** column.

At the top of the central emblem are what Dee refers to as Solar Mercury and Lunar Mercury.

Mercury, the messenger god of the Romans, had wings on his feet and carried a caduceus or staff.

The two Mercuries are visual reflections of each other and they are aiming their pointed wands to **a hole** in the top of the shield.

Sun column

Moon column

They form a triangle with a strange crustacean.
That's Dee humself,
Cancer the Crab.
[Dee's birthday was July 13]

At the bottom of the large egg-shape is Leo the Lion, King Maximillian's birthsign.
Like a lion, Maximillian was also figuratively the "king of the jungle."

Theorem 11

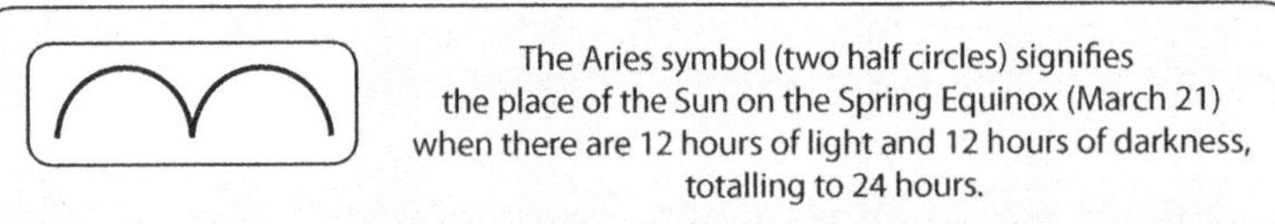

The Aries symbol (two half circles) signifies the place of the Sun on the Spring Equinox (March 21) when there are 12 hours of light and 12 hours of darkness, totalling to 24 hours.

Here, Dee is inferring that the two half circles of the Aries symbol are "12" each, totalling "24".
As we shall see, Dee was aware of the vital importance of 12 and 24 in both geometry and in the realm of number.

From these clues (and others) I was able to decipher the main theme of the *Monas Hieroglyphica:*
The Union of Opposites.

(This is exactly what the present-day researchers had found in the nature of creative people.
They could grasp both sides of a problem simultaneously and come up with a novel idea.)

The principle of the "Union of Opposites" certainly doesn't start with Dee, by any means.

As far back as 600 BC, the Chinese sage Lao Tzu expressed it in the Yin Yang symbol.

Plato, Socrates and their buddies had prolonged discussions about oppositeness.

Aristotle put his spin on what he knew about the Pythagoreans by providing a table of 10 opposites.
(Based on the sacred number of the Pythagorean tetraktys, an equilateral triangle of 10 dots).

Aristotle's table of 10 Pythagorean opposites.

Limited	Unlimited
Odd	Even
Unity	Plurality
Right	Left
Male	Female
At Rest	In Motion
Straight	Curved
Light	Darkness
Good	Evil
Square	Oblong

The Romans expressed the Union of Opposites in their two-headed God, ***Janus***.

A Roman coin with the two faces of Janus

In Medieval days, philosophers expressed the Union of Opposites as an ***ouroborus***, a serpent biting its own tail, making a circle.

The alchemists expressed it as **fire** (an upright triangle) and **water** (an inverted triangle), uniting in a 6-pointed star (or hexagram).

They called the Union of Opposites "**coincidentia oppositorum**."

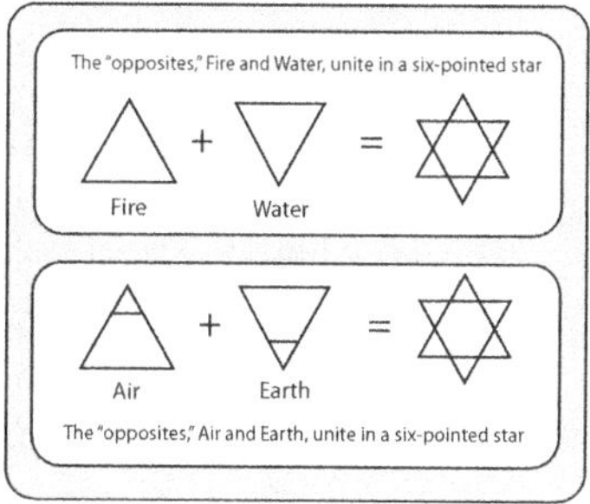
The "opposites," Fire and Water, unite in a six-pointed star
Fire
Water
Air
Earth
The "opposites," Air and Earth, unite in a six-pointed star

The visual oppositeness of yin and yang symbol can even be seen in Gothic Window design.

(Beidermann, *Symbols*, p. 393)

Since Dee's time, many authors have written about "opposites," including:

Immanuel Kant (1724–1804)
Georg Hegel (1770–1831)
Neils Bohr (1885–1962)
Jiddu Krishnamurti (1895–1986)
Claude Levi-Straus (1908–2009)
David Bohm (1917–1992)

Even modern-era poets express the Union of Opposites. Wallace Stevens writes:

"Among twenty snowy mountains, the only moving thing was the eye of a blackbird."

Among the implied opposites in this simple sentence are black-white, small-large, one-many, moving-still, living-nonliving, round-angular. All in one word-image!

tnereffid

When creative consultant Tom Monahan writes about a "tnereffid" way to ideate, he is encouraging "thinking about opposites."

In Theorem 5, Dee tells us that the day of the Moon and Sun were joined, "the LIGHT of the Philosophers was made."

I've portrayed them here as two circles touching, but the Union of Opposites is not a static result, it's an ongoing process.

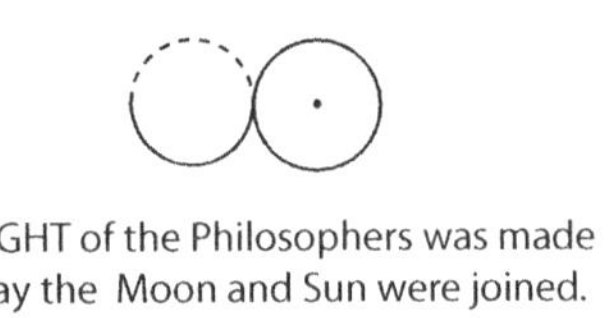
The LIGHT of the Philosophers was made the day the Moon and Sun were joined.

Two things are becoming one,
and that one thing is becoming two.
(concurrently and continuously)

Dee calls this process "Conjunctio" and "Separatio."
Theorem 5 might be visualized this way:

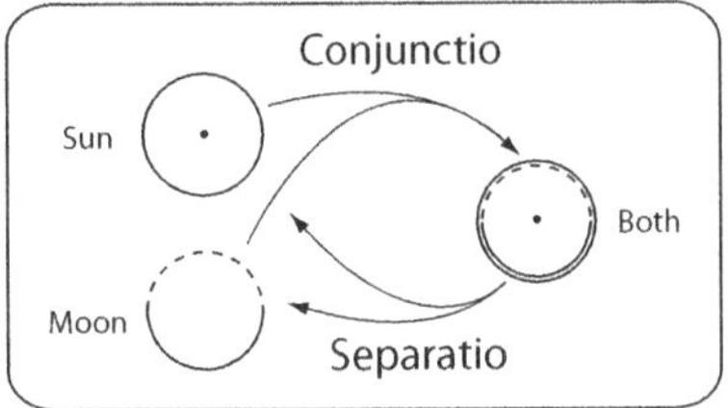

John Dee was well-read and knowledgeable about many things from navigation to law, but above all else, he was a mathematician.

In the *Propaedeumata Aphoristica*, Dee asserts:

"Whatever is in the Universe possesses order, agreement, and similar form with something else."

In the *Monas Hieroglyphica*, Dee drops hints about looking for the idea of Union of Opposites in geometry and in the realm of number.

A simple example is the geometric oppositeness Dee found in the cross.

In Theorems 8 and 16, Dee equates the Pythagorean tetraktys (1+2+3+4=10), to an X (Roman numeral for 10), to an equilateral cross, and to his offset cross.

(In Dee's mind, these 3 versions of the cross all have the same potency.)

Theorems 8 and 16

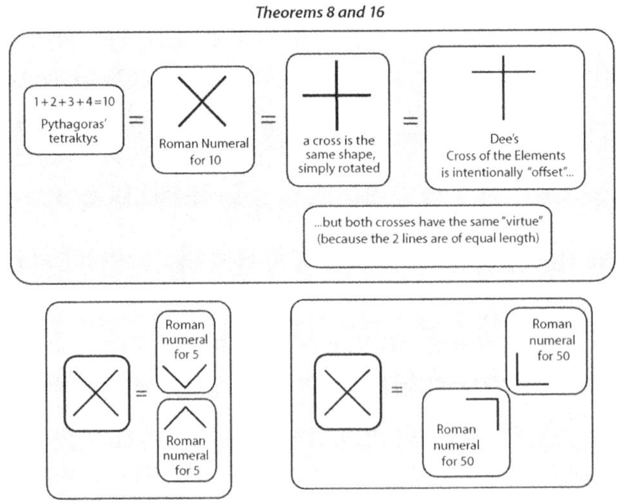

He says the X might be seen as two V's.
(The Roman numeral for 5).

Or even into two L's.
(The Roman numeral for 50)

Theorem 17

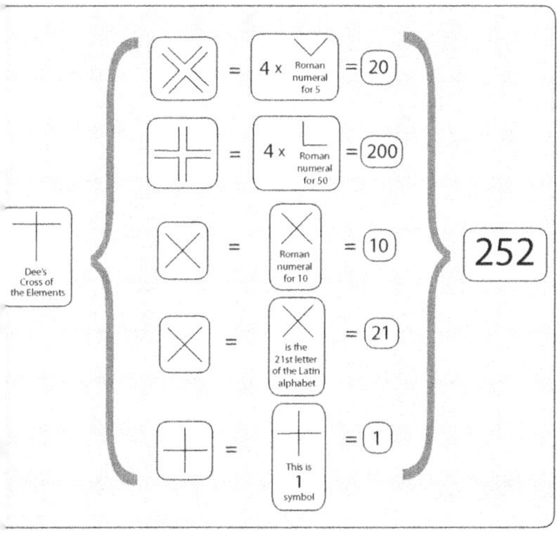

Symbol	=	Meaning	=	Value
X (four V's)	=	4 x Roman numeral for 5	=	20
cross (four L's)	=	4 x Roman numeral for 50	=	200
X	=	Roman numeral for 10	=	10
X	=	is the 21st letter of the Latin alphabet	=	21
+	=	This is 1 symbol	=	1

Dee's Cross of the Elements → 252

In Theorem 17, Dee explains the cross can represent 20, 200, 10, 21, or 1. **These numbers sum to 252.**

From the information in his book, Dee wants us to figure out "2 other logical ways" to arrive at 252.

Here, Dee is punning that the cross, as an X, or two V's, or as two L's, can spell LVX (or LUX, the Latin word for light).

Dee says there are "2 other logical ways" that 252 can be derived "from our premises"

He wants the reader to think about how X separates into either two L's or two V's "because then a LIGHT (**LVX**) will appear."

Aesop's Fable of the "**Eagle and the Dung Beetle**"

Cast of Characters:
The hero: A Scarab Beetle who rolls its eggs in cow dung or horse dung making spherical dungballs.
The villian: An Eagle who lays spherically shaped eggs.
Also starring (with a bit part): A Rabbit
And (playing himself): Jupiter, the chief god of the Romans, (synonymous with the chief Greek god Zeus)

A Rabbit, being chased by an Eagle, begged the Scarab Beetle for help. The Beetle warned the Eagle not to touch the Rabbit. But the Eagle brushed the Beetle away with the sweep if its wing, seized the Rabbit in its talons, and devoured it.

Enraged, the Beetle flew up to the Eagle's nest. Being quite practiced in rolling spherical dungballs, the Beetle rolled the eggs over the lip of the nest and they shattered on the rocks below.

When the Eagle returned to its nest, she was distraught with grief and anger. The following season, the despairing Eagle implored Jupiter to provide her with a safe place to keep her eggs. The great Jupiter allowed her to place the eggs in his lap.

The wily Beetle flew up and deposited some of its spherical dungballs among the eggs. Jupiter noticed the filthy dungballs, was startled, and stood up abruptly. Once again, all the Eagle's eggs were shattered on the ground.

To resolve the whole dispute, Jupiter commanded that the Eagle lay its eggs in early spring, when the Beetles are still asleep in the ground.

In the midst of all this unusual geometry and astronomy, Dee relates one of Aesop's parables (which I have paraphrased above). The moral of the story is that the weak can find clever ways to avenge the powerful, but differences can be resolved. Following the fable, Dee writes: "**I am not trying to play Aesop, But Oedipus**."

Oedipus is famous for his "Riddle of the Sphinx:"
"What goes on four legs in the morning, on two legs at noon, and on three legs in the evening"?
(The answer: A man, who crawls on all fours as a baby, walks on two legs as an adult, and walks with a cane in old age.)

Dee is telling the reader he is using the fable as a riddle **(Oedipus)**, not for its moral message **(Aesop)**.
(Hint: Dee wants the reader to think about how the spherical eggs and dungballs naturally arrange themselves in Jupiter's lap.)

The Greek playwright Aristophanes alludes to Aesop's fable (probably written around 550 BC) in his play *Peace* (written around 400 BC). While attending Saint John's College in Cambridge (from 1542–1545), Dee was the stage manager for a production of *Peace*.

Using a system of hidden ropes and pulleys, Dee had the hero leap off the stage on the back of a giant Beetle and fly up into the rafters. Some of the astonished audience members suspected Dee had used some kind of magic.

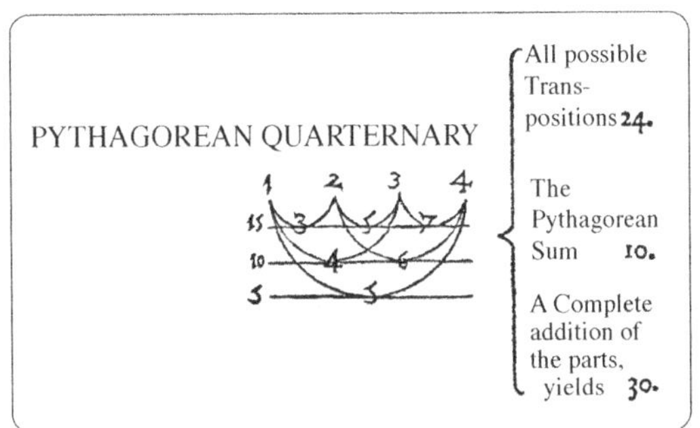

In Theorem 23, Dee compares two "Quaternaries." The **Pythagorean Quaternary** is **1, 2, 3, and 4**.

These mumbers multiply to 24, they sum to 10, and the sum of all the pairings of the parts sums to 30.

Dee has devised his own "**Artificial Quaternary**" which is "1, 2, 3, and then 2 again."

(Nowadays, artificial means fake or unnatural, but in Dee's time it meant artful, skillful, or well-crafted.)

Dee wants us to discover what's so artful about **1, 2, 3, 2**.

They multiply to 12, they sum to 8, and the complete addition of the parts sums to 24.

Here are those numbers 12 and 24 again. Dee even notes that 24 karats is pure gold.

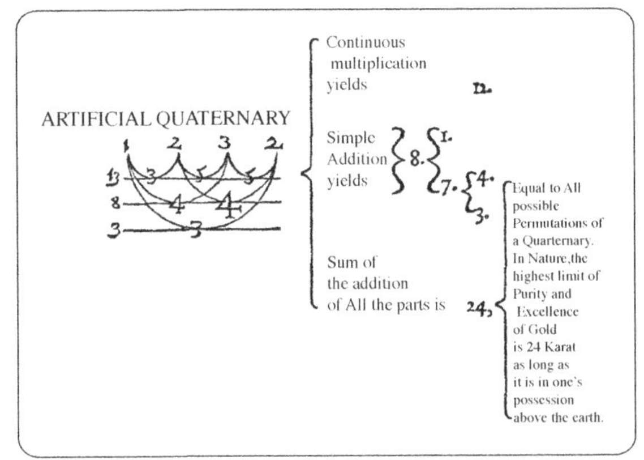

On the left side of what I call the "Artificial Quaternary chart," Dee emphatically claims there are "**certain and Fixed Limits**" in the realm of number.

In the middle are three categories Virtue, Weight, and Time, which incorporate various arrangements of numbers.

Note that Dee list includes 1, 2, 3, 4, 5, 6, 7, 8, 12, 13, 24, and 25.

Why does he omit 9, 10, and 11?

Way down at the bottom is Dee's "Magistral" number or Master number, **252**.

"Lapidification and Fermentation" is Dee's clever was of hinting the "Philosopher's Stone" of number is 252.

What's so special about 252?

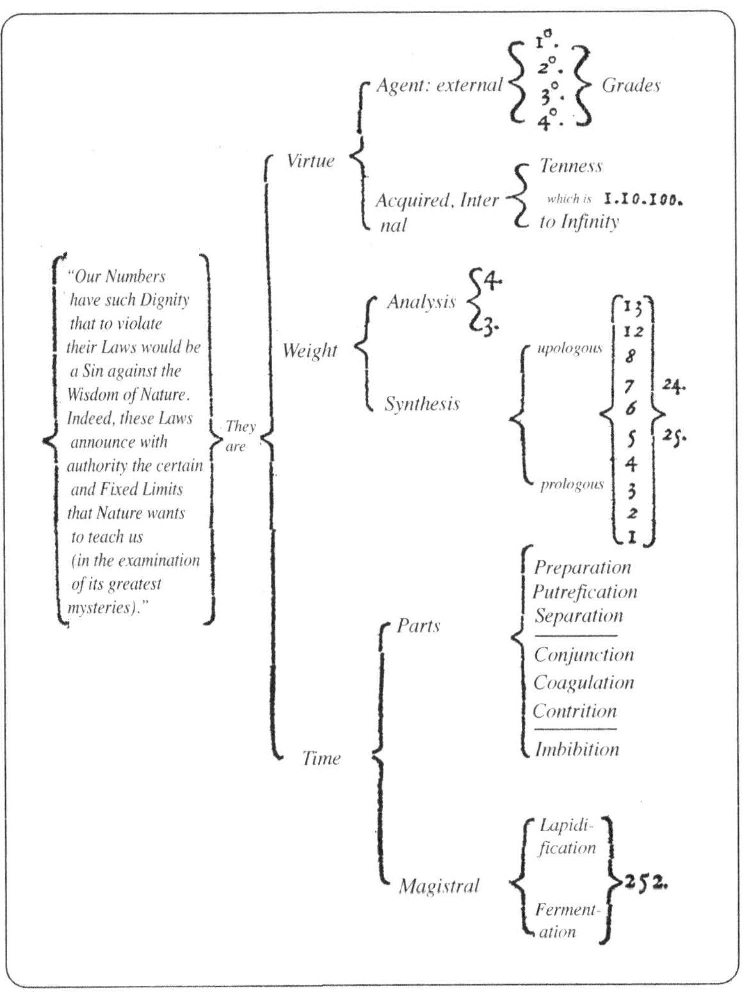

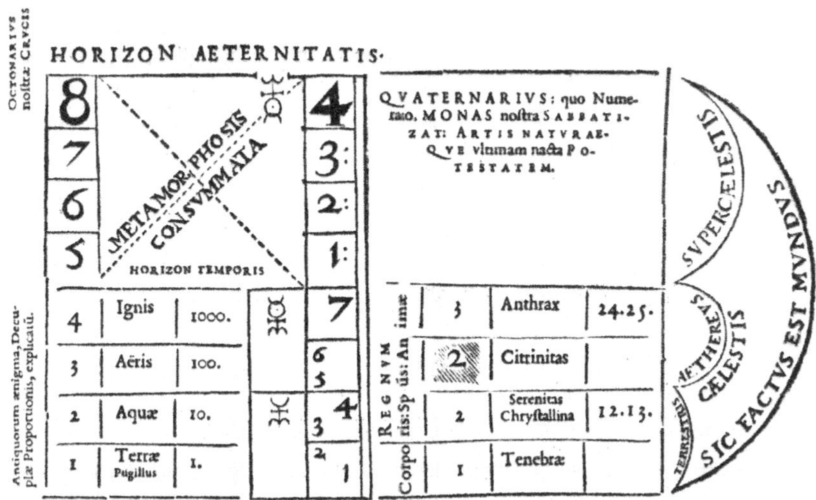

At the end of Theorem 23, Dee presents a chart entitled "Thus the World Was Created."

(How many people do you know that would even attempt to summarize the Creation of the World in a chart?)

The bottom half of the chart (labeled Terrestrial and Aetheic Celestial) is the "Below" part of the world. The upper half (labeled Supercelestial) is the "Above" part of the world.

In the "Above" section, Dee lists, (in bold) **1, 2, 3, 4**, then **5, 6, 7,** and **8**. But in the "Below" section, he only lists 1 through 7.

He also lists various quaternaries, like the Pythagorean Quaternary, the 4 Elements, "1,10,100,1000," his Artificial Quaternary, the colors of 4 alchemical stages, as well as those numbers 12 and 24 (along with 13 and 25).

He uses words like METAMORPHOSIS and CONSUMMATA.

Along the top is the HORIZON OF ETERNITY.

In the upper right, he uses the peculiar word SABBATIZAT.

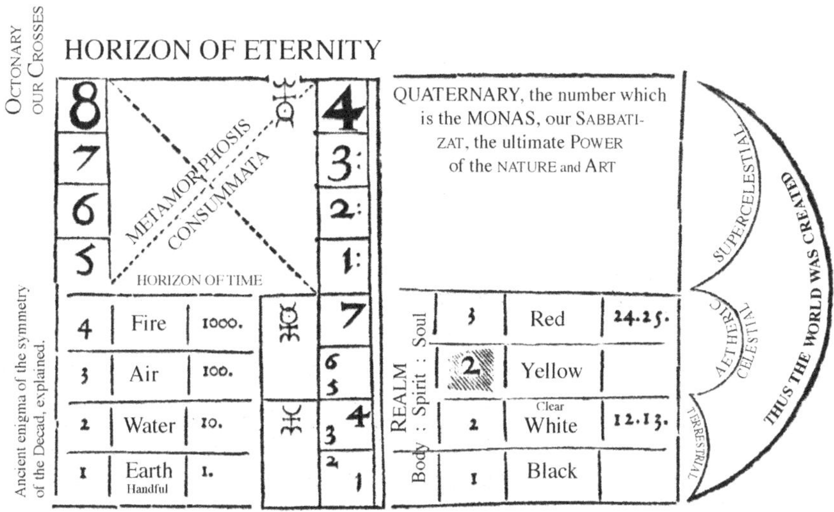

In Theorem 24, he reiterates that the day and night of the equinox total exactly 24 hours. He reiterates that 1 x 2 x 3 x 4 = 24 in the Pythagorean tetractys He also relates several cryptic ways Saint John refers to the number 24 in *Revelations*.

Dee signs his work with an equilateral triangle, his code symbol for himself.

Delta (triangle) is the fourth Greek letter.

The fourth Latin letter is D, pronounced "Dee."
John Dee was a consummate punster and riddlemaker.

Dee's signature
Delta,the fourth Greek letter
like D(ee) is the fourth Latin letter

After much study, I was finally able to understand what this chart (and the whole *Monas Hieroglyphica*) is all about and it's really quite clever. It expresses various rhythms or symmetries found in geometry and number.

Just as Dee suggests, the key to unlocking this puzzle is the number 252. Fortunately, to figure out what 252 meant, I had a tool that historians in the 1800's and 1900's did **not** have.

You know what that tool was?

I googled 252.

I figured if 252 was so important in Dee's cosmology, it might be important in someone else's cosmology.

And guess who popped up when I googled "252 spheres"?

Buckminster Fuller, the geometer and architect who invented the geodesic dome. Unfortunately, Bucky sounded more confusing than Dee:

> "Thus by experimental evidence we may identify the electron with the volume of the regular, unit-vector-radius-edge tetrahedron, the simplest symmetrical structural system in Universe. We may further identify the electron tetrahedral with the maximum possible symmetrical aggregate of concentrically packed, unit-radius spheres symmetrically surrounding a single nucleus – there being [8] new potential nuclei appearing in the three-frequency shell of 92 spheres, which three-frequencies shell, when surrounding embraced by the four-frequency shell of 162 spheres, buries the [8] candidate new nuclei only one shell deep, whereas qualifying as full-fledged nuclei in their own right requires two shells all around each, which [8], newborn nuclei event calls for the fifth-frequency shell of **252 spheres**."

(See what I mean about confusing. In the next few pages, all this will become crystal clear.)

[Warning: the next few chapters involve geometry and mathematics. But fear not! It's all quite simple. Even if you don't feel you have a knack for math, or feel you have forgotten all the geometry you learned in school, you will still be able to understand the next few chapters. (I've explained it to 3rd grade students who have grasped it).

The following chapters might seem like a grand diversion from this story, but they are actually its essence. In the *Monas Hieroglyphica*, Dee actually left us a blueprint for the design if the John Dee Tower of 1583 and clues about his matematical cosmology that he applied later to the design of the original Globe. But it will be totally invisible unless you first understand the startling discoveries Dee made about geometry and number.]

JOHN DEE AND BUCKMINSTER FULLER THOUGHT ALIKE

Richard Buckminster Fuller (1895-1983) was an inventor, philosopher, engineer, and architect. Called by some the Leonardo da Vinci or Benjamin Franklin of the Space Age, he was one of the most important thinkers of the 20th century.

He worked globally and worked fervently suggesting ways "to make man a success in Universe." Born in Milton, Massachusetts in 1895, Bucky got expelled from Harvard twice for partying and "lack of ambition." Bucky explains he was more excited about exploring novel ideas than "memorizing facts."

Bucky became a management trainee at the meat-packing firm Armour and Company in Manhattan. After serving in the Navy during World War II, he got married and went into business with his father-in-law, building houses from a compressed-fiber block they had invented.

In 1927, the company lost its financial backing. Bucky was out of a job. Soon all of his savings were gone and he was falling further and further into debt. Down and out, he started drinking and carousing on the streets of Chicago.

One cold fall night he walked to the shore of Lake Michigan and considered jumping in, swimming as far out as he could far out in the cold water, and ending his life. He knew his wife and baby daughter would live well on the life insurance policy he had taken out.

Suddenly something clicked. He thought, "You don't have the right to eliminate yourself. You do not belong to you. You belong to the Universe." He decided to start a fresh new life, thinking less about himself, and assessing how he could best help all of humanity.

He took a vow of silence for 2 years, speaking only to his wife and daughter. They rented a small room in a cheap hotel in the city's ghetto area. It had one closet and an alcove with a stove and a sink.

Bucky studied great thinkers like DaVinci and Gandhi. To see how nature expressed itself, he studied astronomy, physics, biology, and mathematics. He sensed that nature had certain "pattern integrities," that might not be detectable by the physical senses, but that might be expressed with tangible models. (Sieden, *Buckminster Fuller's Universe: His Life and Work*, pp.22, 88)

Bucky set out to find the geometry of universe,
"**Nature's one comprehensive coordinate system.**"
And he found it!

Bucky's "Spaceship Earth" at Epcot Center

Bucky went on to design cars, maps, houses, buildings, and of course, domes. He is most well-known for inventing the geodesic dome, like Spaceship Earth at Walt Disney World in Orlando.

During the 1960's and 1970's, Bucky gave hundreds of lectures every year at colleges and conferences all over the world. By 1971, he had circumnavigated the globe 37 times.

In 1975, Bucky wrote his 876-page opus ***SYNERGETICS***, *Explorations in the Geometry of Thinking*. It is a synthesis of his discoveries about Nature's coordinate system.

Realizing he still had more to say, in 1979 he followed it up with his 592-page *Synergetics 2*.

Studying the almost 1500 pages of "idiosyncratic, hyphenated prose" of Bucky-speak in the 2 volumes of *Synergetics* is a daunting task. Fortunately, one of his students, Amy Edmondson has done a superb job of summarizing his ideas in ***A Fuller Explanation***, *The Synergetic Geometry of R. Buckminster Fuller.*

It soon became clear to me that John Dee and Buckminster Fuller had both discovered the same thing. It's not that surprising. They were each great geometers. And they were each searching for the same thing, "Nature's operating system."

The world has changed dramatically in the 4 centuries between the mid-1500s and the mid-1900s, but the "Laws of Nature" have stayed the same. They never change.

Nature's operating system

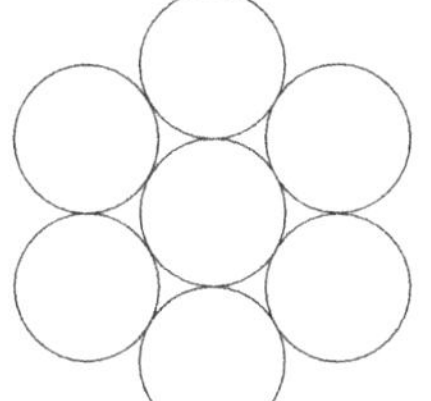

Take one circle.
How many same-sized circles will fit around it?
For example, if put a quarter on a tabletop, how many quarters can you fit around it, so they all touch and fit snugly?

The answer is exactly 6.
Five quarters is not enough
and 7 is too many,
but 6 fit perfectly around 1.

Now let's put a sphere on a flat surface. How many same-sized spheres will fit around it?

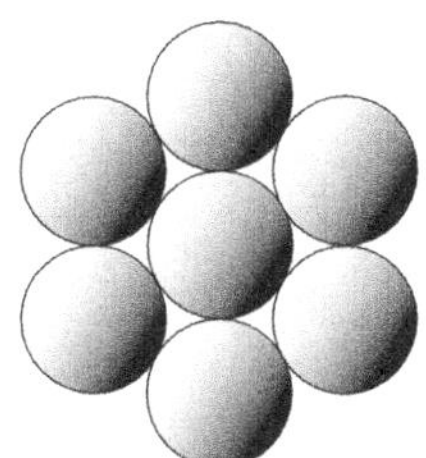

Again the answer is 6. This holds true whether the spheres are marbles, ping-pong balls, bowling balls or planet earths.

Now, instead of using a flat surface, imagine a sphere suspended in space. How many same-sized spheres fit perfectly around it in all directions?

Now the answer is 12.
Eleven is too few, thirteen is too many.
12 spheres fit perfectly around 1.

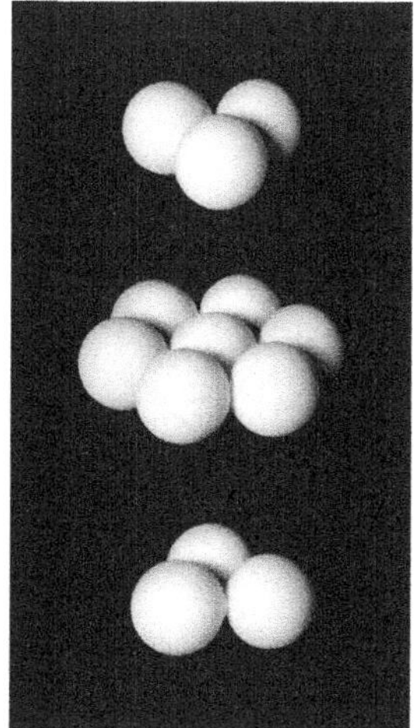

An easy way to envision this is to start with the 6-around-1 arrangement. Then, put three spheres in the nests they create on the top and three more in the nests on the bottom.

(These trios on top and bottom **must** be arranged in opposite direction. For example, here the top triangle of spheres points forwards and the bottom triangle of spheres points backwards.)

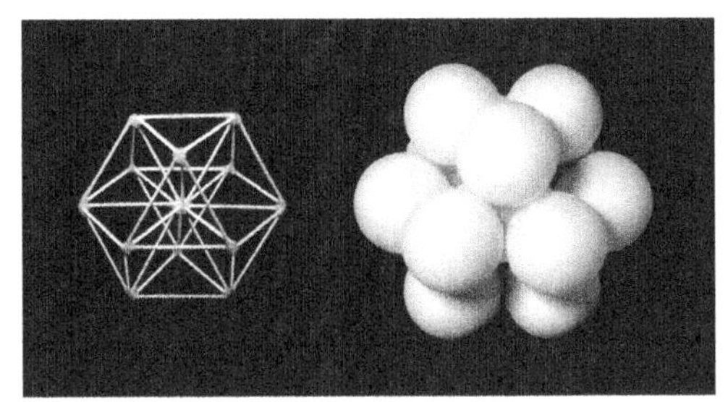

Next, imagine the centerpoints of each of the 12 spheres connecting with the centerpoints of all each of their neighboring spheres (and also with the central sphere).

Let's zoom in for a close up.
Notice that the 12 central radiating lines are the same length as the lines comprising the outer shell (of which there are 24.)

(In other words, I made this model by hot-gluing 36 lollipop sticks that were each 4 inches in length.)

Because the radiating vectors and the outer vectors are equal, Bucky named this shape the "**Vector Equilibrium**."

Bucky loved this shape.
He considered it:
"Nature's operating system."

He even designed a logo for it.

In the closest packing of spheres arrangement, some sides are triangular (made from 3 spheres) and some sides are square (made from 4 spheres).

Notice that each of the 12 outer spheres are "shared" by triangular and square faces.

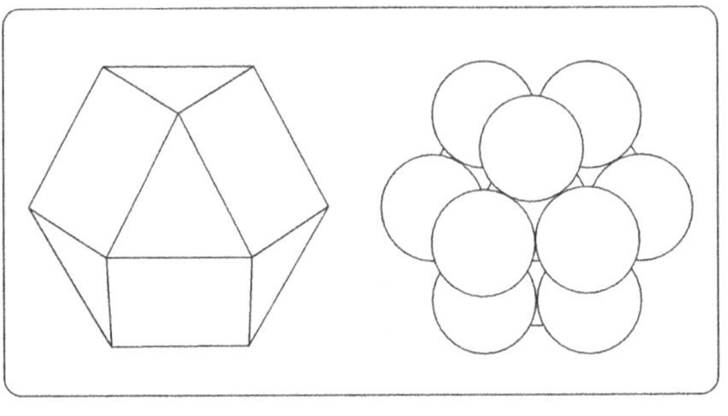

In total, this shape has
8 triangular faces and 6 square faces.
What Bucky called the Vector Equilibrium, other geometers call a cuboctahedron.
This shape was known long before Bucky.

And long before Dee, Heron informs us that even Plato knew about it.

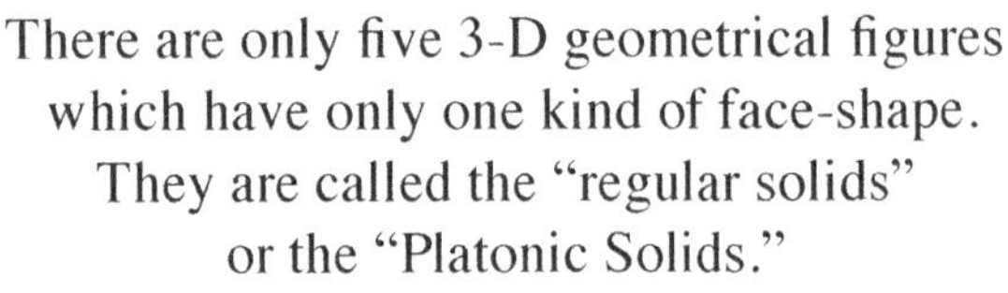

There are only five 3-D geometrical figures which have only one kind of face-shape. They are called the "regular solids" or the "Platonic Solids."

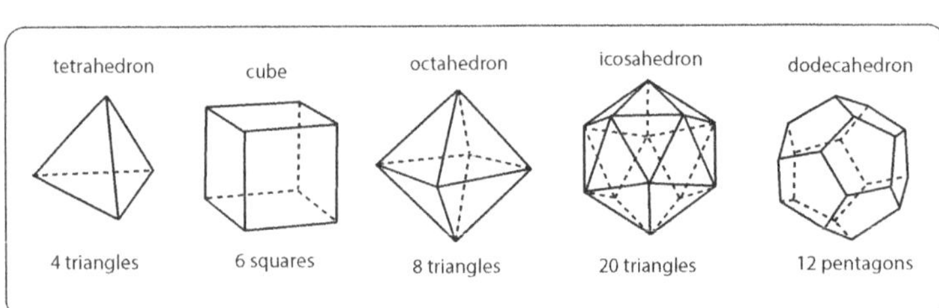

The tetrahedron has 4 triangular faces.
The cube has 6 square faces.
The octahedron has 8 triangular faces.
The icosahedron has 20 triangular faces.
The dodecahedron has 12 pentagonal faces.

Archimedes helped identify a group of "semi-regular solids," which have only 2 or 3 kinds of face-shapes.

As you can see, the cuboctahedron is one of the simplest of the Archimedean Solids.

	types of faces		edges	radiating vertices	total faces
5 "Platonic Solids"	4 triangles	tetrahedron	6	4	4
	8 triangles	octahedron	12	6	8
	20 triangles	icosahedron	30	12	20
	6 squares	cube	12	8	6
	12 pentagons	dodecahedron	30	20	12
13 "Archimedean Solids"	**8 triangles and 6 squares**	**cuboctahedron**	**24**	**12**	**14**
	20 triangles and 12 pentagons	icosidodecahedron	60	30	32
	4 triangles and 4 hexagons	truncated tetrahedron	18	12	8
	8 triangles and 6 octagons	truncated cuboctahedron	36	24	14
	6 squares and 8 hexagons	truncated octahedron	36	24	14
	20 triangles and 12 decagons	truncated dodecahedron	90	60	32
	12 pentagons and 20 hexagons	truncated icosahedron	90	60	32
	8 triangles and 18 squares	rhombicuboctahedron	48	24	26
	12 squares and 8 hexagons and 6 octagons	great rhombicuboctahedron	72	48	26
	20 triangles and 30 squares and 12 pentagons	rhombicosidodecahedron	120	60	62
	30 squares and 20 hexagons and 12 decagons	great rhombicosidodecahedron	180	120	62
	32 triangles and 6 squares	snub cube	60	24	38
	80 triangles and 12 pentagons	snub dodecahedron	150	60	92

length of edge vector / length of radiating vector		
1.6329931619	tetrahedron	5 "Platonic Solids"
1.4142135624	octahedron	
1.0514622242	icosahedron	
1.1547005384	cube	
0.7136441795	dodecahedron	
1.0000000000	**cuboctahedron**	13 "Archimedean Solids"
0.6180339887	icosidodecahedron	
0.8528028654	truncated tetrahedron	
0.5621692754	truncated cuboctahedron	
0.6324555320	truncated octahedron	
0.3367628118	truncated dodecahedron	
0.4035482123	truncated icosahedron	
0.7148134887	rhombicuboctahedron	
0.4314788105	great rhombicuboctahedron	
0.4478379596	rhombicosidodecahedron	
0.2629921751	great rhombicosidodecahedron	
0.7442063312	snub cube	
0.4638568806	snub dodecahedron	

But, here's the remarkable thing: Of of all the Platonic and Archimedean Solids, **only** in the cuboctahedron is the length of the edge vector and the edge of the radiating vector in a 1:1 ratio.

Imagine.
edge vector = radiating vector
Priceless.

The cuboctahedron derives its name from the fact it is the intersection of a cube and an octahedron.

Envision joining these two shapes together, then cutting off all the pointy stellations.

What remains is a cuboctahedron.

(It inherits its square faces from the character of the cube, and its triangular faces from the character of the octahedron.)

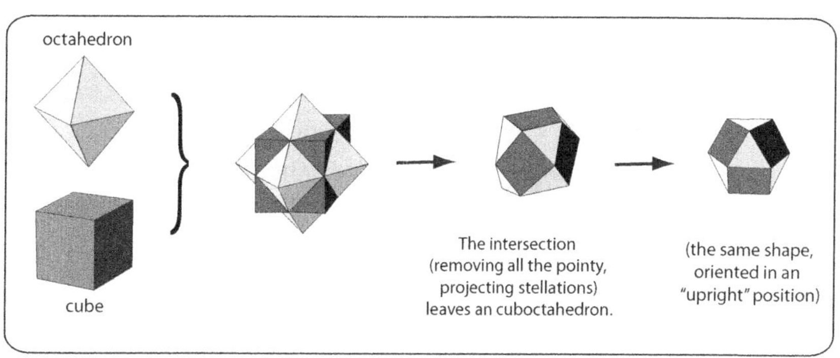
octahedron
cube
The intersection (removing all the pointy, projecting stellations) leaves an cuboctahedron.
(the same shape, oriented in an "upright" position)

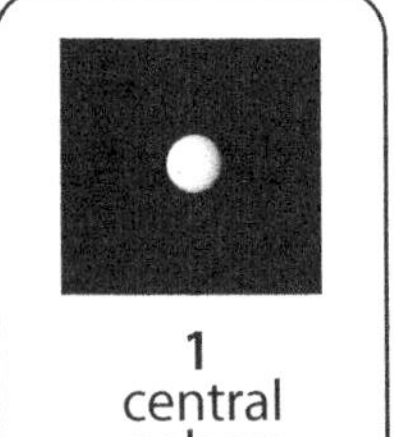

1
central
sphere

We've seen that starting with one sphere ...

... 12 fit perfectly around it.

12
spheres
in
Layer 1

Now, how many spheres do you think will fit perfectly around this cluster of 13 spheres?

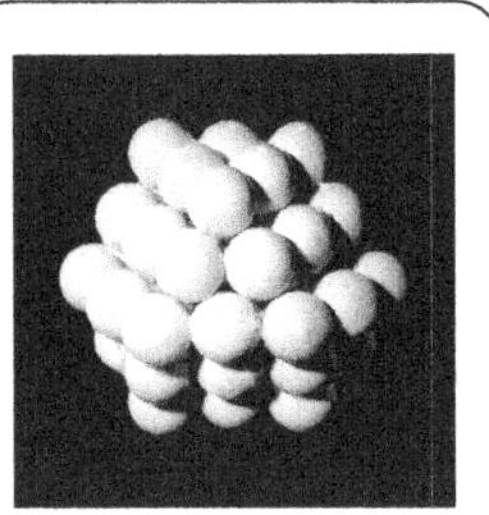

42
spheres
in
Layer 2

This is a littler harder to guess.

The answer is exactly **42.**
But notice it makes an even more well-defined cuboctahedron.

A cluster of 55 total spheres makes the central sphere a "true nucleus."

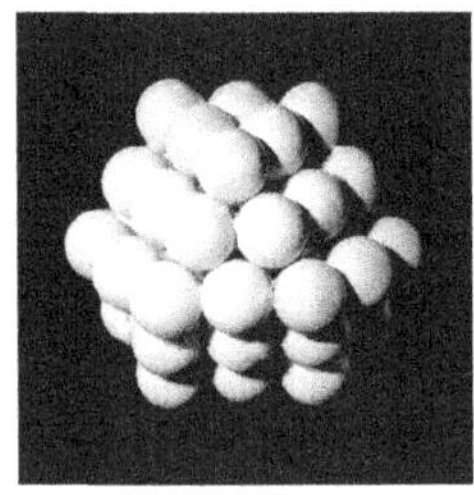

Starting with 1 sphere, plus 12, plus 42 more, making what Bucky calls a "**55-sphere cluster**." At this stage the central sphere finally has become a "true nucleus."

(When only Layer 1 surrounds the central sphere, that nucleus sphere is visible through the gaps between the 12 outer spheres. But after Layer 2, which has 42 more spheres, the central sphere is **not** visible, and it has now become a "true nucleus.")

Now, how many spheres will there be in Layer 3?

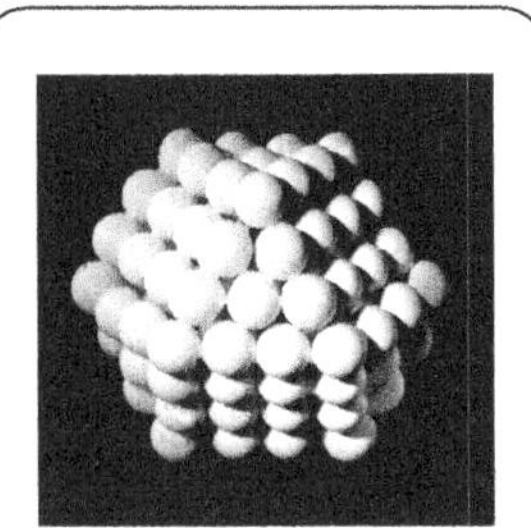

92
spheres
in
Layer 3

The answer is **92**.
And still it makes a cuboctahedral shape.

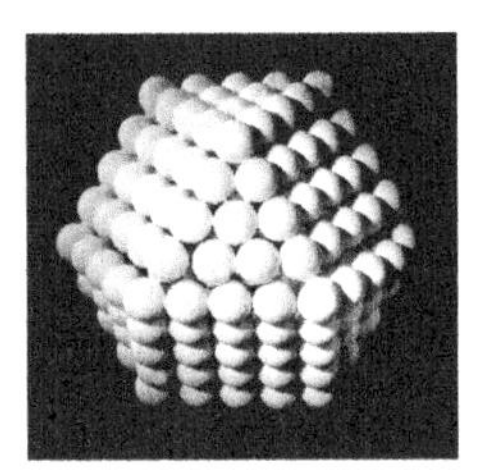

162
spheres
in
Layer 4

How about the next layer?
The answer is **162**, and again the cuboctahedral shape is maintained.

Do you notice anything peculiar about these numbers? Well, they all end in 2. But ignoring the final digit 2 for a moment, the other digits are 1, 4, 9, 16.

Hey, these are the squares of 1, 2, 3, and 4.

Layer 1	**12**
Layer 2	**42**
Layer 3	**92**
Layer 4	**162**

Leonhard Euler

The great mathematician Leonhard Euler discovered this around 1750, and devised this formula for the number of spheres per layer:

Take the Layer number,
square it,
multiply it by 10,
and add 2.

Euler's Formula
for the number of
spheres-per-layer
in the
closest-packing-of-spheres

$$(10\,L^2) + 2$$

L= Layer number

In layer 1, 10 x 1 is 10, plus 2 is 12.
In layer 2, 10 x 4 is 40, plus 2 is 42.
In layer 3, 10 x 9 is 90, plus 2 is 92.
In layer 4, 10 x 16 is 160, plus 2 is 162.
Now, (drum roll, please), how many spheres will there be in layer 5?

	Ten times (the Layer number "squared")...	...Then add 2.
Layer 1	10 x1 = 10	10 +2 = 12
Layer 2	10 X 4 = 40	40 +2 = 42
Layer 3	10 X 9 = 90	90 +2 = 92
Layer 4	10 X 16 = 160	160 +2 = 162

	Ten times (the Layer number "squared")...	...Then add 2.
Layer 5	10 x25 = 10	10 +2 =252

252
spheres
in
Layer 5

5 squared is 25.
10 times 25 is 250,
then adding 2 makes **252**.

Hey, that's Dee's Magistral number!
(It has appeared quite naturally in this basic growth pattern.)

Adding more layers
(like 362, 492, 642, ...)
makes larger and larger cuboctahedrons.

But there's something very special about that layer 5, with its 252 spheres.

Spheres-per-Layer in closest-packing-of-spheres

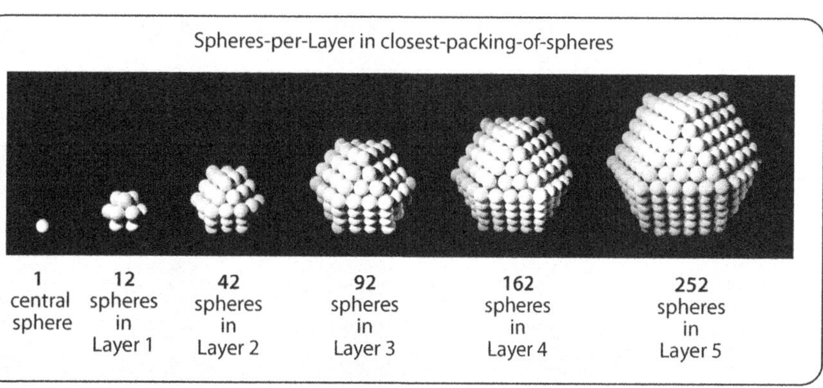

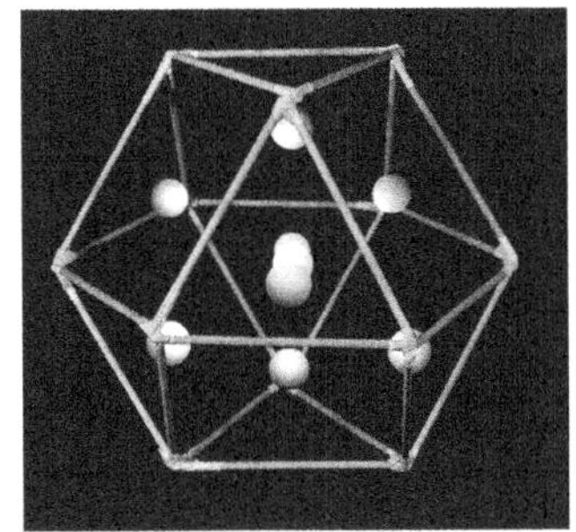

When layer 5 has been reached, 8 of the spheres from layer 3 have enough spheres around them that they are now "true nuclei." It's hard to see their positions without x-ray vision, so I've simulated their positions digitally, along with the original central sphere.

(This is what Bucky was explaining in that confusing paragraph I found when I had googled "252 spheres." If you reread it now, it will make much more sense.)

As we'll see shortly, there's a whole lot more "eightness" going on here than simply these 8 new nuclei.

Four "Bucky bowties" make a cuboctahedron.

Bucky didn't like the term "Platonic solids."
He didn't see these shapes as solid at all.
He saw them as ***energy events***.

Bucky didn't like the word "cuboctahedron" because it defines the shape by its faces. Bucky was more interested in the "vectors."
A vector is simply a line connecting two points.
[The term "vector" is used because technically a "line" extends in 2 directions endlessly.]

vector
point B
point A

And as we've seen, only in the cuboctahedron are the radiating vectors and the edge vectors the same length.

To understand what Bucky means by "equilibrium" (a state in which opposing forces are balanced), let's first start in 2-dimensions.

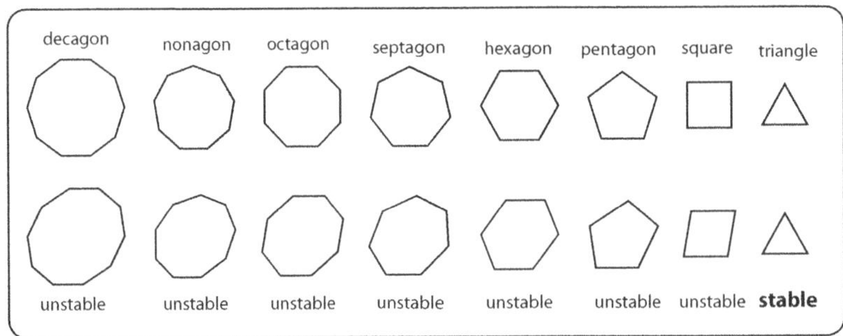

Of all the polyhedra (many-sided shapes), only the triangle is stable.

Using same-sized lollipop sticks and hot glue, if you make models of the triangle, square, pentagon, hexagon, septagon, octagon, etc., you can feel that **only the triangle is completely rigid**.

The others will move at the joining points.
They will not hold their shape.

The equilateral triangle is the simplest 2-D shape.

(Hint: Geometer Dee recognized the wonder of the equilateral triangle–he used it to sign his name.)

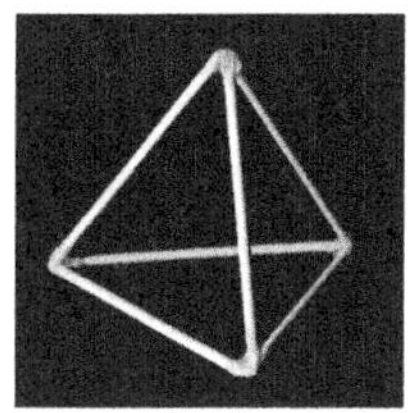

In 3 dimensions, the simplest shape that can be made from triangles is the tetrahedron. In Greek, *tetra* means "four" and *hedron* means "sides." The tetrahedron has 4 identical faces that are each perfect equilateral triangles.

Sometimes the tetrahedron is called a "pyramid," but be aware that it's not the same thing as what I call a "Pyramid of Giza," which has a square base and 4 triangular faces.

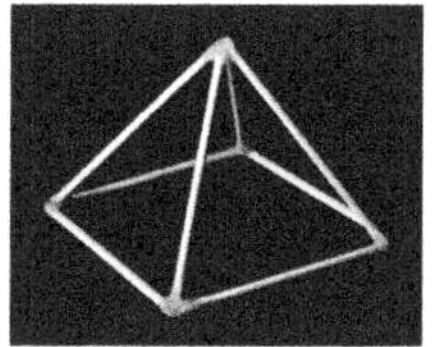

Bucky loved the tetrahedron. He called it the "**simplest structure**" or "**first and simplest subdivision of Universe**" or " **Nature's most economical shape**."

He succinctly declares,
"Six vectors are required for complete multidimensional stability."
(Filler, *Synergetics 1*, Fig 621.10 p. 339)

(Incidentally, John Dee saw the wonders of the tetrahedron as well. He shows Lady Occasion, or Lady Luck, standing on a tetrahedron in the Title page illustration of *General and Rare Memorials pertaining to the Art of Navigation*.)

Tetrahedron on Dee's Title page

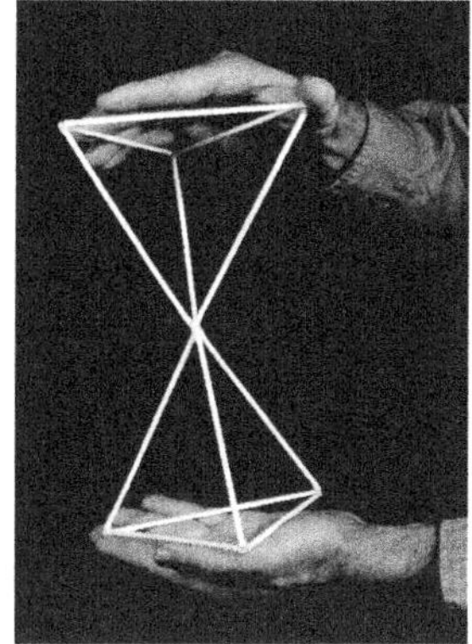

One tetrahedron is nice, but Bucky realized to make an energy event, two tetrahedra are required. And they must be tip-to-tip, with one point in common.

(In the Union of Opposites, it takes two to tango.)

As Bucky frequently wore a Bow tie, I call this shape a "Bucky bowtie."

Bucky frequently wore a bowtie

In a Bucky bowtie, the two tetrahedra **must** be oriented so their edges, align making **three long lines** that each pass through a common point in the middle.

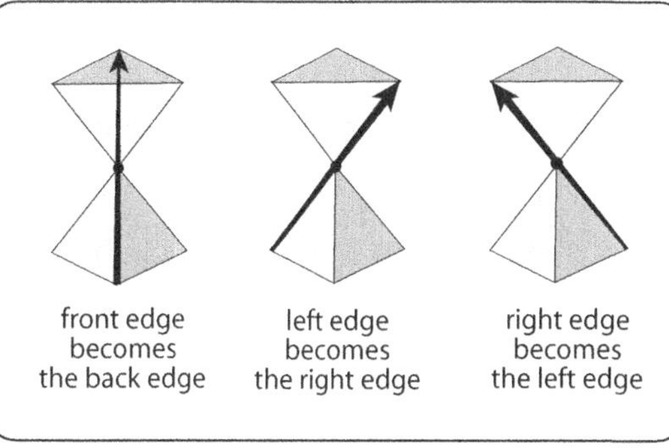

> "The tetrahedron is the only polyhedron,
> the only structural system
> that can be turned inside out and vice versa
> by one energy event."

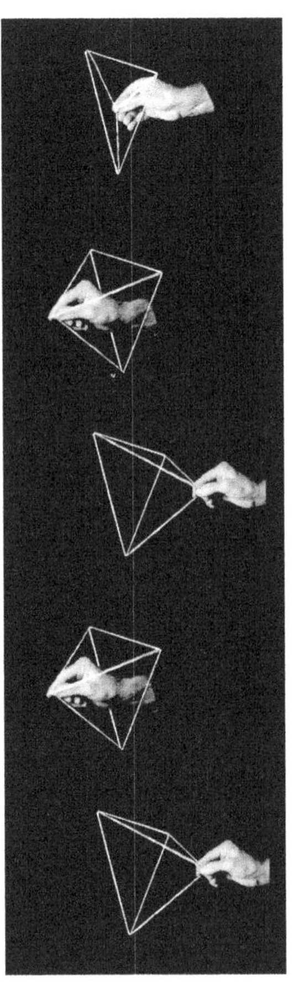

To demonstrate this concept, Bucky welded together three steel rods into a triangle (like the percussion instrument, only fully closed). He attached rubber bands to each of the three corners, then interconnected the bands in the center of the triangle. Holding that center conjunction point in his fingers, he would plunge his hand deep into the triangle forming a tetrahedron (made from 3 rubber band edges and 3 steel edges).

Then he would quickly pull his hand back out of the triangle, making a tetrahedron "pointed" in the opposite direction.

He would plunge his hand back and forth, continuously "inside-outing" the tetrahedron. This pumping action formed what he called "positive and negative tetrahedra" and demonstrated "the essential twoness of a system." (Fuller, *Synergetics 1*, 624.01 and 624.02, p. 341)

Here's another way Bucky demonstrated the "inside-outing" of a tetrahedron. One tetrahedron splits apart at the seams and "opens up like a three-petaled flower bud." In this sequence, the "upward pointing" white tetrahedron morphs into a "downward pointing" black tetrahedron.

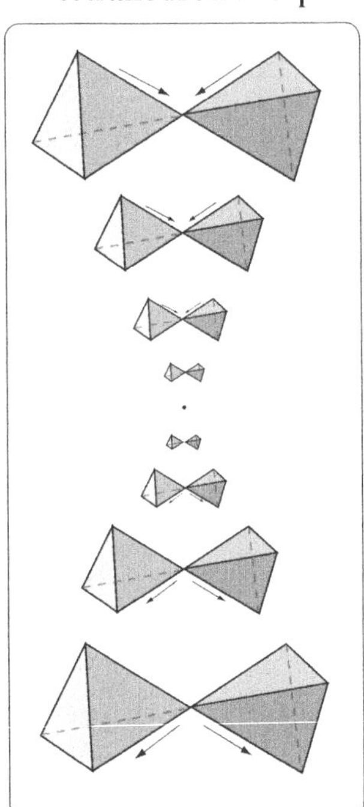

Bucky's "pumping" or "convergence and divergence"

But I think the most insightful way Bucky demonstrates the energy event is with one tetrahedron shrinking, shrinking, shrinking, to a point, then coming out the other side and enlarging into the "opposite" tetrahedron. At the same time, the opposite tetrahedron does the same thing.

You can get a good feel for the "energy event," this two way pumping action of what he calls "convergence and divergence."

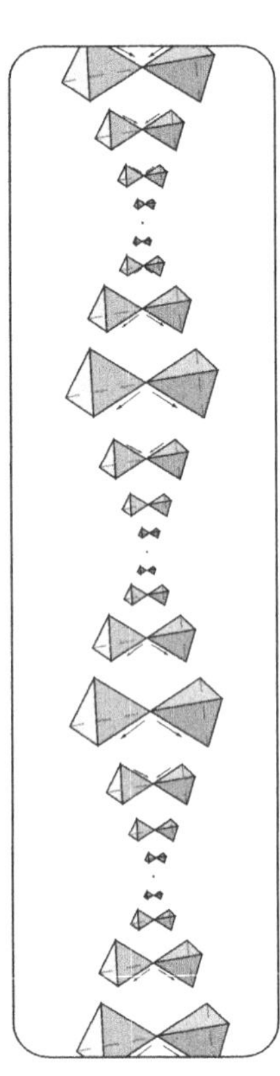

Envision this pumping action as rapid continuous, and going in both directions. It's like an accordion that shrinks to a point, and then expands again, over and over again, every instant, eternally.

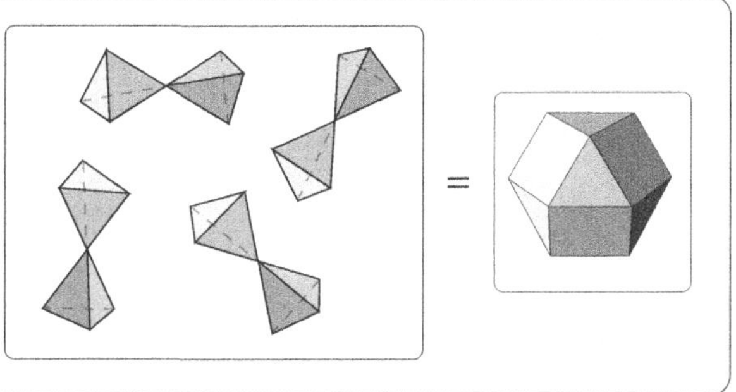
=

4 pairs of tip-to-tip tetrahedra assemble into a cuboctahedron

Now here's the important part.

Four of these Bucky bowties form a cuboctahedron!

(The tops and bottoms of the Bucky bowties make the 8 triangular faces of the cuboctahedron and the spaces between them make the 6 square faces.)

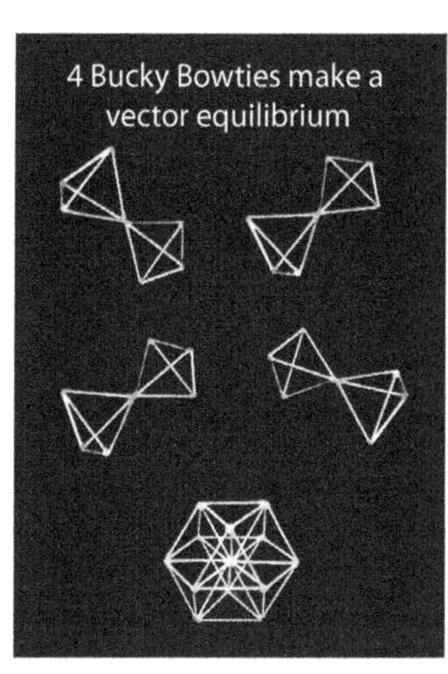
4 Bucky Bowties make a vector equilibrium

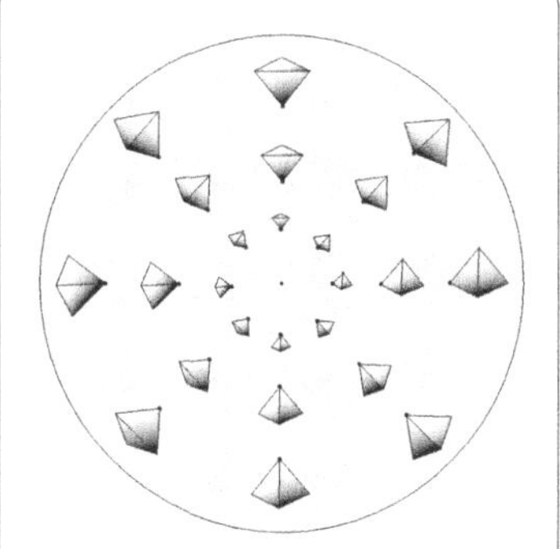

"This locus of vanishment is the nearest to what we mean by a point. The point is the macro-micro switchabout between convergence and divergence."
(Fuller, *Synergetics 1*, 1012.33)

Imagine four Bucky bowtie accordians, all pumping, all contracting, then expanding, all at the same time, through one point in the common center.

Four simultaneous, continual, and eternal energy events passing through a point so infinitesimally small you can't see it, even with an electron microscope.

Bucky poetically calls this central point the **"locus of vanishment."**

Eight tip-to-tip tetrahedra, all shrinking to nothingness at the same time. This glorious event is what Bucky uses to define the simplest thing in all of geometry: **a point.**

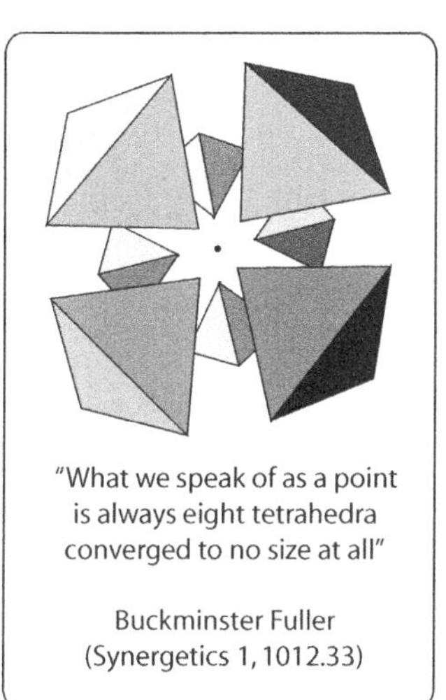

"What we speak of as a point is always eight tetrahedra converged to no size at all"

Buckminster Fuller
(Synergetics 1, 1012.33)

Most people might see the cuboctahedron as just another 3-D shape, perhaps an interesting ornament for a Christmas tree. But to Bucky it was the essence of how Nature's operates.

"A happening is an involuntary experience. You cannot program 'happen.' The vector equilibrium is the minimum operational model of happenings."

(Fuller, *Synergetics I*, sec. 503.01 and 503.03, p. 224)

BUCKMINSTER
FULLER

He even goes a step further with this astounding statement,

"**Pulsation in the vector equilibrium is the nearest thing we will ever know to eternity and god**."

(Fuller, *Synergetics I*, sec. 502.52, p. 224)

Of all the things Bucky explored during his 88-year life on Spaceship Earth, the energy event of this simple shape was the ultimate experience. The quintessence of universe. Eternal and god-like. That's pretty profound.

Rhythm of Geometry = Rhythm of Number

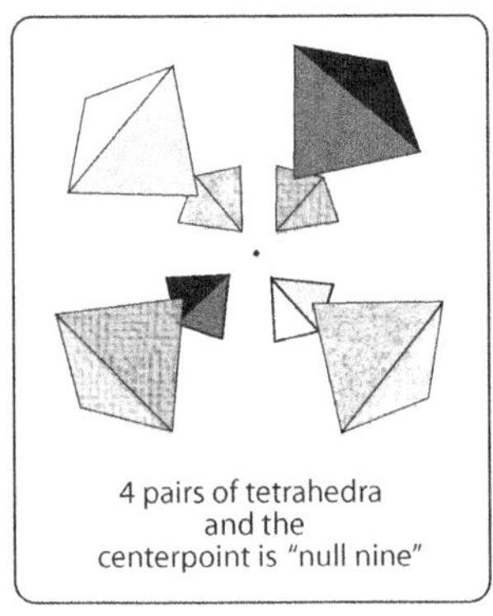
4 pairs of tetrahedra and the centerpoint is "null nine"

Bucky pondered the rhythm of the geometry of the vector equilibrium. Four positive tetrahedra and four negative tetrahedra make an octave of tetrahedra. Then he made a brilliant connection. This was the same rhythm he had seen when working with our Base Ten numbers.

Bucky saw geometry and number as two sides of the same coin. To him, the the "four positive" was like 1, 2, 3, 4, and the "four negative" was like 5, 6, 7, 8.

However, this doesn't account for all the single digits (from which all other numbers are made).

It's missing one digit: the number 9.

Bucky saw that common central point [the very heart of the vector equilibrium] **as the number 9.**

But that central point plays a different role than the 8 tetrahedra in this energy event. Bucky considers the 9 to be more like a "zero." More like a null thing or an empty place.

If all the radiating vectors in a vector equilibrium are like train tracks, that central point is the Grand Central Station, where they all meet up (or pass through).

Bucky asserts that the vector equilibrium has a **"+4, –4, octave; null 9" rhythm.**

In a chapter titled:
Nucleus as Nine = None = Nothing
Bucky writes:

"Nucleus as Nine
that is, non (Latin)
that is, none (English)
that is, nein (German)
that is, neuf (French)
that is, nothing..."

He's pretty clear about it: the center point of the vector equilibrium is the number 9.

He refers to 9 as "zero-nine" or "null nine," suggesting it acts like emptiness, or just plain zero. He calls the vector equilibrium the "**modular domain of the nine-zero-punctuated octave system.**"

What fascinated Bucky was that he found this same "+4, –4, octave; null 9" in the realm of **number.** Bucky remembered a math trick he had learned while training in the accounting department of Armour and Company in Manhattan when he was 25 years old. This was back in 1920, long before hand-calculators had been invented.

The technique called **casting out nines** was used to check if you had done a long multiplication problem correctly. [Perhaps you learned it in math class.]

Casting out nines involves boiling a number down to its "Digital Sum" (that is, the sum of the digits). Bucky called this process "indigging," or finding the "**Indig**" of a number (**in**tegrating its **dig**its).

For example 375 indigs to 15, which further indigs to 6.

Examples of indigging:

24 indigs to 6

913 indigs to 4

90909 indigs to 0

6372815 indigs to 5

4678 indigs to 25, which further indigs to 7

Casting out nines is fun, easy, and useful:

1 Any time the digit 9 appears, cast it out (that is, cross it out, ignore it.)
2 Any combination of digits that add up to 9 can also be cast out.
3 Add up the digits that remain.
4 If the result is a two-digit number, add those two digits together, so it boils down to a single-digit number.

```
 376       7
X 41    4+1=5    7x5=35   3+5=8
 376
1504                      1+1+6 =8
15416
```

These two results should be the same if the original long multiplication was done correctly.

Here's a quick demo of **casting out nines**:

First, indig the two numbers involved in the multiplication problem.

Then multiply these two results together.

Finally, indig that result.

(In this example, the result is 8.)

Next, indig the **product** of the multiplication problem.

(In this example, 15416 also indigs to 8.)

If the two indigged results are equal, you've done your original long multiplication was done correctly.

Amazingly, this "casting out of nines" procedure can also be used to check division, addition, and subtraction problems.

(The only time it doesn't work is if you made a mistake that happened to indig to the same number the correct solution would have indigged to.)

Bucky summarizes,

"From this I saw that nine is zero."

Bucky then made a chart of the indigs in the normal Base-Ten flow of number and found the **same "octave, null 9" rhythm he saw in the vector equilibrium**.

On the left are all the single digits, and 9 is zero.

Next, the numbers 10 through 17 indig to 1, 2, 3, 4 , 5, 6, 7, and 8, and the 18 indigs to zero.

At the bottom of the next column, 27 indigs to zero,

And in the next column, 36 indigs to zero.

This "octave, null nine" rhythm continues endlessly.

Indigging
the normal flow of numbers
reveals an "octave, null nine" rhythm.

1 = **1**	10 = **1**	19 = **1**	28 = **1**	37 = **1**
2 = **2**	11 = **2**	20 = **2**	29 = **2**	38 = **2**
3 = **3**	12 = **3**	21 = **3**	30 = **3**	(...)
4 = **4**	13 = **4**	22 = **4**	31 = **4**	
5 = **5**	14 = **5**	23 = **5**	32 = **5**	
6 = **6**	15 = **6**	24 = **6**	33 = **6**	
7 = **7**	16 = **7**	25 = **7**	34 = **7**	
8 = **8**	17 = **8**	26 = **8**	35 = **8**	
9 = **0**	18 = **0**	27 = **0**	36 = **0**	

Then Bucky made a chart of the **squares** of the normal Base Ten flow of number: 1, 4, 9, 16, 25, etc.

The indigs flow 1407, 7041, zero. Then 1407, 7041 zero again. Then 1407, 7041 zero again, endlessly.

Once again, he found the "octave, null nine" pattern.

Indigging the SQUARES of the normal flow of numbers reveals an "octave, null nine" rhythm.

1 = **1**	100 = **1**	361 = **1**	784 = **1**	1369 = **1**
4 = **4**	121 = **4**	400 = **4**	841 = **4**	1444 = **4**
9 = **0**	144 = **0**	441 = **0**	900 = **0**	(...)
16 = **7**	169 = **7**	484 = **7**	961 = **7**	
25 = **7**	196 = **7**	529 = **7**	1084 = **7**	
36 = **0**	225 = **0**	576 = **0**	1089 = **4**	
49 = **4**	256 = **4**	625 = **4**	1156 = **0**	
64 = **1**	289 = **1**	676 = **1**	1225 = **1**	
81 = **0**	324 = **0**	729 = **0**	1296 = **0**	

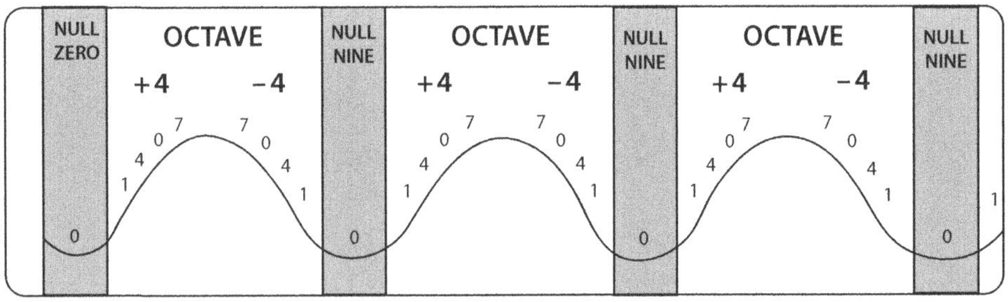

NULL ZERO | OCTAVE +4 −4 | NULL NINE | OCTAVE +4 −4 | NULL NINE | OCTAVE +4 −4 | NULL NINE

0 1 4 0 7 7 0 4 1 0 1 4 0 7 7 0 4 1 0 1 4 0 7 7 0 4 1 0 1

Here is a graphic depiction of this rhythm found by indigging the squares.

Bucky breaks the octave into +4 and −4.

As Bucky puts it:

"Indig congruences demonstrate that nine is zero and that number system is inherently octave..." with an internal rhythm of "four positive and four negative."

He calls it:

"The inherent +4, −4, 0, +4, −4, 0 ⟶ of number"

or the

"+4, −4, octave; null 9" rhythm of number

It's the same rhythm he saw in the vector equilibrium. He saw how Geometry and Number were intrinsically related.

Similarly, John Dee, in his *Preface to Euclid,* emphasizes that all the arts and sciences derive from only two "Principall Mathematical Artes." They are "Geometry" and "Arithmetic."

In short, Bucky discovered in the 1900s the same thing Dee discovered in the 1500s: the closest packing of spheres and its cuboctahedron shape synthesizes with the "+4,–4, octave;null nine" nature of number.

And they were each thrilled with their discovery.

How can I be certain Dee knew about the closest packing of spheres?

Johannes Kepler (in the early 1600's) is generally credited with being the first person to explore the closest-packing-of-spheres. But the wise philosophers of Europe had known about this arrangement for least 50 years.

Girolamo Cardano described the 12-around-1 closest-packing-of-spheres arrangement in his 1550 book about natural phenomena called *De Subtilitate* or "On Subtle Things."

(In 1552, Dee had a meeting with Cardano when the Italian mathematician was visiting London. Not only did Dee have two copies of Cardano's book in his library, he took one with him when he traveled to Prague in 1583. *Subtilitas* literally means "keenness, acuteness, or exactness." In his thick compendium, Cardano explains natural phenomena that go unnoticed by most people, including the behavior of light in a camera obscura.)

Dee cryptically refers to the closest-packing-of-spheres in his *Letter to Maxmillian*, in which he gives advice to those who have studied *Plenum and Vacuo* or "Space and Void."

"They have seen that the Surfaces of Elements, which are in close proximity are coordinated, connected, and Joined Together by a Law (decreed by God Almighty) and Bond (practically Unable to be Loosened) of Nature."

Dee's dramatic wording indicates this was an important concept in his cosmology.

Atomism

As we saw earlier, in Theorem 18 of the *Monas*, Dee relates one of Aesop's parables. A vengeful Scarab Beetle has deposited its dungballs in Jupiter's lap, where the Eagle had left its eggs for safekeeping. Dungballs and eggs (if all the same-sized spheres) will naturally arrange themselves in this closest-packing-of-spheres arrangement.

I'm not suggesting there were exactly 13 spheres arranged in the cuboctahedral pattern in Jupiter's lap. When any large quantity of same-sized spheres close-pack together, in the middle are of the pack are groupings of 13 spheres arranged in the cubocthedral shape.

Indeed, after relating the parable, Dee writes he is acting more like "Aesop" than "Oedipus."

(Oedipus was famous for the Riddle of the Sphinx).

Dee is hinting: This is not a parable, it's a riddle.

My interpretation of Dee's "eggs and dungballs" being "same-sized spheres" might seem conjectural, but not if you understand the bigger picture of Dee's philosophy:

Dee was an Atomist.

Atomism is simply the theory that the universe is made from atoms, which can be neither divided nor destroyed. Dee didn't invent this concept by any means. Atomism goes back to the Greek philosophers:

Anaxagoras (ca. 500 BC – 428 BC),
Leucippus (ca. 425 BC),
his student **Democritus** (ca. 375 BC),
and later, **Epicurus** (ca. 300 BC)

Democritus writes:

"In nature, there is nothing but '*atoma*' (atoms)
and '*kenon*' (void, space, emptiness).**"**

In the Renaissance, great thinkers like Nicholas of Cusa, Marcello Ficino, and Giordano Bruno were influenced by Lucretius' ideas about atomism.

As Andrew Pyle writes in *Atomism and its Critics: from Democritus to Newton*: during the late 1500's and early 1600's, "atomism was becoming very popular and widespread." By the year 1600, the Classical Atomic theory had been thoroughly revived and was the subject of heated controversy. (A. J. Pyle, pp. 224-5)

Robert Kargon, in his 1966 book *Atomism in England, from Hariot to Newton*, prefaces his chapter on Dee's friend, Thomas Harriot, with a few words about John Dee. Kargon calls Dee the "**leading participant in the Platonic-Pythagorean revival of the English Renaissance**."

(Kargon, p. 8)

[Atoms are so small, Dee could never see one closeup. But if he thought atoms were spherical, then all matter would contain cuboctahedral shapes]

More evidence that Dee knew about the cuboctahedron

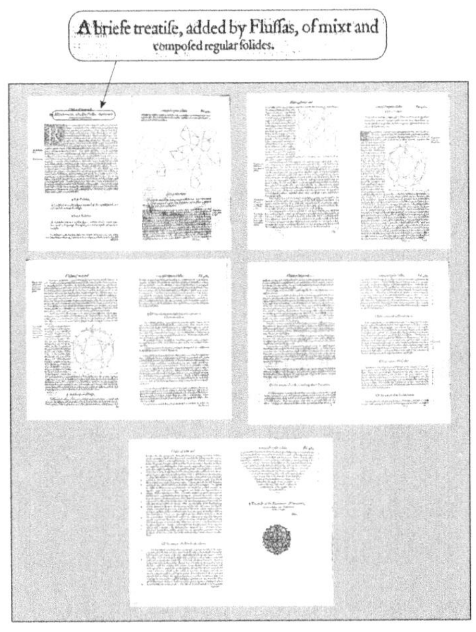

Besides writing the *Preface* to the 1570 first English Edition of Euclid's *Elements*, Dee provided over 150 corollaries and addendums to various propositions. The French expert on Euclid, Francois de Foix (also known as Flussas) provided some as well.

The whole translation of *Elements* is almost 1000 pages long. At the very end, after Book 16, is a *Brief Treatise* by Flussas.

In it, Flussas explains that the intersection of a cube and an octahedron is an "exoctahedron."

(The prefix "ex" is short for "sex" which means "six." So "ex," is simply another name for a six-sided cube. Thus, ex-octahedron means cube-octahedron.)

Exoctahedron, Cuboctahedron, Vector Equilibrium; **they all refer to the exact same shape.**

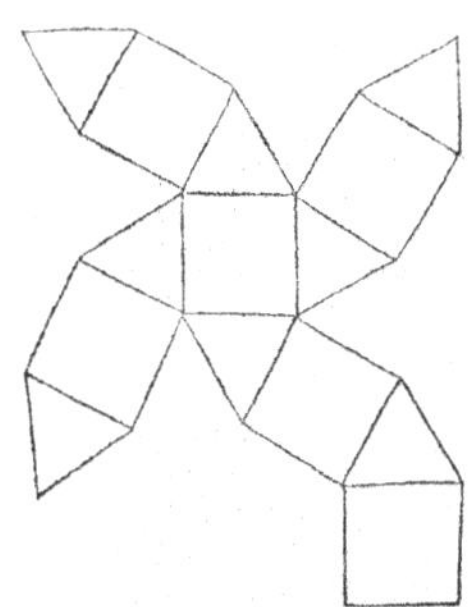

The book even includes a flattened version that can be cut out and shaped into a 3-D cuboctahedron. Note that it it's made from 8 triangles and 6 squares.

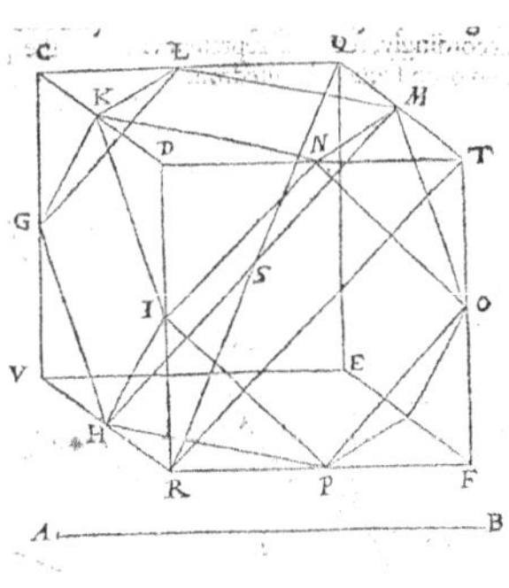

The text also provides a geometric proof of how to make the shape by cutting off the corners of a cube at the middle of its edges.

Dee gives several clues about the cuboctahedron in his "Thus the World Was Created" chart. He knew an astute geometer would recognize that **12**, **13**, **24**, and **25** are all numbers associated with the cuboctahedron:

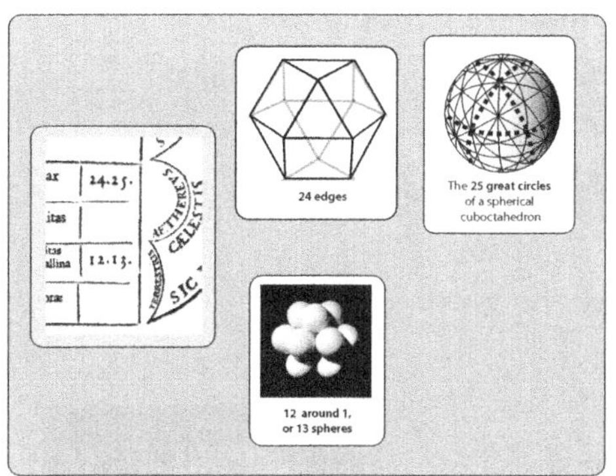

The cuboctahedron's **12** spheres-around-1 arrangement makes a cluster of **13** spheres. The cuboctahedron has exactly **24** edges.

The 25 is a little trickier. If a cuboctahedron is blown up like a balloon, there are exactly **25** "great circles" that pass through the vertices, edge-midpoints, and face-centerpoints.

Dee and his fellow navigator friends were quite familiar with "great circles." They used them to find the shortest route between two places on the spherical globe of the earth.

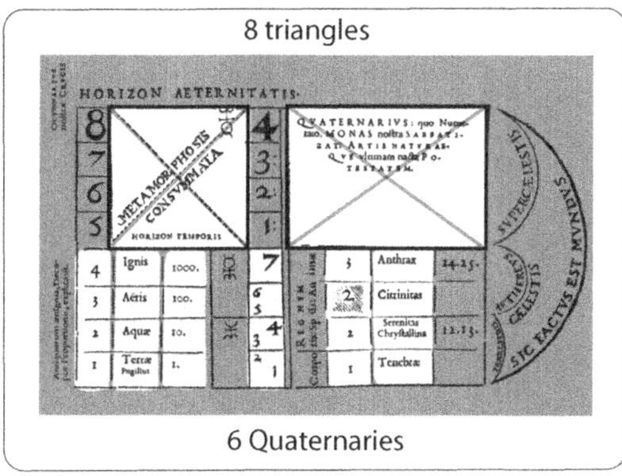

Alchemists like Paracelsus refer to the "**Earthly Quaternary**" and the "**Heavenly Ternary**."

Things "of Earth," are grouped in fours (like the 4 Elements). Things "of Heaven" are in groups of three (like the Holy Trinity).

In the "Below" half of Dee's chart are 6 "quaternaries," or lists containing 4 items.

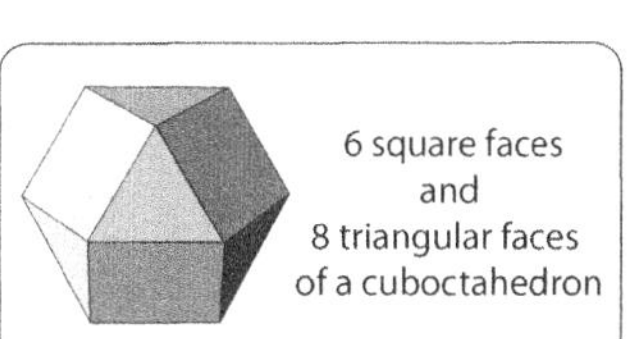

In the "Above" half of the chart, Dee has cryptically hidden 8 triangles.

This is Dee's clever way of hinting at the 6 square faces and the 8 triangular faces of a cuboctahedron.)

How can I be sure Dee knew about the "+4, –4 octave; null 9" nature of number?

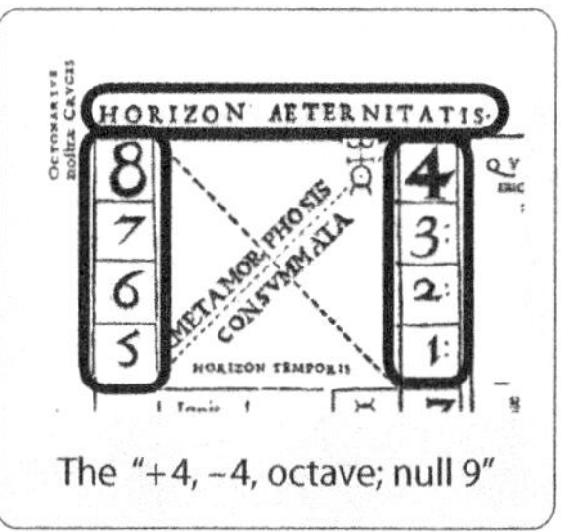

The "+4, –4, octave; null 9"

This one is easy to answer. Dee illustrated it in his "Thus the World Was Created" chart.

The Greeks called 9 the "Horizon Number" because, being the largest single digit, it is on the horizon of a vast sea of multiple-digit numbers.

The digits 1, 2, 3, and 4 are in one grouping. And 5, 6, 7, and 8 are in another. And the two groupings are connected with a large dotted-line X, a symbol of oppositeness.

To conclude, Dee and Bucky both saw the wonders of the cuboctahedron. They each saw that it was made from 4 pairs of tip-to-tip tetrahedra, with a null ninth centerpoint.

One of Bucky's favorite maxims: "Unity is plural and at minimum two."

"Unity is plural" might seem like a contradiction in terms. "Unity" seems as though it means wholeness, or oneness. And "plural" is anything but oneness.

So let's take a sphere as an example. Bucky saw that in order for it to be a sphere, it has to have an outside and an inside. Outsidedness is convex, and insidedness is concave.

How you see the sphere depends on if you're outside it or inside it.

To humans, the surface of the earth is convex. But to an earthworm or a fish, the surface of the world is concave.

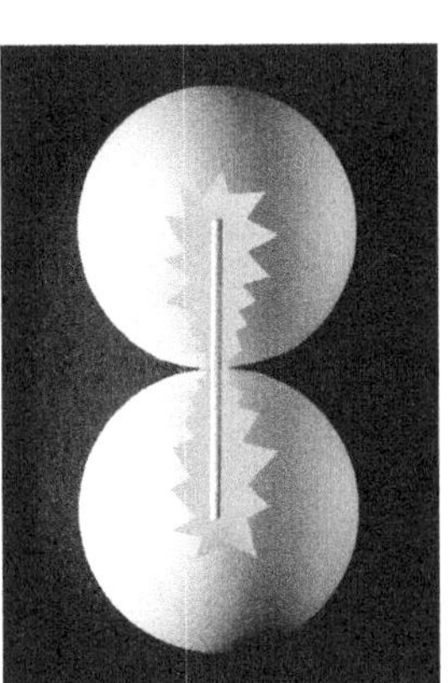

As another example, let's take a line, (in this case a lollipop stick). Most of us see a line as one thing.

But Bucky saw a line as a vector connecting two endpoints.

These endpoints are the centers of two same-sized spheres that are tangent to each other.

To Bucky, a line was an energy event between two things.

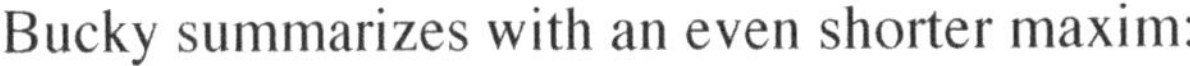

Bucky summarizes with an even shorter maxim:

"Unity=2"

Well, this is exactly how Dee saw things.
The main theme of the *Monas Hieroglyphica* is the Sun and the Moon becoming one. The Union of Opposites.

Dee and Bucky were on the same wavelength. They both fervently searched to find Nature's laws. They were both skilled geometers. And they both found the same things.

Bucky called himself a "**comprehensivist**," someone who ties together various fields of knowledge.
Dee was a **polymath**, a philosopher wise in many fields of learning.

Bucky saw himself as a "**citizen of Spaceship Earth**."
Dee called himself a "**cosmopilite**," meaning "citizen of the world."
(Dee's birthday was July 13 and, curiously, Bucky's birthday was July 12).

Bucky was a brilliant, creative thinker.
And he had the advantage of 300 years of accumulated knowledge over Dee.
But next, we'll see that Dee actually discovered **more** about number than Bucky did!

*(We're halfway through our vacation from the original Globe theater.
Let's switch gears from Geometry to Number.
And we'll discover that they are two sides of the same coin!)*

ROBERT MARSHALL FINDS SYMMETRY IN NUMBER

One of Bucky's followers, Robert Marshall, had a brain for seeing patterns in number and explained his findings to Bucky.

Bucky understood what Marshall had discoverd and was quite excited about it. He asked Marshall if he would publish his findings "in another edition of *Synergetics*." Unfortunately, in 1983, before the project came to fruition, Bucky passed away.

Again, I found Marshall through more googlification of 252. He was in his 70's and living in a small house in Northern California. We corresponded for 10 years until he died. He called his study of the symmetry of number "Syndex." He saw rhythms in number that are invisible to most people.

Marshall was thrilled to explain his discoveries to me. Few scholars besides Bucky were able to see the significance his work.

I was thrilled. I soon realized that Marshall saw numbers the same way Dee saw numbers. Dozens of puzzling parts of the *Monas* became clear.

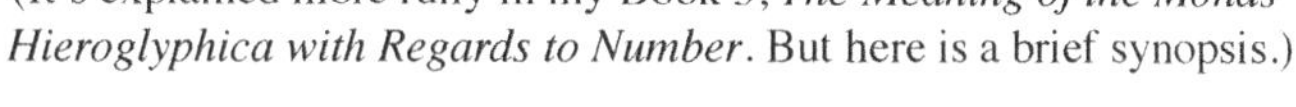
(It's explained more fully in my Book 5, *The Meaning of the Monas Hieroglyphica with Regards to Number*. But here is a brief synopsis.)

Marshall saw numbers differently than most people.

As a child, he had a hard time grasping subtraction of digits.

But when he saw numbers as dots, and some dots were taken away, things were much clearer.

In the 1960's, Bob Marshall was a hippie living in the Haight-Ashbury district of San Francisco – the epicenter of many of the social and cultural changes that were swirling through America.

While studying Eastern religion, he asked a visiting guru how he should proceed in his study of number. The guru was no mathematician, but he recommended that Bob study the number which had been sacred in Indian culture since the days of the ancients – the number 108.

mala
(108 beads)

The Hindus recite the names of 108 deities while counting their mala, a looped string with 108 beads.
There are 108 verses in the Rig Veda.
To the Hindus, 108 represents totality and wholeness.
Even today, some Hindus in India pay lots of rupees to have 108 in their smartphone numbers.

(To my Western-educated mind, 108 seemed as random as 252.
It seemed like 100 would be a better candidate to express wholeness than 108.)

Marshall made a huge spiral of numbers called the "108 Wheel."
The first circle of the spiral went from 1 to 108.
The next circle went from 109 to 216, and onward.
It had 60 cycles that went all the way out to the number 6480.

Marshall's 108 Wheel
(a spiral of 60 cycles up to 6480)

With the wheel as a starting point, Marshall found what he calls an "ancient canon of number." He was quick to add that he didn't discover it. He only claims to have "re-discovered" it, as he was able to discern that it was known to the Ancient Hindus, the Greeks, and even the authors of the Bible.

Why haven't other mathematicians seen what Marshall found? Well, Marshall had a different way of looking at number. Most people see Number as a one-way street. One, two, three, four … and off into infinity. Marshall saw **number as a two way street.** It goes forwards and backwards.

(And backwards doesn't mean the "negative numbers" that go –1, -2, -3, -4, etc. Marshall only worked with the positive integers.)

Marshall found that at certain finite limits, there is **complete symmetry of number**. What does he mean by symmetry of number?

(And could these be the same "fixed limits" of "Nature's Law" that Dee was referring to in his Artificial Quaternary chart?)

Also, Marshall did not consider 1 to be a number. This might sound strange to modern ears. If Joe has 5 apples and sells 4, he has one left. So, one **must** be a number. I live at 321 Main Street. Where am I supposed to tell people I live?

However, math historians will confirm that, up until around 1700, nobody thought one was a number. Greek, Medieval and Renaissance mathematicians saw that "1" acted differently than all the other digits.

Multiply one times any number and the result is the same number.
Divide one into any number and the result is the same number.
Add one to any number, then add another one, then another, and the result is the natural sequence of number.

You can't say these things about 2, or 3, or 4, or any other digit.

As we'll soon see, early mathematician-philosophers considered one to be the "fount" or source of all number.

Marshall's symbol for "retrocity" or "oppositeness"

Marshall also recognized a function that most other mathematicians ignore. He calls it "**retrocity**." It expresses oppositeness.

(From the Latin word *retro*, meaning backwards)

To express it in mathematical notation, Marshall invented the "**retrocity symbol**." He considered the retrocity symbol (which is read as, "is the opposite of") to be as important as other function signs like "=" ("is equal to") or ">" ("is greater than").

To draw it, make a vertical line that ascends, then slowly arches, then descends in the "opposite" direction.

Then add a horizontal line that suggests there is an "interconnection," despite the "opposition."

Here's my artistic interpretation that emphasizes its "Union of Opposites" character.

(There's a positive side and a negative side, but they're united as one symbol.)

An artistic interpretation of Marshall's retrocity symbol

Here are some examples to show how simple it is.

The opposite of 29 is 92.

(As they mirror each other, Marshall calls them "reflective mates.")

The reflective mate of 341 is 143.

The reflective mate of 27956 is 65972.

29 A 92
341 A 143
27956 A 65972

The "opposite" of a number which contains all the same digits is "itself."
For example, the reflective mate of 22 is 22.

8 A 8
22 A 22
77777 A 77777

Here are some examples involving numbers that end in zeros.

The reflective mate of 270 is 072 or simply 72.
The reflective mate of 27,000 is also 72.
The reflective mate of 35,000 is 53.

270 A 72
27000 A 72
35000 A 53

This might seem like a silly number game, but we'll shortly see that it's essential to seeing the natural symmetry of number.

Plus, it's useful shorthand for expressing the "oppositeness" found in many kinds of things.

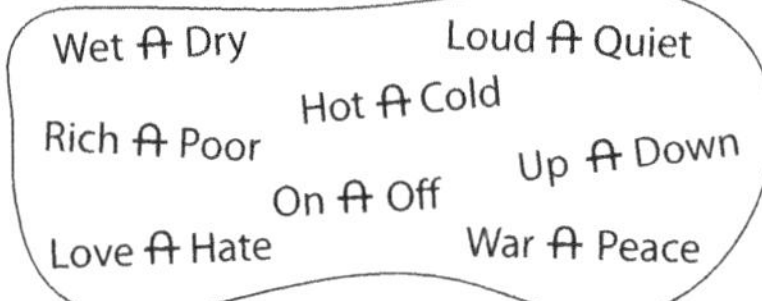

It's obvious that Hot and Cold are opposites, but they are united in the sense they are both aspects of temperature.

Wet and Dry are both aspects of humidity.
Loud and Quiet are both aspects of sound.

My initial reaction was that you can't simply ignore place value like that. For example, the 2 in 29 really represents 20, not 2. Then I recalled how place value was ignored in the "indigging" Bucky did in the "casting out of nines" to check long multiplication.

The idea of ignoring place value opens up a world of number not many people have explored. And in it, wonderful symmetries can be seen. This might sound mysteriously mystical, but perfect symmetry can be easily seen on the chart of numbers you learned in grade school.

	1	2	3	4	5	6	7	8	9
10	11	12	13	14	15	16	17	18	19
20	21	22	23	24	25	26	27	28	29
30	31	32	33	34	35	36	37	38	39
40	41	42	43	44	45	46	47	48	49
50	51	52	53	54	55	56	57	58	59
60	61	62	63	64	65	66	67	68	69
70	71	72	73	74	75	76	77	78	79
80	81	82	83	84	85	86	87	88	89
90	91	92	93	94	95	96	97	98	99

This square chart includes all the single and double-digit numbers.

(Note that it ends with 99, because 100 is a triple-digit number.)

Across the horizontal rows are the single digits, the teens, the twenties, the thirties, etc. Looking vertically down the columns, they all end in 0, or 1, or 2, etc.

To see the perfect symmetry more clearly, allow me to make a few non-destructive adjustments to the chart.

First, let's look at it backwards, like the way Hebrew or Chinese is read.

Now the 10, 20, 30, etc. column is on the right.

9	8	7	6	5	4	3	2	1	
19	18	17	16	15	14	13	12	11	10
29	28	27	26	25	24	23	22	21	20
39	38	37	36	35	34	33	32	31	30
49	48	47	46	45	44	43	42	41	40
59	58	57	56	55	54	53	52	51	50
69	68	67	66	65	64	63	62	61	60
79	78	77	76	75	74	73	72	71	70
89	88	87	86	85	84	83	82	81	80
99	98	97	96	95	94	93	92	91	90

Next, let's rotate it
45 degrees counter-clockwise,
making the square into a diamond.

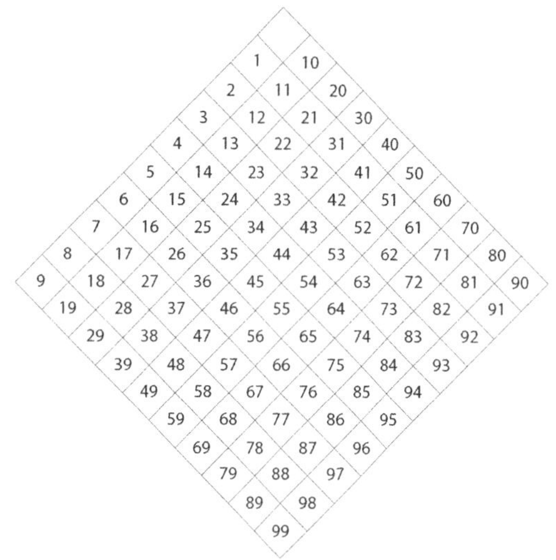

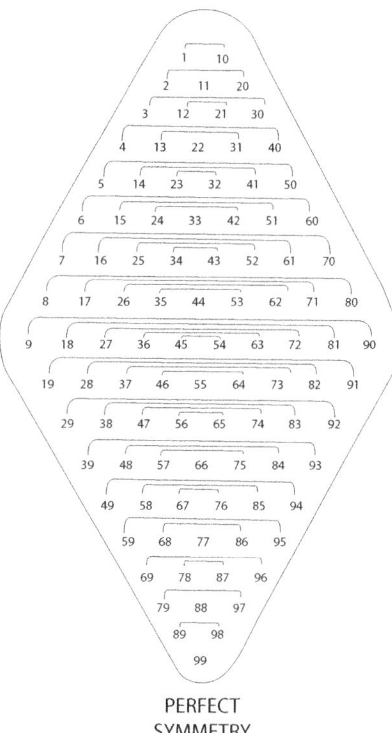

PERFECT SYMMETRY

Then, let's stretch it vertically to make room for brackets which connect various reflective mates.

Look. Every number on the left side of the chart has a reflective mate on the right side!

The chart has **perfect symmetry**!
Like the wings of a butterfly!

There is complete retrocity!

The numbers on the central vertical spine of the chart (11, 22, 33, etc.) don't have partners because they are reflective mates of themselves!
(For example, the opposite of 77 is 77.)

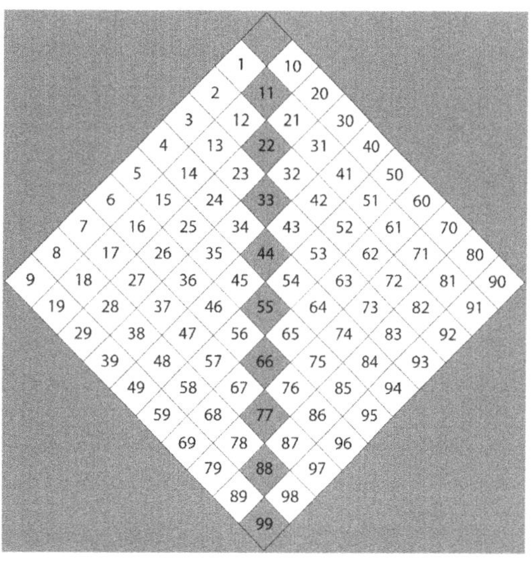

The numbers "11, 22, 33, 44, 55, 66, 77, 88, and 99" are all multiples of 11,
so I call them the "**11 Wave**."
Marshall refers to these numbers as **palindromes** (or palindromic numbers).
(They're similar to palindromic words that read the same forwards as backwards, like level, kayak, or racecar)

Marshall calls the reflective pairs which contain two different numbers "**transpalindromes**."
(If you put a mirror right down the spine of this chart, splitting the palindromes in half,
you can see the perfect symmetry of the whole chart.)

Who knew numbers had such splendor!

It appears as though the **11 Wave** rules the chart.
But not so fast. There's another wave that's just as important.

It's the **9 Wave**, which runs horizontally across the middle of the chart (the multiples of 9).
On the far left is 9.
On the far right is 90.

In them between are 4 transpalindromic pairs, (18 and 81), (27 and 72), (36 and 63), and (45 and 54).

Seeing the 90 as that "null 9th thing," Bucky's "+4, –4, octave; null 9" rhythm is clearly evident.

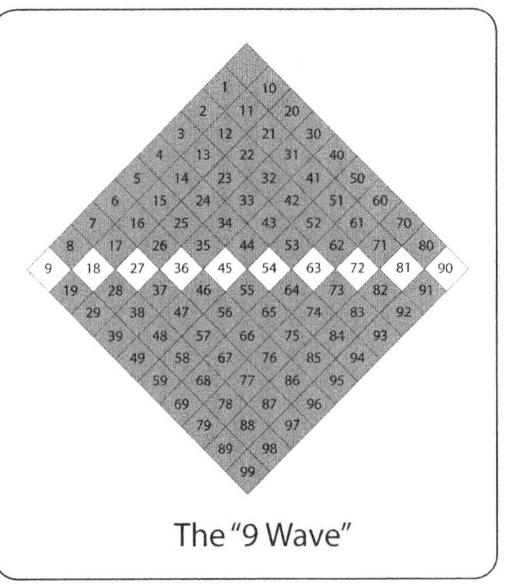

The "9 Wave"

Marshall calls 9 the **transpalindromizer** and 11 the **palindromizer**.

9 10 11
nine ten eleven

Incidentally, similar symmetries can be found in other Bases besides our Base Ten System.

The transpalindromizer is always one digit less than the Base number.

The palindromizer is always one more than the Base number.

(But only Base Ten makes this "octave, null 9" rhythm, and I believe it was for this reason Base Ten was selected by the ancients. And not because man has 10 fingers. But that's a longer story)

The Cycloflex

The "northwest edge" of the "butterfly chart" expresses Bucky's rhythm "+ 4, –4, octave; null nine" (in the single-digit range of number).

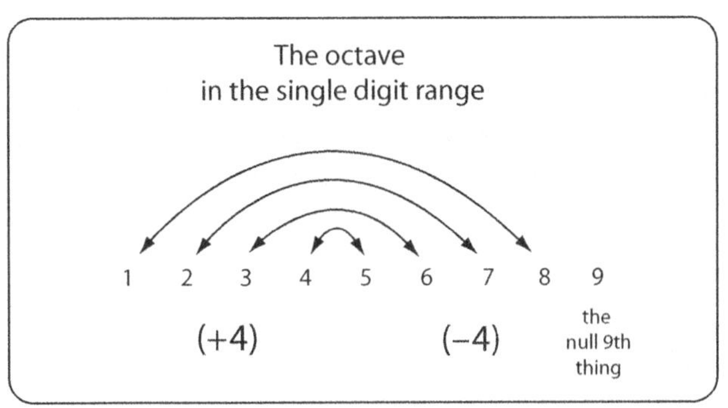

And the middle horizontal row also expresses Bucky's rhythm "+ 4, –4, octave; null nine" (in the two-digit range of number).

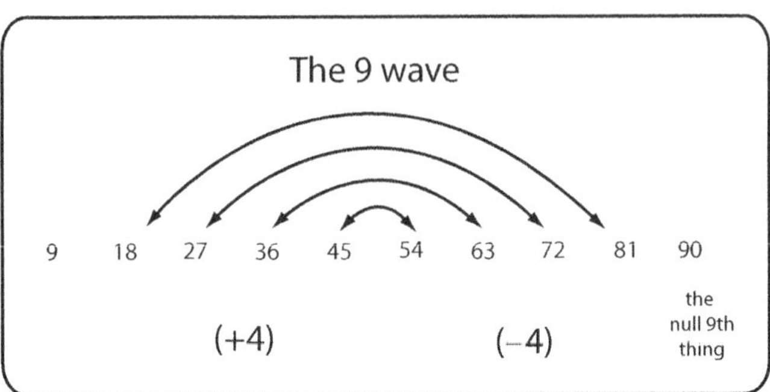

Multiplying 9 times 11 makes 99, which is the largest double-digit number.
The three-digit range of numbers is ruled by the multiples of 99:
198, 297, 396, 495, 594, 693, 792, 891 and 990,
or what I call the "**99 Wave**."

You can see that
198 and 891 are reflective mates,
297 and 792 are reflective mates, etc.

They beat out the same
"+4, –4 octave, null nine" rhythm.

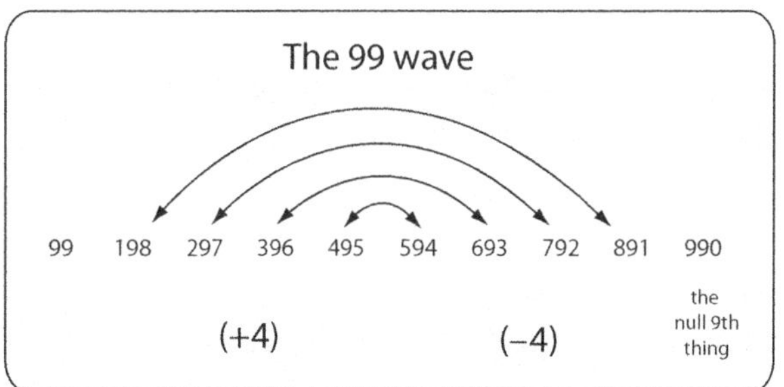

What Marshall meant by
"number is a two-way street"
now becomes a lot clearer.

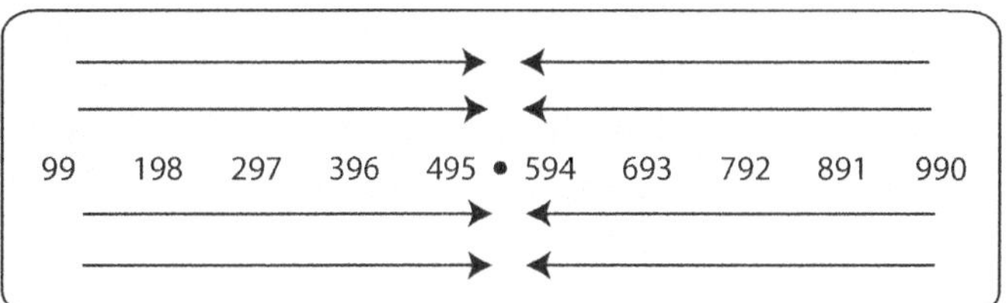

Next, 99 times 11 is 1089,
and the **1089 Wave** rules the
range of the 4-digit numbers.

However, a curious thing happens.
A "nave" or central-point is born.
It's the palindromic number 5445.

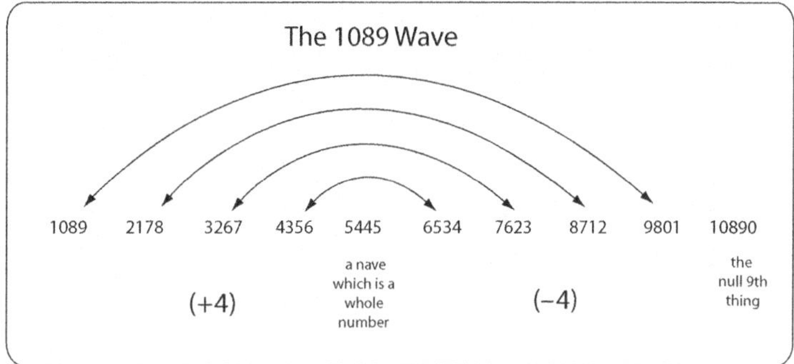

That nave of 5445 causes the
5-digit range to be ruled by 10890.

The **10890 Wave** also exhibits
perfect symmetry and has Bucky's
"+4, –4 octave; null nine" rhythm.

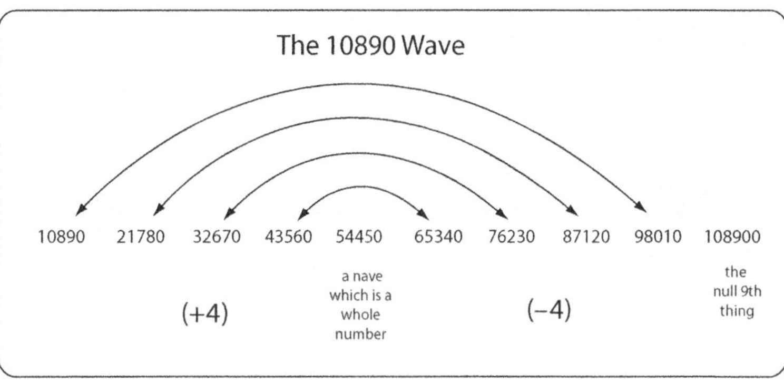

This same "+4,–4 octave; null nine" rhythm continues through the **108900 Wave**,
the **1089000 Wave**, the **10890000 Wave**, etc. (You get the picture).

Marshall referred to this number rhythm as the "**Cycloflex**."
As you **cycle** through the number ranges, numbers **flex** back on themselves.
(Dee called this number rhythm "Consummata," which is Latin for "to make perfect" or "to complete.")

What does all this have to do with Dee?

Note that all of the single-digit numbers are palindromes.
For example, the reflective mate of 6 is 6.
The reflective mate of the palindrome 11 is 11.
That makes 12 and 21 the "**first** transpalindromic pair."

And guess what **12 times 21** equals?

252

Dee's Magistral number.

Putting the hand calculator aside and doing this as "long multiplication" reveals how 252 is made from 12 and 24, two of Dee's favorite numbers.

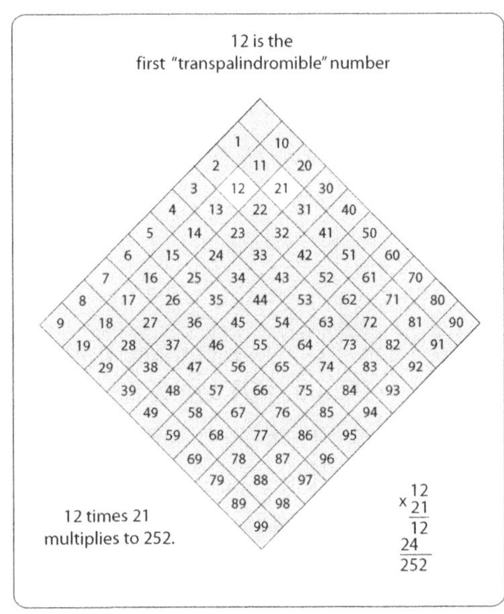

Marshall explored 252 even deeper and found this amazing relationship. The squares of 12 and 21 are transpalindromes themselves: 144 and 441.

$$12^2 = 144$$
} the difference is 108
$$12 \times 21 = 252$$
} the difference is189
$$21^2 = 441$$

Also, the difference between 252 and 144 is 108 (the sacred number of the Hindus pops up again).

Marshall calls this the relationship the "Syndex pretzel"

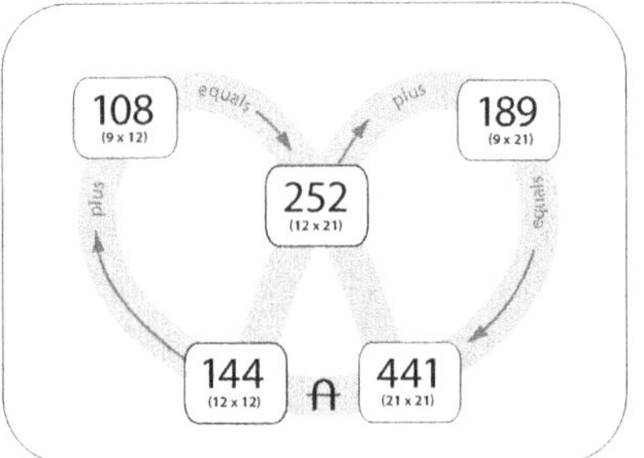

Pascal's Triangle

I call 252 a "nexus number," because its always in the middle of things. Mathematicians will want to explore its prominent position in what is called Pascal's Triangle. When we separate even numbers from odd numbers, right in the center of the large triangular patch of even numbers is 252.

(Pascal's Triangle was known long before Pascal, and Dee definitely knew about it. Dee even uses the "1, 7, 21, 35, 35, 21, 7, 1" row to calculate probabilities in Aphorism 116 of his 1558 *Propaedeumata Aphoristica*.)

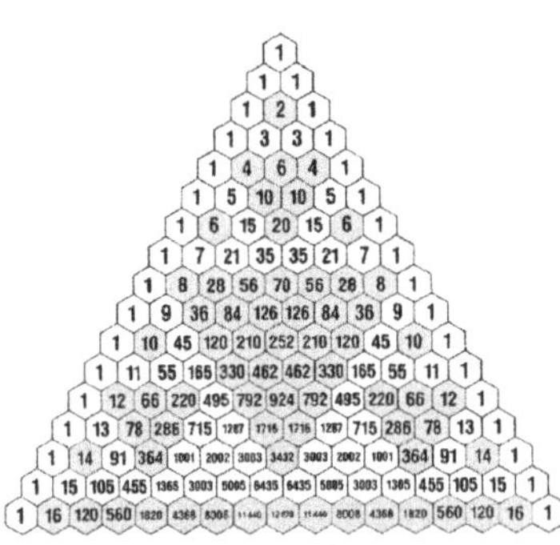
Pascal's Triangle
(with even numbers in grey)

The Holotomic Sequence

Marshall found **another** great sequence that flows through number whose members show the "symmetry of number" in a different way.

He calls them the "**Holotomes.**"

This word is a composite of the Greek word *holo,* which means "whole," and *tome,* which means "book."

Marshall sees them as "whole-books" because each is a complete "book" of numbers, each of which exhibits perfect symmetry.

Plus, contained within each holotome are the symmetries of all the holotomes which precede it.

(This will become clearer in a moment when we look at "number wheels.")

To find these symmetrical books of number we must "Think like a Renaissance man." And remember, Renaissance men didn't consider "one" to be a number.

One is Not a Number

In *History of Mathematics*, D.E. Smith declared:

"Not until modern times was unity considered a number. Euclid defined number as a quantity made up of units..."

(D.E. Smith, *History of Mathematics*, II, p. 26)

Aristotle wrote in *Physics,*

"The smallest number in the strict sense of the word 'number' is two."

(*Aristotle*, edited by Richard McKeon, *Physics*, Book 3, Ch. 11, Section 220, Line 27)

Nicomachus wrote that unity is not a polygonal number, but Boethius interpreted this as meaning that one was not a number. Following Boethius, great mathematicians in the Middle Ages like al-Kwârmizi (ca. 825), Michael Psellus (ca.1075) and Rolandus (ca. 1424) excluded one from the realm of number.

This viewpoint held fast during the Renaissance. The Italian mathmetician Luca Pacioli (ca. 1494) writes, "**...unita nō e numero...**"

The German mathematician Theodoricus Tzwivel (ca.1505), writes:

"Unitas em numeus non est. Sed fons et origo numerorum,"

"Unity is not a number, but the fount and origin of number."

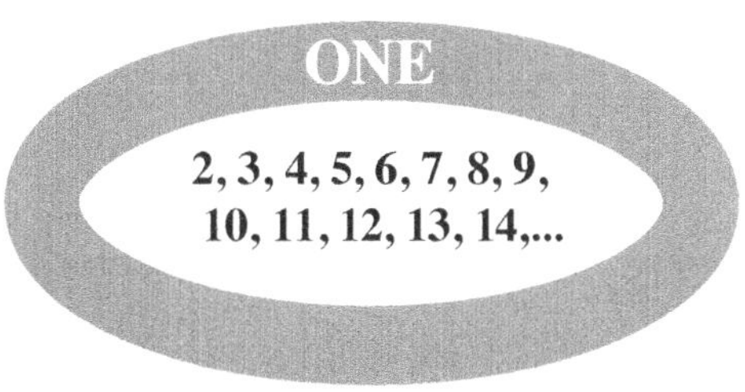

ONE

2, 3, 4, 5, 6, 7, 8, 9, 10, 11, 12, 13, 14,...

Dee writes in his 1570 *Preface to Euclid*,

"We consider a Unit to be a Mathematical thing, though it be no number, as it is indivisible."

(Dee, *Preface*, p. j.)

Humphrey Baker, one of Dee's contemporaries in England, writes,

"**an unitie is no number, but the beginning and original of number**."

Towards the end of the 1500's, mathematicians like Simon Stevin (1585) and Petrus Ramus debated whether it was all a question of semantics. Stevin writes,

"...if from 3 we take 1, 3 does not remain, hence 1 is not no number,"

[He used a "double negative" for emphasis]

Eventually, Stevins' admittedly logical train of thought caught on.
But to grasp why earlier mathmeticians didn't consider one to be a number,
we must explore the ultimate example of oppositeness.
Are you ready.

Nothing A Everything

"Nothing is the opposite of Everything"
Whoa. That's a pretty big concept.
(Don't worry, I'm not going to get all philosophical on you)
Let's look at it mathematically.

The "Nothing" (or the void) is 0.
The "Everything" is 1.
(As all numbers flow from the well-spring of 1.)

As Marshall writes,
"You cannot have matter without space.
An object cannot exist unless it has a place to be.
And you cannot have both, then, without reversal."

Marshall coined an term for this group of 3 things:
the "**Prenumerical Tertiary Singularity**."

"Prenumerical" in the sense that it comes "before numbers" (2, 3, 4...)
"Tertiary" because there are "3 things" involved.
And "Singularity" because "they all work together."

What we normally think of as "one,"
Marshall saw as a collection of three things:

"zero-retrocity-one"

He used a triangle to depict the "Prenumerical Tertiary Singularity."

And to simplify, he shortened the mouthful "zero-retrocity-one" to the pithier term,"zero-one."

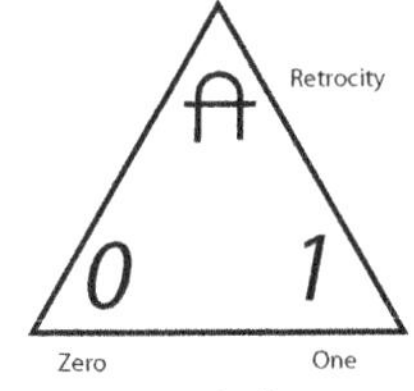

Marshall's
"Prenumerical Tertiary Singularity"

What I call "The Birth of Number"

Let's start with that first important step from "zero-one" to two.

The energy of the "zero-one" generates special number 2.
Marshall calls 2 the "symmetrical aspect" of "zero-one."
Let's label 2 as "symmetry."

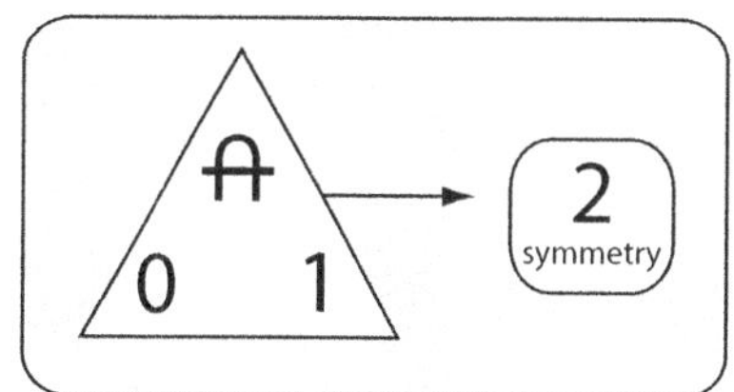

Envision this "symmetry" energy echoing further out into the number realm, to 4, 8, 16, 32, 64, 128 ... and beyond.

But let's confine this analysis to just the single digits (out of which all other numbers are made)..

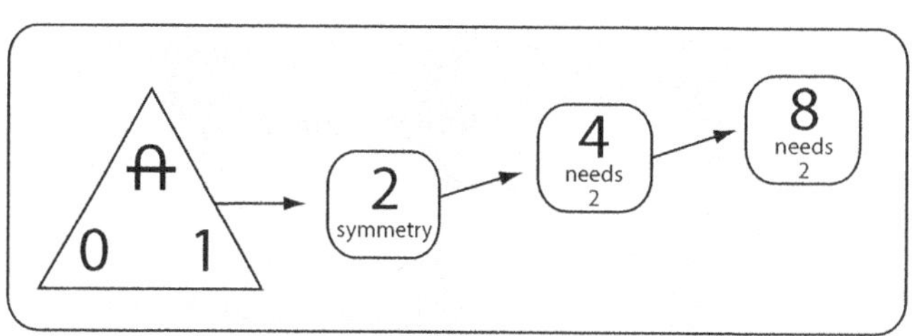

In making 4, number 2 already exists, so (as I express it) 4 only "needs 2."

Similarly, as 4 now exists, 8 only "needs 2."

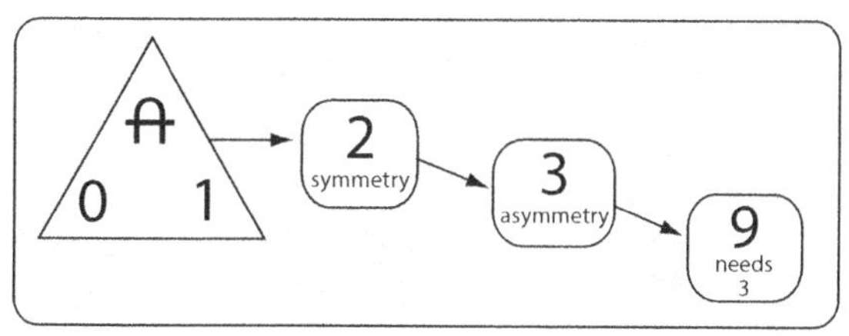

Now that 2 exists, it has another special power.
Along with "zero-one," it generates 3.
I call the number 3 "asymmetry."

[For example, if 3 people are playing tennis together, there will always be an asymmetrical arrangement.]

This "asymmetrical 3" beams its energy into the number realm, making 9, 27, 81, 243, 729, 2187, ...

Again, let's restrict this study to the single-digits.
Because 3 now exists, 9 only "needs 3."

This leads to what I call the "tussle" between 3 and 4

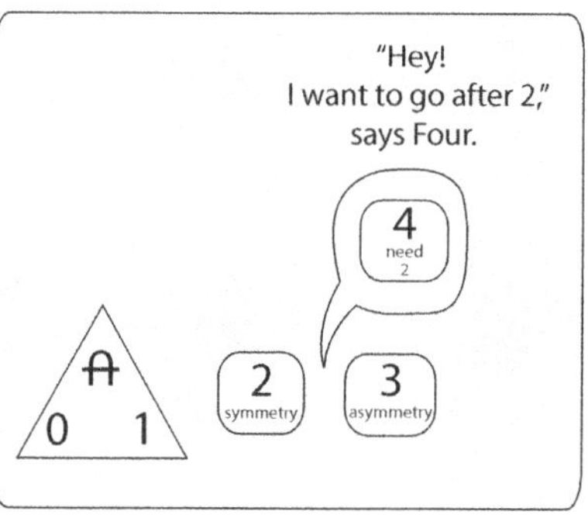

The number 2 has generated two things:
2's close relative, 4,
and 2's neighbor, 3.

Both 4 and 3 are vying for position to follow immediately after 2.

Both have good reasons to claim the spot.

Who wins?

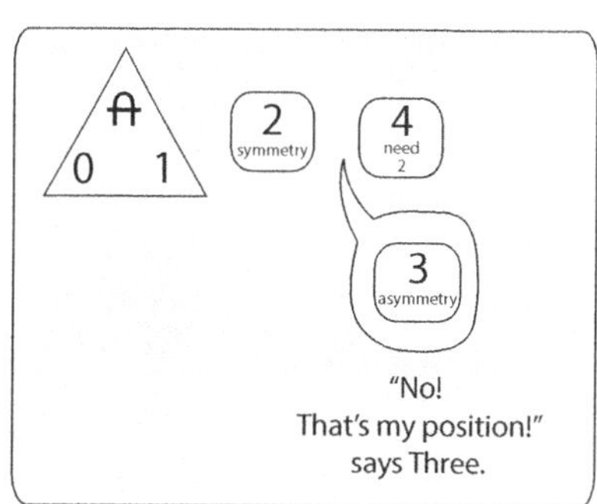

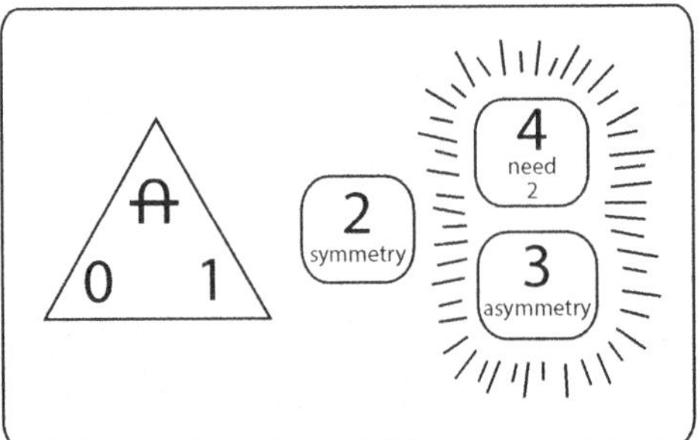

This interaction between the Quaternary and the Ternary has huge ramifications in geometry and number.

This tension between 3 and 4 can be seen physically in the cuboctahedron.
The triangular faces "tussle" with the square faces.

Also, there 6 square faces and 8 triangular faces making a 6:8 ratio, which reduces to a 3:4 ratio.

The cuboctahedron is a display of 3 and 4 in a spherical wrestling match.

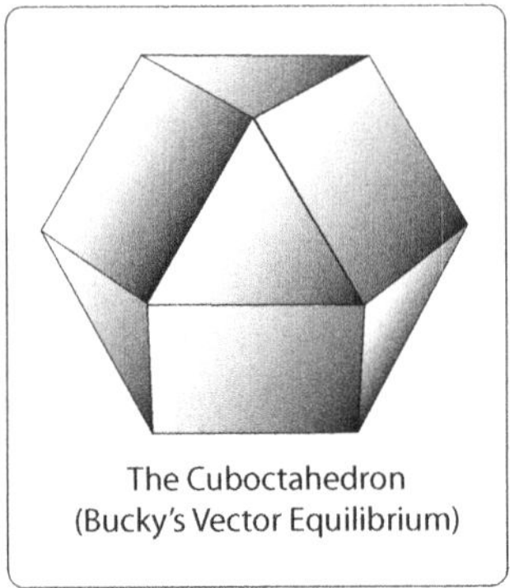

The Cuboctahedron
(Bucky's Vector Equilibrium)

In Theorems 6 and 20 of the *Monas*, Dee cryptically refers to this friendly tension between 3 and 4.

He says the Cross of his Monas symbol can be seen as either "Ternary" (two lines and their common point) or "Quaternary"(four lines).

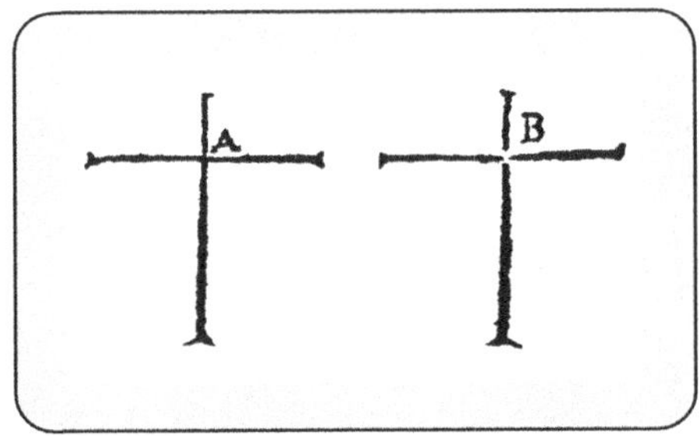

Propædeumata Aphoriſtica
IOANNIS DEE, LONDINENSIS,
De Præſtantioribus quibuſdam
Naturæ Virtutibus.

SVPERCAELESTES RORETIS AQVAE.
ET TERRA FRVCTVM DABIT SVVM.

QVATER NARIVS
IN TERNARIO CONQVIESCENS.

Dee tells us the results of the "tussle" in one of his favorite axioms:

Quaternarius In Ternario Conquiescens

"The Quaternary Rests in the Ternary."

(If the 4 had won the tussle, the Ternary would be resting in the Quaternary.)

(Dee, *Propaedeumata Aphoristica*, Title page of the 1568 edition)

QVATER NARIVS
IN TERNARIO CONQVIESCENS.

Number historian Michael Schneider writes,

"A fundamental map of ourselves is found in the mathematical intimacy between the Triad and the Tetrad.
The ancient mathematical philosophers saw themselves wherever three and four mingle."

(Schneider, Michael, *Beginner's Guide to Constructing the Universe, the Mathematical Archetypes of Nature, Art, and Science*, p. 89; an enlightening book about the qualities of each of the single digits)

So here's where the story now stands.

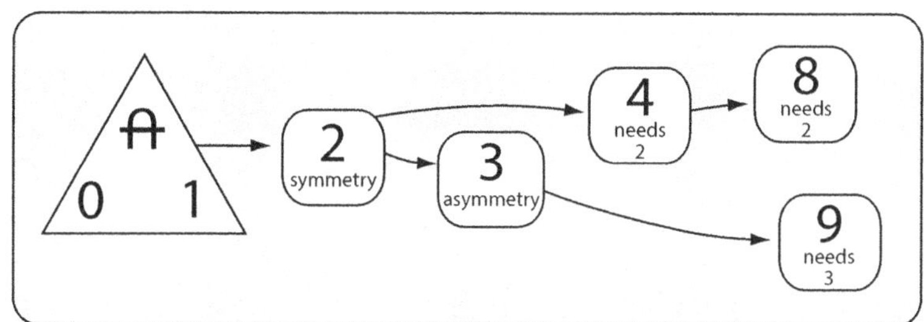

Next, we might add the number 6. But, 2 and 3 already exist, and
2 x 3 = 6,
so 6 already exists.

In other words, 6 "needs nothing,"

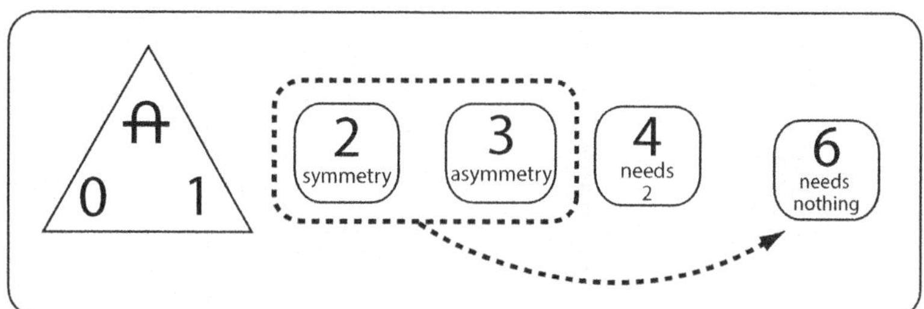

Then 8 and 9 battle it out for the next position. The winner is 8, because it is related to 2, which was born before 3 (the relative of 9).

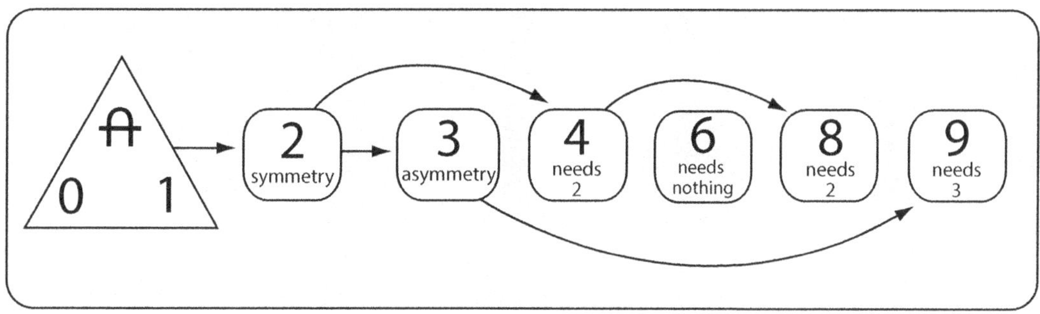

Finally, those prime numbers 5 and 7 can be added to the sequence. They linger at the tail end because they are not related to either symmetrical 2 or asymmetrical 3.

And 5 beats out 7 because it's a lower number.

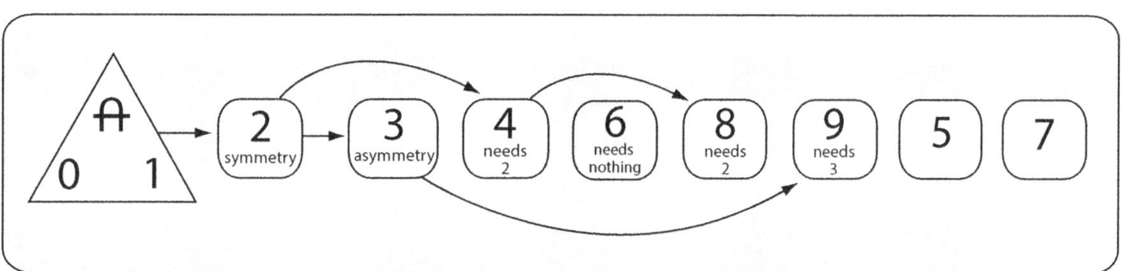

Now that we have accounted for all the single digits,
let's look only at their "essences," or only at what they "need."
Continuous multiplication of these "essences" generates the beginning of what Marshall calls the Holotomic sequence:
12, 24, 72, 360, and 2520.

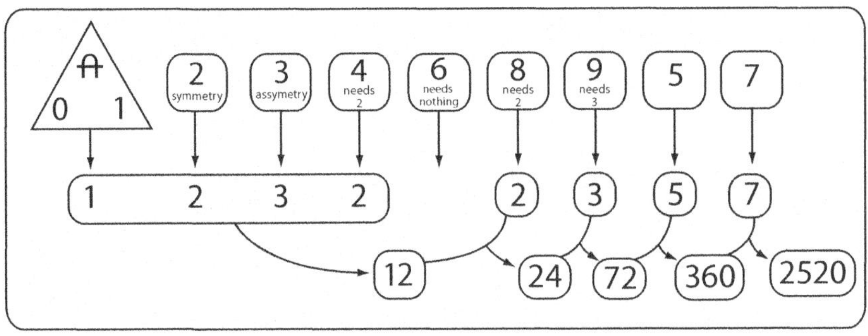

Why not just use the natural order of digits 1, 2, 3, 4, 5, 6, 7, 8, 9?
Well, some of the numbers that result, (60, 420, and 840), are **not** Holotomes.
They do not symmetrically arrange the prime numbers they contain.
(More on how to see this in a moment.)

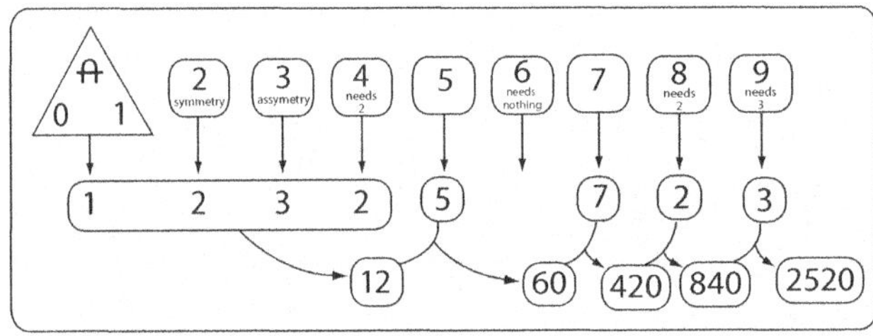

Here's a summary of the creation of the Holotomes:

From the source of retrocity,"zero-one,"
blossoms symmetrical 2 and asymmetrical 3,
and then their relatives (4, 6, 8, and 9),
and then the primes (5 and 7).

So the simplified recipe for the Holotomes is:
"12 times the primes."

Here's a more dramatic way of envisioning the Metamorphosis sequence
It begins at the source, "zero-one," and it spins its way out into the realm of number.

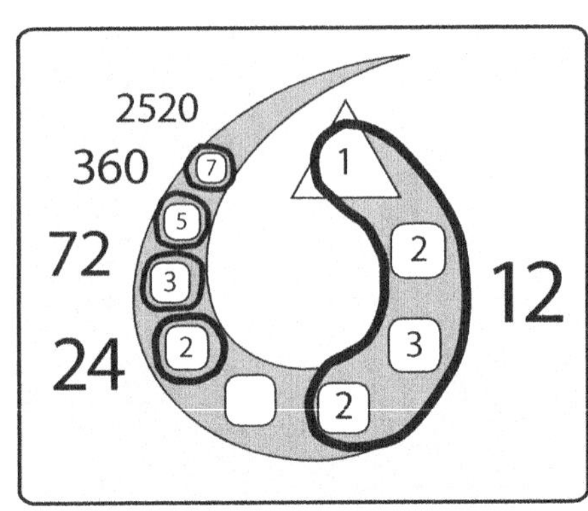

Even More Holotomic Numbers

But the Holotomes don't stop at 2520.
We can continue to multiply by the primes
(in their consecutive order).

Note that "Holotome H" (6126120)
is in the 6 million range.

Next "Holotome I" jumps into
the 116 million range.

And next, "Holotome J" is in the 2 billion range.
And they continue onward in giant steps.
As Bucky said,
numbers are organized in octaves.
So we can assume something special happens
when we have a "octave of Holotomes."

An octave of Holotomes brings us to 6126120.

12	Holotome A
12 x 2 = 24	Holotome B
24 x 3 = 72	Holotome C
72 x 5 = 360	Holotome D
360 X 7 = 2520	Holotome E
2520 x 11 = 27720	Holotome F
27720 x 13 = 360360	Holotome G
360360 x 17 = 6126120	Holotome H
6126120 x 19 = 116396280	Holotome I
116396280 X 23 = 2677114440	Holotome J

Let's look at the "twelveness" inherent in the first few Holotomes.
24 is, of course, two dozen.

72 is half of 144 (which is 12 squared).

The ancients rounded off a year to 360
days and used 12 months of 30 days each
(adding 4-5 days at the end as needed).

6126120	360
360360	72
27720	24
2520	12

The first octave
of Holotomes

The next Holotome, 2520, is perhaps the most spectacular of all.
You might have noticed that it is 10 times Dee's Magistral number, 252.

But even more importantly, seeing it with Marshall's "retrocity,"
the **reflective mate of 2520 is 0252**, or simply **252**.

Nature's most
economical number

2520

(the lowest number
be divisible by all the single digits
1, 2, 3, 4, 5, 6, 7, 8, and 9)

But 2520 is even more important than that.

**2520 is the lowest number that is
divisible by all the single digits!**

Marshall admired it so much he called it the "Auric
Number," in the sense that it has a certain aura about it.

Here are all the single digits and the numbers
by which they need to be multiplied to arrive at 2520.

1 x 2520 = 2520
2 x 1260 = 2520
3 x 840 = 2520
4 x 630 = 2520
5 x 504 = 2520
6 x 420 = 2520
7 x 360 = 2520
8 x 315 = 2520
9 x 280 = 2520

Some of Dee's cryptic references to 2520

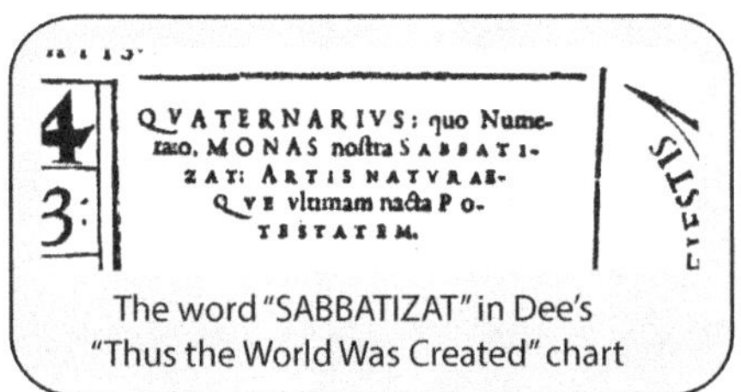
QVATERNARIVS: quo Numerato, MONAS nostra SABBATIZAT: ARTIS NATVRAE-QVE vlumam nacta Potestatem.

The word "SABBATIZAT" in Dee's "Thus the World Was Created" chart

Dee loved the number 2520 cryptically refers to it in many ways in the *Monas Hieroglyphica*, Dee calls it the "Sabbatizat," which, in Hebrew, means a period of seven years. The ancients rounded the year off to 360 days. So, 360 days x 7 years equals 2520 days.

(and added four or five intercalary years to smooth things out at the end of the year)

One of the most references is when Dee tells King Maximilian that his mind has been pregnant with the ideas of the *Monas Hieroglyphica* for "seven years." He contemplated how he could beat express his cosmology for one "Sabbatizat."

quem Annos prius continuos Septem, Mente gestaui mea,

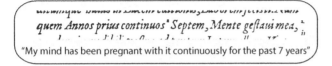

"My mind has been pregnant with it continuously for the past 7 years"

(Remember, this "7 x 360 = 2520" is the exact same multiplication step used in the Holotomic Sequence.)

If you have one circle, how many same size circles fit around it, touching their neighbors and touching the central circle?

The answer is exactly 6. The closest packing of circles is 6-around-1.

Five is too few, and seven is too many. The six outer circles, plus the central circle makes seven circles.

If each of these circles is 360 degrees, that makes a total of 2520 degrees.

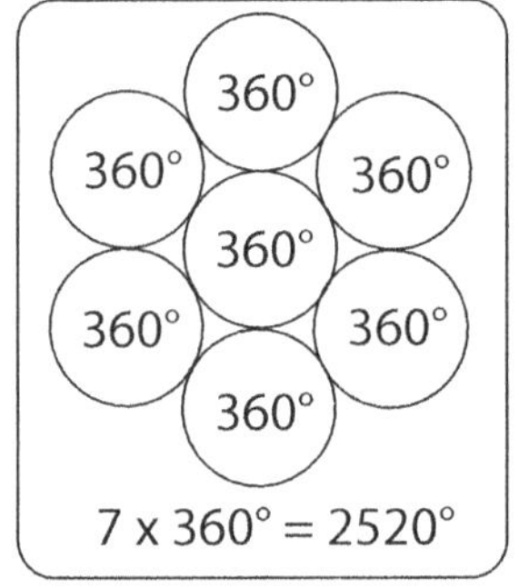

7 x 360° = 2520°

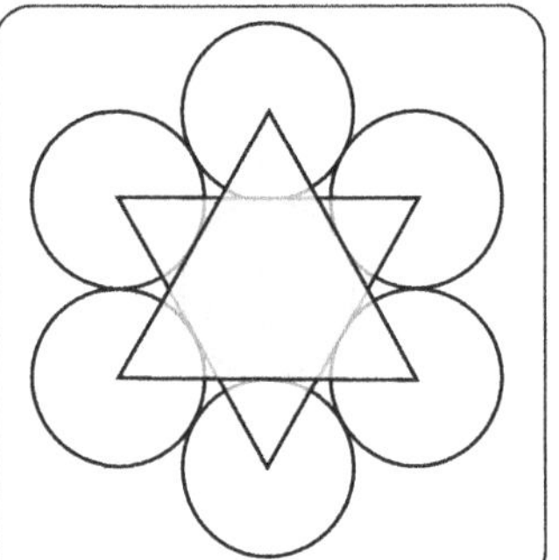

Note that connecting the center points of the outer circles with the two equilateral triangles forms a hexagram star tangent in in six places to the central circle.

(A lucid expression of geometrical "oppositeness," which the alchemists called "fire" and water")

In Theorem, 18 Dee cryptically alludes to the 7 circles in what I call his "Egg diagram."

Each circle represents the orbit of one of the seven planets

(from the top: Saturn, Jupiter, Mars, Sun, Venus, Mercury, and Moon).

And, of course, seven orbits, times 360 degrees per orbit, equals 2520 degrees.

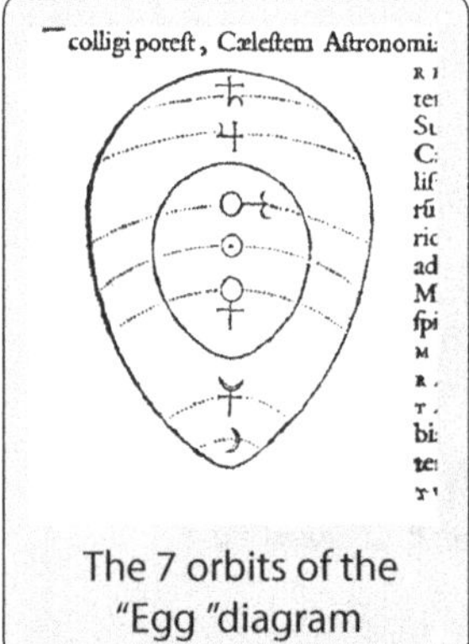

The 7 orbits of the "Egg "diagram

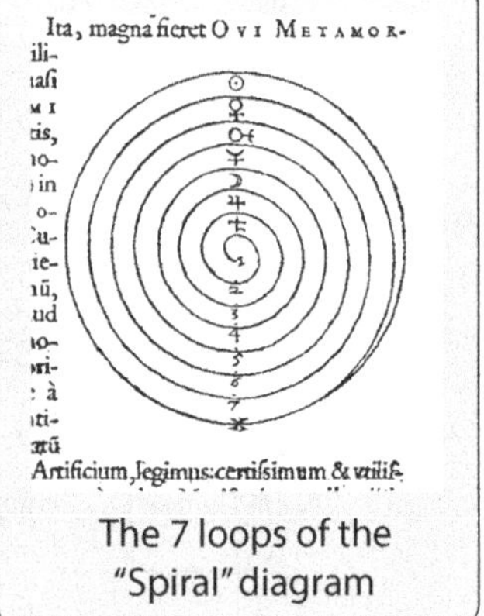

The 7 loops of the "Spiral" diagram

In the same Theorem, John Dee cryptically suggests that the parts of the egg can be mixed by "Spiral Revolutions," which he illustrates with the seven planetary symbols. Again, (7 loops x 360 degrees = 2520°).

Dee cleverly calls his diagram the "Metamorphosis of the Egg."

(You may be suspecting that 2520 is Dee's "rare gift" to Maximilian.

Think again. His gift is even **more** special than 2520.)

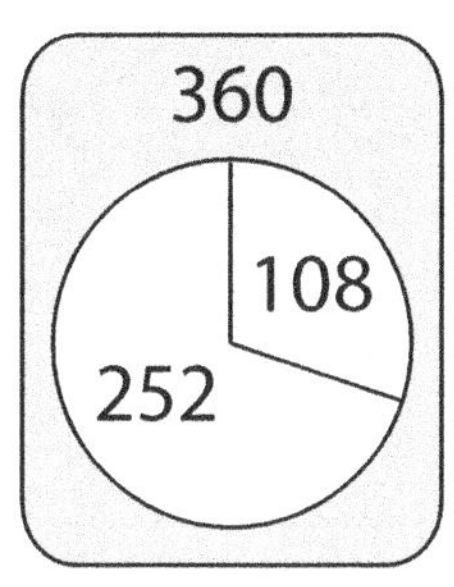

The Holotomic number 360 is pretty special as well.
It's the number of degrees in a circle.

As we've seen, it's also important in a way
I call "**East meets West**."
Add that ancient Hindu number **108** to Dee's
Magistral number **252** and what do you get?

The answer is **360**, a perfect circle.

(Both 108 and 252 represent the same symmetrical
nature of number, in slightly different ways.)

The perfect symmetry of the Holotomes can be seen in "number wheels"

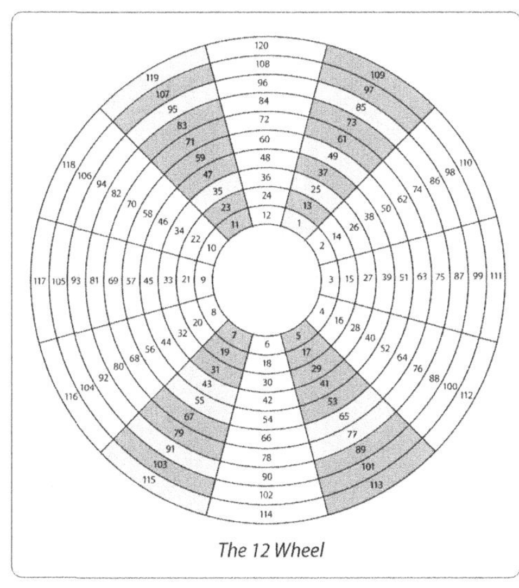
The 12 Wheel

One way to see the symmetrical nature of the Holotomes is by depicting them as wheels. This is what I call the **12 Wheel**.

It's a spiral of numbers from 1 to 12, then the next circle goes from 13 to 24, then 25 to 36, etc. All the prime numbers in the chart have been shaded in **dark** gray.

All the primes fall in only 4 of the 12 radians.

(In these number wheels, the only two primes which I do not shade in dark gray are 2 and 3. As you can see, no other primes ever fall in their radians anyway.)

For the sake of comparison, here's the 18 Wheel.
It **is** symmetrical across the vertical axis, but **not** across the horizontal axis.
(In other words, the left side reflects the right side, but the top half does not reflect the bottom half.)

Number 18 is not a Holotome, but the number 12 is a Holotome.

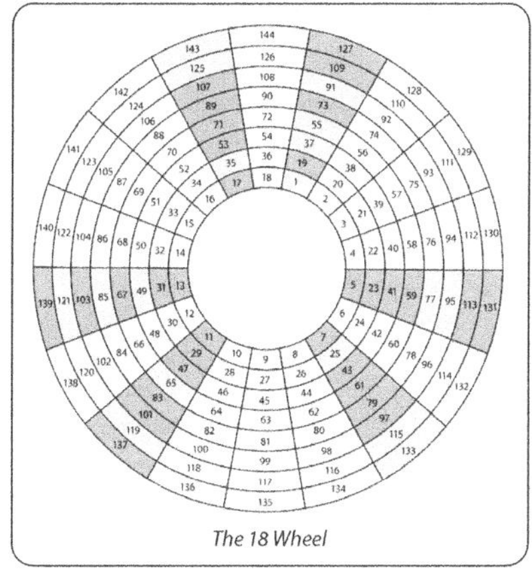
The 18 Wheel

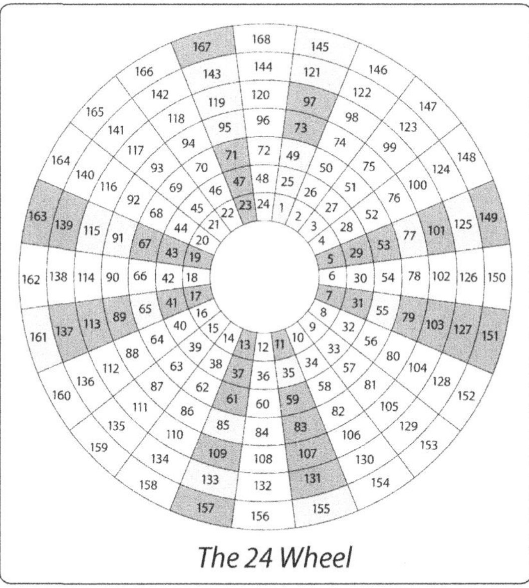
The 24 Wheel

The **24 wheel**.
is like a Maltese Cross,
with perfect horizontal
and vertical symmetry.

For comparison,
here is the 30 wheel.

It **is** symmetrical across
the vertical axis,
but **not** across the
horizontal axis. Thus
30 is not a holotome).

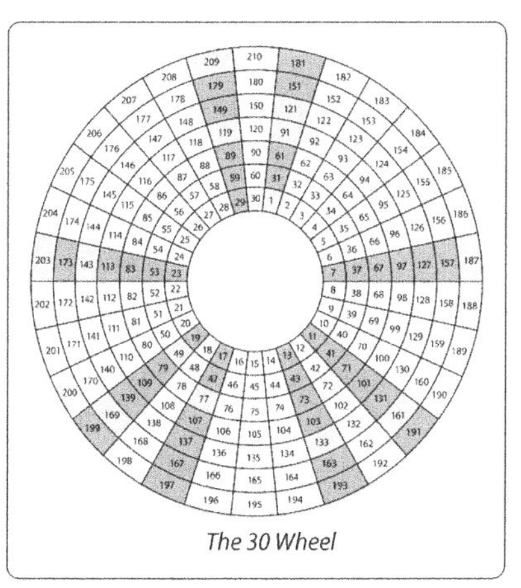
The 30 Wheel

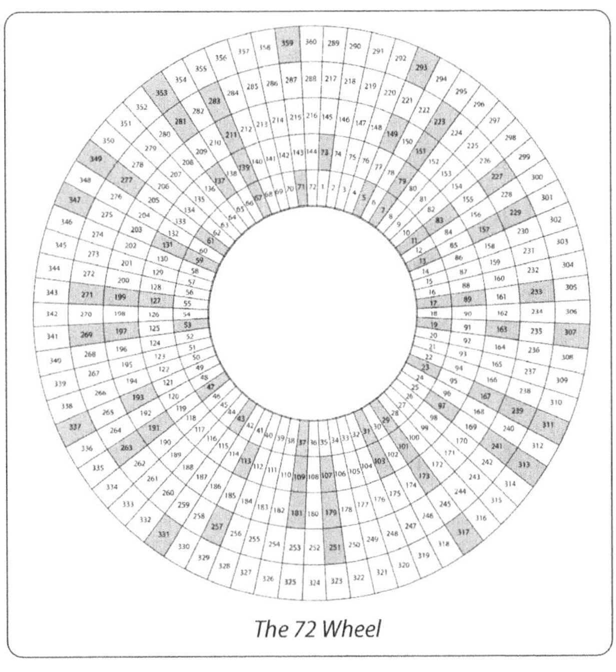
The 72 Wheel

The symmetry of the **72 Wheel** is a little hard to discern.

So in this diagram, the radians which contain prime numbers are fully colored in gray.

It's a **sunburst** of perfect **symmetry**!

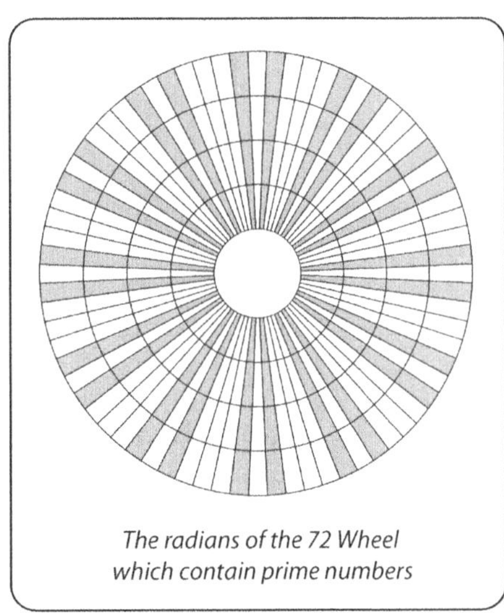
The radians of the 72 Wheel which contain prime numbers

In my **360 Wheel** shown here, the radians are too thin to be able to include numbers, but you can see the perfect symmetrical distribution of the radians containing prime numbers.

The **2520 Wheel** is just as symmetrical, only it's 7 times as big as the 360 wheel.

(It's too detailed to show here, as are the Wheels for all the larger Holotomes.)

As mentioned earlier, each Holotome incorporates all the symmetries of the Holotomes which precede it.

(Caveat: These wheels help us see the symmetrical nature of the Holotomes, but are not an empirical test as to whether a number is a Holotome or not. For example, because of the awesome symmetry in the 72 wheel, half of the 72 wheel or the "36 wheel" is also perfectly symmetrical. And twice the 72 wheel, or the "144 wheel" is perfectly symmetrical as well.)

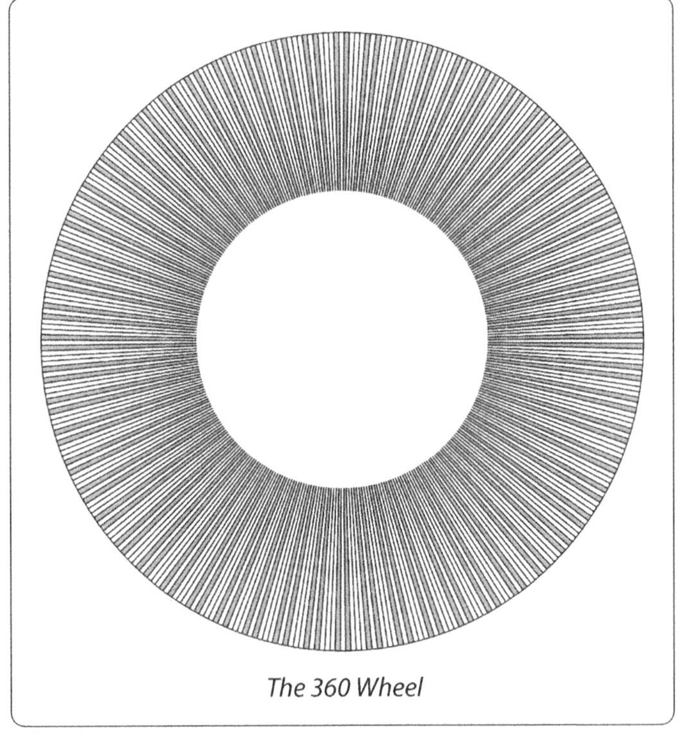
The 360 Wheel

2520
The Great Eagle

To celebrate the wonderful symmetry of the 2520 Wheel (which incorporates all the single digits), Marshall calls 2520 "**The Great Eagle**."

Its two wings of 1260 each are perfect reflections of each other.

This chart of the first octave of Holotomes shows little boxes with their divisors. Starting down on the bottom right, 12 is divisible by 2, 3, 4, and 6.

Through 24, 72, and 360, more divisors are added to the box. When we reach 2520, the box is filled with the first "octave, null nine" of number.

Proceeding upwards, more divisors get added until, at 6126120, the **second** "octave, null 9" of numbers, **up to the number 18**, is included.

Well, almost all. Look closely.
Notice that the **16** is missing.
The number 6126120 is evenly divisible by all the numbers from 1 to 18, **except 16**.
How are we to deal with this fly in the ointment?

6126120	360
360360	72
27720	24
2520	12

6126120 divided by 16 is 382882.5
Because this result ends in .5,
it's obvious that the number which is
"2 times 6126120" **will** be divisible by 16
(and thus be divisible by all the numbers up to 18.)

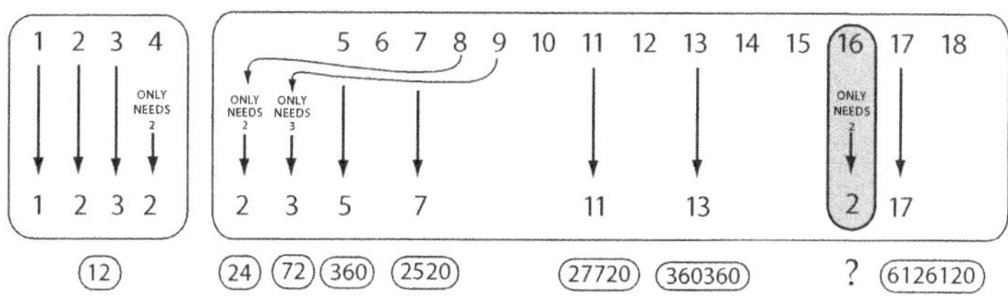

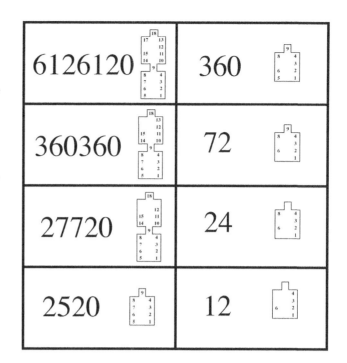

Now.... drum roll please... "6126120 times 2" is this glorious number:

12252240

Ignoring place value, look who we can find in here. There of two of Dee's favorite numbers, the first two Holotomes, 12 and 24. And there's Dee's Magistral number 252.
(Or by using that zero, there's the Sabbatizat or the Great Eagle, 2520)

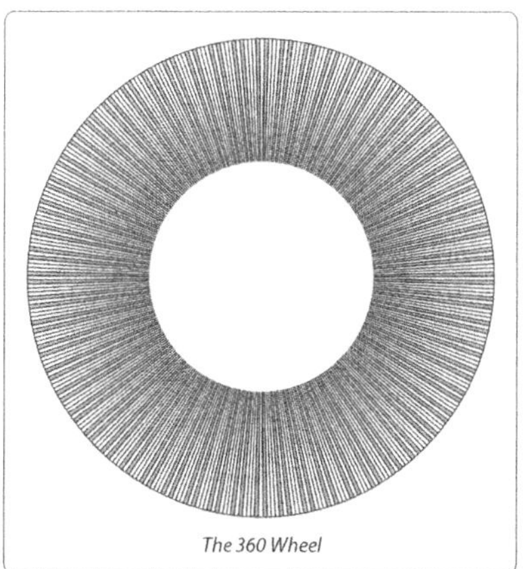
The 360 Wheel

12 252 24 0

Try to imagine what the **12252240 Wheel** would look like.
It would exhibit the same perfect symmetry like the 360 Wheel, only it would have over 12 million radians!

Being the lowest number divisible by all the numbers up to 18 (which is two "octave, null nines" of number).
Yes, 12252240 is truly a **rare** number.

Indeed, 12252240 is Dee's "rare gift" to Maximillian, the King of the Holy Roman Empire!

That's his gift to the King? A measly number? Well, yes, but it's no ordinary number. To a mathematician who sees the symmetries in number, it's very, very special. Dee even prefaces his *Letter to Maximillian* this way:

"This gift is so extremely rare and of great goodness that the warm feelings I have for your Majesty should not be held in contempt, even though it is so small in size."

("small in size" meaning it's only a number, it's not something like a grand sculpture made from gold and silver festooned with precious gems)

Here's a summary of how we reached this glorious Number.

12252240	
x 2 =	
6126120	360
360360	72
27720	24
2520	12

Marshall was so excited about 12252240, he called it the "**Even Greater Eagle**."
[It has two symmetrical wings of 6216120 each.]

12252240
The Even Greater Eagle

Marshall also refers to 12252240 as the "**Encapsulation Number**" because it symmetrically "encapsulates" two octaves of number.

In the *Preface to Euclid,* Dee cryptically refers to 12252240 as the "**Exemplar number of all things Numerable**."
[An "Exemplar" is something which serves as an excellent model (a fitting term for 12252240.]

The word numerable means "able to be counted."
[Of course, there are many numbers higher than 12252240. But this number, way up in the 12 million range, is already pushing the limits of what a man could actually count. There are about a million grains in a handful of sand. Try counting over 12 handfuls.]

To summarize, Dee (in the 1500s) saw the same thing Marshall saw (in the 1900s). They just gave different names to what they found.

Two of the most puzzling words in Dee's "Thus the World Was Created" chart are "Metamorphosis" and "Consummata."

In his final chart, he places them along the dotted-line X, prominently in the middle of his "1, 2, 3, 4 and 5, 6, 7, 8" octave.

Marshall's "Holotomic Sequence" is what Dee calls "METAMORPHOSIS."
Marshall's "Cycloflex" is what Dee calls "CONSUMMATA."

Robert Marshall's names:		*John Dee's names*
Cycloflex	"+4, –4, octave; null 9" rhythm of the 9 Wave, 99 Wave, 1089 Wave,...	Consummata
Holotomes	12 times the primes 12, 24, 72, 360, 2520...	Metamorphosis
Auric number	2520	Sabbatizat
Encapsulation number	12252240	Exemplar number

The Cycloflex (9 Wave, 99 Wave, 1089 Wave,...) and the Holotomes (12, 24, 72, 360, 2520...) exhibit symmetry in different ways.

It might not seem like these two great sequences are related. But they are!

This chart is but one way to see that the Holotomes and the Cycloflex are synchronous.

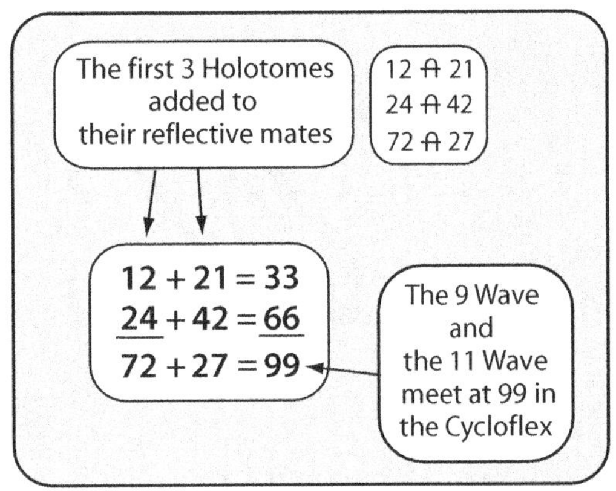

The first 3 Holotomes (12, 24, and 72) are added to their reflective mates (21, 42, and 27).

12 + 21 makes 33
24 + 42 makes 66
33 + 66 total to 99

Amazingly, 72 + 27 also sum to 99.

We started with three **Holotomes,** and ended up with 99, a key number in the **Cycloflex**.

In the *Monas*, Dee's most obvious clue about the Metamorphosis numbers is his Artificial Quaternary (1, 2, 3, 2)

Dee is teaching us how to look for the "essence" of number. Everyone knows the normal flow is "1, 2, 3, 4," but, as 2 already exists, the 4 "only needs 2."

Continue this line of thought with the rest of the single digits (as we did earlier) and the Metamorphosis sequence appears before your eyes.

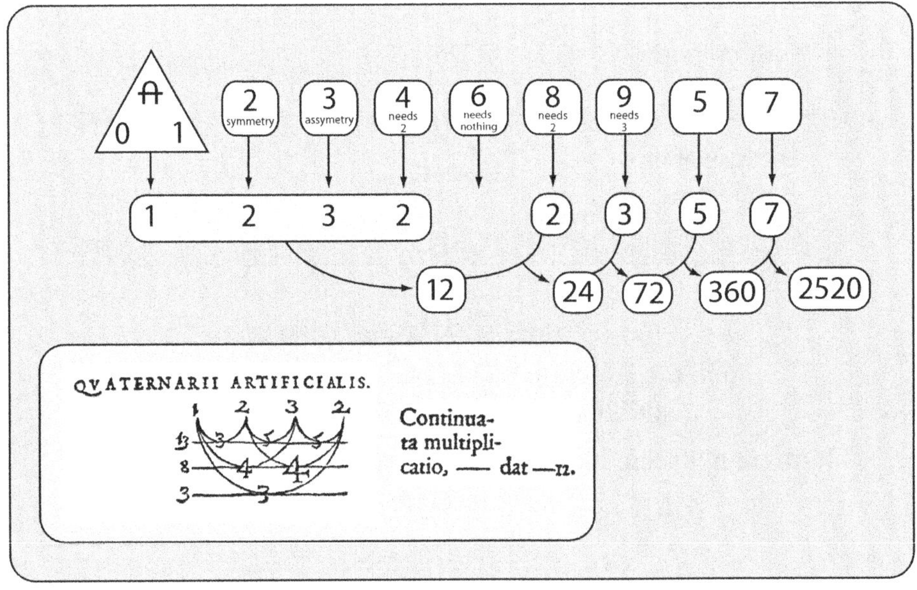

The Ancient canon of number both Dee and Marshall "re-discovered" has been known for a long time

Dee wasn't the only person who understood the ancient canon of number involving 252, the Holotomes and the Cycloflex. The German metallurgist and alchemist Pantheus, writes that the "number of days" is 252. Dee heavily annotated his copy of Pantheus' *Voarchadumia* (*Gold Making*) and makes reference to the book in the *Monas Hieroglyphica*.

Robert Marshall found that the ancient Hindus knew about the canon and that's why number 108 was so special to them. The Yugas, the Hindu's long-calendar-time-periods, are all multiples of number 108.

108
SACRED
HINDU
NUMBER

Marshall asserts that Plato knew about 2520 and cryptically refers to it in *Laws*. Plato recommends the population of his "Ideal City" be **5040** people **(twice 2520)** because the populace could be subdivided in so many ways.

In the Bible, Saint John seems to be making a cryptic reference to 2520 in *Revelation*, by writing that the "woman went into the wilderness" for **1260** days **(half of 2520)**.

Marshall claims other authors of the Bible knew about the canon of number as well. In the last chapter of the Gospel of John (21:1–14), Jesus helps Saint Peter with the "miraculous catch of 153 fish. This seems like such a strange number to pick. Perhaps they actually counted the fish in the net or on the deck of the boat, but why not just say "about 150" or "three barrels."

With his vision for number symmetry, Robert Marshall recognized 153 as a number which relates to 252 and to the Cycloflex.

The reflective mate of 153 is 351.
Added together they make 504.
Divide by two, and their average is 252.
This averaging calculation involves an important number in the Cycloflex: 99, the largest two-digit number.
99 is the product of 9 (of 9 Wave fame) and 11 (of 11 Wave fame).

In short, 153+99=252
Furthermore, 252+99=351

The transpalindromes 153 and 351, are each 99 away from 252.

153 (fish)
+ 99
252
+99
351

Dee also hints that he has figured out ***Plato's Number***, an obscure reference to a number Plato makes in *Republic* (Book 8:546). The explanation is too long to relate here, but Plato actually refers to two numbers. Following Dee, I have determined that Plato's "number of divine births" is 2520, and his "number of human births" is 360, which Plato wittily refers to as "a geometrical number." (See my Book 7, *Dee's Decad of Shapes and Plato's Number*)

Brief Visual Summary

This is just a sampling of Dee's cryptic cleverness in the *Monas Hieroglyphica*. I call it "the book of 100 riddles." Once you catch his mathematical drift, it's not that obscure at all.

In summary, there are two great rhythms that flow through the realm of number:

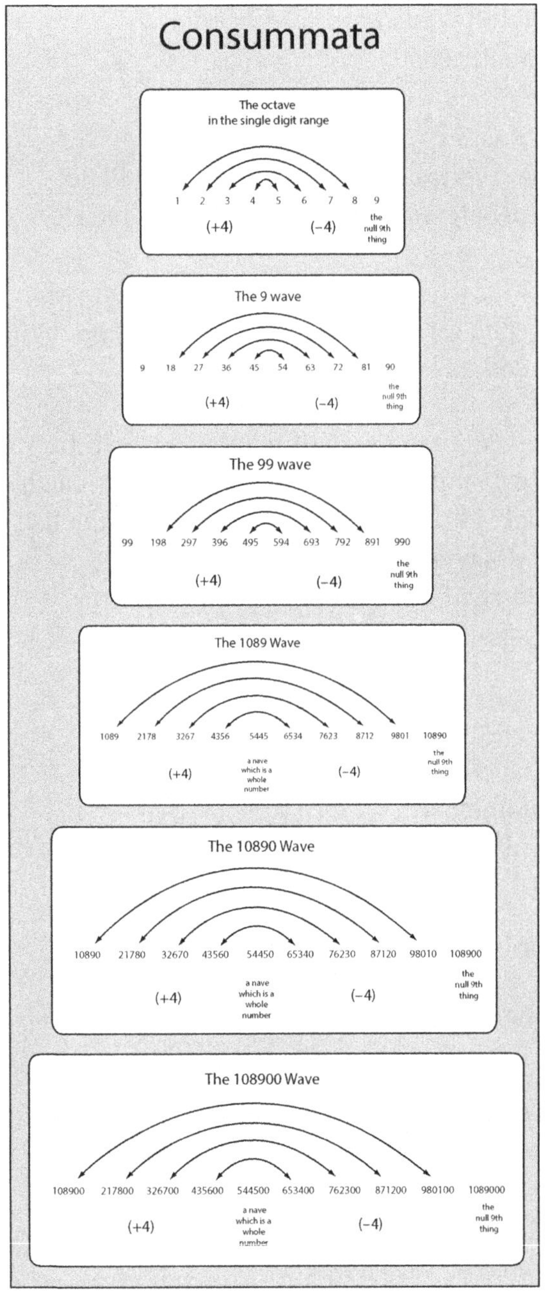

Consummata
(the +4, -4, octave, null nine rhythm)
and
Metamorphosis
("12 times the primes," or 12, 24, 72, 360, 2520...)

The "+4, –4, octave; null nine" rhythm of CONSUMMATA

The METAMORPHOSIS sequence

12	Holotome A
12 x 2 = 24	Holotome B
24 x 3 = 72	Holotome C
72 x 5 = 360	Holotome D
360 X 7 = 2520	Holotome E
2520 x 11 = 27720	Holotome F
27720 x 13 = 360360	Holotome G
360360 x 17 = 6126120	Holotome H
6126120 x 19 = 116396280	Holotome I
116396280 X 23 = 2677114440	Holotome J

Dee defines all the known "Mathematicall Artes"

In the 1600s and 1700s, many scholars praised John Dee's "*Preface*" to the first English translation of Euclid's *Elements.*

Dee explains each of the 18 great arts and sciences known at the time of the (including Perspective, Astronomy, Music, Cosmology, Astrology, Horology, Architecture, and Navigation) But he refers to them all as "Derivative Arts."

He explains that they derive from two things: "Arithmetic and Geometry." Dee explains that these are the "Principal Arts, and he adds, "(there are only two)". Dee was a total math geek. To Dee (as well as other Neo-Platonists), the Universe was made from number and shape. Dee tells us there is only one thing that has one foot in the terrestrial realm and the other foot in the Supercelestial realm: Number.

The wealthy merchant Henry Billingsley, who later became Lord Mayor of London, gets credit for the first English translation of Euclid.

But John Dee added many complex addendums and corollaries to many of Euclid's 465 propositions. Some short commentaries by Dee's European contemporaries have also been added.

¶ Of the inſcriptions and circumſcriptions of an Icoſidodecahedron.

An Icoſidodecahedron may containe the other fiue regular bodyes. For it will receaue the angles of a Dodecahedron, in the centres of the triangles which ſubtend the ſolide angles of the Dodecahedron: which ſolide angles are 20. in nũber, and are placed in the ſame order in which the ſolide angles of the Dodecahedron taken away or ſubtended by them, are. And by that reaſon it ſhall receaue a Cube and a Pyramis contayned in the Dodecahedron: when as the angles of the one are ſet in the angles of the other.

An Icoſidodecahedron receaueth an Octohedron, in the angles cutting the ſixe oppoſite ſections of the Dodecahedron, euen as if it were a ſimple Dodecahedron.

And it containeth an Icoſahedron, placing the 12. angles of the Icoſahedron in the ſelfe ſame centres of the 12. Pentagons.

It may alſo by the ſame reaſon be inſcribed in euery one of the fiue regular bodies: namely, in a Pyramis, if ye place 4. triangular baſes concentricall with 4. baſes of the Pyramis, after the ſame maner, that ye inſcribed an Icoſahedrõ in a Pyramis. So likewiſe may it be inſcribed in an Octohedron, if ye make 8. baſes thereof concentricall with the 8. baſes of the Octohedron. It ſhall alſo be inſcribed in a Cube, if ye place the angles which receaue the Octohedron inſcribed in it, in the centres of the baſes of the Cube. Moreouer, ye ſhall inſcribe it in an Icoſahedron, when the triangles compaſed in of the Pentagon baſes, are concentricall with the triangles, which make a ſolide angle of the Icoſahedron. Finally, it ſhall be inſcribed in a Dodecahedron, if ye place euery one of the angles thereof in the midle ſections of the ſides of the Dodecahedron, according to the order of the conſtructi-

To give you an example, above is a description of the "Inscriptions and Circumscriptions of an Icosidodecahedron."

(This means the sphere tangent to the inside and the sphere tangent to the outside of this three-dimensional Archimedean solid, which has 20 triangular faces and 12 pentagonal faces. Heavy stuff.)

Flußas, of mixt and

in the baſes of the cube, be ſquares: and they ſhall be ſixe in number, according to the nũber of the baſes of the cube. Agayne foraſmuch as the triangle K I N ſubtendeth the ſolide angle D of the cube, and likewiſe the triangle K G L the ſolide angle C, & ſo the reſt, which ſubtend the eight ſolide angles of the cube: and theſe triangles are equall and equilater, namely, being made of equall ſides & they are the limmits or borders of the ſquares, and the ſquares the limmits or borders of thẽ, as hath before bene proued: wherefore L-MNOPHGK is an exoctohedrõ, by the diffinition, and is equilater, for it is contayned of equall ſubtendent lines: it is alſo equiangle, for euery ſolide angle thereof, is contayned vnder two ſuperficiall angles of two ſquares, and two ſuperficiall angles of two equilater triangles.

That the exoctohedron is contayned in a ſphere. And now foraſmuch as the oppoſite ſides and diameters of the baſes of the cube are parallels, the playne extended by the right lines Q T, V R, ſhall be a paralleogramme. And for that alſo in that playne lyeth Q R the diameter of the cube, and in the ſame playne alſo is the line M H, which diuideth the ſayd playne into two equall parts, and alſo coupleth the oppoſite angles of the exoctohedron this line M H therefore diuideth the diameter into two equall partes, by the corollary of the 34. of the firſt, and alſo diuideth it ſelfe in the ſame poynt, which let be S, into two equall partes, by the 4 of the firſt. And by the ſame reaſon may we proue that the reſt of the lines, which couple the oppoſite angles of the exoctohedron, doo in S the centre of the cube diuide the one the other into two equall parts. For euery one of the angles of the exoctohedron are ſet in euery one of the baſes of the cube. Wherefore making the centre the poynt S, and the ſpace S H or S M; deſcribe a ſphere, and it ſhall touch euery one of the angles equediſtant from the poynt S.

That the exoctohedron is contayned in the ſphere geuen. And foraſmuch as A B the diameter of the ſphere geuen, is put equall to the diameter of the baſe of the cube, namely, to the line R T, and the ſame line R T is equall to the line M H, by the 33. of the firſt: which line M H coupling the oppoſite angles of the exoctohedron, is drawne by the centre: wherefore it is the diameter of the ſphere geuen which contayneth the exoctohedron.

That the diameter of the ſphere is double to the ſide of the exoctohedron. Finally foraſmuch as in the triangle R F T, the line P O doth cutte the ſides into two equall partes, it ſhall cutte them proportionally with the baſes, namely, as F R is to F P, ſo ſhall R T be to P O, by the 2. of the ſixth. But F R is double to F-P, by ſuppoſition: wherefore R T, or the diameter H M, is alſo double to the line P O the ſide of the exoctohedron. Wherefore we haue deſcribed an equilater & equiangle exoctohedron, and comprehended it in a ſphere geuen, and haue proued that the diameter of the ſphere is double to the ſide of the exoctohedron.

The

The construction of a cuboctahedron from a cube and an octahedron in the 1570 first English translation of Euclid's Elements

As we've seen, there is even a chapter on how to construct the cuboctahedron geometrically from a cube and an octahedron.

And they even provide a template you can cut out and fold to make your own paper model.

Dee was friends with the great mathematicians on the continent, Reinier Gemma Frisius, Gerard Mercator, Oronce Fine, Pedro Nuñez, and he provided the Italian mathematician Frederico Commandino with a rare book on Arab geometry, which Commandino published.

Dee even gave lectures on Euclid at Reims University in Paris to overflow crowds of students.

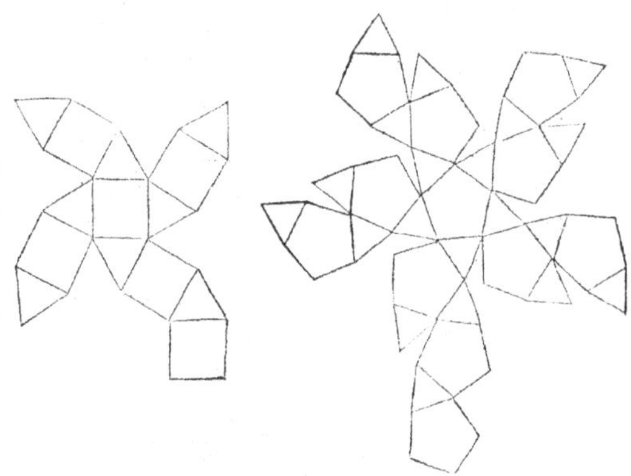

The first Probleme.

To describe an equilater and equiangle exoctohedron, and to contayne it in a sphere geuen: and to proue that the diameter of the sphere is double to the side of the sayd exoctohedron.

Suppose that there be a sphere geuen, whose diameter let be A B. And about the diameter A B let there be described a square by the sixth of the fourth: and vpon the square let there be described a cube by the 15. of the thirtenth: which let be C D E F Q T V R: and let the diameter thereof be Q R, and the centre S. And diuide the sides of the cube into two equall partes, in the poyntes G, H, I, K, L, M, N, O, P. &c. And couple the middle sections by the right lines I N, N O, O P, P I and such like, which subtend the angles of the squares or bases of the cube: and they are equall by the 4. first, and containe right angles, as the angle N I P. For the angle NID which is at the base of the Isosceles triangle N D I, is the halfe of a right angle, and so likewise is the opposite angle R I P. Wherefore the residue N I P is a right angle, and so the rest. Wherefore N I P O is a square. And by the same reason shall the rest N M L K, K G H I &c. inscribed

Construction of the exocto-hedron.

DDD.ij. in

Fold-up model of the cuboctahedron and icosidodecahedron from the 1570 first English translation of Euclid's *Elements*

Dee was also the navigational advisor to all the great Elizabethan explorers. No long distance voyager would dare leave London without consulting Dee about his "charts and rutters."

Around 1570, Dee invented what he called the "Paradoxical Compass" which help sailors navigate the North Atlantic, where the longitude lines converge. He provided a thick compendium of charts that accompanied his compass.

Dee was the expert

I don't think would be unfair to say that in the late 1500s Dee was the most skilled mathematician in England.

Dee wrote over 40 books, most of them on science and mathematics. Needless to say Dee was a prodigious talent and, I suggest, a photographic memory.

All of this material on Dee and Geometry is setting the stage for my analysis of the Globe drawings from The Byrom Collection. Without a firm grounding in Dee's mathematical cosmology, all his clever clues will be invisible.

But first we must explore of another important facet of "1, 2, 3, 4."

It's an idea that was near and dear to both the ancient mathematicians and to Renaissance mathematicians like Dee.

But there is one more thing you need to know about:

"THE GREATEST AND MOST PERFECT HARMONY"

The Story of 1, 2, 3, 4

Flashback to around 500 BC. Legend has it that Pythagoras was passing by a blacksmith's shop and heard a variety of different sounds caused by hammers banging away on anvils. He went inside and found the various sounds were produced by the differently-sized anvils.

Returning to his house, he experimented with various-sized hammers, bells, glasses of water, strings under tension, and flutes to find the most harmonious sounds and the numerical proportions they expressed.

He summarized his discoveries with his famous **tetraktys**, upon which the followers of Pythagoras would swear their oaths.

It's deceptively simple: a triangular shape with four rows of dots (1, 2, 3, 4), making a total of 10 dots in total.

(In Greek, *tetra* means four.)

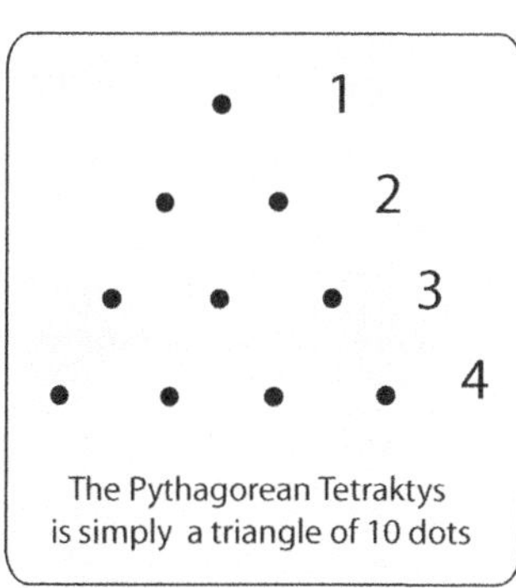

The Pythagorean Tetraktys is simply a triangle of 10 dots

Which, of course, Dee reminds us of in Theorem 23.

The middle result here is *Summa Pythagorica*, or "the Pythagorean Sum," 10.

(Remember, the tetraktys forms an equilateral triangle, the same symbol Dee used to sign his name.)

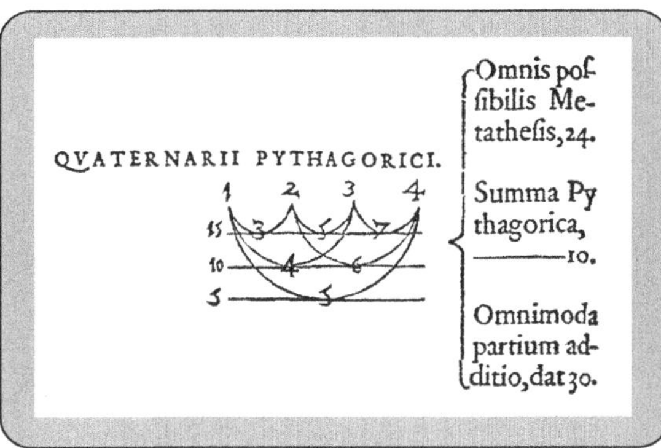

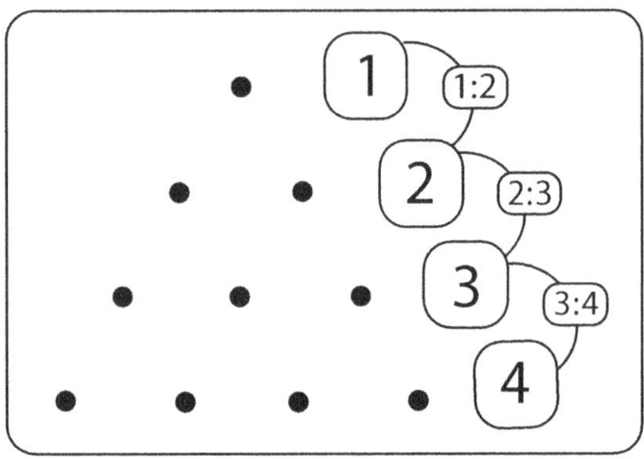

But what Pythagoras and Dee really want us to explore are the ratios between the various rows: (1 to 2), (2 to 3), and (3 to 4).

Nicomachus of Gerasa wrote the famous math text called *Introduction to Arithmetic* around 100 AD.

Around 500 AD, Boethius translated it into Latin.

It was the **most popular math text for 1000 years**,

(From the time of the Neoplatonists, through the Middle Ages and into the Renaissance.)

The *Introduction to Arithmetic* explains how Pythagoras and his followers felt the universe was arranged according to the attunement of the ratios (1:2), (2:3), and (3:4).

They could hear these beautiful harmonies in music as *diapason, diapente and diatessaron*,

(the musical octave, the fifth, and the fourth, shown here on a modern keyboard)

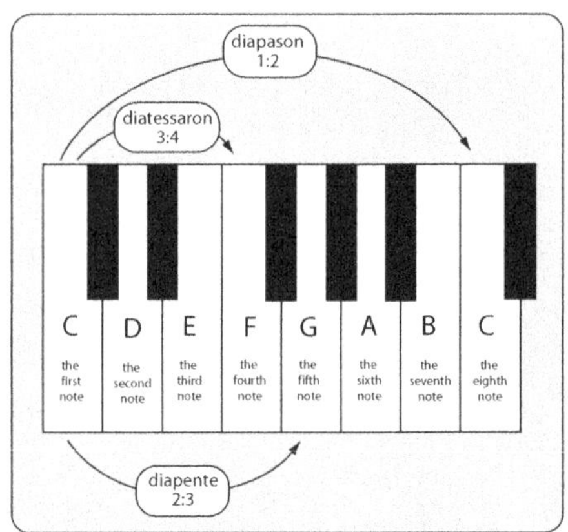

The "greatest and most perfect harmony"

In the last section of the last chapter in their texts,
Nicomachus and Boethius reveal what they call
the "**greatest and most perfect harmony**."
It involves the relationships between
the numbers **6, 8, 9,** and **12**.

(At the top here) The ratio **1:2** can be seen in 6:12
(At the bottom) The ratio **2:3** can be seen in both 6:9 and 8:12
(And in the middle) The ratio **3:4** can be seen in both 6:8 and 9:12
Pure harmony! Hmmmm!

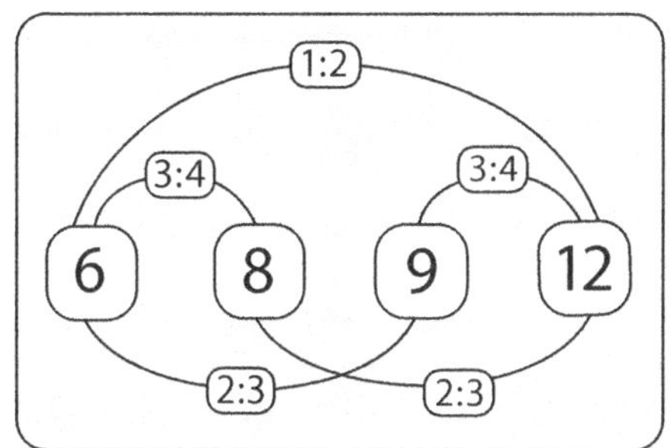

These 3 harmonies were important to Renaissance artists and geometers as well.

Raphael's famous *School of Athens*, a 26-foot wide fresco in the Vatican, depicts all the "superstars" of antiquity.

Under the central arch are Plato and Aristotle.

Various groupings of students are clustered around Epicurius, Socrates, Strabo, Euclid and Pythagoras.

Averroes (Arab translator of Greek works, ca.1175 AD)

Hypatia of Alexandria (famous woman mathmetician, ca. 400 AD)

Boethius holding his *Introduction to Arithmetic* with 3 book clasps visible on the back cover (ca. 525 AD)

Nicomachus peering (ca. 125 AD)

Pythagoras writing (ca. 500 BC)

diagram of "the greatest and most perfect harmony"

Let's zoom in on the group of mathematicians.

Peering around the closest shoulder of Pythagoras is **Nicomachus**.

Standing on the right side, holding his influential text, *Introduction to Arithmetic,* is **Boethius**.

A young student is propping up a tablet in front of Pythagoras.

Let's zoom in even closer.

close up view of
"the greatest and
most perfect harmony"

Written in Greek on the diagram are the words
diatessaron, diapente, and diapason.

Across the top is *epogdoon*, or the 8:9 ratio,
the ratio describing a single increment of "tone."

(The Greeks expressed it as 9:8, an octave plus an eighth-of-an-octave is nine)

At the bottom is the Pythagorean tetraktys along with an X,
which is not Greek, but Latin, as X is the Roman Numeral for 10.

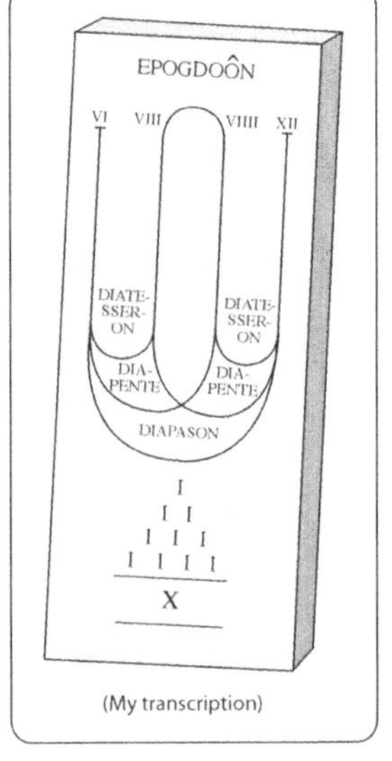

(My transcription)

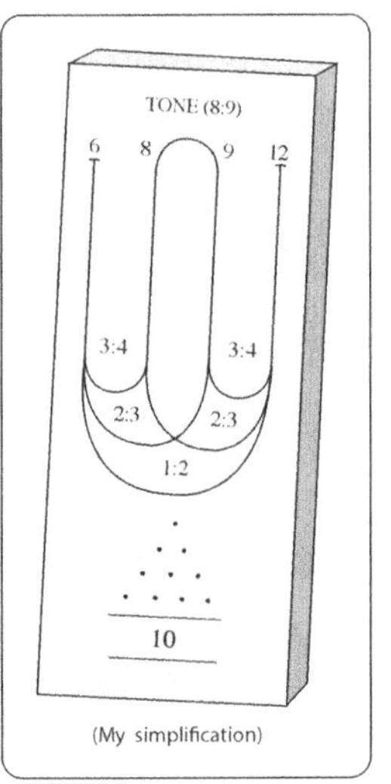

(My simplification)

The tablet is a lot easier
to visualize when the ratios
are expressed with numerals.

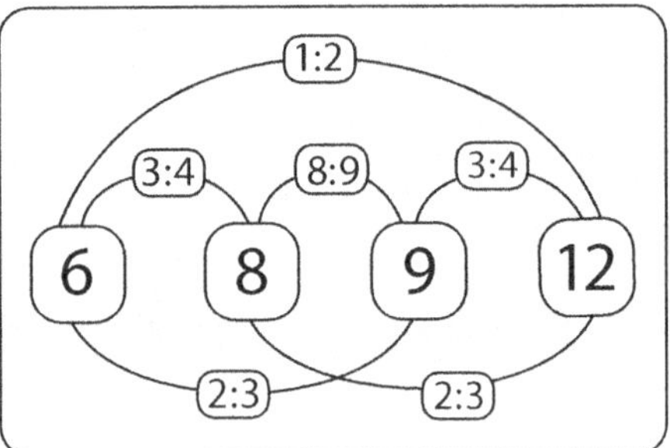

Raphael is depicting the same thing
I show in my modern illustrations.

The 3 ratios the Pythagorean tetraktys are also
implied by the greatest and most perfect harmony,
comprised of the numbers 6, 8, 9, 12.

(It's likely that Raphael incorporated these ratios into the proportions of various parts of his fresco, and he was subtly providing us with his recipe.)

Raphael was not alone. Many great Italian Renaissance
painters, sculptors, and architects glorified their
works with these three harmonic ratios.

Not only did Dee include the Pythagorean Quaternary (1, 2 , 3, 4)
in the "Below" half of his "Thus the World Was Created" chart,
he also put (1, 2 , 3, 4) in the "Above" half of the chart.

Dee makes a very subtle reference to the
proportions (1:2), (2:3), and (3:4) by putting **colons**
after the digits 1, 2, and 3 (but not after the 4).

Incidentally, Dee is credited as being the first mathematician
to use a colon as a symbol to express proportion.

(Florian Cajori, *A History of Mathematical Notations*, p.168)

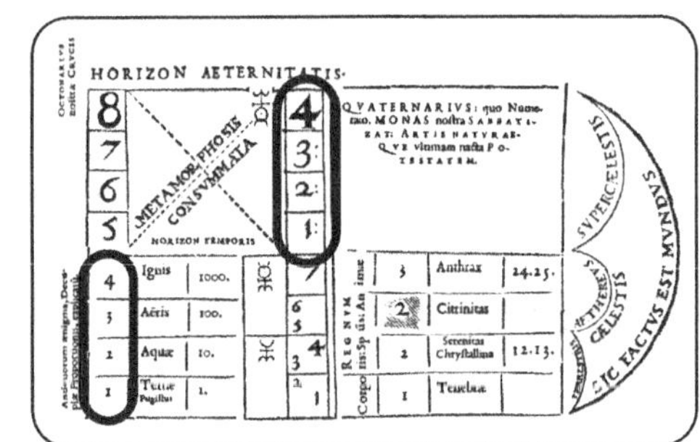

Hidden Metamorphosis (12, 24, 72, 360) and Pythagorean Harmonies (1:2, 2:3, 3:4) in Dee's "Thus the World was Created" Chart

Once I understood how important these three harmonious ratios were to Pythagoras, Nicomachus, Boethius, and Raphael, I searched for traces of them in the *Monas Hieroglyphica*.

I didn't have to look far.

I noticed that the height-to-width proportion of the Title page illustration was 4:3.

Then, I noticed that the rectangular part of Dee's summary chart was in the height-to-width proportion of 2:3.

Hurriedly, I flipped through the Dee's book to find an illustration in the proportion of 1:2, or 2:1. But none were to be found.

It seemed like the Monas symbol might be the proportion 2:1, but making a grid based on Dee's specifications, I found it was 9:4

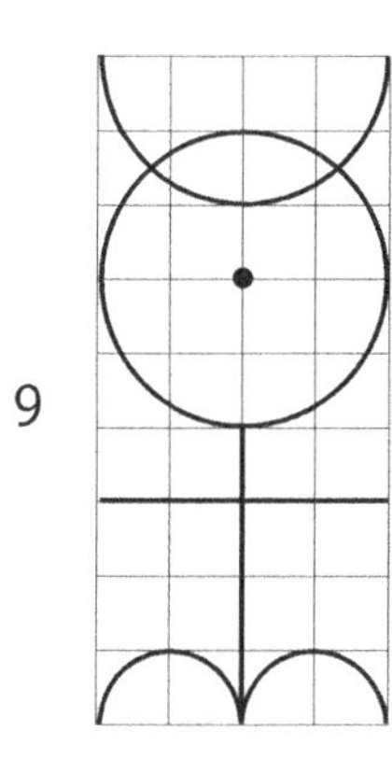

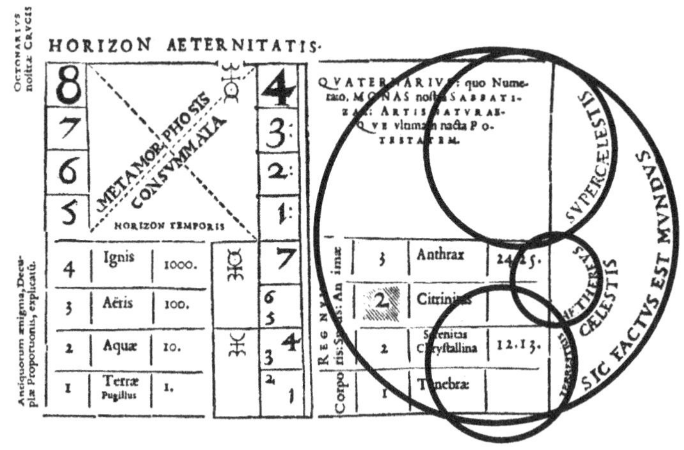

I thought that maybe if the large arc that bracketed the right end of the chart was completed, I could find the 1:2 proportion, but this was not the case.

I completed the arcs of the 3 smaller brackets, but still no 1:2 ratio.

Then I noticed something unusual about the segments Dee had made.

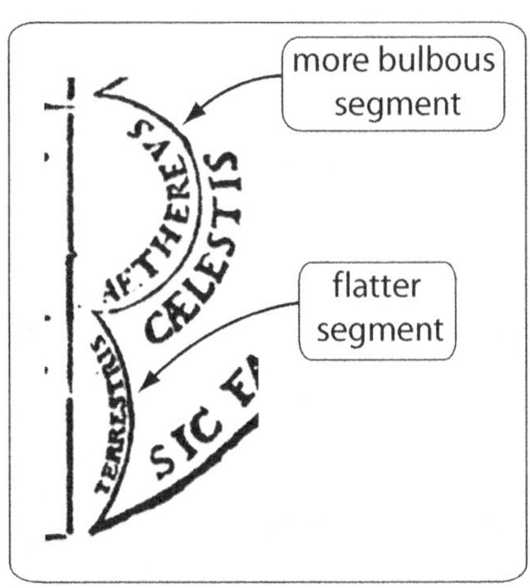

The Terrestrial segment was unusually flat, especially when compared with the Aetheric Celestial segment, which was quite bulbous.

(A segment is the area within a circle that is cut off by a chord.)

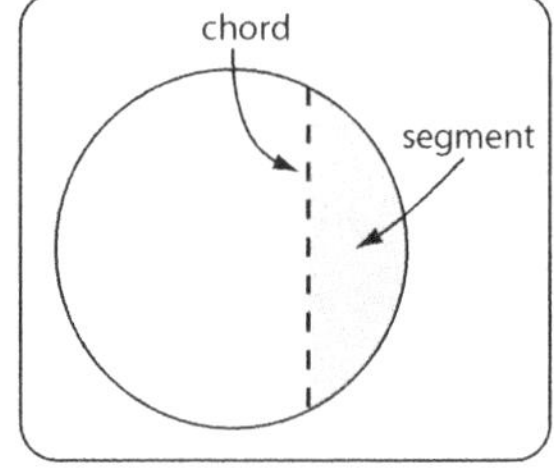

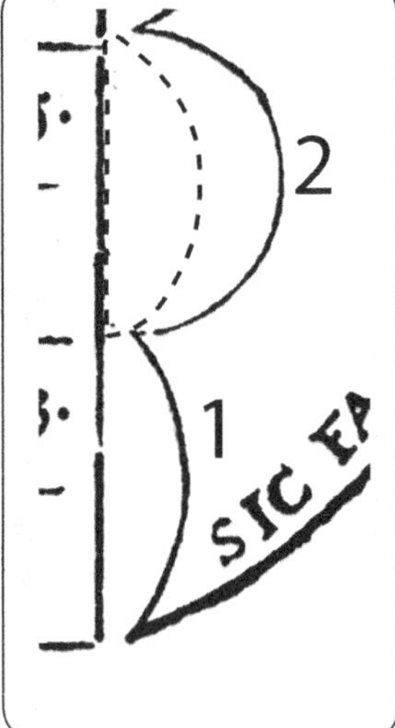

Throughout text of the *Monas Hieroglyphica*, Dee drops hints about the numbers 12 and 24.

Describing the Aries symbol in Theorem 11, he writes that on the first day of Aries (the Spring Equinox) there are exactly **12** hours of daylight and **12** hours of darkness, totaling to **24** hours.

I also knew that 12 and 24 were the first two members of the Metamorphosis sequence.

Eyeballing their areas, it seemed like I could fit two of the flat Terrestrial segments into the bulbous Aetheric Celestial segment. I had found a 1:2 ratio.

[But wait, there's more to Dee's geometric clue-game.]

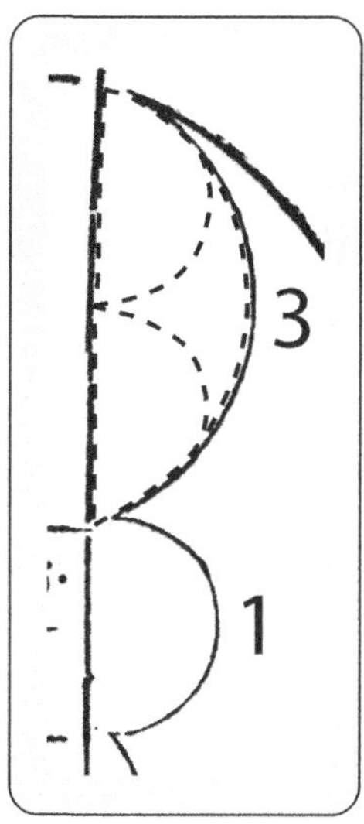

Next, I discovered that the area of the Supercelestial segment was about 3 times the size of the Aetheric Celestial segment. This was following the recipe of the Metamorphosis sequence.

(12 times 2 is 24), then (24 times 3 is 72).

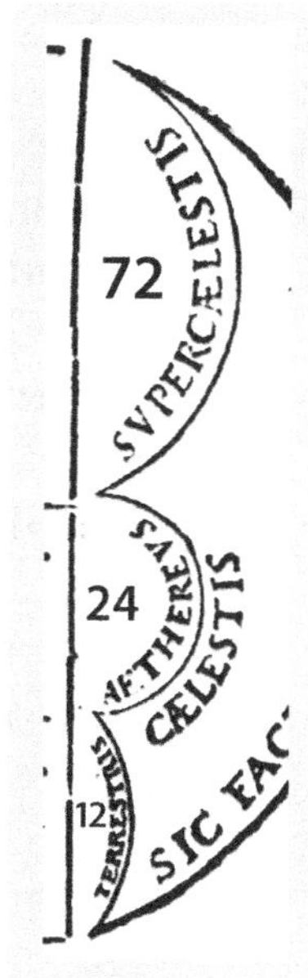

This also made sense symbolically. Kabbalistic tradition holds that there are 72 angels, so 72 is certainly a fitting number for the Supercelestial realm.

As they are involved in the earth/sun dance, 12 and 24 are fitting numbers for the Terrestrial and Aetheric Celestial realms.

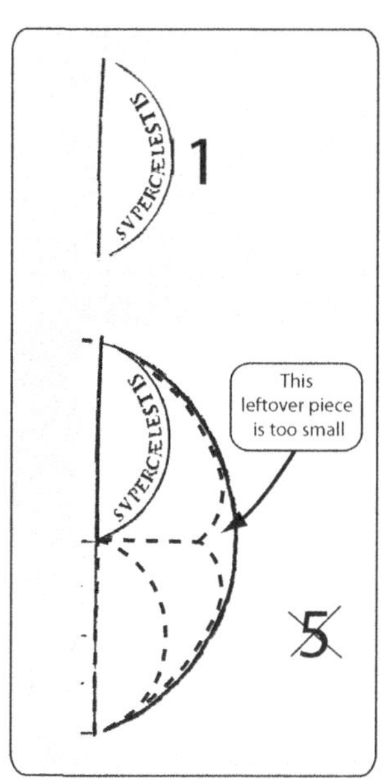

It seemed likely that the largest, encompassing bracket would make a segment 5 times the size of the Supercelestial segment.

But this time I was wrong.

No matter how I tried to estimate it, four Supercelestial segment areas fit fine, but there just was no way that five would fit.

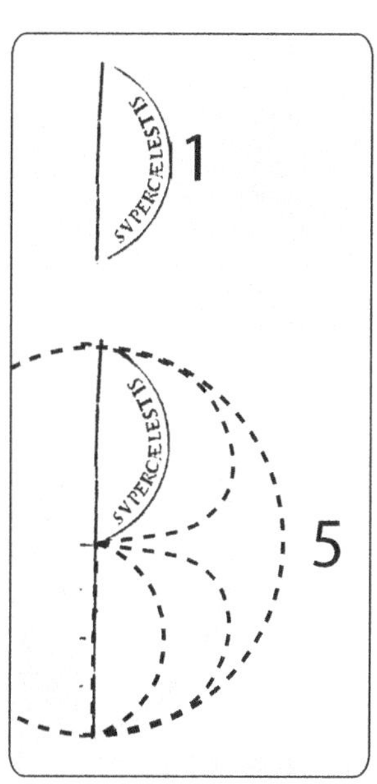

I tried to determine just how large that large segment would have to be so that it would accommodate 5 Supercelestial segments.

I realized it needed to extend out to be a **complete half circle**.

Hey! A half-circle was Dee's symbol for the Moon!

(And it also makes the letter D, the sound of Dee's last name.)

One of the main themes of the *Monas* is the Sun and the (full) Moon, two circles. And now, two circles fit the proportions perfectly. I've "greyed-in" the area that I added. It even looks like a crescent moon!

I call my revised chart the "**ballooned Thus the World Was Created chart**." Admittedly, I have changed the proportions of Dee's 450 year old chart, but this is what Dee wanted the reader to do. It's Dee's geometric riddle.

He left several confirming clues that this was his intent. The point of tangency of the two circles is aligned with his Artificial Quaternary. And in the Artificial Quaternary, the number 2 is curiously **larger** than the rest of the digits.

2

1

Dee's
Artificial
Quaternary

(Dee made the large "2" appear to be a mistake by putting diagonal hatch marks around it. But this large "2" was printed on the "engraving pass" through the press. The three other digits were printed on the "letter-press pass" through the press. The clever Dee made an "intentional mistake" to cryptically emphasize the large "2," hinting at the 2 big circles he wants us to find.)

When I found this next confirming clue,
I knew I was on the right track.
The sum of 12 + 24 + 72 is 108.

In order for whole segment area to be 360,
the rest of the area must be 252,
which is Dee's Magistral number!

It's clearly there, but cleverly
invisible to most readers.

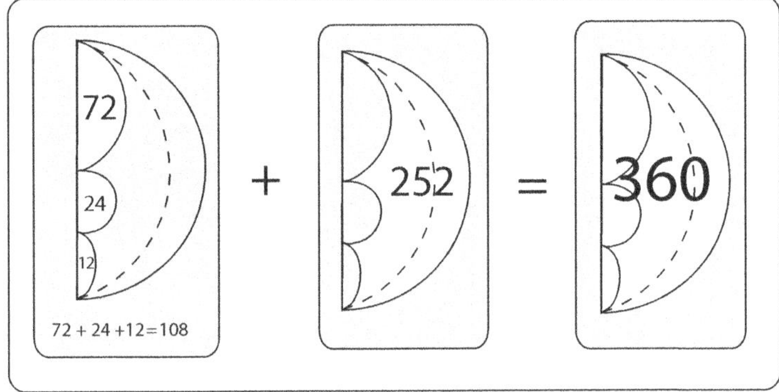

The "Two Circles" or "Two Rings"

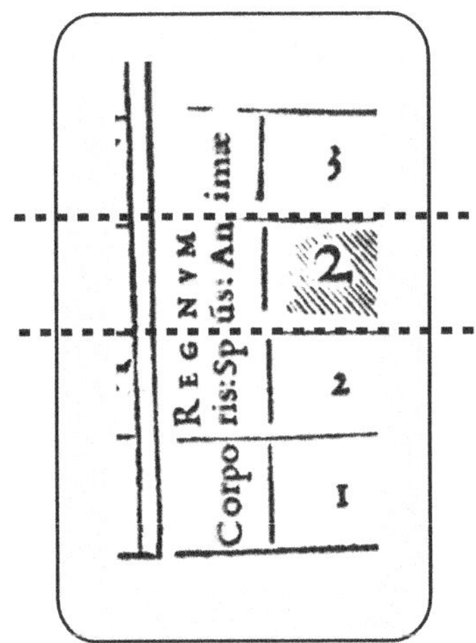

Immediately to the left of this "enlarged 2," Dee writes "REGNUM: Corporis, Sp[irit]ūs, Animae," which means "REIGN: Body, Spirit, Soul."

Dee has omitted several letters and arranged it so the letters "us:An" align with the "enlarged 2."

This is a jumbled-letter clue for the Latin word ***Anus*** which means "ring" (Anus is a shortened version of the Latin word ***Annulus***, which also means "ring.").

The idea of "2 Rings" (like the 2 circles Dee wants us to find)
relates to a famous parable in one of John Dee's favorite books, Plato's *Republic*.

Plato relates the classic tale of the Ring of Gyges. A poor shepherd named Gyges finds a gold ring that has the power to make its owner invisible.

He uses his power to kill the King, marry the Queen, usurp the throne, and become a tyrant.

(There actually was a King of Lydia named Gyges who is known as the "world's first tyrant." Incidentally, J. R. R. Tolkien modernized the tale of the Ring of Gyges with the "One Ring," a magic ring owned by Bilbo Baggins in *The Lord of the Rings*.)

After relating the tale of the Ring of Gyges, Plato's character Glaucon debates with the wise Socrates.

Socrates poses the question: What if there were **two** rings of invisibility?

One given to an **unjust** man,
The other given to a **just** man.

Glaucon replies that the **unjust** man would use it to become rich. But if the **just** man had the power of invisibility and didn't use it, his comrades as would consider him to be a "most miserable and utter fool."

In short, Glaucon asserts that anyone would be unjust given the opportunity and given immunity from getting caught.

This leads to a long discussion between Socrates and Glaucon and about justice and injustice.

Throughout the *Monas Hieroglyphica*, there are subtle references to the tale of Gyges and the two rings of Glaucon.

In the *Letter to Maximillian,* Dee rants about justice and injustice.

He uses the word TYRANT (TYRANNOS) prominently in one of his illustrations.

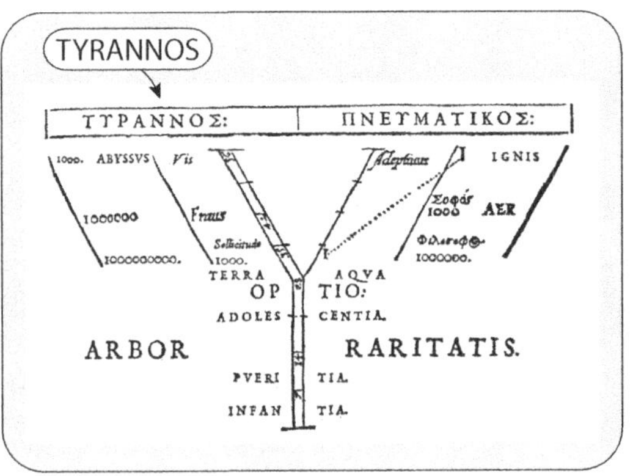

Dee even tells Maximillian he is, "offering him a MAGIC **parable**"

Dee hints,
"...he who nourished the MONAD will First Go Away
into a METAMORPHOSIS, and afterwards, will
very rarely be seen by the eyes of Mortals.
This, O Great King, is the true
INVISIBILITY of the MAGI..."

In short, the "**two rings of Glaucon**" are the "**two circles**" Dee wants us to find. They are the overall design plan for his chart.

(And also perhaps the simplest possible geometric representation of the Union of Opposites. The Sun and the Moon.)

Most importantly, two tangent circles fit in a rectangle that is has a height-to-width proportion of **1:2.**

I had found the missing 1:2 ratio.

The Metamorphosis numbers were the key that had unlocked the door.

Now I had a full inventory of those three wonderful ratios (1:2), (2:3), and (3:4).

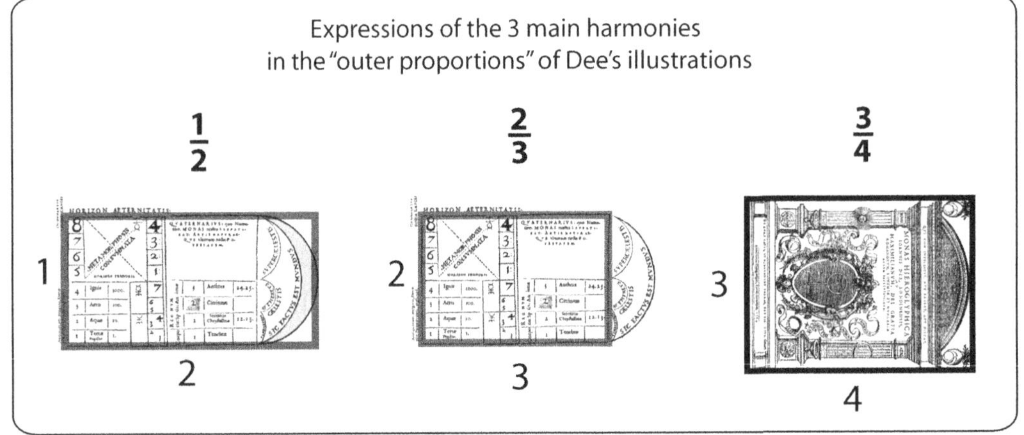

John Dee used the Metamorphosis numbers to select the most propitious day for Queen Elizabeth I coronation

On November 17, 1558, Queen Mary I died. John Dee was asked by Elizabeth I to select the most propitious day for her coronation. He picked January 15, 1559.

January 15 incorporates three of Dee's Metamorphosis numbers.

January is the first of the **12** months.

January 15 is 1/**24** of a year.

As each day has 24 hours, January 15 is **360** hours from the start of the new year or January 1.

(15 × 24 = 360)

Dee had determined that January 15 was a special day at least two years earlier. On January 15, 1556 had he presented his "*Supplication to Queen Mary for the Recovery and Preservation of Ancient Writers and Monuments*." Dee even offered to contribute many of the books to this proposed "Royal Library."

The shortsighted Queen Mary rejected Dee's plan. It was until much later that the British Library was established, which now contains about 14 million books.

Was Dee even interested in architecture and theater design?

Here are two excerpts from Dee's explanation of the "Arte of Architecture" in his 1570 *Preface* to the first English translation of Euclid's *Elements*. The full 3 1/2 pages of text can be found in the Appendix of this book.

(As well as my modernization from Dee's original Elizabethan English).

"I consider an Architect to be that man who (by sure and marvelous reason and method) has the skill to devise (using his own mind and Imagination) and accomplish, by the movement of weighty material and the joining and framing together of bodies, that which is most beneficial for the worthiest needs of Man.

To be able to perform these things, he must have an understanding and knowledge of the highest and most worthy disciplines."

Also, in describing the "Arte of Architecture," Dee discusses theater acoustics:

"And an Architect must know Music in order to understand both Regular Music and Mathematical Music. This will help him fine tune the springs of Balists, Catapults, and Scorpions.

[a balist shoot heavy darts and a scorpion is a small catapult operated by one person].

Likewise, in Theatres, Bronze Vessels are placed in niches beneath the seats using mathematical principles. The Greeks called them echeia.

[êxô means "a returned sound or a ringing sound," from which we get the word echo.]

They are distributed in various places throughout the circular Theatre according to the Musical Harmonies of Diatessaron, Diapente, and Diapason.

[The musical fourth, fifth, and octave or the ratios 3:4, 2:3, and 1:2]

The actor's voice, projected from the stage, would be amplified when it strikes these vessels, allowing the audience to hear a richer and more pleasing sound."

(Dee, *Preface*, p. diiij. and d.iij verso)

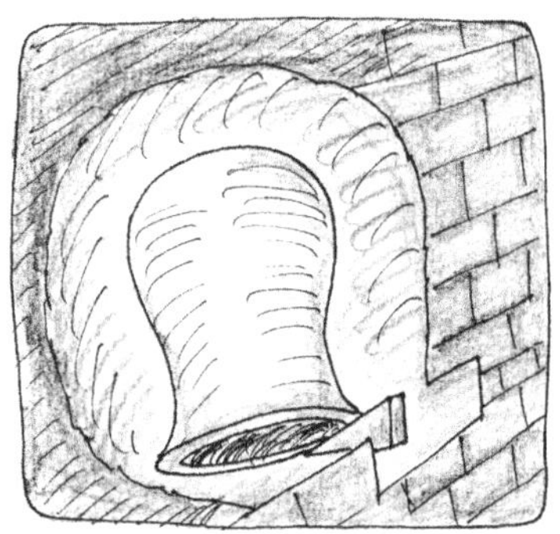

Greek "sounding vessel", as described by Vitruvius

In his book *On Architecture* (ca. 40 BC) Vitruvius explains that brass acoustic vessels which amplified various tones were placed in small cave-like chambers in appropriate places in a theater, in accordance to the three main musical ratios 1:2, 2:3, and 3:4.

I'm not suggesting Dee actually designed *echeia* for the original Globe, but we should definitely be on the lookout for these three ratios, 1:2, 2:3, and 3:4, in Dee's theater plans.

The "sounding vessels" were placed in small chambers scattered throughout the theater to improve acoustics.

So, let's get to it. Our little holiday is over.

You now know more about Dee's mathematical cosmology than 99.999% of the world.

You are well-equipped to understand Dee's numerous mathematical, geometric and word riddles in his plans for the original Globe.

The Harmonious Tiring House

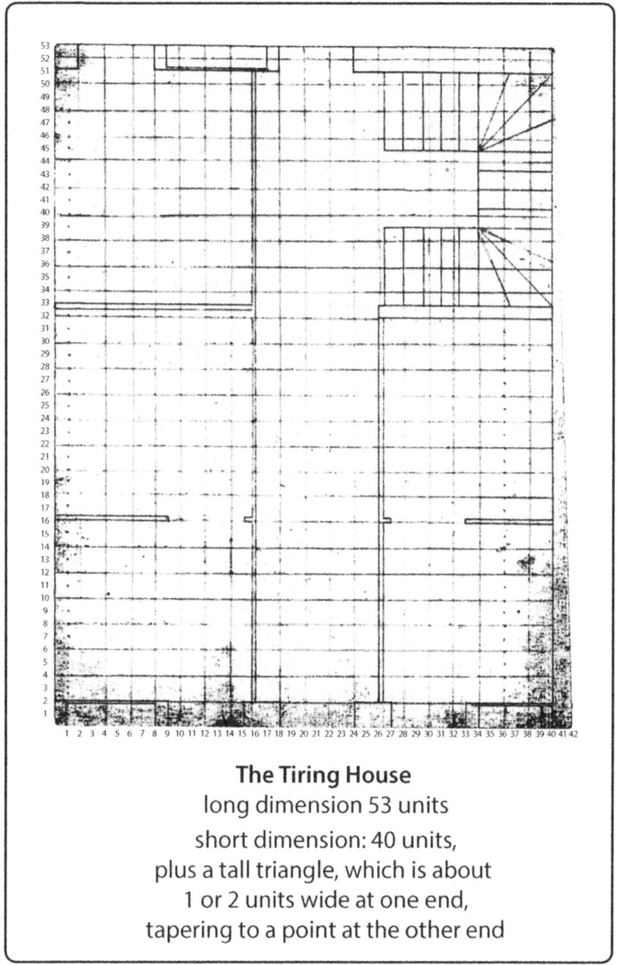

The Tiring House
long dimension 53 units
short dimension: 40 units,
plus a tall triangle, which is about
1 or 2 units wide at one end,
tapering to a point at the other end

The first day back from vacation, always requires a little "read-justment" time. So before exploring the three main diagrams relating to the Globe theater (the "overview" plan, the "side-view" plan, and the "parametric" or the combination of two views), let's tackle the Tiring House plan.

The Tiring House is the "backstage" area where props were stored and where actors changed into their costumes.

It's an odd little diagram. There is no apparent symmetry. The rooms in the left side are larger than the rooms of the right side, and the central corridor is not dead center.

There are five rooms plus a stairwell. The room on the upper left is the largest. Strangely it has a door to the outside, but it has no interior doors. Perhaps it was the "General Office," where outside visitors could enter, yet not gain access to the rest of the facility.

Notice that this "General Office" has exterior walls that are about 2 feet thick on each side of the doorway.

There are pinpricks running vertically near the left and right edges. There are two pinpricks for each grid square. However, let's stick with the pinpricks for our measuring units. The space between two adjacent pinpricks is one "unit," which is probably also one "foot."

The long dimension of the Tiring House appears to be 53 units. But there's something very odd about the width. At the bottom it measures about 41 to 42 units (41.5?), but tapers 40 units the top. This obliquity is created by an tall, thin triangle on the right-hand edge.

Who the heck would design an asymmetrical and crooked building? The answer is: Someone who is trying to hide clues about harmony.

Harmony? It looks downright unharmonious to me!
The answer is: The clues are hidden in the unharmoniousness.

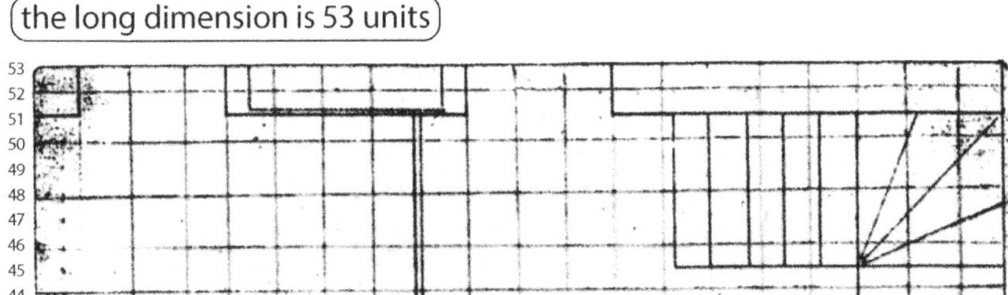

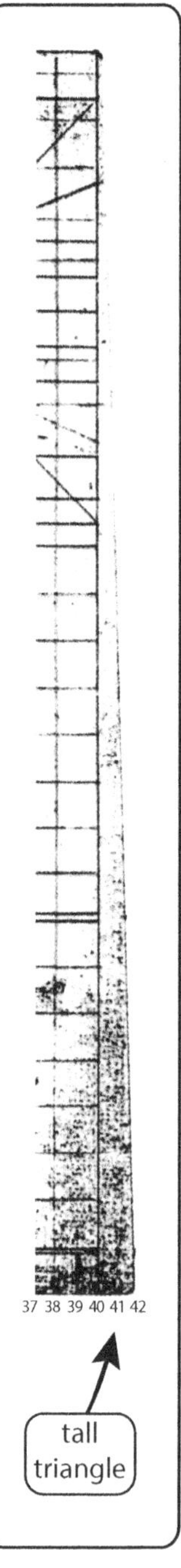

Let's ignore that perplexing tall triangle along the right edge for a moment and consider the whole building to be 40 units wide (as it is at the top).

Determining the long dimension of the building is challenging as well. The long dimension appears to be about 26.5 grid squares, which is 53 units tall.

That's strange, as 53 is a prime number; it's not evenly divisible by 2, 3, 4, 5, 6, or anything other than itself and 1.

(Of course, 53 is actually divisible by *any* number lower than itself, but the result would always involve a fraction.)

Why didn't Dee pick a number that has lots of factors, like 53's neighbor, 54.

(Composite number 54 is divisible by 2, 3, 6, 9,18, and 27).

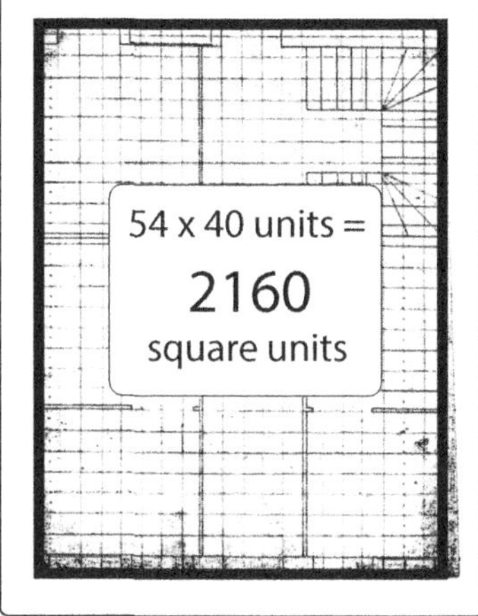

Joy Hancox was puzzled by this discrepancy as well. So in her book, she gives both figures, 53 and 54. Let's set aside the 53 for a moment.

(I promise we'll return, as it's a huge clue.)

Let's consider the long dimension to be 54. Though we arrived here creatively, a "long dimension to short dimension" ratio of 54 x 40 units makes a total area of **2160** square units. Now there's a stellar composite number. It has 40 factors, including all the single digits except the number 7.

(This is actually a "clue by omission," as we shall later see, the Greeks called 7 the "virgin number.")

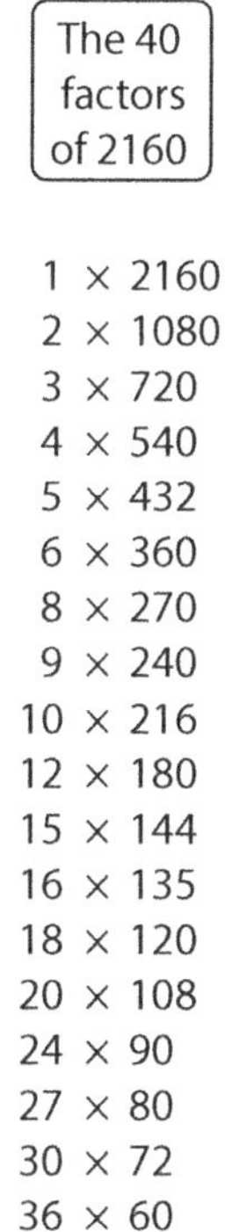

The 40 factors of 2160

1 × 2160	
2 × 1080	
3 × 720	
4 × 540	
5 × 432	
6 × 360	
8 × 270	
9 × 240	
10 × 216	
12 × 180	
15 × 144	
16 × 135	
18 × 120	
20 × 108	
24 × 90	
27 × 80	
30 × 72	
36 × 60	
40 × 54	
45 × 48	

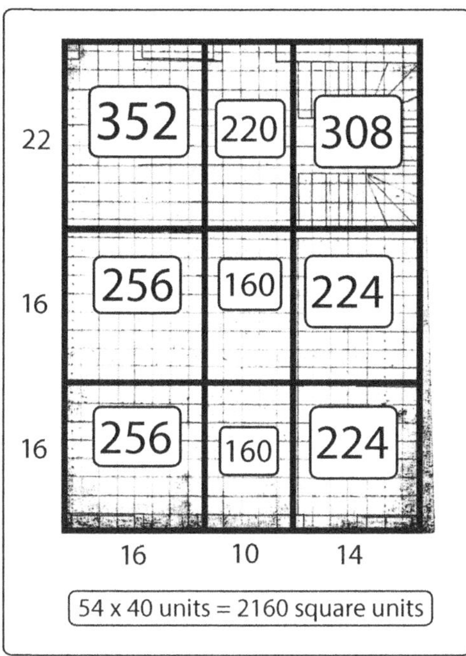

To show all the whole numbers, I divided the whole plan into nine sections, the five rooms, the stairwell, and three parts of the corridor.

Only four numbers are utilized for all the room dimensions: 10, 14, 16, and 22.

If the whole 54 x 40 plan has 1260 square feet, why didn't Dee simply make nine equal sections of 240 each?

One reason is that 54 divided by 3 equals 18
(which is a whole number),
but dividing 40 by 3 equals 13.333
(which is **not** a whole number).

(True 13.333 feet is "13 feet 4 inches," but carpenters would prefer whole feet to inches when they have a whole theater to build, and on a deadline no less.)

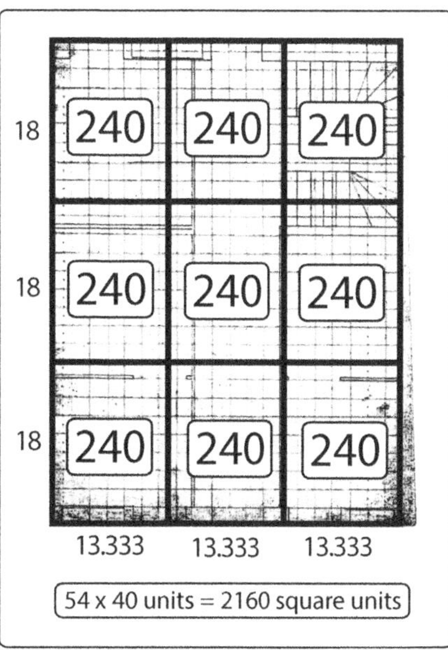

But the real reason for all this dimensional weirdness is that Dee wanted cryptically incorporate the Pythagorean harmonies 1:2, 2:3, and 3:4 into his design!

To explain what I mean, let's talk percentages.
1:2 can be seen as 1/2, which is 50%,
2:3 can be seen as 2/3, which is 66.666%,
and 3:4 can be seen as 3/4, which is 75%.

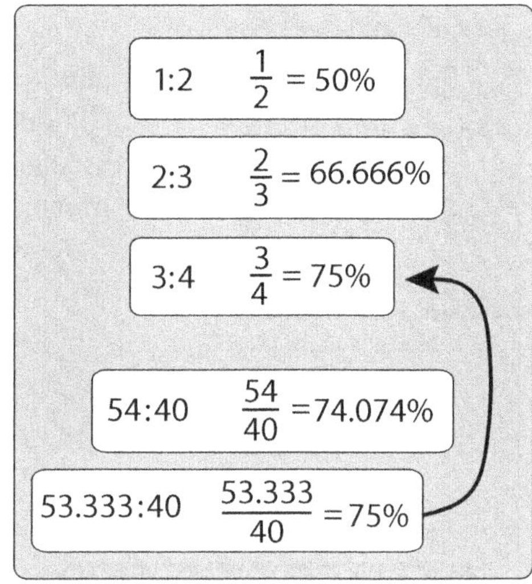

However 40 is 74.074% of 54. (This result might seem random and insignificant, but this is actually the first clue that Dee wants us to find.)

This 74.074% is not exactly 75%, but it's pretty close. In other words, for the Tiring House to have a 3:4 long dimension: short dimension proportion, given the width of 40, the height needs to be 53.333 feet (3/4 = 40/53.33)

(Despite the fact that 53.333 x 40 units has an area of 2133.333 square units, which is obviously not a whole number.)

Hey, 53.333 is pretty close to 53, which is the long dimension of the drawing, estimated by counting the pinpricks.

In short, John Dee gives us two long dimensions, for two different reasons. The "**54**" is divisible in numerous ways, to allow the various room dimensions to be whole numbers.

What Joy and I both originally considered to be "53," Dee really intended to be **53.333**, giving the whole building a harmonious **3:4** "short to long dimension" proportion.

Dee is telling **two** geometric stories at the same time: The first involves, 54, a "whole number" rectangle that can be divided up nicely. And 40 x 53.333, a 3:4 rectangle, which the Greeks called *diatessaron*, and the Romans called *sesquitertia*.(And the interval that musicians call a "fourth.")

John Dee loved four to three

How can I be so sure that Dee wants us to see the Tiring House plan as a 3:4 rectangle? Because he has a track record of using the 3:4 proportion!

Title page of John Dee's 1558
Propaedeumata Aphoristica
(Preparatory Aphorisms)

Dee used the 3:4 proportion in the overall dimensions of the Title page of his 1564 *Monas Hieroglyphica*, his most cherished work.
(In other diagrams in the *Monas Hieroglyphica*, Dee conceals the ratios 1:2 and 2:3)

And 7 years earlier, he had used the 3:4 proportion for the Title page of his 1558 *Propaedeumata Aphoristica*, which contains 120 "*Preparatory Aphorisms*" on astronomy and physics.

And I'm sure it occurred John Dee that the number of letters in his "last name": "first name" is 3:4.

Title page of John Dee's 1564
Monas Hieroglyphica
(Sacred Symbol of Oneness)

Summary (almost)

To summarize, Dee provides 2 "measures" of the Tiring House so he can involve two different types of mathematical harmony. (Double duty! Two for the price of one!)

There's another reason I'm certain this is what Dee is up to. It's because Dee's hiding a **third measure** of the Tiring House! And it expresses **even more** hidden harmonies! To find it, we just have to follow Dee's trail of clues.

The difference between the long dimension of 54 and the long dimension of 53.333 is .666
(which is easier seen as "2/3 of a unit").

If the short dimension of the Tiring House along the top edge is 40 units, that long, thin, horizontal rectangle of "no man's land" is .666 x 40 or 26.666 square units.
(2/3 x 40 = 26.666)

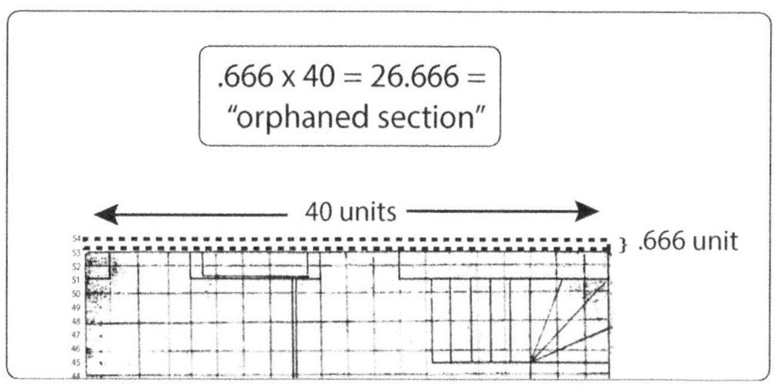

The long, thin rectangle at the top is included in the 54 x 40 rectangle, but "abandoned" by the 53.333 x 40 unit rectangle. I call it the "**orphaned section**." Having "missing" pieces is not very "concinnitas"
(meaning where every part must contribute to the whole).
One must not take from Peter without giving to Paul. Or in this case, we might ask, "Where's Waldo? Do you know where the missing 26.666 square unit section is?

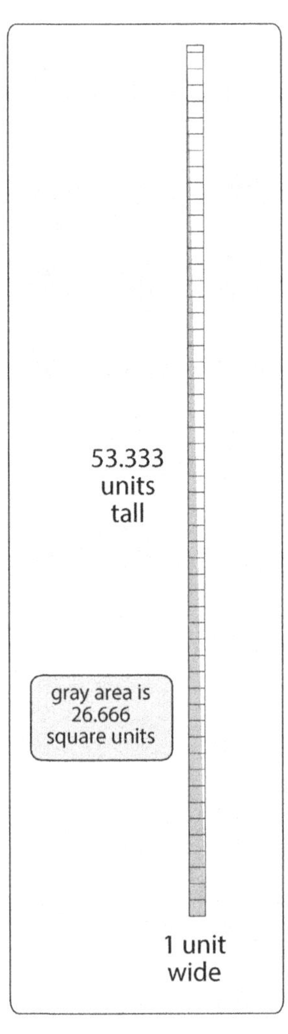

It's that "tall triangle" along the right edge that we've been ignoring all this time!

Picture a stack of "1 unit by 1 unit squares" piled 53.333 units high. If you draw a diagonal from one corner to the opposite corner, it makes two tall triangles (one is upside down from the other).

In Geometry 101, you learned that the diagonal of a rectangle divides that rectangle into two sections of equal area.

And propitiously, half of 53.333 square units is 26.666 square units. **The "orphaned section" from the top is found on the side!**

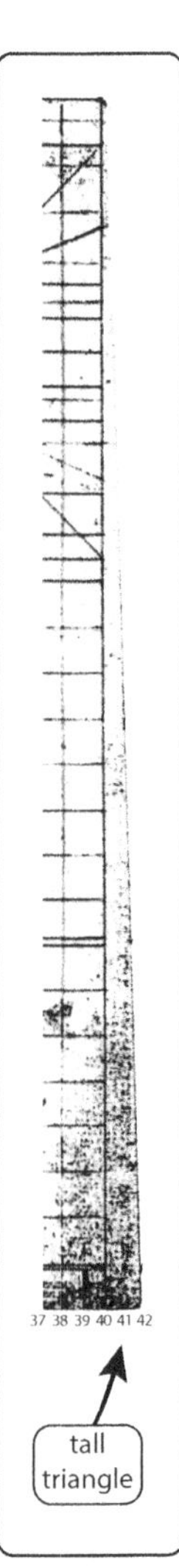

.666 x 40 = 26.666 =
"orphaned section"

40 units

.666 unit

The top "orphaned section" is .666 (or 2/3 of a unit) tall by 40 wide, which equals **26.666 square units**.

The tall, triangular "orphaned section" along the right edge is 50% of 53.333, which is **26.666 square units**.

To summarize, as a confirming clue that he wants us to see two rectangles (53.333 x 40, and 54 x 40), Dee moved the "orphaned section" to the side, by adding a "sliver" which is 1 unit wide at the bottom, and tapers to nothing at the top.

So Dee seems to be suggesting a "**third rectangle**!" He could be hinting at **53.333 x 41** or **54 x 41**. Which one do you think he is suggesting?

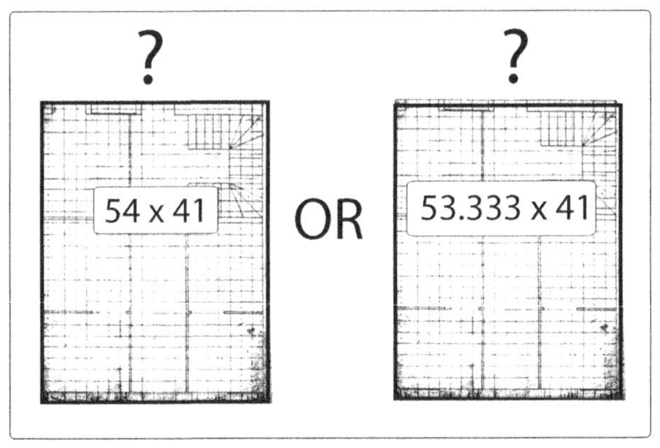

The answer is... **Neither**!
He's hinting at an entirely different rectangle.
Can you guess what it is?

The Door Clue

Dee hides his next clue in the three doorways that enter onto the stage.

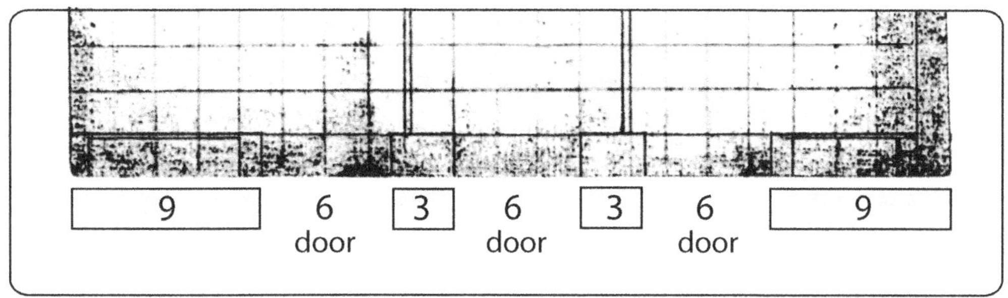

Inside the Tiring House, though the corridor is asymmetrically located. And the left rooms are wider than the right rooms (16 units wide verses 14 units wide). However, the symmetry of three doorways suggests to me there is overall symmetry of the facade. The doorways are each separated from their neighbors by 3 feet. The section to the far left is 9 units wide. So to maintain symmetry, the section on the right side must also be 9 units wide.

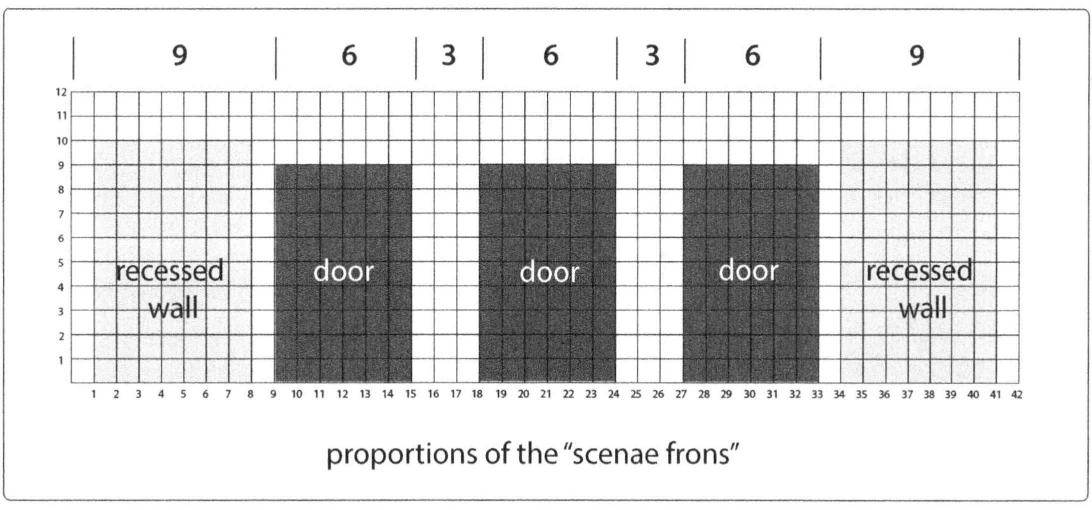

proportions of the "scenae frons"

Thus Dee wants the front facade (*scaenae frons*) of the Tiring House to be 42 units wide. We started with 40, then added the tall triangle to make 41. Where we going to get another foot to make 42? This is where Dee fudges a little bit. One foot on a 42-foot facade is only about 2.38%. Dee seems to just add it on. But for good reason. He wants us to discover another fascinating number.

This "increase" from 40 to 42 would require that the tall triangle be two units wide at the bottom, tapering to nothing at the top. That would give it an area of 26.666 x 2 or 53.333 square units.

However, that's double the size of the missing area! It's 26.666 square units too much. Dee seems to ignore this discrepancy. This extra 26.666, compared to the whole area of the Tiring House plan (54 x 40 = 2160) is only about 1.2% (26.666/2160 = .0123456...)

In the actual building, this approximately 1.2% is hardly noticeable. It would give the carpenters (or probably puzzled) a little more width or substance of this tall triangle. "About 1 foot" isn't that much if the beams you are using are 8 to 12 inches thick and that "side section" is a part of a wall that few people will see anyway.

Concealing universal-magical-mathematical-harmonic-wonders in architecture is more important to Dee then making the carpenter's job too easy. What do I mean by mathematical wonders?

A hidden mathematical gem, .0123456790123456790123...

Well, a moment ago, I divided 26.666/2160 and got the result, .0123456..., which I thought was a weird result: "zero and the first 6 digits, all in consecutive order.

So I went online to one of the free "Big Integer Calculator" sites and typed in 26.66666666666666666...
(plus I typed in about 150 more sixes), divided by 2160.
The result was:
.012345679012345679012345679012345679
012345679012345679 ...

$\frac{26.6666...}{2160}$ = .012345679012345679
012345679012345679
012345679012345679
012345679012345679
012345679012345679
012345679012345679
012345679012345679
012345679012345679
012345679012345679
012345679012345679
012345679012345679
012345679012345679
012345679012345679
012345679012345679 ...

What an amazing thing, an infinitely repeating decimal of
"zero and all the single digits, in their consecutive order.
Except the number 8 is nowhere to be found.
Searching for the root cause of this anomaly, I divided 26.666 and 2160 each by 2.
The results were 13.333 and 1080. So I divided each of these by 10.
The results were 1.333 and 108. In short, **1.333/108** = .012345679012345679...

Wow! One of Pythagoras' sacred harmonies (**4:3**=1.33),
divided by the sacred number of the ancient Hindus (**108**),
makes this crazy repeating decimal with all the digits except 8.
The ancient West, meets the ancient East, in Dee's plan for Shakespeare's Globe.

Actually, we can boil this equation, 1.333/108 = .012345679012345679... down even more.

As three quarters of 108 is 81, we can divide 1 by 81 and get the same result 1/81=.012345679012345679...

$$\frac{1.333...}{108} = \frac{1}{81} = .012345679...$$

Remember, 81 is an important number in the "9 Wave" of Dee's Consummata. It is only 9 away from 90, and these are the "null numbers "in the single-digit and double-digit range, respectively.

Also, the reflective mate of 81 is 18. And as we'll soon see, 18 is a key number in the Globe design (hint: it has to do with height).

A brief explanation of where the 8 is hiding

Incidentally, modern mathematicians can easily explain why the 8 is "missing" in .012345679 ... It's not called the "odometer effect." Things really proceed ...7, 8, 9 10, 11,12 ... , but as we represent 10, 11, 12, etc. as "double digits,"and there's only room for one digit, the digit "1" in 10 "carries forward" to mate with the 9 that precedes it.

Now, that 9+1 adds to 10 and the "1 "in that 10 is "carried forward" to mate with the 8. That 1+8 makes 9, and that's the 9 we see in .012345679... And its the reason why the 8 is missing. (And no more "carrying forward" is required.)

In short, if we used a single digit for 10, let's say the letter A, and 11 was B, and 12 was C, then 1/81 *would* include the 8. It would be, .0123456789ABCDEFGH...

If we had an infinite amount of single-digit symbols, 26.666/2160 or 1/81 equals the whole realm of number, arranged in its proper sequence. Dee would have found *that* fascinating.

Renaissance mathematicians had a different kind of system to express decimals. The decimal point as we know it today, was introduced in 1616 by the Scotsman, John Napier.

But back in 1585, one of Dee's contemporaries, Simon Stevin of Bruges had published *De Thiende* (*On Tenths*), publicly explaining something skilled mathematicians of that era already knew how to add, subtract, multiply, and divide using decimals.

Even if Dee wasn't aware of all this decimal stuff, he certainly knew there was something special about 2160.

Half of 2160 is 1080. A tenth of that is 108. And 108 plus Dee's Magisterial number, 252, makes 360, a perfect circle.

108	sacred number of the East
+252	sacred number of the West
360	a perfect circle

It's much more than just a plan for a crooked building

So, what looked like an asymmetrical, crooked building design holds hidden mathematical secrets. Dee has designed what (in Latin) is called an *aedificium*, "a building that instructs."

Mathematical harmonies described on paper are nice, but when incorporated in a building, they become experiential and can transform the human spirit.

I found two more mathematical reasons why I'm certain Dee wanted the front facade to be 42 feet wide. I call the reasons "3:6:9" and "9 x Dee's Magisterial number." Let me explain these two strange answers.

Part of the caption on the "close-up" plan for the Globe reads "**3:6:9 a rule for itt**." These are the three numbers involved in the proportion of the front facade!

The doors are each 6 units wide. And there's a 3-foot section between each of the doors. And a 9-foot section to the left and to the right. Remember, this facade is the "back drop" that the audience sees behind the actors, for all the plays.

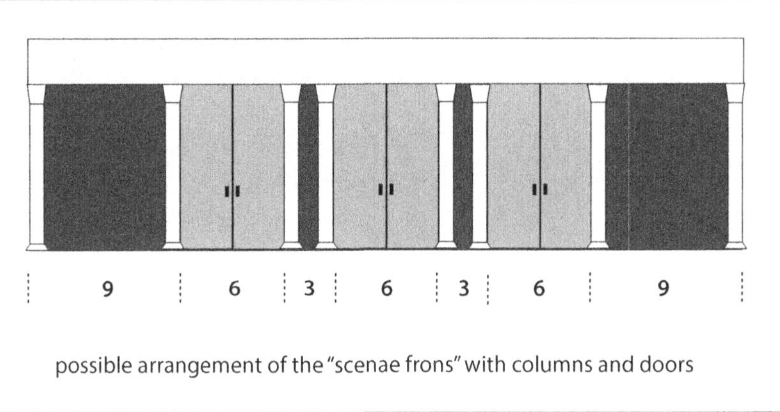

possible arrangement of the "scenae frons" with columns and doors

Dee was a big fan of Leon Battista Alberti, who in 1452 wrote ten books *On the Art of Building* (based on Vitruvius' *Ten Books*, written in 25 BC).

Alberti recommended that openings, like windows and doors, have a height:width ratio of 3:2.

(In other words, the height should be 1.5 times the width).

If Dee followed Alberti's harmonious guideline, the doors would be 9 feet tall. This makes yet another representation of 9 on the facade.

Thus, we could definitely say "**3:6:9**" is included in "**a rule for itt**."

(This proportion, which reduces down to 1:2:3, will also be found elsewhere in the Globe design plans.)

The third measure of the Tiring House is 54 x 42

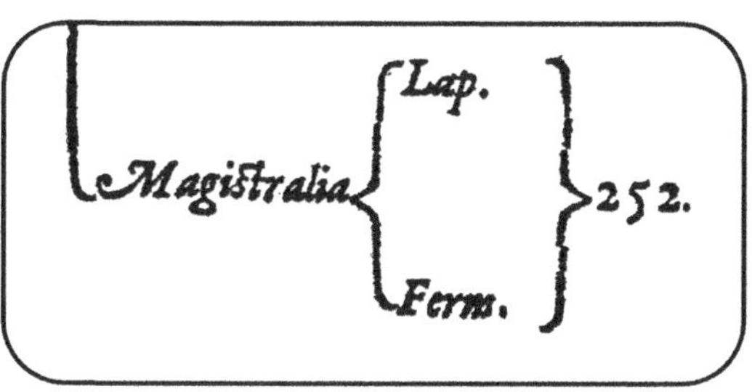

The second reason I'm sure Dee wanted us to see "42" as one of the widths of the Tiring House has a do the number 252.

In the *Monas Hieroglyphica*, Dee calls this number the " Magisterial" number. He cryptically adds "Lap… Firm," which is short for "Lapidification … Fermentation," or the "Philosopher's Stone" of Number.

Here's how 252 is involved:

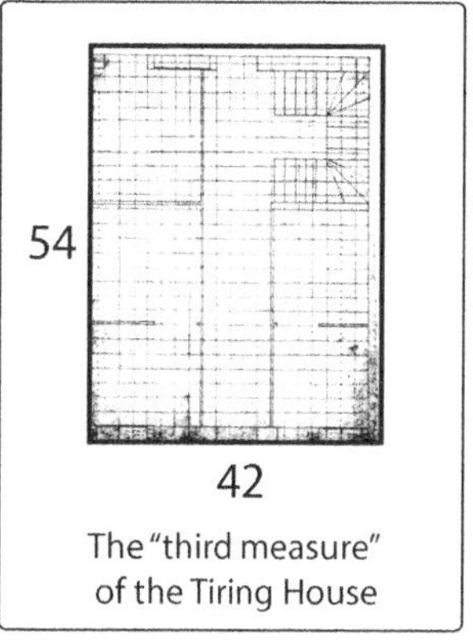

The "third measure" of the Tiring House

The "third measure" of the Tiring House that Dee wants us to see (besides 54 x 40 and 53.333 x 40) is **54 x 42**.

Dee wouldn't want us to see a rectangle with a crooked side. He would want us to see a right-angled rectangle, which is 54 x 42.

And the total square area of a plan that is 54 x 42 units is **2268** square units.

Wow! This number, 2268, is pretty close to 2520, which has the distinction of being the lowest number divisible by all the single digits. Why didn't Dee simply make the Tiring House 2520 square feet?

(He could have made it 54 x 45. That would be 2520 square feet.)

Well, 2268 is pretty special in its own way, for several different reasons. One is that 2268 is **36 x 63**, (two more members of that "9 wave" that keeps popping up)

$$
\begin{array}{r} 2520 \\ -\ 2268 \\ \hline 252 \end{array}
$$

Another reason is that the difference between 2520 and 2268 is…
You guessed it…
252,
Dee's Magisterial number.

Seen another way, as 2520 is 10 x 252, this "area" number, 2268, is 9 x 252.

Hey, if we divide the Tiring House into nine equal parts, as before, they will each be 252!

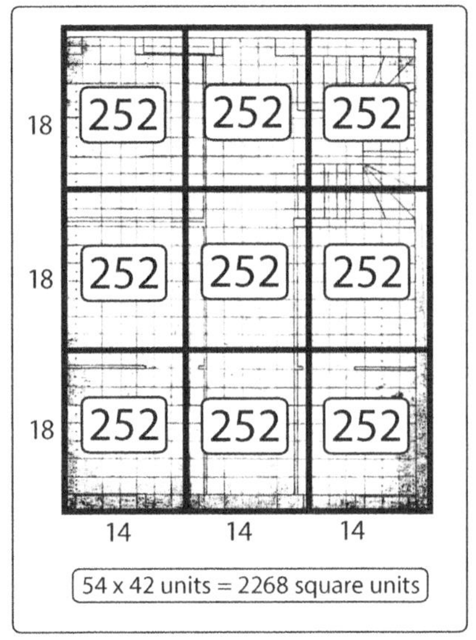

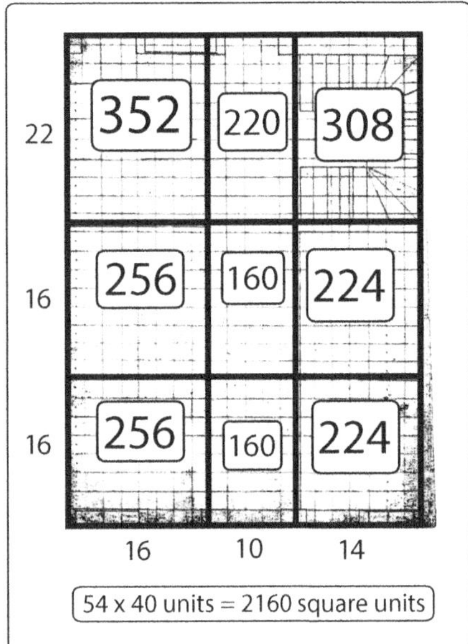

But alas, Dee did not divide the Tiring House symmetrically; he divided it in a weird way, and herein lies another harmony.

Can you find it?
It has to do with the ratio 2:3.
But Dee hid it really well.

Using any of the 3 measures of the Tiring House, the interior walls do not break up the interior into "1/3 and 2/3" sections, either horizontally or vertically.

So then where did Dee hide the ratio 2:3? To find it you must realize there are two kinds of ratios: "part-to-whole" and "part-to-part ratios."

Thus far, we've been looking for the "2:3 part-to-whole ratio." In other words, "1/3 of one whole" plus "2/3 of one whole" equals "one whole."

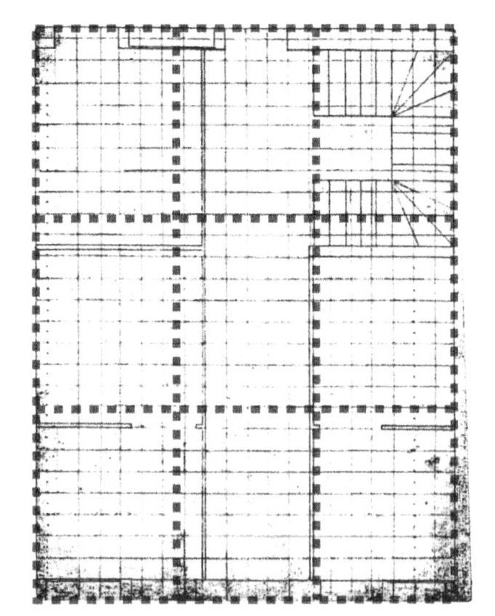
The interior walls do not divide the interior by 1/3 and 2/3 sections, either horizontally or vertically

Instead we need to look for the "2:3 part-to-part ratio," in which "two parts" are compared to "three parts."

To get "two parts compared to "three parts," we really have to divide the whole into "five parts"

An easy way to see this is "2/5 is two thirds of 3/5." Or an even easier way to see it is "40% is two thirds of 60%".

Well, 40% of 54 is 21.6
And 60% of 54 is 32.4
(And indeed, 21.6 : 32.4 = 2:3)

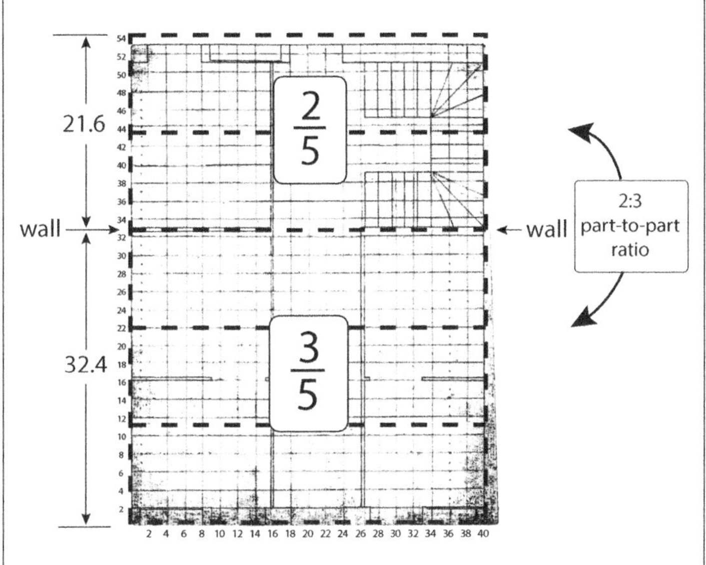

And if we count up 32.4 pin-pricks from the stage end of the Tiring House, guess what we find: the interior wall of what I call the "general office."

This makes the long dimension of the "general office" **21.6 units**.

This "general office" interior wall is aligned with the interior wall, which encloses the stairwell on the right. This "2/5 section of the Tiring House" is **two thirds** of "3/5 of the Tiring House."

In his Tiring House, Dee has cleverly concealed the 2:3 ratio inside and the 3:4 in the overall outside dimensions. **It's house of mathematical harmonies.**

Incidentally, there is another way the inside and outside dimensions connect. We've just seen that the long dimension of the "general office" is 21.6 units.

And we've seen that the 54 x 40 measure for the Tiring House is 2160. These measures are related, in the sense that 100 x 21.6 = 2160. Yet another thread in Dee's intricate mathematical web.

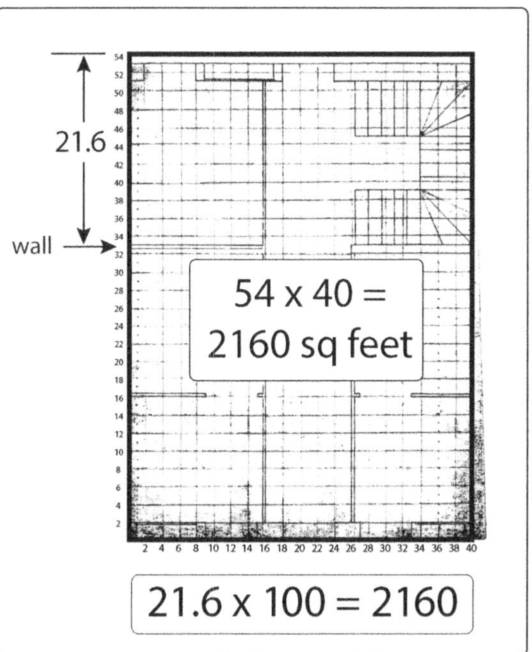

To summarize, Dee hides "three measures for the Tiring House (54 x 40), (53.333 x 40), and (54 x 42), so the structure is imbued with the harmonies of 3:4 and 2:3. Yet the stage still looks symmetrical, based on 3:6:9, which is really 1:2:3.

We can reduce this 3:6 ratio to the 1:2 ratio. And we can reduce the 6:9 ratio to the 2:3 ratio. More hidden harmonies!

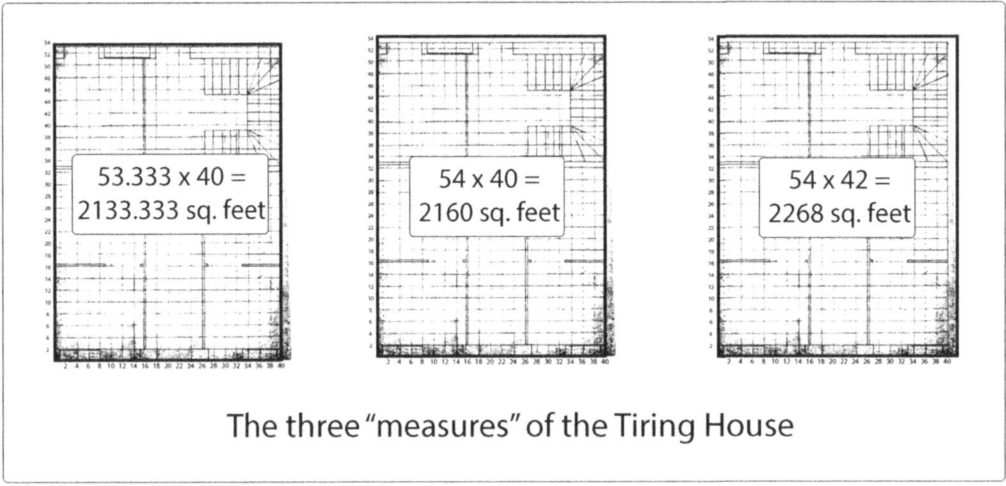

The three "measures" of the Tiring House

So which one did the carpenters build? Probably the largest, 54 by 42, as it would contain all the other secret harmonies. Why didn't Dee simply say make the Tiring House 54 by 42? Because there would be no lessons learned.

A well-hidden clue in the stairwell

As there is a winding stairway on the plan with 22 steps, one might assume that the second floor has the same layout as the first.

One change in the second story layout might be in the area near the stage, which was the balcony where Juliet would look down at Romeo, also somehow accommodated a seating area for about a dozen dignitaries called the "Lord's room."

Furthermore, just as there are three galleries around the Starr's Mall, one might also assume there were three levels in the Tiring House. Thus, there will be another set of 22 stairs in this stairwell brought you from Story 2 to Story 3.

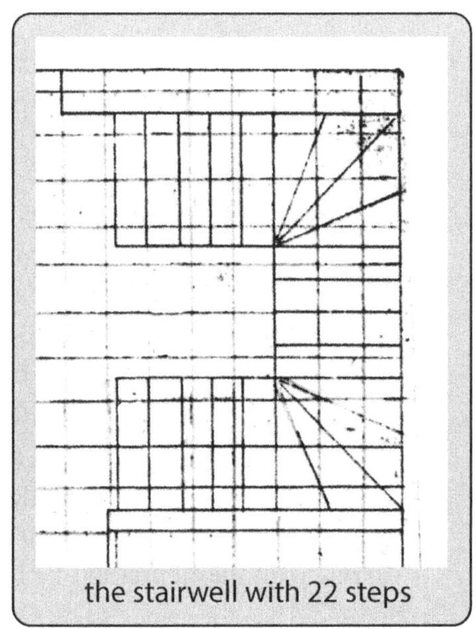

the stairwell with 22 steps

Above the third story would be the eaves, but old illustrations show that there were some "mini-houses" and flagpole tower atop the Tiring House. (We will explore those features later.)

Also, as the stage was about 6 feet off the ground, I suggest the first floor of the Tiring House was 6 feet off the ground. Thus, actors wouldn't have to race up the steps to get on stage and raced down the steps when they exited. Stairs are hazardous when bustling about with long capes and gowns.

Plus, a 6 foot "space under the raised first floor" would provide 2160 square feet more for storage. And it would allow for a passageway so actors could make surprise entrances through any number of trapdoors on the stage.

Indeed, if the actual floor of Story 1 was 6 feet above ground, that would require a short flight of exterior steps to get into the "general office" door and through the "end-of-the-corridor" door." That's not a big deal.

In fact, the "end-of-the-corridor" door might even have had a ramp, allowing really-large props to be wheeled, from outside, right through the Tiring house, and onto the stage, with no steps involved. The stage hands would really appreciate that!

Let's return to the large stairwell.
I call it "large" because each of the stairs
is 6 feet wide. (I used the pinpricks as ruler.)

Modern stairways are usually only about 4 feet wide.

Perhaps this was jumbo-sized to allow for two-way traffic, or to move heavy props or furniture that might require 4 people to carry.

Most modern stairways have about an 8-inch rise and a 10-inch tread depth. But these stairs treads have a depth of about 18 inches. (Again, using the pinpricks to measure.)

I estimate stair treads that wide would have **a rise of 10 inches**.

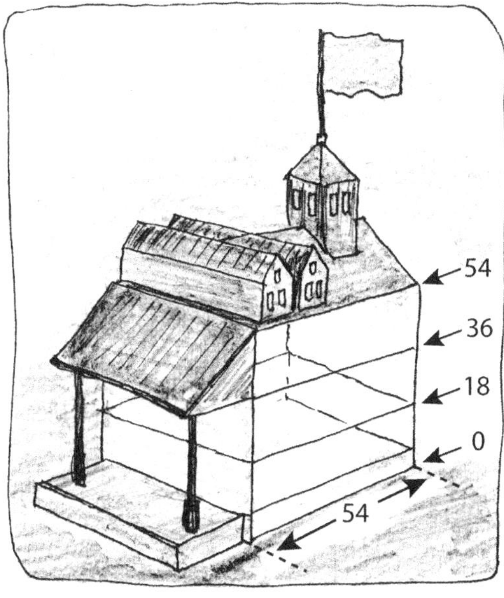

So, if each of the 22 steps was 10 inches tall, that totals to 220 inches, which is **18.333 feet**.

I suggest the height of Story 1, Story 2, and Story 3 of the Tiring House were **each 18 feet tall**.

And for all three stories, 3 x 18 equals **54** feet of height.

Hey, 54, that's the same as one of the long dimensions of the Tiring House!

Height = length. That means each of the 2 side-walls of the Tiring House was a perfect square.

(As we'll soon see, the "square" plays a big role in the 3 other drawings for the Globe)

Admittedly, my "10-inch stair rise" is an estimate, and thus my "18 feet per story" is an estimate, but later will see more clues indicating that 18 feet of height per story is what Dee intended.

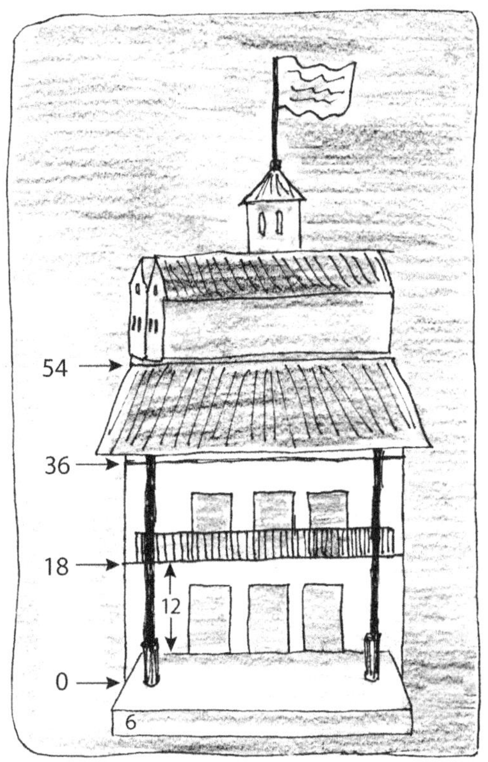

Phew, studying just the Tiring House can be tiring. But if you thought that was mathe-magical, wait till you see the surprises Dee has in store for us on the "overview" plan, the "side-view" elevation, and "parametric" drawings!

THE CRYPTIC MEANING OF THE LONG, THIN TRIANGLE

Eudoxus of Cnidus (408-355 BC)

Eudoxus (408-355 BC) was a Greek astronomer and mathematician from Cnidos, a Greek colony on the coastline of Asia Minor, near the Isle of Rhodes.

His actual writings are no longer extant, but we learn about him through other scholars like Hipparchus, Archimedes, Euclid, and, later, Diogenes Laertius.

The name Eudoxus actually means "of good repute" or "honored, or "well-thought-of," as *eu* means "good" and *doxa* means "belief, opinion or thought."

(The Latin name *Benedictus* has the same meaning.)

With Achines, his father, Eudoxus studied the sun, the moon, the constellations, and the erratic movements of the planets. In his teens, Eudoxus sailed to Tarentum (a Greek colony on the heel of Italy) to study mathematics with the Pythagorean scholar, Archytas. Then, he sailed to Sicily to study medicine with Philiston.

At age 23, Eudoxus journeyed to Heliopolis to study astronomy and mathematics with Egyptian priests. Later, he returned to Athens and became part of Plato's Academy, even becoming headmaster when Plato was on leave.

But Eudoxus and Plato had their disagreements. Eudoxus maintained that Forms were the physical ingredients in the perceptible objects around us. Plato felt Forms were unchangeable and eternal, while perceptible objects were changeable and, thus, only imperfect copies.

Eventually, Eudoxus returned to his hometown of Cnidus to settle down. He got married, had four children and taught until he died at age of 53.

Eudoxus' "method of exhaustion"

Eudoxus' ideas on mathematical proportions laid the groundwork for Book 5 and Book 12 of Euclid's *Elements*. The earlier, "Pythagorean theory of proportion" only dealt with "commensurable magnitudes," or magnitudes whose ratios could be expressed by whole numbers.

With a little help from his predecessor, Antiphon, Eudoxus devised a way to also incorporate "incommensurable magnitudes," by treating them entirely by geometry (and he still managed to avoid the issue of irrational numbers).

Eudoxus' trick was later (in the 1700's) called the "*mèthod des anciens*," or "*methodicus exhaustionibus*," which means " the method of exhaustion." (The Latin word, *exhaustionibus* means "by a draining out.")

Eudoxus' used this technique to get a close approximation of the area of a circle. Oddly, it's a geometric way of side-stepping that irrational number, pi, yet it actually leads to an excellent approximation of pi.

It's obvious that the area of a given circle will be larger than the area of an square inscribed within that circle. And because they are made up of straight lines, it's easy to find the areas of polygons like squares or octagons.

As we'll see, an inscribed square is only about **63%** of the area of its circum-circle. That's not very close.

An inscribed octagon is about **90%** of the area of its circumcircle. That's getting closer.

A 16-gon is **97.449%** of its circumcircle.
A 32-gon is **99.358%** of its circumcircle,
And a 64-gon is **99.839%** of its circumcircle.

You get the idea. The difference between these successive polygons and the circle fairly rapidly becomes "exhausted." Thus you can obtain a good "lower limit" for the area of the circle.

To find the "upper limit" for the area of the circle, a similar procedure can be used. Simply fit a square around the circle, then an octagon around the circle," etc....

When you the average of the "lower limit" and the "upper limit," you get a close approximation of the area of the circle, and thus of pi.

The visual explanation for this method of exhaustion involves slicing a polygon into equal triangles, then lining the triangles up side-by-side. But a row of tangent tee-pees doesn't look much like a circle.

There is a clearer way to visually compare the circle with its inscribed polygon. And guess what it involves: long, thin triangles, similar to the long, thin triangle Dee slapped onto the side of the otherwise-rectilinear Tiring House.

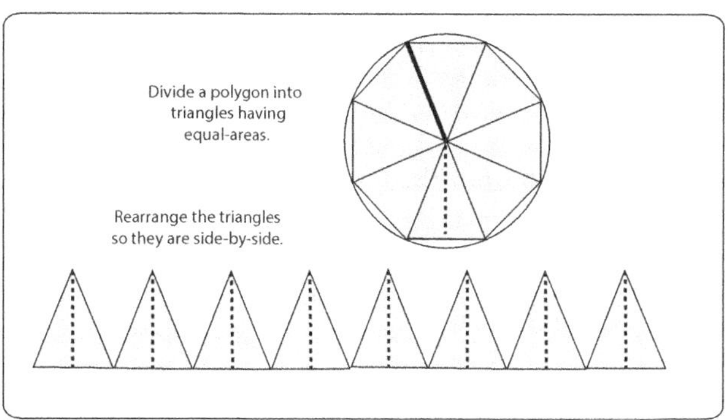

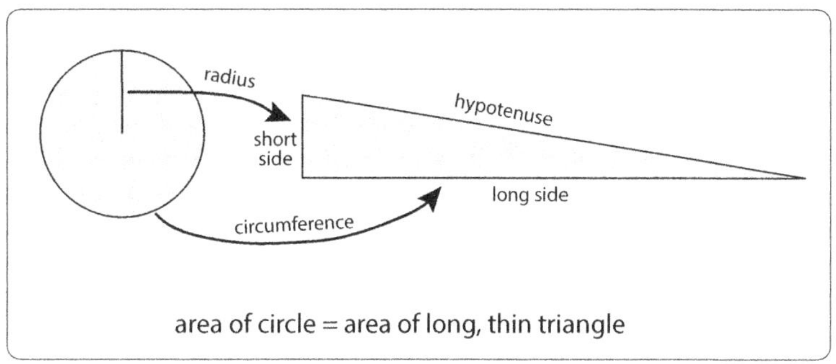

Archimedes proved that the area of a circle is equal to that of a long, thin right angle triangle, whose short side equals the radius of the circle and whose long side equals the circumference of the circle.

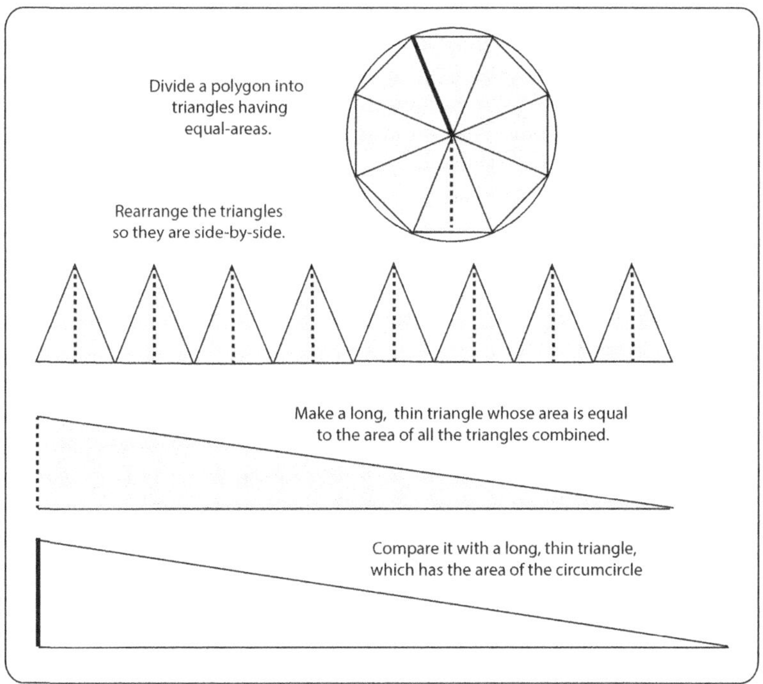

Well, we can easily convert our row of side-by-side triangles into one of these long, thin triangles.

The **height** of one of the triangles becomes the short side of the long, thin triangle.

And the **base** of the row of triangles becomes the long dimension of the long, thin triangle.

Now, we can compare this long, thin triangle, with a long, thin triangle which has the same area as the circumcircle.

This will all become clearer with a few examples.

An inscribed square is about 63% of its circumcircle

Let's start with a circle with a **given radius of 10**.
A big "X" chops the inscribed square into four triangles.
The height of each of these triangles (shown with a dotted line) is called an "**apothem**."
(*apo* means "away" and *tithenai* means "a place")

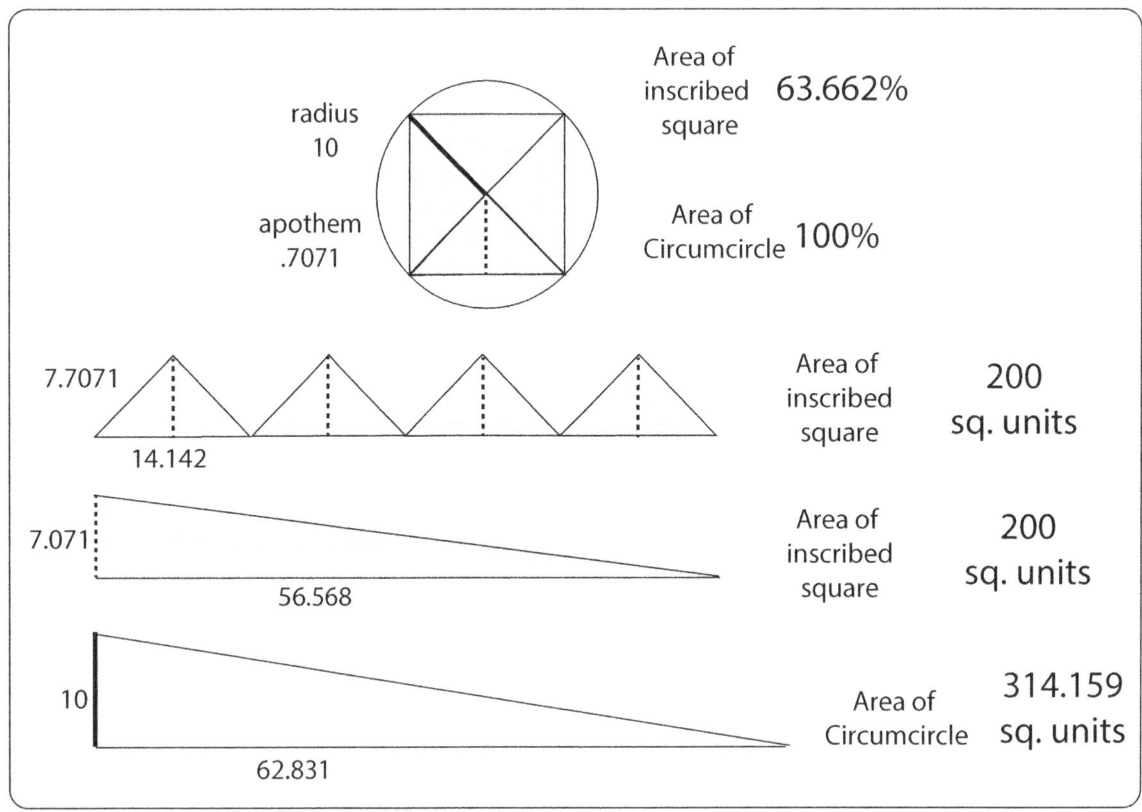

First, we'll "unwrap" the four triangles and line them up side-by-side. The height of each is the apothem. And "the base of all four triangles combined" is the perimeter of the original square

The total area of these four triangles equals the area of a long thin triangle whose short side is the apothem and whose long side is the square's perimeter.

The area of this inscribed square is 200 square units. That's only about **63%** of 314.149, the area of the circumcircle with its radius of 10.

63% is not very close to 100%. So, let's follow the same procedure with an octagon.

An inscribed octagon is about 90% of its circumcircle

This time eight triangles are converted into one long, thin triangle, and compared to the circle. The area of an inscribed octagon is about 90% of the area of its circumcircle.

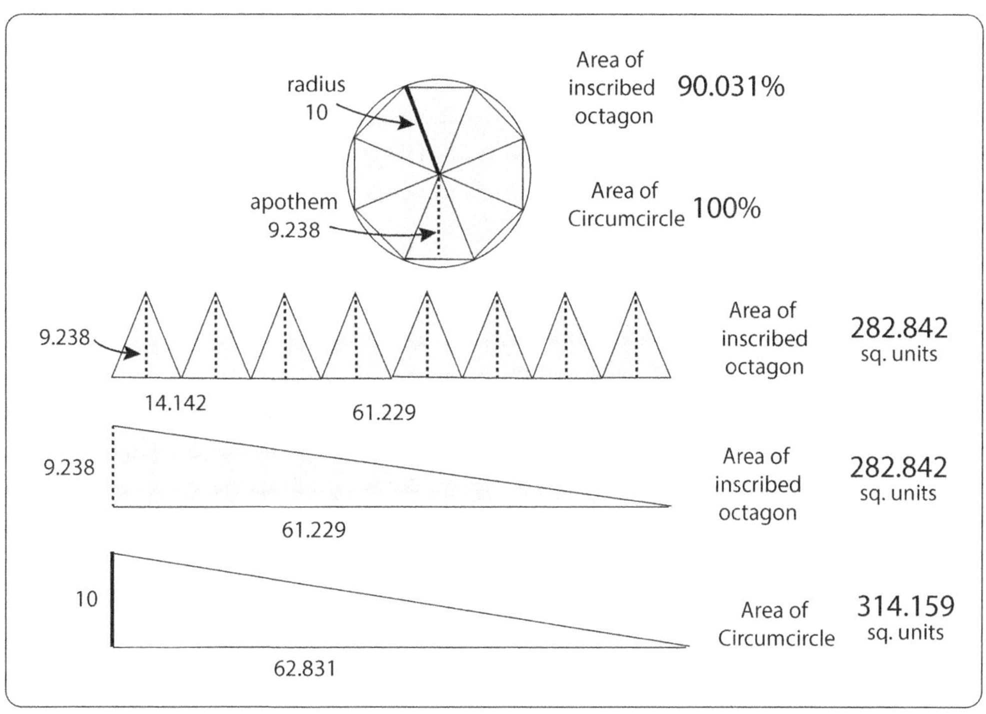

An inscribed 16-gon is about 97.445% of its circumcircle

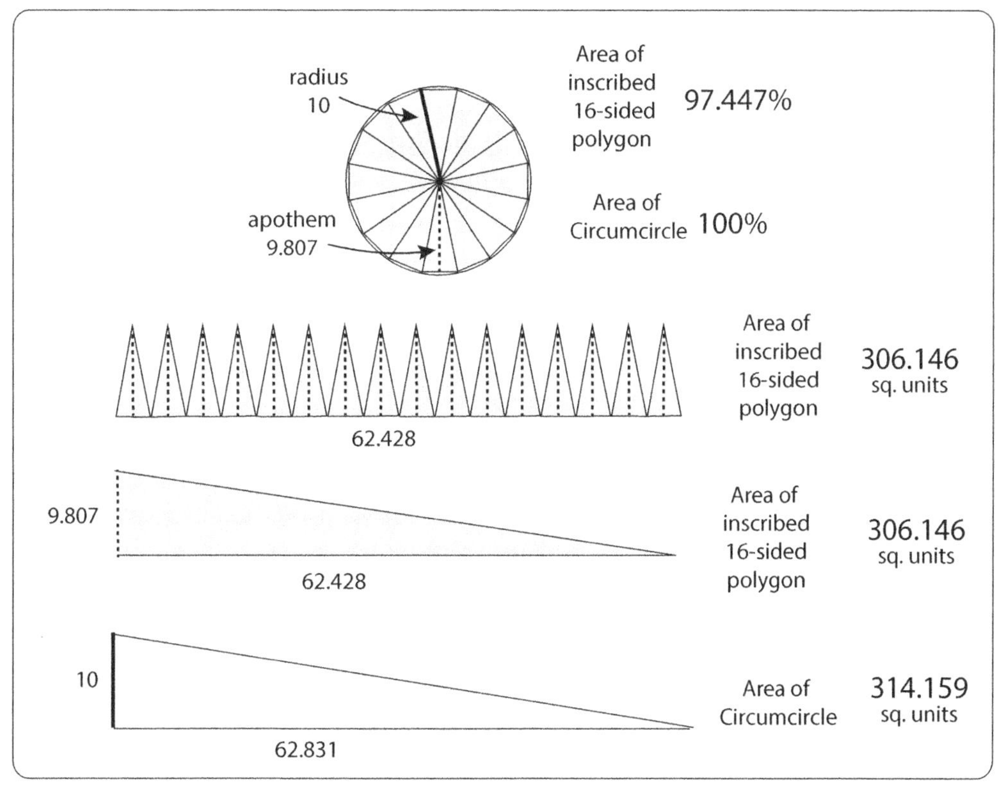

An inscribed 32-gon is about 99.358% of its circumcircle

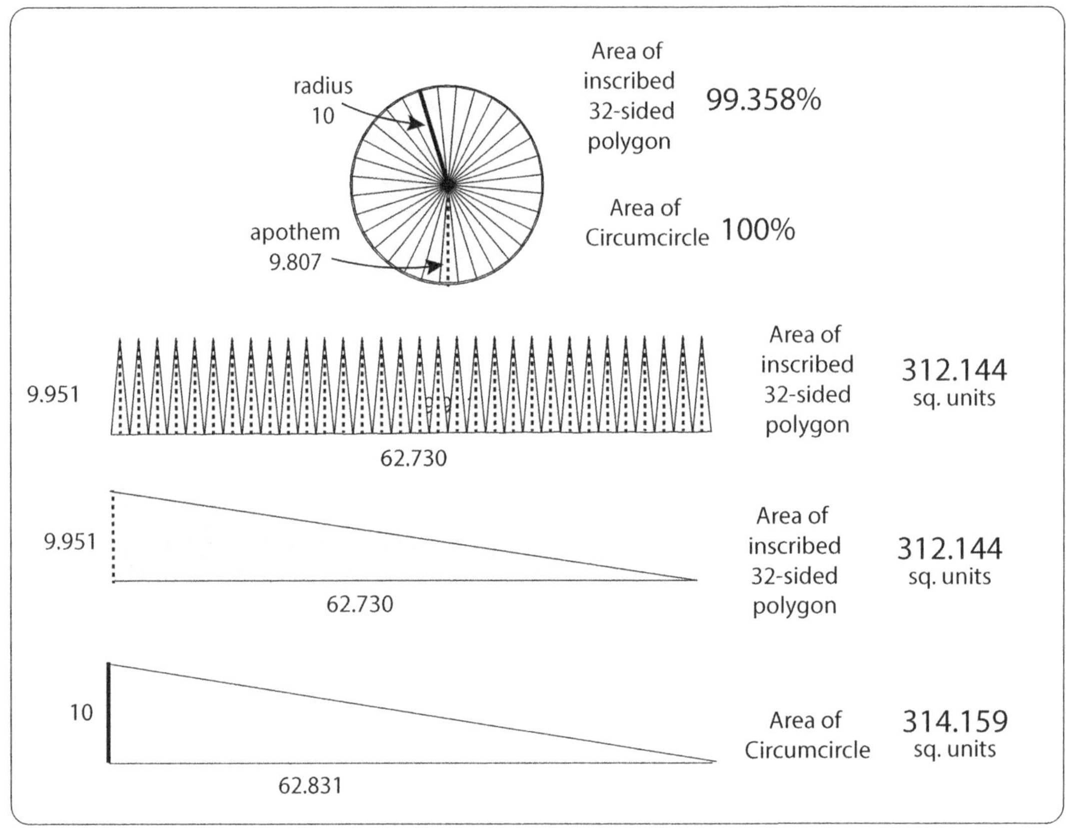

Area of Circumcircle	100%
Area of inscribed:	
square	63.661%
octagon	90.003%
16-gon	97.449%
32-gon	99.358%
64-gon	99.839%
128-gon	99.958%
256-gon	99.989%
512-gon	99.997%
1028-gon	99.999%

This chart summarizes the progress of the "exhaustion."

By the time we get to the 1028-gon, we're within .001% of the area of the circumcircle. Now, that's pretty close.

Archimedes estimates pi using Eudoxus' method

Following Eudoxus, Archimedes used a similar method of exhaustion to arrive at a number for pi. But Archimedes started with a hexagon, then a dodecagon, then a 24-gon, then a 48-gon, and finally a 96-gon.

Archimedes deduced pi was between 3.1408 and 3.1429

(Not bad Archie, pi is actually 3.14159...).

The whole-number-preferring Archimedes actually referred to these limits as 223/71 and 22/7 respectively.

Mathematicians "exhausted" things for centuries

Eudoxus' method of exhaustion was applied by Euclid and Archimedes to find volumes of three-dimensional shapes like spheres, cylinders, and cones, and to help solve the puzzling problem of "squaring the circle."

Eudoxus' method of exhaustion led to the development of calculus in the 1600s, 1700s, and 1800s.

Dee was an experienced Eudoxian "exhauster"

By attaching that strange long thin triangle to the side of his Tiring House drawing, John Dee is giving a clue for what he has in store for us in his other Globe diagrams: stories of inscribed circles, squares, and octagons; and a story about "squaring the circle."

The area of Dee's long, thin Tiring House triangle is 26.666. A circle with an area of 26.666 sq. units has a radius of 4.1202 units, and a diameter of 8.2404 units.

I don't think Dee is necessarily thinking that we should search for such a circle, but I think he's using the long, thin triangle metaphorically to suggest that Eudoxus' "method of exhaustion" is related to other drawings.

Remember, this long, thin triangle is Dee's way of incorporating the "third measure" of the Tiring House, which is 54 x 42.

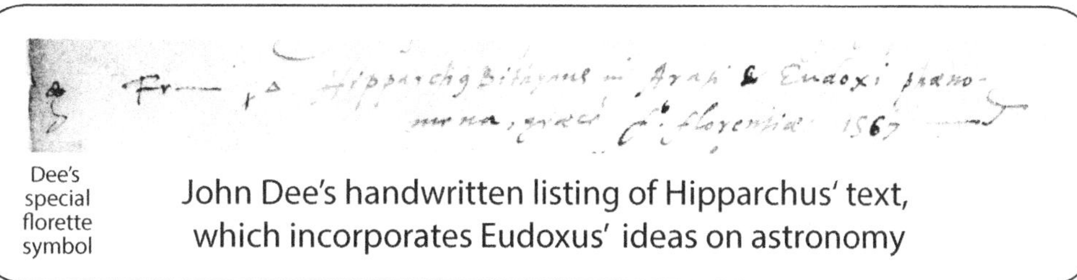

Dee's special florette symbol

John Dee's handwritten listing of Hipparchus' text, which incorporates Eudoxus' ideas on astronomy

Incidentally, John Dee owned a copy of a text by Hipparchus of Bithynia (now Iznik, Turkey), which incorporates "phenomena" described by the "Arabs" and "Eudoxi," written in Greek, and printed in Florence in 1567.

Of the thousands of books and manuscripts that Dee listed in 1583, it's one of only a handful which is marked with a special symbol: a florette made from three circles and a long, twisty stem.

Summary

To summarize, Dee knew that mathematicians who had worked with Eudoxus' "method of exhaustion" would recognize the "long, thin triangle."

It's partially a hint that we should employ the "method of exhaustion" in one of the of the other Globe drawings, to find the area of a circle. Specifically, a circle which is equal to a square (in area).

But Dee makes use of "long, thin triangle" in other ways. And I don't mean as a design plan for his "long, white beard." One usage is to help him conceal some magic numbers in the Tiring House plan!

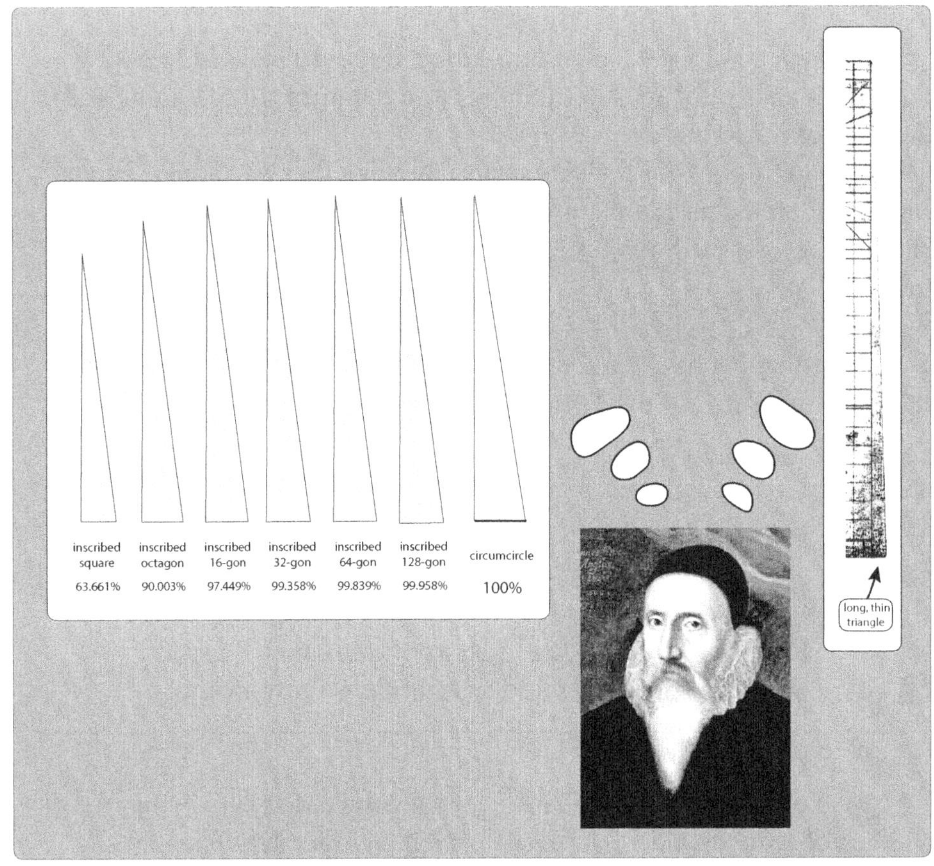

The hidden harmonies in the numbers Dee used for the Tiring House

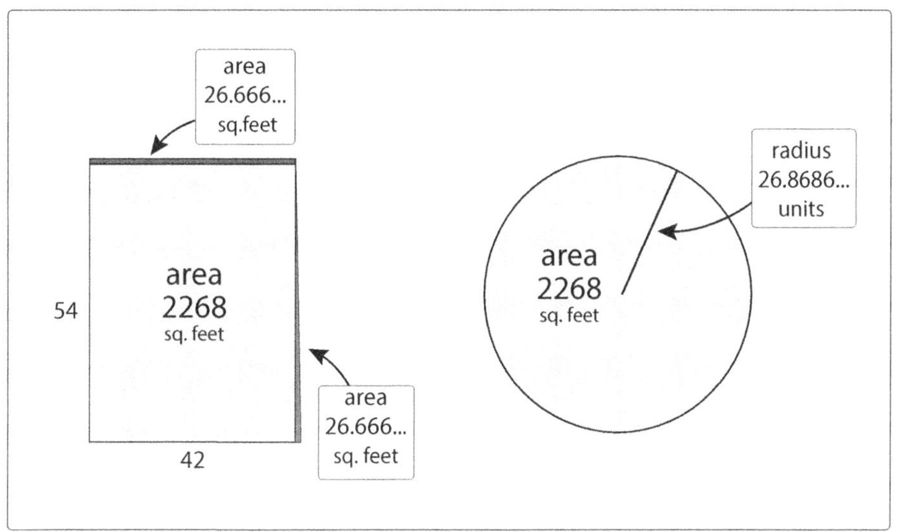

In a very unusual way, Dee seems to be confirming that he wants us to see this "third measure." This 54 x 42 measure is suggested by the long, thin triangle and the proportions of the front facade, with its three doors. Here's how:

First we found the missing "orphaned section" of 26.666 at the top of the Tiring House was the "long, thin triangle," one measure of which was also 26.666.

Next, we saw the 54 x 42 measure of the Tiring House has an area of 2268 (that special number, which elegantly is 252 less than 2520).

Now, a circle which has an area of 2268, has a radius of 26.8686

Hey! That number 26.8686 is pretty close to 26.666.
(The difference between the two numbers is less than one percent. Actually .75%)

26.6666....
26.8686....
2268

Curiously, all of these numbers are made from the digits 2, 6, and 8.

It's interesting that all of these numbers 26.666, 2268, and 26.8686 are all made from the digits 2, 6, and 8. Plus, they are all even numbers, multiples of 2)

Granted, 26.666 is a area (comprised of square units) and 26.8686 is a radius (just comprised of units).

And indeed, areas and lengths are quite different. But it's uncanny that these numbers are so closely to each other and so "digitally" interrelated. Surely, Dee would have found this unusual as well.

By contrast, the 54 x 40 "measure" has an area of 2160.
A circle with an area of 2160 has a radius of 26.221
(That's about 1.6% of 26.666)

The 53.333 x 40 "measure" has an area of 213.333.
A circle with an area of 213.333 has a radius of 26.058
(That's about 2.2% of 26.666)

Neither of these results is as close to 26.666 as 2.8686 is.
(As we've seen, it's only .75%)

More curious ratios (with a little help from the Monas symbol)

This idea of comparing two numbers, one of which is **length**, (in units) and the other is **area** (in square units) is indeed unorthodox.

But knowing John Dee was unorthodox, I decided to allow for this possibility in Dee's work. And auspiciously, this opened another door into finding even more harmonies hidden in the Tiring House plan.

Here's a summary of a few things I had already discovered:

The numbers involved in one "measure" of the Tiring House is **53.333 x 40**.

And the area of the "orphaned section," or one measure of the long, thin triangle" is **26.666**

Hey! Even though 53.333 is "length," and 26.666 is "area" it's amazing that one is double the other.

I had already discovered that the proportion, **40:53.333**, was equivalent to the ratio **3:4**.

And I realized the ratio **26.666:53.333** was **1:2**

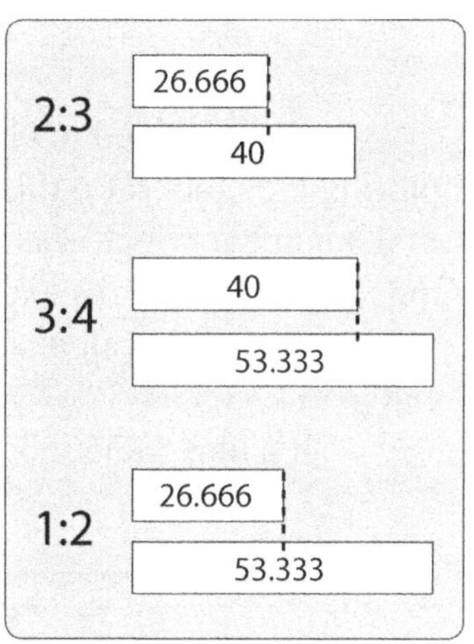

Having studied the interrelationships of the Pythagorean harmonies, I knew **2/3** x **3/4 = 1/2**

(or 66% of 75% is 50%).

Thus, **26.666/40** must be the ratio **2:3**.

(And my hand calculator confirmed it.)

$$\frac{2}{3} \times \frac{3}{4} = \frac{1}{2}$$

$$\frac{26.666}{40} \times \frac{40}{53.333} = \frac{26.666}{53.333}$$

In short, Dee's numbers are an expression of **2/3** x **3/4 = 1/2**

With these three harmonies involved, it occurred to me that I had the makings of Nicomachus' "greatest and most perfect harmony."

Except I seemed to be missing a number. That's not a challenging problem to solve. The "missing number" is involved in two of the ratios (3:4 and 2:3).

So I multiplied 26.666 x 4/3.

The result was **35.555555....** Initially, I was a bit disappointed. I was hoping that the result was a whole number (like 36), instead of being another irrational, repeating decimal.

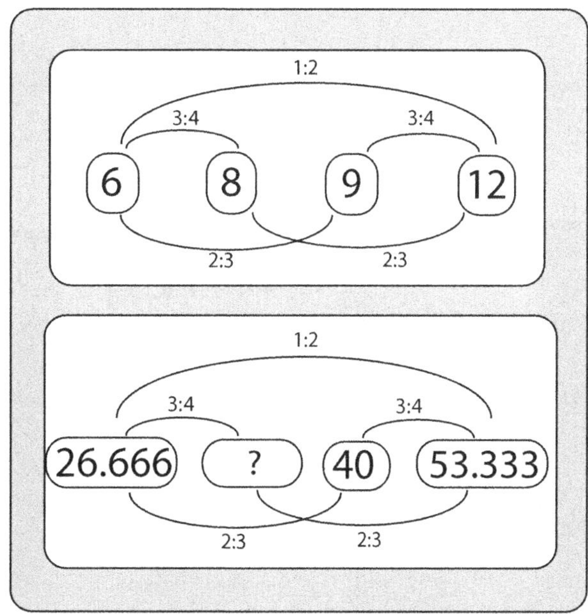

So, I decided to check my math by starting with 53.333 and exploring the other ratio this missing number was involved in. I wanted to find a number which was 2/3 of 53.333. So I multiplied 53.333 x .666 and indeed, the answer, as expected, was 35.55555....

But while calculating at these numbers I realized something special about 35.55555...

It's like 53.33333... , only "inside-out."

$$\frac{53.3333333...}{35.5555555...} = \frac{2}{3}$$

Look at this crazy fraction that reduces nicely to 2/3.

The reflective mate of 35 is 53, but irrational numbers don't really have reflective mates. Yet somehow these digits all reflect each other.

When the 5 looks in the mirror, it sees a 3; and when the 3 looks in the mirror, it sees of 5. Suddenly, I was glad that the result wasn't 36, but was this weird number, 35.55555....

I know this would have enthralled Dee. But it also, made me realize there was an unsolved part of this puzzle that tied all of these numbers together.

$$\frac{26.666}{6} = 4.44444...$$

$$\frac{1}{4.44444...} = .225$$

Because they are woven in a Nicomachean symphony, I knew Dee's four numbers were ultimately multiples of 6, 8, 9, and 12. So I divided 6 into 26.666 and the result was 4.444.

Again, I was initially disappointed at getting another irrational number. (Even the fraction 40/9, which is made from whole numbers, resulted in 4.444.)

So, I began to explore 4.444. I decided to find its reciprocal or 1/4.444.... The result was .225. Finally, I was dealing with a number that didn't fly off to infinity.

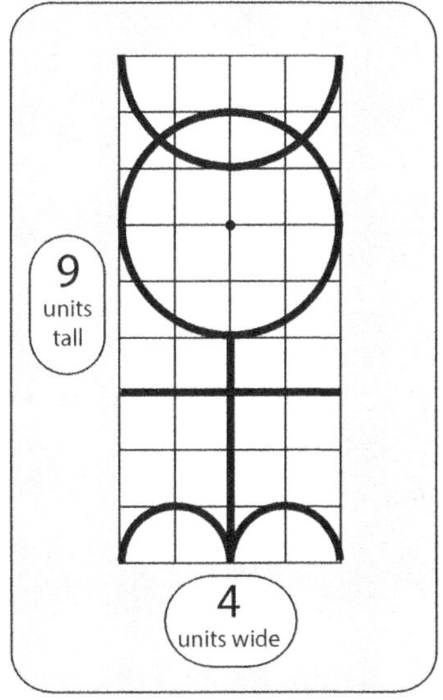

Then, suddenly it occurred to me. These numbers, 4.444 and .225, are related to .444 and 2.25. And I recognized them as the fractions, 4/9 and 9/4. Why?

Because these are the proportions of Dee's beloved Monas symbol!

In short, "6, 8, 9, and 12,"
times the Monas symbol's
"height:width" proportion,
times 10,
makes key numbers in Dee's Tiring House measurements:

$$6 \times \frac{4}{9} \times 10 = \frac{240}{9} = 26.666$$

$$8 \times \frac{4}{9} \times 10 = \frac{320}{9} = 35.555$$

$$9 \times \frac{4}{9} \times 10 = \frac{360}{9} = 40$$

$$12 \times \frac{4}{9} \times 10 = \frac{480}{9} = 53.333$$

A clue in the results: 240, 320, 360, and 480

Another important equivalency of 6, 8, 9, and 12 is hidden in the previus chart: 24, 32, 36, and 48. Here's how:

The various multiplications yield the numbers 240, 320, 360, and 480, each divided by 9. (As we'll later see, the number 9 plays a key role in the "parametric" drawing of the Globe.)

Reducing 240, 320, 360, and 480 by a factor of 10 (indtead of 9) makes 24, 32, 36, and 48.

I immediately recognized the numbers, **24, 32, 36, and 48** from my reconstruction of the John Dee Tower of 1583. (Quite simply, they are the harmonic friends "6, 8, 9, and 12," each multiplied by 4.)

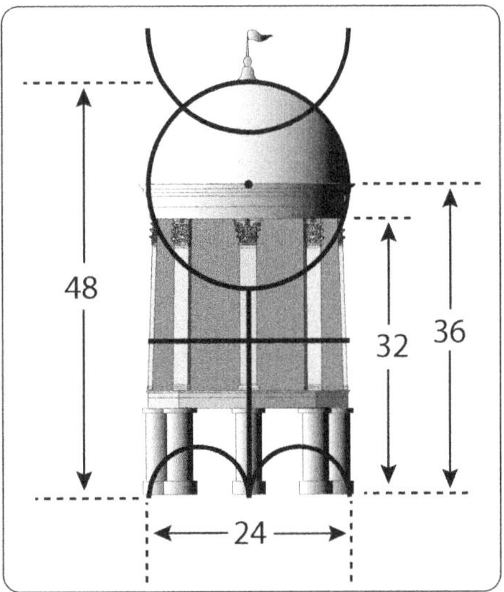

The width of the cylinder above the columns is 24.
The height to the bottom of the entablature is 32 feet.
The height to the top of the entablature is 36 feet.
And the height to the top of the dome is 48 feet.

And similarly, the Monas symbol is involved. In this case, it's the "side-view" elevation of the Tower.

Dee's architectural designs seem to be riffs on the same mathematical theme. A theme Dee felt was supreme.

Here's a graphic way of expressing what Dee is integrating into the Tiring House drawing. It's pretty eclectic, but it's pretty amazing.

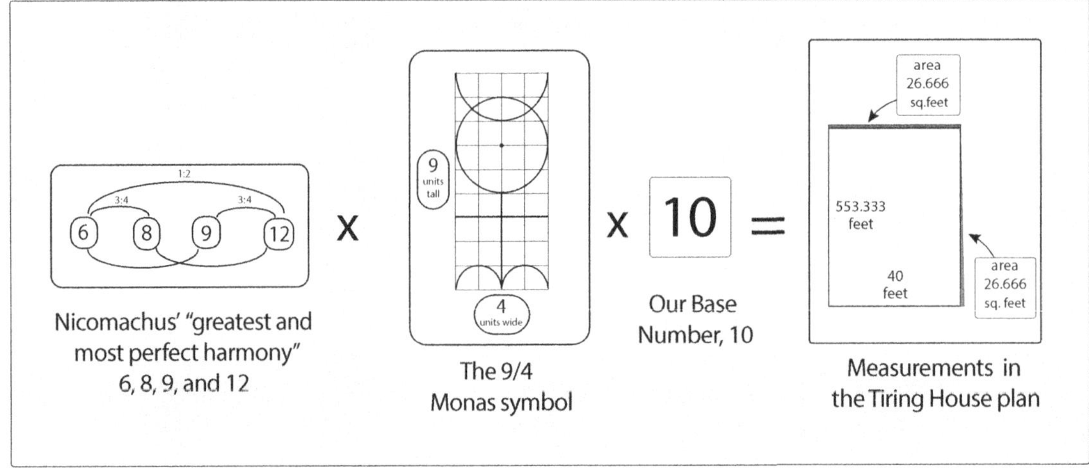

THE "CLOSE-UP" PLAN FITS IN THE "OVERVIEW" PLAN

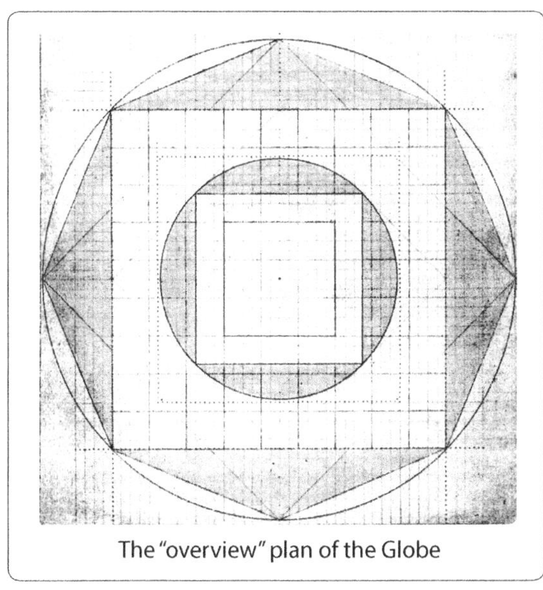

The "overview" plan of the Globe

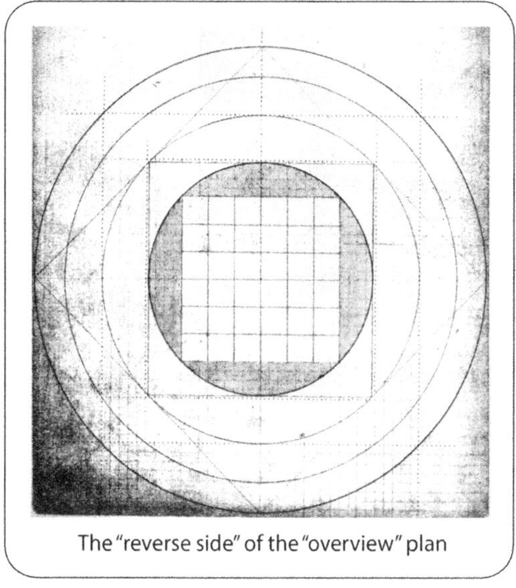

The "reverse side" of the "overview" plan

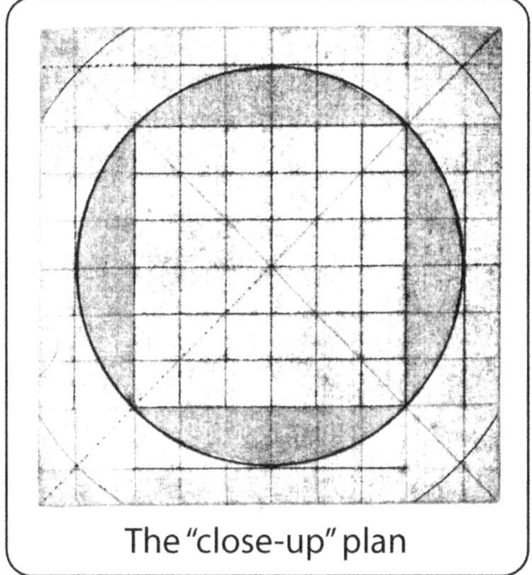

The "close-up" plan

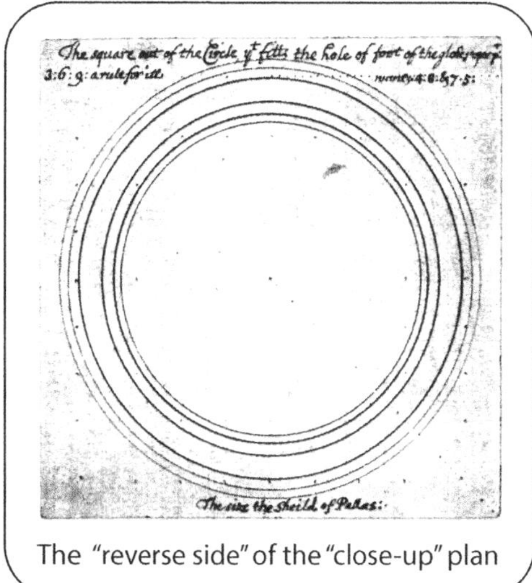

The "reverse side" of the "close-up" plan

The front side of the "close-up" plan looks identical to the center of the "reverse side" of the "overview" plan. It's easy to see the correlation.

The "reverse side" of the "close-up" plan, with its 6 circles, seems different than all the rest. And it's chock-full of cryptic clues.

But before exploring it, here's a brief review of what we learned earlier about the "overview" plan.

The "halvings" of the squares and circles of the "overview" diagram can be boiled down to these two simple formulas:

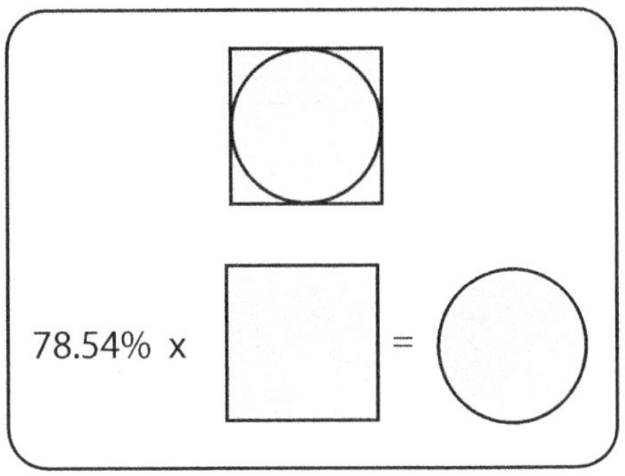

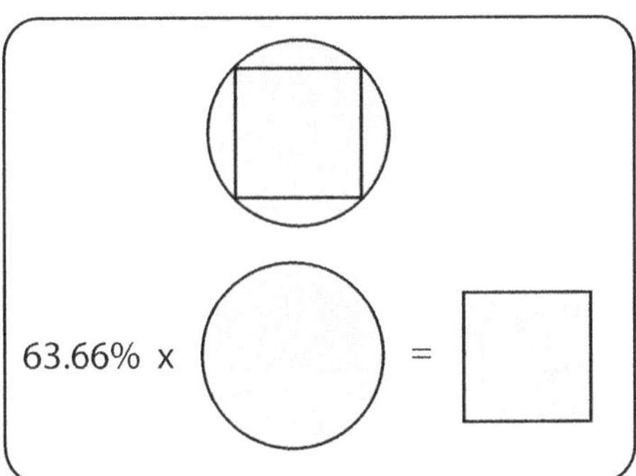

To find the area of a circle inscribed in a square, multiply the area of the square by 78.54%.

(Because, $\pi/4 = .7854$

To find the area of a square inscribed in a circle multiply the area of the square by 63.66%.

(Because, $2/\pi = .6366$)

Halvings of squares on the "overview" plan:

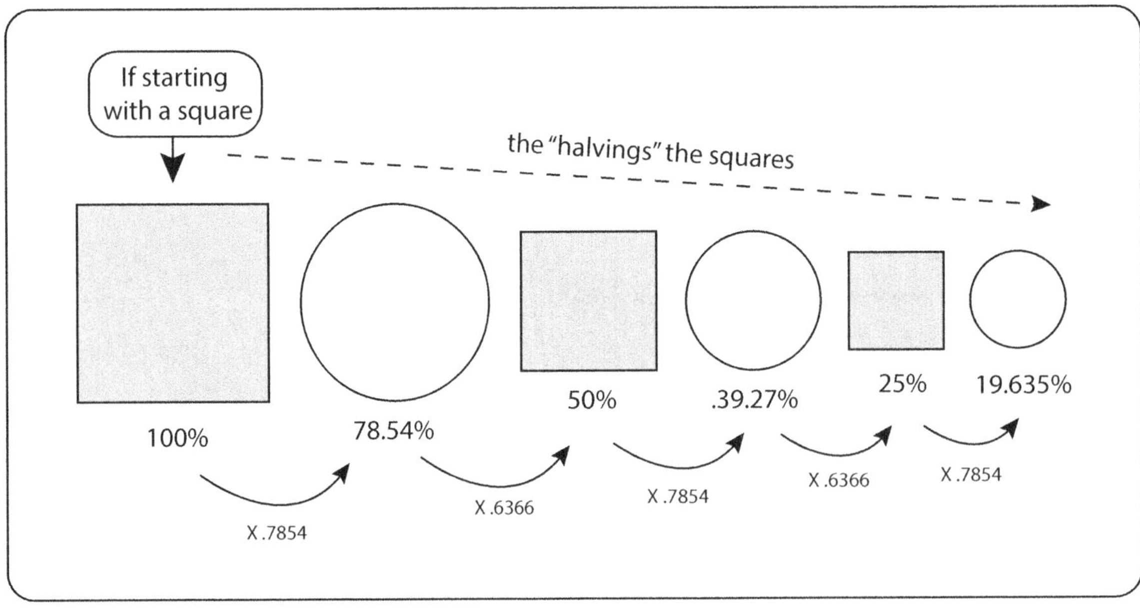

Halvings of circles on the "overview" plan:

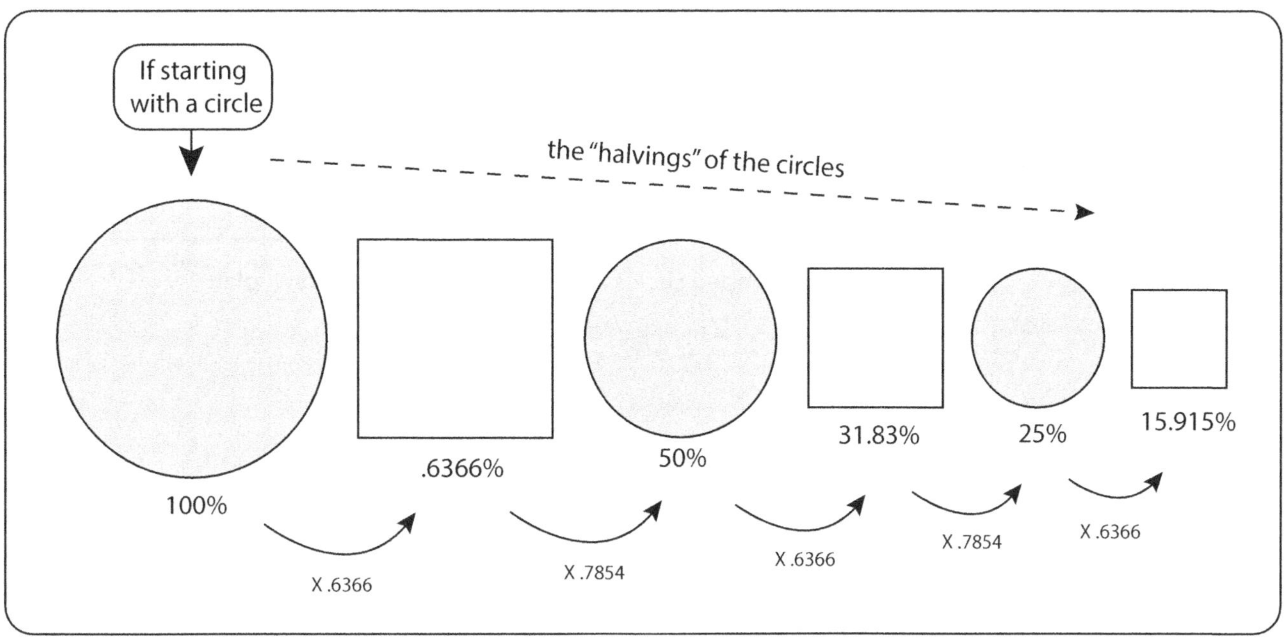

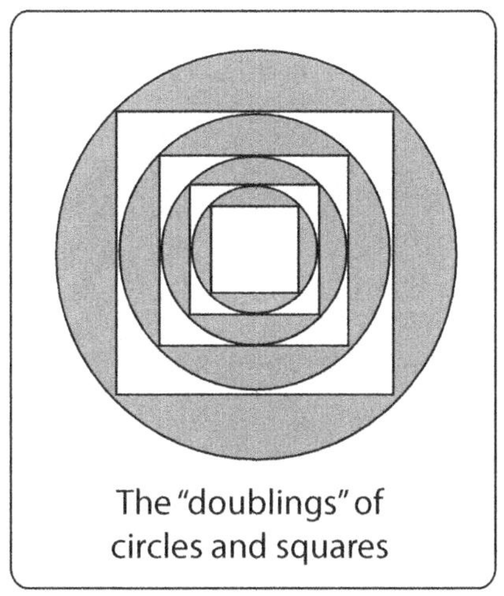
The "doublings" of circles and squares

All these circles and squares superimposed looks radioactive.

A more extended view

To see more clearly the "doublings" in the "overview" plan, let's extend the procession to the left and to the right.

Here are all the concentric circles and squares:
(Some are drawn by Dee, others are implied).

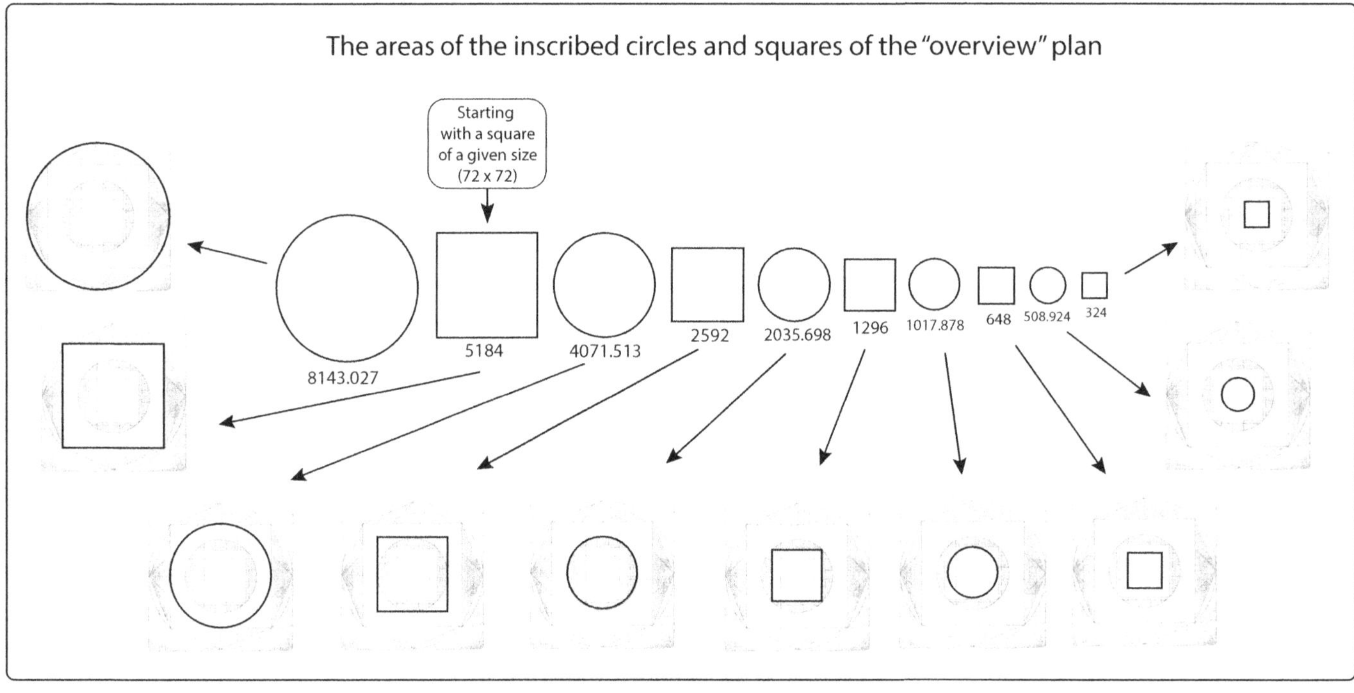

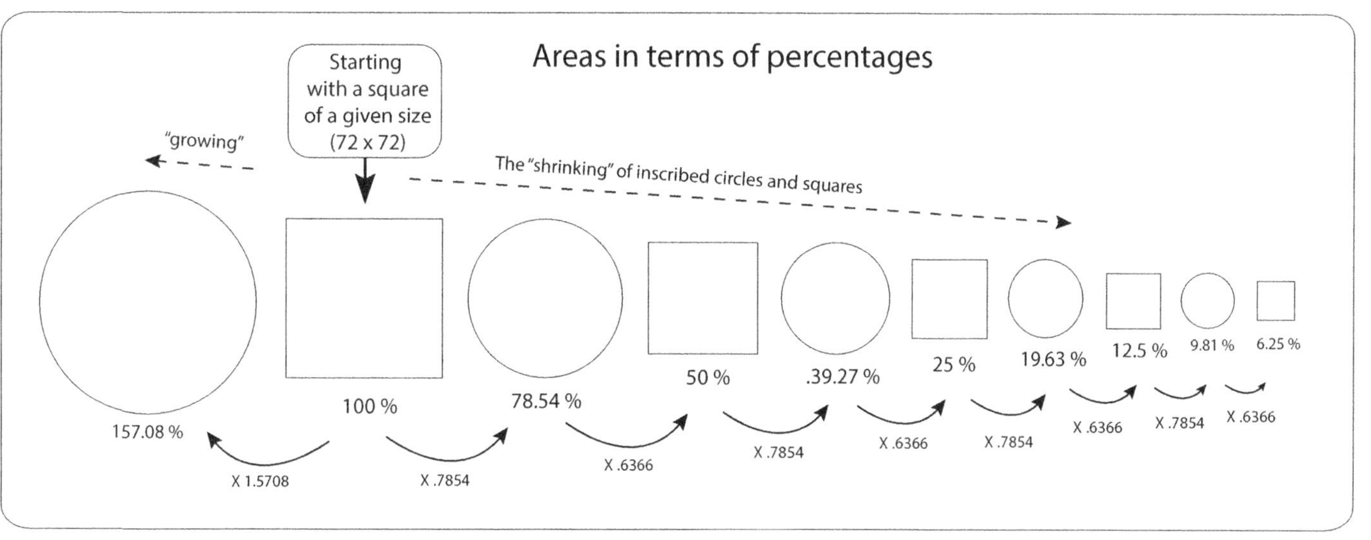

The "given" or starting point of this exploration is the 72 x 72 square.

(On Dee's "overview" plan, it's clearly marked, and even has the 72-pinprick measuring ruler superimposed vertically along its left edge.)

The 72 x 72 square's circumcircle has an area 157.08 times the area of the 72 x 72 square.

(Mathematically, $\pi/2$ equals 1.5708
Or seen another way $2/\pi$ equals .6366
And 1/.6366 equals 1.5708)

The "halvings" of the squares proceed:
100%,
50%,
25%,
12.5%,
6.25%

The "halvings" of the circles proceed:
157.08%,
78.54%,
39.27%,
19.63%,
9.81%

Both the front and the reverse sides of the"close-up" plan fit into the "overview" plan.

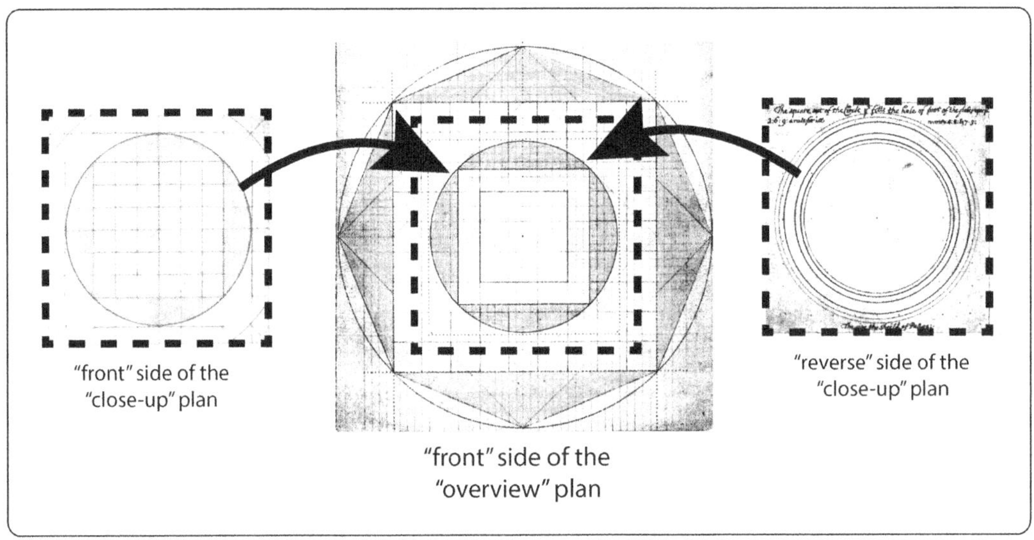

The key to undertanding what these doublings are all about, we must first explore the "close-up" plan in depth.

A SEVENTH CIRCLE APPEARS IN THE "CLOSE-UP" PLAN OF THE GLOBE

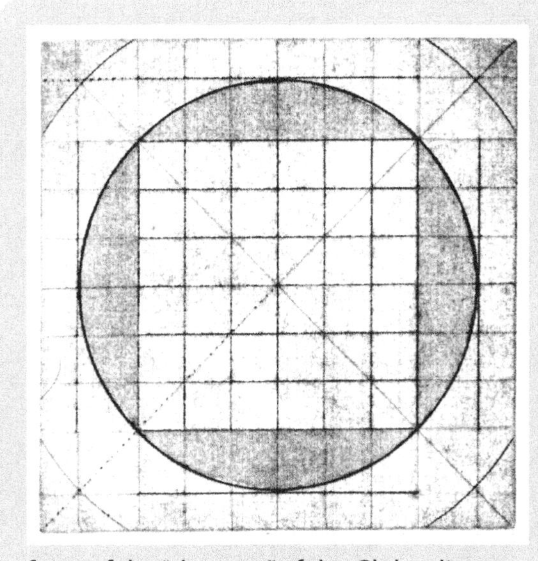

front of the "close-up" of the Globe diagram

The main features on the front of the "close up" plan are a "6 x 6" white grid, circumscribed by a circle.

It's sort of like an all-white checkerboard that just barely fits on a round table. Each of the grid lines has six pinpricks, so the "6 x 6" grid is actually a "36 unit x 36 unit" grid.

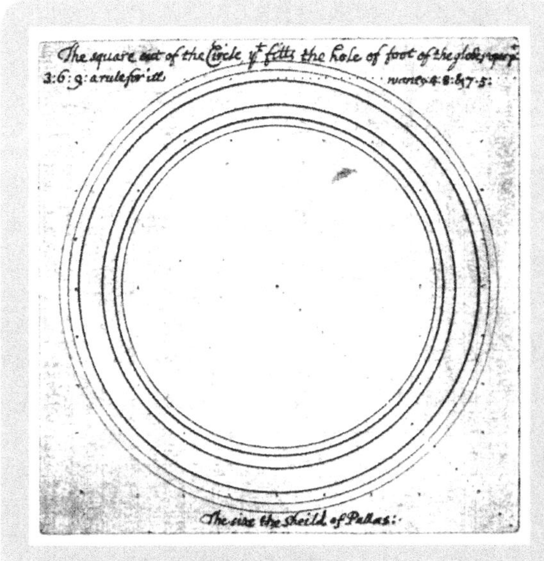

back of the "close-up" of the Globe diagram

And on the "reverse side," there are no vertical or horizontal lines to be seen – only concentric circles – sort of like a doughnut with six racing stripes.

And along the top of the "reverse side" is handwritten:
"The square out of the Circle, yt fitts the hole of foot of the globes uper pt"

The next line is a numerical clue:
"3:6:9: a rule for itt............varies 4:8:&7·5:"

And along the bottom it reads:
"The size the Sheild of Pallas"

The whole card only about 3.5 inches tall by 3.5 inches wide.

(By comparison, a poker-size playing card is 3.5 inches tall by 2.5 inches wide.)

The "front" diagram and the "reverse" diagram obviously relate to each other because they share pinprick measuring holes and share a common center point.

But you cannot see both sides at the same time. (If the paper upon which it was drawn were light enough, perhaps both images would appear "superimposed" when put on the lightbox.)

Instead of using a lightbox, I did it digitally. I scanned both images, superimposed them and made the upper image semi-transparent by setting that layer's opacity to 50% in Photoshop.

The "round table top" plus the "6 racing stripes" made 7 concentric circles! Wow! Just like the orbits of the 7 planets! And "7 circles" x "360 degrees each" = 2520 degrees! I sensed I was on the right track.

(The 1 circle that got added to the 6 circles is the black, thickest circle that touches the corners of the white square.)

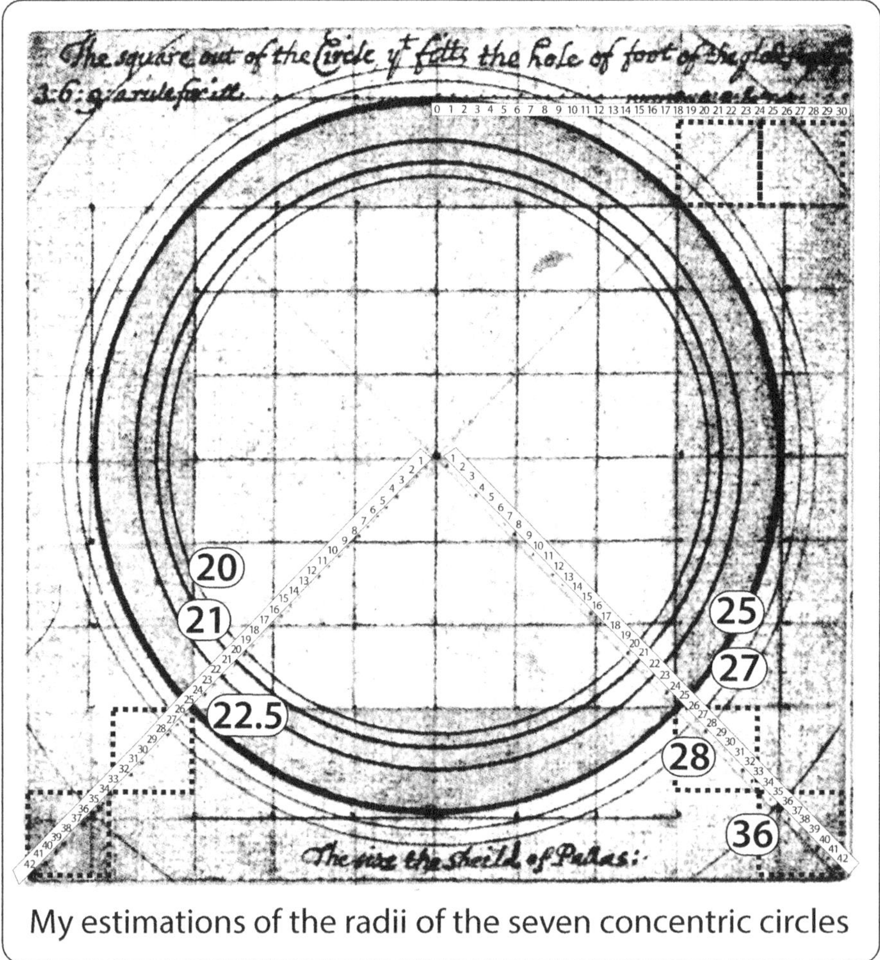

My estimations of the radii of the seven concentric circles

First, I investigated the pinpricked measuring scales. Based on the measuring scale on the top right, it was clear that each of the main grids of the white square is subdivided into six parts. (In the upper right, I've added two black "dotted-line" squares to clarify my measurements)

This is the same scale used in the lower diagonals. (Here as well, I've added some black "dotted-line" squares to clarify the measurements.)

Next, I "eyeballed" the radius of each of the 7 concentric circles. The radii of the "inner" group of three circles, I estimated, were **20** units, **21** units, and **22.5** units respectively. The "middle group of three," I estimated were **25**, **26.5**, and **28**. And the "outer circle" seemed to have a radius of **36**.

It didn't take me long to discover that my estimating in "whole numbers" was an "irrational" path to take. Here's why:

All geometry students learn the Pythagorean Theorem : In a right-angled rectangle, "height squared" times "width squared" equals the "hypotenuse squared." As its height equals its width, the square is a special kind of rectangle, .

If a square has a "height of one unit" and a "width of one unit," the hypotenuse will be "the square root of two" units. In decimal equivalent of √2 is 1.41421356237… and it continues on randomly, apparently forever. Mathematicians have calculated it out to 10 million digits and they still haven't found the end. It can be estimated by 99/70, but for my computations I have simply used 1.4142...

The point is this: Even if we choose a "whole number" for the sides of the square, the hypotenuse will always be "an irrational number."

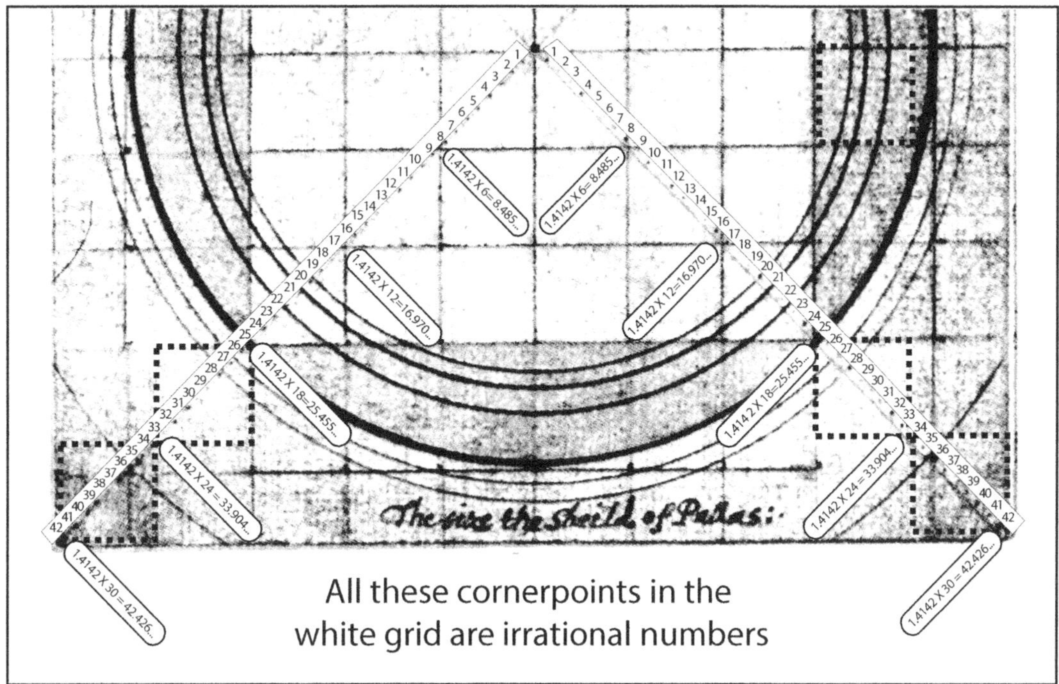

All these cornerpoints in the white grid are irrational numbers

To clarify, let's zoom into the center of the diagram. Each of the grid squares is actually "6 units tall" by "6 units wide." So the hypotenuse (or the diagonal) of one grid square would be 6 x 1.4142, which equals 8.485. And if you look closely, this corresponds pretty well with the diagram.

(The corner of the grid square is *between* the 8 pinprick and the 9 pinprick.)

Extending further, the hypotenuse of a 2 x 2 grid (which is 12 by 12 units) is 16.970.

(This is "almost 17," just as it appears on the illustration.)

A 3 x 3 grid (which is 18 by 18 units) has a hypotenuse (diagonal) of 25.455… units.

(This black, thickest circle is the "edge of the round tabletop" from the "front side" of the "close-up" plan.)

Next, a grid of 4 x 4 (which is 24 by 24 units) makes a hypotenuse of 33.904… units.

And finally, a grid of 5 x 5 (which is 30 by 30 units) makes a hypotenuse of 42.426… units.

(And not 42, as it seems by just looking at the diagram.)

Is Dee riddling with the word "square?

Let's return to the black thickest circumcircle which I had "estimated" was 25 units, but which is actually 25.455... units.

Dee is making a geometric/visual riddle here to throw the unsuspecting a red herring. In the title, "The square out of the Circle," the word "square" is not capitalized, but the word "Circle" is. The emphasis is on Circle and the most prominent circle is that black, thickest round-tabletop-circumcircle.

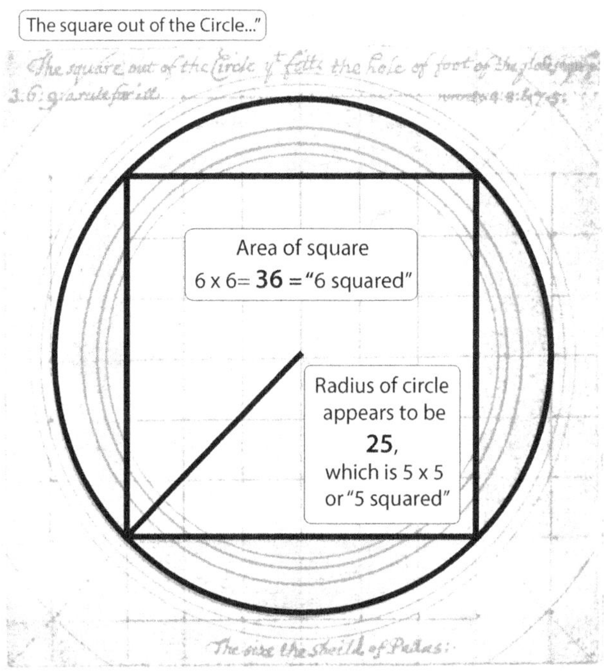

One might first think the riddle is about the word "**square**." The white square is a grid of 36, which is "**6 squared**." To the casual observer, the black circumcircle appears to have a radius of "25," which is "**5 squared**."

The casual observer might conclude Dee is riddling about "square numbers" (25 and 36). But Dee knew that a head-scratching mathematician would soon realize the radius of the black circumcircle is actually 25.455...

The long history of "squaring the circle"

There is a whole lot of history behind Dee's phrase. Ancient geometers posed this problem: **Using only a finite number of steps with compass and straightedge, construct a square with the same areas as a given circle.**

Attempts to "square the circle" go back to the Babylonians, Egyptians, and the Greeks. Aristophanes mentions the geometric puzzle in his play "*The Birds*."

Florian Cajori, in *History of Mathematics*, explains there was renewed interest in "squaring the circle" in the 1400s. New postulations were made by like Nicolas Cusanus (Italian) and Regiomontanus (German).

Interest continued into the 1500s, with mathematicians like Oronce Finé (French) and Pedro Núñez (Portuguese).

John Dee was friends with both of these expert mathematicians. Most likely, John Dee spent hours with compass and straightedge in hand, pondering the classic problem as well.

Incidentally, in 1557 influenza swept across England and Dee caught it. Feeling he was about to die, he appointed Pedro Núñez as his literary executor. (Even though Núñez lived in Portugal.)

From Oronce Finé and Gerard Mercator, John Dee learned enough geography that he could make his own map of North America in 1580. (Mathematician and cartographer Gerard Mercator, in a sense, squared the circle" (or sphere) by putting latitude and longitude lines on his famous globes).

In 1855, the artist and mathematician Lewis Carroll wrote about the "squaring the circle."

In 1882, Ferdinand von Lindemann proved that pi was not only irrational, but also transcendental, meaning it can even be expressed by an equation. Finally, once and for all, there was proof that you can't "square the circle" using a finite number of steps with compass and straightedge. Since then, the term, "squaring the circle" has been used as a metaphor for "trying to do the impossible."

"trying to do the impossible" .... sounds like fun

Impossible wasn't about to stop me! I'm an irrational, transcendental artist.... and I have Photoshop!

On a 48 x 48 unit grid, I made a 36 x 36 unit square.

(Within the 36 x 36 square, I put bold lines every six units to make it easier to visualize the various areas.)

Then I drew a circle that "seemed" to be the same size as the 36 x 36 square. I quickly realized I had to make the "fingernail clipping" equal to the "dog ear." The fingernail clipping" is what I call the thin curved segment of circle that extends beyond the square. The "dog ear" is the small "corner-triangle" of the square that extends out beyond the circle.

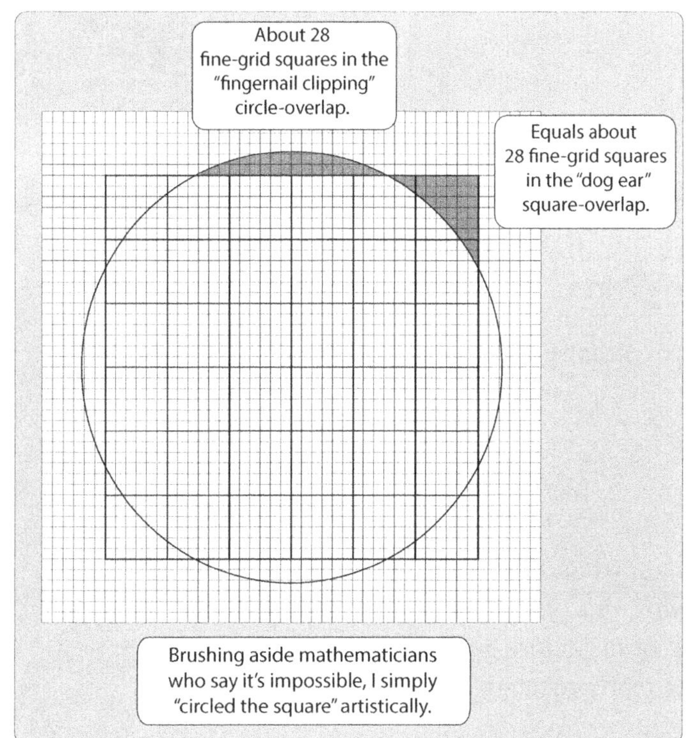
About 28 fine-grid squares in the "fingernail clipping" circle-overlap.
Equals about 28 fine-grid squares in the "dog ear" square-overlap.
Brushing aside mathematicians who say it's impossible, I simply "circled the square" artistically.

By using a fine grid, I could count the number of grid squares in the "fingernail clipping" and the "dog ear" to see if they were equal.

After a few guesstimations and readjustments, I had squared the circle (at least visually).

My inner-mathematician knew I had not actually "squared the circle," but my inner-artist didn't care.

I suspected Dee might had walked the same steps I just walked ... And then concealed this artistic "**square = circle**" on his "close-up" plan!

The burning question became: which of the seven circles did Dee use to demonstrate the "squaring of the circle"?

The Seven Circular Contestants

There were 7 possibilities. I call the innermost circle "Circle 1," and the outermost one "Circle 7."
"Circles 4, 5, 6, and 7" were instantly disqualified because the square fits inside each of them. But "Circles 1, 2, and 3" all make various "fingernail clippings and dog ears" with the white square.
And the winner proved to be ....

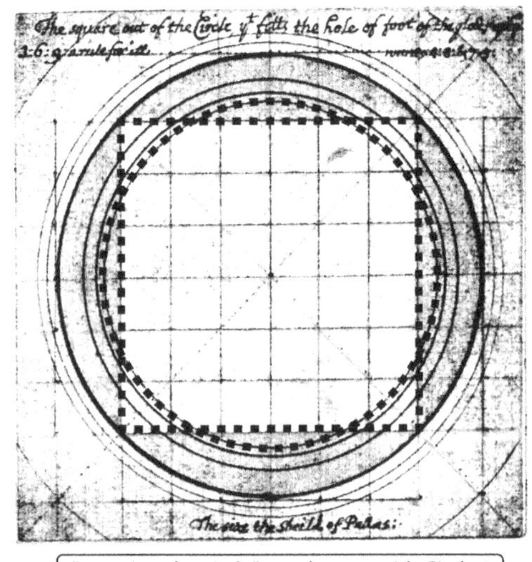

"squaring the circle" matches up with Circle 1

.... **Circle 1, the innermost circle!**

My artful "squaring the circle" matched perfectly with Circle 1, John Dee's artful "squaring the circle."
(And they were done over 400 years apart.)

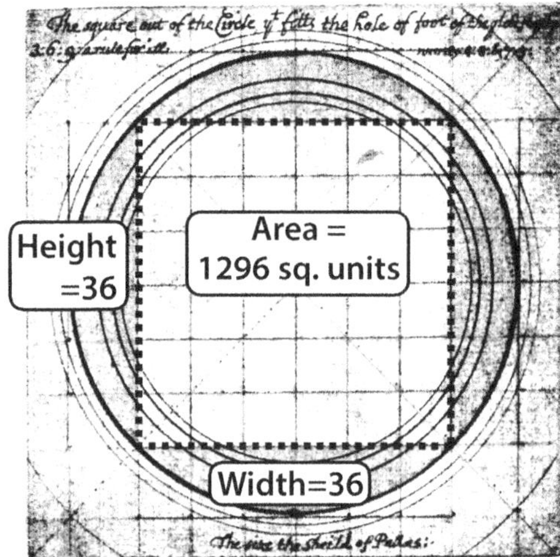

As the height and width of the white square are each 36 units, its area is 1296 square units.

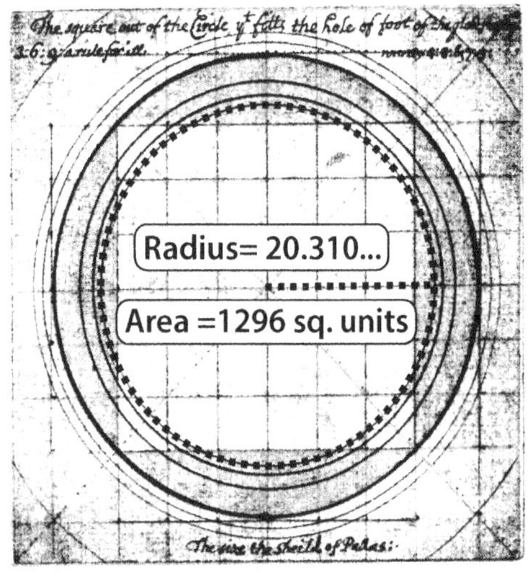

If the circle has the same area, 1296 units, it has a radius of 20.310... units.
(Simply divide the area by pi, then find the square root.)

What I had earlier guessed was 20 units, was actually 20.310.... units.

To summarize, when John Dee wrote
" ***The square out of the Circle...***"
at the top of his "close-up" plan,
he really meant it.

Did Dee also "double" the "squaring of the circle"?

As the remaining 6 circles were all larger than Circle 1, might Dee have also depicted the "doubling" the "squaring of the circle"?

Doubling 1296 results in 2592.
Dividing by pi and finding the square root, I found that such a circle would have a radius of 28.723… units.

That's pretty darn close to **Circle 6**, which I had previously estimated, by observation, to be 28 units in radius.

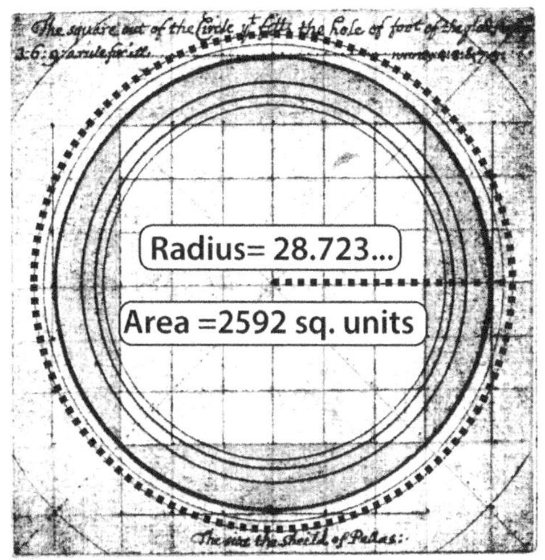

Did Dee also "triple" the "squaring of the circle"?

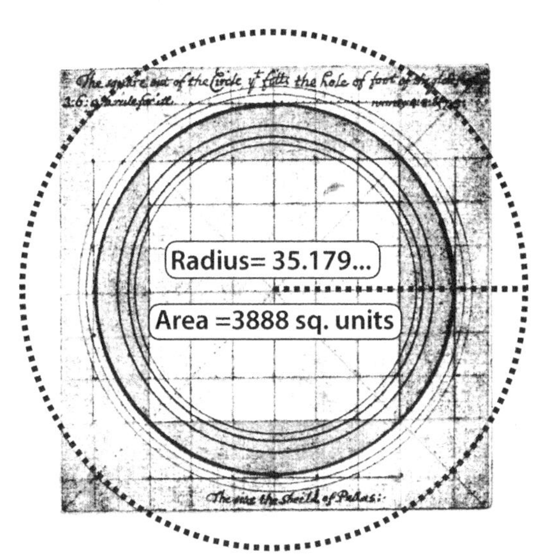

I was on a roll. Did Dee also "triple" the "squaring of the circle" by making an even larger circle with an area of 1296 x 3 = 3888 square units?

Calculating mathematically, such a circle would have a radius of 35.129 units.
That's pretty darn close to **Circle 7**, which I had earlier estimated was around 36 units in radius.

Circle 7 is somewhat disguised, as it's so large it runs off the paper.

Wow! Dee had "squared the circle,"
then doubled it,
then tripled it.

And Circles 1, 6, and 7 were "disguised" by the loud visual ringing of all seven circles.

The area of Dee's "square = circle" is 1296 sq. units.
Double 1296 is 2592 sq. units.
And triple 1296 is 3888 sq. units.

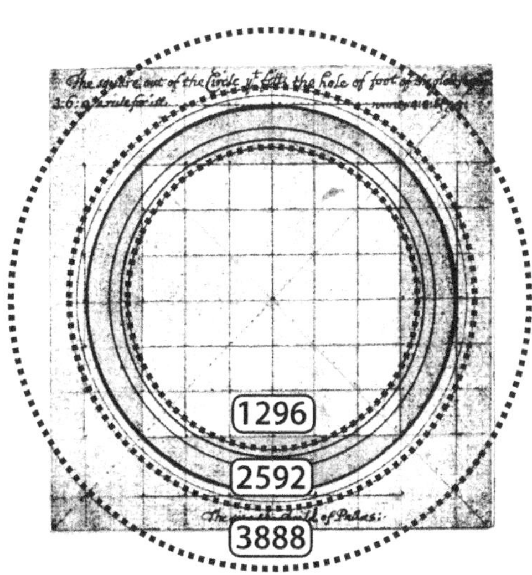

2592 is special in many ways

When the number 2592 popped up as the area of the "double-sized" circle, it rang a bell. The number 2592 had come up frequently in my discussions with Robert Marshall and in my geometric studies of Dee's works.

2520 + 72 = 2592

It's the sum of two of the Metamorphosis numbers: 2520 + 72 = 2592.

35 x 72 = 2520
36 x 70 = 2520

A more revealing path to 2592 relates to this pair of equations that Marshall considered quite important:
35 x 72 = 2520
36 x 72 = 2520

36 x 72= 2592

The way 2592 relates is:
36 x 72 = 2592

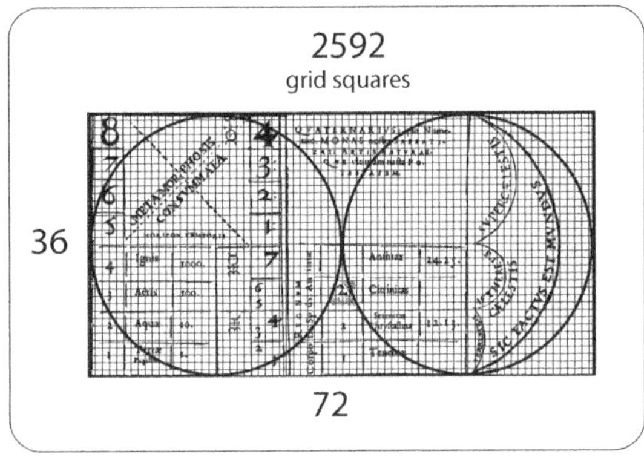

The special thing about this equation is that 36 and 72 are in the 1:2 proportion. It's very likely John Dee based his "ballooned Thus the World Was Created" chart on a 36 X 72 grid, which would make a total of 2592 grid squares.

Also, Dee was an expert astronomer, and 2592 is closely related with the Precession of the Equinoxes. Aside from "daily rotation" and "yearly revolution," the earth exhibits a third motion, which completes itself in a much longer time frame.

Because of the slight wobble of the earth, the stars of the zodiac appeared to precess (or move backwards to the east) by 1 degree every 72 years.

As there are 360 degrees in a circle, the full circuit of the Precision of the Equinoxes is 360 degrees x 72 years = 25920 years.

This 25920, of course, is 10 x 2592.

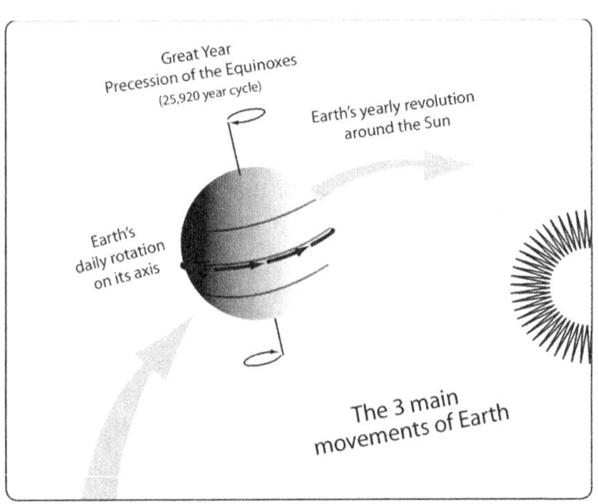

From about 2000 BC to 1 BC,
we were in Aries.

From 1 A.D. to the present time
we have been in Pisces.

And we'll soon be entering,
the "Age of Aquarius."
(If you haven't already heard).

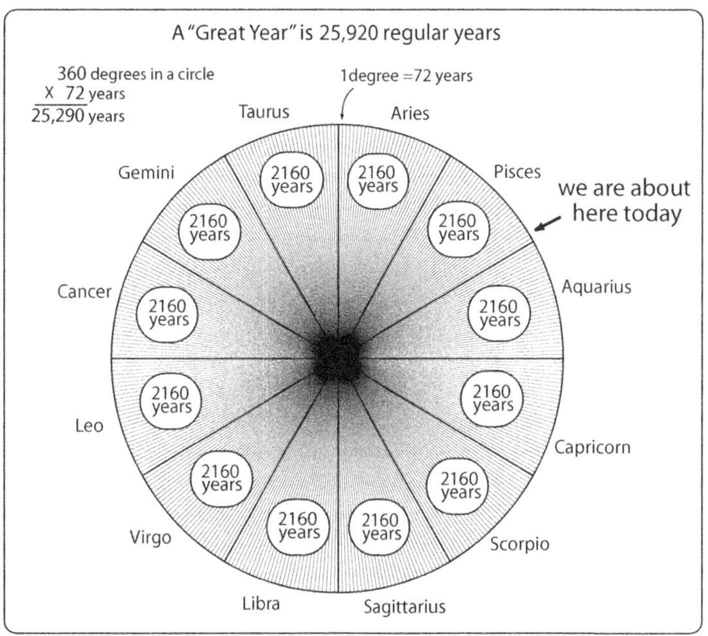

Hipparchus

Around 150 BC, Hipparchus knew about this cycle by studying the "backdrop" of stars every year at dawn on the Spring Equinox, the "First of Aries."

In 1545, Copernicus estimated that the precession cycle was 25920 years.

Not only did John Dee own Copernicus' text, *On the Revolutions of the Heavenly Spheres*, Dee himself wrote about Precession of the Equinoxes in Aphorism 75 of his 1558 *Propaedeumata Aphoristica*:

"However, all of the fixed stars are subject to an extremely slow Movement to the East, along the Ecliptic."
John Dee, 1558

Hindu "Brahma Month"
259, 200, 000, 000 years

Around 1500 BC, long before Hipparchus, the Hindus of India designed a "really long" calendar system. They call the period of 259,200,000,000 years a "Brahma Month."

Ignore all the zeros and you've got 2592.

As you can see 2952 has been special number for a long time.

It relates to "Metamorphosis" in Mathematics, and "Precession" in Astronomy, and Dee was perhaps the most knowledgeable Elizabethan on these two subjects.

Finding 2952 here in the "doubling" of the "squaring of the circle" helped confirm to me that Dee was the mastermind behind these Globe drawings.

The Zodiac in the Globe theater

This "close-up" illustration we have been studying is the plan for the Starr's Mall, where the groundlings stood. It was called the Starr's Mall as it was open to the stars at night and the sun in the day.

Not only that, Joy Hancox suggests, (and I agree) that the underside of the roof over the stage was probably painted with, you guessed it... the zodiacal signs of the ecliptic. After all, that false ceiling that projected over the stage was called "The Heavens."

(Joy Hancox found that William Cecil's grand home at Theobalds had the 12 signs of the zodiac, with individual stars, painted on the ceiling.)

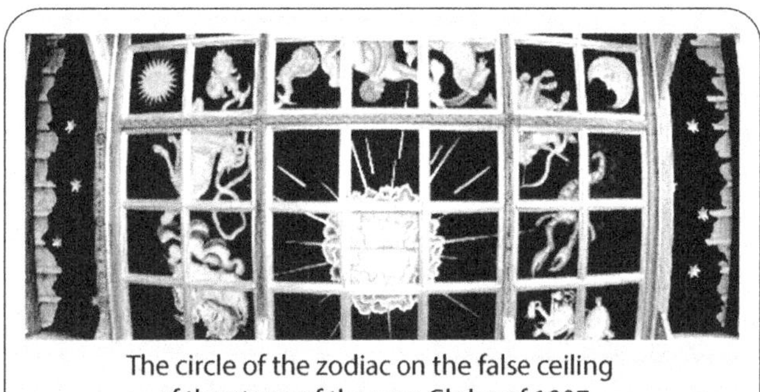

The circle of the zodiac on the false ceiling of the stage of the new Globe of 1997

The reproduction of the Globe Theater, which opened in 1997, has the Sun, the Moon, and the Zodiacal signs painted on the ceiling of "The Heavens."

In summary, the groundlings would look up at the actors, and beyond they would see the zodiac ceiling. That's the "Above" or "Heavens."

"Below" their feet they stood in an area one tenth the size of the Precession of the Equinoxes, the 25920 year dance of the earth with respect to the fixed stars.

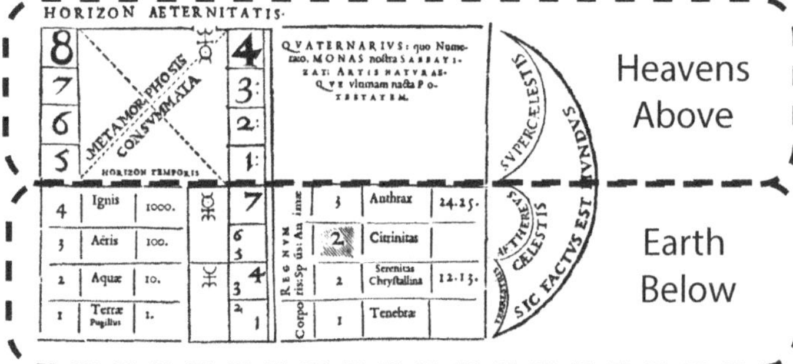

This motif is just like Dee's "Thus the World Was Created" chart, which is divided into the Above (Supercelestial) and Below (Aetheric Celestial and Terrestrial).

As Above, So Below.
Macrocosm and Microcosm.
Heaven and Earth.

What's more amazing is the numbers are the same:
The ballooned "Thus the World Was Created" chart,
with a "36 by 72" grid, is 2592 grid-squares.
That makes the "Above" and the Below" sections
each "18 by 36," or 1296 grid squares.

All these numbers, 18, 36, 72, 1296, and 2595
are prominent in the Globe drawings.

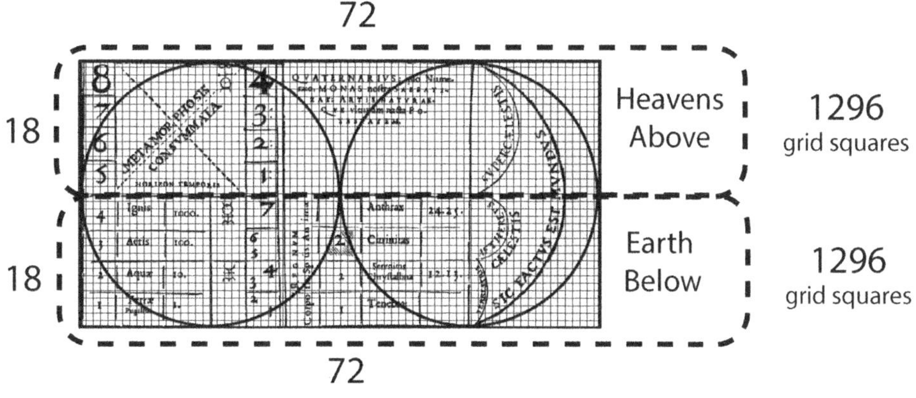

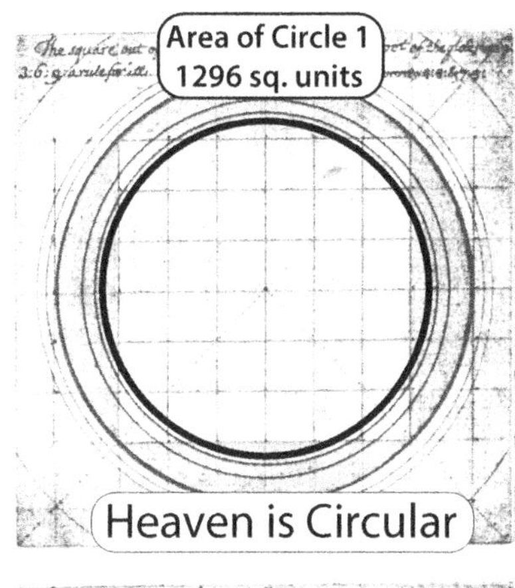

And in the "close-up" diagram,
Circle 1 has an area of
1296 square units.

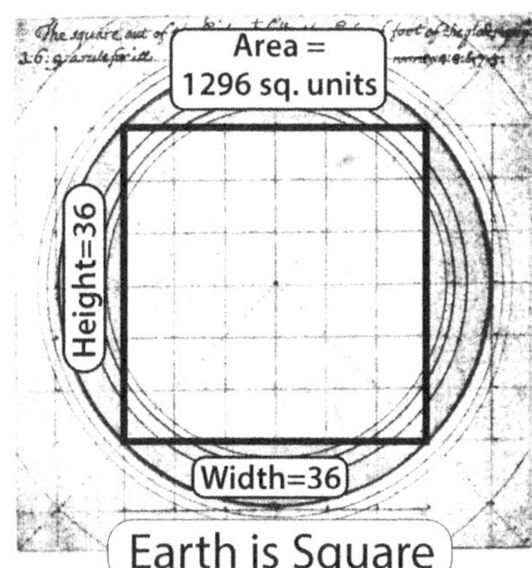

And the 36 by 36 white
square has an area of
1296 square units.

And in the Hermetic tradition,
Heaven is circular and Earth is square.

This stuff is pure Dee.

Finding 1296, 2952, and 3888 in the
"squaring of the circle," the doubling, and the tripling
really convinced me this plan was conceived by
astronomer/mathematician/polymath John Dee.

But there was another reason I knew Dee's concentric circle
"close-up" plan is about what I call "1x, 2x, and 3x."

Another confirming clue

The card is small.
The hand-drawn circles had a margin of error.
There were still several circles unaccounted for.

How could I be so absolutely certain that
this doubling and tripling is *really*
what Dee had in mind?

Because he tells us!

Along the top it reads,
"3:6:9 is the plan for itt..."

This "**3:6:9**" can be reduced down to the ratio "**1:2:3**,"
which is about the simplest expression
of doubling and tripling you can find!

How the "overview" and "close-up" plans sync together

Remember that the "overview diagram" was a progression of "halvings" of the areas of inscribed squares and inscribed circles, starting with the 72 x 72 unit square.

Dee doesn't actually draw all these squares and circles on his diagram, but they can be geometrically deduced from those he does show.

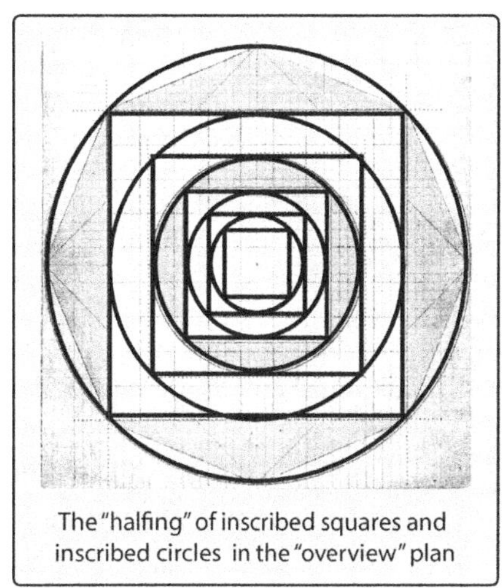

The "halfing" of inscribed squares and inscribed circles in the "overview" plan

The areas of the inscribed circles and squares of the "overview" plan

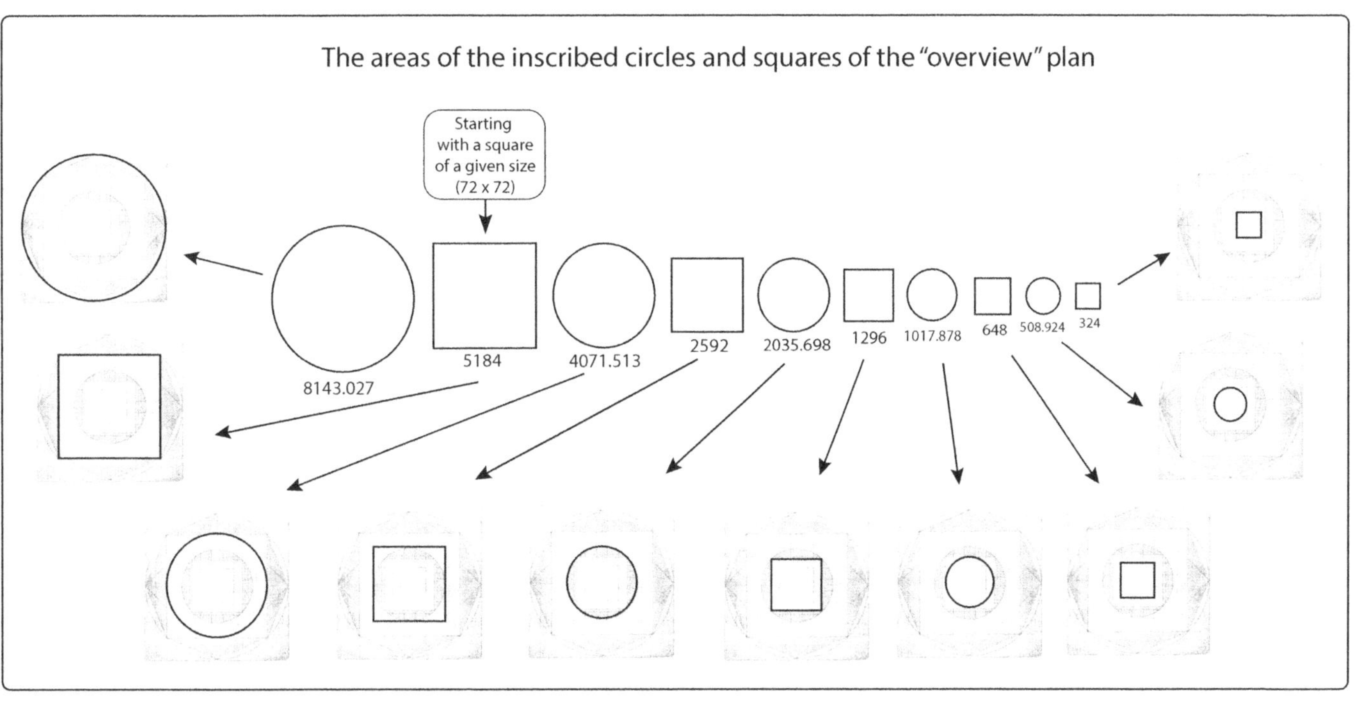

Here the "halvings" of the circles are inter-leafed
with the "halvings" of the squares.

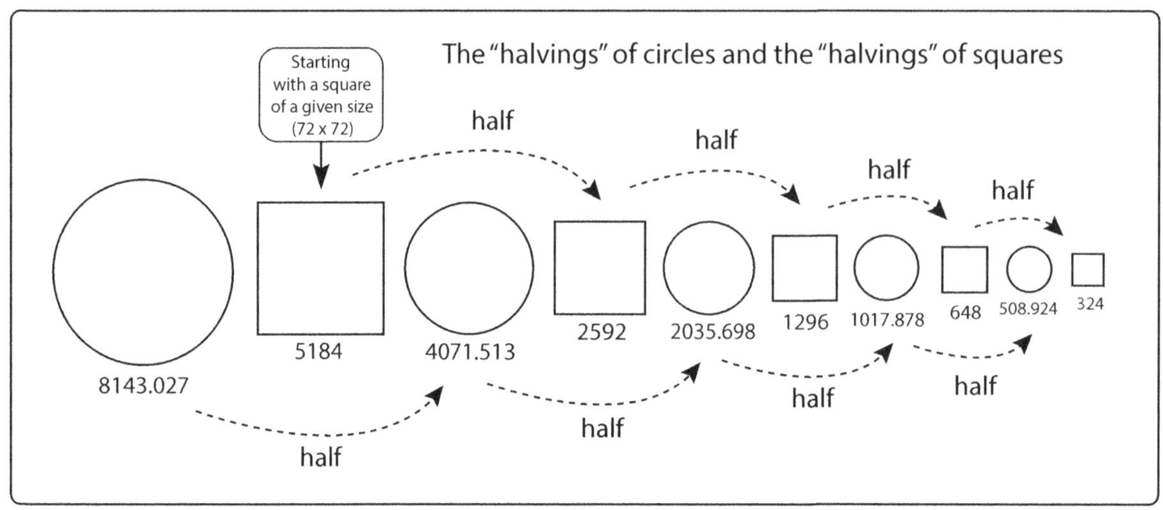

And we've more recently seen that the "close-up" plan (somewhat cryptically) portrays the doubling, and tripling of the "square = circle" (with Circles 1, 6, and 7).

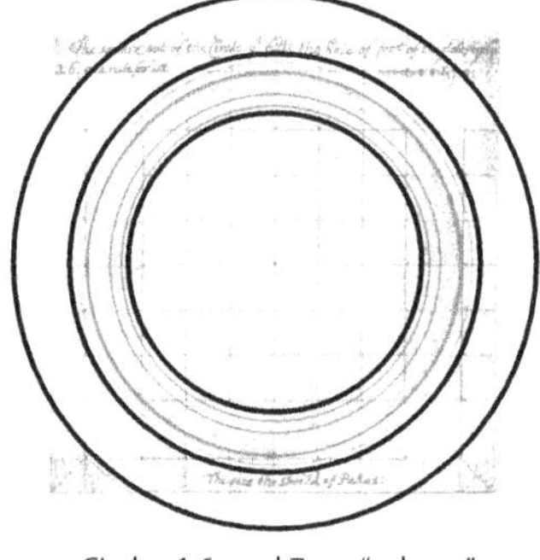
Circles 1,6, and 7 are "echoes"

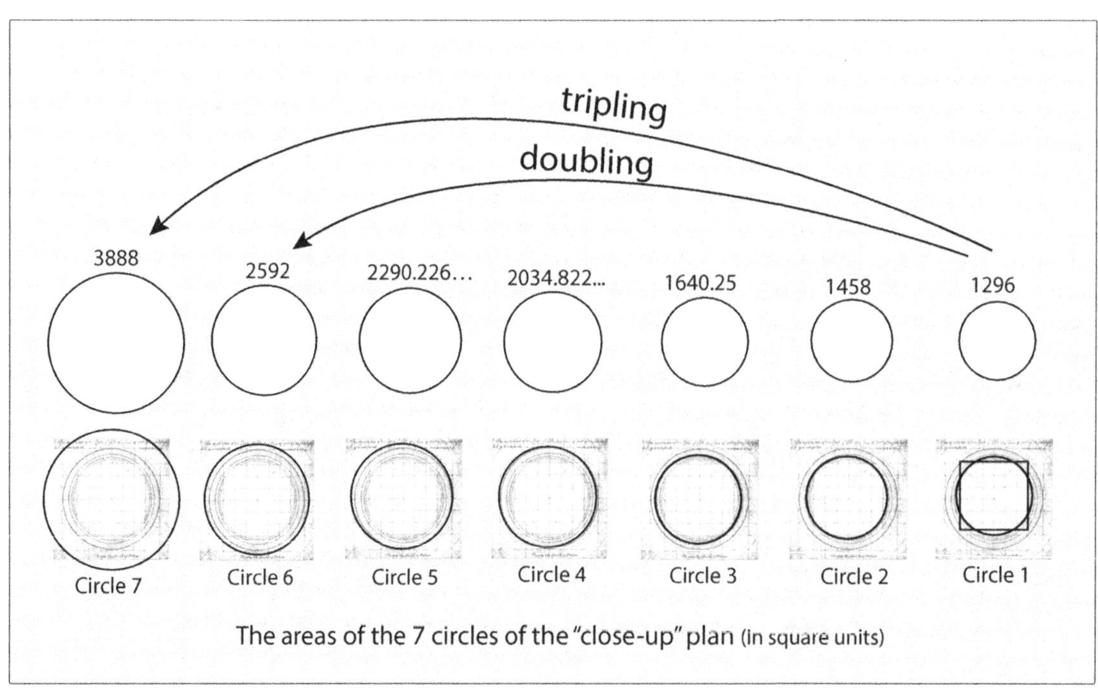

The areas of the 7 circles of the "close-up" plan (in square units)

This illustration shows how the "overview" diagram and the "close-up" diagram sync together.

(Don't be intimidated by this combination drawing, we'll review it a step at a time.)

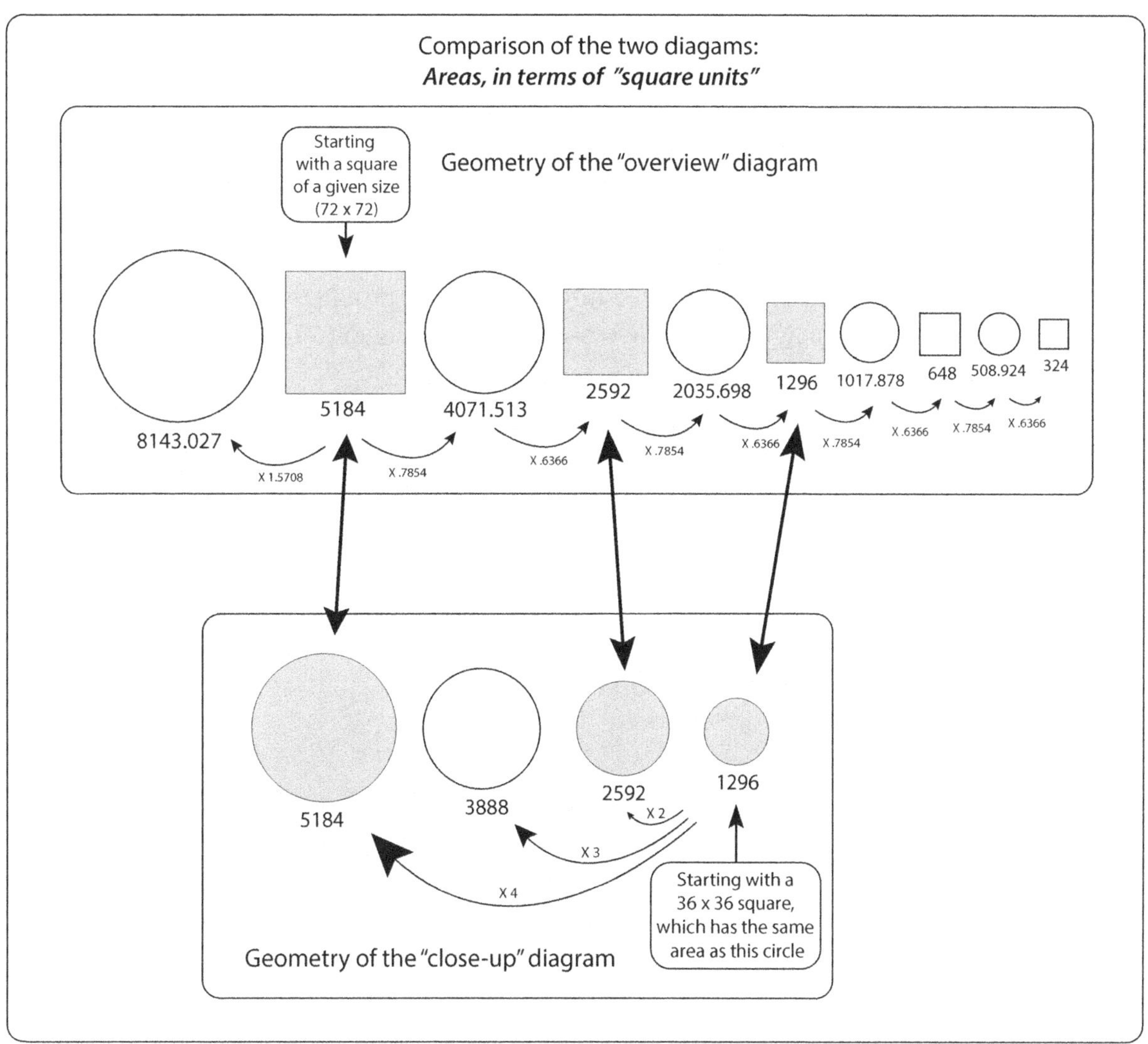

The 100% circle = The 100% square

Locate the 1296 square (in the "overview") and the 1296 circle (in the "close-up").

Dee has shown us "square = circle"
by using the 36 x 36 white square (1296 square units)
and the Circle 1 (also 1296 square units).

The 200% circle = The 200% square

Locate the 2592 square (in the "overview") and the 2592 circle (in the "close-up").

In his "close-up" diagram, Dee has drawn Circle 6, which has 2592 square units.

Correspondingly, in the "overview" diagram he has hinted about a
50.911 x 50.911 square, which has an area of 2592 square units.

(The "hint" is Dee's 52 x 52 dotted-line square, which is NOT QUITE tangent to the gray circle in the diagram. Calculating geometrically, the gray circle's circumscribing square is actually 50.911 X 50.911)

The 400% circle = The 400% square

(We'll investigate "The 300% circle = 300% square" in a moment.)

Locate the 5184 square (in the "overview") and the 5184 circle (in the "close-up").

In the "overview" diagram, the 72 x 72 square Dee drew has an area of 5184.

A circle with an area of 5184 would be way too big to fit on the "close-up" diagram, but it can be deduced from the information Dee provides. As 4 x 1296 = 5184, we might imagine a "circle = square" involving the 72 x 72 square.

There is no 300% circle = The 300% square but there is a 300% circle ≈ 72 x 72 square incircle

On the "close-up" plan, Dee has drawn Circle 7, the tripling of the 1296 Circle.

(It is only partially seen, being clipped off north, south, east, and west).

Circle 7 has an area of 3880 square units.

(3 x 1296 = 3888)

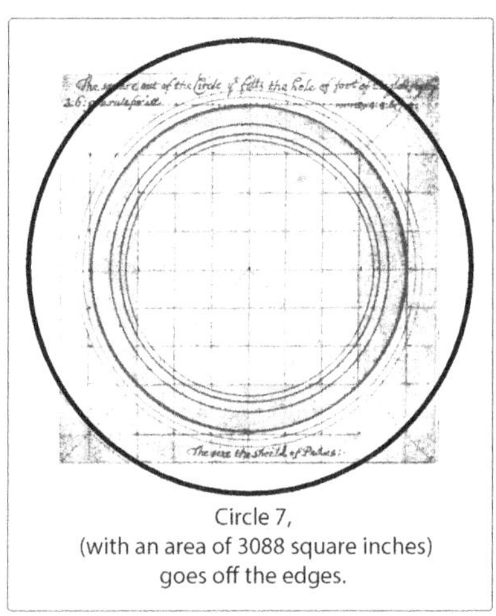

Circle 7,
(with an area of 3088 square inches)
goes off the edges.

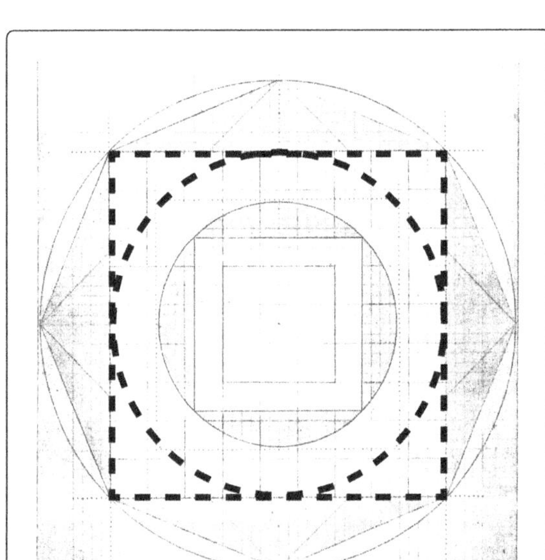

The "incircle" of the 72 X72 square has an area of 4071.503 square units

On the "overview plan Dee has *not* drawn a circle inscribed inside the 72 x 72 square.

But as the whole diagram is about inscribed squares and inscribed circles, it is certainly implied.

Such an "incircle" of the 72 x 72 square would have an area of 4071.513 square units.

Thes two circles are approximately the same size!

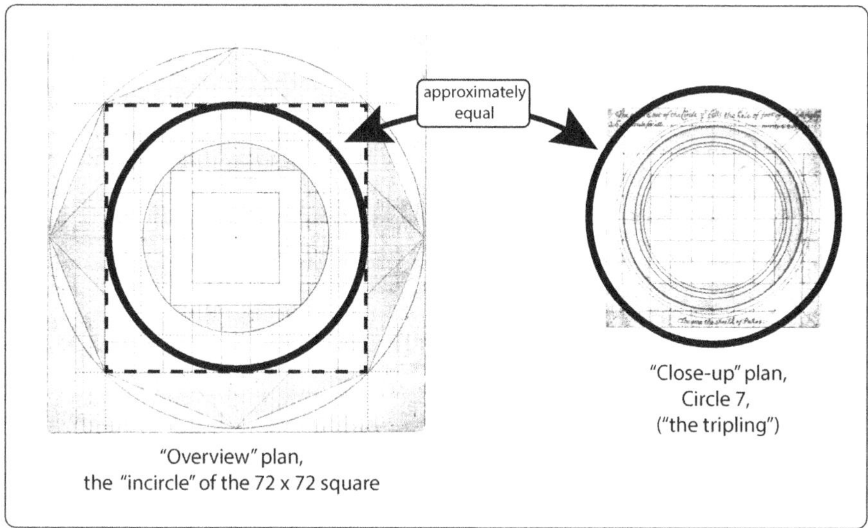

"Close-up" plan, Circle 7, ("the tripling")

"Overview" plan, the "incircle" of the 72 x 72 square

Although it might not seem like it, this 4017.513 is pretty close to 3888 (which is the area of Circle 7).

The difference is only about 125.513 square units, which is only **about 3%** (of 4017.513).

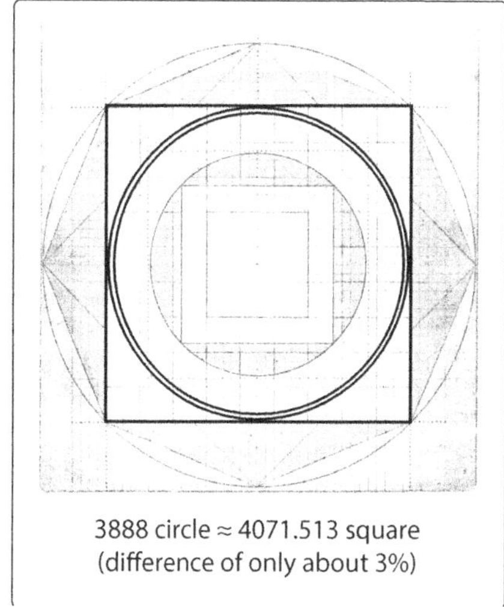

3888 circle ≈ 4071.513 square (difference of only about 3%)

3888 circle ≈ 4071.513 square
(difference of only about 3%)

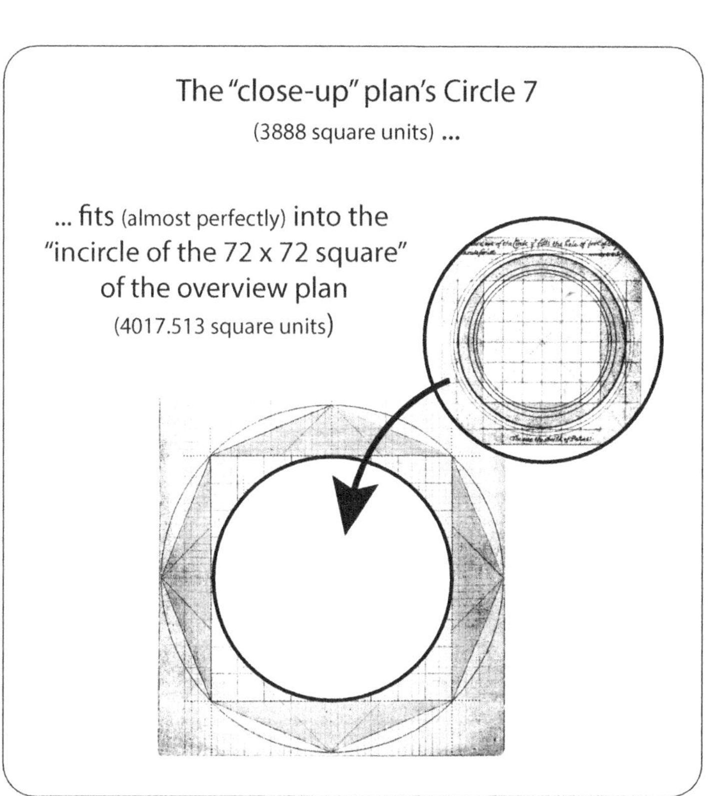

The "close-up" plan's Circle 7
(3888 square units) ...
... fits (almost perfectly) into the
"incircle of the 72 x 72 square"
of the overview plan
(4017.513 square units)

In short, the area of the tripling of the "square = circle" (on the "close-up" plan), is almost exactly equal to (except by about 3%) the incircle of the 72 x 72 square (on the "overview" plan).

This is how the two designs sync up!

It's how the close-up diagram fits in the overview diagram.

It's how the Starr's Mall fits into the wooden viewing gallery which surrounds it.

Here's a comparison of the two diagrams showing the areas of the various circles and squares, in terms of "square units."

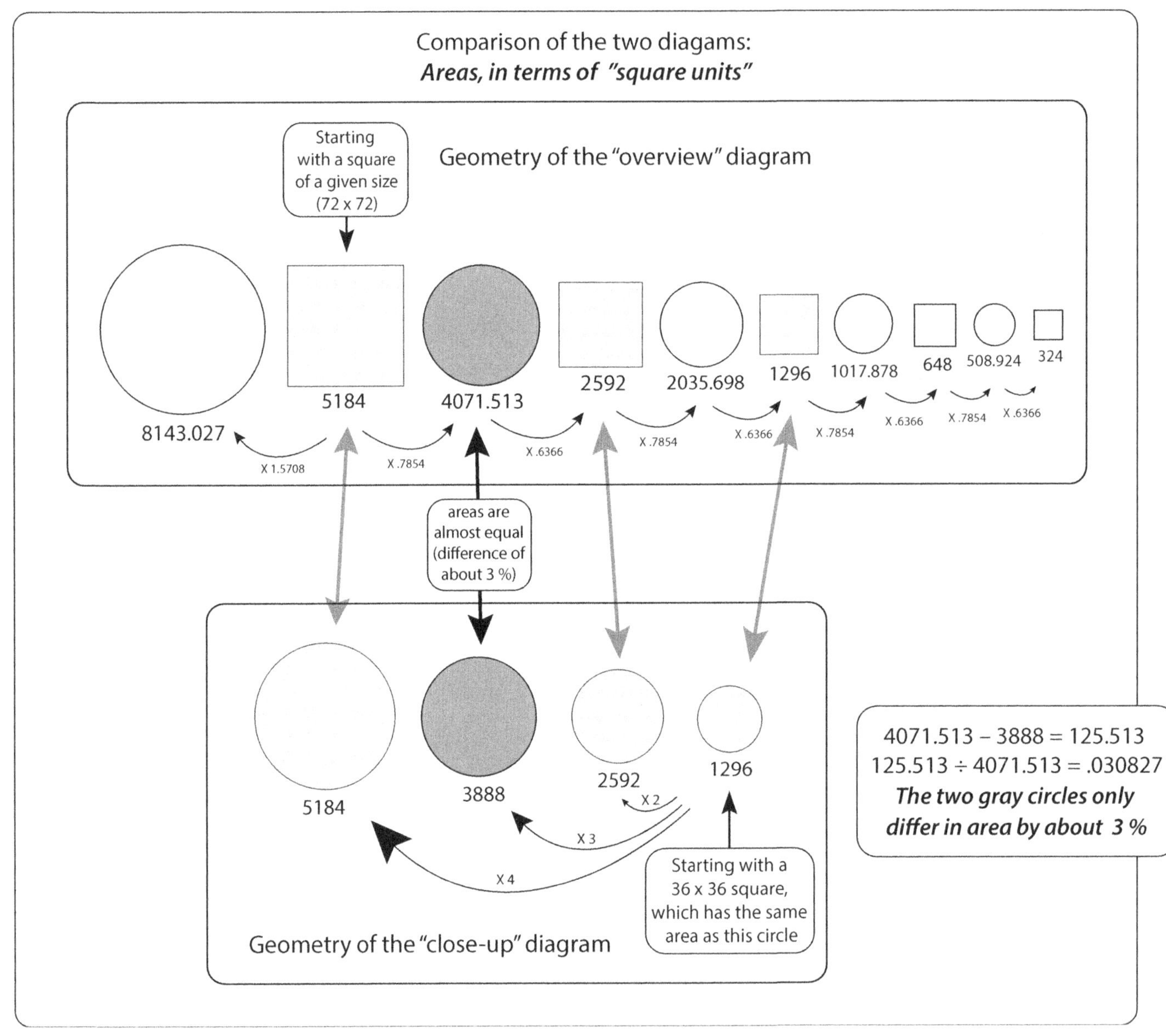

The same comparison, using diameters and diagonals to see the "sync"

So far, we've been dealing with the areas of squares and circles. But areas are hard to wrap your head around. Let's view this "syncronization" in terms of something more discernible: "diameters of circles" and "diagonals of squares."

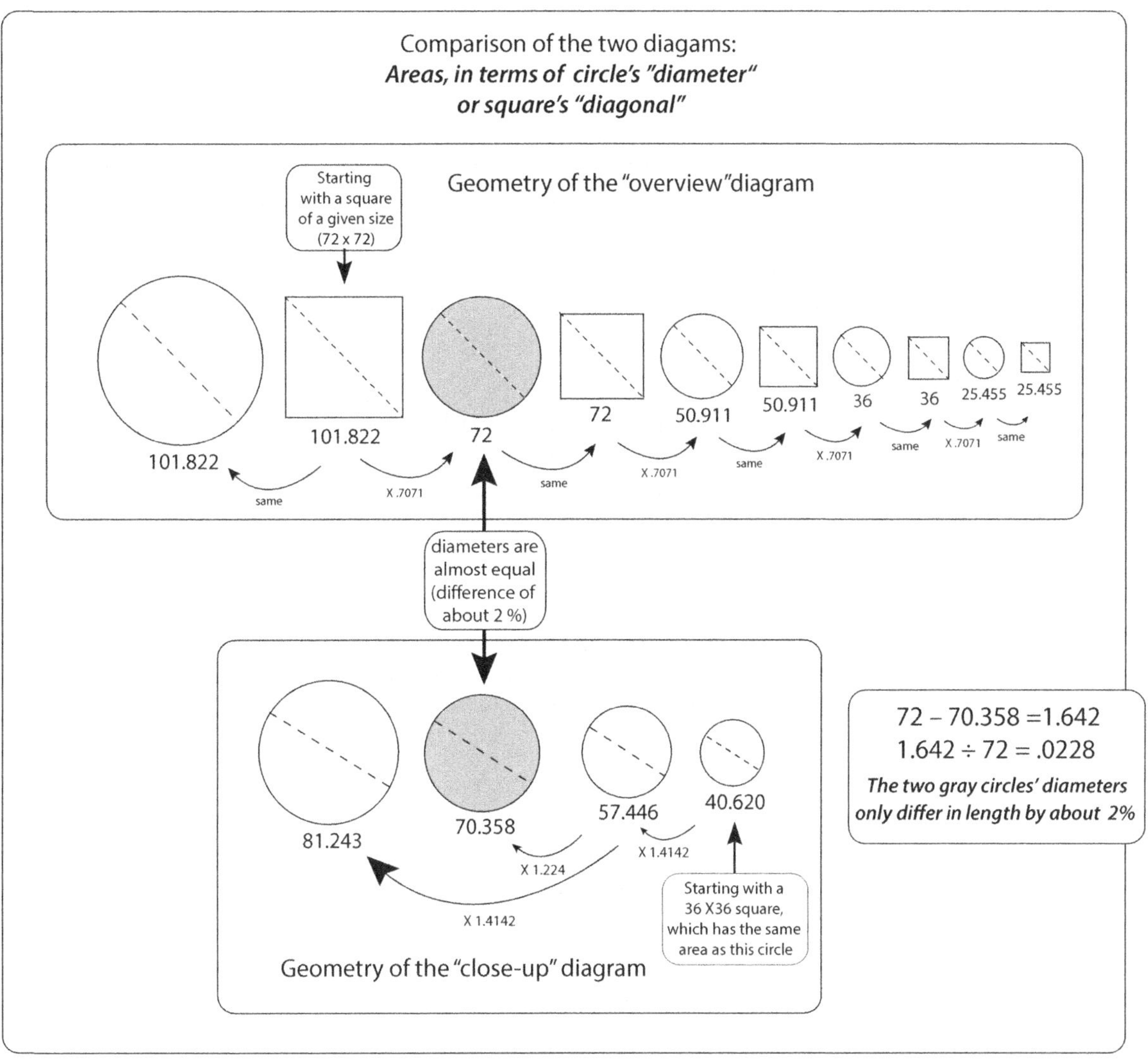

On the "close-up" diagram, the diameter of Circle 7 (the tripling of Circle 1) is 70.358 units. On the "overview" diagram, the diameter of the incircle of the 72 x 72 square is 72 units. The difference between 70.358 and 72 is 1.642 units. That's a difference of only about 2%.

If we consider a unit to be a foot, the difference between 72 and 70.358 is less than 2 feet.

As the circular Starr's Mall in the middle of the circular wooden galleries, that's only about one foot on each side.

The whole Globe theater has a diameter of 101.822, so one foot on each side of the Starr's Mall is not a very big deal.

(In case you were wondering, the reason this "diameter discrepancy" is only 2% is that the calculation of the 3% "area discrepancy" involves the "squaring" of numbers.)

The same comparison, using radii to see the "sync"

Instead of areas or diameters, let's look at this "syncronization" in terms of radii (of circles) and half-diagonals (of squares).

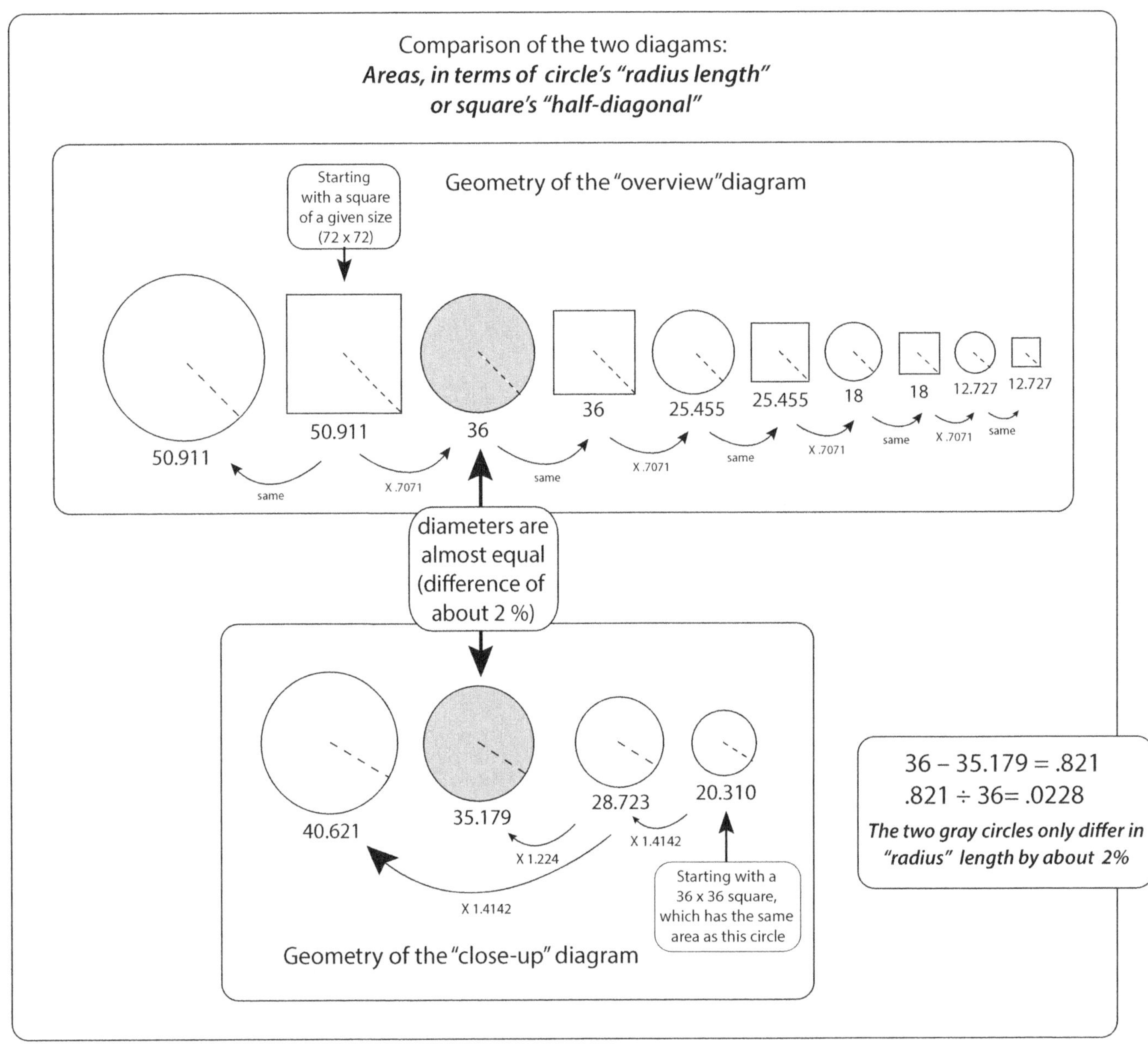

On the "close-up" plan, the radius of Circle 6 (the tripling of circle 1) is 35.079 feet.

On the "overview" plan, the inner circle of the 72 x 72 square has a diameter of 36 feet.

The difference between 35.179 and 36 is only .821, or about 9 1/2 inches. That's not much at all.

(Again about a 2% discrepancy)

A one-sentence summary

John Dee was an expert on Euclid *Elements of Geometry*.
After describing various "definitions," Euclid posed "propositions,"
then mathematically proved them.
The proofs are universal.
They hold true at any scale.
And anytime. And anywhere.

Here's a general postulate of what Dee seems to be trying to prove (or at least visually demonstrate) in the "overview" and "close-up" diagrams:

If the area of a circle is equal to the area of a square (or Square A = Circle A),

the area "three times as large" as Circle A (or Square A) is approximately* equal to

the "incircle" of a much larger square, which is four times the area of Square A (or Circle A).

*(The difference in area is only about 3%.)

Or more simply:

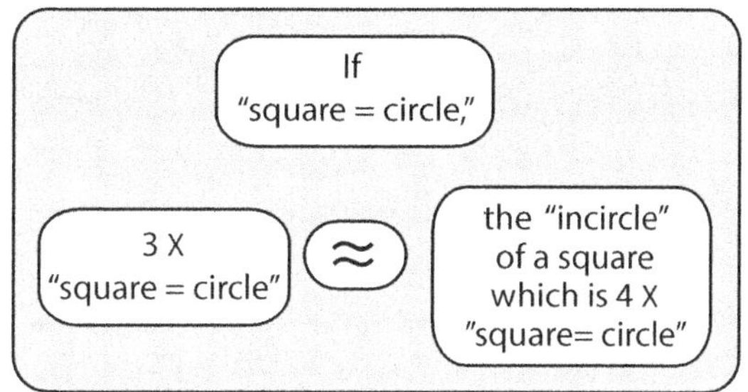

Here's my graphic summary of Dee's apparent proposition.

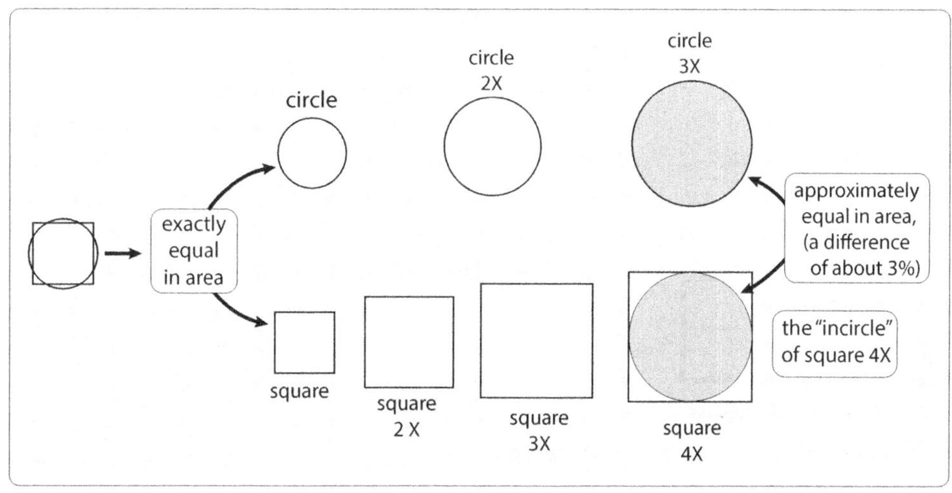

"Ternary-Heaven" and "Quaternary-Earth"

In the graphic summary just shown, notice there are 3 circles and 4 squares.

The idea of involving 3 circles and 4 squares resonates with Dee's mathematical cosmology in another way.

Let's imagine all three circles of equal size, and all four squares with of the same equal size.

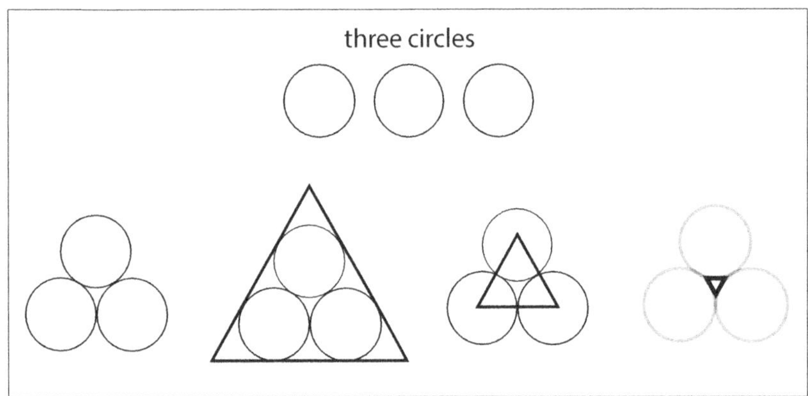

The closest-packing of three circles makes an equilateral triangle of circles. This equilateral triangle can be seen by connecting the three center points.

Or it can be seen by circumscribing a triangle around the three circles.

Or even by inscribing an upside-down equilateral triangle in island in the middle.

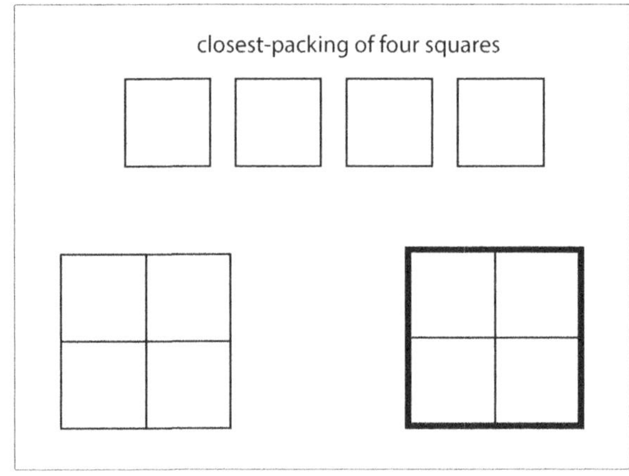

The closest-packing of 4 squares makes a large square with an area that is four times one of the original squares.

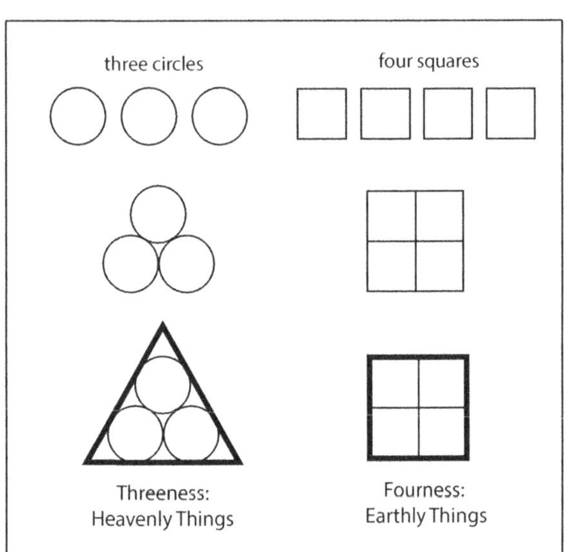

Suddenly, instead of circles and squares, we're dealing with triangles and squares!

And in John Dee's cosmology, just as **circles** are "Heavenly"and squares are "Earthly," **triangles** are seen as "Heavenly" and squares are "Earthly."

("Circle = heavenly" is an idea that comes from classical Greek and Roman times.

"Triangle = heavenly" derives from Medieval and Renaissance iconography, in which the triangle symbolizes the Christian Trinity.

John Dee's Renaissance Neoplatonic philosophy was an amalgamation of classical thought and Christian doctrine.)

In his fascinating book mentioned earlier, *A Beginners Guide to Constructing the Universe, The Mathematical Archetypes of Nature, Art, and Science, a Voyage from 1 to 10,* in a chapter called "FOUR CORNERS OF THE YOUNIVERSE," (pp. 89-91), author Michael S. Schneider writes:

"The common theme in worldwide mythology is the human as microcosm, a miniature model of the whole universe. Now dismissed as primitive, this view was long considered a key to the understanding of the Self. The ancient philosophers saw their lives arranged according to nature's own harmonies, for in nature, geometry, and their spiritual lives they discovered the same principles

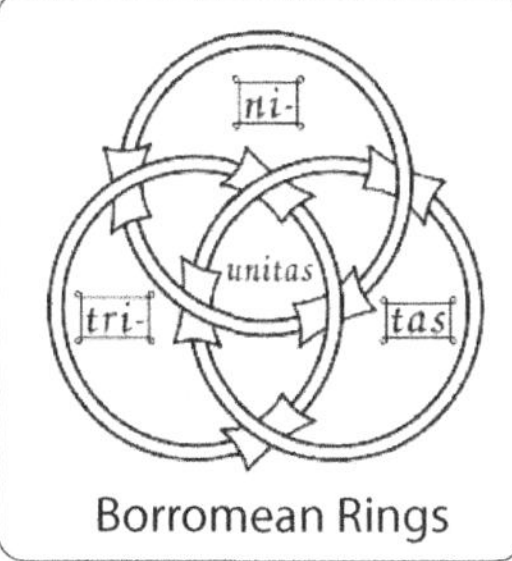

Borromean Rings

A fundamental map of ourselves is found in the mathematical intimacy between the Triad and the Tetrad. The ancient mathematical philosophers saw themselves wherever three and four mingle. Three Borromean Rings intersect at four secondary spaces, just as lights three primary colors blend to produce four more.

This simultaneity of three and four is a simple blueprint of ourselves: the triangle denoting a divine trinity 'above,' and deep within, and below it a square unfolding the four elements of familiar human nature and body outward."

"A triangle above the square in art and architecture traditionally represents our deepest design nature over the four 'elements' of our human nature. Few would suspect anything special about the design of doors, windows, and roofs. So common are weight supporting triangular roofs and lentils over rectangular facades, doors, windows, and porticos that we hardly notice them.

"triangle over square"
Temple of Nereidas
in ancient Athens

But this is just the effect the enlightened architects of ancient times wanted for embedding esoteric instruction about the self. The architecture itself, its proportion and ornamentation held the esoteric teaching in plain sight, a reminder of their divinity to those initiated in the timeless wisdom that speaks of self-knowledge and spiritual transformation.

Copies of ancient architecture are scattered throughout our cities. The wisdom-teaching is still evident to those who notice and can read it. But this century's trend in urban architecture has been simply to hang walls on skyscraping steel frames.

Triangular lintels are no longer used to support weight and pass along the traditional teachings that, until recently, had endured for thousands of years. By allowing the square and cube to eclipse the divine triangle from common site, we've replaced a valuable body of knowledge with soulless architecture." (Michael S. Schneider, *A Beginner's Guide* ..., pp. 89-91)

Illustration entitled "Monas or the One" from Michael Maier's 1617 alchemical embem book, *Atalanta Fugiens,* with triangle, square, and circles

Many mathematical alchemists have been fascinated by "squaring the circle" and the idea of "Fourness resting in Threeness. Here's an illustration entitled "Monas or the One" from Michael Maier's 1617 alchemical emblem book, *Atalanta Fugiens*.

A geometer measures the radius of a circle. In the circle is a triangle. In the triangle is a square. And in the square is a circle.

Dee loved the integration of Fourness and Threeness

Illustration from the front cover of John Dee's 1568 "second edition" of the *Propaedeumata Aphoristica*

Relating threeness and fourness is at the heart of John Dee's mathematical cosmology

On the front cover of his 1568 second edition of the Propaedeumata Aphoristica, Dee writes, "*Quaternarius In Ternario Conquiescence*," which means "The Quaternary Rests in the Ternary."

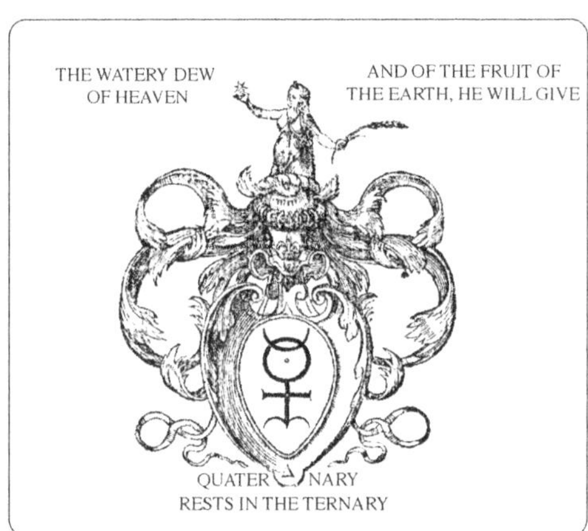

(My translation from Dee's Latin)

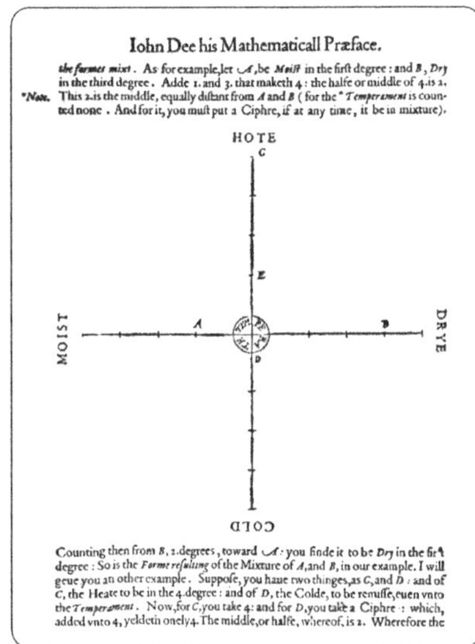

Iohn Dee his Mathematicall Præface.

the formes mixt. As for example, let A, be *Moist* in the first degree: and B, *Dry* in the third degree. Adde 1. and 3. that maketh 4: the halfe or middle of 4. is 2. *Note.* This 2. is the middle, equally distant from A and B (for the *Temperament* is counted none. And for it, you must put a Ciphre, if at any time, it be in mixture).

Counting then from B, 2. degrees, toward A: you finde it to be *Dry* in the first degree: So is the *Forme resulting* of the Mixture of A, and B, in our example. I will geue you an other example. Suppose, you haue two thinges, as C, and D: and of C, the Heate to be in the 4. degree: and of D, the Colde, to be remisse, euen vnto the *Temperament*. Now, for C, you take 4: and for D, you take a Ciphre: which, added vnto 4, yeldeth onely 4. The middle, or halfe, whereof, is 2. Wherefore the

The "Arte of Graduation," from John Dee's 1570 *Preface to Euclid*

The Fourness of Earthly things rests in the Ternary of Heavenly things.

The Fourness of Earthly things can be seen in the four Elements: Fire, Air, Earth, and Water, or the four cardinal directions, North, South, East, and West.

It can be seen in John Dee's "Art of Graduation" in his *Preface to Euclid*, which involves the opposites "hot and cold" and "wet and dry."

The Threeness of Heavenly things can be seen in the "3-persons-in-one" Christian Trinity: Father, Son, and Holy Ghost.

(Though at times Protestant, and at times Catholic, Dee was always a devout Christian.)

In Theorem 20 of his *Monas Hieroglyphica*, Dee discusses the Cross of the Elements: " Thus, we clearly DEMONSTRATE: the QUATERNARY RESTS IN THE TERNARY." He tells us his offset Cross can be seen as "3 things" (two lines and their intersection point) or "4 things" (four lines).

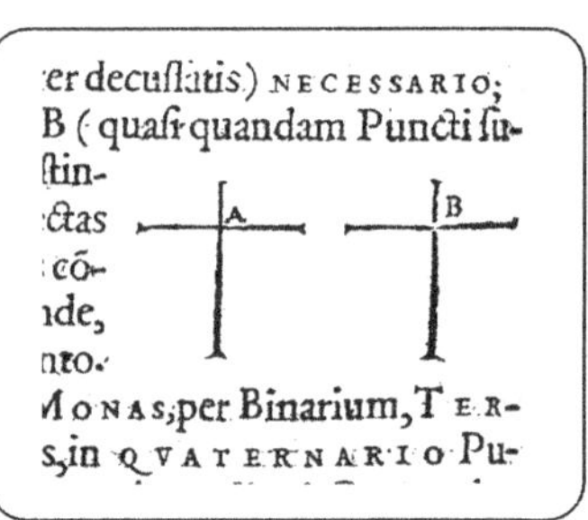

er decussatis) NECESSARIO;
B (quasi quandam Puncti su-
stin-
ctas
cō-
ide,
nro.
MONAS, per Binarium, TER-
S, in QVATERNARIO Pu-

A Cross as Ternary.
B Cross as Quaternary.

And speaking of "closest-packing of circles,"
Threeness and Fourness can be seen in the
cuboctahedron, the very framework
of the closest-packing-of-spheres.

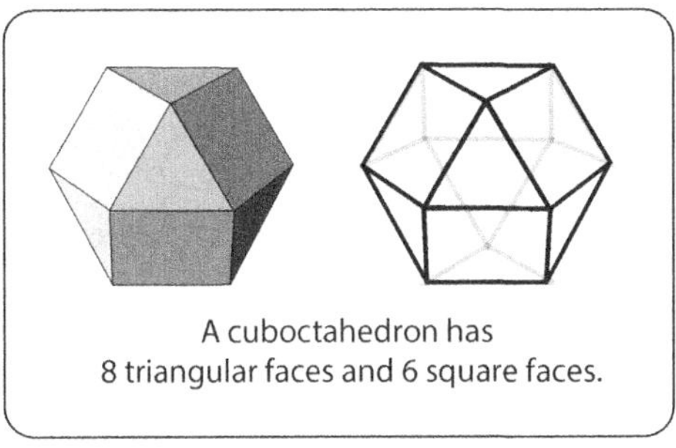
A cuboctahedron has
8 triangular faces and 6 square faces.

The cuboctahedron has only two kinds of faces: triangular and square.

There are 6 square faces and 8 triangular faces. The ratio of 6:8 is equivalent to 3:4. The whole cuboctahedron is suffused with Threeness and Fourness.

The 8 triangular faces are the ones made from the four Bucky bowties, ("the four pairs of tip-to-tip tetrahedra"). They are more important than the 6 squares that fit into the spaces between the 8 triangular faces.
Thus, Fourness rests **in** Threeness. "*Quaternarius In Ternario Conquiescence*"

Dee cleverly hides this idea in his
"Thus the World Was Created" chart.

In the "Above" half of the chart he draws a dotted-line X,
implying another dotted line X just to the right.
These two X's make eight triangles.

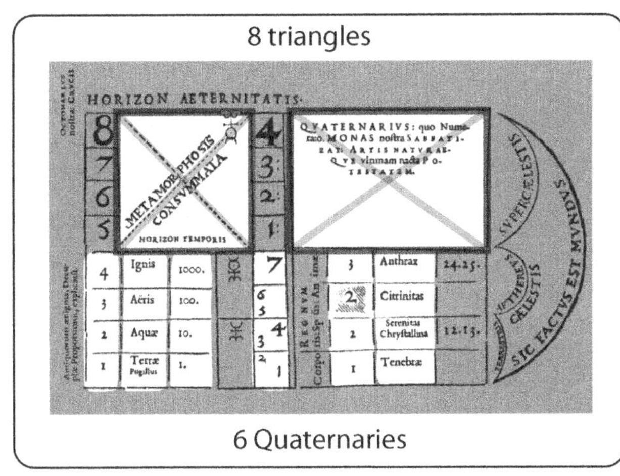

=

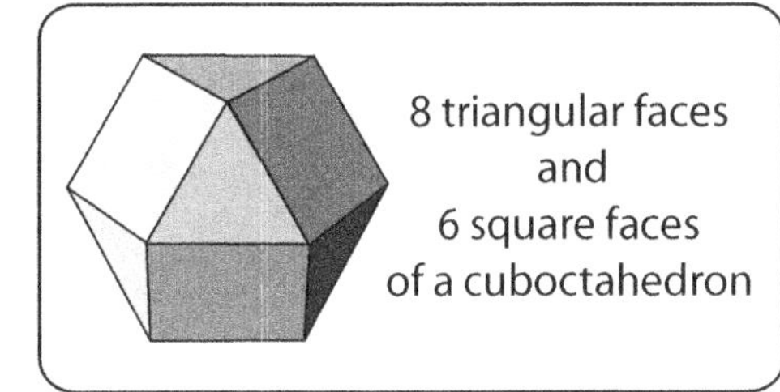
8 triangular faces
and
6 square faces
of a cuboctahedron

In the "Below" half of the chart, he lists 6 quaternaries:

the Pythagorean Quaternary (1, 2, 3, 4),
the four Elements (Fire, Air, Earth and Water);
the heart of our Base-10 numbering system (1, 10, 100, 1000);
the digits from 1 to 7 (1 and 2), (3 and 4), (5 and 6), and (7 all alone)
Dee's own Artificial Quaternary (1, 2, 2, 3)
the 4 alchemical stages (black, clear, yellow, and red)

The whole chart expresses
"Threeness Above and Fourness Below."

Dee even jumbles the letters of his axiom, "***Quaternarius In Ternario Conquiescence***" in the chart in Theorem 23 with the words: "***Agens: externa; Acquisita, Interna***."

Granted, some of the letters have to be used twice. And the letter "o" does not appear, but the "o's" can be seen as the circular "degree symbols" embraced by the brackets, just to the right.

Dee's jumbled-letter clue for *"Quaternarius In Ternario Conquiescens"*

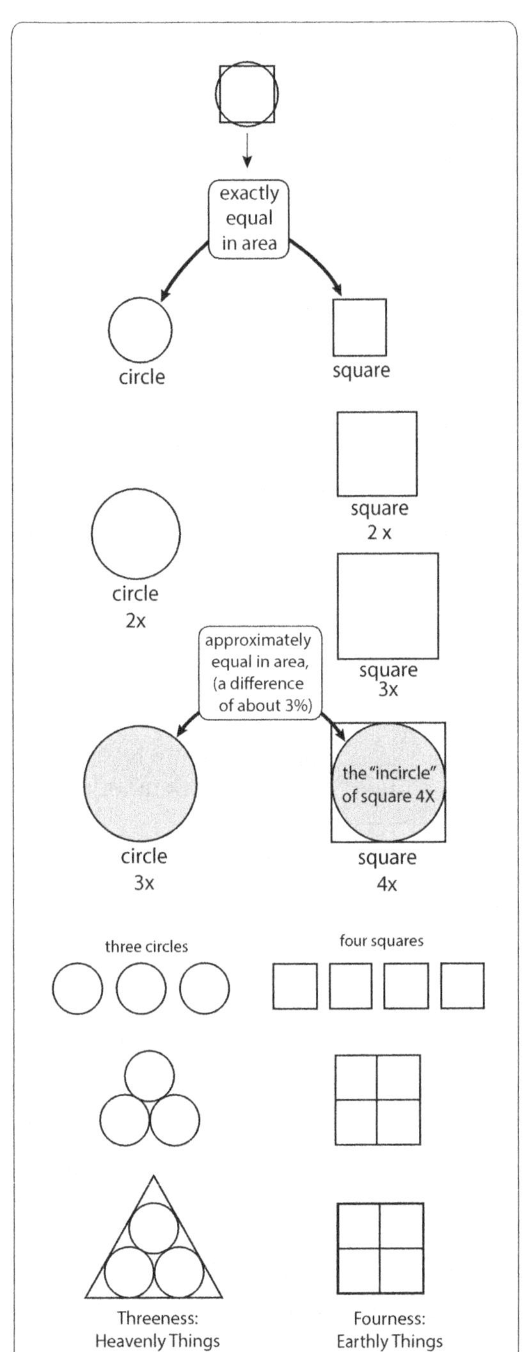

To summarize, the way Dee's two rhythms involving circles and squares sync up, basically incorporates three circles and four squares. Three same-size circles form an equilateral triangle. Four same-size squares form a big square.

Triangles are Heavenly. Squares are Earthly. The Globe theater design connects Heaven and Earth.

To John Dee, a public theater, a setting to share wisdom, would be a microcosm of the macrocosm of the Universe. As Above, so Below.

Dee expresses his spiritual beliefs geometrically. Even though the average theatergoer wouldn't be able to comprehend the underlying geometry, Dee knew they would sense something special was going on.

The words of greatest playwright in Elizabethan England, William Shakespeare, would be made even more enchanting in this harmonically designed theater-in-the-round.

When I hear the word "globe,"
I think of a "spherical earth-map,"
depicting oceans and continents.

Engraving by Camille Flammarion
in his book, *L'atmosphère : météorologie populaire*
Paris, 1888

But "globe" (from the Latin word *globus*)
actually means anything spherical.

Even though the ancient philosophers
considered "Earthly things" square,
they knew the earth was spherical.

But they also saw the Heavens as spherical
(actually a number of concentric spheres).

The Latin word Dee used, *MUNDUS*, can mean either
"world" or "dome," as in the Heavenly dome.

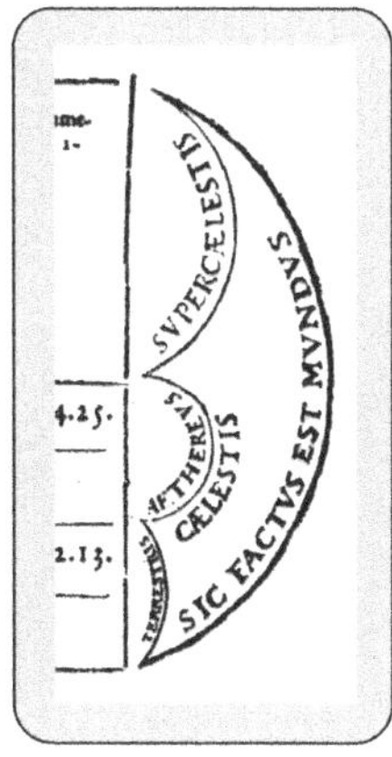

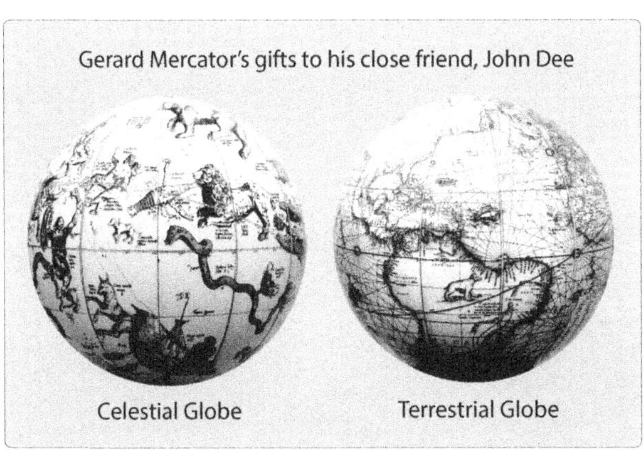

Gerard Mercator's gifts to his close friend, John Dee

In 1552, when John Dee returned home
to England after studying in the Louvain,
he brought with him two
24-inch diameter globes.

They were a gift from his best friend,
the famous cartographer Gerard Mercator.

One was an earth globe and the other
was a celestial globe, depicting the
bright stars and constellations.

One globe was Earth. The other was Heaven.

The overall philosophical design of the theater was to connect
Heaven and Earth. And there's one word that's appropriate for both:
Globe.

WHAT ABOUT CIRCLES 2, 3, AND 5?

It's obvious that Circle 4 is the circumcircle of the white square.

And it was relatively easy to discover that the areas of Circles 1, 6, and 7 are in the proportion of 1:2:3.

But what about Circles 2, 3, and 5? Were they only inserted to disguise the geometric interrelationships of the other circles?

Not likely. Including superfluous things was not John Dee's style.

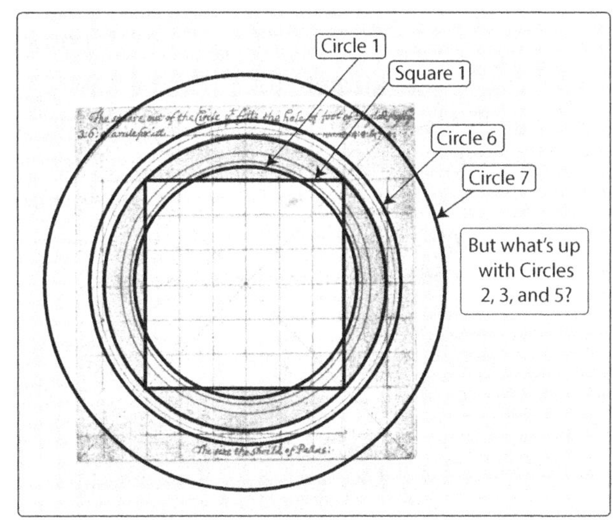

John Dee (ca. 1599)
learned from Leon Battista Alberti (ca. 1486),
who learned from Vitruvius (ca. 25 BC) that:

"Beauty is that reasoned harmony of all the parts within a body, so that nothing may be added, taken away, or altered, but for the worse."

(Leon Battista Alberti, *On The Art of Building in Ten Books*, translated by Rykwert, Leach, and Tavernor, Book IV, Chapter 11:2, (Cambridge MA and London, The MIT Press, 1997)

Alberti had a word for this elegant correspondence of all parts to the whole:
concinnitas,
which is pronounced con-chin-ee-tass.
(from the Latin word *concinnus*, meaning "skillfully put together.")

It took a little deeper thinking to find out what Dee was trying to say with Circles 2, 3, 5. But what I found was a fascinating geometric coincidence involving shape, number and, strangely enough, music.

Here's the "really short" summary of Dee's discovery

Draw Square 1 and Circle 1 with equal areas.
Draw Circle 4, which is the circumcircle of Square 1.
Draw Circle 6, which has twice the area of Circle 1.
Two "tones" out beyond Circle 4 brings you to Circle 6!!!!

Don't be concerned if this doesn't make sense. You're probably be wondering, "What the heck is a "tone"?

This only the "really short" summary. We'll walk through it slowly, thrice more: once using percentages, once using actual areas and once on the piano.

"Tone" is simply 9/8

The idea of "tone" can be most easily seen in the "greatest and most perfect harmony," made famous by Nicomachus (ca. 125 AD) and Boethius (ca. 525 AD).

Notice that the numbers 6 and 12 each relate to **three** other numbers.

But 8 and 9 only relate to **two** other numbers!

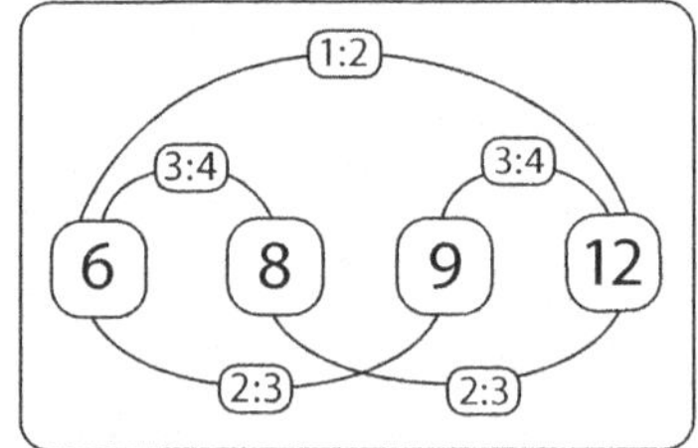

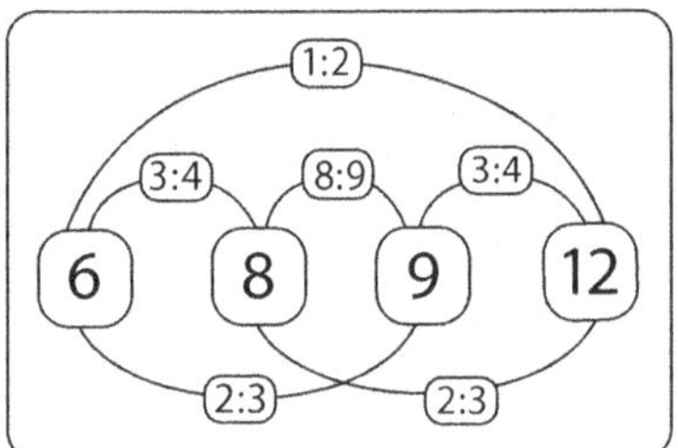

The "missing ratio" here is 8:9.

The Greeks didn't like fractions. They preferred to deal with whole numbers. They saw 8:9 as 9:8, in the sense that "nine is one more than eight."

Their name for 9:8 is *epogdoon*, which reflects this thinking. *Epi* means "one more than" and *ogdoon* means "eight."

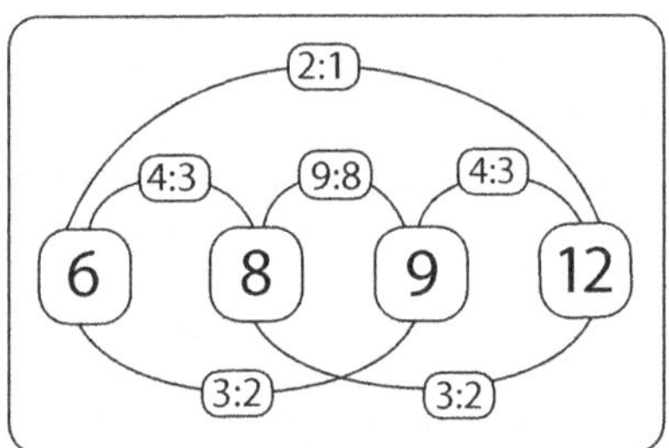

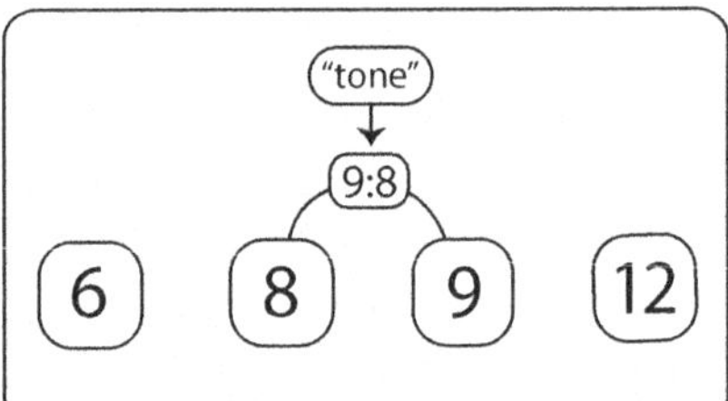

There are 8 tones in an octave of tones.
Thus, each tone is 1/8 of an octave.
So, 8/8 (a whole octave) plus 1/8 (one tone) makes 9/8.

The "longer" story of Dee's discovery (seen in terms of "percentages")

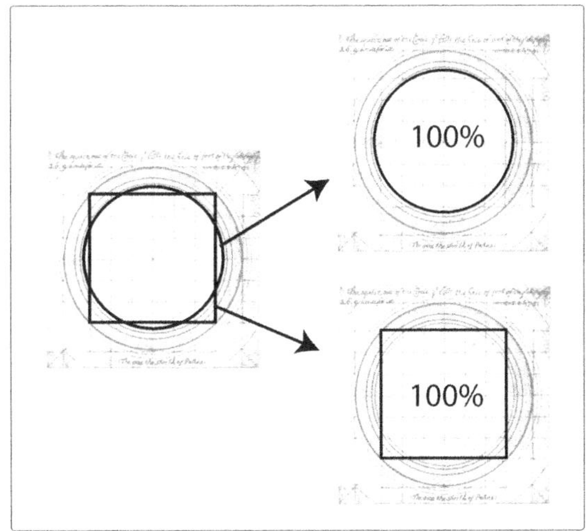

Let's start with
Circle 1 and Square 1,
which are equal in area.

Then, concentrically draw Circle 6, with an area twice the size of Circle 1.

(This is easy to do, as Circle 6's radius is simply √2, or 1.4142, times the radius of Circle 1.)

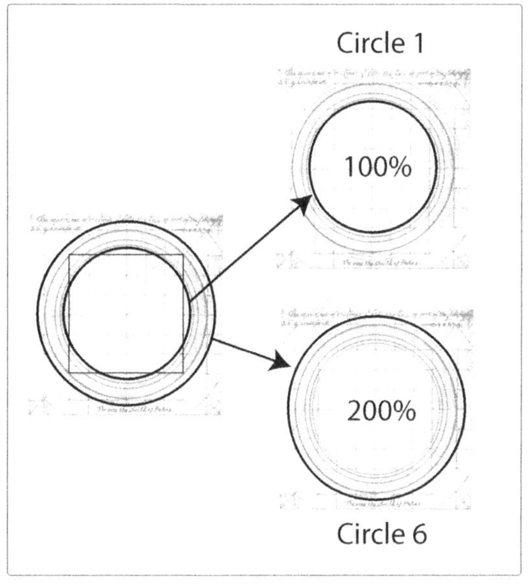

If we consider Circle 1, to be "our measuring standard" or "100%," then Circle 6 has an area of 200%.

Remember that amount: 200%. As we proceed, it will become our "target."

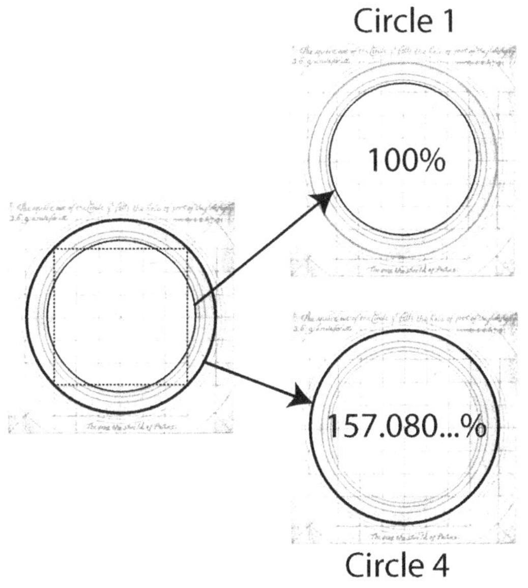

Circle 4, the circumcircle around Square 1, will be 157.08 % larger than Square 1

(or Square 1's "twin-in-area," Circle 1).

Numberwise,
157.08% represents how much larger π is, when compared with the number 2.

(3.1416 ÷ 2 = 1.5708)

Let's shift gears and use **Circle 4** as a starting point.

(Remember, Circle 4 is the circumcircle of the 36 by 36 unit white square.)

We're going to "expand" Circle 4" twice by a musical "tone."

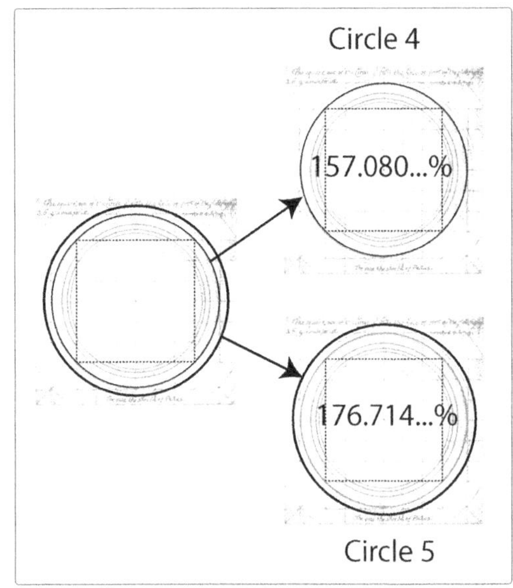

As there are eight notes in the octave, each note is 1/8 of the octave.

To increase a number by a "tone" we multiply it by the epogdoon, or 9/8, or **1.125**

So, to expand Circle 4, which has an area of 157.08%, we multiply it by 1.125. The result is 176.714%.

And guess what! This is the size of **Circle 5**!

Next, we'll expand Circle 5 by a "tone." Multiplying 176.714% by 1.125, the result is 198.803%.

This **198.803%** is essentially 199%. You can't get much closer to our target of **200%**!!!

(Remember, our **200% target** was Circle 6, which has twice the area of Circle 1.)

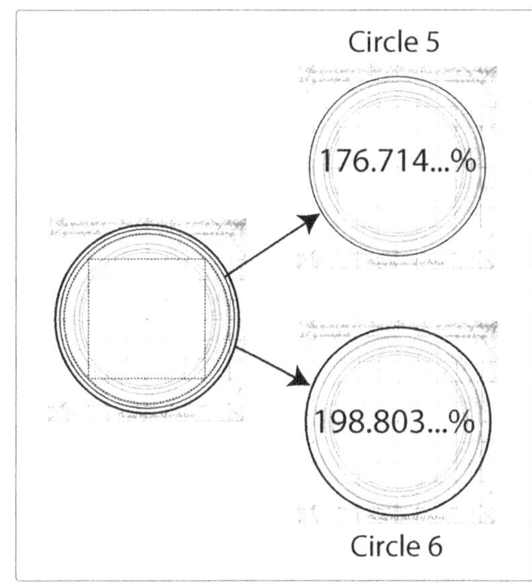

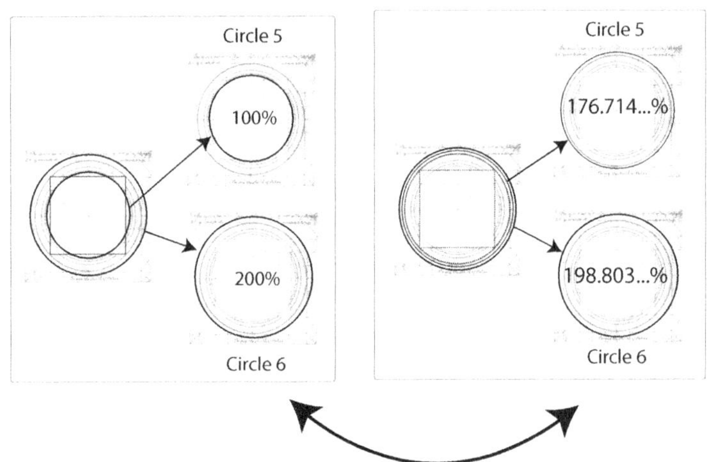

These two results are within 1% of each other.

Comparing 199% to 200% means were only "off target" by about one half of a percentage point.

If you saw new suit with a price tag of $199 on it, and someone asked you how much it cost, you would probably say, "200 bucks."

Seen another way, 198.803 compared to 200 is like 99.4 compared to 100, or 99.4%

(Even Ivory soap doesn't get any purer than that.)

It's just an amazing coincidence.... and it delighted Dee

I'm not suggesting that "two tones" beyond Circle 1 is *exactly equal* to Circle 6 (indeed, 198.08 is not exactly 200).

And the discrepancy was not caused by my "rounding off" some of the numbers involved, like π or √2.

The closeness of 198.803% and 200% here is simply a **mathematical coincidence**. It's one that Dee most likely discovered on his own. And he was thrilled enough to use as a centerpiece of his geometrical architectural masterwork.

Dee plants big fat clues about these"two tones." To see them, instead of percentages, let's look at the actual numbers involved.

The same "longer" story of Dee's discovery (this time, seen in terms of actual dimensions)

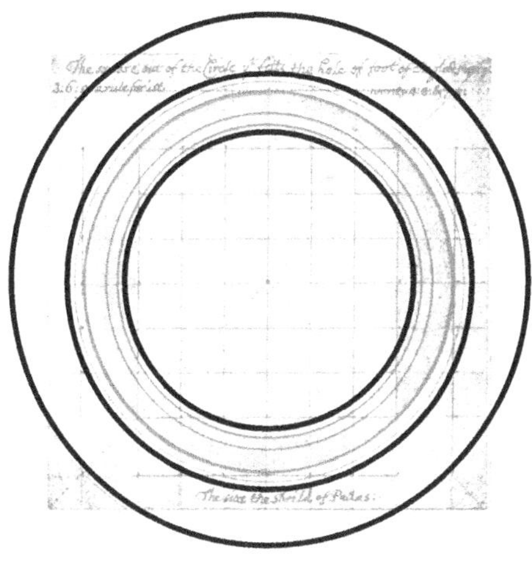

Circles 1,6, and 7 are "echoes"

Just to review, the "big picture" idea here is the doubling and tripling of Circle 1.

Circle is 36 units tall by 36 units wide, or 1296 square units. It's twin, Circle 1, also has an area of 1296 square units.

Circle 6 contains twice the area of Circle 1, an area of 2592 square units. And Circle 7, which is three times the area of Circle 1, has an area of 3888 square units.

When seen alone, these 3 circles suggest radiating sound, or three concentric waves emanating from a pebble tossed in a still pond.

This time, instead of doubling **Circle 1**, let's just increase it by a "tone."

1296 square units times 1.125 makes 1458 square units. This is **Circle 2**.

Next, let's increase Circle 2 by a "tone." 1458 square units times 1.125 makes 1640.25 square units. This is **Circle 3.**

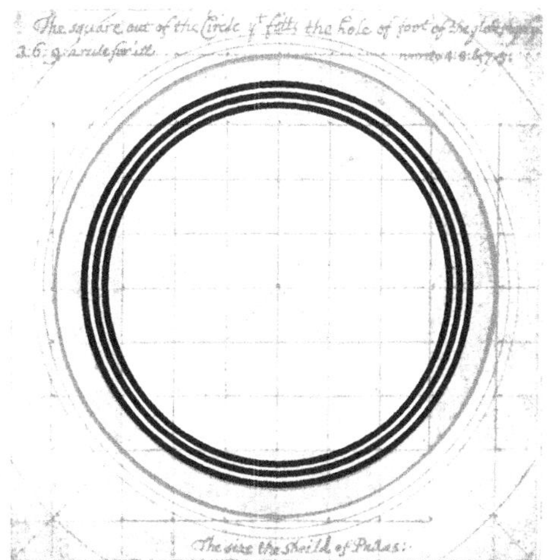

Circle 1 increased by a "tone" = Circle 2
Circle 2 increaded by a "tone" = Circle 3

There is yet another instance of "increasing by two tones," involving Circles 4, 5, and 6

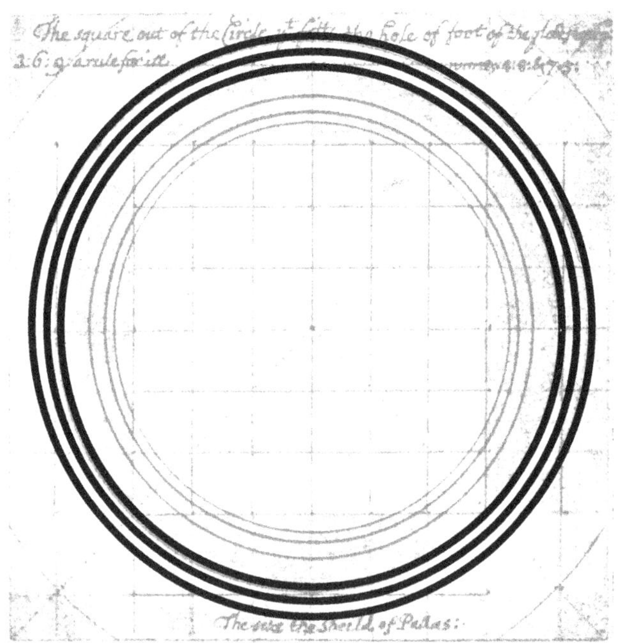

Circle 4 increased by a "tone" = Circle 5
Circle 5 increaded by a "tone" = Circle 6

This "increasing by two tones" is the same thing Dee also does starting with **Circle 4,** (which is the circumcircle of the 36 x 36 unit white square.)

Circle 4's area, 2034.822... times 1.125 makes 2290.226, which is **Circle 5**

Next, Circle 5 times 1.125 makes 2576.504... This is not exactly is equal to **Circle 6,** which we found earlier was 2592.

But it's pretty darn close.

2576.504... is 99.4% of 2502 (as we just saw when reviewing the percentages).

In other words, Dee is increasing **Circle 1** by two tones (making **Circles 2 and 3**) as a CLUE that he wants the reader to increase the circumcircle (that round-tabletop, black, thickest circle) or **Circle 4** by two tones (making **Circles 5 and 6**).

And when the reader gets to Circle 6, he realizes:
Hey, that's just about the same size as the "doubling of Circle 1."

In short, **Circle 6 is involved in two different patterns of growth:** the "doubling of Circle 1" and the "two-tone increase from Circle 4."

Here's another graphic way of expressing what Dee is trying to tell us about his very heart of the Globe theater.

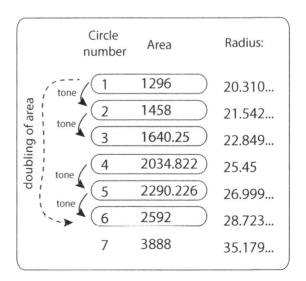

Circle number	Area	Radius:
1	1296	20.310...
2	1458	21.542...
3	1640.25	22.849...
4	2034.822	25.45
5	2290.226	26.999...
6	2592	28.723...
7	3888	35.179...

The same "longer story" in terms of differences of radii

Just looking at the playing-card-sized illustration, it's not easy to visually compare the various circles by area or by radius length.

A more revealing way to see the pattern is to look at the **differences** between the neighboring radii.

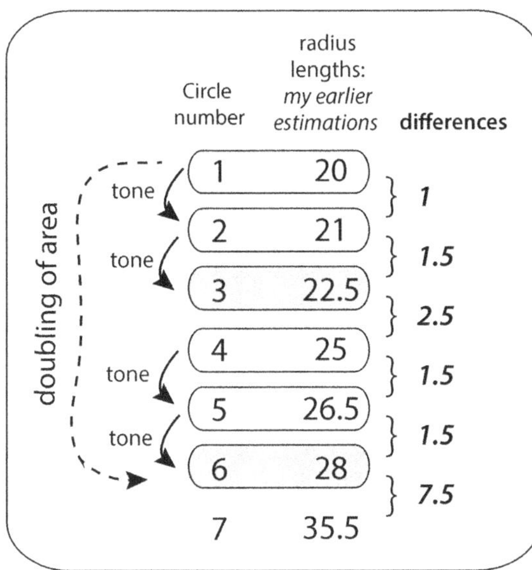

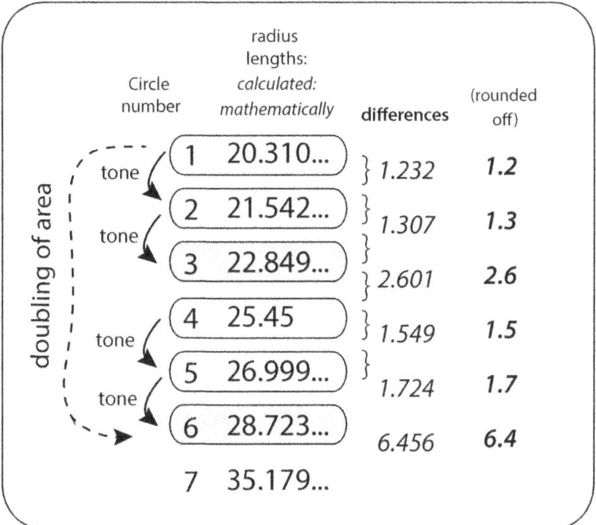

Explanation of any discrepancies

There are several possible reasons that my **visual** estimations vary slightly from my **mathematical** calculations.

1 The illustration is diminutive, the height of a playing card, with units (between pinpricks) only about 1/16 of an inch.

2 This may be "copy" of the original artwork, reproduced as faithfully as the reproducer knew how.

3 While working out all the details, it's most likely Dee originally drew this larger. Then he reduced it so it could be used as the "close-up" plan, thereby keeping the "overview" plan to a reasonable size.

4 Dee was forcing us to do the math. He wasn't concerned that "the vulgar" wouldn't fully comprehend his work.

But the most important thing is:
the pattern, the rhythm,
the interrelationships between the 7 circles.

Centuries after it was drawn, Dee's music
of the seven circles can still be heard.

Boiling John Dee's discovery into one sentence

The following premise might seem obvious, but it's important to clarify it before we boil John Dee's wondrous discovery into one sentence:

That is, if the area of a circle equals the area of a square, doubling the area of the circle can be seen in 3 ways:
"two circles,"
"square plus circle,"
or "two squares."

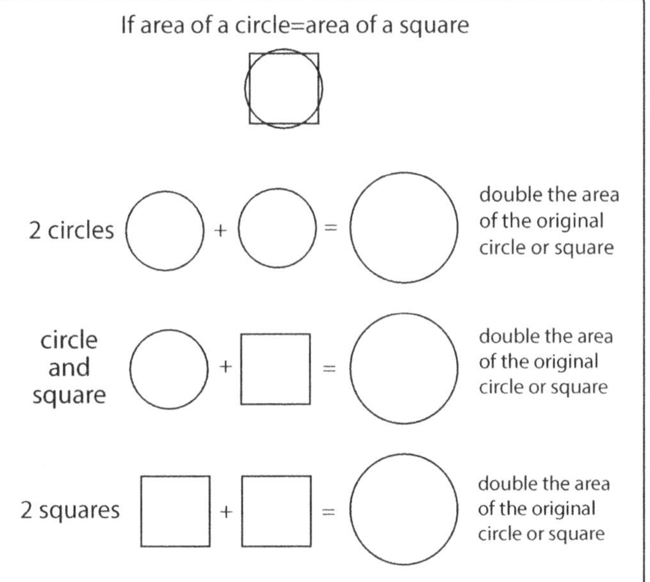

So one sentence, here's what Dee is trying to tell us:

Doubling the area of a square almost exactly equals the area of that square's circumcircle raised by two "tones."

Or as one simple graphic:

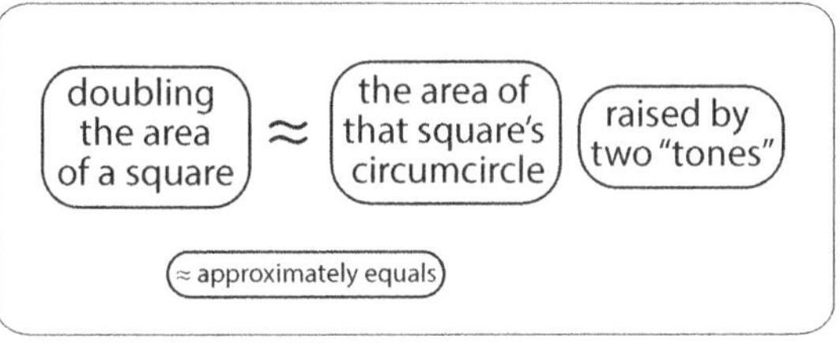

Boiling John Dee's discovery into one equation

Here's how this looks mathematically. That 99.4% is pretty darn close to 100%

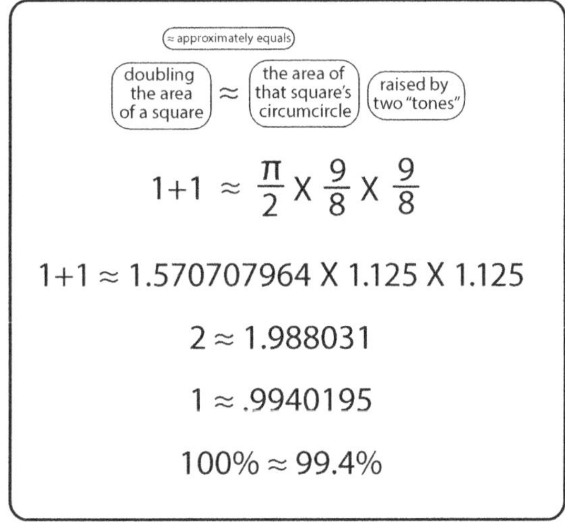

Conclusion

These 7 seemingly random circles tell several different geometric stories, but they are challenging to see, because Dee has grouped them all together

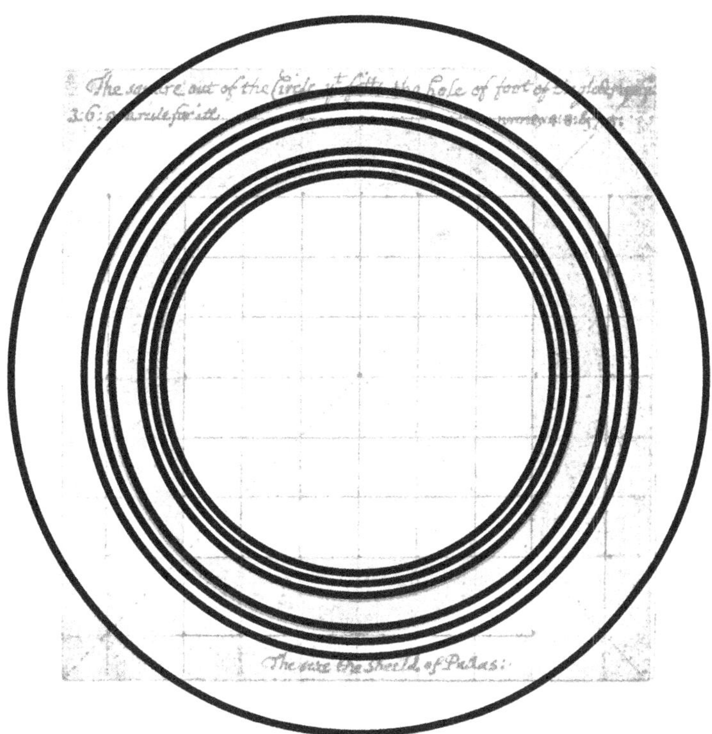

Dee's Seven Circles

SHHHH....
ITT'S IS A SECRET

The clue that helped me realize that
"Circle 1 doubled makes Circle 6" and
"Circle 1 tripled makes Circle 7" is the
caption written at the top of the card:
"3:6:9 is a rule for itt"

3	1	100%
6	2	200%
9	3	300%

As we've seen, the ratios 3:6:9
can be reduced to **1:2:3**, which is an
expression of doubling and tripling.
This might also be seen as "100%:200%:300%"

In a creative way,
this "1:2:3" rhythm can also be seen in the word "**itt**."
This is a peculiar way to way to spell the word "**it**."

This "**itt**" mirrors, in sight and sound, the word
"**fitts**," which is used in the first line of the caption.

The *Oxford English Dictionary* shows that the Old English
spelling of "**fitt**" (for the word "**fit**") was used in Elizabethan times.

But the last time the Old English spelling of "**itt**" (for the word "**it**")
was used, was back in 1400. And then it was spelled "**itte**."
(The year 1400 would be about 200 years before the time of the 1599 Globe.)

This all smelled like a "clever-Dee-clue" to me.

The lowercase letter "**i**" is essentially
a vertical line with a dot on top.
An uppercase letter "**I**" is just a vertical line.

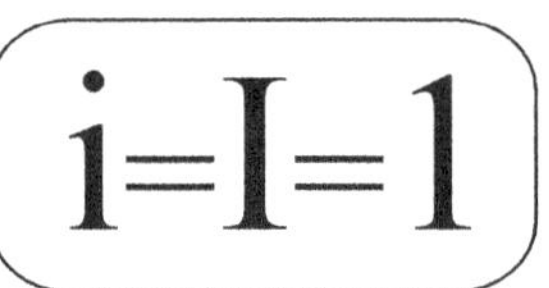

Ignoring serifs, both the lowercase"**i**" and
uppercase "**I**" are pretty much identical
with the Arabic numeral for one, that is, "**1**."

i	1
t	t(wo)
t	t(hree)

Seeing the "**i**" as a one,
suddenly it became apparent
that "**tt**" represented the
numbers "**t**wo and **t**hree."

To express all
this visually:

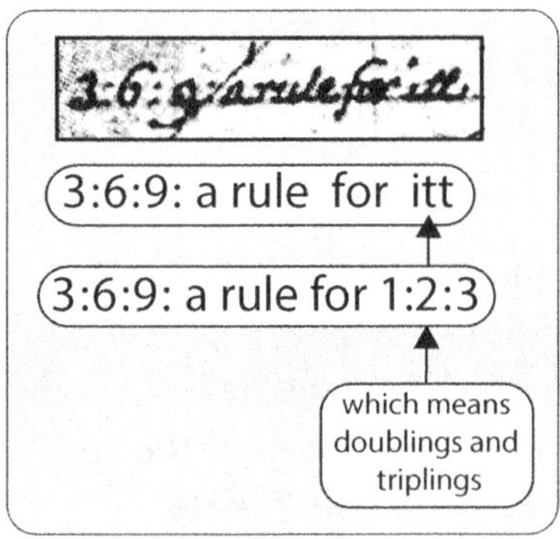

Would Dee actually hidden a clue like this? You betcha.

In the *Monas Hieroglyphica*, Dee tells us that he likes to use three secret coding techniques:

"Gematria" (a number code in which certain letters represent certain numbers)

"Notariacon" (the first letters of the phrase are combined to spell a new word, sort of like an acronym)

"Tzyruph" (certain letters, jumbled, form different words)

Having seen examples of these in my previous studies of Dee's works, I was not surprised to find one in this pithy caption to a brilliantly conceived geometrical puzzle.

This clue is part "Gematria" and part "Notariacon." Though not a full "Gematria" number code, it does associate numbers with letters. Though not a full example of Notariacon (**o**ne, **t**wo, **t**hree should be "**ott**"), two of the three letters ("**t**wo" and "**t**hree") do act as acronyms.

Dee amused himself by finding ways to put things before the readers' eyes, yet have them invisible to most. Dee was among the best, but wasn't just him. Clever concealment was part of the Elizabethan cultural milieu. (If you don't believe me, study the puns of Shakespeare or read *Elizabethan Silent Language*, by Mary E. Hazard.)

GLYPHICA. 28

CORONIS) adorant; dicentes: Dignus es Domine accipere GLORIAM & HONOREM, & VIRTVTEM: QVIA, TV, CREASTI OMNIA: Et propter VOLVNTATEM TVAM SVNT: ET CREATA SVNT. AMEN, DICIT LITERA QVARTA, Δ:

Cui, DEVS, Voluntatem Habilitatemque dedit, Diuinum hoc Mysterium, æternis Sic consignare Literarum Monimentis: Laboresq́, hosce Suos, placidissimè absoluere, Ianuarij 25: die eiusdem 13, Inchoatos:

An. 1564. Antwerpia.

IN TELLECTVS IVDICAT VERITATEM

Contektus ad Punctum.

Vulgaris, Hic, Oculus CALIGABIT, DIFFIDETQVE *plurimùm.*

ANTVERPIÆ

EXCVDEBAT GVLIELMVS SILVIVS, REGIVS TYPOGRAPHVS: PRIDIE CALEND. APRILIS. AN. 1564.

Final page of Dee's 1564
Monas Hieroglyphica

A similar clue in the Monas Hieroglyphica

This "itt"=123 clue is similar to the clue in the emblem on the final page of the *Monas Hieroglyphica*,

Inside a circle Dee writes:
"**InTeLlectus iudicat veritatem**,"
meaning
"**Let intellect be the judge of truth**."

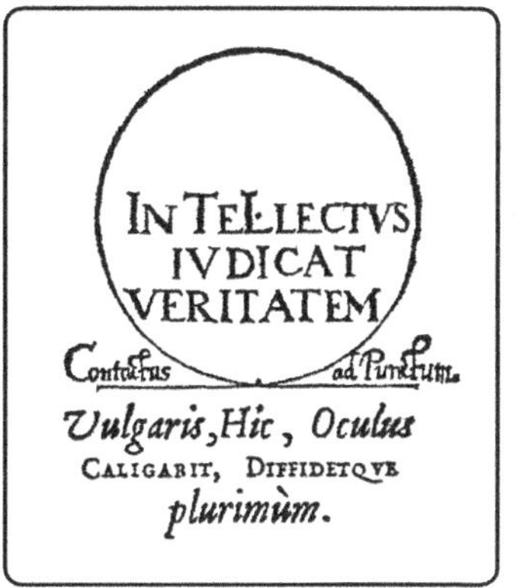

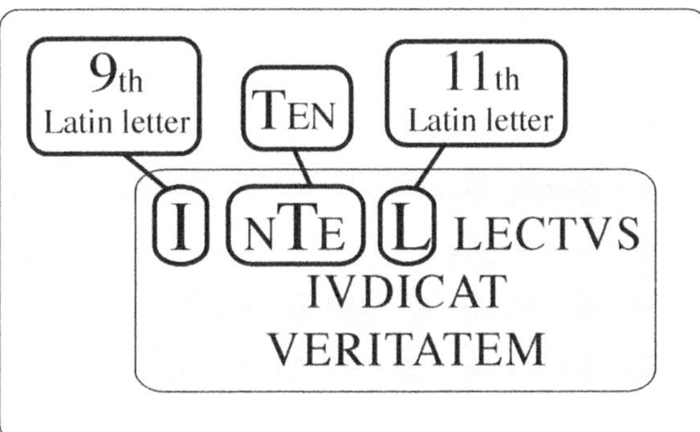

Notice that the only large capital letters are "I, T, and L."
Dee is cryptically expressing the numbers 9, 10, 11.

In the letters, "InTeL," the "I"= 9., the "L"=11,
And "in between" are the letters "Ten."

This sequence is at the heart of Consummata, as
9 is The Transpalindromizer (9 Wave),
10 is our Base Number, and
11 is The Palindromizer (11 Wave).

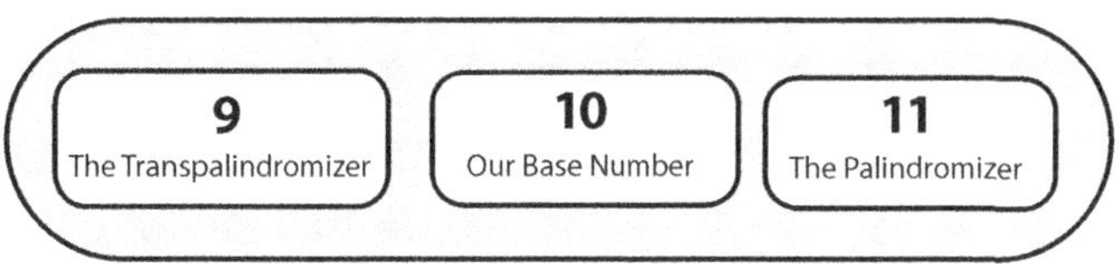

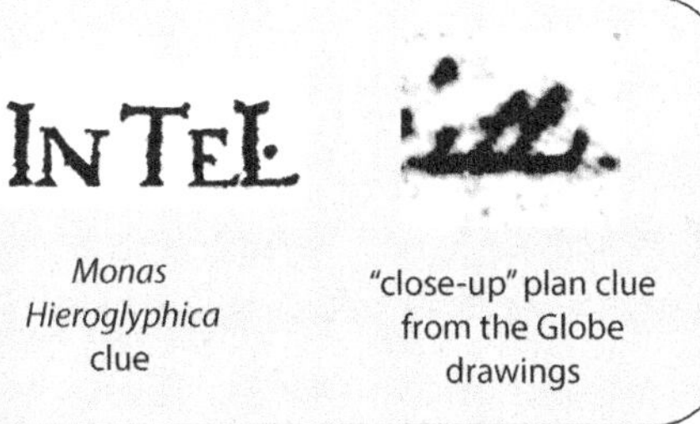

Monas Hieroglyphica clue

"close-up" plan clue from the Globe drawings

Though deciphered differently, these clues are amazingly similar.
Both clues are on captions to geometric drawings
Both clues involve a group of three letters. (ITL and itt).
Both clues share first two letters, and in the same order, the "i" and one "t."

Dee conceived of the "ITL" clue before 1564.
Perhaps he had "Monas on the mind" when he later planted the "itt" clue.

Maybe he's even hinting at a connection here:
"**Let intellect be the judge of the truth**" of my 7 Circle plan.

But was actually another (even bigger) clue that actually tipped me off that "itt" was "1:2:3"

To the far right of "***3:6:9, a rule for itt***," seemingly connected by a row of pin-pricks, is written "***varies 4:8: & 7·5:***" What could that mean?

Interestingly, among these numbers, we can find 4 + 8 = 12, and 7 + 5 = 12, (just as 3 + 9 = 12).

The number 12 is an important number in the chart, as the width of two white grid squares is 12 units.

But there are no plus signs shown; only proportion signs and a dot. There must be something more going on.

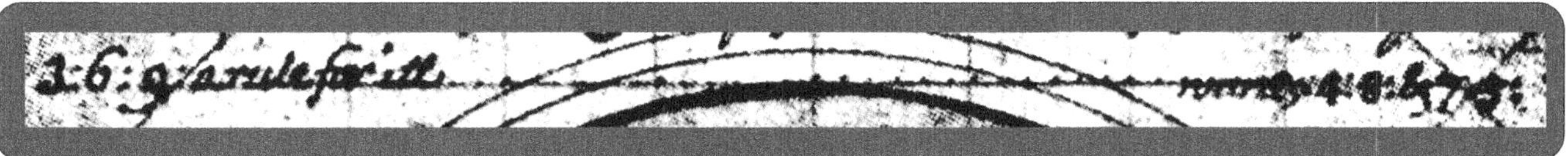

The "**varies 4:8**" part seems to suggests the ratio 4:8, which is 1:2, a "variation" of the 3:6 ratio written on the left edge of the card.

But that doesn't explain the last bit, "***: & 7·5:***"

It occurred to me that this "number phrase" was an inventory of the single-digit numbers. In other words, the phrase "**3:6:9: a rule for it.......varies 4:8: & 7·5:**" includes the numbers **3, 4, 5, 6, 7, 8** , and **9**.

Only the digits **1** and **2** are missing.

But 1 and 2 can be easily found ... in many ways

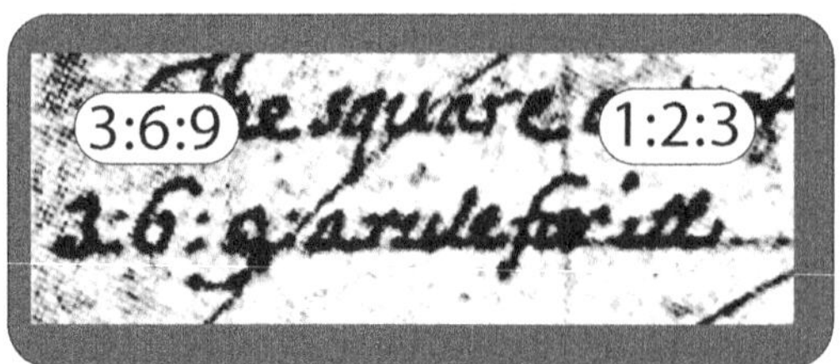

As we've seen, they are cryptically expressed by the word "**itt**"= **1:2:3**.

If Dee already has the numeral 3 in his "sentence of numbers," why did he need the second "**t**" in "**itt**"?
It seems as thought that would be duplicating that numeral 3?
Well, if he had just written "**it**" for "**1 and 2**," it wouldn't be much of a riddle.

When you see something that's "not quite right" in Dee's work, it's never a mistake. It's always an important clue. Dee was a perfectionist.

For example, in one of his number puzzles in the "Thus the World was Created" chart of the *Monas Hieroglyphica*, Dee made the number "2" look like a printer's error. But Dee's "intentional error" turns out to be a huge clue.

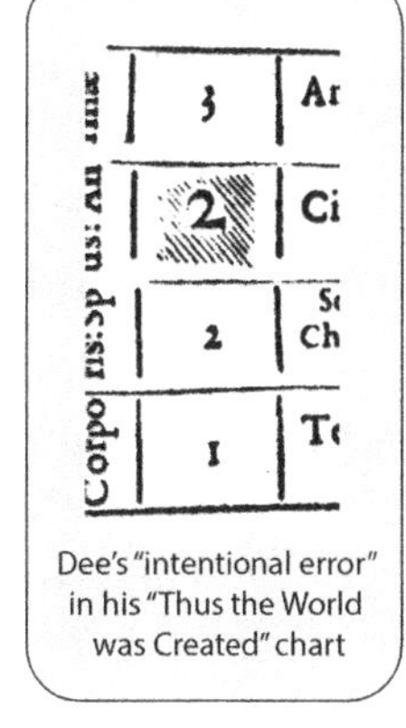
Dee's "intentional error" in his "Thus the World was Created" chart

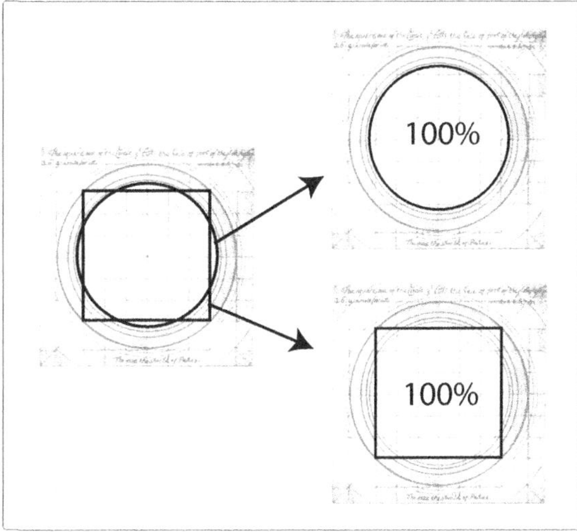

Besides, those "missing digits," 1 and 2 are being shouted loudly by the whole diagram!

The very concept of "squaring the circle," is that "1 area" is applied to "2 very different shapes." In short, "100% +100% = 200%."

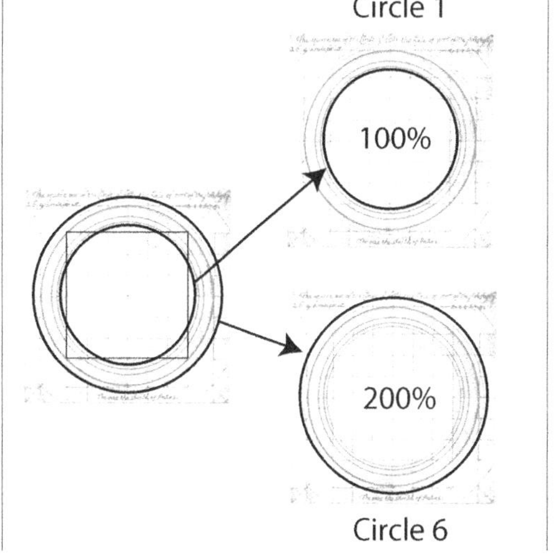

Yet another a geometric expression of 1:2 is the way Circle 6 is a "doubling" of the area of Circle 1. Or 100% x 2 = 200%

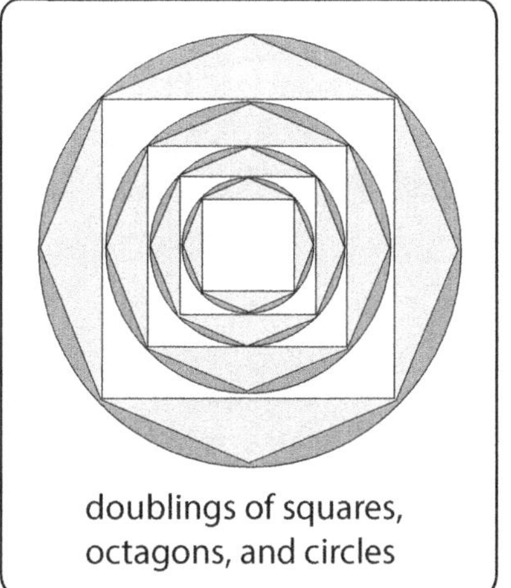
doublings of squares, octagons, and circles

Moreover, the ratio 1:2 is implied by all the "doublings" of the squares, octagons, and circles we saw in the "overview" plan, which organically grows from the "close-up" plan.

What's the big deal about a full inventory of numbers?

First of all, from this inventory "**1, 2, 3, 4, 5, 6, 7, 8, 9**" (and also 0, our symbol of "nothingness") all the numbers can be made.

Every number, in the hundreds, thousands, millions, even gazillions, is made from this merry band of single digits.

...78395938237616561719304957263485238457986459409274508729587168741235975626 73...

Secondly, look at the order in which these numbers are presented:
3, 6, 9, 4, 8, 7, 5,
The prime numbers
7 and 5 come at the very end.

This is an echo of the "birth of number, which leads to the formation of Metamorphosis. Note how the primes, 5 and 7, come at the **end** of each series.

The visible numbers on the geometric Globe drawing

3, 6, 9, 4, 8, 7, 5

1, 2, 3, 4, 6, 8, 9, 5, 7

The "birth of number" leading to "Metamorphosis"

How "3, 6, 9, 4, 8, 7, 5" echoes Metamorphosis

Remember how we saw growth of number deriving from "symmetrical twoness,"
(That is, 2, 4, 8, 16, 32...)

And a different growth from "asymmetrical threeness,"
(That is, 3, 9, 27, 81...)

2:4:8:16...

3:9:27:81...

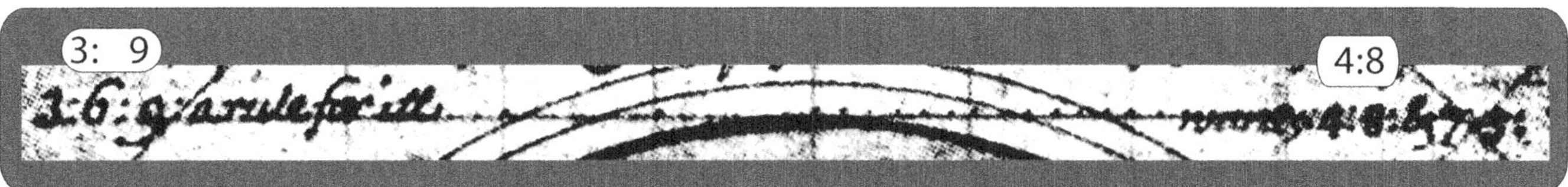

Well, here, in the phrase,
"3:6:9: a rule for it.......varies 4:8:& 7·5:"
Dee has included the ratios "**4:8**" and "**3:9**"

(By putting a "6:" in the middle of "3:6:9"
Dee has somewhat disguised the "3:9" ratio.)

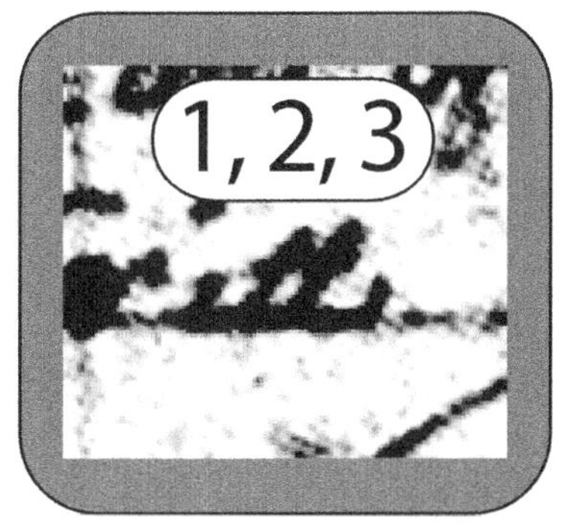

In the "**itt**" clue, Dee has included the three "superstars" that begin the growth of numbers: **1, 2,** and **3**.

To Dee "**1**" represented all numbers, or the "whole" from which all numbers flowed.

The multiples of "**2**" include half of all the numbers in the universe.

And the multiples of "**3**" include a third of all the numbers in the universe.

Admittedly, the sequence "3, 6, 9, 1, 2, 3, 4, 8, 9, 7, and 5" is *not* exactly the same as "1, 2, 3, 4, 6, 8, 9, 5, 7."

But there are enough similarities, that anyone who understands Metamorphosis will see the correlation.

Remember, Dee's "Thus the World Was Created" chart summarizes his entire mathematical cosmology.

And in the Supercelestial area of the chart, embracing the word "Metamorphosis," are all the single digits: 1, 2, 3, 4, 5, 6, 7, 8.

And cryptically, just above them all is the number 9, which the Greeks called "Horizon,"just before vast expanse of multiple-digit numbers.

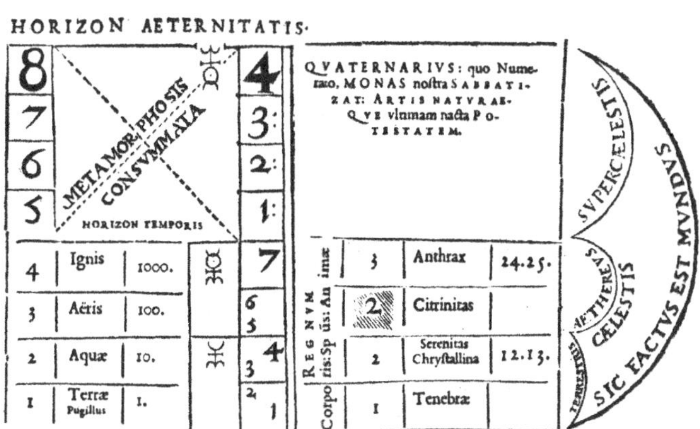

In short, as Dee's caption,

"3:6:9: a rule for it.......varies 4:8:& 7·5:"

expresses the "Birth of Number" in Metamorphosis.

Thus, it also incorporates all the magic of the Metamorphosis sequence.

Remember, multiplying the "essences" of the "Birth of Numbers" leads to 12, 24, 72, 360, 2520,..., numbers in which the primes are organized in perfect symmetry!

But there is still another aspect of Dee's mathematical cosmology hidden in "3:6:9: a rule for itt.......varies 4:8:& 7·5:"

And oddly enough, the biggest clue is: the colons. Let me explain:

Besides ending with the primes, 7 and 5, the Globe caption sequence contains the digits 1, 2, 3, 4.

They are in the proper order and they are precisely in the *middle* of the sequence "3, 6, 9, **1, 2, 3, 4**, 8, 7, 5."

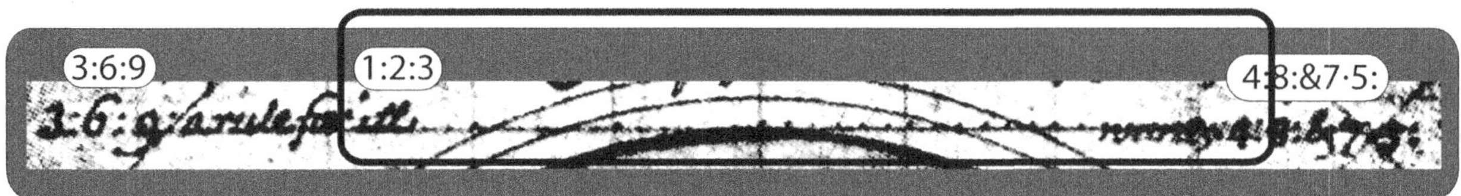

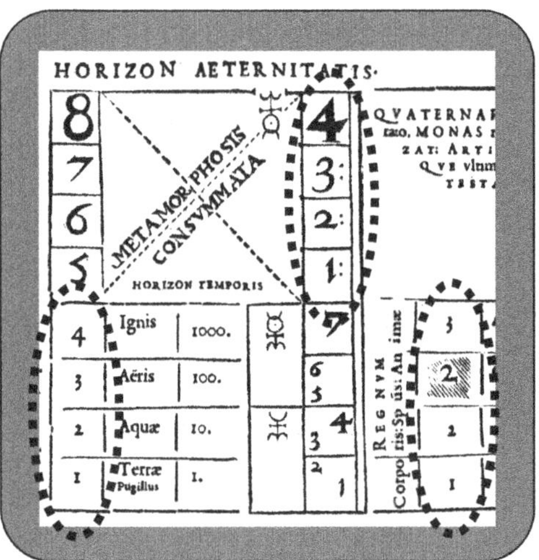

This sequence is of major importance in Dee's cosmology. He shows it in three places in his "Thus the World Was Created" chart.

One of them is actually Dee's Artificial Quaternary, (1, 2, 3, 2), which relates closely to the Pythagorean Quaternary, (1, 2, 3, 4).

In the top part of the chart, in the 1, 2, 3, 4 sequence, there are colons following the digits 1, 2, and 3, but not after the digit 4.

Dee is cryptically suggesting the proportion **1:2:3:4**, which, visually speaking, is the Pythagorean tetractys.

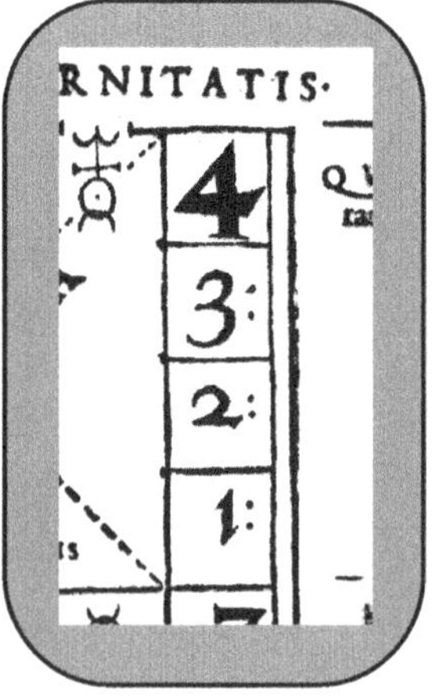

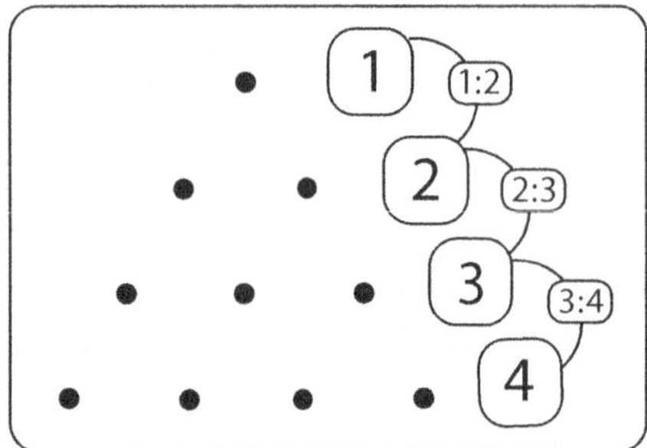

And as we've seen, the relationships between the four rows of the Pythagorean tetractys are the harmonies **1:2**, **2:3**, and **3:4**.

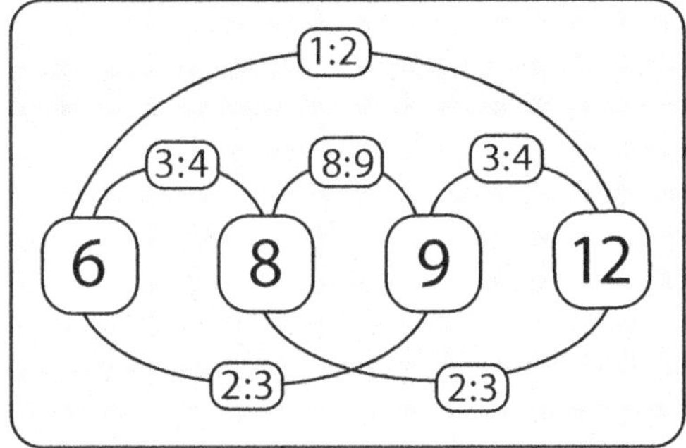

And Nichomachus saw how these ratios can be found in the "greatest and most perfect ratio" involving the numbers 6, 8, 9, 12.

And of course in the midst of Nichomachus' ratios is 9/8 or "tone," which is a major aspect of the interrelationships of the "7 concentric circles" of the Globe diagram.

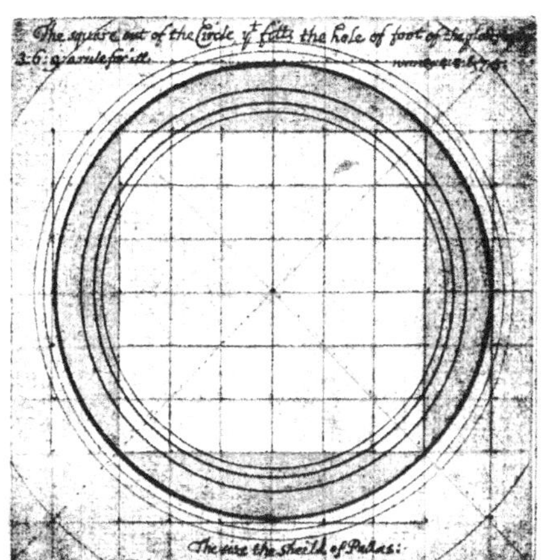

You're probably getting the picture. These Globe diagrams and the "Thus the World Was Created" chart are two slightly different ways of expressing the same mathematical cosmology: The harmony Dee saw in shape and in number.

When I first started researching Dee's cosmology, I wondered if Dee might have known about the use of the colon to denote proportion. Was it invented before or after Dee's time?

The best book on the subject: Florian Cajori's *A History of Mathematical Notation*. And guess what it said on page 168?

The "**first usage of the colon**" in math was credited to **John Dee**.

Not only did he know about it, he invented it!

John Dee and the first use of the colon in math

Cajori thinks the use of the notation started off out as "rhetorical marks used in the text" as shown in the bottom right of this excerpt from the 1570 first English translation of Euclid's *Elements* (Book 5, Definition 7).

conuerſion of proportion, and of ſome euerſion of proportion. Likewyſe in numbers, as 9.to 6, ſo 12.to 8. eyther proportion is ſeſquialtera: the exceſſe of 9.the antecedent of the firſt proportion aboue 6. the conſequent of the ſame is 3: the exceſſe of 12. the antecedent of the ſecond proportion aboue 8.the conſequent of the ſame,is 4: now cōpare the antecedent of the firſt proportion 9. as antecedēt to 3. the exceſſe therof aboue 6. the conſequēt, as to his conſequent, likewiſe compare 12. the antecedent of the ſecond proportion as antecedent to 4.the exceſſe therof aboue 8.the conſequent,as to his conſequent: ſo ſhall your numbers be in thys order by conuerſion of proportion : as 9.to 3: ſo 12.to 4: for either proportion is triple.

9 . 6 : 12 . 8
9 . 3 : 12 . 4

First ever use of the colon to denote proportion, by John Dee, Book 5, Definition 7, First English translation of Euclid's Elements.

uent,as to his conſequent: ſo ſhall
f proportion : as 9.to 3: ſo 12.to 4:

Dee's text showing the colon

Just as in the caption of the Globe diagram, the proportion marks are used in the context of a sentence.

Dee is merely citing an example of proportion here, but it's interesting that his example involves the numbers 3, 6, and 9, and he is comparing them to the numbers involving 4 and 8.

This is very similar to what's going on in the Globe caption, which starts off with 3:6:9 and proceeds to 4:8.

9 . 6 : 12 . 8
9 . 3 : 12 . 4

Dee's first use of the colon in math

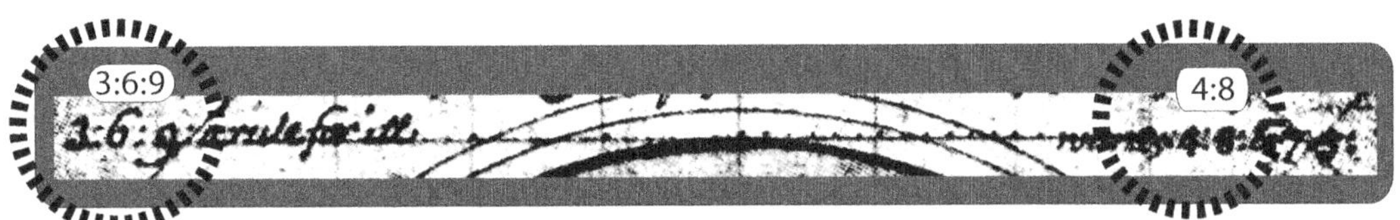

Incidentally, Dee's (:) colon clue in the "Thus the World Was Created" chart is disguised by the visual busy-ness of the chart.

But it's actually easier for us moderns to see the clue than it would be for Elizabethans. Why? Because John Dee had just invented it, so it wasn't in common use yet.

(Dee would be amused that the colon is now used as the eyes of a smiley face emoticon :)

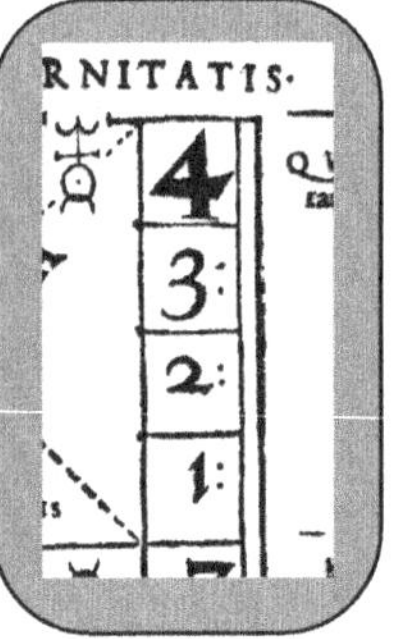

But notice in the "Below" half of the chart, Dee has no colons, and only has the digits 1 through 7, omitting digits 8 or 9.

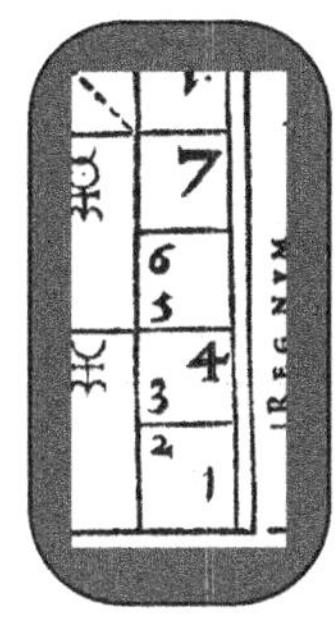

He labels the "Below" half of the chart the "Aetheric Celestial" (the wandering stars: Sun, Moon, and five planets) and the "Terrestrial" (the sub-lunar realm or the Earthly things).

The digits 1 to 7 in the "Below" half of his chart = 7 circles = orbits of the 7 planets = 2520

Dee's "close-up plan" and his "overview" plan for the Globe theater are each **floor plans**. The floor is "earth. Terra firma.

And the "close-up plan" has seven circles.

(Just like the digits 1 through 7 in the "Below" half of his chart shown above)

Dee loved seven circles. Although each of the 7 circles on the "close-up" plan have different areas, they each have 360 degrees, making a total of 2520 degrees. (360 x 7 = 2520)

Remember, 2520 is a key number in Dee's Metamorphosis sequence. It's the lowest number divisible by all the single digits. And 2520 is a reflective mate of 252, John Dee's Magisterial Number.

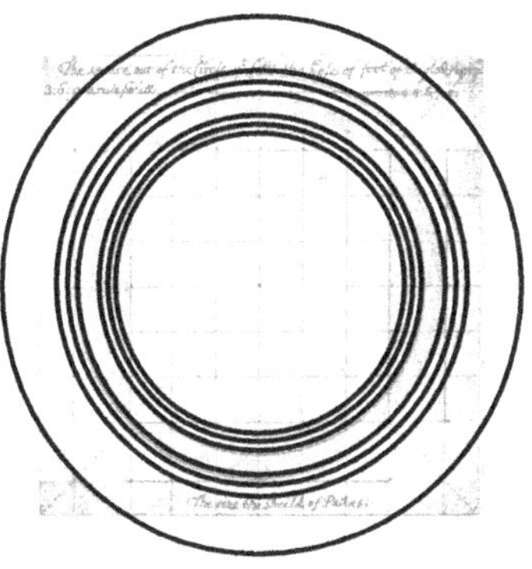

Dee's Seven Circles

Seven same-sized circles form closest-packing-of-circles

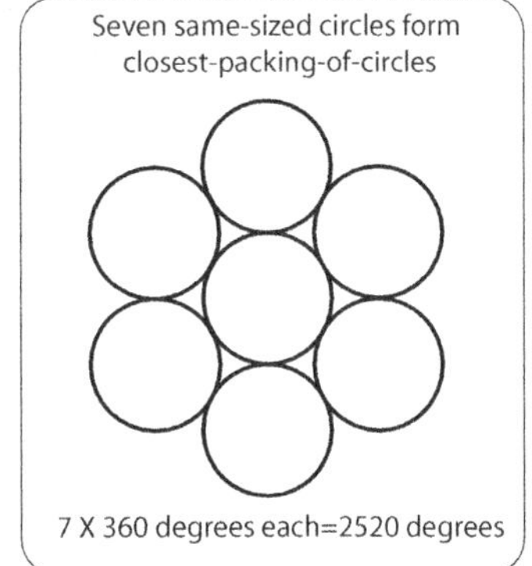

7 X 360 degrees each=2520 degrees

If the 7 circles were all the same size, it would be an expression of the 6-around-1 "closest packing" of 7 same-sized circles. A 2520 florette.

In the *Monas Hieroglyphica*, Dee makes cryptic visual references to 7 x 360 = 2520.

The spiral "Metamorphosis of the Egg" diagram has 7 loops of 360 degrees, totalling to 2520 degrees.

The "Egg" diagram has the orbits of the 7 planets.

Visual references to 7 circles in John Dee's *Monas Hieroglyphica*

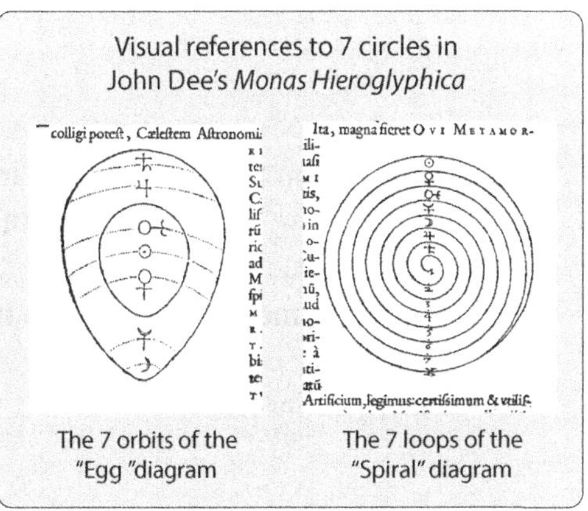

The 7 orbits of the "Egg "diagram

The 7 loops of the "Spiral" diagram

But it's not just 2520. Dee's "close-up" drawing incorporates Metamorphosis numbers 12, 24, 72, and 360 as well.

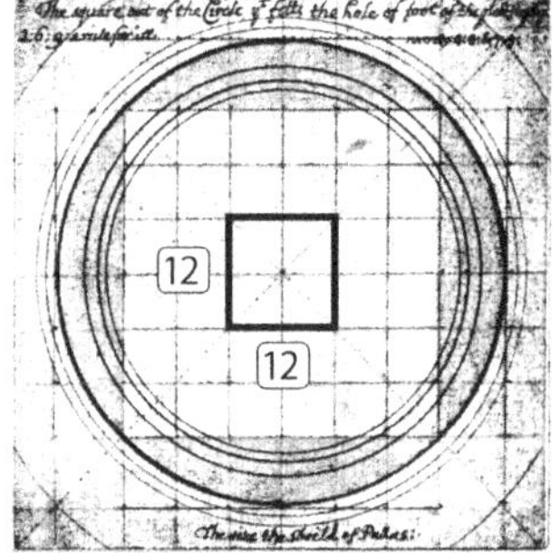

Four white grid squares is 12 units by 12 units.

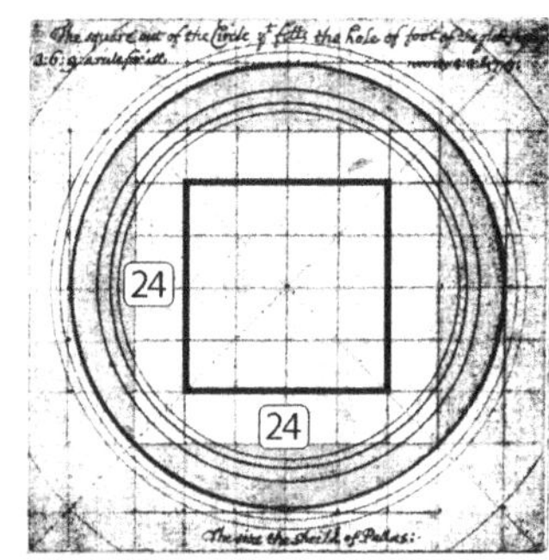

Sixteen white grid squares is 24 units by 24 units.

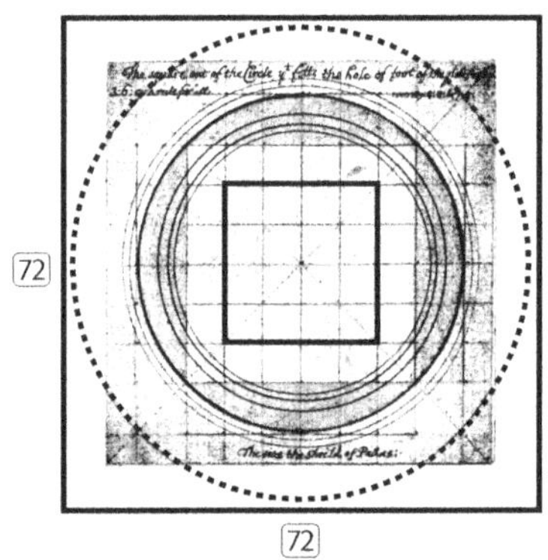

The square just outside Circle 7 is 72 units by 72 units.

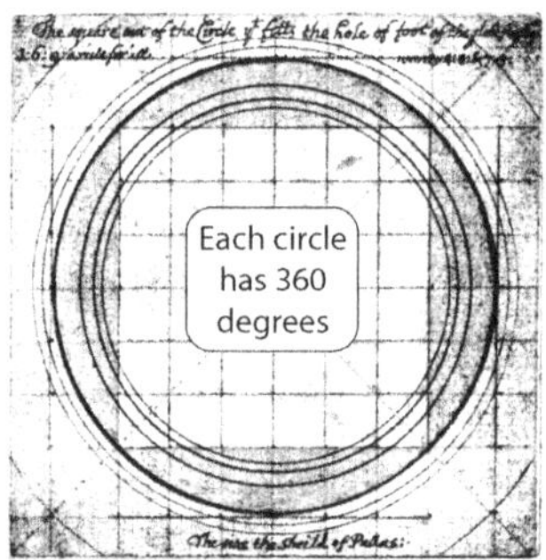

Each circle has 360 degrees.

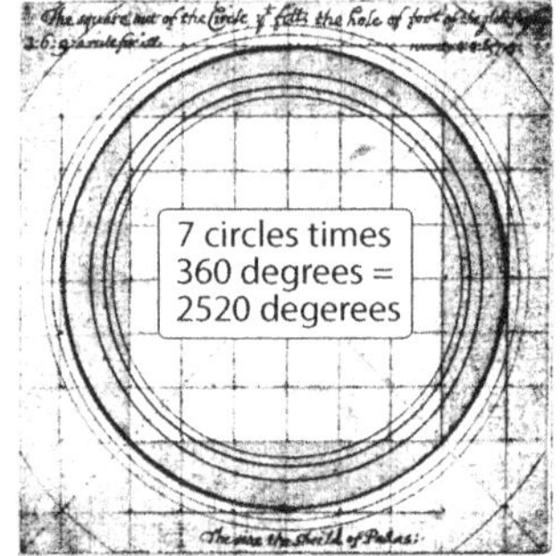

And 7 circles totals 2520 degrees.

To summarize, his "7 circles" clue is another example of why I say the Globe diagram has Dee written all over it.

Dee is merely walking us through the same mathematical cosmology via slightly different paths.

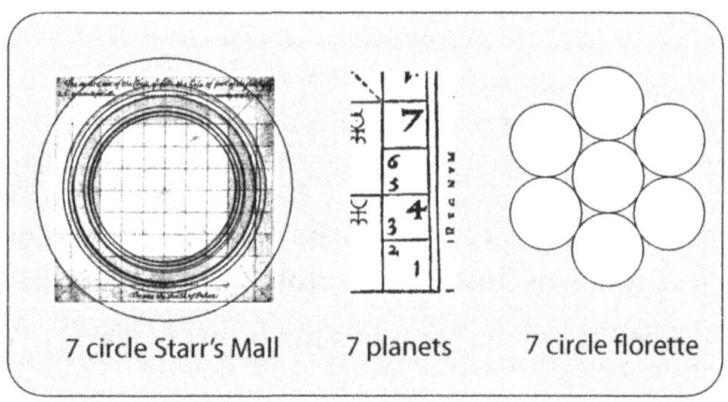

Dee not only invented symbols, he coined words

By the way, after Dee's use of the colon in 1570, it was adopted and popularized by William Oughtred (1574-1660) in his *Clavis Mathematicae* (*Key to Mathematics*). Oughtred invented the "X" symbol for multiplication, as well as the slide rule, which is all about proportions.

The idea that John Dee was an inventor of symbols is not that unusual. The *Oxford English Dictionary* will tell you John Dee was the "first to use in a printed English book," 144 different words, many of which Dee derived from his thorough knowledge of Greek, Latin, and the Romance Languages.

Among Dee's 144 words are:

ante meridiem (before noon)
British Isles
burning glass (a convex lens that can concentrate the sun's rays)
calculate
catoptric (use of mirrors)
dialing (using sundials)
experimenter
gnomonical (measurement of time with a sundial)
harmonist (someone who judges music by sound, like the Greeks did)
canonist (one who judged music by mathematical relations)
horometry (the science of measuring time)
lunular (crescent shaped)
mechanically,
optical (relating to light)
microcosmical
model (a scale model, like of a ship)
perspective glass (spy glass or hand-held telescope)
pilotage (skill in piloting a vessel)
primovant (the primium mobile, sphere of the fixed stars)
sesquialter (the 2:3 ratio)
solsticy (the solstice)
starshine (like sunshine or moonshine, only from a star)
tactical (the use of strategy in war)
trochilic (the use of pulleys and wheels)
unit (the numeral "one")
vertex (each anglular point of a polyhedron)
verticality (when a sun or star is at its zenith)
watch-clock (a clock accurate to minutes and seconds)

Guess what Dee's word "varies" means.... (hint: it begins with M)

Dee's word "**varies**" might simply be an odd spelling of the word "various," in the sense, "Here are 'various' other numbers, besides 3:6:9."

Indeed, the Latin adjective ***varius***, does mean "various." But the *Oxford English Dictionary* indicates the word "**various**" wasn't used in England until after around 1620. And even then, it's spelled with always with an "**-ious,**" never with an "**-ies**."

The word"**varies**" might also be a form of the word "to vary" meaning to change or to diversify." (From the Latin verb, ***vario***)

The Lewis and Short Latin Dictionary explains that the verb ***vario*** was also used to mean "**changed**" or "**metamorphosed**."

The dictionary even provides an example: Chapter 12, line 559 of Ovid's well-known work – you guessed it – **Metamorphosis**.

Ovid tells us the Greek god Periclymenus could "transform" into many shapes. The Latin reads "*formas* ***variatus*** *in omni*, (word-for-word meaning: form, transform, into, many)

Periclymenus, disguised as an eagle, is killed by Hercules' arrow

In Book 12 of Ovid's *Metamorphosis*, Periclymenos transformed himself into an eagle to disguise himself. But nonetheless he was killed by an arrow from Hercules' bow, during an attack Pylos, on the southern coast of Greece.

To "transform into another shape" is "metamorphosis" – a theme that was so important to Ovid, he made it his book title! *Metamorphosis* was Ovid's magnum opus, a poetic compilation of 250 classical myths. It has been considered by many to be one of the most influential works in Western culture. It influenced Chaucer, Shakespeare, and Dante.

The Greek word *metamorphosis* is made from *meta*, meaning "after," and *morphe*, meaning "shape." The word "metamorphosis" entered the English language in the mid-1500's, when fresh translations of Ovid's text were published.

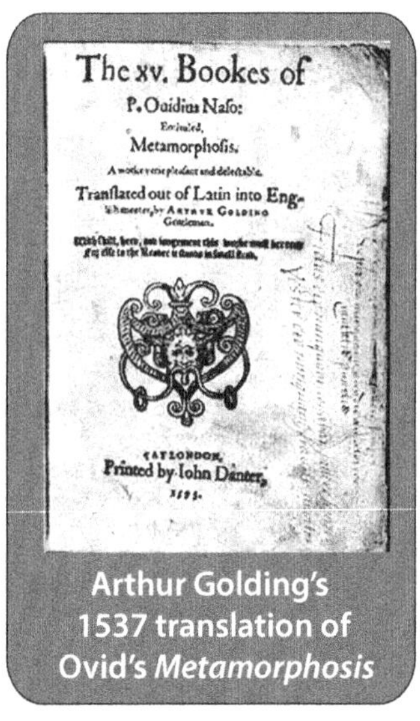
The xv. Bookes of
P. Ouidius Naso:
Metamorphosis.
Translated out of Latin into Eng-
Gentleman.
Printed by Iohn Danter,

Arthur Golding's 1537 translation of Ovid's *Metamorphosis*

Dee must have been a big fan of Ovid's masterwork.
When Dee compiled his library inventory in 1583,
he had four copies of *Metamorphosis*.

[Books 24, 715, 716, and 717 of *John Dee's Library Catalog*,
edited by Julian Roberts and Andrew Watson;
(London, Bibliographical Society, 1990)]

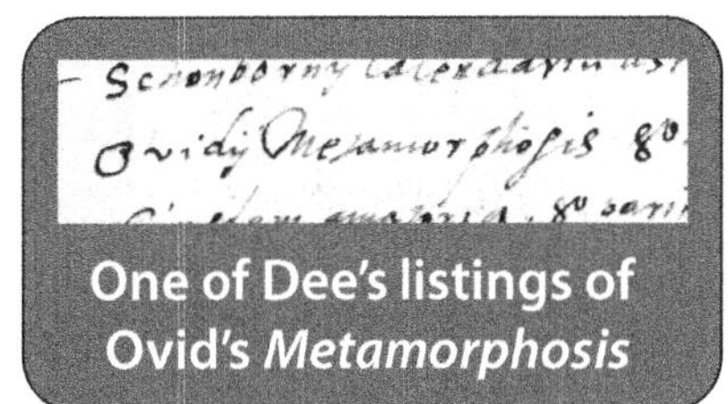
One of Dee's listings of Ovid's *Metamorphosis*

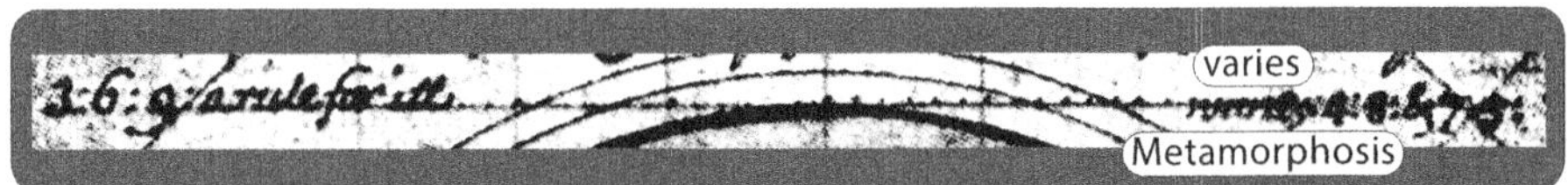

The point is this:
Dee's word "***varies***" is a code word for "Metamorphosis."

Metamorphosis is the 12, 24, 72, 360, 2520, ... sequence
which results from the "Birth of the Single Digits,
"1, 2, 3, 4, 6, 8, 9, 5, 7,"
which is darn close to the
"3, 6, 9, 1, 2, 3, 4, 8, 7, 5"
on the Globe drawing.

A little more evidence of vario

(Dee liked the word various. In the *Monas Hieroglyphica*, only a
handful of words are written IN ALL LARGE CAPITAL LETTERS.
On page "19 recto" Dee fully capitalizes the words
INDICIO VARIO, which mean "VARIOUS EVIDENCE."
All the capitalized words in the book are VARIOUS EVIDENCE, or clues,
that work together to help explain Dee's Union of Opposites theme.
Dee was big fan of various forms of *vario*.)

FITERI COGIMVR MORTALES: SI MAXIMA
TERRENA SECRETA ET ARCANA, VNIVS IS-
TIVS PVNCTI, A ME, (AT IN TVO LVMINE)
LOCATI ET EXAMINATI, INDICIO VA-
RIO, EXPLICARI ET FIDELISSIME DEMON-
STRARI QVEANT? PVNCTI videlicet, in TERNA-

What does the title, "The size the Sheild of Pallas" mean?

At the bottom of the "close-up" diagram is the title *"The size the Sheild of Pallas:·"* To figure out this word-play puzzle, let's journey back to ancient Greece.

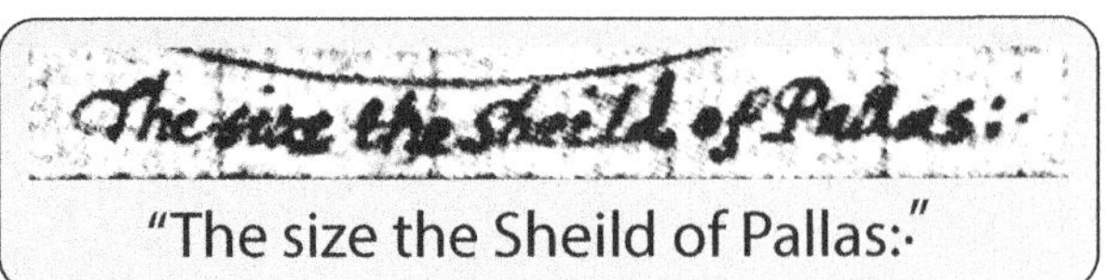

"The size the Sheild of Pallas:·"

Athena sprouting from the head of Zeus, ca. 535 BC

In Greek mythology, Athena was born, in full armor and ready for battle, from the head of Zeus. When Athena and her friend Pallas were young girls, they liked to play war-games.

One day, Athena accidentally killed Pallas. Athena felt terrible. So, to honor her friend she appended the name Pallas to he name.

Pallas Athena remained a virgin, never marrying. Pallas means "unmarried maiden" or "virgin."

Pallas Athena became the goddess of wisdom, of arts and crafts, of mathematics and skill, and she was also a war goddess (with a focus on wise tactics, rather than brutal killing).

Pallas Athena with her shield by Lucas van Leyden, ca. 1520

The Parthenon in Athens or the Temple of Pallas Athena *Parthenos* and Pallas both mean "virgin"

Athena is the patron goddess of her namesake city-state, Athens. And on a high plateau in the middle of their main city, the Athenians built a huge temple to honor her: The Parthenon.

(Parthenon is a form of the word *parthenos*, which also means "a virgin.")

In the Parthenon, “the temple of the virgin goddess,” the Greeks built a huge statue of Pallas Athena. The statue was destroyed long ago.

But in Nashville, Tennessee, in 1897, a full-scale replica of the Parthenon was built. The only thing inside is a colossal, 42-foot-tall statue of Pallas Athena, modeled on descriptions of the one in Athens. With her left hand, she is supporting her trusty “shield of Pallas Athena.”

Pallas Athene with shield, in the reproduction of the Parthenon in Nashville, Tennessee

Queen Elizabeth I and the Three Goddesses, by Hans Eworth, 1569. The central goddess is Pallas Athena

In Elizabethan England, Queen Elizabeth was venerated as “Athena.” She was as courageous as any English King had been in defending the state (though she favored peaceful strategies).

Also, Elizabeth was proud of being a “virgin queen.” She considered the subjects of the realm to be her family.

(Although many of her courtiers would have preferred she married in order to perpetuate the Tudor line of succession.)

So the term “***The size the Sheild of Pallas:·***” on this Globe drawing seems to be associating the theater architecture with Queen Elizabeth, the Virgin Queen.
(It’s also where the states of Virginia and West Virginia got their names.)

The Globe theater was to be a public Playhouse, a place where Elizabethan culture, inspired by the goddess Queen, could be nurtured and grow.

This “association with Queen Elizabeth” might *seem* to solve the riddle of “***The size the Sheild of Pallas:·***” but it’s really a red herring, an easy solution, meant to appease the casual reader.

Rehearsal at the Swan Theater in 1596

The word "size" might mean "dimension, proportion, magnitude, or scale." But the English word "size" derives from the French word "assise," or in English, "assize," which means a "rule, regulation, ordinance, assessment, or an established order"

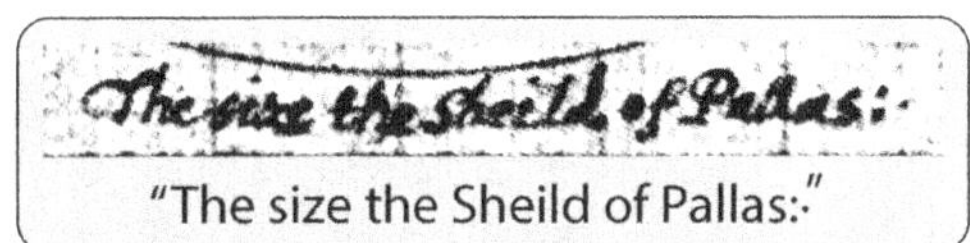
"The size the Sheild of Pallas:·"

The word "shield" is spelled oddly as "sheild,"
But that was not uncommon, as the English had borrowed the Dutch word **shild** (meaning to divide or separate) and Elizabethans sometimes spelled it in other ways, like "**sheelde**" or "**scheilde**."

The number symbolism in "The Size the Shield of Pallas"

As we've seen, the caption on the top of the "close-up" diagram is riddled with clues about number. And the diagram itself is all about number.

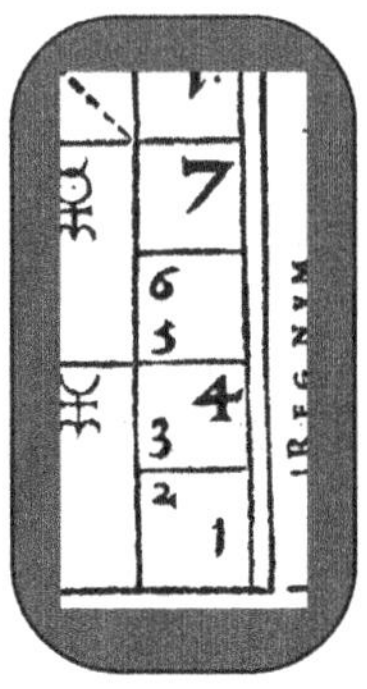

Dee was not only brilliant mathematician, he was a sharp-witted wordsmith. It would be just like Dee to incorporate number symbolism in the title, "*The size the Sheild of Pallas:·*"

Specifically, I think Dee was symbolizing the number 7, the largest number in the single-digit column of the "Below" half of his "Thus the World Was Created" chart.

1 2 3 4 5 6 **7** 8 9
"the virgin number"

The Greeks called 7 "the Virgin number" because it's a prime number which is not divisible by, or even related to, any of the other single digits.
(Except, of course, "1," but "1" was special as it was the "fount of number." Every number is divisible by 1.)

Most of the other single digits have interrelations, like "2, 4, 6, 8" or "3, 6, 9."
Number 5 is also prime, but it's closely related to 10, which the Greeks considered a "return to oneness."
Only 7 truly stands alone.

The idea that "Pallas Athena = number 7" goes back 2400 years!

In the *Mystery of Numbers*, Annemarie Schimmel quotes Philolaus (ca. 400 BC), who wrote that the number 7 is:

"comparable to the goddess Athena, the leader and ruler of all things, eternal as a deity, steady, immobile, similar only to itself, different from all others."

7=virgin=Pallas Athena

The “virgin goddess,” “Pallas Athena,” “the virgin number 7,” “the 7 planets’ orbits,” “the 7 circles,” and even “2520.” Dee would have seen these all of these things as the same thing.

Note that Dee wrote “The size the Sheild of **Pallas**.” He did not write: “The size the Sheild of **Pallas Athena**.”

Yet he is definitely *not* referring to Athena’s playmate, who died young (and apparently had no shield). Dee is indeed referring to Athena, but he abbreviated it to the “Sheild of Pallas” which is, quite literally, “the Sheild of the Virgin.”

So the full expression “***The size the Sheild of Pallas:·***,” can be seen as something like, “***The Shield of the Virgin Number 7,***” or “***The Rule of the 7 Circles.***”

This cleverness is pure Dee.

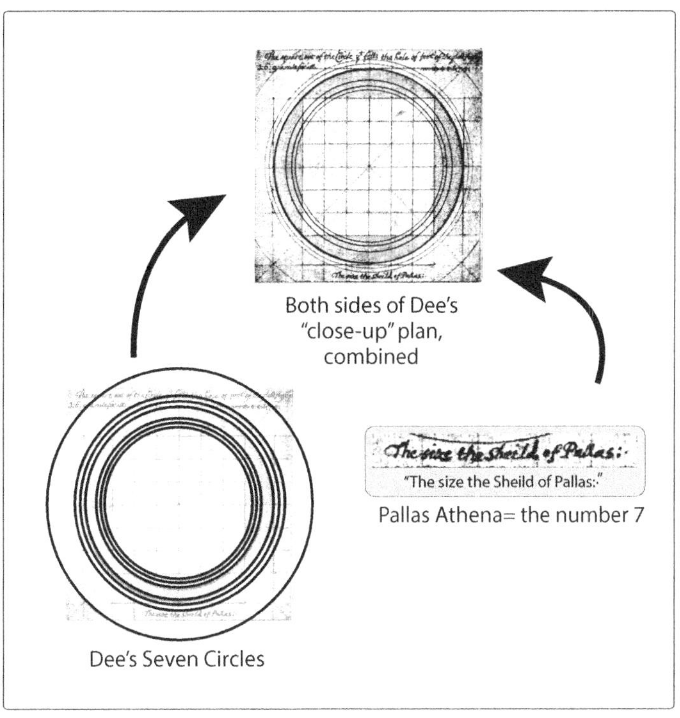

John Dee writes about the Art of Architecture

Citing Leon Battista Alberti's *On the Art Of Building* (Book 1, Chapter 1), John Dee writes the following, in his 1570 Preface to the first English translation of Euclid's *Elements*:

"The whole Feat of Architecture in building consists of Lineaments [proportions of the parts] and Framing [structure and engineering]. The whole intent and purpose of lineaments lies in determining the best way of coordinating and joining all the lines and angles that define all the faces of the building.

The function of the lineaments is to prescribe an appropriate location, precise numbers, proper scale, and elegant order for the whole building as well as for its various parts. Thus the entire form* and appearance of a building may depend upon the lineaments."

[John Dee, *Preface to Euclid*, p. d.iiij, (London, John Daye, 1577)]

may be able to performe theſe thinges, he hath nede of atteynyng and knowledge
of the beſt, and moſt worthy thynges. &c. The whole Feate of Architecture in
buildyng, conſiſteth in Lineamentes, and in Framyng. And the whole power
and ſkill of Lineamentes, tendeth to this: that the right and abſolute way may
be had, of Coaptyng and ioyning Lines and angles: by which, the face of the buil-
dyng or frame, may be comprehended and concluded. And it is the property of
Lineamentes, to preſcribe vnto buildynges, and euery part of them, an apt place,
& certaine nūber: a worthy maner, and a ſemely order: that, ſo, ẏ whole forme
and figure of the buildyng, may reſt in the very Lineamentes. &c. And we may * The Immaterialitie of perfect Archіtecture.
*preſcribe in mynde and imagination the whole formes, * all materiall ſtuffe be-*
yng ſecluded. Which point we ſhall atteyne, by Notyng and forepointyng the an-
gles and lines by a ſure and certaine direction and connexion. Seyng then, theſe

To Dee, Architecture and Mathematics were both spiritual

And in the margin, Dee writes. ***The Immateriality of perfect Architecture.**

In other words, architecture involves stone, mortar, and wood, but the ideal, the "perfect Architecture" is "immaterial," it involves ideas.

By "immaterial," Dee's certainly doesn't mean "unimportant." He means "not-material." Or spiritual as opposed to physical.

And Dee felt mathematics (geometry and number) was spiritual.

A hidden riddle about the size of the Globe

Realizing that Dee's "close-up" plan caption was riddled with riddles, I turned my attention to the part that reads, ***"yt fitts the whole of foot of the globes uper pt"***

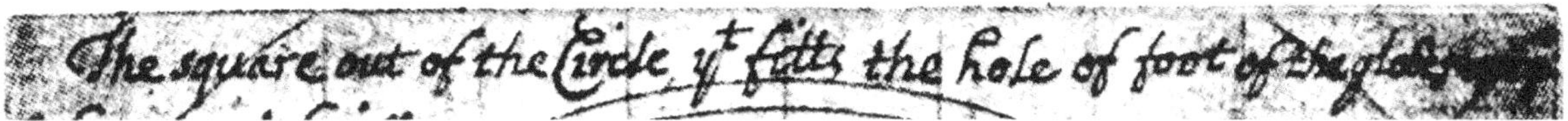

It's true that the open-air Starr's Mall is a like a "hole" in the midst of the balconies of the gallery. But "hole" seemed like an unusual word to use. Holes, like holes in socks, or rabbit holes, are empty spaces.

The most obvious interpretation of this phrase might be, **"that which fits the 'hole,' whose outer perimeter is at the 'foot' of the 'upper part' of the globe."**

In other words, **"that which fits the Starr's Mall area, which extends to the foot of the surrounding seating gallery."**

Or expressed even more concisely, **"this 'close-up' drawing fits into the doughnut hole of the 'overview' drawing."**

Yes, the 70.248 diameter Circle 7 of the "close-up" drawing does indeed fit into the 72 diameter circle in the "overview" drawing. But not perfectly. There's a little wiggle room.

If we subtract 70.248 feet from 72 feet, the difference is 1.752 feet. That's a little over "1 foot, 9 inches," or little more than 21 inches. That's almost 2 feet!

Why would Dee want to combine two drawings that didn't precisely match?

First, it didn't really matter if they matched, because the 70.248 diameter circle was only the open-air section.

But the main reason is that Dee wanted the Globe to be fully based on the special number 72, a key number in Metamorphosis.

Dee skillfully meshes two geometric stories

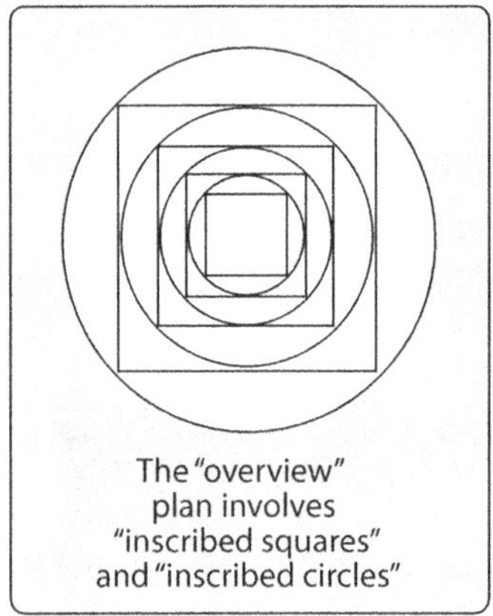

The "overview" plan involves "inscribed squares" and "inscribed circles"

Dee's phrase
" square out of the Circle"
can be interpreted in two ways.

One story involves
"inscribed circles
and inscribed squares."

The other story involves a
"square equal to a circle."

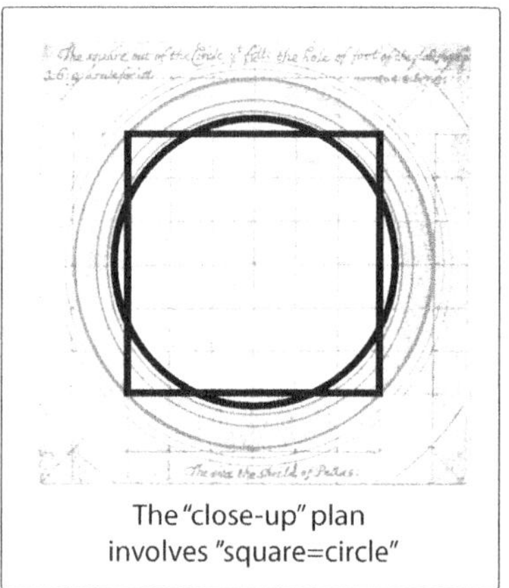

The "close-up" plan involves "square=circle"

The "overview" plan is story about "halvings" of inscribed squares and inscribed circles, starting with the 72 x 72 square working inwards.

The "close-up" plan story is of a "squaring the circle" starting with the 36 x 36 grid, finding an equal sized circle, and then working outwards, doubling, then tripling the circle.

The inward progression of one geometric story magically corresponds (almost perfectly) with another, quite different, outward geometric story.

The idea that these two rhythms sync together (within a few percentage points) is the essence of Dee's Globe design.

As we've seen, "tripling a circle which equals a "36 X 36 square"
doesn't lead to a perfect 72 foot diameter circle.
But amazingly, it leads to one pretty darn close: 70.248 diameter.

To resolve the situation, Dee could have abandoned
one of his two references to 72 and just had either
outgrowths from "tripling a circle which equals a 36 x 36 square"
or **ingrowths** of the "halvings starting from a 72 x 72 square.

But no. Dee wanted to involve the number 72 in his
outgrowth story and in his completely different **ingrowth** story.

Being off by 21 inches for the Starr's Mall was
small price to pay for a design which incorporated
two sensational geometric stories.

And Dee even (cryptically) explains this to us.
Have you figured out how?

Dee's pun about the meshing of the two geometrical stories

Let's round off that 1.752 foot discrepancy (or 21 inches) to an even "2 feet."

As the close-up diagram "**fits**" into the "**hole**" of the overview diagram,
that means it's really only one "**foot**" on each side of the "**whole**" diameter.

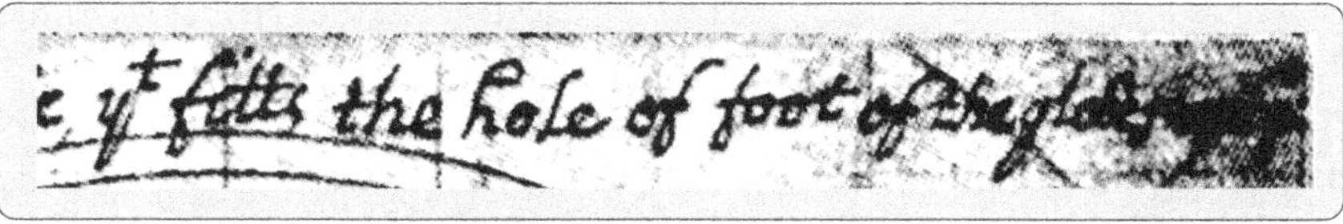

Do you get the riddle?

Dee's phrase:
"Yt fitts the hole of foot of the globes uper part."

My interpretation:
"That which **"fits"** the **"whole"** is **"off"** by a **"foot"** compared to the upper part**."**

It's a triple pun:
hole = whole (they sound the same)
of = off (they sound somewhat the same)
foot (the base of) **= foot** (12 inches)

You think I might be stretching things a bit here.
But Dee was an inveterate riddler, and I've
decoded quite a few of his clever clues.

This one is right up his alley.

But wait.
There's an even deeper riddle hidden in Dee's caption. It's a poetry pun

John Dee was not renowned as a great poet. But he did to compose several poems to accompany his lengthy treatises

For example, Dee wrote a poem to dedicate his *General and Rare Memorials to the Part of Navigation* to Sir Christopher Hatton, a Privy Counsellor and one of the wealthiest men in court.

Some scholars criticize Dee's poetry as " doggerel," meaning it has "imprecise rhymes" or "intentional misordering of words to force correct meter." But we're not here to judge artistic merit. We're here to get a sense of Dee's poetic (and punning) style.

In the third line of the fifth stanza, Dee writes, **"That * Redy friend, can witness be"**

And in footnote the margin, Dee writes " *** E. D. Esq.**"
Esq. is short for Esquire, or Sir, and the initials E. D. refer to Dee's close friend and patron, Sir Edward Dyer.

The word "**Redy**" is a jumbled word clue for "**Dyer**."

Dee's poem in his book, *General and Rare Memorials to the Perfect Art of Navigation*

TO THE RIGHT WORSHIPFVL M. CHRISTOPHER Hatton, Esquyer, Capitayn of her Maiesties *Garde, and Ientleman of her Priuy Chamber.*

YF Priuat wealth, be leef and deere,
To any VVight, of Brytish Soyl:
Ought Publik Weale *, haue any peere?*
To that, is due, all Wealth and Toyl.

Anno. 1576. *Wherof, such Lore as I (of * late,)*
Haue lernd, and for Security,
By Godly means, to Garde *this State,*
To you I send, now, carefully.

Unto the Gardians, most wise,
And Sacred Senat, or Chief Powr,
I durst not offer this Aduise,
(So homely writ,) for fear of Lowr.

But, at your will, and discreet choyce,
To keep by you, or to imparte,
I leaue this zealous Publik voyce:
You will accept so simple parte.

M. Instructors freend did warrant me,
You would so do, as he did his:
E. D. Esq. *That ** Redy *freend, can witnes be,*
For Higher States, what written is:

Of Gratefulnes, due Argument.
Yf greeuous wound, of sklandrous Darte,
At length to cure, they will be bent,
M. Instructor, then, will doo his parte,

In ernest wise, I know right well:
No Merit shall forgotten ly.
Thus much, I thought, was good to tell:
God graunt you Blis, aboue the Sky.

In the fifth stanza, Dee puns on the name of his friend, Edward Dyer

**That Redy freend...*

*E.D. Esq.

Another poem by John Dee

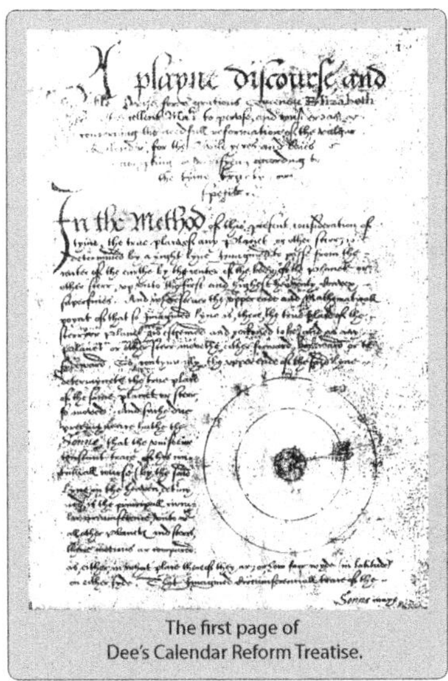
The first page of
Dee's Calendar Reform Treatise.

Here are the words of the poem Dee wrote to introduce his Calendar Reform Treatise of 1582, urging Queen Elizabeth to adopt reforms similar to the Gregorian Calendar Reform of 1583.

(This work only exists in manuscript form, and the handwriting is challenging to read.)

Notice that the second stanza has four lines all ending in the letter "s" (superfluous, hypothesis, odious, and amiss)

And in the third stanza Dee rhymes "time" with "crime, and "**writ**" with "**fit**."

Does the word "**fit**" ring a bell?

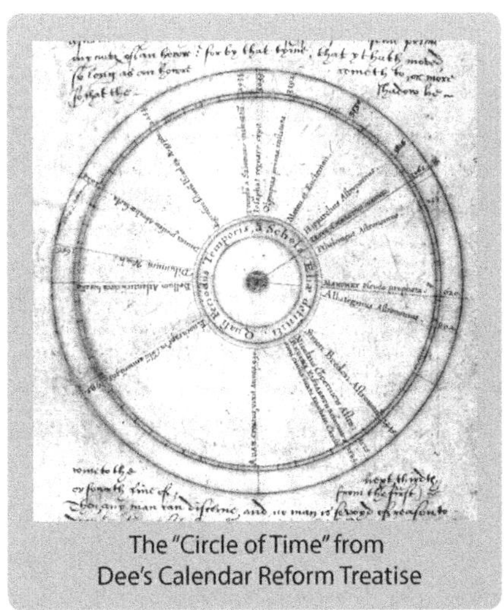
The "Circle of Time" from
Dee's Calendar Reform Treatise

John Dee's poem
to Queen Elizabeth
in his 1582
Calendar Reform Treatise

As Caesar and Sosigenes,
The vulgar calendar did make.
So Caesar's Peer, our true Empress,
To Dee, his work she didt betake.

To find the Days superfluous,
(Which Caesar's false hypothesis,
Had Bred, to Nature, odious)
Wherein, he found eleven amiss.

For he, from Christ, Chief Root of time
The time did try, by heavenly writ:
No Council can deem this a crime
From Christ, to us, true time to fit.

Elizabeth our Empress bright,
Who in the year of eighty three,
Thus made the truth come to light,
And Civil year with heaven agree.

But eighty four, the Pattern is
Of Christ's birth year, and so for ay?
Each Bissext shall fall little miss,
To show the Sunn of Christ's birth day.

Three hundred years, shall not remove,
The Sun, one day, from this new match.
Nature, no more shall us reprove
Her golden time, for all to watch.

The God of might, our father dear,
Whose reign no time can comprehend,
Good time our Elizabeth grant here
And Bliss eternal, at her end.

Amen

In the third
stanza, Dee
rhymes
"writ" with "fit"

That word "**fit**" is the same word, "**fitts,**" (which rhymes with "**itt**"), that Dee used in the caption of the "close-up" plan of Globe theater.

I also noticed that the phrase "**globe's uper pt**" is not only a weird spelling, but it likewise ends in the letter "**t.**"

But alas, the ending of the caption is simply numbers, so there is no "**t.**"

Then it struck me. What about 8? The word "**eight**" ends in the letter "**t**".

So I morphed Dee's caption into a four-line poem:

> The square out of the circle, yt fitts
> the hole of foot of the globes uper pt.
> 3:6:9 a rule for itt
> varies 4:8 ("eight")
> :& 7· 5:·

It felt like I was on the right track.

The endings "**t**" sounds of "**fitts**," "**pt**" (part), "**itt**," and **eight**" all seemed to rhyme. But there was a problem. The very last section, "**: & 7·5:·**" gets left out.

It's unlike Dee to include something that's superfluous, something that's not a part of the whole. It's not *concinnitas*.

The ampersand (**&**) seemed to be suggesting "**and also**," as if this extraneous bit was still somehow integrated with rest of the poem.

That left the digits 7 and 5, which are primes. Then it clicked!

The numbers 7 and 5 multiply to 35.

7 X 5 = 35

And as we've seen, the radius of the largest circle in the "close-up" plan, Circle 7, is **35.179** units.

That's pretty darn close to **36**.

(The difference between 36 feet and 35.179 feet is .821 feet, which is about 10 inches)

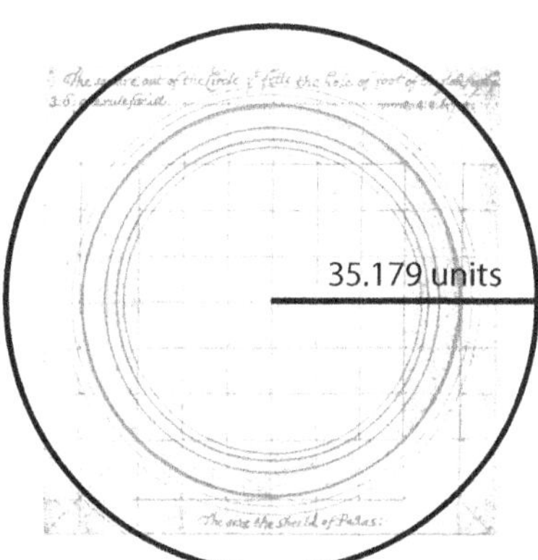

A raduis of 35.179 is close to a radius of 36.
(Just like a diameter of 70.358
is close to a diameter of 72)

The diameter of Circle 7 is 70.358 feet. As we've seen, this is about "one foot" less (on each side) than the 72 foot interior diameter of the "overview" plan. That's what the "hole of the foot = **the whole is off by a foot**" riddle is all about.

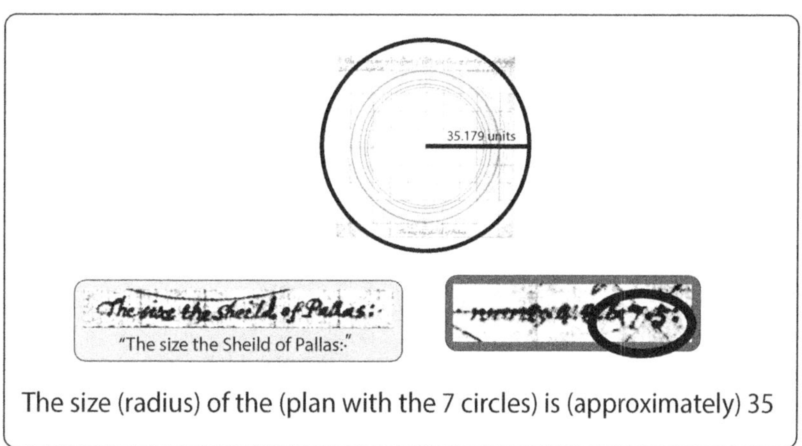

The size (radius) of the (plan with the 7 circles) is (approximately) 35

In other words, in his title, Dee is telling us "the **size** of the shield of Pallas" is 7×5, or 35." The idea of "size" can be interpreted as area, diameter, or radius.

So we might read this as "the radius of the diagram with the seven (the Virgin number) circles is 35."

It's a clever poetic and numerical riddle. Dee loved mixing numbers and letters like this.

And the riddle involves a technique Dee was quite fond of: hiding a "clue by omission." (Leaving 7 and 5 out of the rhyming poem.)

Even the format of Dee's riddle is a riddle

The caption on Dee's "close-up" plan was not something that Dee just came up with off the top of his head. He worked long and hard to make every word, letter, number and symbol count. And most of them have a double-meaning.

On top of that, Dee has invented his own unusual riddle format: It's a **poem,** which oddly incorporates **numbers** and **words,** which is intentionally disguised as a mere **sentence**.

Remember, today we consider riddles to be child's play. But in Elizabethan times, riddling was a sign of intelligence. And Dee was proud to strut his stuff.

To summarize, what appears to be a simple caption is a power-packed compilation of clues. It's riddled with riddles.

OLD ILLUSTRATIONS OF THE GLOBE AND THE THEATRE

The Theatre, just north of the City

In London, during the plague of 1564, 1000 people died every week. Eight years later, in 1572, when the epidemic started to spread again, the Mayor and Corporation of London formally banned all public gatherings, including plays.

This prompted impresarios like actor/manager James Burbage to construct theaters just outside the city limits. Shoreditch, just beyond the northern border of the City of London, was already notorious for the its gaming houses and brothels. In 1576, in this "suburb of sin," James Burbage constructed a playhouse named the ***Theatre***.

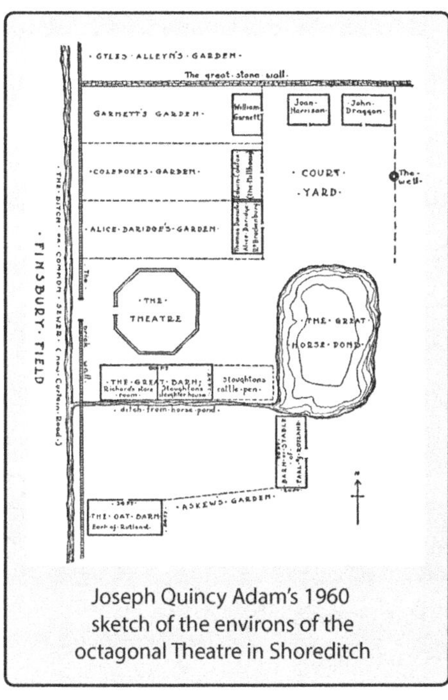

Joseph Quincy Adam's 1960 sketch of the environs of the octagonal Theatre in Shoreditch

As Joseph Quincy Adams describes in his 1960 book *Shakespearean Playhouses* the Theater's location was, "Near from where the ditch from the Horse Pond empties into the ditch called the "common sewer." (Pew!)

In the following year, 1576, another playhouse called the Curtain was built just up the road.

England's first arts and entertainment district had been born.

Twenty years later, the Burbage Family was being sued by Giles Allen, the landowner. Burbage's lease had expired and Giles Allen felt he owned the building that had been built on his land.

So, on the night of December 28, 1598, (while Giles Allen was away celebrating the holidays in his country home) Burbage hired carpenter Peter Street to dismantle the entire Theater and move its girts, beams, and rafters to Street's yard.

The following spring, the wood was ferried across the Thames and was used in the construction of the original Globe.

The tall building (directly above the man and his horse), may be the Theater, before it became the Globe.

Here is an unknown artist's *View of the Cittye of London from the North towards the Sowth*, done sometime around 1599. The tall, three-story building in the mid-ground could be either the Theater or the Curtain. Notice that it appears to be about as tall as it is wide.

The structures on the left and right might be staircases leading to the galleries, or perhaps they are part of full width of the building. On top above the roof line is a tower surmounted by a large flag.

The Globe, south of the City

In 1616, the Dutch engraver and mapmaker, Claes Janszoon Visscher, (1586-1652) drew a panorama of what London looked like in the year 1600.

(The part shown here is the midsection; the original is over 6.5 feet long.)

In the background, the palaces, mansions, and churches (the largest is Saint Paul's) of the City of London are clearly depicted. In the foreground. on the south bank of the Thames are the Swan, the Bear Garden and the Globe (encircled).

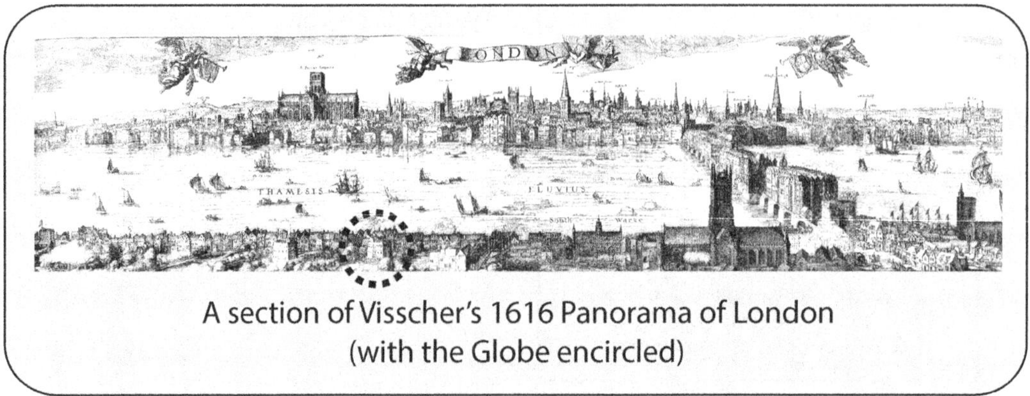

A section of Visscher's 1616 Panorama of London (with the Globe encircled)

Some recent scholars claim Visscher's illustration is mislabeled, inaccurate, and unreliable. Others claim Visscher's work is very accurate and the Globe was indeed octagonal, as shown. (For discussion, see Joy Hancox, *Kingdom For A Stage*, p. 133-135)

Close-up of the original Globe from Visscher's 1616 panorama

To me, Visscher's depiction looks very similar to the Theatre (or the Curtain) drawing. The building is 3 stories tall, about as tall as it is wide.

At the top are 2 small buildings and a taller flagpole tower, supporting a tall flag.

Just to the left of the original Globe is the Bear Garden, where bulldogs and mastiffs were pitted against bears and bulls.
(Spanish Bullfighting is a vestige of this form of "entertainment.")

The Bear Garden, from Visscher's 1616 panorama

Note the two people in the foreground restraining a collared animal.

Though it's only two stories, the whole side-view elevation is still close to a 1:1 square.
The building on the rooftop is small, about half the size of the flag.

The Swan theater, from Visscher's 1616 panorama

On the extreme left edge of the section of Visscher's map shown previously is the Swan. It also has a roof top building with a large flag. Notice that the long sides of the rooftop building are parallel (not perpendicular) to the exterior wall.

Visscher knock-offs

Other artists, basing their engravings on Visscher's illustration, have depicted the Globe in the same way: about as tall as it is wide, small roof top buildings, a tower with pitched roof, and a big flag.

In 1814, by Charles Turner made a mezzotint of Francis Delaram's (1590-1627) portrait of King James I on horseback. Beyond the King is the City of London as it looked when he took the throne in 1603.

King James I of England (and VI of Scotland) by Charles Turner, after Francis Delaram (1590-1627)

Under the horse are the Bear Garden (left edge), the circular Rose (all white) and the original Globe (about in the center).

Close-up view of the Bear Garden (left), the Rose (center) and Globe (right) in Francis Delaram's portrait of King James I

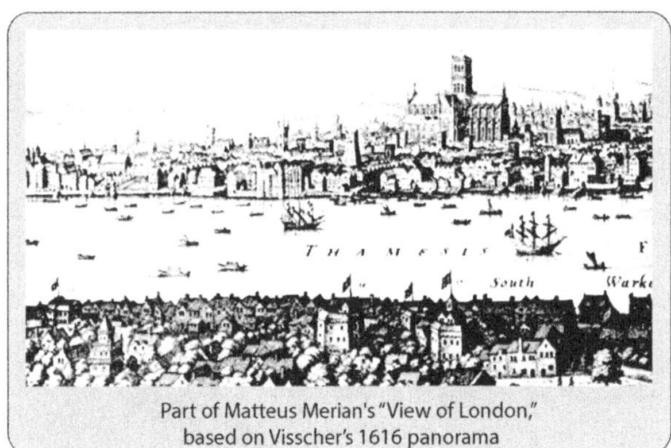

Part of Matteus Merian's "View of London," based on Visscher's 1616 panorama

Above is a section from Mattäus Merian's *View of London*, showing the Bankside playhouses. Merian's panorama depicts London as it was around 1612. It was mainly based on Visscher's *Panorama of London*, with some features derived from other sources. (Printed in Ludvig Gottfried's *Neuwe Archontologia Cosmica*, Frankfurt am Mayn, 1638)

This enlargement of the Globe shows the two small rooftop buildings, the tower, and the flag, much like Visscher's illustration.

Close-up of the Globe from Matteus Merion's copy of Visscher's 1616 panorama

Another copy of Visscher's 1616 depiction of the original Globe (Artist Unknown)

Here are two more much clearer engravings, done by Unknown Artists, but both again appear to be copy of Visscher's depiction.

The drawing on the right has omits the windows on story 1, but has the two small structures and the flag tower above the roof line.

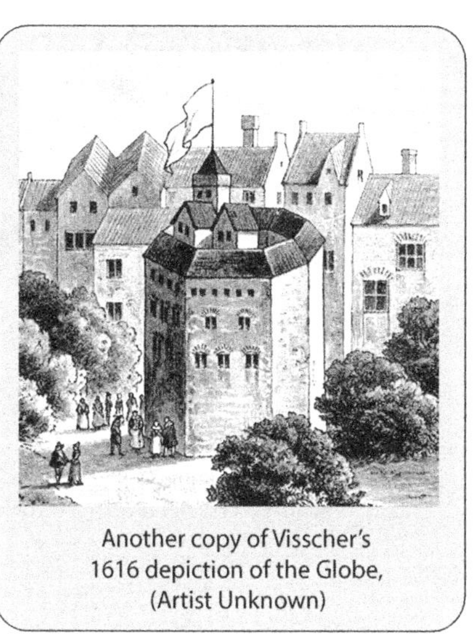
Another copy of Visscher's 1616 depiction of the Globe, (Artist Unknown)

A calamitous conflagration. Then, the "second" Globe.

On June 29, 1613, during a dramatic performance of Henry VIII, a theatrical canon misfired, igniting thatching, then the wooden beams. Soon the whole theater was ablaze. Within an hour the whole wooden structure had burned to the ground.

Fortunately, no one was killed or even injured – except for one fellow whose pants caught on fire – but the flame was quickly doused with beer.

Within a year, by June 1614, the "second" Globe theater had been built, reportedly on the foundation of the original.

It remained open for 28 more years, until 1642, when the Puritans closed down all of the theaters in London. Around 1644, the second Globe was demolished to make way for tenements. The end of an era.

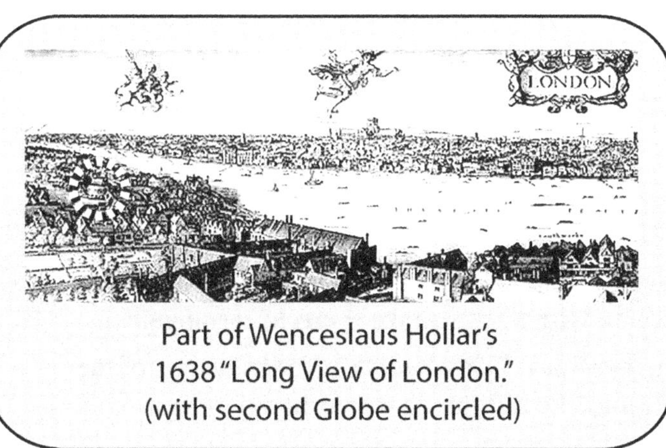

Part of Wenceslaus Hollar's 1638 "Long View of London." (with second Globe encircled)

Around 1638, Wenceslaus Hollar of Antwerp drew his preliminary sketch for his nine-foot-long "Long View of London."

It includes the second Globe and the Bear Garden, but Hollar accidentally reversed the labels of the two buildings.

The (properly labeled) close-up the second Globe, from Wenceslaus Hollar's 1638 "Long View of London."

Zooming in on the (here, properly labled) "second" Globe Theater, it seems much wider than it is tall.

The rooftop structures are larger, with the gable ends facing the Starr's Mall. The top of the tower now sports a small "onion dome."

The second Globe seems different than the first. Did some "Jacobean Fire Marshall" create new building guidelines, thus altering the harmonic Elizabethan geometries of the original?

John Dee wisdom was not appreciated by King James I, and besides, Dee died in 1608, four years before the original Globe burned down.

What was Dee really trying to express in the Theatre and the original Globe?

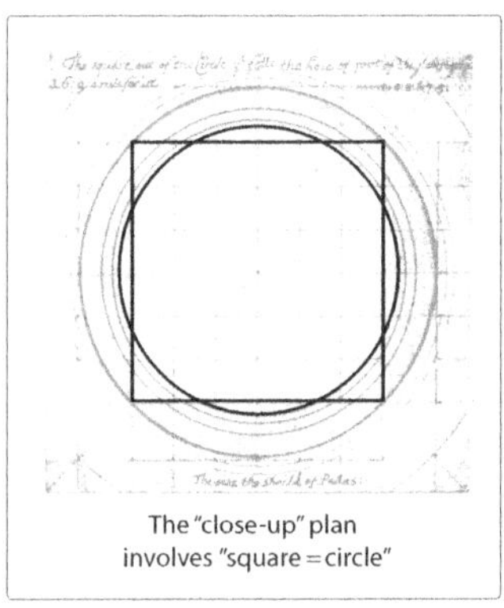
The "close-up" plan involves "square = circle"

Let's return to John Dee's "close-up" plan and the overriding 2D geometrical concept for the original Globe: **"square = circle**."

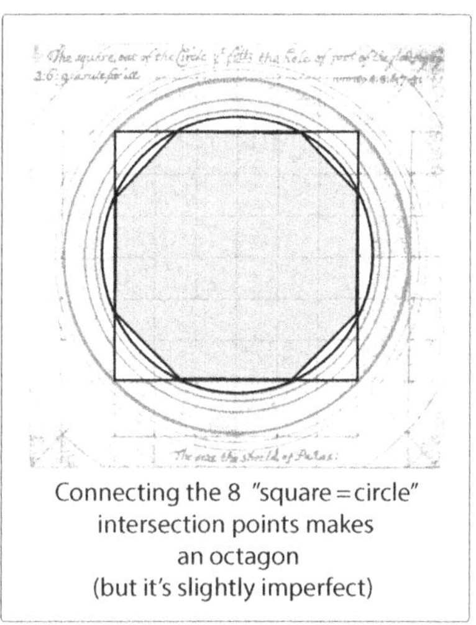
Connecting the 8 "square = circle" intersection points makes an octagon (but it's slightly imperfect)

The square and the circle have eight points of intersection. Connect each point with its two neighbors and what have you got?
An octagon!
Admittedly, it's *not* a mathematically perfect octagon. If you look closely, the "N, E, S, and W" sides are slightly longer than the "NE, SE, SW, and NW" sides, but it still looks pretty octagonal.

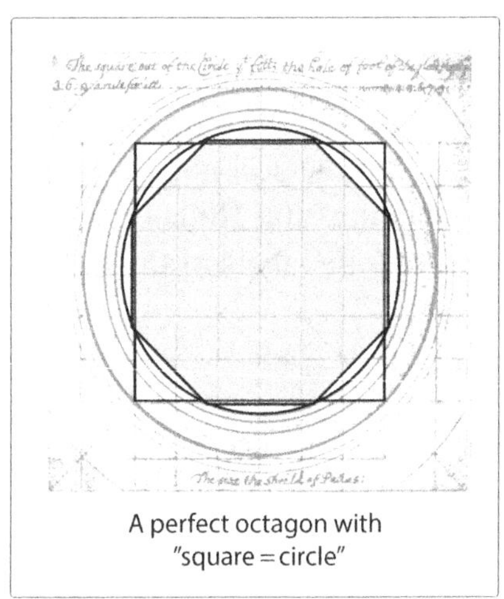
A perfect octagon with "square = circle"

Here's what a perfect **octagon** looks like in conjunction with this "**square = circle**" arrangement.

With thicker lines, like the thick wooden beams of the skeletal frame, the difference would barely be noticeable.

(Much like the barely noticeable differences we saw in the doublings or triplings on Dee's "close-up" plan.)

The octagon is a metaphor for the "Union of Earth (square) and Heaven (circle)"

To understand the dramatic play involving square, octagon and circle, let's do a deeper character study. The octagon is a nice "middle" stage between the square and the circle.

Of course there are many degrees of "middle stages" as we proceed "polygonally" towards the perfection of the circle. But as 4 x 2 = 8, the octagon is intrinsically related to square.

(In Sanskrit, *o-cata* means"twice four." This became *octa* in Greek and *octo* in Latin.)

The only character "less round" than the square is the triangle.

(We'll soon see triangle plays more than a supporting role on this philosophical story of shape.)

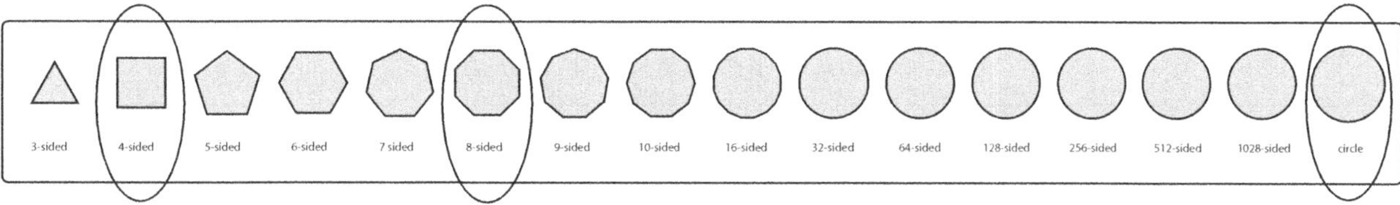

Octagonal Buildings throughout History

The octagonal Church of the Holy Sepulchre, Cambridge, England, ca.1130 (Dee attended St. Johns College, directly across the street)

The octagon is a metaphor for the "**Union**" of Earth (square) and Heaven (circle). This is not, by any means, a novel concept originated by Dee. Many architects throughout history have hinted at this conjunction between the supernatural and the terrestrial with octagonal buildings, for example:

ca. 75 BC, Tower of the Winds in Athens

ca. 520 AD, Mausoleum of Theodoric in Ravenna, Italy,

ca. 690 AD, Dome of the Rock in Jerusalem

ca. 800 AD, Palatine Chapel in Aachen, Germany

ca. 1100, Baptistery of San Giovanni, in Florence

ca. 1130 AD, Church of the Holy Sepulchre in Cambridge, England

ca. 1240 AD, Castle Del Monte in Apulia, Italy,

The medieval Chapterhouses of Salisbury, Wells, and York Cathedrals in England,

And, I might also add, John Dee Tower of 1583 in Newport, Rhode Island

The octagonal Tower of the Winds, a horologium (a building that keeps track of time) in Athens, Greece, built around 50 BC

The octagonal Baptistery of San Giovanni, Florence, Italy, ca.1100

The octagonal John Dee Tower of 1583 in Newport, Rhode Island

Summary

Geometrically and philosophically the octagon represents the unity of the square and the circle. Dee's clever design for the original Globe incorporates both the octagon and the square = circle.

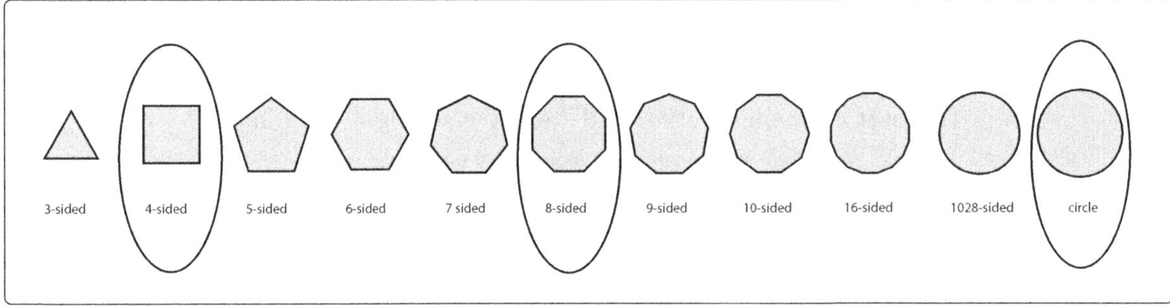

What was the height of the original Globe Theater?

Among the drawings of the Byrom Collection are several "parametric" drawings, meaning they combine an "overview" plan and a "side-view" or "elevation" plan in one drawing.

Based on the specific "parametric" plan Joy believes represents the original Globe, she concludes that the height of the theater was 36 feet (not including the roof or towers).

There were three floors in the original Globe. Americans refer to these as "floor 1, floor 2," and floor 3." The English call them the "ground floor, floor 1, and floor 2." To simplify, I'll refer to them as "story 1, story 2, and story 3."

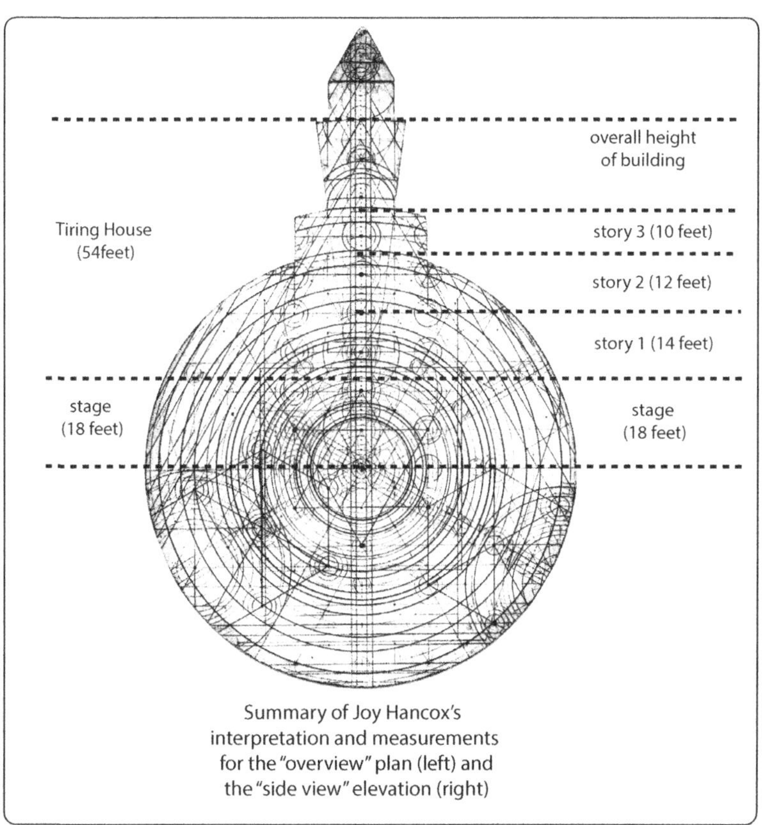

Summary of Joy Hancox's interpretation and measurements for the "overview" plan (left) and the "side view" elevation (right)

Joy suggests "story 1" was 14 feet tall, story 2 was 12 feet tall, and story 3 was 10 feet tall, totaling 36 feet. Adding 18 feet for the roof, the total becomes 54 feet.

Joy noticed this 54 feet of height (in elevation) reflects the 54-foot long dimension of the Tiring House (in plan).

These various height estimates seem reasonable for two good reasons, but, to me, they seem slightly off because of "a third thing."

Reason 1

The Globe and the Fortune were built by the same master carpenter, Peter Streete, with a year of each other. Though they have many similarities, they also have differences.

The Globe was octagonal with a side-to-side width of 72 feet. That makes a footprint of **4294.56** square feet.

The Fortune was square, **80 feet by 80 feet**, so its footprint would contain **6400** square feet. This means the Fortune's footprint was about **1.5 times** that of the Globe's. Or the Globe's footprint was two-thirds the size of the Fortune's.

Fortunately, the contract for the Fortune still exists, and it calls for the builder to mimic some of the details of the Globe.

Here are some of the specifications (my bold)**:**

Foundation.

A good, sure, and strong foundation, of piles, brick, lime, and sand, both without and within, to be wrought one foot of assize at the least above the ground.

Frame.

The frame of the said house to be set square, and to contain **fourscore foot** of lawful assize every way square without, and **fifty-five foot** of like assize square every way within.

Materials.

And shall also make all the said frame in every point for scantlings larger and bigger in assize than the scantlings of the said new-erected house called the Globe.

Exterior.

To be sufficiently enclosed without with lath, lime, and hair.

Stairs.

With such like stairs, conveyances, and divisions, without and within, as are made and contrived in and to the late erected playhouse ... called the Globe.... And the staircases thereof to be sufficiently enclosed without with lath, lime, and hair.

Height of galleries

And the said frame to contain three stories in height; the first, or lower story to contain **twelve foot** of lawful assize in height; the second story **eleven foot** of lawful assize in height; and the third, or upper story, to contain **nine foot** of lawful assize in height.

Breadth of galleries

All which stories shall contain **twelve foot** of lawful assize in breadth throughout. Besides a jutty forward in either of the said two upper stories of **ten inches** of lawful assize.

Protection of lowest gallery

The lower story of the said frame withinside ... [to be] paled in below with good, strong, and sufficient new oaken boards.... And the said lower story to be also laid over and fenced with strong iron pikes.

Divisions of galleries

With four convenient divisions for gentlemen's rooms, and other sufficient and convenient divisions for two-penny rooms.... And the gentlemen's rooms and two-penny rooms to be ceiled with lath, lime, and hair.

Seats

With necessary seats to be placed and set, as well in those rooms as throughout all the rest of the galleries.

Stage

With a stage and tiring-house to be made, erected, and set up within the said frame; with a shadow or cover over the said stage. Which stage shall be placed and set (as also the staircases of the said frame) in such sort as is prefigured in a plot thereof drawn. [The plot has been lost.] And which stage shall contain in length **forty and three foot** of lawful assize, and in breadth to extend to the middle of the yard of the said house. The same stage to be paled in below with good, strong, and sufficient new oaken boards.... And the said stage to be in all other proportions contrived and fashioned like unto the stage of the said playhouse called the Globe.... And the said ... stage ... to be covered with tile, and to have a sufficient gutter of lead to carry and convey the water from the covering of the said stage to fall backwards.

Tiring-house

With convenient windows and lights, glazed, to the said tiring-house.

Flooring.

And all the floors of the said galleries, stories, and stage to be boarded with good and sufficient new deal boards, of the whole thickness where need shall be.

Columns

All the principal and main posts of the said frame and stage forward shall be square, and wrought pilaster-wise, with carved proportions called satyrs to be placed and set on the top of every of the said posts. [A satyr is a Greek woodland diety, which is part human and part horse or goat.]

Roof

And the said frame, stage, and staircases to be covered with tile.

Miscellaneous.

To be in all other contrivations, conveyances, fashions, thing and things, effected, finished, and done, according to the manner and fashion of the said house called the Globe.

[Joseph Quincy Adams, *Shakespearean Playhouses: A History of English Theatres from the Beginnings to the Restoration*, (Gloucester MA, Peter Smith, 1960) pp. 274-277 (or Teddington, UK, Echo Library, 2008) reprinting, pp. 118-120]

The term "scantlings" comes from the old French word *escantillon*, which means "sample." It means that the lumber is of a "prescribed size that fits a set of standard dimensions." In other words, compared to the original Globe, all the posts, beams and girts for the Fortune should be beefed-up too make it more substantial.

The Fortune's specifications indicate story 1 was to be **12 feet** tall, story 2 to be **11 feet** tall, and story 3 to be **9 feet** tall.

To summarize, Joy Hancox's estimation of "54 feet" to the top of the roof is quite reasonable.
Her "3 stories estimate" of **14 +12 + 10 = 36** (not including the roof)
is reasonably close to
the Fortune contract's **12 +11 + 9 = 32** (not including the roof)

Reason 2

The second good reason the height of the original Globe theater might be 54 feet (to the top of the roof) has it do with Leon Battista Alberti's interpretation of Greek and Roman theaters, (which was based on the writings of Vitruvius).

In Book 8, Chapter 7, of *On the Art of Building*, Alberti writes,:
"**Most theaters were given a height equal to the width of the central area**."
Granted, Alberti seems to be more referring to the large ancient amphitheaters, whose "central area" is the area between the stage and the first row of seats (what we might call the "orchestra").

The width of the "central area" or the Starr's Mall of the original Globe is **50.9 feet**.
An (equal) height of 50.9 feet **is reasonably close** to Joy Hancox's height estimation of **54 feet**.

However, there's a "Third Thing"

But there's a third thing–and it's the reason why I feel the height of the original Globe was **much taller** than 54 feet. The reason is simple: it looks taller in the illustrations of that era.

Let's return to the ca. 1599 "*View of the Cittye of London from the North looking south towards the Sowth*."

In the middle-ground is a tall building, which is thought to be the Theater.

(Some suggest it might have been the Curtain, which was just down the street, but either way they were most likely very similar.)

The tall building (directly above the man and his horse), may be the Theater, before it became the Globe.

If the Theater was 72 feet wide and 54 feet high, the "side-view" elevation of such a building would be a **3:4 horizontal rectangle.**

(As 54 feet is 75% of 72 feet.)

However, such a rectangle is much wider than the way the Theater is depicted in the illustration.

To me, the Theater looks as though it would fit in a **square**.

(Like, for example, a square 72 feet wide by 72 feet tall).

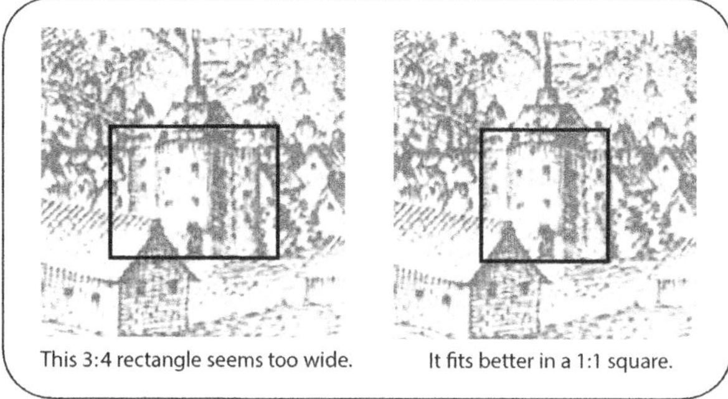

This 3:4 rectangle seems too wide. It fits better in a 1:1 square.

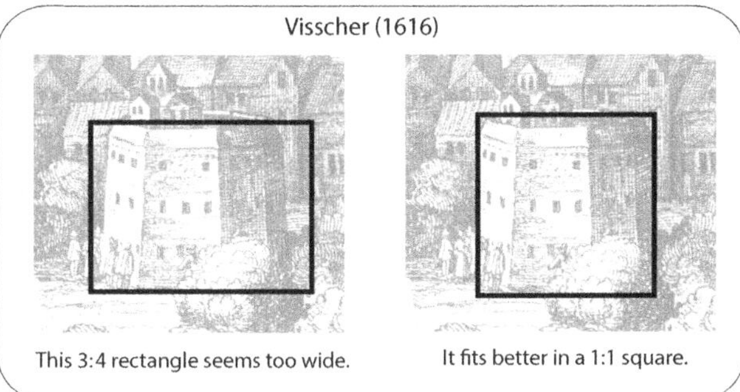

Visscher (1616)

This 3:4 rectangle seems too wide. It fits better in a 1:1 square.

The same applies to Visscher's 1616 depiction of the original Globe, constructed on the south bank of the Thames from the old beams from the Theater.

The 3:4 rectangle is way too wide. But a 1:1 square fits nicely.

Incidentally, Visscher has depicted the sides is tapering a bit towards the top. There could be several reasons for this. First he might have wanted to make it seem like the building was tall and introduced this parallax for artistic effect (to make it "feel" tall).

Or the building might have originally had a slight *entasis*, a technique of a tapering architecture to accommodate the optical illusion of the sides not being straight.

(Incidentally, the cylinder of stone-and mortar Tower in Newport, Rhode Island was built with *entasis*)

Or perhaps the tapering is a reflection of the 10-inch jutting of the floors in the interior. However, offsetting the floors so the whole structure "leaned inwards"would require a lot more work for the carpenters than simply having a vertical exterior wall.

I think the tapering was probably Visscher's artistic styling, However, it doesn't seem likely Visscher would have altered the overall proportions significantly in his depiction.

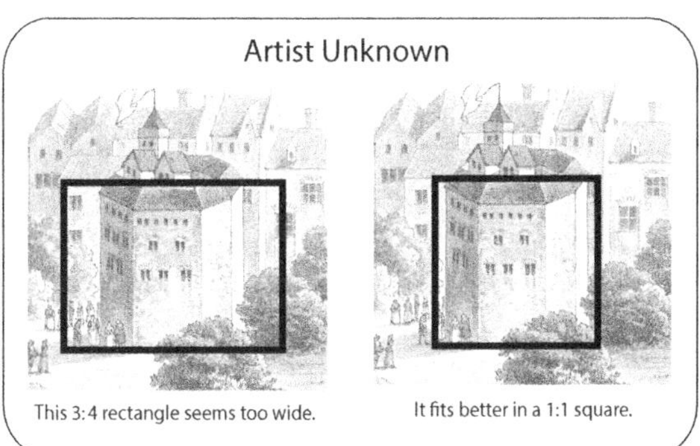

Artist Unknown

This 3:4 rectangle seems too wide. It fits better in a 1:1 square.

Artist Unknown

This 3:4 rectangle seems too wide. It fits better in a 1:1 square.

And the illustrators who seemed to have derived their work from Visscher's 1616 illustration all depicted the Globe as having an approximately **"1:1 side view,"** but definitely not a **"3:4 side view."**

After the original Globe burned down and the second Globe was reconstructed, it's thought they used the exact same foundation.

However, the depiction of the second Globe, done by Wenceslaus Hollar in 1647 shows a building that is closer to a "**3:4 ratio**" than a "**1:1 ratio**."

On the "second" Globe, the 3:4 rectangle fits better than a 1:1 square.

(Perhaps the "South Bank Fire Department" informed the theater owners that they couldn't shoot water 72 feet high. And, as they had done in the Fortune, the thatching on the roof of the second Globe was probably replaced by tiles).

Even though some scholars doubt that Visscher's drawing is an accurate depiction of the original Globe, it seemed to me like the closest thing to a "primary document" available.

So I wondered how a "square-proportioned" Globe might correlate with the Byrom Collection drawings and what I had learned about John Dee's mathematical cosmology by studying his writings and (what I refer to as) the John Dee Tower of 1583.

What's so special about a cube? Lots of things.

Thinking in three dimensions instead of two, Joy Hancox's "height: width: depth" estimation would be **54:72:72**
(or 3:4:4, a short square box).

We might imagine the octagonal galleries fitting inside this space.

But, as per **my hypothesis**, based on the old illustrations, the "height: width: depth" would be **72:72:72** (or a 1:1:1 cube).

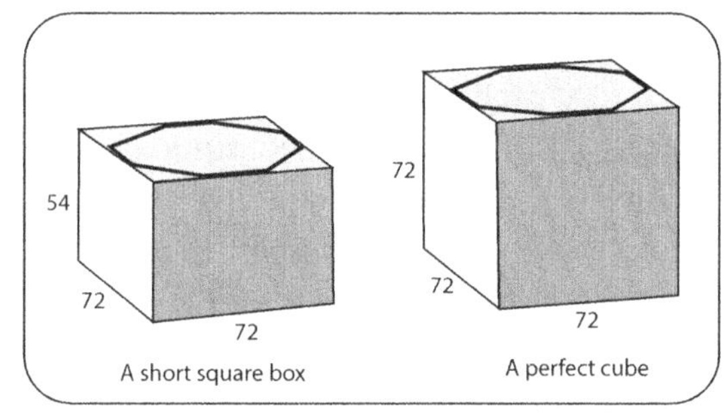

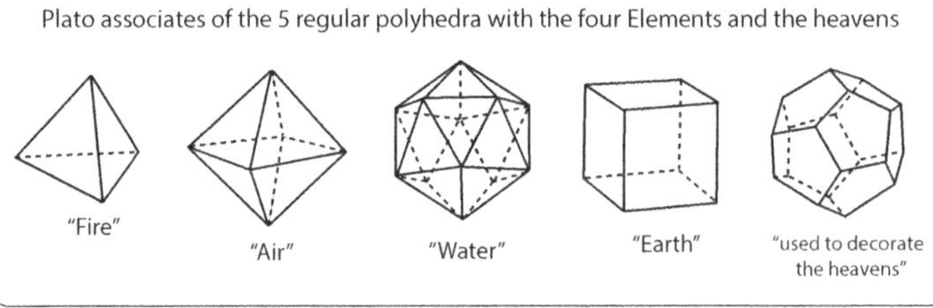

A cube would be a thrilling solution for John Dee for several profound reasons: First, **the cube** is one of the Platonic solids.

(There are only 5 regular 3-D shapes with only one kind of face: the tetrahedron, the octahedron, the cube, the icosahedron, and the dodecahedron)

Plato associated the tetrahedron with Fire,
the octahedron with Air,
the icosahedron with Water, and the
dodecahedron with the "embroidering of the heavens,"
and the **cube** with ... (you guessed it) ...
Earth.

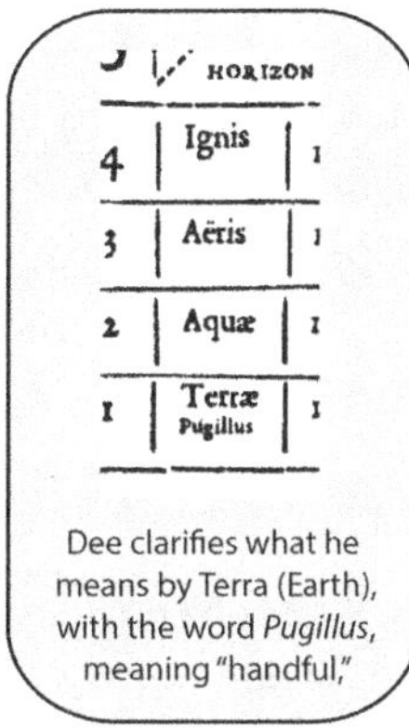

Dee clarifies what he means by Terra (Earth), with the word *Pugillus*, meaning "handful,"

As one of the four Elements, this "Earth" really refers to "dirt" definition of "Earth," as opposed to the "globe-with-oceans-and-continents" definition of "Earth."

Dee makes this distinction in his "Thus the World Was Created" chart of the *Monas Hieroglyphica*, referring to Earth as *Pugillus*, meaning "a handful" (of dirt).

(Like our word, "pugilist," or boxer, who only uses his hands).

In alchemical symbolism, there's a strong "**square = earth**" connection (in 2D), in the symbolism of the ancients there is a strong "**cube = earth**" connection (in 3D).

Something else is special about the cube

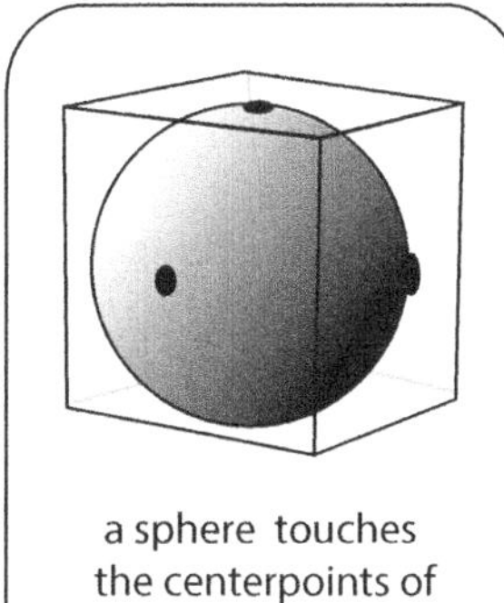
a sphere touches the centerpoints of the cube's 6 faces

There's an even more profound symbolism in the 1:1:1 cube (as opposed to the 3:4:4 box-shape).

Do you know what fits perfectly inside a cube?
A **sphere**!
The sphere will be tangent to the center points of each of the cube's six faces (four sides, top and bottom).

a globe ... just like the Globe (theater)

And what's another, more common name for a sphere?

The very name of the theater:
"**Globe**."

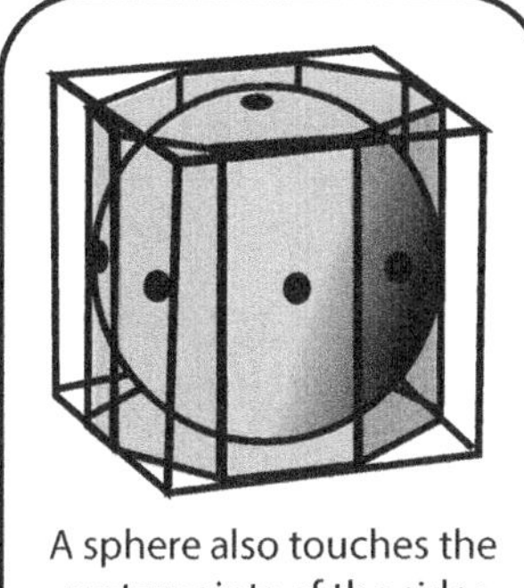
A sphere also touches the centerpoints of the sides of an octagonal cylinder

True, the original Globe was made from the dismantled beams of the Theater, but perhaps John Dee designed the Theater as well.

True, the Theater and the original Globe are not cubes or spheres, but are **octagonal cylinders**. However that's just as exciting.

A sphere with a diameter of 72, which is inside a "72-tall by 72-wide" octagonal cylinder, is tangent to the centers of the eight faces, and also the octagonal cylinder's top and bottom!

All this interweaving of three-dimensional shapes was very much a part of Dee's Euclidean mathematical philosophy.

Books 11, 12, and 13 of Euclid's *Elements* (to which Dee adds corollaries and addendums in the 1570 first English translation of Euclid's *Elements*) are all about the interrelationships between various 3D shapes: cones, cylinders, pyramids, prisms, spheres, and cubes, as well as the octahedron, icosahedron, and dodecahedron.

For example, Book 13, Proposition 15, reads:

"To construct a cube and comprehend it in a sphere, like the pyramid; and to prove that the square on the diameter of the sphere is triple the square on the side of the cube."

(This takes a few re-readings just to figure out what Euclid is saying, never mind setting out to prove it.)

The idea of an **octagonal cylinder** (72 tall by 72 wide) fitting in a perfect **cube** (72 tall X 72 wide by 72 deep) and containing **sphere** (72 diameter) would have Dee dancing around his library.

Imagine. Three-dimensional mathematical geometry encapsulated in a home for the performance of verbal, musical, and choreographic arts. Now that would be harmonious!

The proportions of the new (1997) Globe

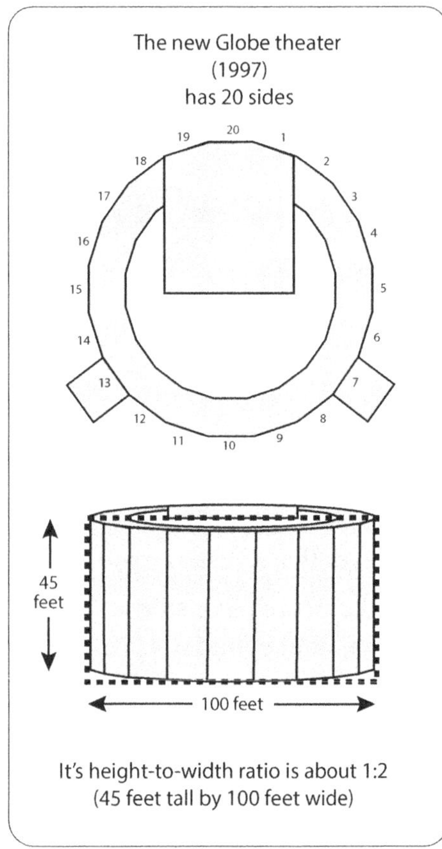

Let's flash forward to 1997, when the "new" Globe was constructed, about 750 feet from the site of the original theaters.

Excavations done in 1988-89 suggest the second Globe was polygonal, and not round, as depicted by Hollar.

The "new" Globe has 20 sides, and a diameter of 100 feet.

It's 33 feet high (to the eaves), with a 12 foot roof, making it 45 feet tall overall.

This makes it's height: width ratio about 1:2. That's more squat than the 3:4 "second" Globe, and much more squat of the 1:1 "original" Globe (based on the old illustrations).

I think the original Globe was intimate, classical and harmoniously proportioned

The new Globe theater has a capacity of 1600 people, (including 700 groundlings.) This 20-sided polygon, with a 100-foot diameter, has an area of 7919.22 square feet.

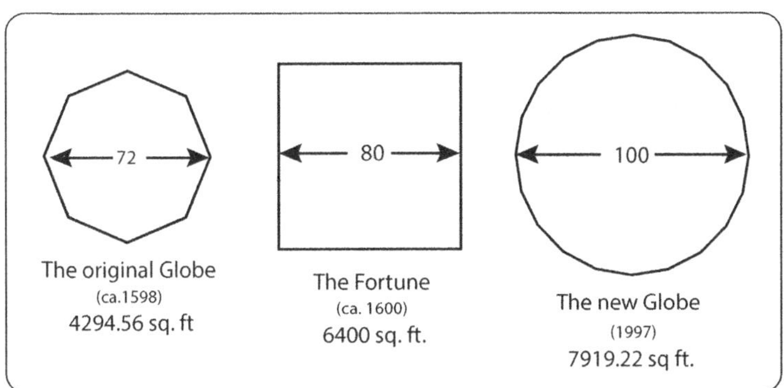

The original Globe (ca.1598) 4294.56 sq. ft
The Fortune (ca. 1600) 6400 sq. ft.
The new Globe (1997) 7919.22 sq ft.

That's much larger than footprint of the original Fortune, which was of **6400** square feet.

And it's almost double the footprint of the original Globe, which was **4294.56** square feet. I think the original Globe had a very intimate interior.

On the exterior of the new Globe, the beams are exposed, as was the style of many Elizabethan homes. However, a theater is not a house.

My conjecture is that the original Globe exterior was fully plastered and "sgraffitoed," or faux-painted to make it look like marble or stonework. This decorative technique was quite popular all across Europe during the Renaissance.

Dee was trying to introduce a Renaissance revival of classical architecture to Londoners. Even though the original Globe was made from wood, I think Dee would have wanted it to echo the design of Greek and Roman theaters, as discussed by his favorite architects, Alberti and Vitruvius. The decorative elements would express classical themes and the overall shape would express classical proportions. To me, the satyrs on the pilasters (flat columns) in the Fortune suggest a classical decor for the original Globe as well.

In discussing the "Arte of Architecture" in his 1570 *Preface to Euclid*, John Dee quotes Leon Battista Alberti: "Lineaments [proportions] have nothing to do with the particular material the building is made from."

Then Dee comments: "We thank you, Master Alberti. By setting aside the material stuff of the building, you have appropriately given your Art (and your description of it) is a Mathematical perfection that involves thinking about order, number, form, figure, and symmetry." (John Dee, 1570 *Preface to Euclid*, p. d iii.j, my transcription)

Forgive my redundancy, but to understand my interpretation of the original Globe, it's important to really understand Dee's mindset about Architecture, so take a moment to contemplate each word in Dee's phrase:

"a Mathematical perfection that involves thinking about order, number, form, figure, and symmetry."

My hypothesis is that the height of each of the 3 stories was 18 feet

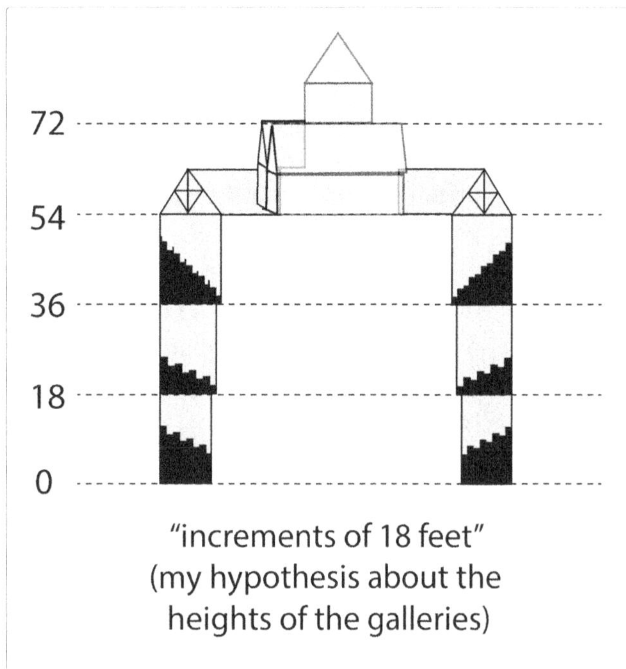

"increments of 18 feet"
(my hypothesis about the heights of the galleries)

Based on the old illustrations, if the height of the Globe was 72 feet to top of the roof, I wondered how Dee would have distributed the various heights if the floors inside?

As 72 divided by 4 is 18,
I suggest that story 1, story 2, and story 3, were each 18 feet tall (totaling 54 feet).

And to the peak to the small buildings on the roof was another 18 feet.
(totaling to 72 feet)

Eighteen feet might seem rather tall, as we moderns are used to rooms that are 8-10 feet tall. In the original Globe, if there were four rows of benches, and the back 3 rows were "stepped up" by 2 feet each, the eyes of six-foot person standing in the back row would be about 12 feet above ground level. This leaves about leaving 6 feet of headroom. That's not an inordinate amount in a crowded space with dozens of other theatergoers around.

However, I think the front row of seats of "story 1" must have been raised up about 6 feet, otherwise the view of those "high-paying" seated patrons would be blocked by the "less-paying" groundlings standing in the Starr's Mall.

This 4-6 foot rise is not unreasonable if, as I suggest, the Globe's stage was also 6 feet above the ground.

In Book 8, Chapter 7 of the *Art of Building*, Leon Battista-Alberti says the height of a stage should be 5 feet, but "on occasion raised as high as six cubits."

As a cubit is 1.5 feet, he's saying the stage in a classical theater might be anywhere from 5 to 9 feet off the ground.

With this 6-foot rise of "story 1," a six-foot person standing in the back row would now barely have any headroom at all. Suddenly, 18 feet doesn't seem very tall.

In story 3, the four rows of seats would probably be even steeper than in stories 1 and 2, so those seated in the back rows with a clear line of sight down to the stage. But here, height would not be a problem, as above the third story would be an "attic" space under the eaves that would be quite open, airy and would "catch" the sound emanating from the stage, like an giant ear.

With three 18-foot galleries, it might seem as though the folks in the back row of "story 3" would be too far away to see and hear the action.

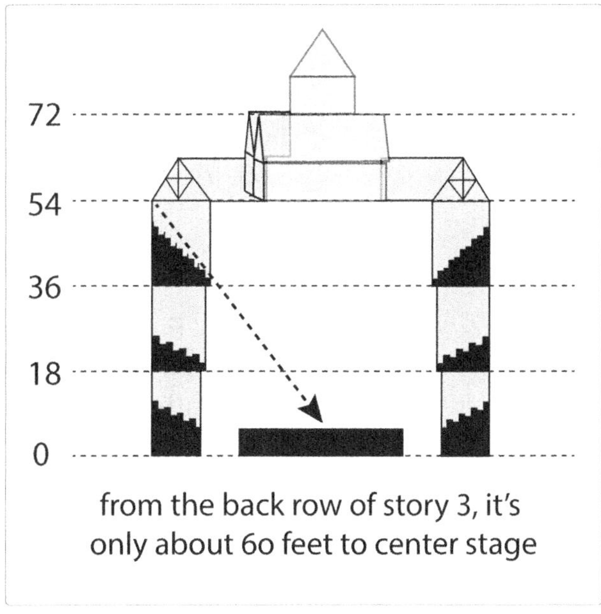

from the back row of story 3, it's only about 60 feet to center stage

But in actuality, this would only put these back-seaters about 60 feet from center stage.

Sixty feet is only 20 yards.

That's closer than even the front-row-balcony seats in many modern-day theaters.

To ease the cramped quarters, often the second and third stories jutted out more into this Starr's Mall area (or they "jettied," as the British say).

The second story might have been 12.5 feet in depth and the third story 13.5 feet in depth.

This might have allowed for five rows of benches up in the "cheap seats" of story 3.
(what American's call the "bleachers" in a baseball park.)

In short, providing ample height (18 feet) for each story would make up for the skimpy depth (10 to 13.5 feet) of each of the seating galleries.

Again, my idea of a 72-foot tall and by 72-foot wide octagonal cylinder is based on the old illustrations, but it also provides a simple, but well-integrated, way to read the "parametric" illustration of the Globe:

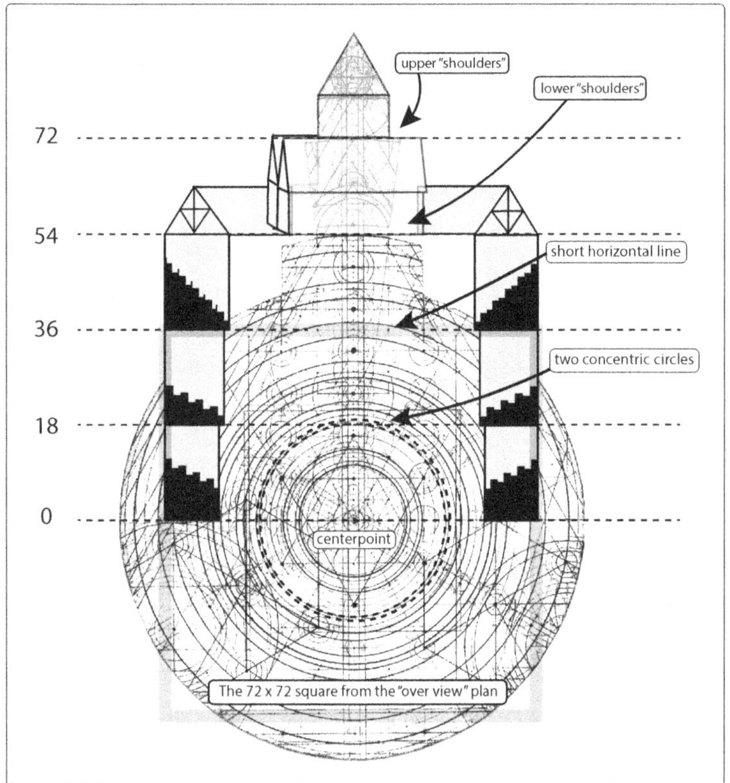

The "height" is measured up from the center point (where the pinpricks start).

The "72 line" is exactly where the **upper "shoulders"** are on the parametric drawing.

The "54 line" is right where the (wider) **lower "shoulders"** are.

The "36 line" is aligned with a **"short horizontal line"** on the parametric, which corresponds with the **"72 x 72 square"** of the "overview" drawing.

And the "18 line" aligns where Dee has drawn **2 concentric circles** unusually close together.

And way up at the top of the parametric drawing, left over, is an equilateral triangle on a rectangular base, a perfect representation of the Tower seen rising above the roof line in the drawings of Visscher and his copyists.

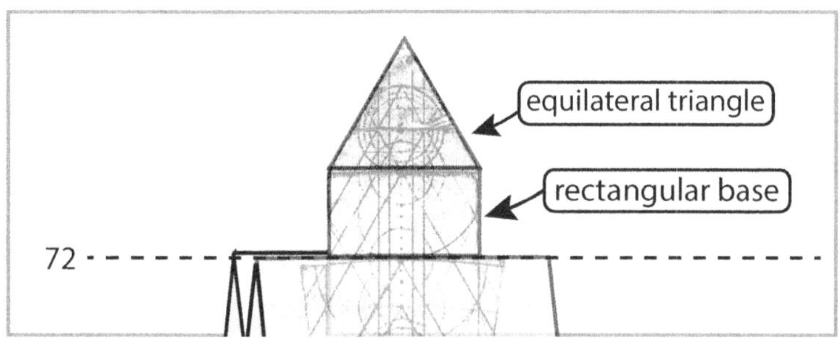

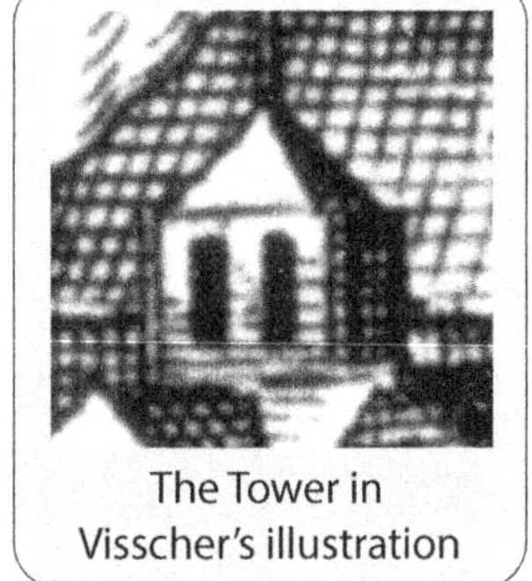
The Tower in Visscher's illustration

Visually, this tower helps give the octagonal cylinder more "vertical lift." It acts sort of like a church steeple, or the tip of a rocket at Cape Kennedy.

By contrast, a more horizontal or squat building inherently has much less visual "lift," like a heavy football stadium or a sprawling "big box" store.

So sorry John, but a dome isn't in the budget

Incidentally, I'm pretty sure that if Dee could if have figured a way to structurally add a 72-foot diameter wooden dome, he would have. Vitruvius and Alberti both explained that circular temples usually have domes. Though made of masonry, Brunelleschi had put a 150-foot-diameter dome of the Florence Cathedral a century earlier.

I believe the John Dee Tower of 1583 in Newport, Rhode Island originally had a 24-foot diameter stone-and-mortar dome. If you rotate Dee's "Thus the World was Created" chart 90 degrees counterclockwise, at the top is Dee's word "MUNDUS" which can mean either "WORLD or DOME."

(Buckminster Fuller could have given John Dee some structural tips about a lightweight geodesic dome.)

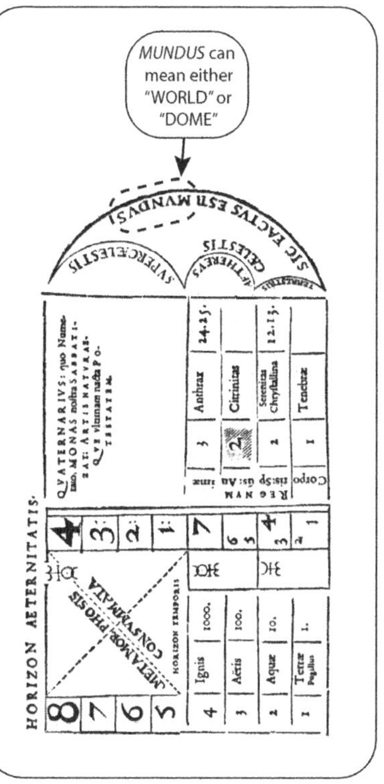

An explosion of geometry rocks the Globe!

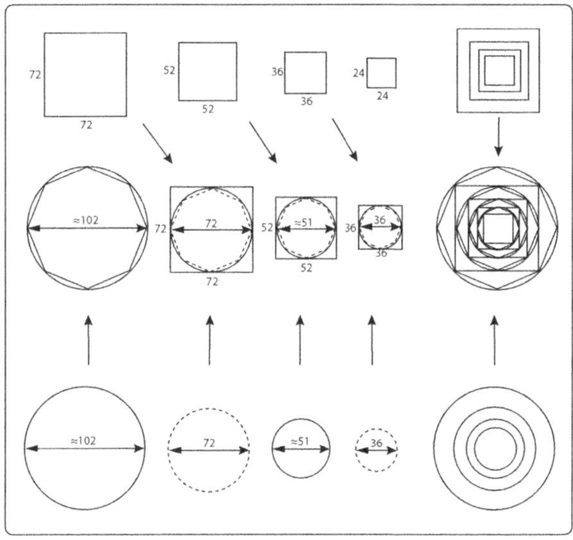

"Halvings and doublings" of the circles, octagons and squares in the plan of the Globe

Just as the "overview" plan has a progression or doublings (or halvings) of the areas of **circles, octagons, and squares**, we might now imagine the doublings (or halvings) of the areas of **spheres, octagonal cylinders, and cubes**.

Envision a 6-foot sphere, like a weather balloon, suspended, dead center in the middle of the original Globe, above the Starr's Mall.

(This digital illustration actually uses a 1595 sketch of the "thrust stage" of the Swan, but that's o.k., as we're using our imaginations.)

Now, imagine an octagonal cylinder around the weather balloon.

And around that,
a cube-shaped box.

Next, imagine that whole assembly inside a **larger** weather balloon.

Then another octagonal cylinder.

Then another cube-shaped box.

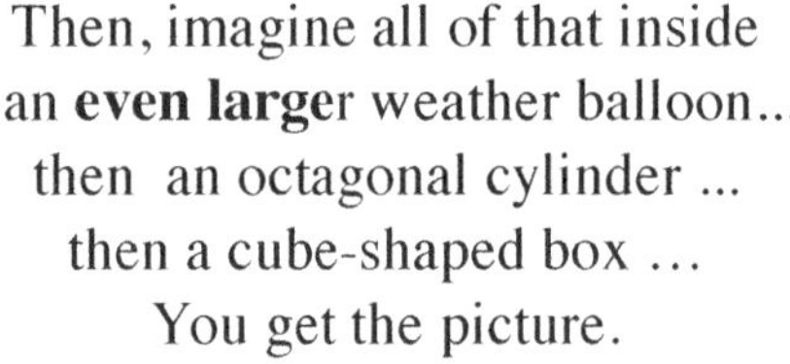

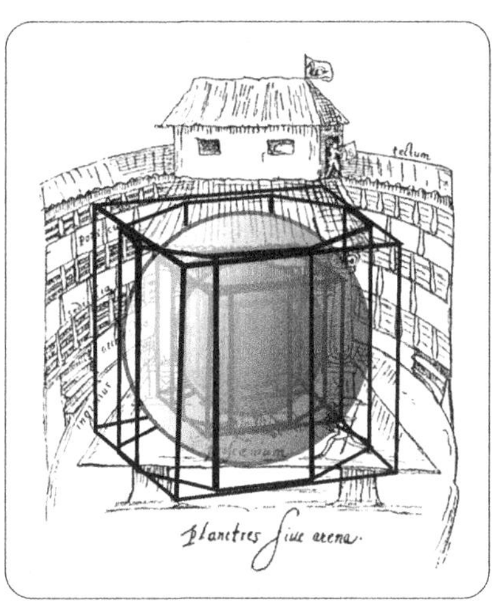

Then, imagine all of that inside
an **even larger** weather balloon...
then an octagonal cylinder ...
then a cube-shaped box ...
You get the picture.

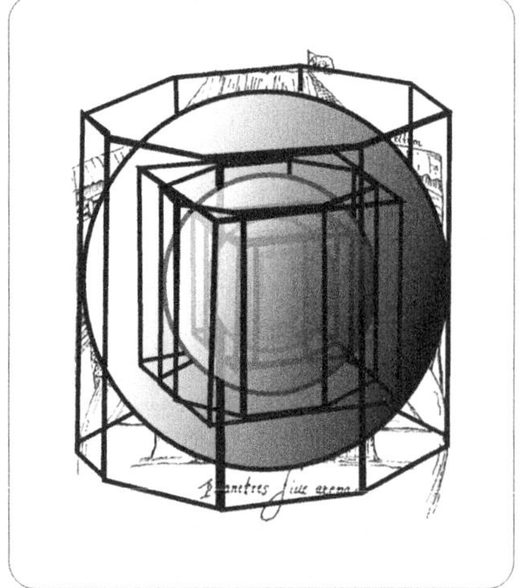

From the first weather balloon outwards its like an explosion of expanding shapes ...

until you get to the octagonal cylinder of the wooden walls of the original Globe.

In fact, we might even continue this progressive geometry further outwards, because the news of the Globe's plays spread through the city, through England, through Europe, an even through time, as Shakespeare is still immensely popular today.

The radiant power of geometrical symmetry of these most basic shapes broadcasts the stories of humanity to the world. Sounds bizarre, but I believe this would have been John Dee's thought process. He called himself a "cosmopolite," which is Greek for "citizen of the world."

Is there a "hidden octahedron" in the Globe as well?

One of the most amazing characteristics of the five Platonic solids is that certain pairs of them are "**duals**" of each other.

The octahedron and the cube are **duals**.

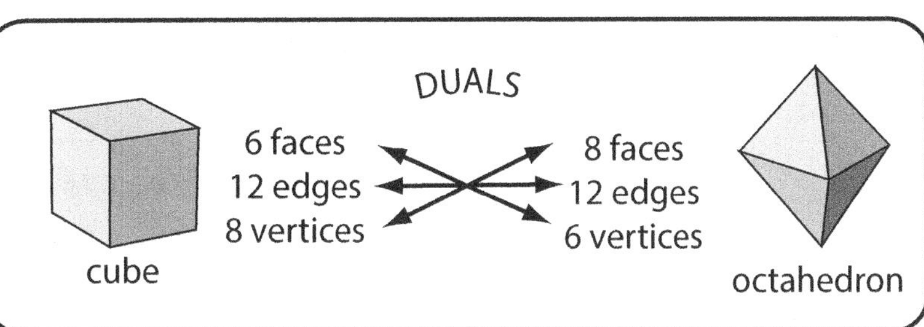

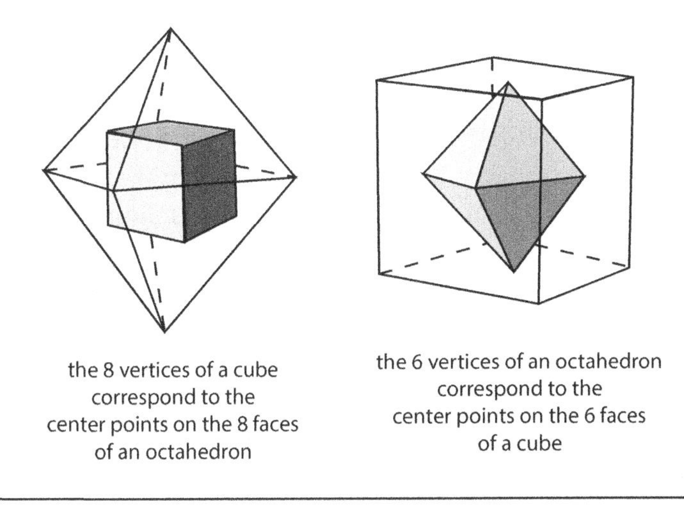

the 8 vertices of a cube correspond to the center points on the 8 faces of an octahedron

the 6 vertices of an octahedron correspond to the center points on the 6 faces of a cube

Basically this means you can fit a octahedron inside a cube, and the octahedron's 6 vertices will touch all 6 center points of the faces of the cube.

Conversely, you can fit a cube inside an octahedron, and the cube's 8 vertices will touch the center points of all 8 faces of the octahedron.

Similarly, the icosahedron is the **dual** of the dodecahedron.

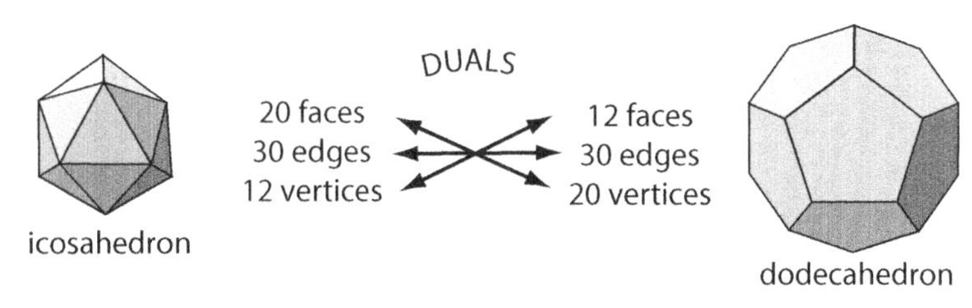

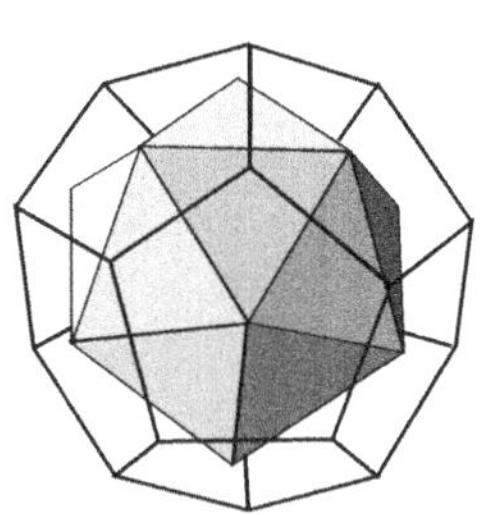

the 12 vertices of an icosahedron correspond to the center points on the 12 faces of a dodecahedron

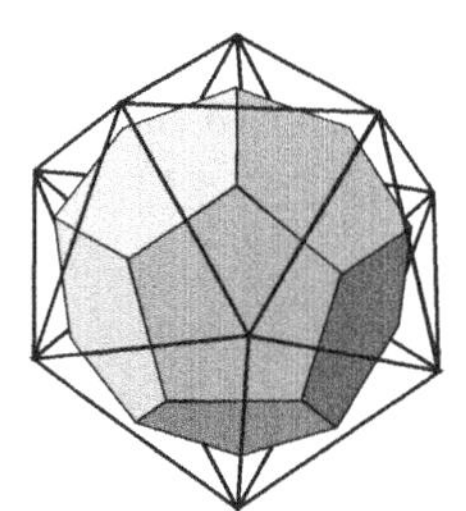

the 20 vertices of an dodecahedron correspond to the center points on the 20 faces of a icosahedron

The 12 vertices of an icosahedron, inside a dodecahedron, will touch the center points of each of the 12 faces of the dodecahedron.

Conversely, the 20 vertices of a dodecahedron, inside an icosahedron, will touch the center points of the 20 sides of the dodecahedron.

(I bet you can't say that 5 times fast.)

And amazingly, the tetrahedron is a **dual** of itself.

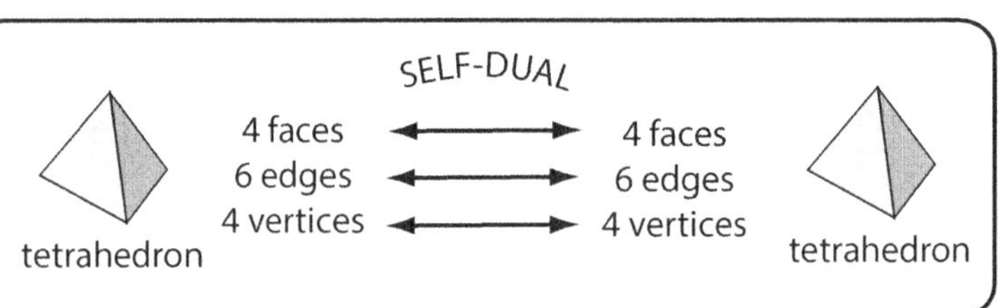

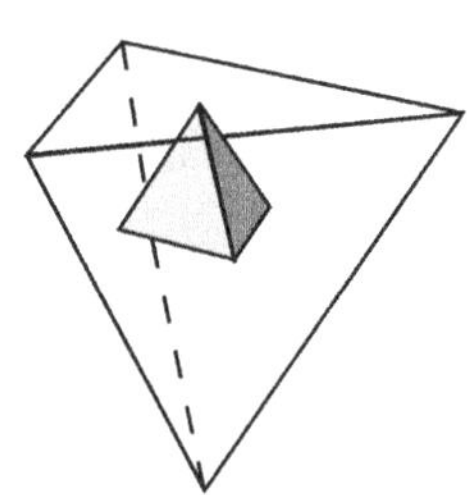

the 4 vertices of a "inverted" tetrahedron correspond to the 4 center points on the faces of an "upright" tetrahedron

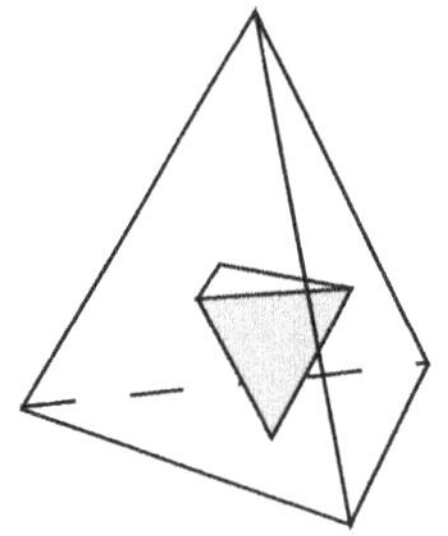

the 4 vertices of an "upright" tetrahedron correspond to the face center points on the faces of an "inverted" tetrahedron

An inverted tetrahedron fits inside a larger upright tetrahedron in such a way that the 4 vertices of the inverted tetrahedron touch the center points of the 4 faces of the upright tetrahedron.

And vice versa.

(In Latin, "vice versa" actually means "in-turned position," which is exactly what's going on here)

So, let's return to the octahedron, which fits inside the cube, and touches the center points of the 6 faces of the cube.

As we've seen, a sphere inside a cube will also touch the center points of the six faces of the cube.

But here's something special:

This "internal sphere" is tangent to the cube in the **exact same six places** the "internal octahedron" is.

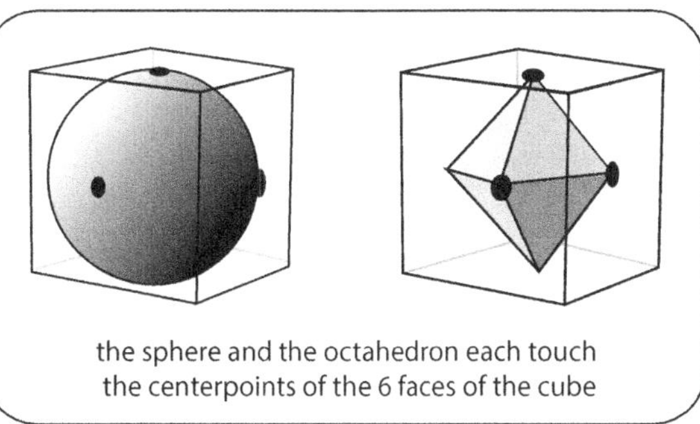

the sphere and the octahedron each touch the centerpoints of the 6 faces of the cube

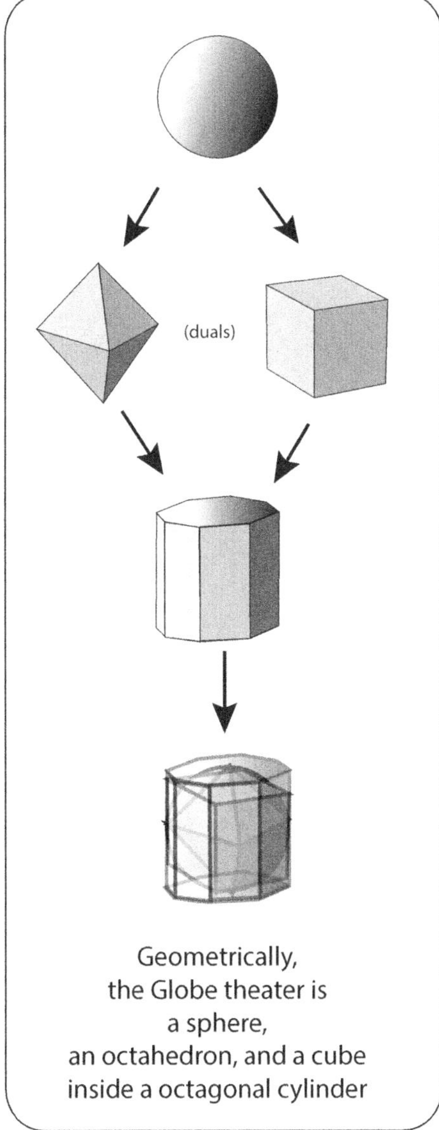

Geometrically, the Globe theater is a sphere, an octahedron, and a cube inside a octagonal cylinder

In other words, the octahedron fits beautifully in Dee's whole three-dimensional geometrical scheme for the original Globe.

This is all very nice conceptually, but how could I prove it?

Certainly if this was Dee's intent, he would have left numerous confirming clues. That was Dee's style.

CURIOUS CUT LINES AND FOLD LINES IN THE PARAMETRIC DRAWING

Let's return to the "parametric drawing" of the Byrom Collection which combines an "overview" plan with a "side-view"plan.

We'll explore all the circles and lines later, but first let's analyze the "cut lines" and "fold lines" at on the "neck" of this bottle-shaped drawing.

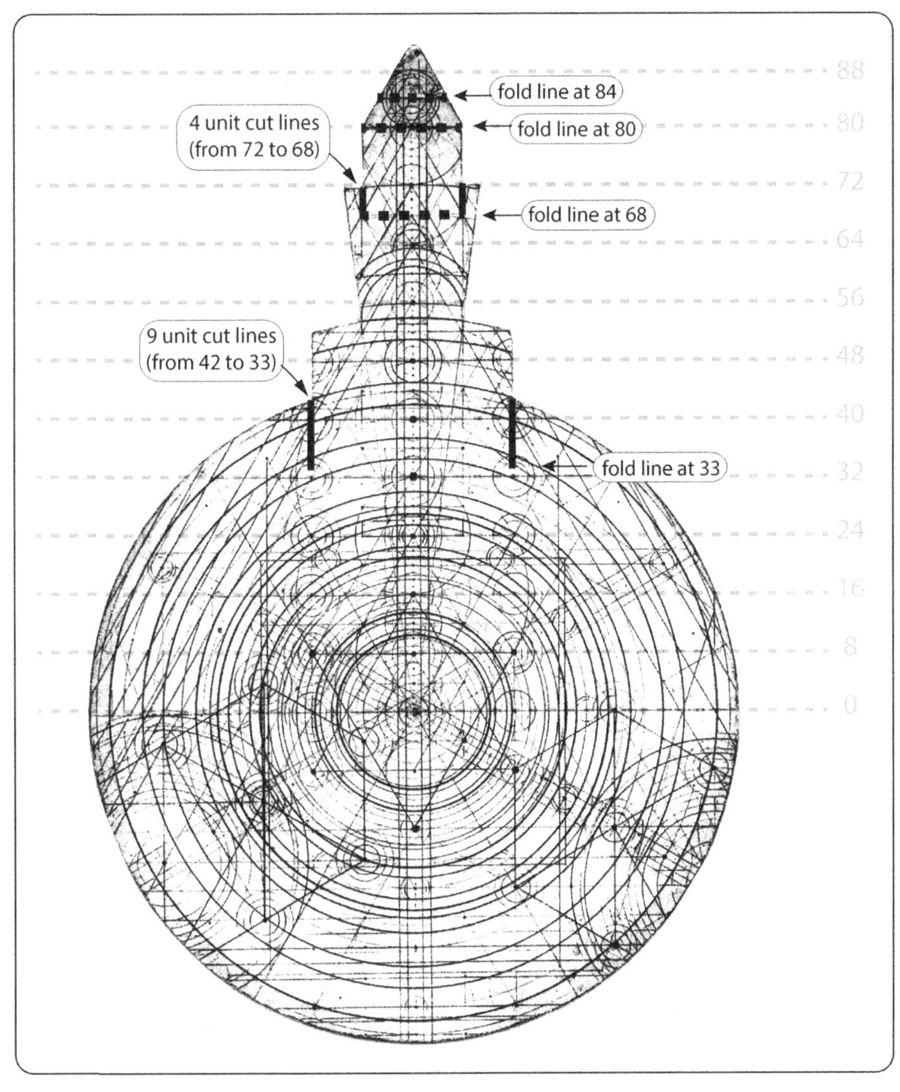

In the equilateral triangle at the top, there are marks left from folding, at a height of **84 and 80**.

Below them are two vertical cut lines, each 4 units long (**from 72 to 68**).

At **68**, there is also a fold line.

Below that are two cut lines, each 9 units long (**from 42 to 33**).

And there's a fold line at **33**.

To understand what this was all about, I enlarged a photocopy of the drawing, made the cutlines, and folded it.

Using the 4-unit cutlines and folding at the "68 line"

By using the 4-unit cutlines and folding at the "68 line," the vertical part looked like a little house.

By using the 9-unit cutlines and folding at the "33 line," the vertical part looks like a church with a steeple.

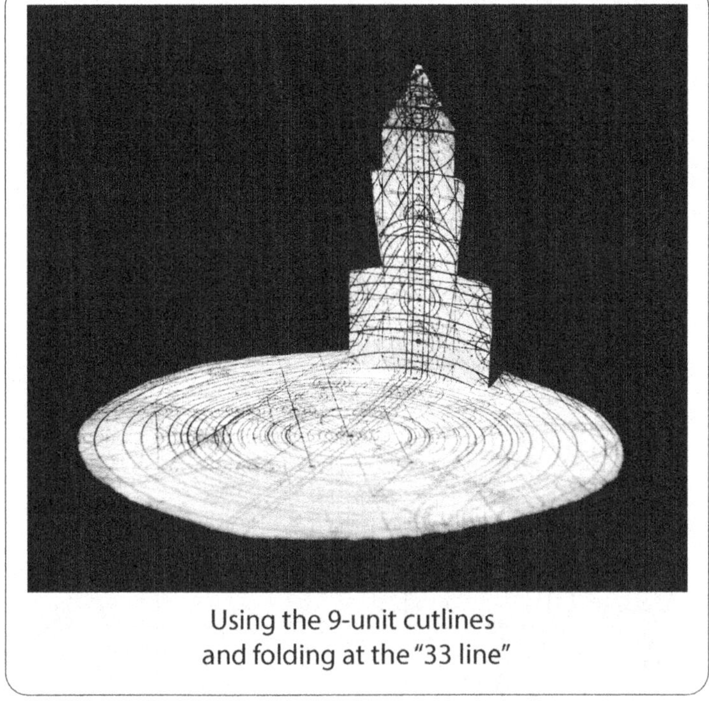
Using the 9-unit cutlines and folding at the "33 line"

This folding was interesting, but didn't seem to further my hypothesis that there was a huge invisible octahedron in the original Globe. However, there is a cryptic clue here about a different "hidden octahedron."

To see it, let's first look at another important relationship between the octahedron and the square (besides the fact that they are duals).

THE HIDDEN OCTAHEDRON?

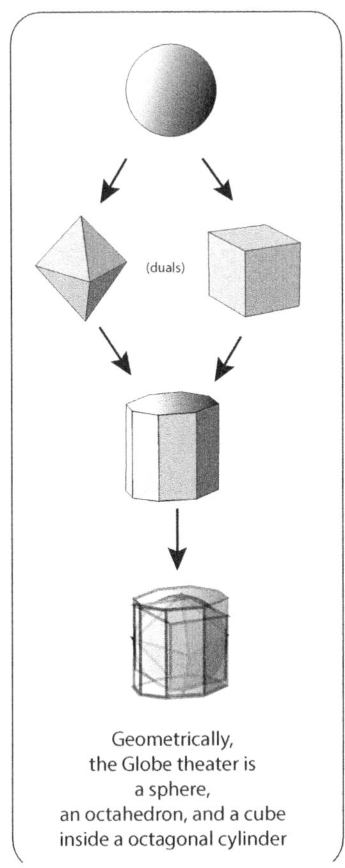

Geometrically,
the Globe theater is
a sphere,
an octahedron, and a cube
inside a octagonal cylinder

My hypothesis was that John Dee designed to Globe theater around these geometric shapes:

1. Sphere: 72 feet in diameter
2. Cube: 72 feet x 72 feet x 72 feet
3. Octahedron: 72 feet in diameter.
4. Octagonal cylinder: 72 feet in diameter and 72 feet tall

That's a pretty bold hypothesis – but I knew Dee was a bold thinker. Still, I needed more proof.

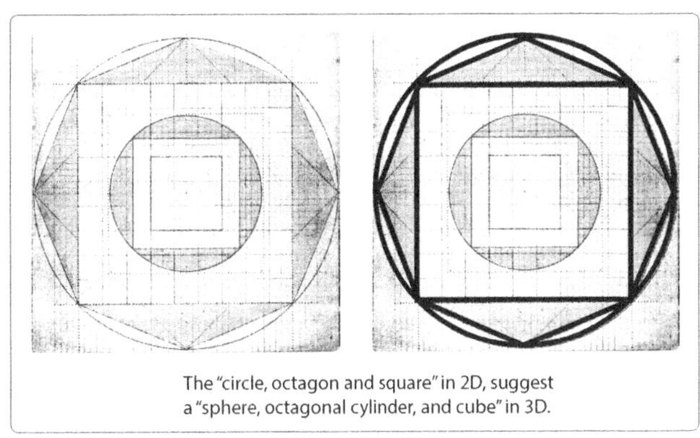

The "circle, octagon and square" in 2D, suggest a "sphere, octagonal cylinder, and cube" in 3D.

On the "overview" plan, the 3D **sphere, octagonal cylinder, cube**, are implied by the 2-D **circle, octagon, and square**.

But the octahedron is different. An octahedron like a sandwich of two Pyramids of Giza, most frequently depicted as balancing on a point, like a top.

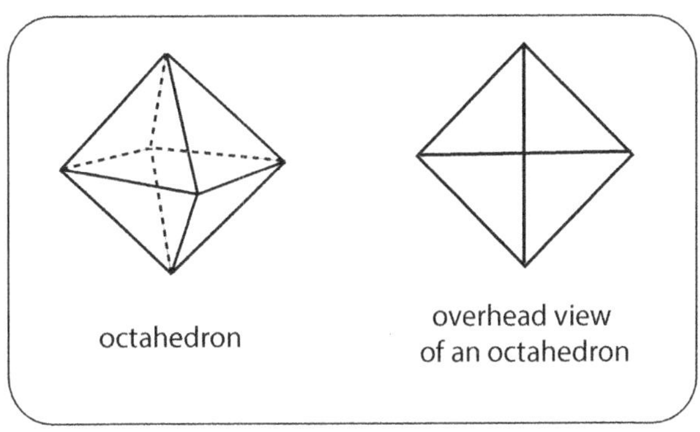

Looking straight-on to any of the octagon's 8 vertices (as, for example, in a "bird's-eye view"), an octahedron looks like a **square** or more descriptively, a **diamond**.

As the octahedron and the cube are duals, an octahedron's 6 vertices will touch the center points of the 6 faces of a cube.

Seen from above, this would look like a "diamond in a square."

And just such an arrangement can be seen on Dee's "overview" plan!

There's a faint, but distinct, diamond within the 72 x 72 white square.

(And it's tangent to the circumcircle of the 36 x 36 white square.)

(Admittedly, this diamond is hardly proof of an octahedron. It's Dee's hint to search deeper.)

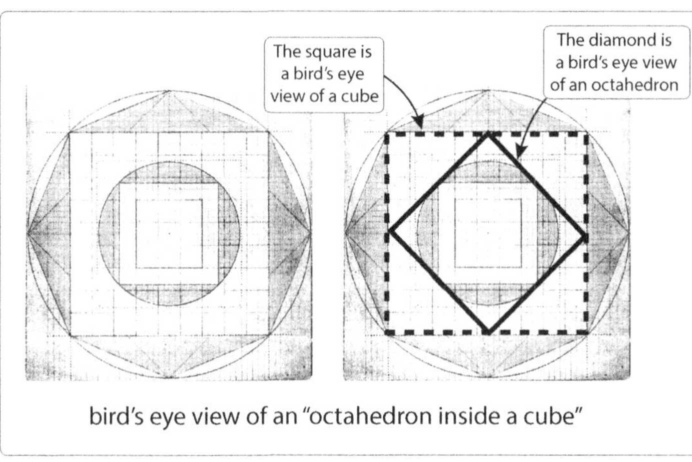
The square is a bird's eye view of a cube
The diamond is a bird's eye view of an octahedron
bird's eye view of an "octahedron inside a cube"

The wedding of a cube and an octahedron = a cuboctahedron

Seen as duals, the ocathedron fits in the cube, and the cube fits in the octahedron. But there's a third arrangement: the intersection of an octahedron and a cube.

With the intersection,
some of the octahedron extends beyond the cube,
and
some of the cube extends beyond the octahedron

If you cut off all the pointy stellations,
what remains is a cuboctahedron.

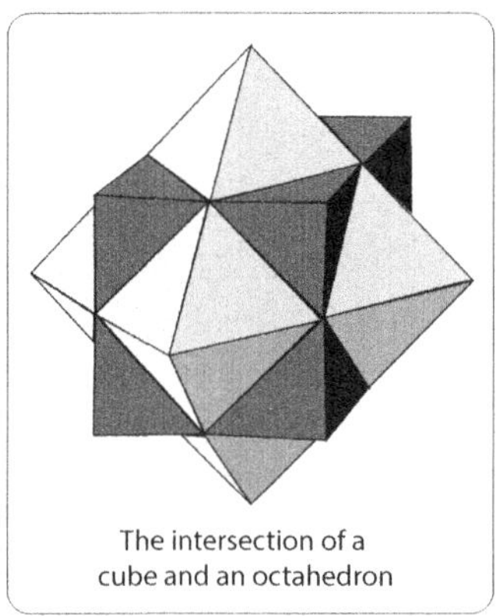
The intersection of a cube and an octahedron

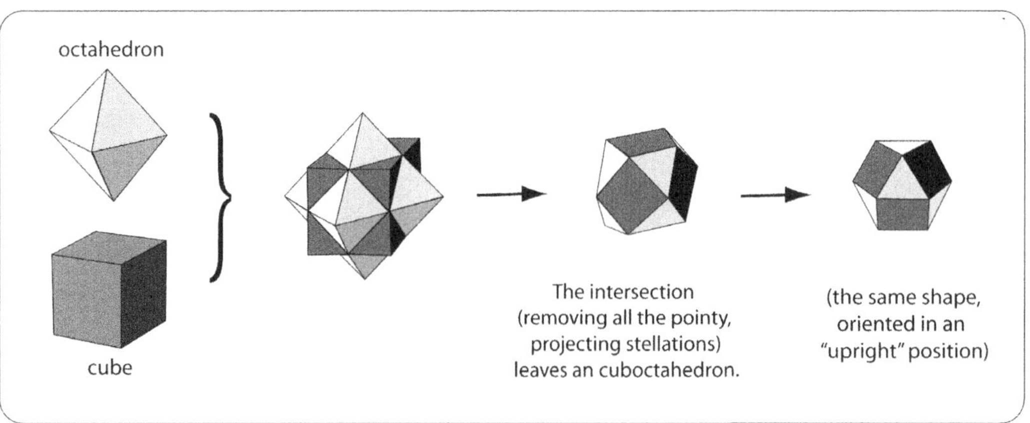
octahedron
cube
The intersection (removing all the pointy, projecting stellations) leaves an cuboctahedron.
(the same shape, oriented in an "upright" position)

We'll return to the cuboctahedron in a moment, but first let's envision a bird's-eye view of a cube and an octahedron intersecting.

A bird's-eye view of a the intersection of a cube and an octahedron looks like two superimposed squares, one rotated 90 degrees from the other.

And that's exactly what Dee has drawn on the "overview" plan.

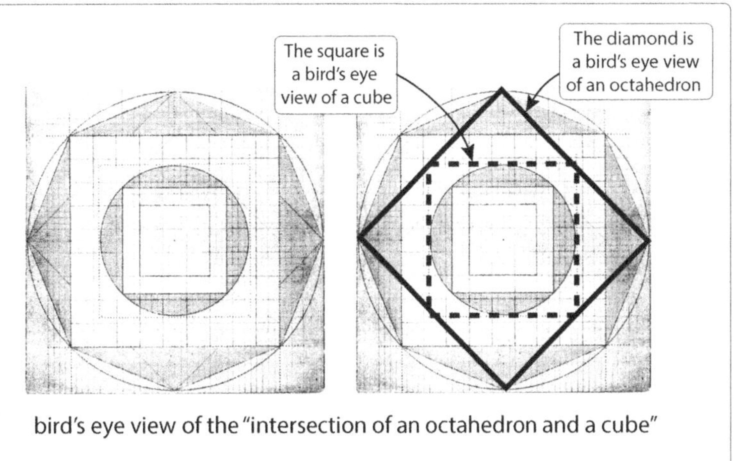

The square is a bird's eye view of a cube
The diamond is a bird's eye view of an octahedron

bird's eye view of the "intersection of an octahedron and a cube"

Admittedly, my deriving 3D shapes from 2D shapes is a nice idea, but it's hardly incontrovertable proof this is what Dee had in mind.

While mulling this over,
suddenly the hidden octahedron appeared!
It's hidden in the parametric drawing, but it was Visscher's 1616 illustration of the Globe that helped me find it.

The roof of the tall tower is a half octahedron!

It looks just like the top "pointy stellation" we just sliced off the octahedron when making the cuboctahedron!

Could this roof be a half-octahedron?

I realize sounds speculative. Any small building would have an angled roof to allow the rain and snow to slide off. And I could hardly ascertain from Visscher's drawing if the angles were exactly correct to make an perfect octahedron.

A **perfect octahedron** must have 8 faces that are equilateral triangles (3 equal angles of 60°, 60°, and 60°). And the internal angles of each face must be at an angle of 120° to each of its neighboring faces. Irregular octagons that are "too flat" or "too pointy" simply won't do.

The parametric drawing has a perfect equilateral triangle at the top. And that's what you see when looking directly "face on" to any side of an octagon.

But the parametric drawing is a "elevation, or a "side-view" plan. And looking straight-on to one edge of an octahedron, **you will definitely not "see" an equilateral triangle.**

As the equilateral triangle is "leaning backwards" to be part of the sloping roof, the height of the side-view of this triangle would appear to be **70.71%** of the equilateral "face on" view. (70.71% is $1/\sqrt{2}$)

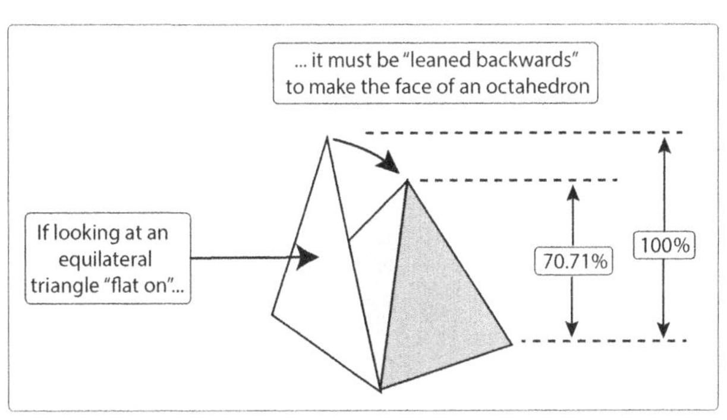

... it must be "leaned backwards" to make the face of an octahedron
If looking at an equilateral triangle "flat on"...
70.71%
100%

Despite this rather significant problem, this idea of a "half-octahedral roof" still intrigued me. I pushed onward.

In time, my efforts were rewarded. I soon discovered this rooftop was the key to unlocking a **great secret** about the various heights of the Globe theater, hidden cryptically in the whole parametric drawing. Here's the story:

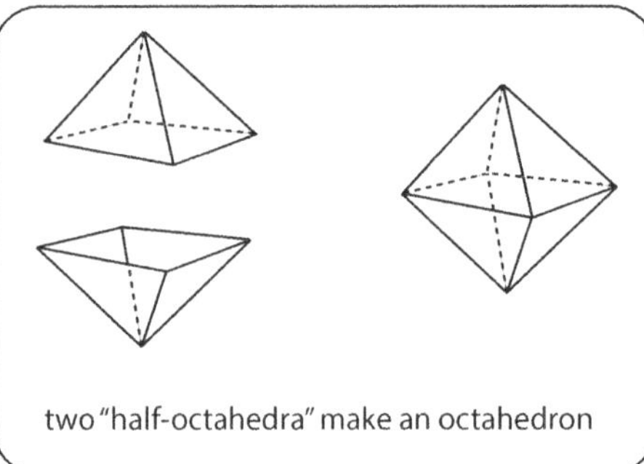

two "half-octahedra" make an octahedron

The function of the "half-octahedral" rooftop

I switched gears from thinking about this from this perplexing equilateral triangle problem and thought about the small tower itself. It was not ornamental. In fact, it served a very important function. It was the support for the **flagpole**. And the pole held the **flag**.

For Elizabethan theaters, the flag was like a modern-day advertising billboard. There were no Elizabethan newspapers, only the occasional broadside or pamphlet.

A flag, sometimes illustrated or with a fewwords, was raised the morning of the performance. White flags for comedies, black flags for tragedies, and red flags (like blood) for plays about history.

The flag of the Globe had to be large enough for Londoners to see from across the Thames River. And prior to that, the flag at the Theater had to be large enough to be seen from Moorgate, the northern entry to the city.

The 1612 book "*Curtain-Drawer of the World*" explains:

"*Each play-house advanceth his flagge in the aire, wither quickly at the wavering thereof are summoned whole troops of men, women, and children.*"

(www.bardstage.org/globe–theater–flags.htm)

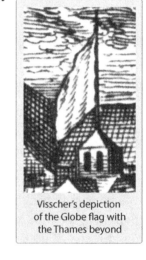

Visscher's depiction of the Globe flag with the Thames beyond

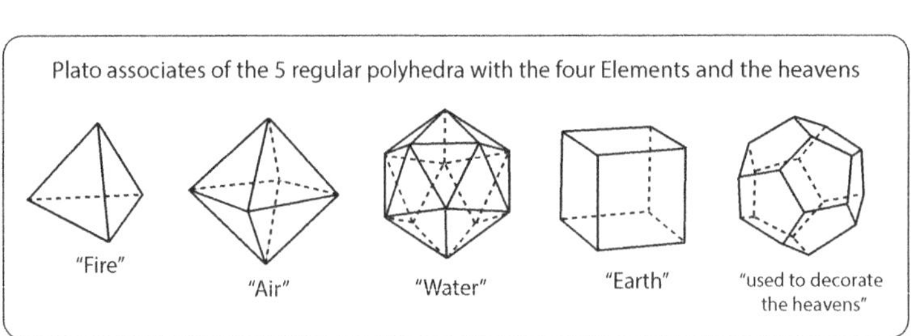

Plato associates of the 5 regular polyhedra with the four Elements and the heavens

I liked the sound of that word: "aire."

Plato had associated the octahedron with the Element of Air.

A big flag requires a tall flagpole. And a tall flagpole requires substantial support. Judging from Visscher's illustration, I estimated the flagpole was 18 feet tall. And the flag was about 12 feet tall by 18 feet wide. That's pretty big.

ship masts go through the decks to the keel

Just like the mast of a Elizabethan galleon, a 18-foot flagpole would be made from the trunk of a tall conifer (they grow straight). I estimate at the base it might be 8 to 9 inches thick.

Because sails are designed to catch powerful winds wind, ship masts must extend down through all the decks to be solidly attached to the keel.

As flags fly along with the breeze, flagpoles don't need to be quite as sturdy. But still, a flag whipped by a fierce wind requires substantial support. You wouldn't want the flagpole tumbling to the Starr's Mall.

The bottom of the flagpole had to be securely fastened in some fashion to the wood frame of the Tiring House. It might have even extended one floor down into the attic of the Tiring House for sturdier support. Either way, the internal structure of the flagpole tower had to be built to be strong. Undoubtedly, there would be some kind of triangulated arrangement of thick support beams.

At the apex of the tower, there must have been substantial "collar," not just to hold the flagpole steady, but also to securely connect the four sections of the roof together.

The illustrations from the 1600s are too small to provide clues, so I enlarged the very top of the parametric drawing. The upper tip was quite rounded off, the left side was worn more than the right, almost as if something had been torn off over the ages.

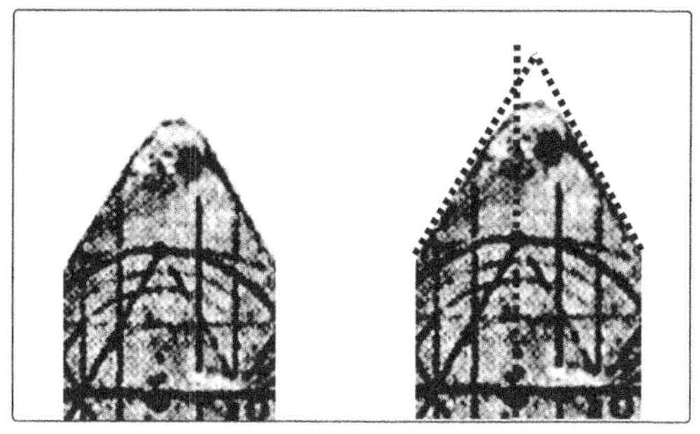
The tip of the parametric drawing is slightly "off axis" and quite worn

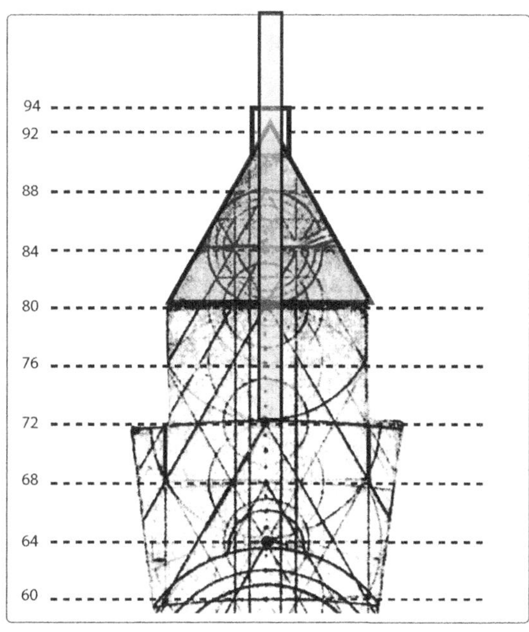

I estimated that the height of the roof, including the flagpole collar was about 94 units tall.

But still, that didn't account for the problem that the "side-view" of a half-octahedron is **not** an equilateral triangle.

To find the height of a half-octahedron, let's first look at the **three equal-sized squares** which make up the octahedron.

From the viewpoint shown here, you can see a horizontal square, as well as two vertical squares, which are at right angles to each other.

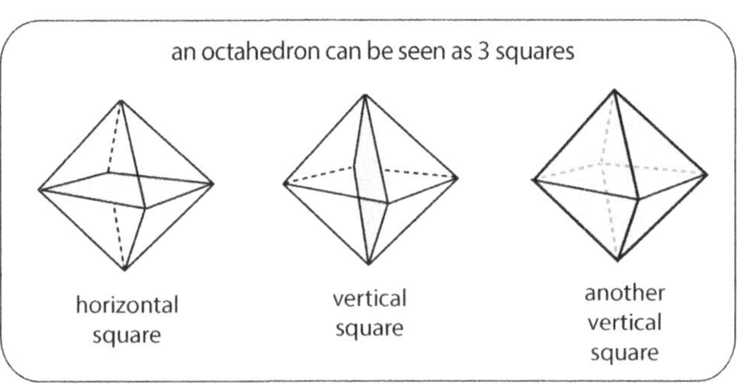

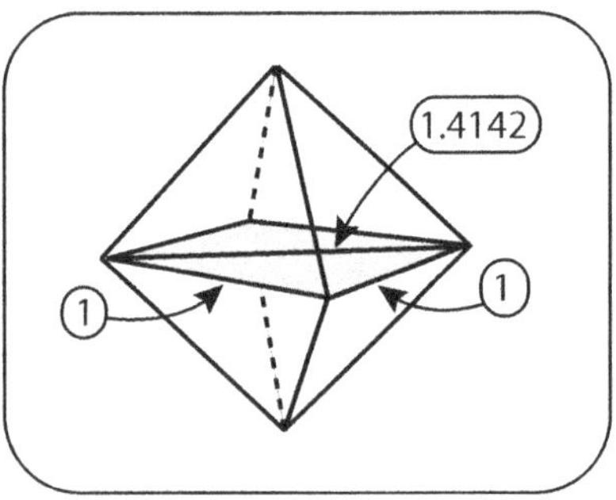

If each of the sides of the horizontal square is "1," the diagonal is 1.4142 (which is √2).

The center point divides the diagonal into 2 pieces, each .7071 on length.

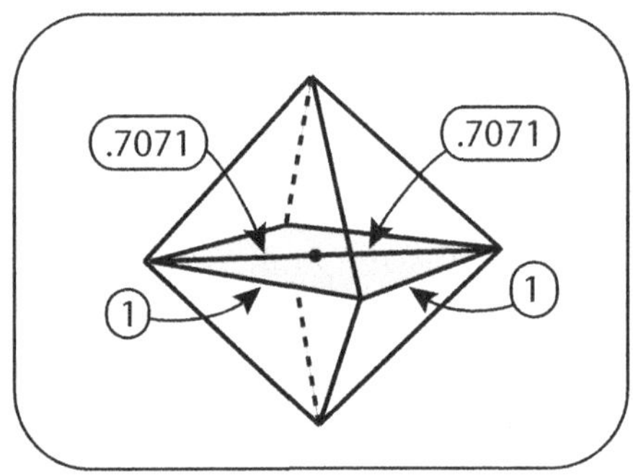

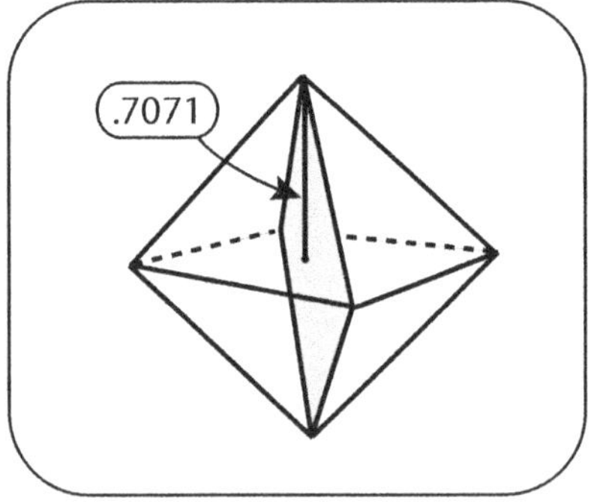

This vertical square is the same size as the horizontal square.

So the height of this half-octahedron is .7071.

Now, if we chose the sides of the octahedron to all be 14 units (as Dee did) all these "radiating vectors" are **9.899** units long.

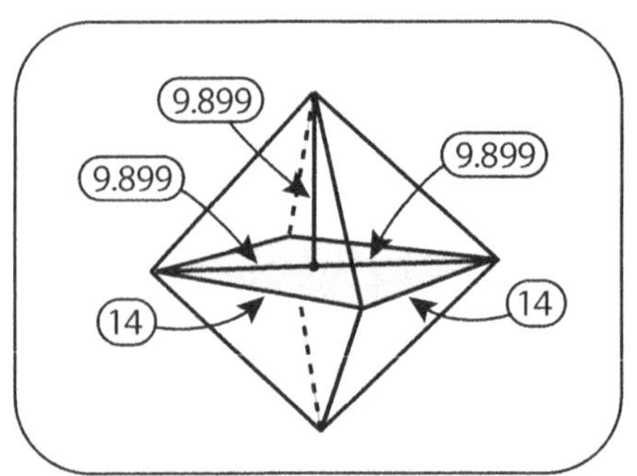

Hey, **.9899** is surprisingly close to **10**.
(It's only off by about 1%.)

If we had used **14.142** for sides of the horizontal square, the height of the half-octahedron would be **exactly 10**.

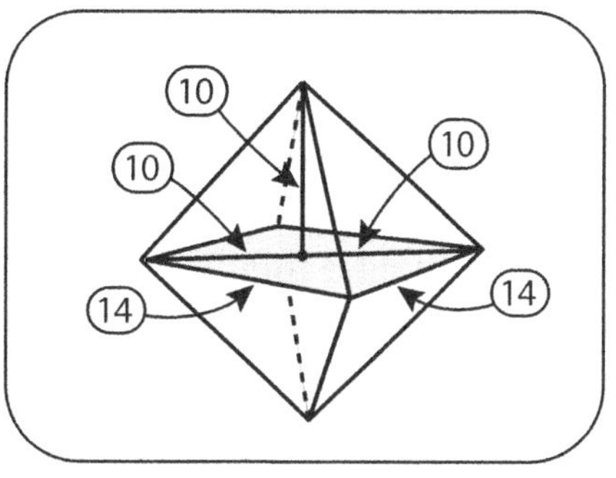

to a creative geometer like Dee, 1.4142 is a lot like 14

Then I realized. Dee did this all on purpose! He made the width of the flagpole tower to be 14, so it's height would be 10 (within 1%).

Dee dealt with √2 so much in his geometry, he saw the similarity between 1.4142 and 14.

They are a factor of 10 apart (within 1%).

(The reason I recognized that John Dee was playing this "1.4 is like 14" riddle is because I was a professional photographer for 40 years.

To double the amount of light coming through a 1-foot diameter window, you make a 1.4-foot diameter window. To double the light again, you make a 2-foot diameter window. To double the light again you make a 2.8-foot diameter window. In short, to double the amount of light, you multiply by √2 or 1.4142.

Well, these are the apertures or "f-stops" you see on photography lenses: 1, 1.4, 2, 2.8, 4, 5.6, 8, 11, 16, 22, 32...)

Yes. Dee did indeed want us to see the roof of the flagpole tower as a perfect half-octahedron.

And to me, its presence suggests that Dee wanted us to see a huge octahedron filling the Globe!

(mating with the huge cube, inside a huge octagonal cylinder, inside a sphere)

But Dee left an even better clue about the half-octahedron

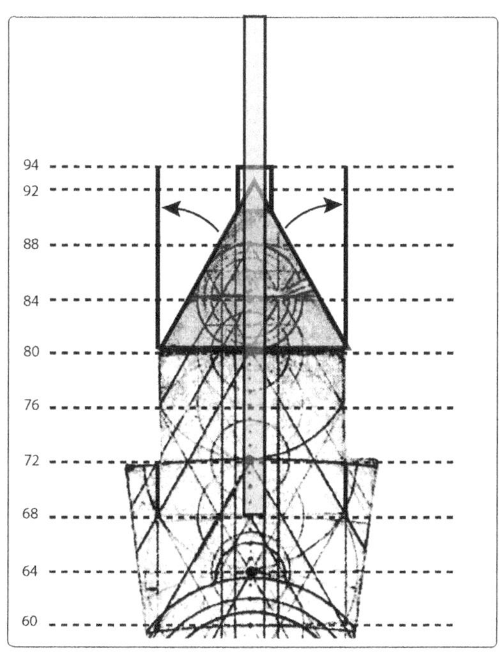

If we take either of the two upper sides of the equilateral triangle and swing them each "outwards," so they become vertical, they extend to the "94 line" (which is 14 units above the "80 line").

But still, if the drawing shows 14 feet and the side-view of a half octahedron only needs to be 10 feet, how are we to account for those 4 feet we just lost?

How does Dee graphically indicate this "4 foot loss."

The answer is:

The “folds.”
Recall that Joy Hancox noticed “score lines” or horizontal fold lines across the “80 line” and the “84 line.”

If you make and **in-fold** at the “80 line” and make **out-fold** at the “84 line,” you make a little 4-unit “step.”

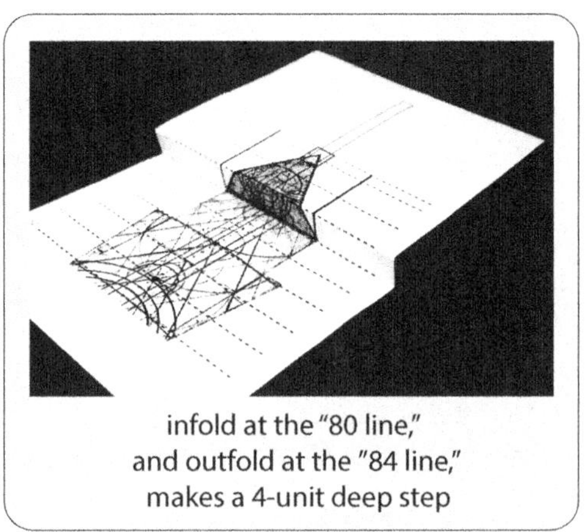

infold at the "80 line," and outfold at the "84 line," makes a 4-unit deep step

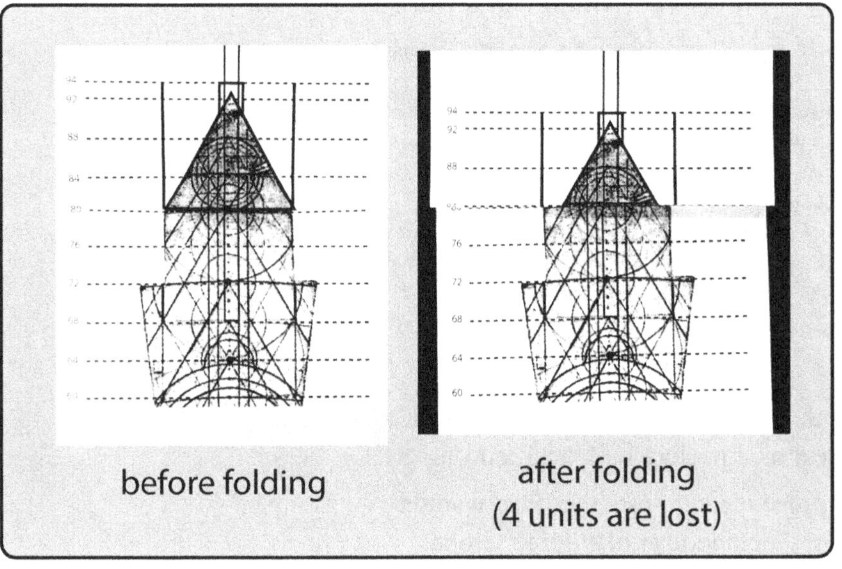

before folding

after folding (4 units are lost)

Viewing exactly straight-on to the illustration (so the step can’t be seen), the flagpole tower has instantly decreased in height by 4 units. (84 – 80 = 4).

This “step-process” creates a triangle which is not very wide. However it’s obvious the roof line must extend to the edge of a building.

So I have added black lines to indicate how this equilateral triangle is really intended to be an **isosceles triangle** (in this “revised” side-view).

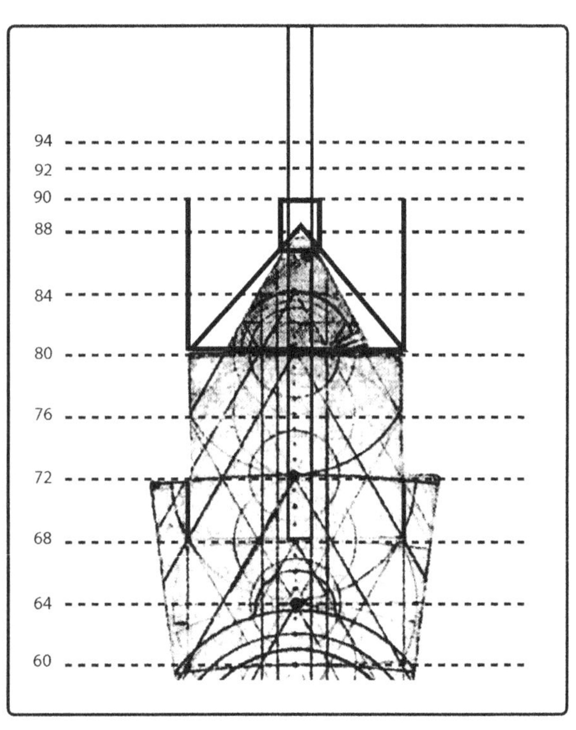

Would John Dee really have done a geometric "fold trick" like this?

You bet your sweet bippy he would have. He loved folding geometric figures. One cannot firmly grasp the sophisticated interrelationships between three-dimensional Euclidean geometric shapes, like Dee did, without making models.

Did I mention John Dee was the first person to use the word "model" in a printed book in the English language? He derived "model" from the French word *modelle* and the Italian word *modello*. (*Oxford English Dictionary*, model)

Using the 4-unit cutlines and folding at the "68 line"

We've seen how he employed other fold lines (and cut lines) to show the vertical aspect of the Globe.

Using the 9-unit cutlines and folding at the "33 line"

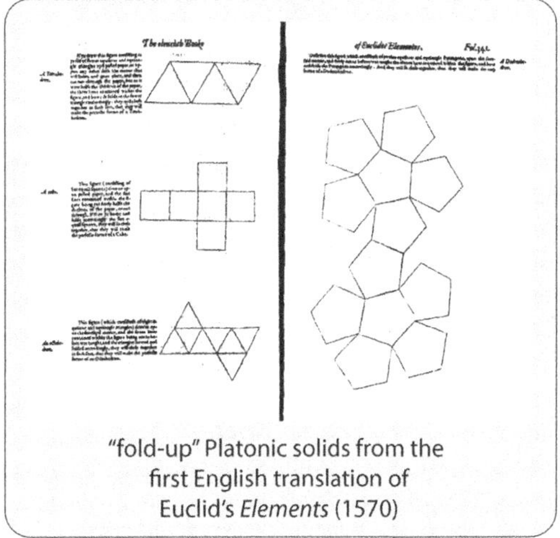

"fold-up" Platonic solids from the first English translation of Euclid's *Elements* (1570)

In the 1570 English translation of Euclid's *Elements*, there are 2-D drawings of various Platonic and Archimedean solids that the reader can cut out and fold into 3-D models.

I recognized this fold gimmick as one of Dee's signature cryptic tricks because of another fold trick I deciphered on the back cover his 1564 *Monas Hieroglyphica*.

It depicts a fancy shield or emblem, proudly displaying his Monas symbol. Above that are the letters YHVH, the ancient Hebrew name for God. Above that is a woman holding a seven-pointed star. Swirling symmetrically to both sides are strangely elongated leaves. And up at the top are two captions.

The left caption reads (translating from the Latin) "The Watery Dew of Heaven" and the right caption reads, "And the Fruit of the Earth He Will Give."

Oddly, both captions are rotated 90 degrees from normal. And also, they are upside-down from each other.

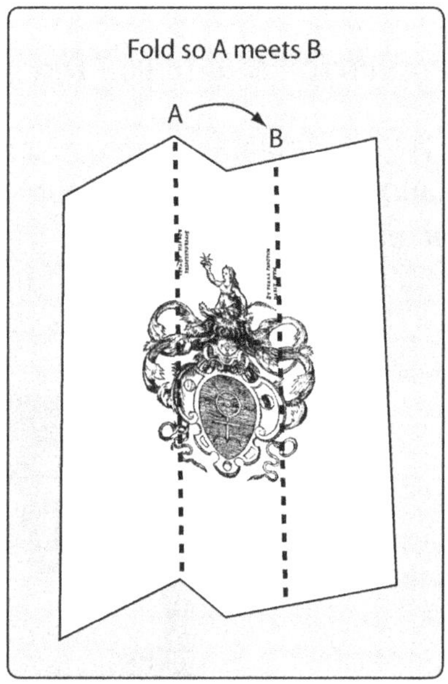

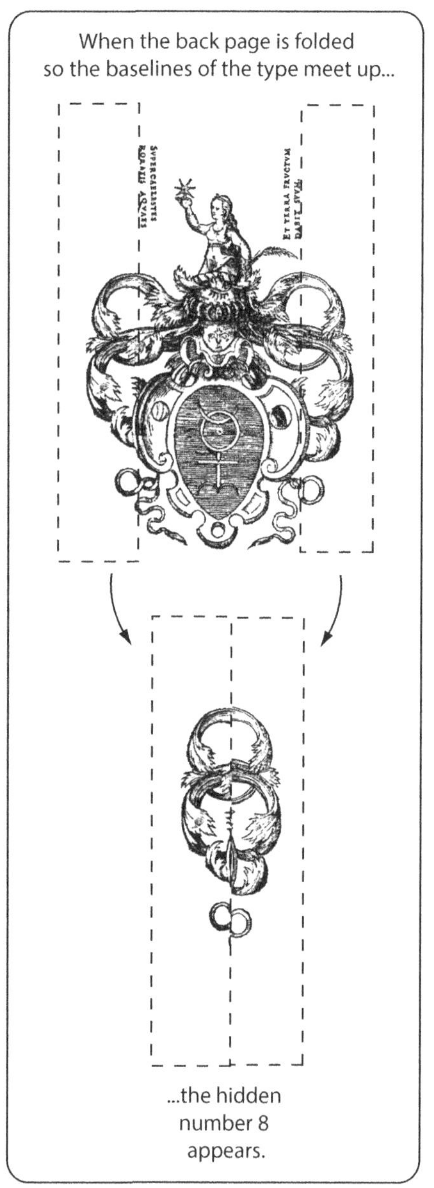

When the back page is folded
so the baselines of the type meet up...
...the hidden
number 8
appears.

If you make two folds, so that the baseline of the left caption aligns with the baseline of the right caption, the flowing leaves make **the shape of the figure 8**.

And one of the main themes of the *Monas Hieroglyphica* is **eightness**, or the **octave**, as in the "+4, –4, octave, null nine" rhythm of Consummata.

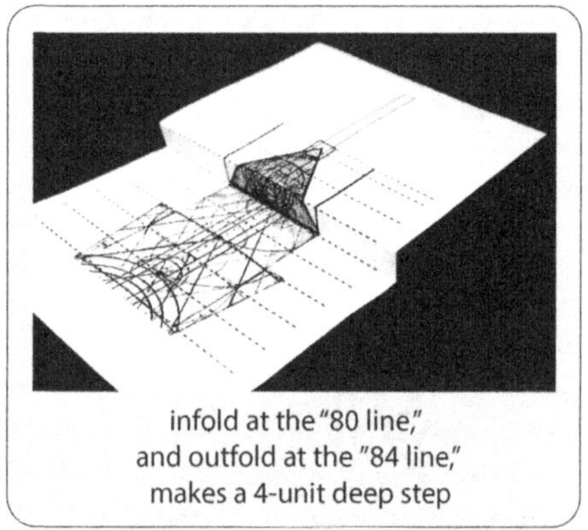

infold at the "80 line," and outfold at the "84 line," makes a 4-unit deep step

Oh yes, the clever "4 unit folding" to transform an equilateral triangle "face-on" view into a "side view" of the half octahedron was pure Dee. One hundred percent.

One might wonder why Dee didn't draw simply the parametric with a squatter triangle (10 units tall) in the first place. Well, then all the riddle-hinting about the "half-octahedron" would hardly be as effective.

And, to me, this half-octahedron roof implies a the huge implied octahedron filling the whole theater. (along with cube, octagonal cylinder, and sphere).

How can I be so sure of all these half- octahedra clues?

Because (as I promised to explain) this little "4-unit reduction" is also the key that unlocks the door of understanding the whole parametric drawing. And it's pure Dee. It's the heart of his mathematical cosmology.

If the height the building,
up to the top of the flagpole collar, was 94 units,
and we "lost" 4 units with this folding trick,
the height would be 90 units.

There's something special about 90.
To find out, let's look at all this in another way.

Starting with the 8-foot tall base of the flagpole tower,
and we add the 10-foot tall "half-octahedron" roof
(to the top of the flagpole collar),
that makes the whole flagpole tower 18 feet tall.

On the parametric, this 18-foot tall
section starts from the "72 line"
and goes up to the "90 line."

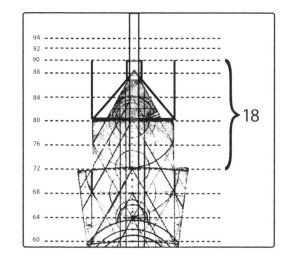

Hey, that's the same as the other 18-unit heights of the floors of the galleries and the Tiring House!

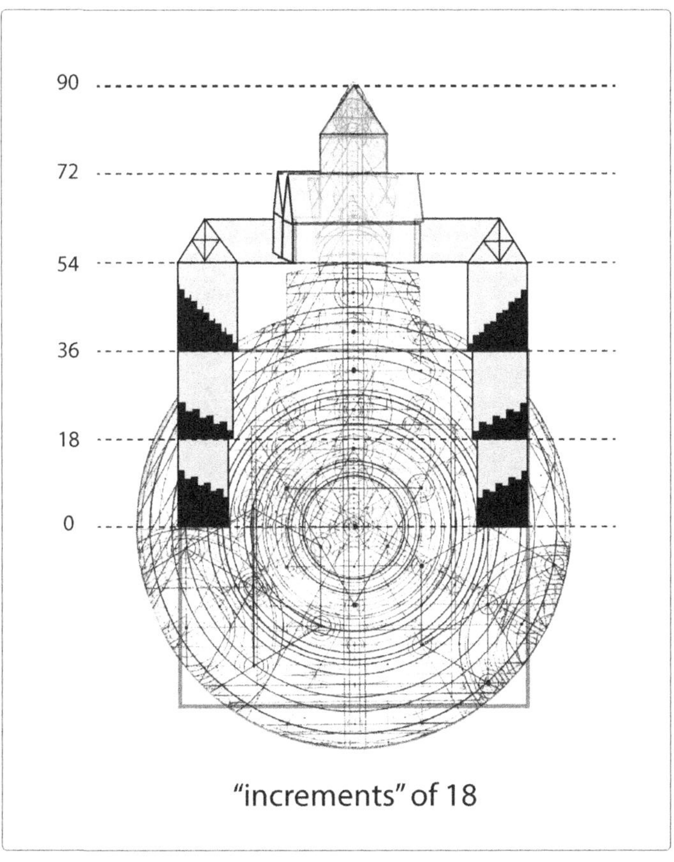

"increments" of 18

Remember, Story 1 goes up to the "**18 line**."

Story 2 goes up to the "**36 line**."

Story 3 goes up to the "**54 line**."

And the small buildings at the top of the Tiring House go up to the "**72 line**."

And now, the flagpole tower goes up to the "90 line!"

Admittedly, way back at the beginning, it was simply my hypothesis that the sections were all 18-units tall. And indeed, it's still a hypothesis. I haven't really proved anything yet.... Until now.

Seeing all these numbers together rang a bell (18, 36, 54, 72, 90). Not only are they all very "composite" numbers (they each have numerous factors), they are also all multiples of 9. (Do you see where this is headed?)

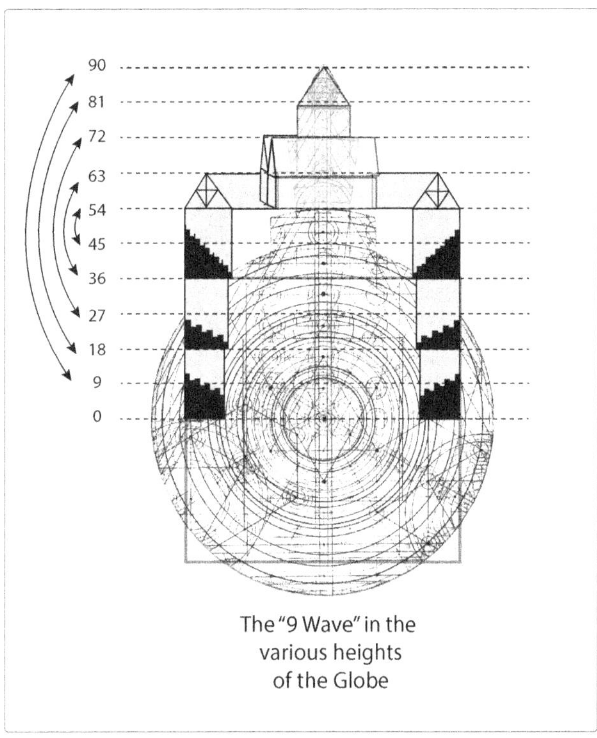

The "9 Wave" in the various heights of the Globe

Let's put "mid-lines" in between all these various heights.

These "halfway marks" fall at 9, 27, 45, 63, and 81.

Suddenly, we have the "9 wave," the rhythm that John Dee found in number and called "Consummata" (meaning "to make perfect").

The "9 wave" is the middle, horizontal row in the diamond-shaped arrangement of single-digit and double-digit numbers.

The "9 wave" is comprised of five sets of "reflective mates," (or transpalindromes) (09 and 90), (18 and 81), (27 and 72), (36 and 63), and (45 and 54).

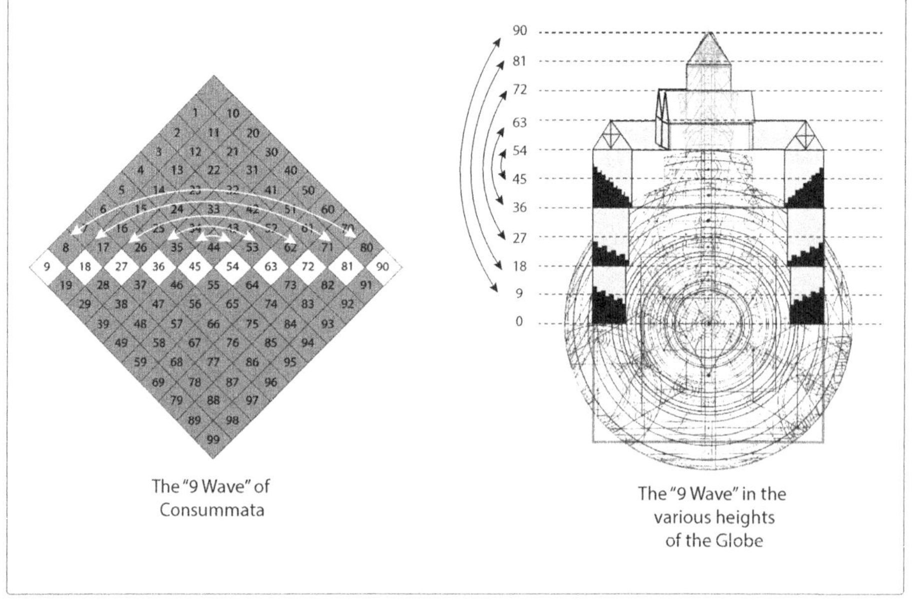

The "9 Wave" of Consummata

The "9 Wave" in the various heights of the Globe

According to Dee's
"Thus the World was Created" chart
in the *Monas Hieroglyphica*,
it's the pattern found in the
"Supercelestial" realm or the
"Above" half of his chart.

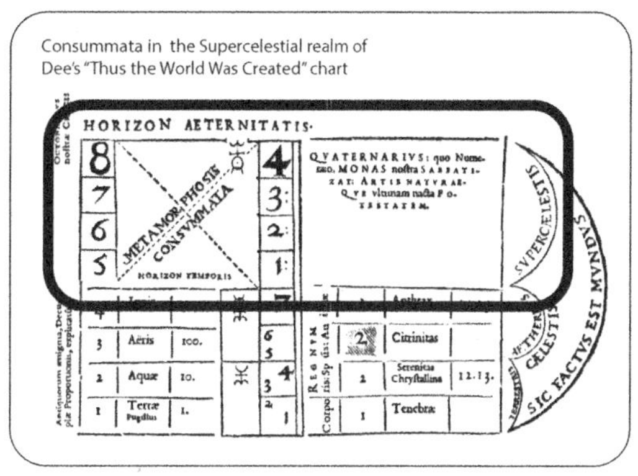

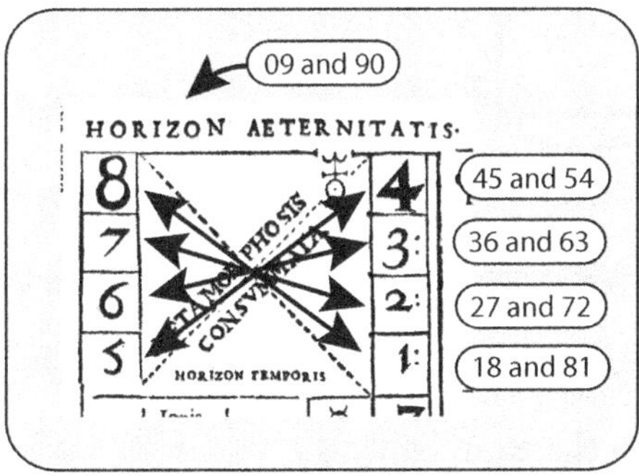

Dee's "dotted-line X" is a hint that he wants us to see
(18 and 81), (27 and 72), (36 and 63), and (45 and 54).
And the "Horizon of Eternity" is 9 (and also 90).

The Greeks called 9 the "Horizon Number,"
as it's on the horizon before all of multiple-digit numbers.

The number 9 is the "null number" in the single-digit range
and 90 is the "null number" in the two-digit range.
And they are reflective mates: (09 and 90).

Disguising the "9 wave" with the "8 wave." Pretty sneaky.

The method John Dee used to
conceal this "9 wave" was to
organize the "measuring tool"
(or the "vertical row of pinpricks")
with the **"8 wave."**

The extra large black dots
(there are also small concentric circles around them)
mark measures of 8, 16, 24, 32, 40,
48, 56, 64, 72, 80, and 88.
(Notice how Dee stops just shy of 90.)

All of these members of the
"8 wave" are entirely different
from the members of the "9 wave,"
except for 72 (which, of course, is 8 x 9).

Dee's used of the "8 wave" as a
red herring, designed to throw
the casual observer off track.

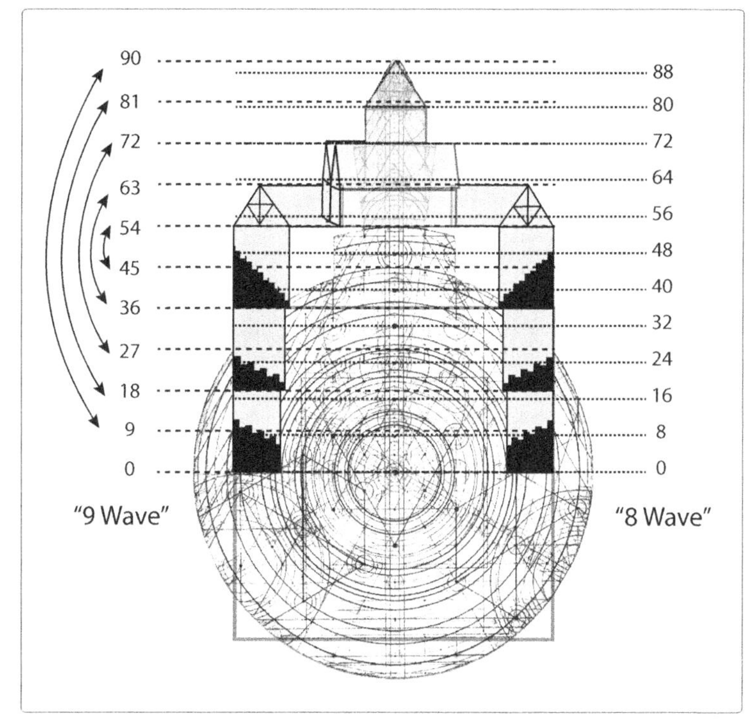

(Well, not entirely. As we seen, there is an important relationship between eight and nine. The Greeks called this relationship "epogdoon," which means "one more than eight."

This extra "one eighth of an octave" in music is called a "tone." So there indeed is a strong relationship between the "8 wave" and the "9 wave." And the place they "sync up" is 72.)

How can I be so sure that John Dee wants us to see that "9 wave"?
Because these uses the members of the "9 wave" in other dimensions in the theater:

1. The 36 x 36 white square that fits in the Starr's Mall.

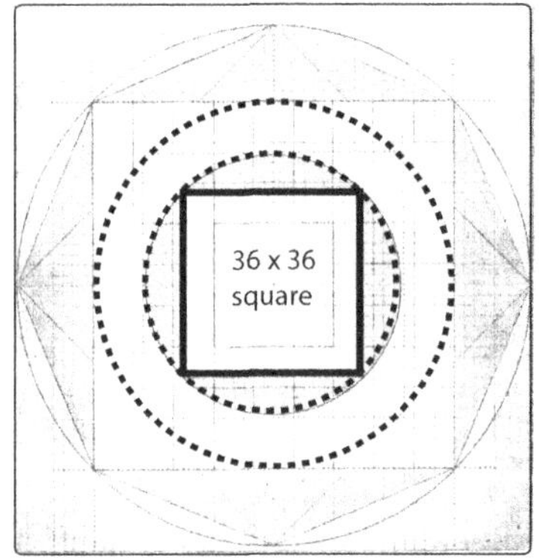

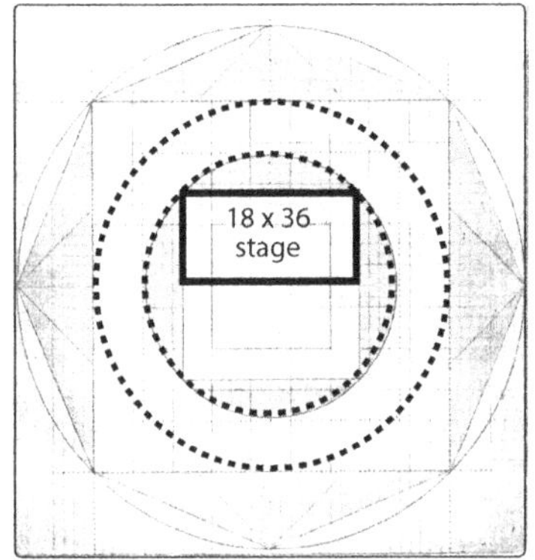

2. The 18 X 36 stage that juts out into the Starr's Mall.

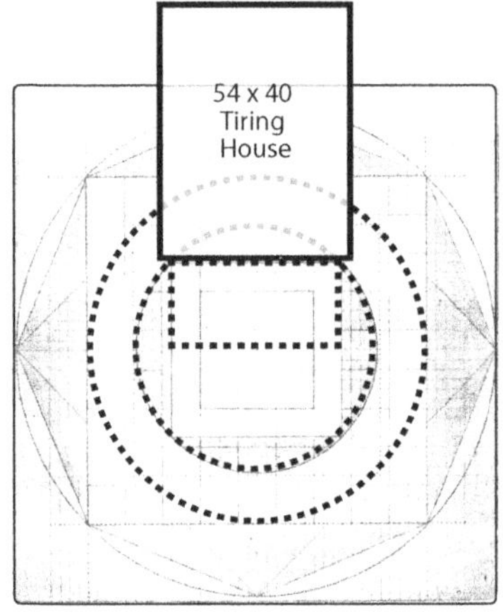

3. The 54 length is involved in two of the three measurements of the Tiring House, "54 x 40" and "54 x 42."

(But not "53.33 x 40," that's a different harmony, the ratio 4:3)

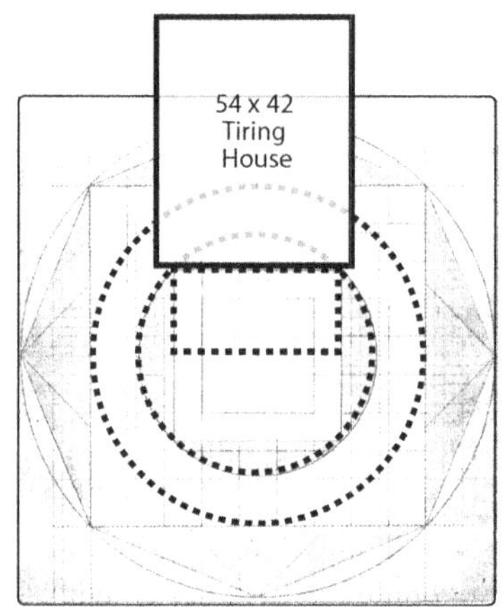

4. The 72 x 72 square in the "overview" plan, into which fits a 72-diameter circle or a 72-diameter octagon.

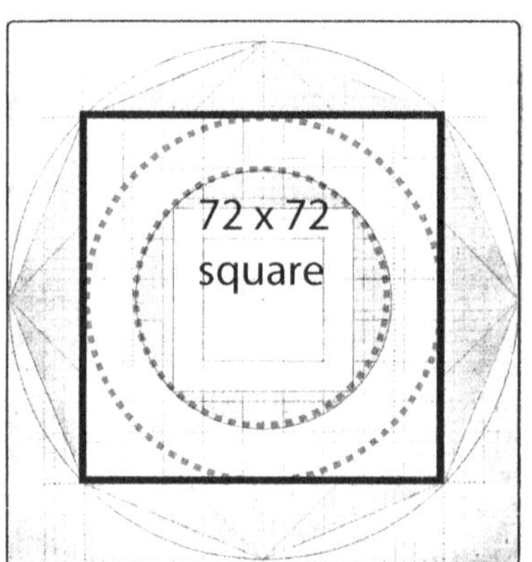

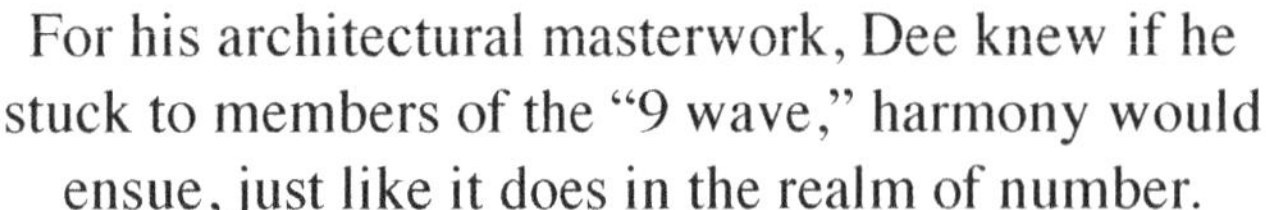
For his architectural masterwork, Dee knew if he stuck to members of the "9 wave," harmony would ensue, just like it does in the realm of number.

Another reason I'm sure Dee was hiding the "9 wave": the sacred number 108

There's another reason I'm certain John Dee used the "9 wave" of Consummata as the measuring rule for the various heights in the Globe theater.

Based on the old illustrations, I estimated the flagpole was 18 feet tall.

If this "visible part" of the flagpole is measured from the top of the flagpole collar upwards, it puts the top of the flagpole at 108 feet. (90 + 18 = 108).

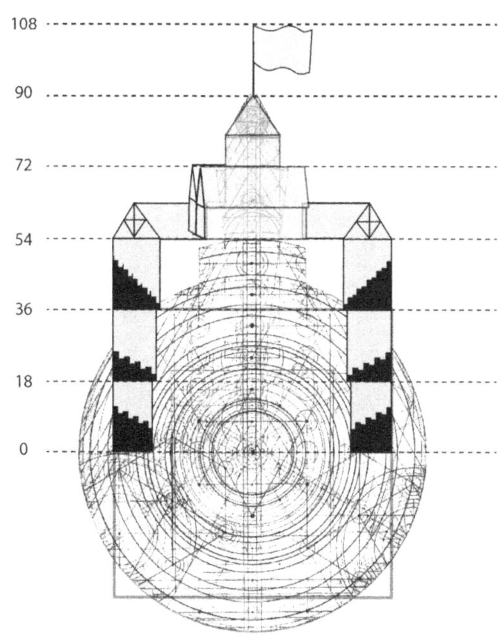

108

I recognized **108** as a number which was sacred to the ancient (and current) Hindus.

In a Hindu *Mala* (similar to Rosary Beads) there are **108** beads. They built their sacred fireplaces with **108** bricks. There are 54 letters in the Sanskrit alphabet. Each has masculine and feminine (shiva and shakti), so 54 x 2= **108** letters. Also, **108** is an intrinsic part of the Hindu calendar system, the Yugas. Even today, Indians pay large sums of rupees to have **108** in their mobile phone numbers.

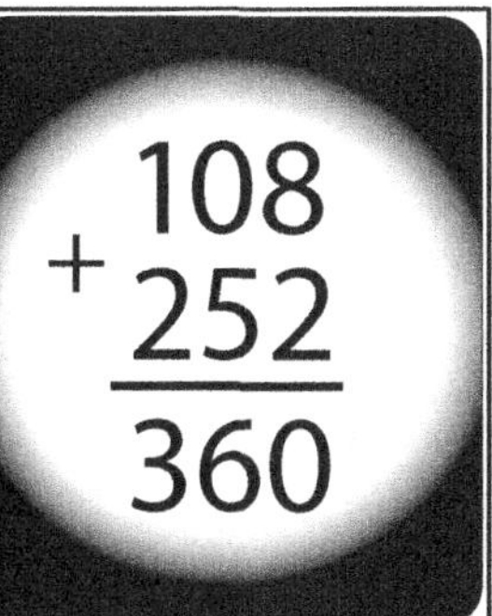

I call **108** "the sacred number of the East." I call John Dee's "Magisterial number," **252**, the "sacred number of the West."

And when you add 108 to 252, what do you get?

360

A perfect circle.

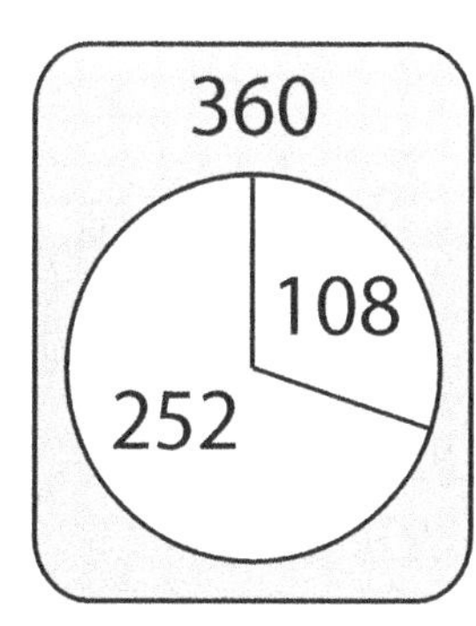

In other words, 108 and 252 are both expressions of the same rhythms found in number.
(Dee's "Metamorphosis" and "Consummata," and more)

These numerical rhythms were known to the ancient Hindus, In the 1500s, John Dee (and, most likely, others) learned about them.

In the late 1900s, Robert Marshall discovered these rhythms independently in his own number explorations. And he explained them to me.

Here's another way to see the relationship between 108, 252 and more of Dee's favorite numbers

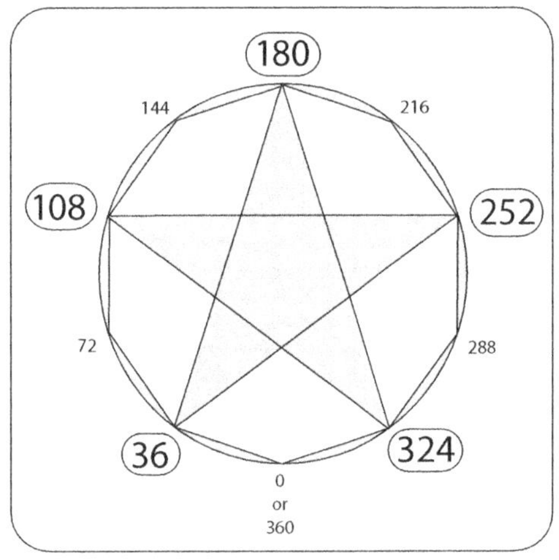

The numbers 108 and 252 are prominent in a pentagram star (like a Sheriff's badge or the Texaco gas logo).

If you proceed clockwise counting, starting from the bottom, the "upper, left arm" is 108° and the "upper, right arm" is 252°.

Things become clearer when the pentagram star is seen in a decagon.

The 108° is 3/10 of 360°

And the 252° is 7/10 of 360°

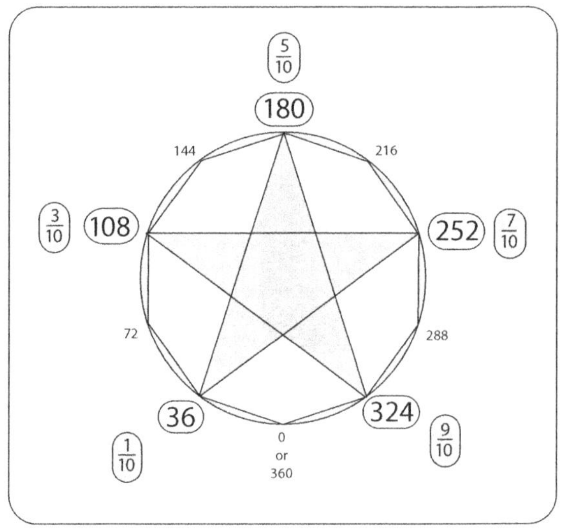

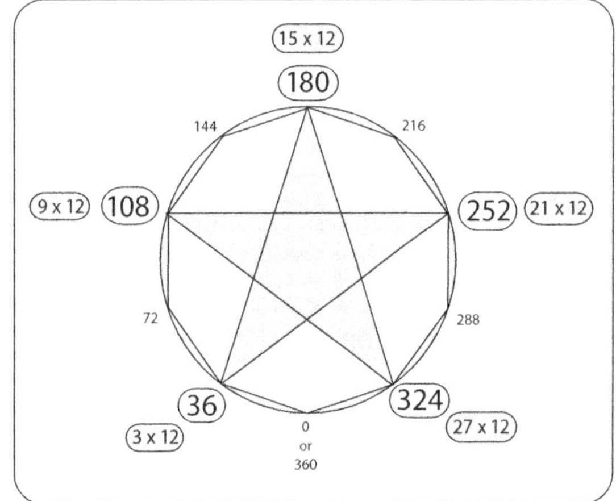

More relationships become apparent when these numbers are seen as multiples of 12.

The number 108 is that notorious "null nine," times the first Metamorphosis number, 12.

And of course, 252 is 12 times its reflective mate, 21. (12 and 21 are first transpalindromic pair)

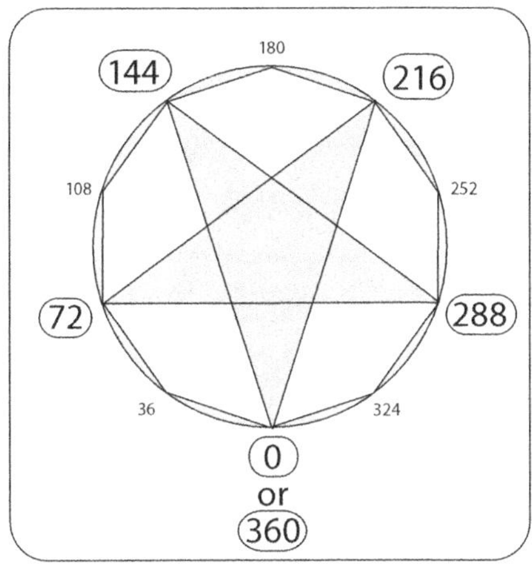

The numbers highlighted by an inverted pentagram relate to the original Globe design as well.

Here we have 72, as in the "72 x 72" unit square of the "overview" plan.

And 144 is a gross, or 12 x 12.

And 288 is twice 144.

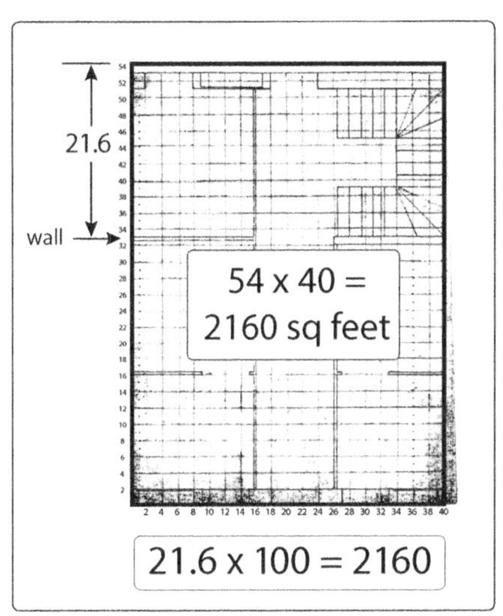

Though 216 itself hasn't popped up yet, its close relatives 2160 and 21.6 certainly have.

The 54 x 40 measure of the Tiring House contains 2160 square units.

And the long dimension of the "General Office" in the Tiring House is 21.6 feet.

(The number 216 is notable in other ways. In Book VIII of *Republic*, Plato mentions that 216 is the smallest cube that is also the sum of three cubes. (3 cubed + 4 cubed + 5 cubed = 6 cubed) or (27 + 64 + 125 = 216).

In the Kabbalistic tradition, there are 72 Angels or 72 Hebrew names of God. As each name is comprised of 3 letters, there are a total of 216 letters in the Shemhamphorasch

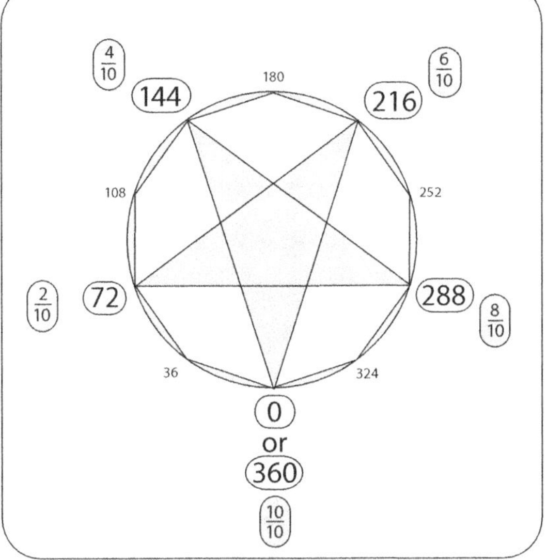

Here are these numbers expressed as fractions of 10.

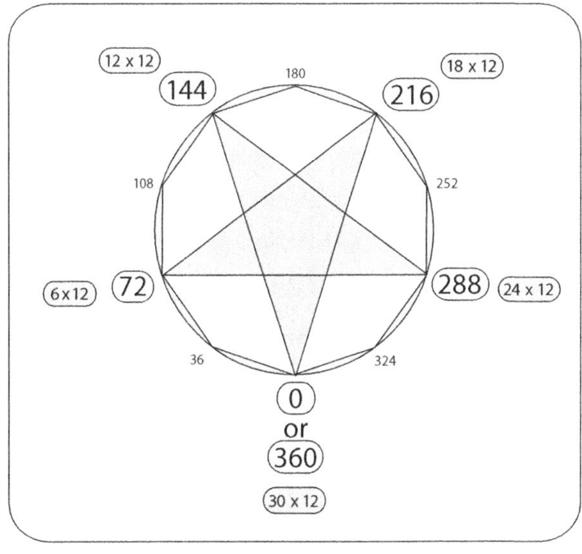

And here they are as multiples of 12.

Some of these "10 parts of 360" numbers are also the internal and external angles in the geometry of the pentagram star.

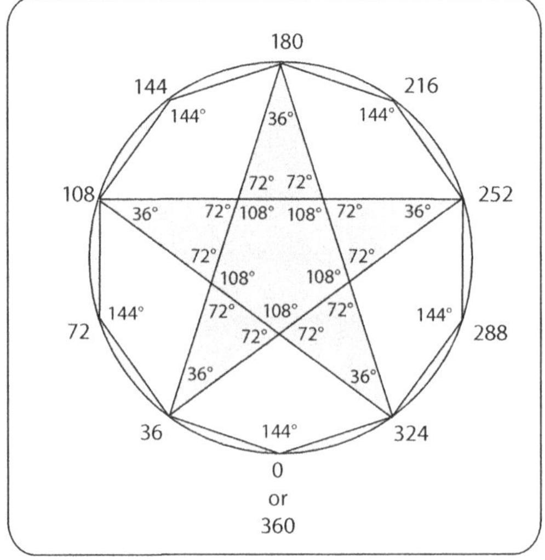

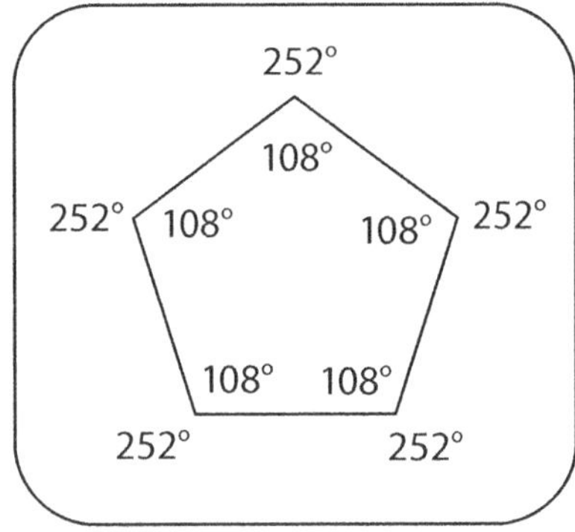

This leads to seeing an example of 108 + 252 = 360.
The five internal angles of a pentagram are each 108°.
The five external angles of a pentagram are each 252°.
East meets West.

Conclusions

Not only has John Dee incorporated all the harmony of Consummata in the Globe, the "stepping-back-by-4 units-fold" to bring "94-down-to-90" proves that he was incorporating the "half-octahedron" in the Tower.

And "As Above, So Below,"
this half-octahedron suggests that
indeed the huge octahedron is implied.
(Along with the huge octagonal cylinder, the huge square, and a huge sphere.)

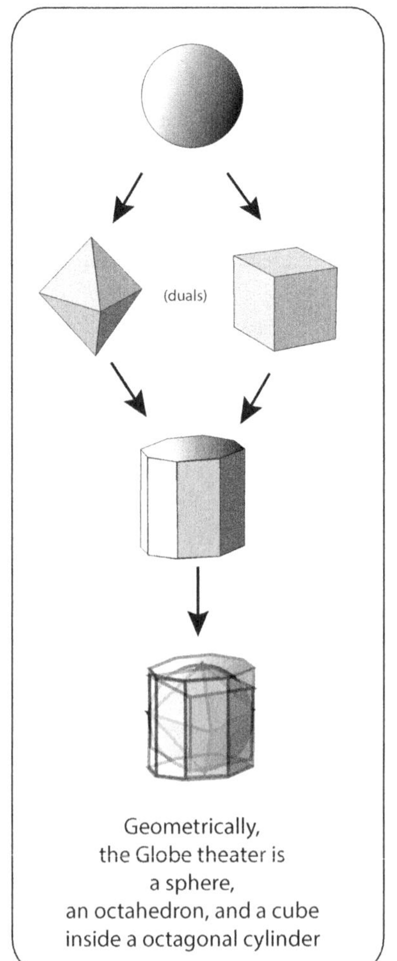

Geometrically,
the Globe theater is
a sphere,
an octahedron, and a cube
inside a octagonal cylinder

A Fuller proof

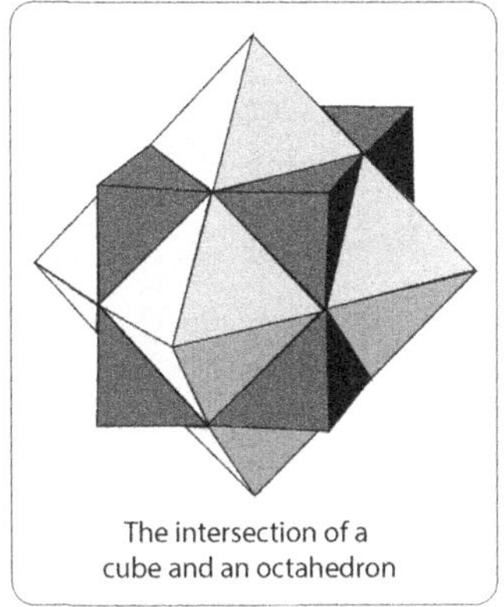
The intersection of a cube and an octahedron

As we've seen, the intersection
of a cube and an octahedron
is a cuboctahedron,
a favorite three-dimensional shape
of John Dee and Buckminster Fuller.

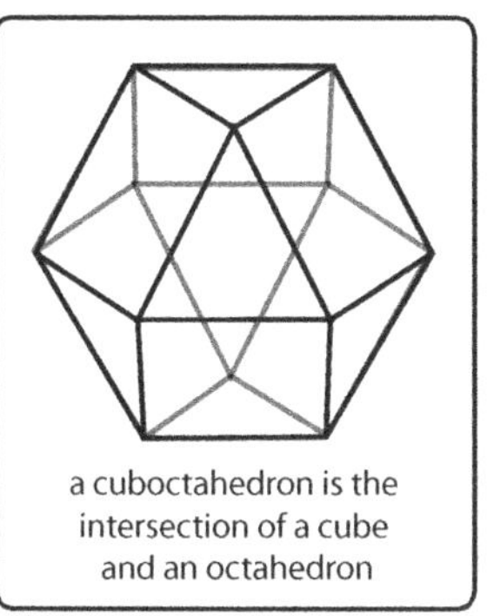
a cuboctahedron is the intersection of a cube and an octahedron

The cuboctahedron is the growth pattern of the closest-packing-of-spheres.

And the fifth layer of closest-packing-of-spheres contains 252 spheres, John Dee's "Magisterial" number.

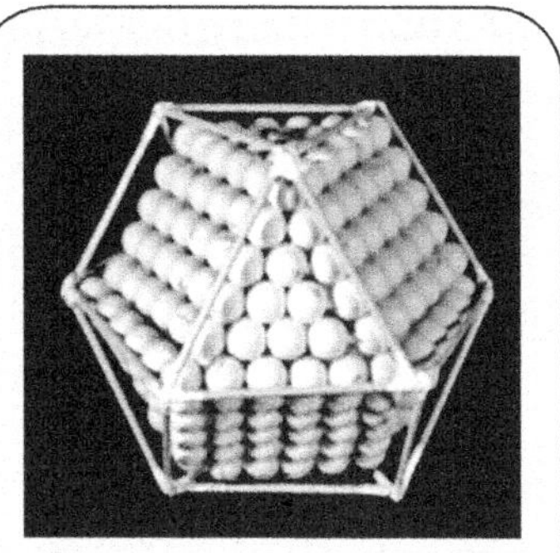
252 spheres close-packed in a cuboctahedral arrangement

The Globe is a symphony in three-dimensional geometric harmony!

The ground plan **sings**:
"**square – octagon – sphere**."

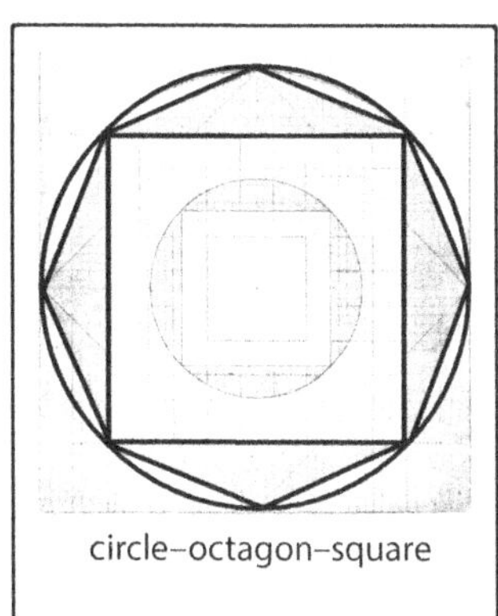
circle–octagon–square

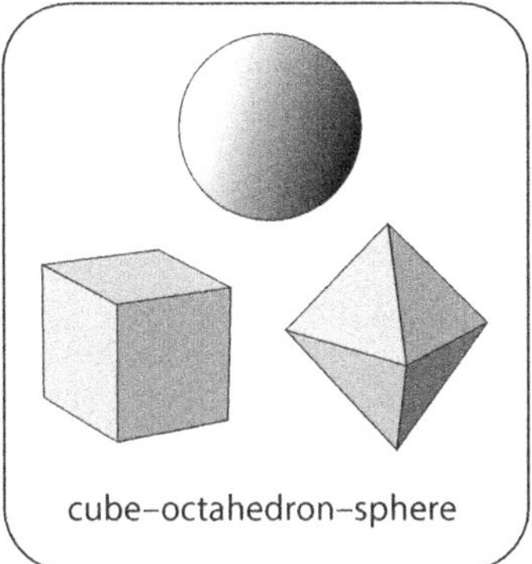
cube–octahedron–sphere

And the whole three-dimensional shape **sings**:
"**cube – octahedron – sphere**."

And this whole symphony takes place in
the octagonal cylinder of the Globe theater.

Dee is the equilateral triangle

There's another important reason I'm certain John Dee intended us to see a giant octahedron in the Globe theater
(and the "half octahedron" roof of the flagpole tower).

An octahedron is made from 8 equilateral triangles. That's it. An octave of triangles.

At the very end of the *Monas Hieroglyphica* Dee writes, "**Amen, says the fourth letter**." And under it, he draws an **equilateral triangle**.

AMEN, DICIT
LITERA QVARTA,
Δ:

"Amen says the fourth letter, Δ"

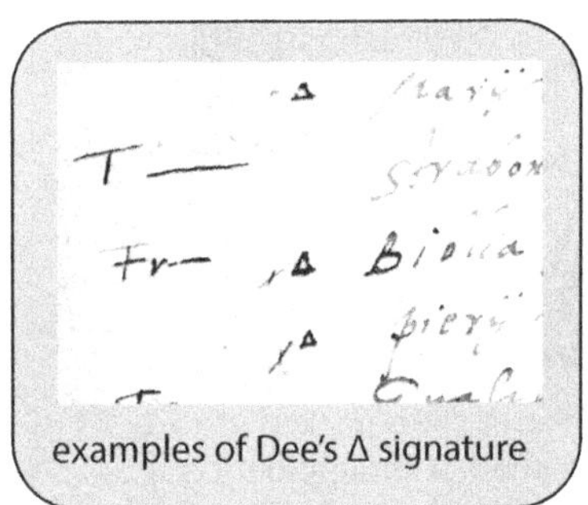
examples of Dee's Δ signature

Well, the fourth letter of Latin, "D," is pronounced "Dee," which is his last name.

And the fourth letter in Greek is "Delta," an equilateral triangle.

John Dee signed his name with a triangle many times in his writings
(especially in his diary and his 1583 list of his 4000 library books and manuscripts).

This equilateral triangle was Dee's "signature."

Thus, the "hidden octahedron" in the Globe theater is Dee's signature, eight times over.

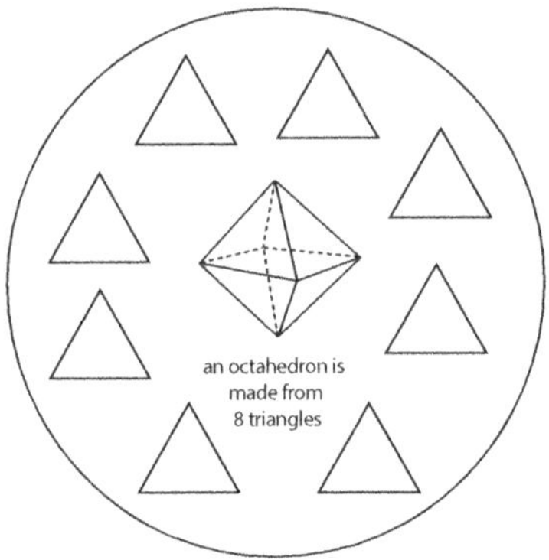

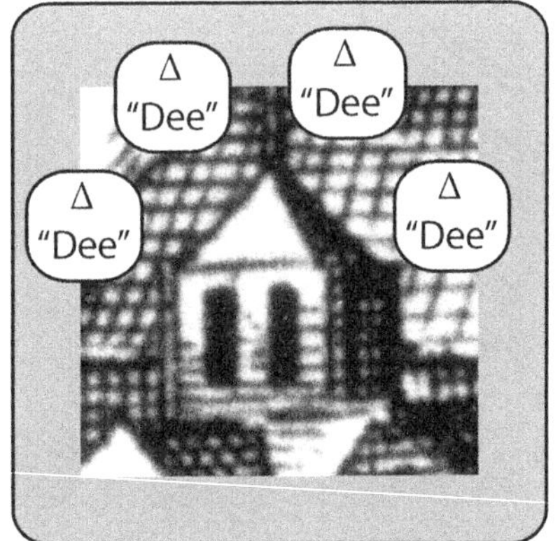

More visibly, each of the 4 equilateral triangles that make up the half-octahedral roof of the flagpole tower is John Dee's signature.

He cryptically signed his work, for all Londoners to see!

But to Elizabethan theatergoers who didn't understand Dee and his geometric philosophy, all of this would be invisible.

The Flagpole Tower is Dee's initials, I.D. (Ioannes Dee)

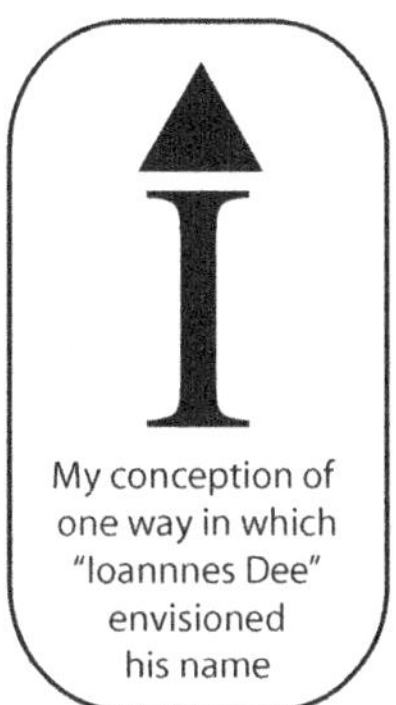

My conception of one way in which "Ioannnes Dee" envisioned his name

The reason I believe the equilateral triangle (or actually, all four of them) on top of the flagpole tower represents "Dee" is because the lower part of the flagpole tower is like the letter "I."

The whole thing reads "I.D."

These are the initials of Ioannes Dee!

Flagpole tower as John Dee's initials, "I. D."

What leads me to believe Dee "signed" his architectural masterpiece?

Because Dee had a habit of cryptically signing all his works!

John Dee's "Cancer the Crab" signature on the Title page of his *Monas Hieroglyphica*

On the cover of the *Monas Hieroglyphica,* Dee depicts himself as Cancer the Crab, his birth sign.

Dee signed the Title page of his 1558 *Propaedeumata Aphoristica* with his initials, I. D., Ioannes Dee.

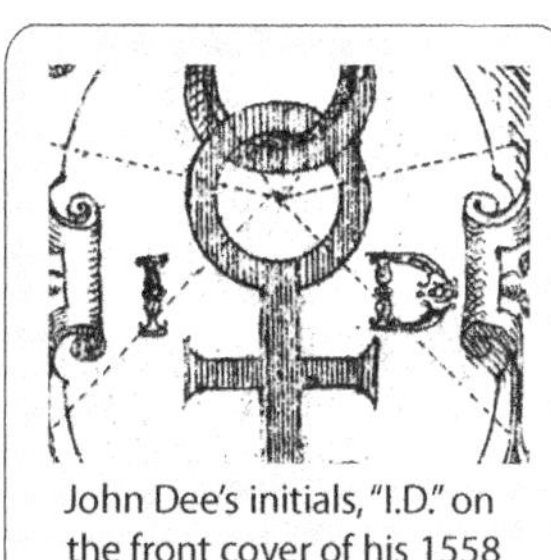

John Dee's initials, "I.D." on the front cover of his 1558 *Propaedeumata Aphoristica*

Dee was a mathematics whiz as well as a navigational expert.

The Title Page illustration of *General and Rare Memorials* is riddled with riddles, but here's how he hid his initials.

(The full Title page is shown on page 25 of this book.)

Along the left edge of the illustration is a vertical lineup of 4 soldiers brandishing fire. Above them, in the ocean, is a lineup of 4 ships.

Dee hides the "+4,–4, octave, null nine" rhythm of Consummata

This is the "+ 4, – 4, octave" of Consummata. And the Horizon line is the "null nine."

The Greeks called nine the "Horizon" number because it's on the horizon before all the multiple digit numbers.

So the horizon is "9." And the ninth letter of the Latin alphabet is "I."

Dee uses the simplest "Gematria" number code in the *Monas Hieroglyphica*: (A = 1, B = 2, C = 3, etc.)

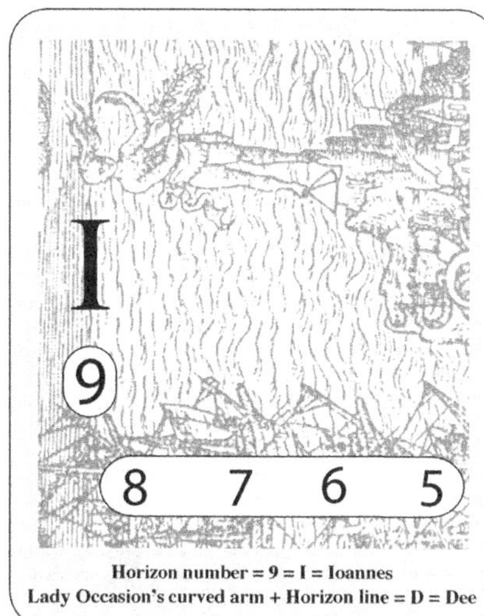

Horizon number = 9 = I = Ioannes
Lady Occasion's curved arm + Horizon line = D = Dee

As I = 9, the Horizon is the letter "I." And appropriately, it's a straight line, just like an uppercase "I" is essentially a straight line.

If the horizon is "I," where's the "D"?

Dee hid the "D" in different two ways.
If you look closely at Lady Occasion's arm, it's not the normal two straight lines that meet at the elbow.

The whole arm is like a semicircle.
The finger tips touch the horizon line.

The horizon "line" and Lady Occasion's semicircular arm form the letter "D."
"I" (horizon) + "D" (arm and horizon) = "I.D."

Horizon number = 9 = I = Ioannes
Lady Occasion's curved arm + Horizon line = D = Dee

Dee's tetrahedron on the Title page of *General and Rare Memorials* is four Δ's or four "D's"

The other way he hid his name is with the tetrahedron upon which Lady Occasion is perched.

The tetrahedron is actually 4 "D's."

But the "most similar" example to Dee's signature in the Globe is on his other work of architecture, the John Dee Tower of 1583.

In the center of the west-southwest exterior arch is a "triangular stone" on top of a "tall, vertical, rectangular stone."

This "keystone signature" even has the same relationship of geometrical shapes the flagpole tower of the Globe has:

A small triangle that sits atop a tall, vertical, rectangle.

John Dee's initials, "I.D." in the exterior of the west-southwest arch of the John Dee Tower of 1583

My conception of one way in which "Ioannnes Dee" envisioned his name

There's no doubt my mind Dee intended the flagpole tower of the original Globe to be his signature.

Flagpole tower as John Dee's initials, "I. D."

More about John Dee's initials in the rocks of the John Dee Tower of 1583

part of John Dee's 1580 map of North America

You may be thinking, "There are thousands of rocks in the Tower, one of them is bound to look triangular."

Well, it's not only its distinctively triangular shape that's important. It's in a prominent location in the keystone area of the exterior of the west-southwest arch.

This compass direction looks out over the mouth of what was called, in 1583, the "Dee River" (now Narragansett Bay). Remember, Dee's name was the triangle.

And just 15 miles offshore is a triangular island (now called Block Island), which points to the mouth of the Dee River. Dee even includes this triangular island on his 1580 Map of North America, as well as his 1582 Map of the Northern Hemisphere.

(It's a visual pun: triangle + river = Dee River)

There is something else that suggests the "triangular rock" and the "tall, vertical, rectangular rock" are a symbol: in the neighboring arch is an even more distinctive symbol.

The "Sun Stone and the "stone with shoulders," a representation of the Monas symbol

In the center of the exterior of the west-northwest arch is a round rock about the size of a bowling ball. You can't tell from this black and white photograph, but it's the only red rock in the vicinity.

Beneath it is a stone with cut shoulders, which I claim was fashioned by man, using hammer and chisel.

West Window

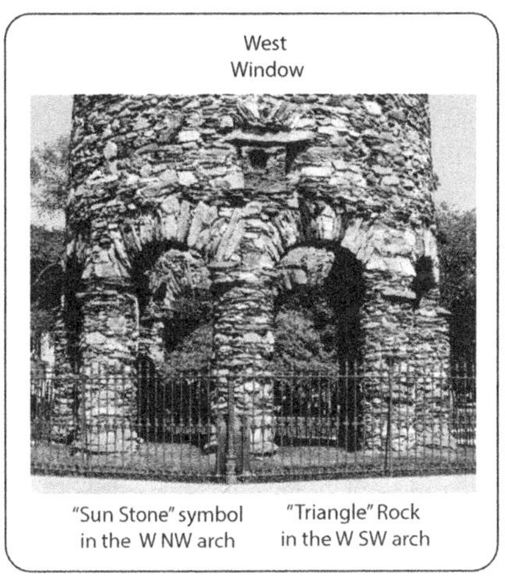
"Sun Stone" symbol in the W NW arch

"Triangle" Rock in the W SW arch

The "Sun Stone and the "stone with shoulders," a representation of the Monas symbol

The cryptic representation of the Monas symbol

I suggest these two rocks are a representation of Dee's Monas symbol. The "Sun Stone" is the "Sun circle," and the "shoulders" align with the arms of the Dee's "offset cross."

As the proportions of the Tower were based on the Monas symbol, this is a hidden blueprint for the Tower, built right into the Tower.

(Very Dee.)

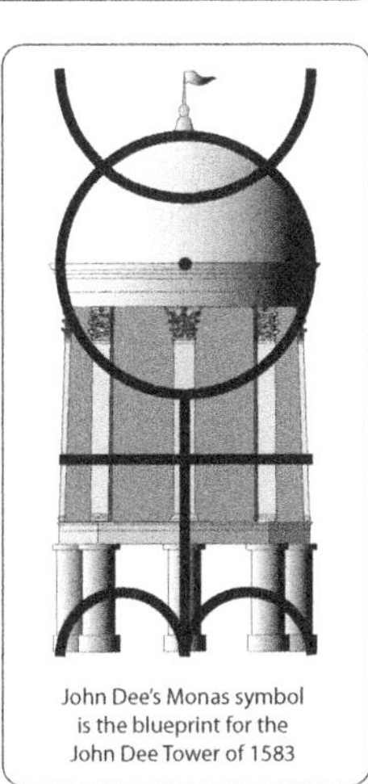
John Dee's Monas symbol is the blueprint for the John Dee Tower of 1583

But there's something even more amazing about this "Sun Stone" and "rock with shoulders." The Tower is about 2 feet thick, and on the interior of that same west-northwest arch is a large egg-shaped rock.

It's larger than any of the other rocks in any of the interior arches. In other words, the Monas symbol and this egg-shaped rock are back-to-back in the same arch.

Just after dawn, on and around the Winter Solstice, the sun streams through the South window, through the Tower, out the West window, and can be seen and can be seen from the northwest corner of the park.

(This alignment was discovered in the early 1990's by William Penhallow, a Professor of Astronomy and Physics at the University of Rhode Island.)

Sunlight coming through two of the three windows in the first-floor room just after dawn on the Winter Solstice.

The egg-shaped rock that gets illuminated on the Winter Solstice

A little later, the patch of sunlight streaming through the South window, slowly moves down and across the western interior wall, and at 9:00 AM, it illuminates the egg-shaped rock.

It's very dramatic. It looks like a spotlight, just on that rock.

[This solar alignment was shown on the History 2 Channel episode of *America Unearthed* entitled "America's Oldest Secret," (They are referring to the Tower.)]

The progress of the patch of light that illuminates the egg-shaped rock

To reiterate, the "Monas symbol rocks" and the "egg-shaped rock" are back-to-back in the same arch. Now, look at the front cover of John Dee's *Monas Hieroglyphica*. Contained in the egg-shape is the Monas symbol.

(Dee was big on egg metaphors.)

To me, the egg-shaped rock illumination confirms the "Sun Stone" and the "rock with shoulders" is the Monas symbol. And the Monas symbol confirms that the "triangular rock and the tall, vertical, rectangular rock" represent John Dee's signature.

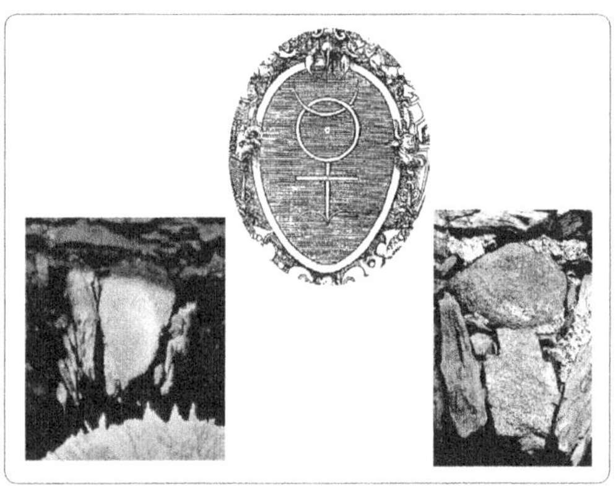

Dee cryptically signed all his works. And had fun doing it.

In light of all the ways Dee cleverly hid his name in his works, the idea that the flagpole tower of the original Globe is Dee's initials is not unusual at all.

THE CLEVER CLUES IN THE CUTLINES

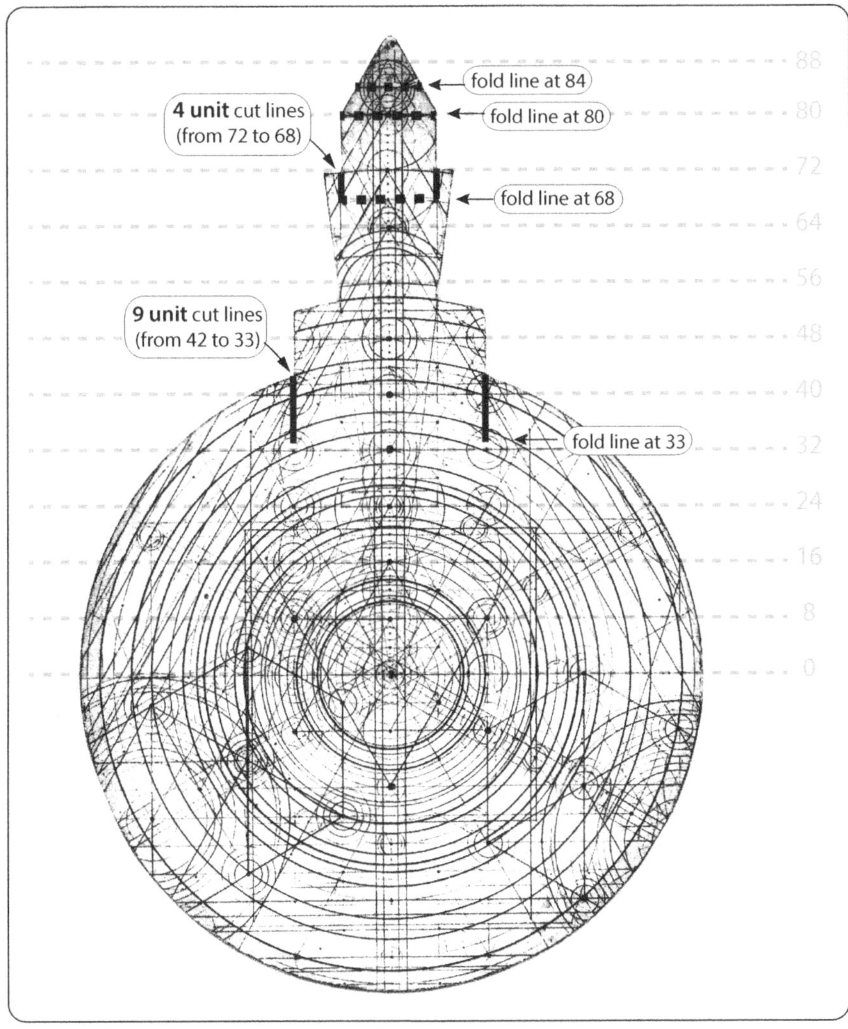

What is the significance of the **4-unit** cutline (from 72 to 68) and the **9-unit** cutline (from 42 to 33).

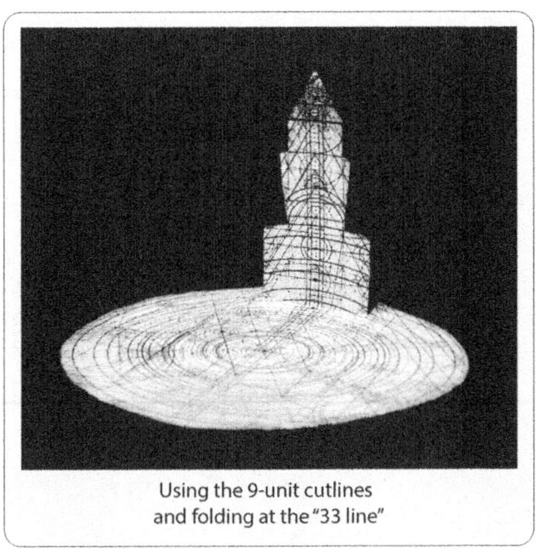

Using the 9-unit cutlines and folding at the "33 line"

At first, I thought that the lengths **4** and **9** were arbitrary, that they were just intended to show that the parametric was intended to be seen as a "side-view" plan, as well as an "overview" plan.

I thought perhaps the 4-unit cuts were somehow involved with the "4-unit in-fold and out-fold step" riddle explored earlier.

Or perhaps 4-units was simply a random length chosen to indicate that the top part of the diagram could be folded to verticalize the flagpole tower.

Using the 4-unit cutlines and folding at the "68 line"

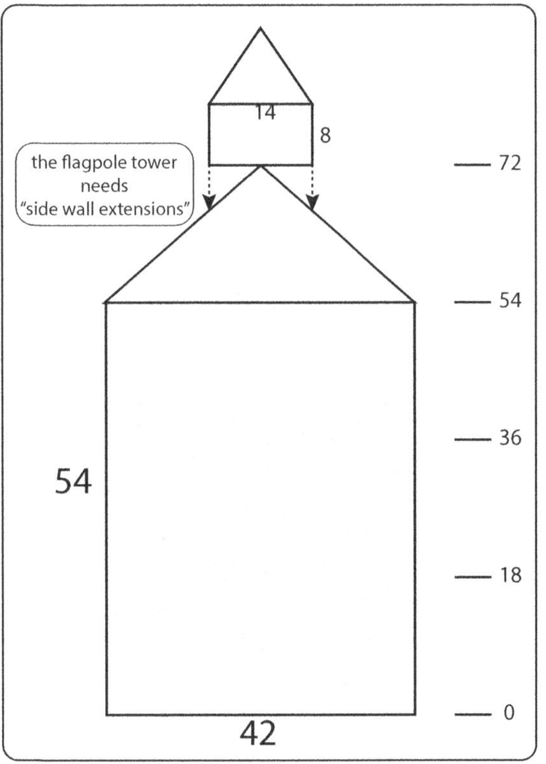

Then I deduced a third possibility, which is a strange combination of things (quite Dee-like).

The 14-unit wide flagpole tower can't just balance on top of the angled ridgeline of the much wider Tiring House roof. It needs "side supports" or legs which extend down to the angled side of the roof.

To geometrically find the length of these "side supports," we first need to know the width of the Tiring House.

But as there are three measures of the Tiring House (53.33 x 40, 54 x 40, and 54 x 42), which width should we choose?

(The number 42 seemed the likelier candidate, as among its factors are 6 and 7, numbers that divide evenly into 18 and 21 respectively.)

So if the width of the Tiring House is 42, half of the width is 21. And the height of the gable up to the ridge line of the roof is 18
(the same as the other two small roof buildings roof-buildings)

As these numbers, 18 and 21, are each divisible by three, the ratio 18:21 can be reduced to 6:7.

Well, we know the flagpole tower is 14 feet wide, so half of 14 equals 7 units.

Now we have two "similar" right triangles
(as they share a hypotenuse).
So calculating geometrically,
the height of the "side supports" must be 6 units.

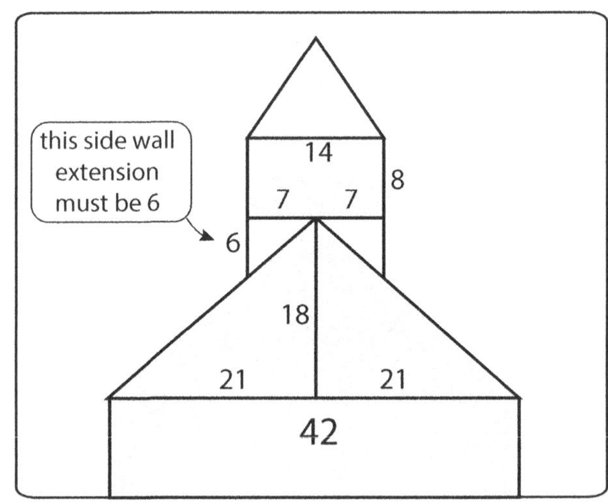

But there's is a discrepancy here.

The side supports need to be **6 units long**, but the length of the cutline in the illustration is only **4 units long**.

The cutline is only 2/3 the length it needs if it represents this "side wall extension." What's going on here?

Remember, the parametric drawing incorporates not just the elevation "side view," but also the "overview" plan.

So, let's switch gears and review the "overview"diagram

If the stage has a width of 18, and the Tiring House has a length of 54, that puts the outer edge of the Tiring House at the 72 line, exactly where the cutline begins at the upper shoulders."

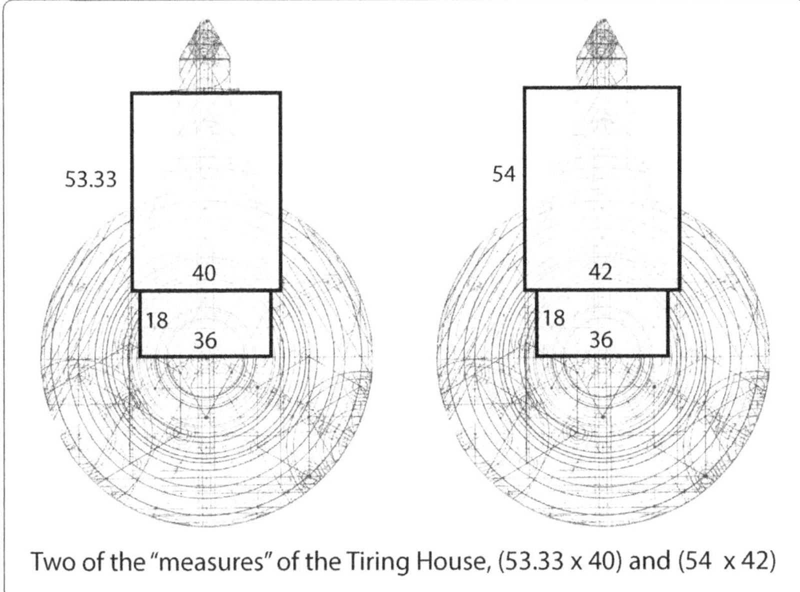

Two of the "measures" of the Tiring House, (53.33 x 40) and (54 x 42)

But remember, there are three possible dimensions of the Tiring House, (55.33 x 40), (54 x 40), and (54 x 42), and they involve two different lengths, (53.33 and 54).

Perhaps this difference is what the cutline is all about.

However, 54 – 53.33 = .66, which is only "2/3 of a unit," much shorter than the "4 units" shown. An apparent dead end.

Perhaps these dead ends both work **in tandem** to resolve each other!

Perhaps Dee wanted to creatively express **both** "the flagpole tower side extension length **(6 units)** and the "difference between the two Tiring House lengths **(.66 of a unit)** **at the same time.**

When you multiply 6 x .66, the result is **4**, **exactly the length of the cut marks!**.

Just as the parametric shows both elevation and plan, the "elevation discrepancy" and the "plan discrepancy" **are combined into one drawing!**

This is a very creative and clever solution. And that's what Dee was – creative and clever.

The width of the stage and the Tiring House are shown in the parametric drawing

The parametric drawing contains a dizzying array of about 40 concentric circles.

But if you look closely, you can see that the measures for the width of the stage (**36 units**) and the two different widths of the Tiring House (**40** units and **42 units**) are emphasized graphically. Here's how:

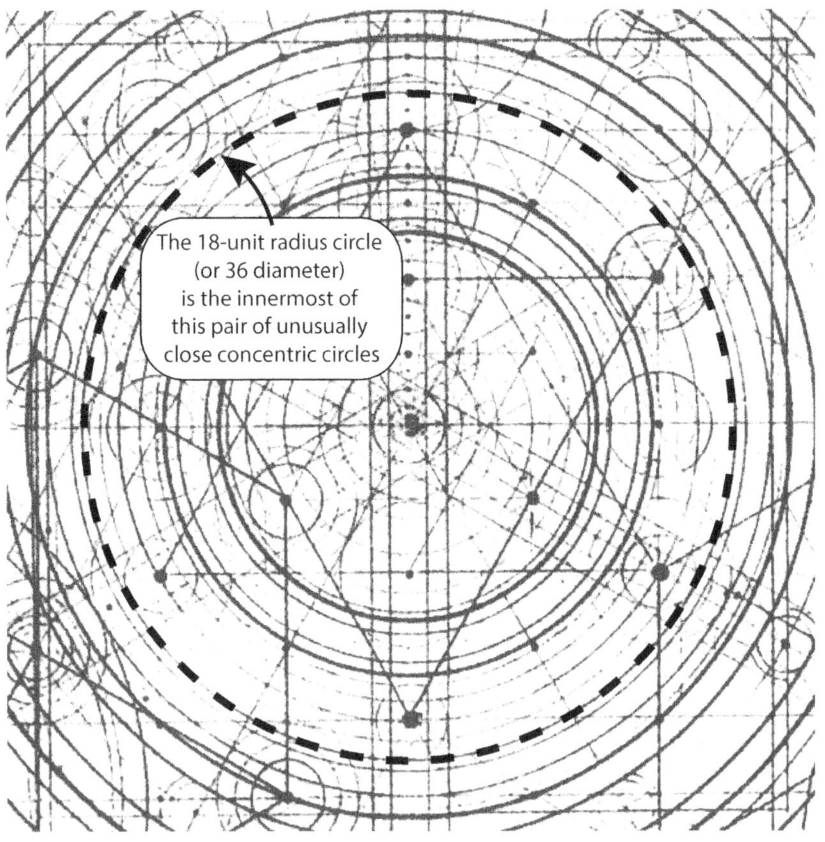

The 18-unit radius circle
(or 36 diameter)
is the innermost of
this pair of unusually
close concentric circles

As the pinpricks originate from the central point, they measure radii.

So if the three widths (36, 40, and 42) are indicated by "diameters" of circles, we need to look for circles with radii of 18, 20, and 21.

Starting from the center point, counting upwards by 18 pinpricks, the **18-unit radius circle** (or 36-unit diameter circle) is the innermost of the **"two unusually-close concentric circles"** in that area of the diagram.

The upper half of the 36 x 36 square is 18 x 36. This represents the stage of the Globe theater. (Ground zero for Shakespeare).

The 18 x 36 rectangular
stage of the Globe theater

Starting from the center point, counting upwards 20 pinpricks, the **20**-unit radius circle touches the **innermost** of "two very-close-together" squares drawn on the parametric.

And the **21**-unit radius circle touches the **outermost** of these "two very-close-together" squares.

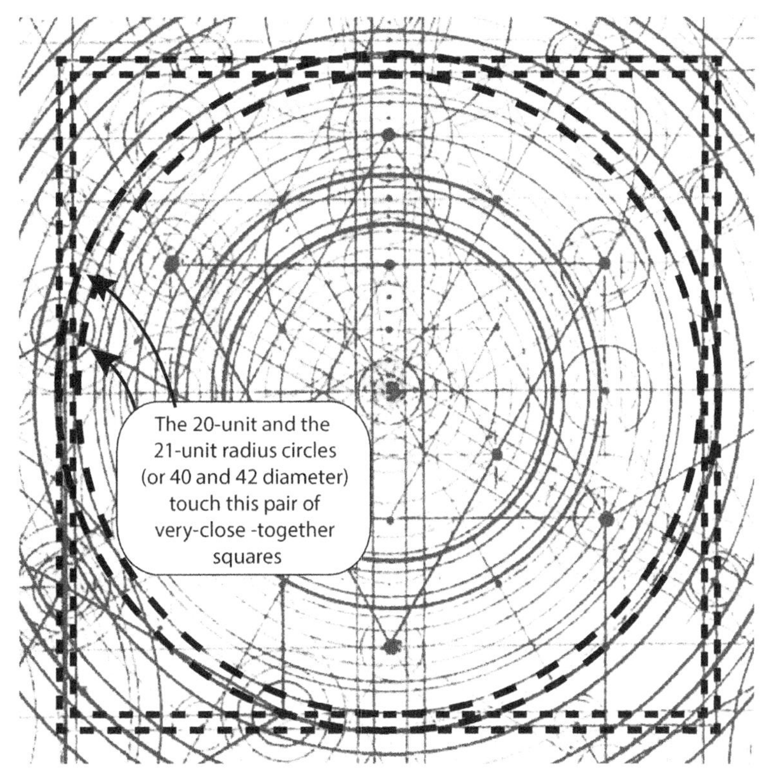

The 20-unit and the 21-unit radius circles (or 40 and 42 diameter) touch this pair of very-close -together squares

54 x 40 "overview" of the Tiring House

54

40

inner circle and inner square

So the width of the innermost square is 40 and the width of the outermost square is 42.

These are the two widths used in the "3 different measures" of the Tiring House.

To the left is the 54 x 40 Tiring House version.

And to the right is the 54 x 42 Tiring House version.

Remember, this 42 is the width of the "scaenae frons," with its three doors.

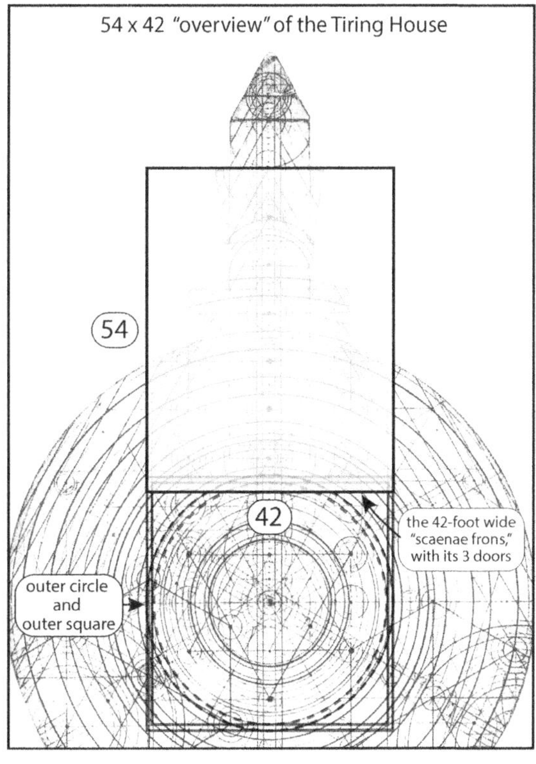

54 x 42 "overview" of the Tiring House
54
42
the 42-foot wide "scaenae frons," with its 3 doors
outer circle and outer square

Now it's easy to see how the horizontal "overview" plan
and the vertical "side-view" elevation "sync up."

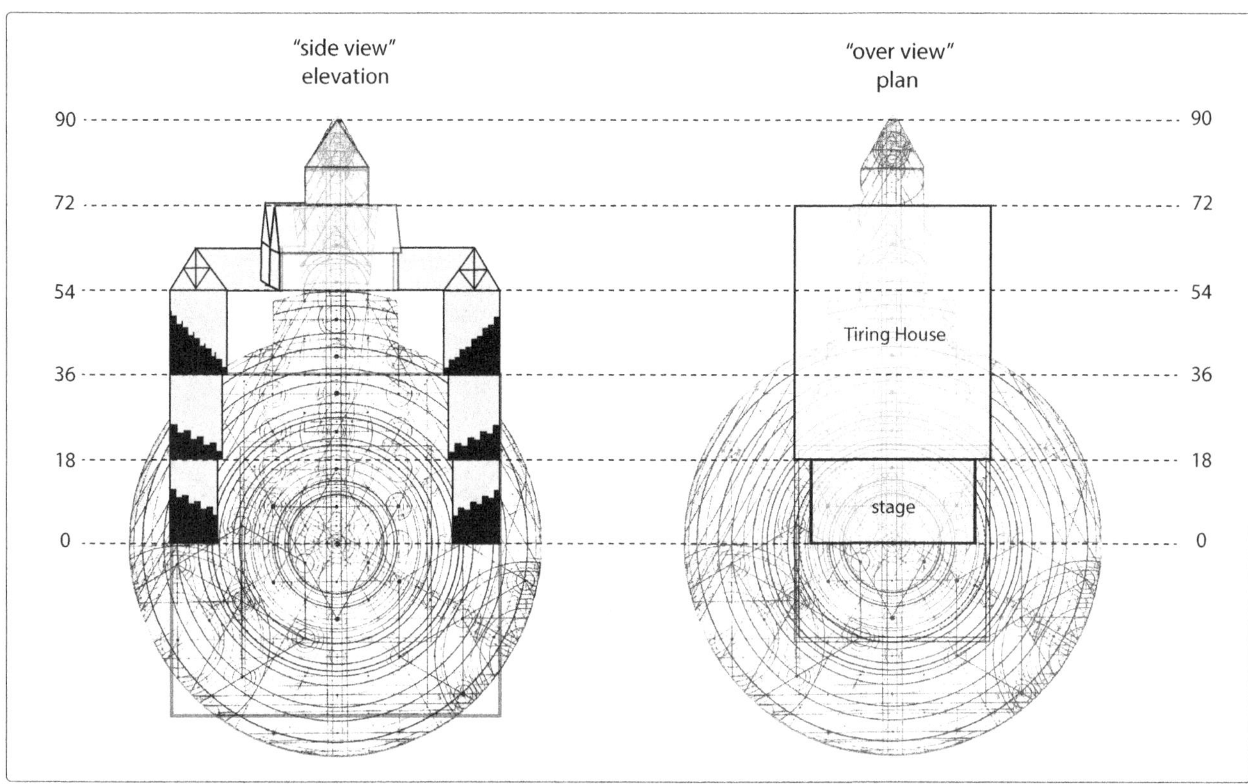

In the "side view" elevation plan," the "18, 36, and 54 lines" mark the height of stories 1, 2, and 3.

The "72 line" marks the roof line of the two small buildings atop the Tiring House. (18 +18 +18+18 =72)

(This "72 line" also marks where the flagpole tower meets the ridge line of the Tiring House roof).

In the "overview" plan, the 18 corresponds with the "scaenae frons" end of the stage.

The "72 line" marks the outermost wall of the Tiring House. (18 + 54 = 72)

Dee makes one drawing work for two different views, vertical and horizontal! A double-duty plan. Pretty darn clever.

More "sync" with 36 and 54

There are actually several more ways Dee's "overview and "side view" plans "sync up."

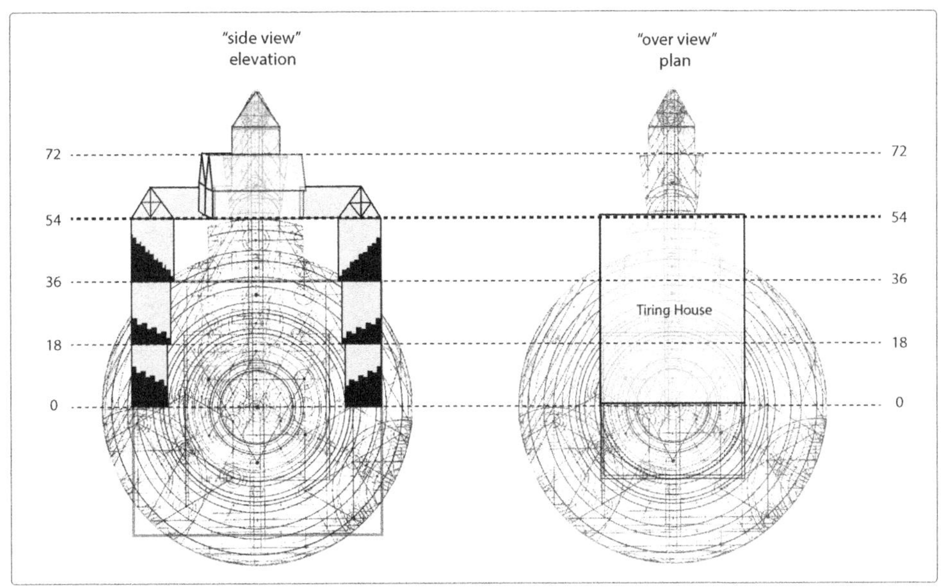

On the "overview" plan, let's temporarily move the Tiring House down to the center point of the concentric circles.

Now, the Tiring House's 54-unit length syncs up with the 54-unit height of the galleries (to the ceiling of Story 3) in the "side-view" elevation.

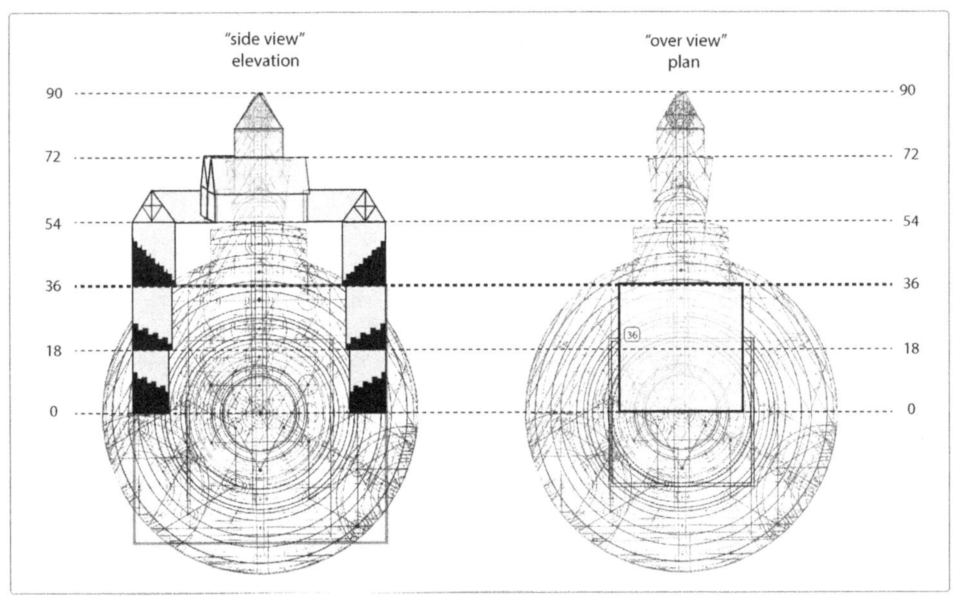

Let's temporarily move the 36 x 36 square "upwards," so it "sits" on the center point of the concentric circles.

Now, its 36-unit length syncs up with the 36-unit height of the floor of story 3 (or the ceiling of story 2) in the "side-view" plan.

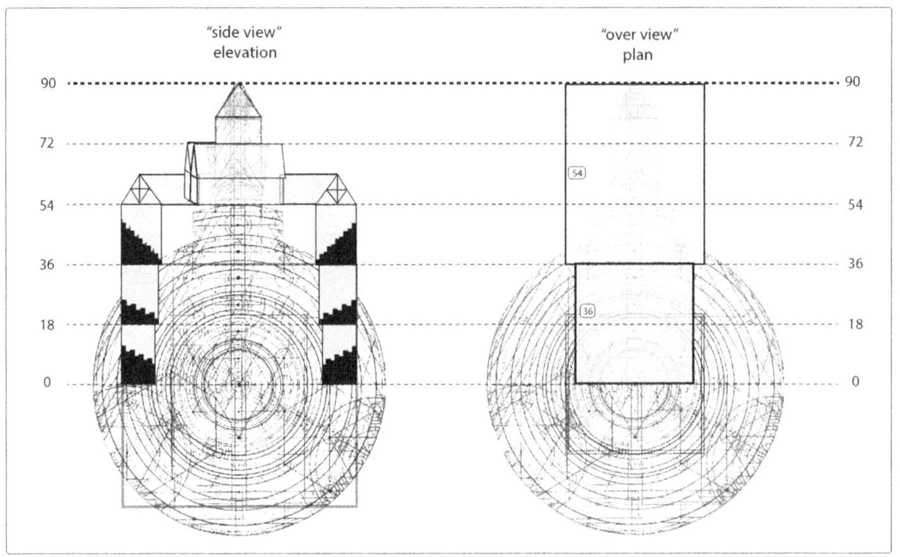

And, of course, we might pile up the 54-length Tiring House on top of the 36 square, starting at the center point.

Now the total total length of 90, which is the height to the top of the "flagpole collar."

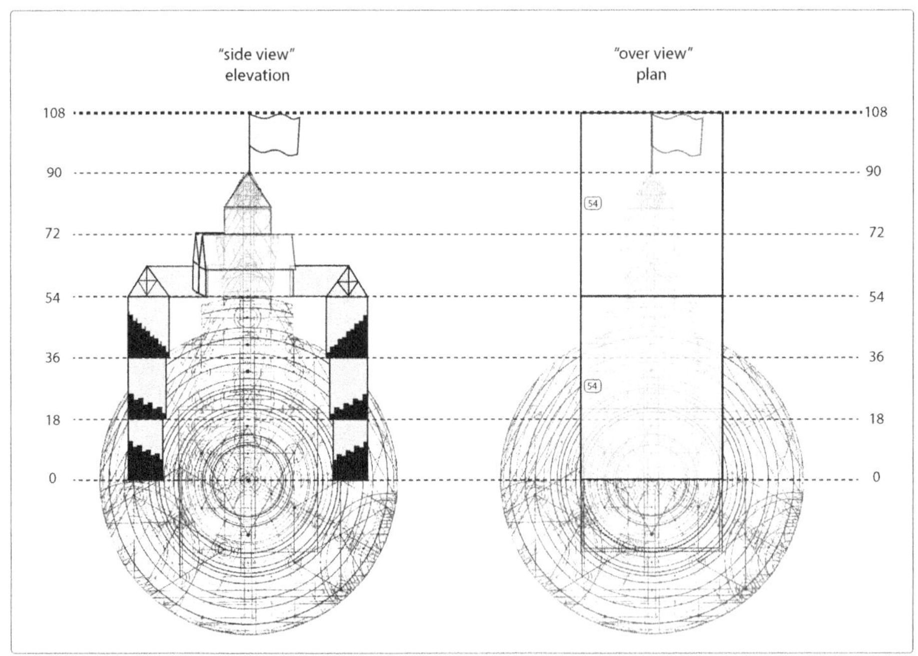

Or we might creatively pile up two 54-length Tiring Houses.

Now, the total length would be 108, which is the height of the whole Globe, including the flagpole.

To summarize, **18, 36, 54**, and **72** are key numbers in **both** the "**side-view**" plan (room heights and roof heights) and the "**overview**" plan (stage and Tiring House lengths). Concinnitas.

The secret meaning of the 9-unit cutlines

The lower pair of the 9-unit long vertical cutlines still perplexed me.

These 9-unit incisions extend from the **42** line to the **33** line.
These are, indeed, important numbers in Dee's mathematical cosmology.

The number 42 is the reflective mate of Metamorphosis number 24.
And 6 x 42 equals 252.

The number 33 is a member of the "11 wave."
It is 1/3 of 99, which is the largest two-digit number.

We've seen the number 42 before, as it's one of the widths of the Tiring House.
But that "odd number," 33, had not popped up in my analysis of the Globe drawings.

Then it all clicked.
The two "4-unit" cut lines represent the "8-wave."
I realized the cut lines were John Dee's depiction of the two different measuring systems for the parametric drawing:
the "**8 wave**" and the "**9 wave**."

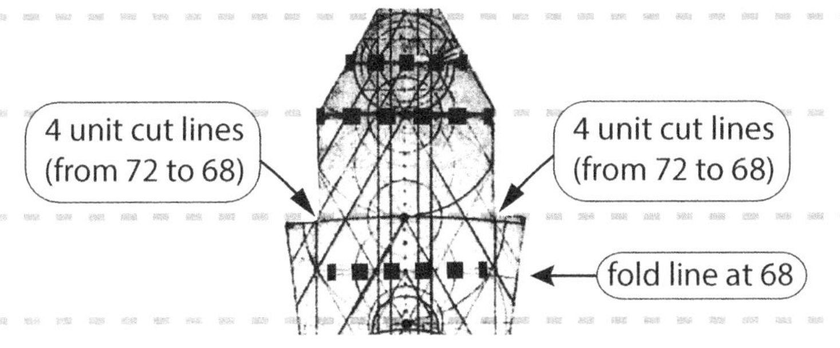

Up above, the pair of 4-unit cut lines added together, make 8, representing the "8 wave."

By using large dots on every eighth pin-prick this is the "measurement system" Dee clearly indicates.

And further below, the "9-unit" cutlines not only suggests the "9 wave," but added together they make 18, which is the height of 6 things:

Story 1, story 2, story 3, the "small structures on the Tiring House roof," the flagpole tower, and the flag!

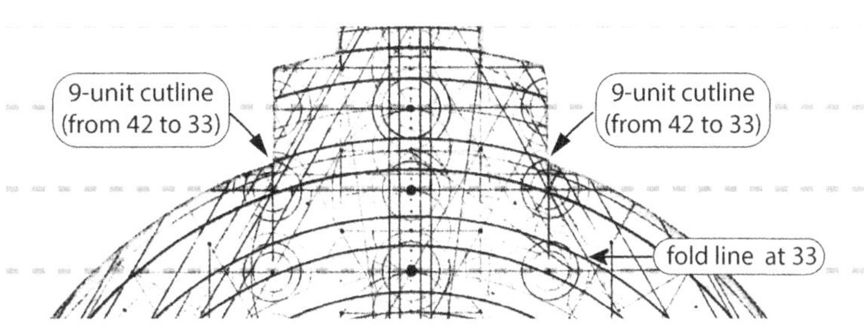

In short, the cut lines are the "rulers" of the diagram.

4/9 is half of 8/9

One way of seeing the comparison of the "8 wave" and the "9 wave" is the ratio 8:9,. As we've seen, the Greeks expressed this important ratio as "9:8," or *epogdoon*, "one eighth more than eight," a musical "tone."

In his works, Dee likes to (cryptically) express this **8:9** relationship with the ratio **4:9**. Certainly, 4:9 and 8:9 are not the same thing, but as 4 is half of 8, much of the magic of the *epogdoon* is maintained.

In a sense, 4:9 is like a "**half tone**," as half of 8/9 is 4/9. In this equation, look what pops up! The numbers **8** and **18**. These are key measures in Dee's parametric drawing!

$$\frac{8}{9} \times \frac{1}{2} = \frac{8}{18} = \frac{4}{9}$$

Very important relationships in number can be seen if you put away the hand calculator. That said, a fresh perspective on a fraction can be seen by finding its decimal equivalent, for example, 4/9 = .4444. And 8/9 = .8888)

$$\frac{4}{3} \times \frac{2}{3} = \frac{8}{9}$$

Another important characteristic of 8:9 is its relationship with the harmonic ratios, 2:3 and 3:4.

So "arithmetically" hidden in this **4:9** ratio are all of Pythagoras' three main harmonies, **1:2, 2:3,** and **3:4**.

(Again, notice the result, 8/18. 8 is the "8 wave." And half of 18, or 9, is the "9 wave.")

$$\frac{4}{3} \times \frac{2}{3} \times \frac{1}{2} = \frac{8}{18} = \frac{4}{9}$$

A special place where Dee hides the ratio 4:9 .... The Monas symbol

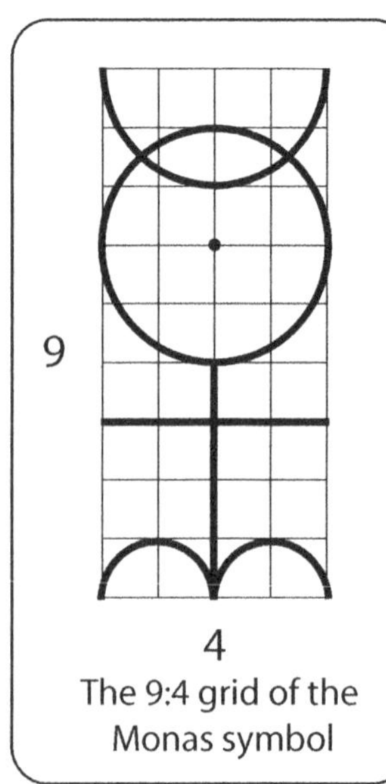

The 9:4 grid of the Monas symbol

I had first thought these "4" and "9" cut line numbers were randomly chosen. But then I remembered how important they were to Dee. They are the width and the height of John Dee's Monas symbol!

As per Dee's exacting specifications in Theorem 23 of the *Monas Hieroglyphica*, the Monas symbol must be **4** units wide by **9** units tall.

(which totals to 36 square units).

Deviate from that ratio, and it's no longer the Monas symbol. It loses its arithmetic and geometric magic.

In short,
the "4 unit:9 unit" cutlines =
the 4 unit:9 unit dimensions
of the Monas symbol.

Same man, Same cosmology.

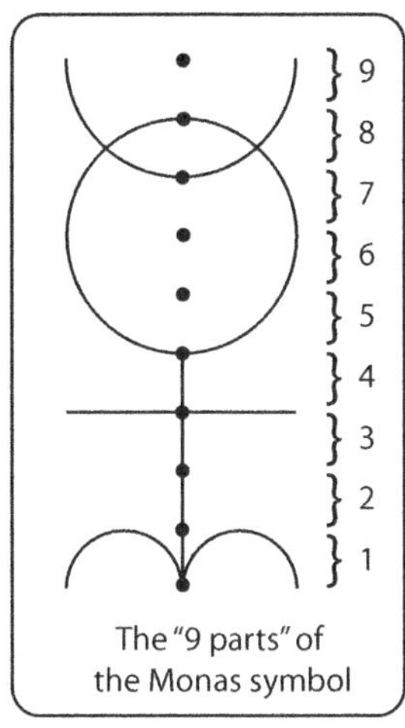

The "9 parts" of the Monas symbol

Here's a clearer way to see the "nine-ness"of the Monas symbol:
The 10 points on its spine connect 9 equal parts.

All Dee's works are permutations of his one holistic mathematical cosmology.

My familiarity with Dee's favorite numbers and shapes gleaned from my extensive analysis of the *Monas Hieroglyphica* and its illustrations is what allowed me to decipher these Globe theater drawings. (I ain't braggin,' I'm just explainin.')

Studying the Globe drawings without first understanding the *Monas Hieroglyphica* is like reading the last chapter of a math text without having started from the first chapter.

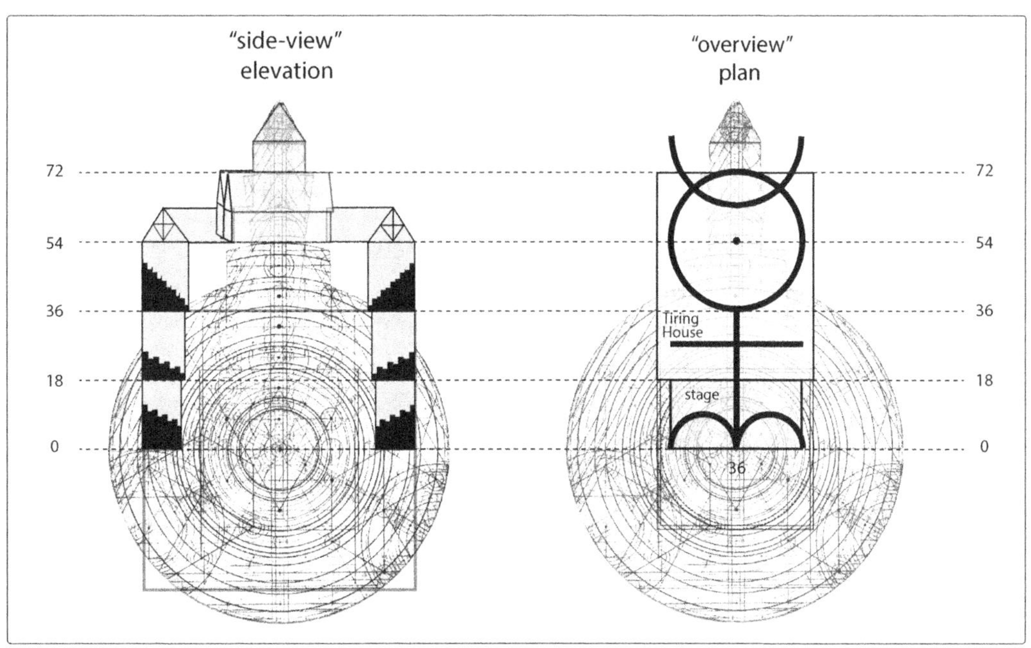

So if the stage is 36 feet wide,
and we align it with a Monas symbol 36 feet wide,
the top of the Sun circle would be at the "72 line,"
(which is the top of the "two small buildings" on the Tiring House roof).

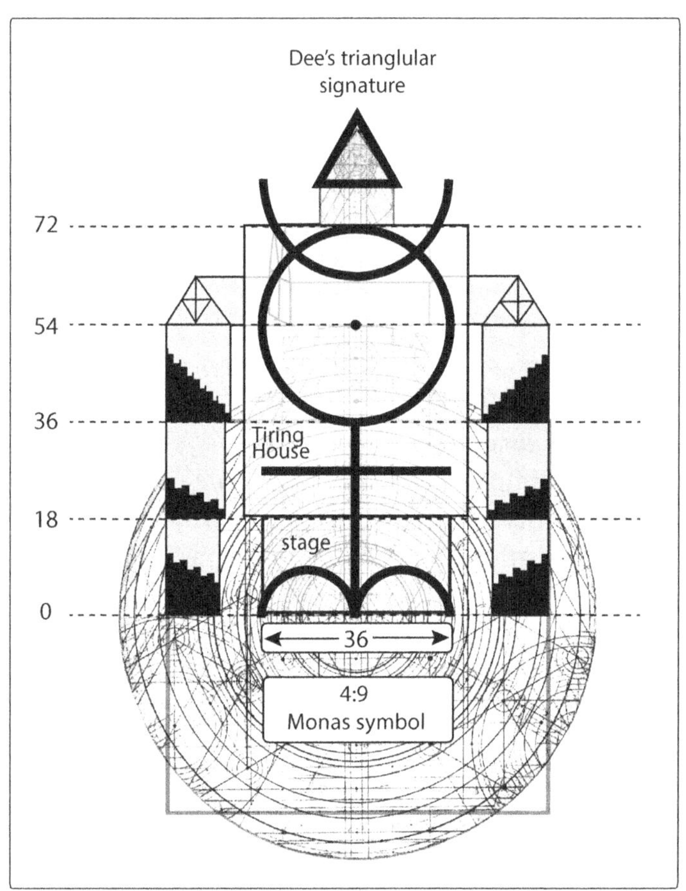

So, if John Dee went to the Globe for a play,
he would see the **Monas symbol** standing
in the middle of the Starr's Mall,
toes on the edge of the stage.

And above that Dee would see his
signature: the equilateral triangle

But these things would be invisible
to just about everyone else.

Conclusion

Remember Dee didn't have to worry about modern building codes, strict fire codes, or handicap accessibility requirements that might have dictated some alterations in his design. In Dee's mind, philosophy, tempered by practicality, was the order of the day.

I realize I seem to have been to be working backwards from an idealized philosophy (huge cube, huge octahedron, huge sphere, huge octagonal cylinder) but that would have been John Dee's starting point as well.

Dee has a talent for hiding his philosophical ideas in graphic form. Over time, clues often get lost. And buildings get destroyed.

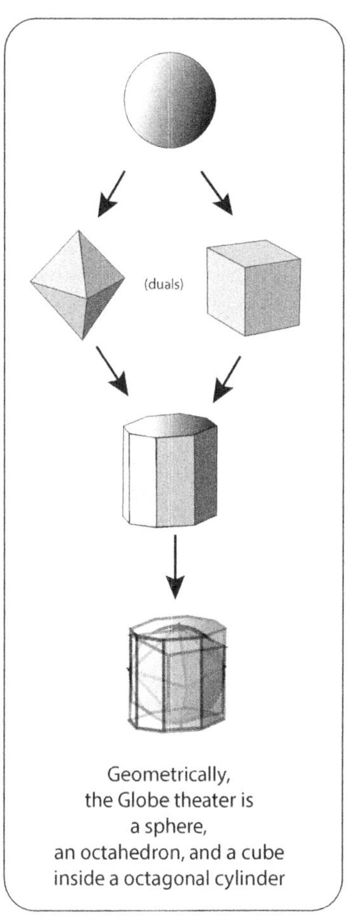

Geometrically, the Globe theater is a sphere, an octahedron, and a cube inside a octagonal cylinder

But there are enough clues in the Byrom Collection drawings that lead me to believe that John Dee started with the "big picture" idea of the interplay of huge geometric shapes. Then he two-dimensionalized the concept in his various drawings.

And along the way, he incorporated other things like the harmonic ratios (1:2, 2:3, 3:4), the doublings and triplings of areas, as well as the marvelous numbers of Metamorphosis.

AS IN THE ORIGINAL GLOBE DESIGN, DEE HID HEAVEN (CIRCLE) AND EARTH (SQUARE) ON THE TITLE PAGE OF HIS 1564 MONAS HIEROGLYPHICA

By studying his other graphic works, we can learn a lot about the ways Dee liked to conceal his cosmology.

Dee's Title page, as printed in 1564

Years ago, when I first started studying the Title page of the *Monas Hieroglyphica*, I noticed the lower parts of the architecture (foundation, columns, entablature) were made from **straight lines and right angles.**

But the upper parts of the architecture (the dome and the urns) were all **rounded** shapes.

Realizing Dee undoubtedly drew the architecture with a straightedge and compass, I tried to locate the center of the circle he used to create the dome.

After a few trial-and-error attempts, I found the center point was just about at the hole of the top of the emblem, exactly where the two figures of Mercury are pointing their spears.

the center point of the circle of the dome

"Something's wrong with Title Page of the Monas Hieroglyphica" (and it's related to the design of the Globe theater)

After years of practice, artists, photographers, and graphic designers become sensitive to things like proportion, visual balance, positive and negative space, and sense of depth.

When I first started pondering Dee's Title page, I said to my photo assistant, "Something wrong with this Title Page."

He replied, "How can you say there's something wrong with the design made in 1564, almost 450 years ago!"

"No. I mean something was *intentionally* done wrong. The designer of this work of art made it look "heavy," so we would see his clue and fix it. Then "harmony" would be restored, and even more "clues" would become apparent.

He interrupted, "Heavy? Harmony? Clues? What are you talking about?

I explained:

From a graphic design point of view, the Title page has three main elements: the architecture, the central emblem, and the type.

To make the other things easier to see, let's temporarily remove all the words and sentences.

Dee's Title page (with type removed)
The emblem is cut off by the jutting bases of the columns

The architecture (except for the dome and the urns above) is rectilinear. It's all straight lines and right angles. But in the central emblem, all the lines are curved. There are no right angles in the shield, the egg-shape, and the flowing ribbons. In fact, there are no angles at all, everything's swirly.

Notice how the central emblem fits nicely between the columns–except down near the bottom. I have encircled where a short part of the flowing ribbons are blocked by the jutting bases of the column (and the tops of the short pedestal below).

This floating, airy emblem is being "pinched" by the solid, rectilinear architecture. It wants to be set free!

I also noticed that the horizontal distance between the two columns is equal to the height of the columns. In other words, the top of the "theater" between the columns is a perfect square.

Furthermore, the overall shape of the central emblem is also a square, of about the same size.

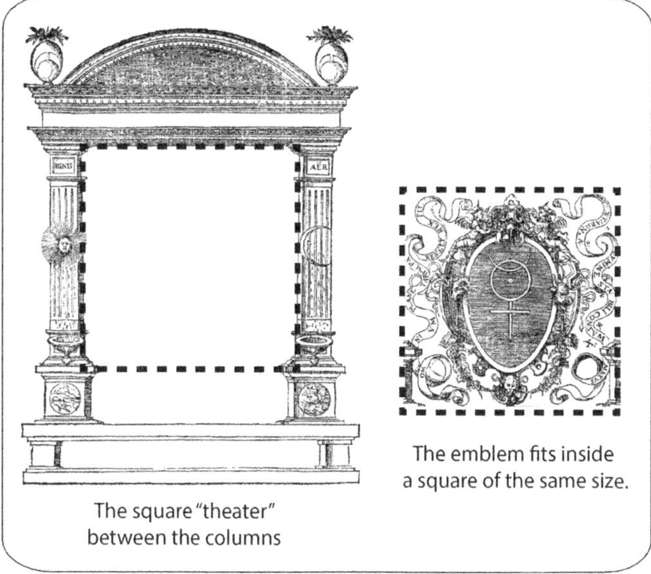

The square "theater" between the columns

The emblem fits inside a square of the same size.

Dee wants us to move the whole central emblem upwards, and suddenly, there is beautiful visual harmony!

The airy emblem floats happily in the theater of the solid columns!

Now, if we put the type back in, the title can still fit above the emblem, and the author's name and dedication fit nicely below.

Even my skeptical photo assistant agreed that my "restored" version looked more harmonious than the original version.

Before

After

More graphic magic and confirming clues

When the emblem is "raised up", lines connecting "Fire and Water" and "Earth and Air," cross at the intersection point of the vertical and horizontal lines of the Cross on Dee's Monas symbol

When the emblem is restored, more wonderful "things" happen.

And these "things" act as "confirming clues" that we're on the right track.

On the capitals of the two columns are the words Ignis and Aër (Fire and Air).

And on the pedestals below are circular illustrations of Earth (hills and mountains) and Water (a mermaid in the sea).

An "X" connecting these 4 Elements **also** crosses the intersection point of the Cross of the Elements of the Monas symbol. How propitious!

(And also a visual pun on the word "cross.")

Also, the center point of the arc of the dome has moved down on the emblem.

The circle's center point is now the crustacean hanging its claws over the top of the egg. Why is that important?

John Dee was born on July 13, 1528. His sign was Cancer in the Crab.

(And King Maximilian was born in August. He is Leo the Lion, picture down below.)

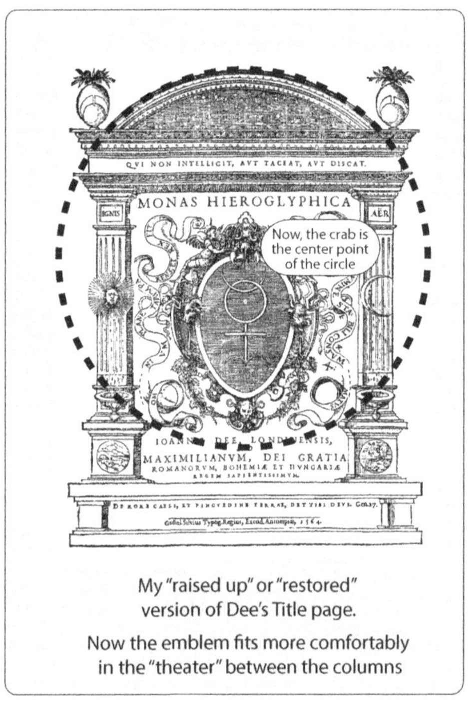

My "raised up" or "restored" version of Dee's Title page.

Now the emblem fits more comfortably in the "theater" between the columns

In short, by centering the circular Dome of the Heavens on his cryptic self-portrait, John Dee seems to be confirming this "restoration" was what he intended (and he's chuckling along with us.)

Dee's dome and his "center point riddle" indicate there's a large **circle** hidden on the Title page.

Also the "theater" between the columns is a large hidden **square**.

Dee seems to be to be relating the "**Heavenly**" **circle** with the "**Earthly**" **square**.

But he doesn't seem to be doing a very good job here. The square doesn't seem to relate to the large circle (in either size or position).

However, Dee connects "circle and square" in a much more subtle (and more clever) way.

If you draw in the diagonals of the square "theater," they cross at the center point of the Sun circle!

He's connecting the **square** "theater" with the smaller "sun **circle** of the Monas symbol," instead of with the Dome circle.

My "raised up" or "restored" version of Dee's Title page.

Now the emblem fits more comfortably in the "theater" between the columns

Heaven=Circle and Earth=Square.

Yes, a strong underlying theme in all of Dee's works is "Heaven-Circle" and "Earth-Square."

It's an underlying theme of John Dee's "Thus the World Was Created" chart (the "Above" half and the "Below" half), the Monas symbol, and much of the text of the *Monas Hieroglyphica*.

It's also an underlying theme of the John Dee Tower 1583.

And, as we've seen, it's also an underlying theme of Dee's design for original Globe theater.

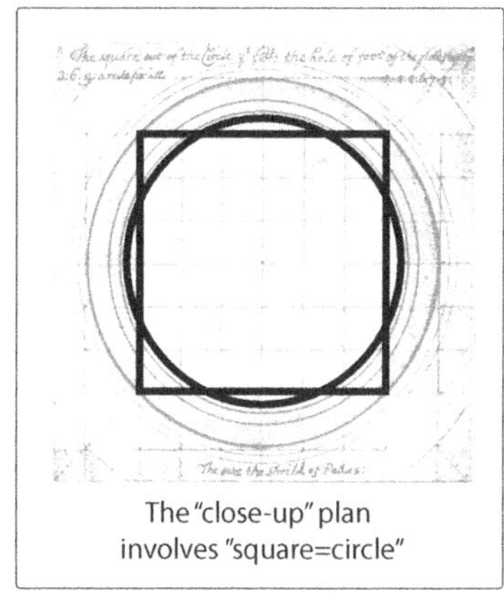

The "close-up" plan involves "square=circle"

The Element of Air (Plato's "octahedron") connects with the Element of Earth (Plato's "cube")

Incidentally, we've seen another theme in the design of the Globe, which is related to the 2D "circle and square."

It's the 3D "Airy," floating octahedron and the solid, "Earthy" cube.

Well, one of the diagonal lines we just drew on the Title page connects the Element of Air (Plato's "octahedron") with the Element of Earth (Plato's "cube").

Remember, the octahedron and the cube have a special relationship. Not only are they are "duals," but their intersection makes a cuboctahedron, the pattern of the closest-packing-of-spheres.

Another representation of the "Airy" octahedron and the "Earthy" cube

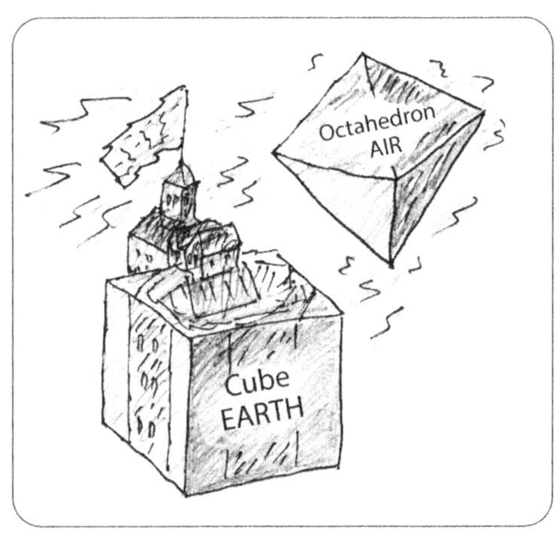

Plato associated with the octahedron with the Element of "Air." It's challenging to depict the idea of "Air" because it's invisible, but the alchemists often symbolized it with smoke, clouds or **wind**.

And sure enough, at the pinnacle of this "half-octahedron" roof is a **giant flag** that not only tells London "there will be a show today," but it also indicates the direction of the "**Air**."

A billowing flag is a symbolic representation of element of "Air." Just like the 72 x 72 x 72 unit cube that fits in the Globe is a representation of "Earth."

I know this geometrical philosophizing sounds a bit fanciful to modern ears. But back in the 1500s, this was a cultural meme.

All the Platonic solids are on Dee's Title page

In fact, we might see all 4 Elements on the Title page. And the fifth, the dodecahedron, Plato associates with "the embroidery of the Heavens," which Dee expresses with the stars in the dome.

This well-integrated story is right in front of everyone's eyes on the Title page, yet to most, it's invisible.

("That's the sign of a good riddle," Dee seems to be saying with sly smile.)

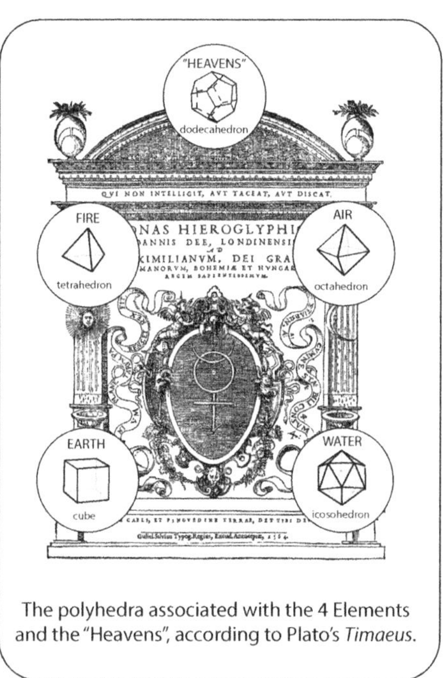

The polyhedra associated with the 4 Elements and the "Heavens", according to Plato's *Timaeus*.

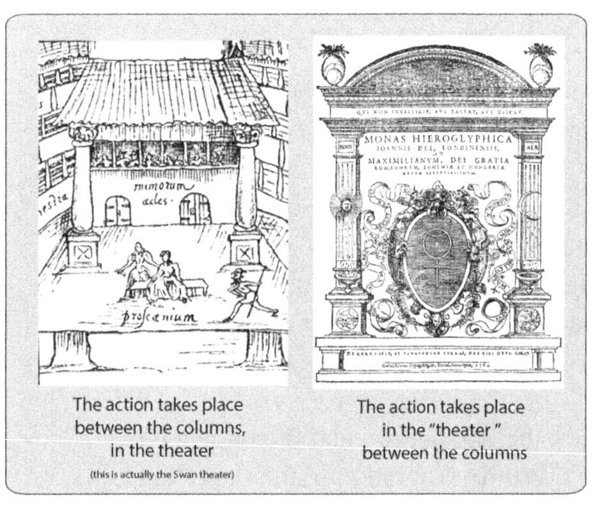

The action takes place between the columns, in the theater

(this is actually the Swan theater)

The action takes place in the "theater" between the columns

By the way, did you catch another strong connection between the Title page illustration and Dee's Globe design?

On the Title page, all the action takes place in the "theater" between the two columns.

In the Globe theater, all the action takes place on stage between the two columns.

(It seems Dee also thought, "All the World's a stage."

JOHN DEE WRITES ABOUT THE "ARTE OF ARCHITECTURE"

As John Dee writes in his 1570 *Preface to Euclid*:

"First remember that I include Architecture among the Mathematical Arts which are Derived from the Principal arts of Arithmetic and Geometry. Realize that some of these arts deal more with Natural things and matter perceptible by the senses, while others draw nearer to Simple and absolute Mathematical Observations."

Dee continues, about architects:

" This worthy profession is garnished, beautified, and stored with many varied skills and fields of knowledge, I do not think that someone can just suddenly proclaim he is an Architect. One must start from childhood and slowly climb the steps of these studies. Only after being trained in Languages, Arts, and Sciences will he be able to reach the high Temple of Architecture.

But to those whom Nature has bestowed such ingenuity, skillfulness, and a good Memory that they have mastered Geometry, Astronomy, Music, and the other Arts, and who have surmounted and pass the calling and state of Architects can finally become Mathematicians. Such men are rarely found."

Dee was an expert mathematician, so by his own definition, he considered himself to be an expert architect.

(John Dee, *Preface to Euclid,* Dee's chapter on the Art of Architecture, pp. d.iij. – d.iiij. verso).

As Dee helped introduce Vitruvius and Leon Battista Alberti to England (in his 1570 *Preface to Euclid)*, Dee would have been the "go-to guy" for a project such as the design of a state-of-the-art theatre in Elizabethan London.

As Joy Hancox writes on page 102 of her book, *The Byrom Collection*:

"The men responsible for the actual construction of the Theater were undoubtedly Elizabethan carpenters, supervised by characters such as Brayne, Burbage, Streete and later, Henslowe; the ideas for its design– the intellectual origins – came from a different level in society altogether. For me the figure of John Dee emerges as the most likely channel for the dissemination of the sophisticated theories behind the circular playhouses of the Bankside.

The polygonal shape of the Theater arises from a Geometric plan. Dee was the leading mathematician in this country at the time, with an international reputation and international contacts... His library was one of the greatest in the country and contained no less than five editions of Vitruvius and two of Alberti's famous treatise on architecture."

The Globe theater and the John Dee Tower of 1583 are "sisters"

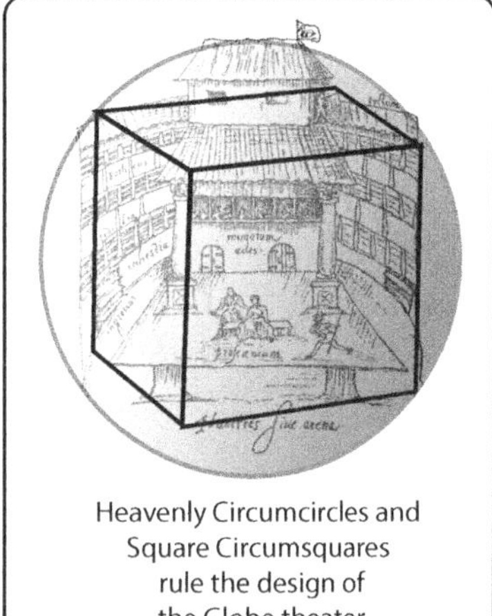

Heavenly Circumcircles and Square Circumsquares rule the design of the Globe theater

John Dee's Globe theater design appears to be based on one sphere, inside a cylinder with 8 sides.

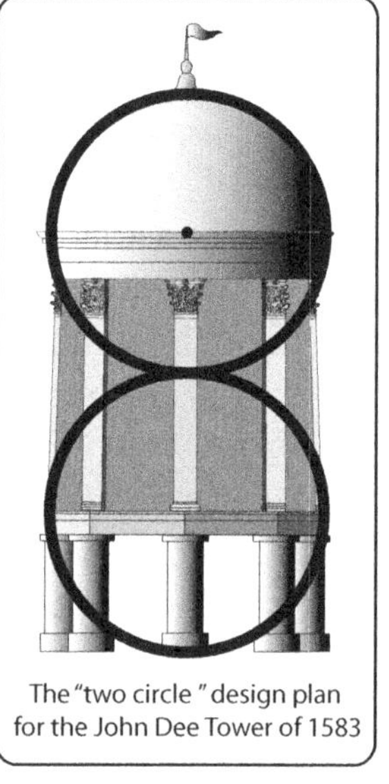

The "two circle" design plan for the John Dee Tower of 1583

John Dee's Tower 1583 is based on two spheres (one on top of the other), with an octagonal base of 8 pillars.

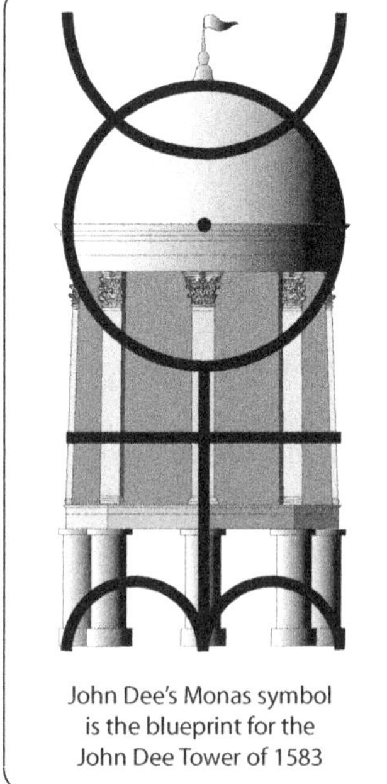

John Dee's Monas symbol is the blueprint for the John Dee Tower of 1583

In different ways, each of these designs represent the Union of Opposites, Heaven and Earth, probably the grandest mathematical/philosophical metaphor one can attempt to express architecturally.

I wouldn't have been able to decipher the Globe drawings without first having understood the design plan of the Newport Tower. Both works of architecture are based on ideas expressed by Dee in the *Monas Hieroglyphica*.

Both these designs came from the same "father." That's why I call the original Globe and the Newport Tower "**sisters**."

EPOGDOON EPILOGUE

This combination "sphere, cube, octagon, and octagonal cylinder" concept is "**frozen music**" of the highest order.

Dee would't have settled for anything less.

Unfortunately, Dee's reputation was stigmatized in the Jacobean and Puritan times after Elizabeth had died, and it has remained tarnished ever since.

Around 1610, while Shakespeare paints *The Tempest*'s Prospero (perhaps based on Dee) in a wise light, Ben Johnson, in *The Alchemist,* satirizes eccentrics like Dee as superstitious fools.

We should all learn more about this man who identified the two great rhythms in number, **Metamorphosis** (The 12, 24, 72, 360, 2520 ... rhythm) and **Consummata** (The "+4, -4, octave, null nine" ... rhythm), not just to find out more clues about the past, but to find out clues about our future.

Sure the Globe theater is famous for Shakespeare and all his brilliance.

But this octagonal playhouse is also famous as an architectural masterpiece.

That's why humanity had the impetus to re-create it over four centuries after it was originally built.

Even if the current "reproduction" is not exact to Dee's explicit specifications, its polygonal shape, its open-air stage, its Starr's Mall, and its Tiring House, still capture most of the magic of the conceptual "wooden O," Dee's Renaissance reworking of a classical amphitheater.

Even if its not fully up to Dee's original specs, by virtue of the fact that a new Globe has been built, John Dee has managed to incorporate a fourth dimension into his 2D and 3D design:
time.

That said, I think a reconstruction of the "original" Globe, based on John Dee's designs found in the Byrom Papers would be ultra-magical.

Admittedly, my analysis is based on my interpretation
of the geometry of the Byrom Collection drawings
(there may be other ways to interpret them)
and upon old illustrations of the Globe
(that may or may not be accurate representations).

But I feel that the "big picture" idea here is brilliant.
It's one that Dee would have felt worthy enough
to encapsulate in his design for a theater.

To me, only the man....
who set the date for Queen Elizabeth's coronation,
who convinced her she had a legal right to most of North America,
who coined the term the British Empire and coined 144 English words,
who was friends with brightest mathematicians and cartographers in Europe,
who was the navigational guide to all the great Elizabethan explorers,
who wrote the proposal for the English Calendar reform,
who added corollaries to Euclid's propositions and invented the colon,
... could have conceived the of such a harmonious design.

No other Englishmen at the time could have come close
to composing this musical geometrical masterpiece.

Dee was a Renaissance man.
Few compare.

"Amen, says the
fourth letter."

APPENDIX
THE "ARTE OF ARCHITECTURE"
(IN JOHN DEE'S OWN WORDS)

This is the Title page of the first English translation of Euclid's *Elements.of Geometry*

The next 4 pages includes Dee's actual explanation of the "Arte of Architecture" from his "very fruitful" Preface to that book.

As Dee's Elizabethan English is a little challenging to read, the final 4 pages is my transliteration or modernization of Dee's words.

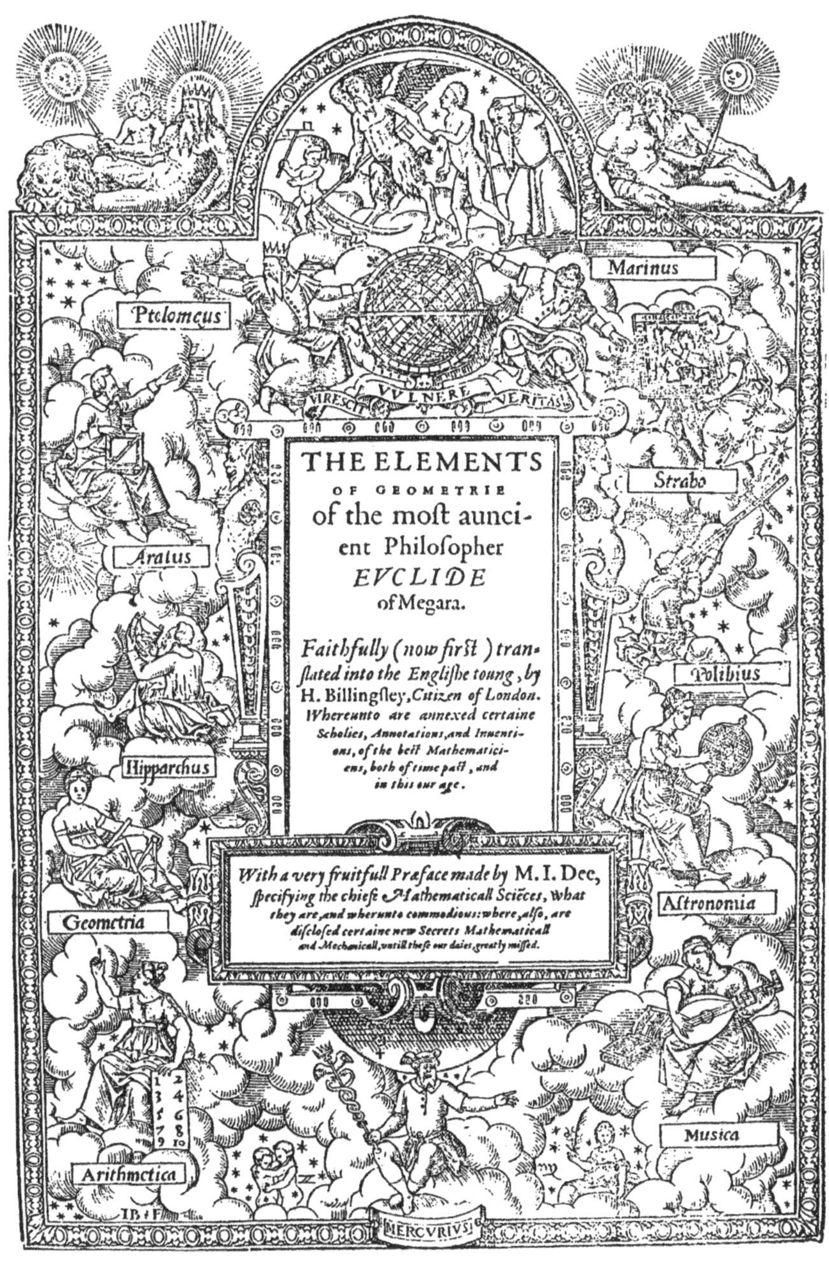

THE ELEMENTS
OF GEOMETRIE
of the moſt aunci-
ent Philoſopher
EVCLIDE
of Megara.

Faithfully (now firſt) tranſlated into the Engliſhe toung, by H. Billingſley, *Citizen of London. Whereunto are annexed certaine Scholies, Annotations, and Inuentions, of the best Mathematicians, both of time paſt, and in this our age.*

With a very fruitfull Præface made by M. I. Dee, *ſpecifying the chiefe Mathematicall Scieces, what they are, and wherunto commodious: where, alſo, are diſcloſed certaine new Secrets Mathematicall and Mechanicall, untill theſe our daies, greatly miſſed.*

Imprinted at London by *Iohn Daye.*

der, or *Paynter*(*&c*)know their Arte,to be commodious.

Architecture,to many may seme not worthy, or not mete, to be reckned among the *Artes Mathematicall*.To whom,I thinke good,to giue some account of my so doyng.Not worthy,(will they say,)bycause it is but for building,of a house, Pallace,Church,Forte,or such like,grosse workes.And you,also, defined the *Artes Mathematicall*,to be such,as dealed with no Materiall or corruptible thing:and also did demonstratiuely procede in their faculty, by Number or Magnitude. First, you see,that I count,here,*Architecture*, among those *Artes Mathematicall*, which are Deriued from the Principals: and you know, that such,may deale with Naturall thinges,and sensible matter. Of which, some draw nerer,to the Simple and absolute Mathematicall Speculation,then other do. And though,the *Architect* procureth, enformeth, & directeth,the *Mechanicien*,to handworke, & the building actuall,of house,Castell,or Pallace, and is chief Iudge of the same: yet, with him selfe(as chief *Master* and *Architect*,) remaineth the Demonstratiue reason and cause, of the Mechaniciens worke: in Lyne,plaine, and Solid: by *Geometricall*, *Arithmeticall*,*Opticall*,*Musicall*, *Astronomicall*,*Cosmographicall* (& to be brief) by all the former Deriued *Artes Mathematicall*, and other Naturall Artes,hable to be confirmed and stablished.If this be so:then, may you thinke,that *Architecture*,hath good and due allowance, in this honest Company of *Artes Mathematicall* Deriuatiue. *An obiection.* *The Answer.*

I will,herein,craue Iudgement of two most perfect *Architectes*: the one, being *Vitruuius*, the Romaine: who did write ten bookes thereof,to the Emperour *Augustus* (in whose daies our Heauenly Archemaster, was borne): and the other, *Leo Baptista Albertus*, a Florentine: who also published ten bookes therof. *Architectura* (sayth *Vitruuius*) *est Scientia pluribus disciplinis & varijs eruditionibus ornata: cuius Iudicio probantur omnia, quæ ab cæteris Artificibus perficiuntur opera*. That is. Architecture, is a Science garnished with many doctrines & diuerse instructions: by whose Iudgement, all workes,by other workmen finished, are Iudged. It followeth.*Ea nascitur ex Fabrica, & Ratiocinatione.&c. Ratiocinatio autem est, quæ,res fabricatas,Solertia ac ratione proportionis,demonstrare atq; explicare potest*. *Architecture,groweth of Framing,and Reasoning.&c. Reasoning,is that,which of thinges framed,with forecast,and proportion: can make demonstration, and manifest declaration*. Againe. *Cùm, in omnibus enim rebus, tùm maximè etiam in Architectura, hæc duo insunt: quod significatur, & quod significat. Significatur proposita res, de qua dicitur: hanc autem Significat Demonstratio, rationibus doctrinarum explicata*. *Forasmuch as, in all thinges: therefore chiefly in Architecture, these two thinges are: the thing signified: and that which signifieth. The thing propounded, whereof we speake, is the thing Signified. But Demonstration,expressed with the reasons of diuerse doctrines,doth signifie the same thing*. After that.*Vt literatus sit, peritus Graphidos,eruditus Geometriæ, & Optices non ignarus: instructus Arithmetica: historias complures nouerit, Philosophos diligenter audiuerit: Musicam sciuerit: Medicinæ non sit ignarus, responsa Iurisperitorũ nouerit: Astrologiam, Cæliq; rationes cognitas habeat*. *An Architect* (sayth he) *ought to vnderstand Languages, to be skilfull of Painting, well instructed in Geometrie, not ignorant of Perspectiue, furnished with Arithmetike, haue knowledge of many histories, and diligently haue heard Philosophers, haue skill of Musike, not ignorant of Physike, know the aunsweres of Lawyers, and haue Astronomie,*

d.iij.

nomie, and the courses Cælestiall, in good knowledge. He geueth reason, orderly, wherefore all these Artes, Doctrines, and Instructions, are requisite in an excellent *Architect.* And (for breuitie) omitting the Latin text, thus he hath. *Secondly, it is behofefull for an Architect to haue the knowledge of Painting: that he may the more easilie fashion out, in patternes painted, the forme of what worke he liketh. And Geometrie, geueth to Architecture many helpes: and first teacheth the Vse of the Rule, and the Cumpasse: wherby (chiefly and easilie) the descriptions of Buildinges, are despatched in Groundplats: and the directions of Squires, Leuells, and Lines. Likewise, by Perspectiue, the Lightes of the heauen, are well led, in the buildinges: from certaine quarters of the world. By Arithmetike, the charges of Buildinges are summed together: the measures are expressed, and the hard questions of Symmetries, are by Geometricall Meanes and Methods discoursed on. &c. Besides this, of the Nature of thinges (which in Greke is called φυσιολογία) Philosophie doth make declaration. Which, it is necessary, for an Architect, with diligence to haue learned: because it hath many and diuers naturall questions: as specially, in Aqueductes. For in their courses, leadinges about, in the leuell ground, and in the mountinges, the naturall Spirites or breathes are ingendred diuers wayes: The hindrances, which they cause, no man can helpe, but he, which out of Philosophie, hath learned the originall causes of thinges. Likewise, who soeuer shall read Ctesibius, or Archimedes bookes, (and of others, who haue written such Rules) can not thinke, as they do: vnlesse he shall haue receaued of Philosophers, instructions in these thinges. And Musike he must nedes know: that he may haue vnderstanding, both of Regular and Mathematicall Musike: that he may temper well his Balistes, Catapultes, and Scorpions. &c. Moreouer, the Brasen Vessels, which in Theatres, are placed by Mathematicall order, in ambries, vnder the steppes: and the diuersities of the soundes (which ẏ Grecians call ἠχεῖα) are ordred according to Musicall Symphonies & Harmonies: being distributed in ẏ Circuites, by Diatessaron, Diapente, and Diapason. That the conuenient voyce, of the players sound, whẽ it came to these preparations, made in order, there being increased: with ẏ increasing, might come more cleare & pleasant, to ẏ eares of the lokers on. &c. And of Astronomie, is knowẽ ẏ East, West, South, and North. The fashion of the heauen, the Æquinox, the Solsticie, and the course of the sterres. Which thinges, vnleast one know: he can not perceiue, any thyng at all, the reason of Horologies. Seyng therfore this ample Science, is garnished, beautified and stored, with so many and sundry skils and knowledges: I thinke, that none can iustly account them selues Architectes, of the suddeyne. But they onely, who from their childes yeares, ascendyng by these degrees of knowledges, beyng fostered vp with the atteynyng of many Languages and Artes, haue wonne to the high Tabernacle of Architecture. &c. And to whom Nature hath giuen such quicke Circumspection, sharpnes of witt, and Memorie, that they may be very absolutely skillfull in Geometrie, Astronomie, Musike, and the rest of the Artes Mathematicall:*

call: Such, surmount and passe the callyng, and state, of Architectes: and are become Mathematiciens. &c. And they are found, seldome. As, in tymes past, was Aristarchus Samius: Philolaus, and Archytas, Tarentynes: Apollonius Pergeus: Eratosthenes Cyreneus: Archimedes, and Scopas, Syracusians. Who also, left to theyr posteritie, many Engines and Gnomonicall workes: by numbers and naturall meanes, inuented and declared. *A Mathematicien.*

Thus much, and the same wordes (in sense) in one onely Chapter of this Incõparable *Architect Vitruuius*, shall you finde. And if you should, but take his boke in your hand, and slightly loke thorough it, you would say straight way: This is *Geometrie, Arithmetike, Astronomie, Musike, Anthropographie, Hydragogie, Horometrie. &c.* and (to cõclude) the Storehouse of all workmãship. Now, let vs listen to our other Iudge, our Florentine, *Leo Baptista*: and narrowly cõsider, how he doth determine of *Architecture. Sed anteq ultra progrediar. &c.* *But before I procede any further* (sayth he) *I thinke, that I ought to expresse, what man I would haue to bee allowed an Architect. For, I will not bryng in place a Carpenter: as though you might Compare him to the Chief Masters of other Artes. For the hand of the Carpenter, is the Architectes Instrument. But I will appoint the Architect to be that man, who hath the skill, (by a certaine and meruailous meanes and way,) both in minde and Imagination to determine: and also in worke to finish: what workes so euer, by motion of waight, and cuppling and framyng together of bodyes, may most aptly be Commodious for the worthiest Vses of Man. And that he may be able to performe these thinges, he hath nede of atteynyng and knowledge of the best, and most worthy thynges. &c. The whole Feate of Architecture in buildyng, consisteth in Lineamentes, and in Framyng. And the whole power and skill of Lineamentes, tendeth to this: that the right and absolute way may be had, of Coaptyng and ioynyng Lines and angles: by which, the face of the buildyng or frame, may be comprehended and concluded. And it is the property of Lineamentes, to prescribe vnto buildynges, and euery part of them, an apt place, & certaine nũber: a worthy maner, and a semely order: that, so, ỹ whole forme and figure of the buildyng, may rest in the very Lineamentes. &c. And we may prescribe in mynde and imagination the whole formes,* all materiall stuffe beyng secluded. Which point we shall atteyne, by Notyng and forepointyng the angles, and lines, by a sure and certaine direction and connexion. Seyng then, these thinges, are thus: Lineamente, shalbe the certaine and constant prescribyng, conceiued in mynde: made in lines and angles: and finished with a learned minde and wyt.* We thanke you Master *Baptist*, that you haue so aptly brought your Arte, and phrase therof, to haue some Mathematicall perfection: by certaine order, nũber, forme, figure, and *Symmetrie* mentall: all naturall & sensible stuffe set a part. Now, then, it is euident, (Gentle reader) how aptely and worthely, I haue preferred *Architecture*, to be bred and fostered vp in the Dominion of the peereles *Princesse, Mathematica*: and to be a naturall Subiect of hers. And the name of *Architecture*, is of the principalitie, which this Science hath, aboue all other Artes. And *Plato* affirmeth, the *Architect* to be *Master* ouer all, that make any worke. Wherupon, he is neither Smith, nor Builder: nor, separately, any Artificer: but the

Vitruuius.

VVho is an Architect.

** The Immaterialitie of perfect Architecture.*

What, Lineament is.

Note.

d.iiij. Hed,

Hed,the Prouost, the Directer,and Iudge of all Artificiall workes, and all Artificers. For,the true *Architect*,is hable to teach,Demonstrate,distribute,describe, and Iudge all workes wrought. And he,onely,searcheth out the causes and reasons of all Artificiall thynges. Thus excellent, is *Architecture*: though few (in our dayes) atteyne thereto : yet may not the Arte, be otherwise thought on, then in very dede it is worthy. Nor we may not,of auncient Artes,make new and imperfect Definitions in our dayes: for scarsitie of Artificers : No more,than we may pynche in,the Definitions of *Wisedome*,or *Honestie*, or of *Frendeshyp* or of *Iustice*. No more will I consent,to Diminish any whit,of the perfection and dignitie, (by iust cause) allowed to absolute *Architecture*. Vnder the Direction of this Arte, are thre principall,necessary *Mechanicall Artes*. Namely , *Howsing* , *Fortification* , and *Naupegie*. *Howsing*, I vnderstand,both for Diuine Seruice,and Mans common vsage: publike, and priuate. Of *Fortification* and *Naupegie*, straunge matter might be told you: But perchaunce,some will be tyred,with this Bederoll, all ready rehearsed: and other some, will nycely nip my grosse and homely discoursing with you : made in post hast : for feare you should wante this true and frendly warnyng, and tast giuyng, of the *Power Mathematicall*. Lyfe is short, and vncertaine : Tymes are perilouse: &c. And still the Printer awayting, for my pen staying : All these thinges,with farder matter of Ingratefulnes, giue me occasion to passe away, to the other Artes remainyng, with all spede possible.

THe Arte of Nauigation, demonstrateth how,by the shortest good way, by the aptest Directió,& in the shortest time, a sufficient Ship,betwene any two places (in passage Nauigable,) assigned: may be códucted: and in all stormes,& naturall disturbances chauncyng, how,to vse the best possible meanes , whereby to recouer the place first assigned. What nede, the *Master Pilote*, hath of other Artes, here before recited,it is easie to know: as, of *Hydrographie*, *Astronomie*, *Astrologie*, and *Horometrie*. Presupposing continually,the common Base,and foundacion of all: namely *Arithmetike* and *Geometrie*. So that,he be hable to vnderstand,and Iudge his own necessary Instrumentes,and furniture Necessary: Whether they be perfectly made or no: and also can,(if nede be) make them, hym selfe. As Quadrantes, The Astronomers Ryng,The Astronomers staffe,The Astrolabe vniuersall. An Hydrographicall Globe. Charts Hydrographicall,true,(not with parallell Meridians). The Common Sea Compas: The Compas of variacion: The Proportionall,and Paradoxall Compasses (of me Inuented,for our two Moscouy Master Pilotes, at the request of the Company) Clockes with spryng: houre,halfe houre,and three houre Sandglasses: & sundry other Instrumétes: And also, be hable,on Globe, or Playne to describe the Paradoxall Compasse : and duely to vse the same,to all maner of purposes, whereto it was inuented. And also, be hable to Calculate the Planetes places for all tymes.

Anno. 1559.

Moreouer, with Sonne Mone or Sterre (or without) be hable to define the Longitude & Latitude of the place, which he is in: So that,the Longitude & Latitude of the place, from which he sayled, be giuen: or by him, be knowne. whereto, appertayneth expert meanes,to be certified euer, of the Ships way. &c. And by foreseing the Rising, Settyng, Nonestedyng, or Midnightyng of certaine tempestuous fixed Sterres : or their Coniunctions, and Anglynges with the Planetes, &c. he ought to haue expert coniecture of Stormes, Tempestes, and Spoutes: and such lyke Meteorologicall effectes, daungerous on Sea. For (as *Plato* sayth,) *Mutationes*,

oppor-

(My modernization of Dee's original Elizabethan English.)

[The Arte of Architecture]

Many might consider it improper to include Architecture among the Mathematical Arts because it is not worthy enough. To them I will provide good reasons why I dare do so. They might point out that I have defined Mathematical Arts as not dealing with material or corruptible things, but dealing with things which can be expressed using Number and Magnitude. They will claim Architecture unworthy because it deals with such gross, material works like the building of a house, Palace, Church or Fort. *An Objection*

First, remember that I include Architecture among the Mathematical Arts which are Derived from the Principal arts of Arithmetic and Geometry. Realize that some of these arts deal more with Natural things and matter perceptible by the senses, while others draw nearer to Simple and absolute Mathematical Observations. *My Response*

The Architect prepares, informs and guides the Mechanician who does the actual handiwork of building a house, Castle or Palace. He is also the final Judge in any decisions that must be made. As the chief master, the Architect is responsible for the Demonstrative reason and cause of the Mechanician's work. Working in Line, Plane, and Solid the Architect's work must be solidly based on the principles of Geometry, Arithmetic, Optics, Music, Astronomy, Cosmography—indeed all the Mathematical Arts in this *Preface*, as well as other Natural Arts.

As it is based on the principles of all these Arts, you can see why it should be include as its own Mathematical Art.

Let's hear from the two men I consider to be the two most perfect Architects:

One is the Roman Vitruvius who wrote *On Architecture* [ca. 25 BC]. He dedicated the *Ten Books* in this work to Emperor Augustus who ruled Rome at the time our Heavenly Archmaster [Jesus] was born. The other is Leon Battista Alberti of Florence, who also published *Ten Books on Architecture* [in 1452].

Vitruvius writes: [in his first sentence of Chapter 1, Book 1]

"Architecture is a science involving many disciplines and various kinds of specialized knowledge. All the work done by the builders is guided by the seasoned judgment of the architect. His expertise grows from practice and reasoning. Reasoning is what declares the final proportions of the work."

Vitruvius continues:

"In all things, but particularly in Architecture, there are two aspects to be considered, the significant and the signifier. The signified is the object spoke about [like a building]. The signifier is the reasoned demonstration based on established principles of knowledge. They are two aspects of the same thing."

Further along in Book 1, Chapter 1, Vitruvius writes:

"An Architect must be familiar with various Languages, skillful in Painting well instructed in Geometry, not ignorant of Perspective, equipped with knowledge of Arithmetic, familiar with History, a diligent student of Philosophy, have skill in Music, be not ignorant of Medicine, understand rules of Law, and have a firm grasp on Astronomy and the courses of Celestial objects."

(d.iij.)

Vitruvius clearly explains why an Architect must be familiar with all these Arts and disciplines:

"It is important for an Architect to have knowledge of Painting so he can more easily illustrate the work he proposes.

Geometry offers many aids to Architecture. First among them is the use of the Rule and Compass to facilitate drawing the building plans. On-site, this geometry is carried out using squares, levels and plumb lines.

Likewise, by Perspective, the Lights of heaven are well-led in the buildings, from certain quarters of the world.

By Arithmetic, the cost of the building is summed up, the measurements are calculated, and the important issues of Symmetry are resolved using Geometric principles and methods.

It is essential to thoroughly study Philosophy because it deals with many varied natural problems about the "Nature of things," which the Greeks call *physiologia.*

One example of this is conducting water through Aqueducts. Parts of the course are downhill, but some are level, and some must actually go over high ground. In each of these situations water pressure will vary. Problems like this can only be solved by someone who has learned the natural causes of things by studying Philosophy.

In addition, anyone who has read the books of Ctesibus and Archimedes (or others who have written down such Rules) will not be able to fully appreciate their meaning unless he has been trained in these subjects by the Philosophers.

And an Architect must know Music in order to understand both Regular Music and Mathematical Music. This will help him fine tune the springs of Balists [which shoot heavy darts], Catapults, and Scorpions [a smaller catapult operated by one person].

Likewise, in Theatres, Bronze Vessels are placed in niches beneath the seats using mathematical principles. The Greeks called the *echeia.*

[êxô means "a returned sound or a ringing sound," from which we get the word echo].

They are distributed in various places throughout the circular Theatre according to the Musical Harmonies of **Diatessaron, Diapente, and Diapason**.

[The musical fourth, fifth, and octave or the ratios 3:4, 2:3, and 1:2]

The actor's voice, projected from the stage, would be amplified when it strikes these vessels, allowing the audience to hear a richer and more pleasing sound.

As for Astronomy, the Architect must know East, West, South and North, and the design of the heavens, the Equinox, the Solstices, and the course of the stars. Anyone who lacks knowledge of these matters will be unable to understand the Art of Horology.

As this worthy profession is garnished, beautified and stored with many varied skills and fields of knowledge, I do not think that someone can just suddenly proclaim he is an Architect. One must start from childhood and slowly climb the steps of these studies. Only after being trained in Languages, Arts, and Sciences will be able to reach the high Temple of Architecture.

But to those whom Nature has bestowed such ingenuity, skillfulness, and a good Memory that they have mastered Geometry, Astronomy, Music and the other Arts, and who have surmounted and passed the calling and state of Architects can finally become Mathematicians. Such men are rarely found, but here are a few examples from times past: Aristarchus of Samos, Philolaus and Archgas of Tarentum, Appolonius of Perga, Eratosthenes of Cyrene, and Archimedes and Scopinas of Syracuse. Using natural laws and mathematical principles they invented many kinds of Machines and Sundials, which they described in their books for the posterity."

A Mathematician

(d.iij. verso)

These words (paraphrased in places) can all be found in one chapter in the Ten Books by the Incomparable Architect Vitruvius. [that is, Chapter 1, Book 1] If you were able to take this book in your hand and glance through it you would immediately agree: This is a Storehouse of all workmanship. It incorporates the Arts of Geometry, Arithmetic, Astronomy, Music, Anthropography, Hydragogy, Horometry and more. *Vitruvius.*

Now let's listen to our other Judge, the Florentine Leon Battista Alberti, and briefly examine his views on Architecture [in his Prologue to Book 1]:

"Before proceeding, I must describe the man I would consider to be an Architect. As other Arts have Chief Masters, you might think the Carpenter to be the Chief Master of Architecture. But this is not so. The Carpenter is but an Instrument of the Architect. *Who is an Architect?*

I consider an Architect to be that man who (by sure and marvelous reason and method) has the skill to devise (using his own mind and Imagination) and accomplish by, the movement of weighty material and the joining and framing together of bodies, that which is most beneficial for the worthiest needs of Man. " " " "

To be able to perform these things, he must have an understanding and knowledge of the highest and most worthy disciplines."

[In Book 1, Chapter 1, Alberti continues:] "The whole Feat of Architecture in building consists of Lineaments [its distinctive lines] and Framing [structure]. The whole intent and purpose of Lineaments lies in determining the best way of coordinating and joining all the lines and angles that define all the faces of the building.

The function of the lineaments is to prescribe an appropriate location, precise numbers, proper scale, and elegant order for the whole building as well as for its various parts. Thus the entire form* and appearance of a building may depend upon the Lineaments. ** The Immateriality of perfect Architecture*

Lineaments have nothing to do with the particular material the building is made from. Building made from different materials can have the same lineaments if they share similar siting, order, and all the lines and angles are similar.

Thus, **Lineaments** are all the precise and correct lines and angles of a building, first conceived in the mind, and then perfected by inspired vision and learned intellect." *What a Lineament is.*

We thank you, Master Alberti. By setting aside the material stuff of the building, you have appropriately given your Art (and your description of it) a Mathematical perfection that involves thinking about order, number, form, figure, and symmetry.

Now, Gentle reader, it is evident why I consider Architecture to have been born and raised in the Dominion of the incomparable Princess Mathematica and to be one of her natural subjects. The word "Architecture" itself helps describe what distinguishes this Science from all the other Arts. " *Note* " "

As Plato affirms, the Architect is the Master of all other workers. He is neither a Smith or a Builder or any other Craftsman. He is the Head, the Provost, the Director, and the Judge of all Artificial works and of all Artificers. The true Architect is able to teach, demonstrate, administer, describe, and Judge all works made. And only he searches out the causes and reasons of all Artificial things.

(d.iiij.)

(d.iiij. verso)

Thus, Architecture is so excellent that, in our days, few endeavor to undertake it. But it should only be thought of as a virtuous pursuit.

Just because we have scarce few Artificers these days doesn't mean we should imperfectly redefine the ancient Arts anymore than we should pinch in the Definition of Wisdom, Honesty, Friendship, or Justice. No more will I consent to Diminish, in anyway, the perfection and legitimate dignity given to absolute Architecture.

Under the direction of this Art are three important Mechanical Arts, Housing, Fortification, and Naupegie [ship building].

Housing incorporates buildings made for Divine Service and for Man's common usage, whether public or private.

Strange matters might also be explained about Fortification and Naupegie. But perchance some will be weary of all this Bede-Roll [lengthy listing or cataloging]. Others might prefer I nicely nip my bulky and unrefined discoursing with you, made in post-haste. I wouldn't want you to lose interest in this true and friendly sampling of Mathematical Power. Life is short and uncertain. Times are perilous. And the Printer is waiting for my pen to stop. So let's proceed to the remaining Arts with all speed possible.

Bibliography

Abraham, Lindy, *A Dictionary of Alchemical Imagery*, (Cambridge, Cambridge University Press, 1998)

Adams, Joseph Quincy, *Shakespearean Playhouses: A History of English Theatres from the Beginnings to the Restoration*, (Gloucester MA, Peter Smith, 1960; or Teddington UK, Echo Library, 2008)

Agrippa, Henry Cornelius, *Three Books of Occult Philosophy,* annotated by Donald Tyson, (St. Paul MN, Llewellyn, 2000)

Alberti, Leon Battista, *De re aedificatoria* (*On Architecture*, or *On the Art of Building*) (ca. 1443-1452)

Alberti, Leon Battista, *De Pictura* (*On Painting* or *On Pictures)* (1435)

Allen, Dr. F. J., *The Ruined Mill, or Round Church of the Norsemen, at Newport, Rhode Island, USA, compared with the Round Church at Cambridge and others in Europe, (*1921) (booklet, 1921, 2011; offprint from the "Cambridge Antiquarian Society's Communications," Volume XXII)

Allen, R. E., *Plato, The Republic*, (New Haven, Yale, 2006)

al-Haitham, Ibn, "Opticae Thesaurus: The Mechanistic Hypothesis and the Scientific Study of Vision," edited by . F. Risnero, in A. C. Crombie (Cambridge, MA: Heffer, 1967)

Archibald, Raymond Clare, *Euclid's Book on Division of Figures* (Cambridge, University Press, 1915)

Aubrey, John, (edited by Oliver L. Dick) *Aubrey's Brief Lives* (Ann Arbor, U. of Michigan, 1962)

Brunner, G. O., "An Unconventional View of Closest Sphere Packings," (1971, *Acta Crystallographica*, A, Part 4, 1971, p. 27)

Caljori, Florian, *A History of Mathematical Notations,* (Mineola NY, Dover, 1993)

Clullee, Nicholas H., *John Dee's Natural Philosophy: Between Science and Religion*, (London and New York, Routledge, 1988)

Smith, George, editor, *Dictionary of National Biography*, (London, Oxford, 1917)

Dee, John, *A Letter Containing a Most Brief Discourse Apologetical*, (London: Peter Short, 1599); transliterated by James A. Egan, in *The Works of John Dee: The Modernizations of John Dee's Main Mathematical Masterpieces* (Newport, RI: Cosmopolite Press, 2010).

Dee, John, *The Diaries of John Dee*, edited by Edward Fenton, (Oxfordshire, Day Books, 2000)

Dee, John: *Monas Hieroglyphica* (Antwerp: Guliemo Silvio, 1564) and translation by James A Egan, in *The Works of John Dee,: The Modernizations of John Dee's Main Mathematical Masterpieces* (Newport, RI: Cosmopolite Press, 2010).

Dee, John , *Preface to Euclid*, in *The Elements of Geometry of the most ancient Philosopher Euclide of Megara*, Henry Billingsley, (London: John Daye, 1577); Preface transliterated by James A Egan, in *The Works of John Dee: The Modernizations of John Dee's Main Mathematical Masterpieces* (Newport, RI: Cosmopolite Press, 2010).

Edmondson, Amy C., *A Fuller Explanation: The Synergetic Geometry of R. Buckminster Fuller,* (Pueblo CO, Emergent World, 2007)

Egan, James Alan, *Elizabethan America: The John Dee Tower of 1583: A Renaissance Horologium in Newport, Rhode Island*, (Newport, RI, Cosmopolite Press, 2010).

Egan, James Alan, *The Works John Dee: The Modernizations of John Dee's Main Mathematical Masterpieces* (Newport, RI: Cosmopolite Press, 2010).

Egan, James A., "Highlights of Research on the Newport Tower," in *The Newport Tower, Arnold to Zeno*, (NEARA, Edgecomb, ME, 2006)

Egan, James A., Nine Books: (Newport, RI, Cosmopolite Press, 2010)
Book One: The John Dee Tower of 1583: A Renaissance Building in Newport, Rhode Island
Book Two: The Works of John Dee: Modernizations of his Main Mathematical Masterpieces
Book Three: The Meaning of the *Monas Hieroglyphica* with Regards to Geometry
Book Four: The Meaning of the *Monas Hieroglyphica* with Regards to Number
Book Five: The Story of 1, 2, 3, 4, and the Proportions of the John Dee Tower
Book Six: The Coronation Date of Queen Elizabeth I and More *Monas* Mathematics
Book Seven: Dee's Decad of Shapes and Plato's Number
Book Eight: John Dee, Governor Benedict Arnold and the Anchor of Hope

Euclid, *Euclid's Elements,* (Santa Fe, Green Lion Press, 2003)

Fenton, Edward, (editor), *The Diaries of John Dee,* (Oxfordshire, Day Books, 2000)

Fernando, Diana T., *The Dictionary of Alchemy: An A-Z of History, People, Definitions,* (London, Vega, 2002)

Fuller, Buckminster, *Synergetics 1: Explorations in the Geometry of Thinking,* (NY, Macmillan, 1975)

Fuller, Buckminster, *Synergetics 2: Explorations in the Geometry of Thinking,* (NY, Macmillan, 1979)

Gilbert, Sir Humphrey, *A New Passage to Cataia, 1576*, (Menston, England, Scolar, 1972)

Godfrey, William S. Jr., "The Archeology of the Old Stone Mill in Newport, Rhode Island," (*American Antiquity*, 1951-2, pp. 120-129)

Goodwin, William B., "The Dee River of 1538 (Now called Narragansett Bay) and its relation to Norumbega." (R. I. Historical Society, *Collections*, April 1934, pp. 38-50)

Grafton, Anthony, *Leon Battista Alberti, Master Builder of the Italian Renaissance* (New York: Hill and Wang, A Division of Farrar, Straus and Giroux, 2000).

Gullberg, Jan, *Mathematics: From the Birth of Numbers*, (New York, Norton, 1997)

Hakluyt, Richard, *The Principal Navigations, Traffiques and Discoveries of the English Nation*, (London, Penguin, 1972)

Hammond, John H., *The Camera Obscura: A Chronicle* (Bristol: Adam Hilger Ltd., 1981)

Hammond, Mary Sayer, "The Camera Obscura: A Chapter in the Prehistory of Photography; Pinhole Photography, Astronomy, Drawing Machines, Kepler, Perspective," (Ph.D. Thesis, Ohio State University, 1986)

Hancox, Joy, *Kingdom For a Stage: Magicians and Aristocrats in the Elizabethan Theatre* (Stroud UK, Sutton Pub. Ltd., 2001)

Hancox, Joy, *The Byrom Collection: And the Globe Theatre Mystery* (London, Jonathan Cape Ltd., 1997)

Hancox, Joy, *The Hidden Chapter: An Investigation into the Custody of Lost Knowledge* (Manchester, Byrom Projects, 2011)

Hancox, Joy, *The Queen's Chameleon: Life of John Byrom: A Study in Conflicting Loyalties* (London, Jonathan Cape Ltd., *1994)*

Hazard, Mary E., *Elizabethan Silent Language* (Lincoln NE and London, University of Nebraska Press, 2000)

Heilbron, J. L., *The Sun in the Church: Cathedrals as Solar Observatories* (Cambridge, MA and London, Harvard University Press, 1999)

Hendrix, John, *Platonic Architectonics: Platonic Philosophies & the Visual Arts,* (NY, Peter Lang, 2004)

Hendrix, John, *The Relation Between Architectural Forms and Philosophical Structures in the Work of Francesco Borromini in Seventeenth-Century Rome*, (Lewiston NY, Edward Mel Press, 2002)

Hockney, David, *Secret Knowledge, Rediscovering the Lost Techniques of the Old Masters* (New York, Penguin, 2001)

Iamblichus, *The Theology of Arithmetic*, trans. by Robin Waterfield, (Phanes Press, Grand Rapids, 1988)

Lewis, Charlton, T. and Short, Charles, *A Latin Dictionary* (Oxford: Clarendon Press, 1991)

Liddell, Henry George, and Scott, Robert, et al. A *Greek-English Lexicon* (Oxford: Clarendon Press, 1996)

MacMillan, Kenneth, *Sovereignity and Possession in the English New World; The Legal Foundations of Empire, 1576-1640,* (Cambridge, Cambridge University, 2006)

MacMillan, Kenneth, with Jennifer Abeles, *John Dee The Limits of the British Empire*, (Westport, CT, Praeger, 2004)

Mancall, Peter C., *Hakluyt's Promise: An Elizabethan's Obsession for an English America* (New Haven, Yale U. Press)

Mann, A.T., *Sacred Architecture* (Rockport, MA, Element Books, 1993)

Marshall, Robert, (personal correspondences about Syndex, 2000-2010)

Masi, Michael, *Boethian Number Theory: A Translation of De Institutione Arithmetica*, (Amsterdam, Editions Rodopi B.V. , 1983)

Means, Philip Ainsworth, *Newport Tower,* (New York, Henry Holt and Co., 1942)

Means, Philip Ainsworth, "The Riddle of Newport Tower," (Boston, *The Christian Science Monitor*, 1943)

Merriman, R.B., "Some Notes on the Treatment of the English Catholics in the Reign of Elizabeth I" *American Historical Review,* (London, Macmillan, 1908)

Mood, Fulmer., "Narragansett Bay and the Dee River, 1583," (R.I. Historical Society, *Collections*, Oct, 1935, p. 97-100)

Nicomachus of Gerasa, *Introduction to Arithmetic*, trans. by Martin L. D'Ooge (Chicago, Encyclopedia Brittanica, 1978)

Nicomachus of Gerasa, *The Manual of Harmonics,* trans. by Flora R. Levin, (Grand Rapids, MI, Phanes Press, 1994)

Parry, Glyn, *The Arch Conjurer of England: John Dee* (New Haven and London, Yale University Press, 2011)

Penhallow, William S., "Astronomical Alignments in the Newport Tower," in *The Newport Tower, Arnold to Zeno*, (NEARA Publications, Edgecomb, ME, 2006)

Poole, Robert, *Time's Alteration,* (London, University College of London Press, 1998)

Quinn, David Beers, *England and the Discovery of America 1461 - 1620*, (London, George Allen & Unwin Ltd, 1974)

Quinn, David Beers, *Sir Humphrey Gilbert and Newfoundland*. (St. Johns, Newfoundland Hist. Society, 1983)

Quinn, David Beers, *The Voyages and Colonizing Enterprises of Sir Humphrey Gilbert* (Vol. I and II, London, Hakluyt Society, 1940)

Reeds, Jim, "Solved–The Ciphers in Book III of Trithemius' Steganographia," (AT&T Labs, NJ, 3/26/98 26, *Cryptologia* 22, 10/98, pp. 291-319)

Renner, Eric and Nancy Spencer, "Pinhole Journal: A Tour of Renaissance Pinhole Sites in Italy," (Vol 14, #1, April 1998)

Renner, Eric and Nancy Spencer, *Pinhole Photography,* (Boston, Focal Press, 2000)

Roberts, Julian and Watson, Andrew, *John Dee's Library Catalogue,* (London, Bibliographical Society, 1990)

Robson, Lloyd, *Newport Begins*, (Newport Historical Society, Newport RI, 1964)

Rohr, Rene R. J., *Sundials: History, Theory, and Practice,* (New York, Dover, 1996)

Rowland, Ingrid D. and Thomas Noble Howe, *Vitruvius: Ten books on Architecture*, (Cambridge, Cambridge U. Press, 1999)

Rykwert, Joseph, Neil Lynch, and Robert Tavernor, *Leon Battista Alberti: on the Art of Building in Ten Books* (1486) (Cambridge, The MIT Press, 1997)

Sacks, David, *Letter Perfect*: *The Marvelous History of Our Alphabet from A to Z,* (NY, Broadway Books, 2003)

Schneider, Michael S., *A Beginner's Guide to Constructing the Universe: The mathematical archetypes of Nature, Art, and Science,* (NY, Harper Perennial, 1994)

Schumaker, Wayne, *Renaissance Curiosa* (Binghamton NY, Center for Medieval and Renaissance Studies, 1982)

Schumaker, Wayne and J. L. Heilbron, *John Dee on Astronomy: Propaedeumata Aphoristica, 1558 and 1568,* (Berkeley, U. Cal, 1978)

Sherman, William H., *John Dee, The Politics of Reading and Writing in the English Renaissance*, (Amherst, U. Mass. Press, 1995)

Sherman, William H., "Putting the British Seas on the Map: John Dee's Imperial Cartography," (*Cartographica*, 35, 1998, pp. 1-10)

Sieden, Lloyd Steven, *Buckminster Fuller's Universe: His Life and Work*, (Cambridge, Perseus Publishing, 1989)

Singman, Jeffrey L., *Daily Life in Elizabethan England*, (Westport, CT and London Greenwood Press)

Smith, Charlotte Fell, *John Dee, 1527-1608*, (Berwick, ME, Ibis Press, 2004)

Smith, D.E., *History of Mathematics*, 2 Volumes, (New York, Dover, 1923)

Smith, E. Baldwin, *The Dome: A Study in the History of Ideas*, (Princeton, Princeton U. Press, 1950)

Smith, Thomas Gordon, *Vitruvius on Architecture*, (New York, Monacelli Press, 2003)

Szonyi, György, *John Dee's Occultism,* (Albany, NY, SUNY, 2004)

Suster, Gerald, *John Dee : Essential Readings* (London, Aquarian Press, 1986)

Szulakowska, Urszula, "John Dee and European Alchemy" (Occasional Paper 21, Durham, Thomas Harriot Seminar,1995)

Tavernor, Robert, *On Alberti and the Art of Building*, (New Haven, Yale U. Press,1998)

Taylor, E.G.R., ed., Original Writings & Correspondence of the Two Richard Hakluyts, 2 vols, (London, The Hakluyt Society, 1935)

Wittkower, Rudolf, *Architectural Principles in the Age of Humanism* (New York and London: W.W. Norton & Company, 1971)

Woodward, Walter William, *Prospero's America: John Winthrop Jr., Alchemy, and the Creation of New England Culture 1606-1676* (Chapel Hill, U.N.C. Press, 2010)

Woolley, Benjamin, *The Queen's Conjurer,* (NY, Henry Holt, 2001)

Wroth, Lawrence C., *The Voyages of Giovanni da Verrazzano: 1524-1528*, (New Haven, Yale University Press,1970)

Yewbrey, Graham, *John Dee and the Sidney Group,* (1981, British Thesis Service, Hull)

My conjectured illustration of John Dee
designing the four plans for the Globe theater

Made in the USA
Monee, IL
07 March 2021

62167759R00162